Ray C. Freeman III

Generic CADD 5.0 Inside & Out

Osborne **McGraw-Hill**

Berkeley New York St. Louis San Francisco
Auckland Bogotá Hamburg London Madrid
Mexico City Milan Montreal New Delhi Panama City
Paris São Paulo Singapore Sydney
Tokyo Toronto

Osborne **McGraw-Hill**
2600 Tenth Street
Berkeley, California 94710
U.S.A.

Osborne **McGraw-Hill** offers software for sale. For information on software, translations, or book distributors outside of the U.S.A., please write to Osborne **McGraw-Hill** at the above address.

This book is printed on recycled paper.

Generic CADD 5.0 Inside & Out

Copyright © 1991 by McGraw-Hill, Inc. All rights reserved. Printed in the United States of America. Except as permitted under the Copyright Act of 1976, no part of this publication may be reproduced or distributed in any form or by any means, or stored in a database or retrieval system, without the prior written permission of the publisher, with the exception that the program listings may be entered, stored, and executed in a computer system, but they may not be reproduced for publication.

34567890 DOC 9987654321

ISBN 0-07-881712-9

Information has been obtained by Osborne **McGraw-Hill** from sources believed to be reliable. However, because of the possibility of human or mechanical error by our sources, Osborne **McGraw-Hill**, or others, Osborne **McGraw-Hill** does not guarantee the accuracy, adequacy, or completeness of any information and is not responsible for any errors or omissions or the results obtained from the use of such information.

Contents

Introduction .... *xvii*

1 The Essence of CAD 1
CAD Program Characteristics 3
    Real World Scale 5
    Real Data Storage 7
    Basic Drawing Elements 9
    Grouping Primitives 10
    Hardware Independence 12
CAD as a Drawing Medium 14

2 The Generic Approach 19
History 20
Generic CADD Versus generic CAD 20
    The Generic CADD Drawing Database 20
    Hardware Support 21
    Coordinates 25
    Hard Copy Output 26
    Simple Entities 27
    Complex Entities 28
    Layers 29
    Drawing Files 32
    Modeling Reality 33

The Look and Feel of Generic CADD 34
    The Generic CADD Screen 34
    Menu Structure 40
    Two-Character Commands 45
    Standard Abbreviations 45
    Editing Shortcuts 47
    How Shall I Command Thee? Let Me Count the Ways... 49

3 Preliminary Considerations 53

Installing Generic CADD 5.0 54
Setting Up CADD to Run on Your Computer 56
Starting Generic CADD 5.0 59
    Loading a Drawing 59
First Things First 60
    Selecting a Unit System 61
    Defining the Drawing Space 65
    Adjusting the Display 67
    Turning on the Grid 68
    Setting the Current Drawing Parameters 71
    Choosing the Layer for Drawing 74
    Coordinate Display Modes 74
    Manual Entry of Coordinates 75

4 Basic Drawing Tasks 79

Your First Drawing: A Room 80
    Drawing a Rectangle 80
    Drawing Another Rectangle 83
    Erasing the Drawing 85
    Using Lines 86
    Typing the Dimensions 88
    Saving the Drawing 89
Your Second Drawing: A Musical Staff 91
    The Drawing Setup 91
    The First Line 92
    Repeating the Line Command 93
    Distance Between Lines 93
    Save the Drawing 94

Your Third Drawing: A Key 94
    Starting Out 94
    The Easy Part 96
    The Round Parts 96
    A Less Powerful Erase Command 99
    Save and Exit to DOS 99
Your Fourth Drawing: A Star 100
    The Drawing Setup 101
    A Five-Sided Figure 101
    Snapping to an Existing Endpoint 102
    Continuing with the NP Command 103
    Erasing the Construction Lines 103
    Save and Exit 104
Adding to Your First Drawing: A Bathroom 105
    Reviewing the Room 105
    Getting Ready to Draw 105
    Adding Lines and Rectangles 106
    Zooming in Closer 107
    Drawing an Ellipse 108
    Another Ellipse: The Sink 109
    More Arcs 110
Your Fifth Drawing: A Site Plan 114
    Starting Up 115
    Drawing the Lines and Rectangles 115
    A Curved Pool 117
    Three Point Circles 119
    Standard Points 121
    Display Without Construction Points 121

5 *Basic Editing Tasks* 123

Editing Command Organization 124
    Methods of Selection 124
    Combined Methods 127
    Editing Functions 128
    Two-Character Commands 137
Editing Example: ROOM 138
    Changing the Shape 138
    Rotating the Fixtures 140
    Reversing the Plan 142

Cutting a Doorway	143
Adding Another Sink	145
Editing While Drawing: MUSIC Revisited	146
Two Lines Are Sometimes All You Need	146
Editing the Rest of the Drawing into Existence	146
Creating a Manuscript Page	147

6 Drawing Aids and Controls 149

The Zoom Commands	150
Displaying the Entire Drawing	150
Zooming In and Out	153
Zooming to a Specified Area	155
Returning to the Last Screen	156
Named Views	158
Getting a Scaled View	159
Moving Around Without Changing Scale	160
Refreshing the Screen	160
Changing the Order of Display	161
The Display Commands	162
The Line Commands	162
Display of Points	166
Rubberbanding	171
The Highlighting Command	172
Display of Coordinates	173
Cursor and Screen Text Display	176
Making More Room on the Screen	183
The Layers Commands	184
The Layer List	186
The Current Layer Command	187
Editing on the Current Layer	187
Selecting Which Layers to Display	190

7 Information and Inquiries 193

The Status Lines	194
More Information: The Screen Flip Command	195
Display Drawing Status	196
List Objects in Drawing	197

Display Assigned Macros	198
Return to Drawing	199
The Measure Command	199
The Distance Option	200
The Area Option	201
The Angle Options	202

8 Complex Entities — 205

What Are Complex Entities?	206
Complex Entities Are Still Just Entities	206
Complex Entities Are Defined Once	207
Placement Parameters	207
Predefined Versus "On the Fly" Complex Entities	209
Components	210
Creating a Component	210
What Really Happened?	215
Setting the Table	216
Real Objects Versus Symbols	223
One Component, One Entity, One Reference Point	224
Exploding a Component	224
Manipulating Component Definitions	228
Text	232
Selecting the Type Style	232
Setting the Spacing	233
Aspect	235
Setting the Text Color	236
Setting the Text Size	236
Setting the Rotation	237
Placing the Text	237
Creating Your Own Fonts	246
Attributes	248
Hatches and Fills	248
Placement Parameters	249
Placing Hatches and Fills	250
Window Hatch and Fill	250
Hatching and Filling Complicated Areas	255

9 Multiple Entities 261
- Bezier Curves 262
  - Placing Multiple Beziers 264
  - Placing Single Beziers 265
  - Editing Bezier Curves 266
- Smart Lines 267
  - Filleted Lines 268
  - Double Lines 269

10 Advanced Drawing and Editing Techniques 277
- Selection Revisited 278
  - The Last Selection Method 279
  - A Special Command: Selection 279
  - The Filter Method 280
  - The Like (=) Function 283
  - Multiple Color Selection 284
- Damage Control 284
  - I Didn't Mean To—The Undo Command 285
  - Yes, I Did Mean To—The Redo Command 286
  - More About the Pack Data Command 287
- Definitions 288
  - Eliminating Ghosts in the Attic with the Definition Unload Command 289
- Additional Editing Functions 290
  - Copying Around a Circle 290
  - A Variety of Effects 294
- The Trim Commands 296
  - Trimming Lines and Arcs 296
  - Extending Lines and Arcs 297
  - Manually Filleting Lines and Arcs 298
  - Chamfering Lines 299
  - Filleting Four Lines at the Same Time 300
  - The Buzz Saw—The Multi-Trim Command 302
- Changing Your Point of Reference 306
  - Uses of the Origin 307
- Making Use of Existing Geometric Properties 308
  - The Snap Commands 309

Eligible Entities	321
Cursor Control	322
Tracking—Starting in the Right Place	322

11 Dimensioning — 327

Associative Dimensions	328
Understanding the Dimensioning Menu	329
Creating a Dimensioning Style	329
Layer and Color	331
Dimensioning Text	332
Tolerance	335
Arrows and Other Line Terminators	336
Extension Lines	340
Dimension Display Variables	341
Linear and Angular Dimension Parameters	345
Leader Shoulder Length	348
Notes on Dimension Scale	350
Placing Dimensions	350
Linear Dimensions	351
Angular Dimensions	352
Radial and Diameter Dimensions	353
Leaders	354
Editing Dimensions	356
Editing Dimension Parameters	356
Moving Dimensions	357
Updating Dimensions	357

12 File Storage and Retrieval — 359

Default Paths	360
The File Paths Command	361
The Individual Path Commands	362
Storing Information	364
Saving Drawing Files	364
Saving Component Files	367
Saving Batch Files	369
Saving Attributes	370
Saving Image Files	370

Saving the Default Parameters with
   the Environment Command 371
Retrieving Information 372
   Loading Drawing Files 372
   Loading Components 376
   Loading Batch Files 378
   Loading Attributes 379
   Loading Image Files 379
The File Selector 380
   The Files Area 380
   Selecting Files 381
   The Directory Tree Area 381
File Selector Commands 382
   The Help (H) Command 382
   The Drive (D) Command 382
   The Filespec (F) Command 382
   The Search (S) Command 383
   The Tag (T) Command 383
   The All (A) Command 383
   The Load (L) Command 384
   The Exit (X) Command 384

13 Printing Your Drawings 385

Basic Concepts 386
   Paper Size 386
   Reducing or Enlarging the Drawing 387
   Telling CADD Where on the Paper to Place Drawings 389
Plotting 389
   Preparation 390
   Plotting Selected Entities 390
Type of Device 390
Where to Send the Data 391
Specifying Page Size 392
Options 392
   Standard Options 392
   Plotter Options 393
   Printer Options 396
   PostScript Options 396
Selecting the View Type 397

	Use Current View	397
	Fit Full Drawing	399
	Specify Scale and Origin	399
	Page Setup	400
	Origin (O)	400
	Scale (S)	401
	Rotate (R)	402
	Fit (F)	402
	Center (C)	402
	Return to Accept	402
	Start Plot	403

14 Using a Digitizer 405

The Digitizer as a Pointing Device	406
Selecting the Active Area	407
Using the Digitizer to Trace Drawings	408
Aligning Paper and Electronic Drawings	409
Tracing	412
Tracing Versus Drawing	412
Using the Digitizer to Select Commands	413
A Menu File	413
Configuring for the Tablet Menu	415
Loading the Digitizer Menu	416
Using the Digitizer Menu	417
Activating More Digitizer Menus	418
Switching Digitizer Menus	418
Loading More Commands	419

15 Customizing Generic CADD 5.0 421

Custom Configurations	422
CONFIG5.FIL	422
ENVIRON.FIL	423
GCADD.DWG	423
Multiple Configurations	424
Clearing Digitizer Menu Areas	426
Macros, Menus, and Batch Files	426
Assigning Macros	427

Custom Menus	428
Batch Files	429
Custom Images	429

16 Programming Generic CADD 5.0 431

Basic Macro Format	432
Command Options	433
Supplying Information	433
Interactive User Input	434
Other Special Characters	435
Directional Toggles	437
Preparation	437
Digitizer Menu Items	438
Video Submenus	438
Conventions	440
Do-Nothing Items	440
Loading a Video Menu	440
Long Menu Items	443
Including Images to Illustrate Menus	444
Some Useful Menu Macros	446
Wall Intersections	446
Openings in Double Lines	449
Setting Variables	449
Macro Tricks	450

17 Communicating with Other Programs 453

Communication Through Drawing Files	454
Sending Drawing Data to Other Software	455
Data Input Through Drawing Files	455
Two-Way Communication	455
Communication Through Batch Files	456
Data Extraction	456
Data Input Through Batch Files	457
Creating a Drawing with a Spreadsheet Program	457
Communication Through Attributes	464
Comma-Separated Value	465
Worksheet Files	466

Extracting Attribute Data	466
Communication Through Image Files	467
Sharing Images in CADD	467
Transferring Images to Other Software	468
Communication Through Print and Plot Files	468

A Related Software 471

Generic 3D (formerly 3D Drafting)	472
AutoConvert	473
Symbols Libraries	473
Type Fonts-I and Type Fonts-II	474
Translator (bundled with Generic CADD for the MAC)	474
CADD Master Ray's CADD PLATTER	475

B Command Summary 477

The Create Entity Commands	478
The Parameter Commands	478
The Toggle Commands	478
The Command Modifier Commands	479
The Edit Objects Commands	479
The Database Modifier Commands	479
The File Input/Output Commands	479
The Define Complex Object Commands	479
The Place Complex Object Commands	480
The Display Modifier Commands	480
The Program Modifier Commands	480
The Inquiry Commands	480

C Glossary 493

Index 519

Acknowledgments

Thanks go to my associates at WORKSHOP 3D Design Studio, both for covering for me while I was writing and for joining me in exploring the possibilities of CADD as a drawing and design tool. Thanks also to all the clients for whom we have made both designs and drawings, and for their acceptance of the electronic medium through which we have chosen to execute their work. Finally, thanks again to the folks at Generic Software for getting it right again, and to those at Osborne/McGraw-Hill whose unenviable task it was to extract this document from me.

Introduction

This is a book about drawing. Just as you use a word processor to write, and you use a spreadsheet to analyze or make projections, so it is that you use a CAD program to draw. Whether you are a new computer user or an experienced CAD veteran, this book will help you learn how to draw with Generic CADD, and to do it well—with ease, speed, accuracy and efficiency.

This book is organized and written to teach the user the concepts and skills required to master Generic CADD 5.0 as a drawing tool. The ideas and techniques discussed in *Generic CADD 5.0 Inside & Out* are the result of several years of experience and experimentation with Generic CADD in both professional and nontechnical applications.

What Is CAD?

This book begins with important conceptual ideas about Computer Aided Design (CAD). Chapter 1 discusses the philosophy behind CAD as a program type and as a drawing medium. This conceptual background will help you to understand exactly what a CAD program does best.

Chapter 2 deals with how these ideas are approached in Generic CADD 5.0. This chapter also examines the drawing screen and its cursor, the menu and its cursor, and the Generic CADD 5.0 command structure and syntax.

Getting Started

Chapter 3 reviews installation, configuration, and data paths. This chapter shows you how to configure Generic CADD 5.0 to run exactly the way that you want it to, by selecting default colors, a unit system, and a drawing size.

Drawing

Chapters 4 through 12 are organized into a number of sample drawing tasks, arranged from the simplest drawings to those that require more complex techniques. Simple drawing commands are introduced in Chapter 4, while basic editing is covered in Chapter 5.

Drawing organization and special drawing aids are the subjects of Chapters 6 and 7, and more complex drawing techniques that deal with complicated drawing tasks are covered in Chapters 8, 9, and 10. Many of the features new to this release of Generic CADD will be found in Chapter 10.

Associative Dimensioning is the topic of Chapter 11. Special consideration is given to customizing the dimensioning functions to draw the way that you do, so that your drawings will look as though you drew them.

Saving and loading your drawings are covered in Chapter 12. Topics include all file input techniques such as moving information from one drawing to another, saving partial drawings, saving and loading your drawing as a screen image only, and saving and loading your drawing to and from ASCII text files to provide for interaction with other software.

Peripheral Devices: Printers, Plotters, and Digitizers

Chapter 13 focuses on getting the drawing from the screen (or, more accurately, the disk) to the paper. Whether you are using a dot matrix printer, laser printer, or a plotter, many of the basic considerations are the same. The specifics of the various output devices are covered as well.

Chapter 14 explains the many uses of a digitizer with Generic CADD 5.0, including its use as a pointing device, a command generator, and a tracing tablet.

Beyond Drawing

The final chapters show how to take advantage of the programmable menu structure, Generic CADD's ability to communicate with other software through a variety of file formats, and the availability of utility software to take up where Generic CADD leaves off.

Appendixes

Three appendixes provide a summary of commands, a guide to available software that may be used with or interfaced to Generic CADD 5.0, and an extensive glossary.

Not everyone who reads this book will be trying to draw the same thing. A drawing program is in many ways more flexible, and the variety of possible applications wider, than most other applications software.

By combining readily applicable techniques with explanations of their conceptual backgrounds, *Generic CADD 5.0 Inside & Out* will lead you to discoveries that you can adapt and use to meet your own drawing needs and enhance your personal drawing style. This is not so much the nature of this book, or even CADD, as it is the nature of drawing.

CHAPTER 1

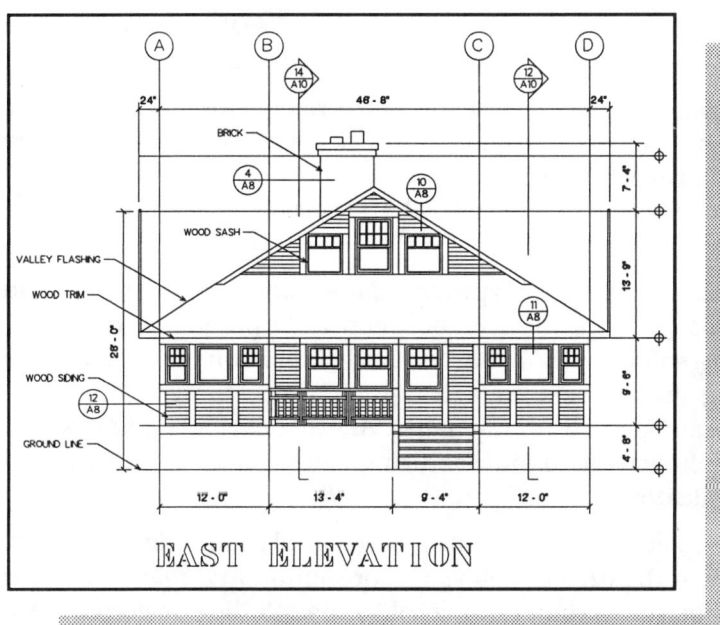

The Essence of CAD

Powerful, inexpensive CAD (an acronym for Computer Aided Design) for microcomputers is a fairly recent phenomenon. This chapter provides a general overview of the basic nature of CAD for the personal computer environment. By taking the time to acquaint yourself with CAD's conceptual foundations, you will be able to apply the detailed information and applications contained in following chapters. Generic CADD 5.0 may be your first exposure to a CAD program, and you may find it to be quite different than you had imagined. If you have experience with more expensive CAD systems, you will be surprised at the many capabilities that Generic CADD 5.0 offers—capabilities that were difficult to find even on powerful mainframe systems only a few years ago. With the low price and easy-to-use features of Generic CADD 5.0, many more people can now take advantage of CAD's technical and creative features.

As you will see, drawing with CAD and drawing by hand are very different processes. If you assume that drawing with CAD will simply mimic the hand drawing process, you will miss many of the conceptual and technical benefits of CAD. In general, the best approach is to pretend that you have never drawn before.

To get the most out of any CAD program, it is important to understand some of the conceptual differences between CAD programs and other types of drawing software. CAD has evolved principally as a technique for representing real objects on a computer. The storage and representation of real and accurate data make CAD an ideal tool for industrial, engineering, architectural, manufacturing, electronic, scientific, and many other applications.

In CAD every object is defined by its location and geometric properties, and every entity in the drawing plays a representational role. A line, for example, might be the perimeter of an object, a fold line or corner, or a change of material, but it almost always represents *something*.

CAD can be classified as a drawing medium or as a type of software. Because CAD is a relatively new drawing process, its inherent characteristics have hardly been explored, much less technically or artistically exploited to their fullest potential. To use any CAD program effectively, however, you must first master it as a program, so that its use becomes second nature. Once you have done this, you will be able to utilize CAD as a drawing medium, which is more interesting and ultimately more useful.

CAD Program Characteristics

The term "Computer Aided Design" is rather broad and often provokes confusion and controversy. Some people prefer words such as "Drawing" or "Drafting," to "Design." However, not every use of the computer for design, drawing, or drafting is considered to be CAD. Over the past several years, a specific technical definition of CAD as a type of computer program has evolved. To understand the characteristics that are unique to CAD, it is helpful to examine both what CAD is and what it is not, by comparing it to other computerized and manual drawing techniques.

Many properties of a CAD program are very different from another class of drawing programs, commonly referred to as *painting programs.* The distinction between these two types of programs does not necessarily make a CAD program better than a painting program, just different. A CAD program is better for certain uses, while a painting program is more useful for other functions. Understanding the difference between the two program types makes it easier to determine which would be more effective for your particular application.

The information that is input, stored, processed, and output by a CAD program is considered real geometric data, rather than graphic data. The data stored by a CAD program represents physical properties (such as an object's actual location, size, edges, and shape) rather than their appearance on the screen. In order to display, print, or otherwise make use of graphic depictions of objects, a CAD program creates these visual images from stored definitions. In contrast, painting programs store data as graphic depictions of these properties, in the form that they appear on the computer screen, as a number of dots called *pixels.* CAD stores data used to create the images that appear on screen. Painting programs store the images themselves.

The difference between the data actually stored when a line is drawn in a CAD program and a line drawn in a painting program is shown in Figures 1-1 and 1-2. Although the user may input similar data in both types of programs (in this example, the location of the two endpoints of a line), the data stored by a CAD program and a painting program are quite different.

4 Generic CADD 5.0 Inside & Out

 A line and its associated data in a CAD program

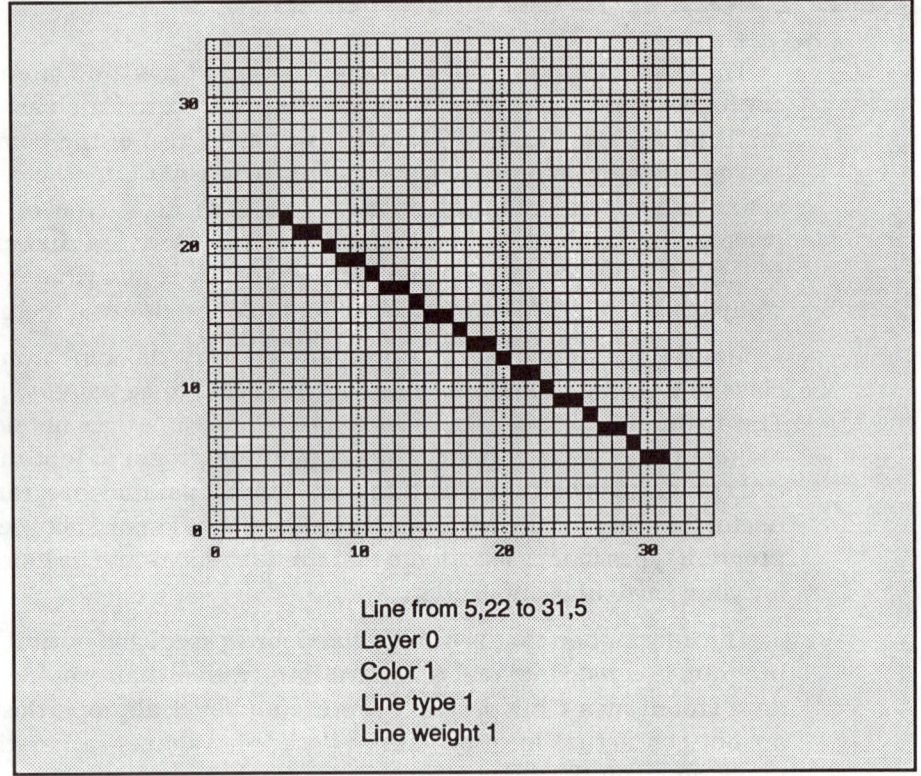

A CAD program stores the location of the two endpoints that you have specified and derives the information regarding which pixels should be turned on each time the line is displayed. A painting program actually stores only the locations of the pixels that represent the line on the screen. This means that a CAD program can calculate the length of a line, its angle, and its X and Y displacements, but a painting program can do none of these things, and in fact doesn't even remember the two endpoints that you specified originally. As you will notice from the figures, the CAD program also stores a number of other defining features of the line, including its color and thickness, which can be changed later if you like.

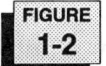

FIGURE 1-2 A line and its associated data in a paint program

5,22;6,21;7,21;8,20;9,19;10,19;
11,18;12,17;13,17;14,16;15,15;
16,15;17,14;18,13;19,13;20,12;
21,11;22,11;23,13;24,9;25,9;
26,8;27,7;28,7;29,6;30,5;31,5;

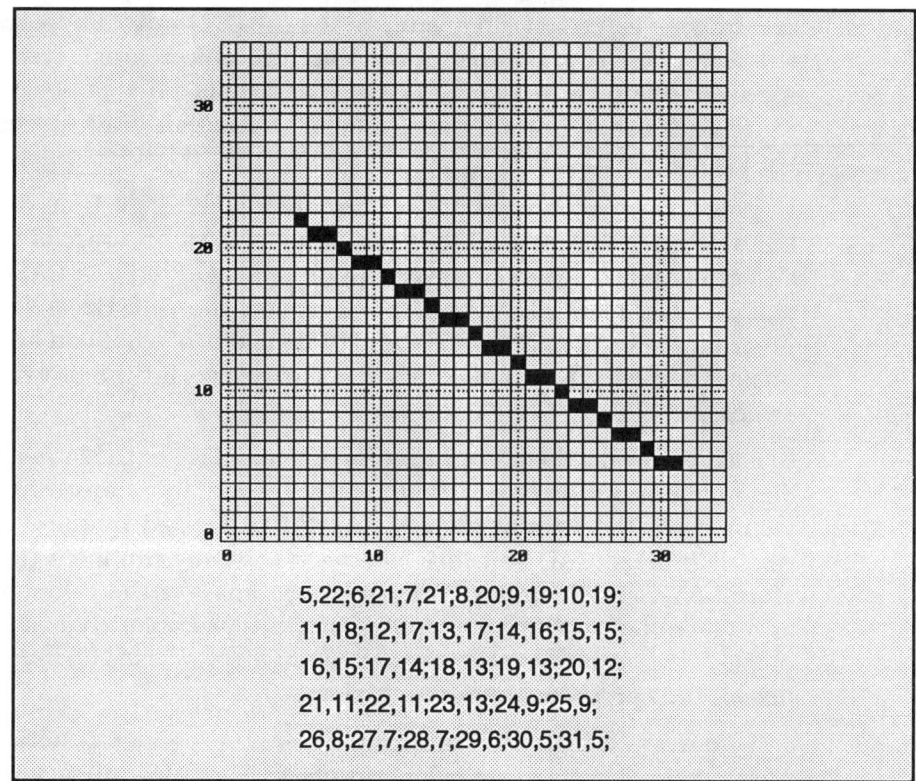

Real World Scale

The part of the real world that you are trying to draw is usually larger or smaller than your computer screen. The standard technique for fitting a drawing onto a sheet of paper is a scale conversion factor. For example, building floor plans are typically drawn at scales of 1/4" = 1'-0", meaning that one-quarter inch on the drawing represents one foot in the real building. Certain types of manufacturing drawings are larger than real life. A scale of 4:1 means that the drawing is four times larger than the actual object.

With a CAD program, this scaling is not necessary. If the object you are drawing is ten feet long, you can tell the CAD program to draw a line ten feet long. You needn't worry that the object must eventually be reduced to fit on a piece of paper or that the screen is only eight inches wide—that's the program's responsibility! You can draw objects in *real world scale* (actual size).

This is one way in which CAD is markedly different from drawing by hand. When you draw by hand, you must always be aware of your scale and either use a scale or conversion units as you draw. A CAD program almost never asks you to do the conversion yourself. Because the CAD program stores the actual sizes and dimensions of what you are drawing rather than its screen image, it can display or print the drawing at *any* scale.

CAD programs do not reduce dimensional data to the lowest common denominator of video resolution, plotter resolution, or any other limiting factor. Only the current display or print is affected by these hardware considerations. CAD software can work with any numbers that can be stored on your computer. Painting programs, on the other hand, are always limited to the *minimum* resolution available, that of the video display. The very premise of a painting program is based on manipulating pixels; CAD programs manipulate data.

To develop a high level of accuracy, CAD programs generally offer a number of methods of specifying numeric data. Most allow you to point to places on the screen, to trace drawings on a digitizer, and to enter coordinates manually by typing dimensions on the keyboard. Generic CADD 5.0 offers all of these forms of data input, as well as others. Of these methods, typing on the keyboard is undoubtedly the most reliable. *Digitizing*, or tracing drawings into the CAD database from a specially designed tablet (called a *digitizer*) that sends coordinate information to the CAD program, can be useful when absolute accuracy is not important or when combined with other automated geometry-adjusting features of CAD software. Pointing on the screen is accurate only when combined with automatic incrementation techniques (such as adjustable tolerances or resolution-enforcing grids), or when referencing existing geometry (such as the center of an existing circle or the end of an existing line).

Real Data Storage

In a CAD program, a line can be one inch long, 12 feet long, 225 feet long, or any other dimension because, as you have seen, a CAD program records the definition of the line rather than its graphic representation. Additional information can be derived from this data depending on your drawing needs.

The stored definition of any object is based on its geometric properties. In the case of a line, the properties are namely that it starts at one point and ends at another. For a circle, the locations of the centerpoint and either the radius or one additional point on the circle are sufficient to generate not only the graphic representation of the circle, but all of its other physical properties as well. Figure 1-3 shows the data associated with and derived from the geometric properties of a circle.

Flexibility of Stored Data

Because CAD programs record geometric properties, you have considerable control over the way this data is displayed and used. You can view the same drawing in various sizes and can query the database for accurate dimensional information derived from the existing geometry of a single object, or from the relationships between objects. You will find

The data associated with or derived from a circle

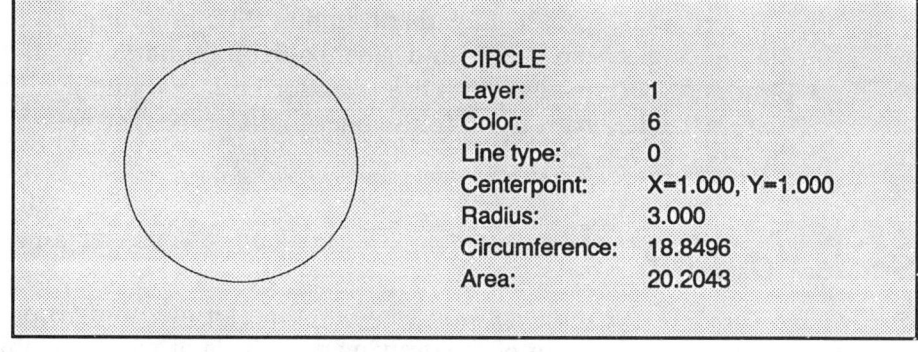

that editing a CAD drawing is crucial to its eventual accuracy. When editing a line, for example, you can move either endpoint, changing the location, length, and angle of the line simultaneously. In addition, the color, thickness, type (solid or dashed), and other properties of the line are always adjustable. These editing capabilities make CAD exceptionally flexible as a drawing tool. When drawing by hand, you have to decide, for example, the thickness and color of a line before you draw it. With a CAD program, you can draw the line first, and then try various color and thickness alternatives.

Real Objects Versus Symbols

Certain CAD drawing tasks seem to break the rule of real world scale. However, if you examine these tasks carefully (see Chapter 8, "Complex Entities"), you will see that they are not actually exceptions.

Many drawings, especially those that will eventually be printed or plotted at other than real world scale, contain two distinct types of information. The lines, circles, arcs, and so on that represent actual objects make up the "real" portion of your drawing and follow the real world scale concept as you would expect. The second type of information, drawing symbols, such as text, arrows, dimensions, and other symbols, are not representations of objects but help to describe these objects. When such symbols are used, the concept of real world scale is irrelevant because the size of these objects is related to the reduced or enlarged scale of the final paper print or plot, not the size of the "real" objects in the drawing.

There is no specific agreement among CAD programs as to how the difference between "real" and "symbolic" information is handled. In Generic CADD, components are used for both real and symbolic information. Generally, it is left to the user to make the distinction and scale objects accordingly.

Scaled Output

All CAD programs contain some method for obtaining proportionally correct scaled output of the drawing data. This provides the final reconciliation between the real world scale of the object and the size of the paper on which you are printing it. Most CAD programs provide a choice between a user-selected scale and automatic scaling. Generic CADD provides a number of automated and user-generated scaling functions as part of its printing and plotting routines.

Basic Drawing Elements

The geometric properties and dimensional data that we have been discussing are created and stored as a series of predefined elements, which are often referred to as *primitives*. So far, a line has been used as the primary example of a primitive. CAD programs include a variety of commands for actually placing a number of these primitives (including circles and arcs, among others) and additional commands for combining and editing these primitives once they are placed. These commands vary among CAD programs.

To understand the concept of primitives, compare the basic facets of a CAD program, which creates, edits, and processes drawing data, to a word processing program, which creates, edits, and processes written data. In a typical English-language word processor, letters, numbers, and punctuation symbols may be considered the primitives for that type of software. These primitives are placed into the document by moving a cursor to a desired location and typing the characters on a keyboard. These characters are then manipulated through combinations of editing keystrokes. Often, the editing process adds no new characters, but merely manipulates existing ones. However, you can't edit a document until you have created at least part of it with a few characters.

In a CAD program, primitives take the form of lines, circles, arcs, points, ellipses, curves of various types, and other basic geometric shapes. Normally, a number of these primitives are placed into a drawing by moving a cursor to a desired location and then selecting commands, either from a menu or by typing them on a keyboard. Figure 1-4 shows a number of primitives common to most CAD programs.

Just as the writer is limited to the 26 letters of the alphabet, ten numeric digits, and a finite number of punctuation marks, the CAD drafter is limited to the primitives provided by a particular CAD program. As might be expected, CAD programs are less standard in regard to the number and type of primitives than word processors, which are based on an accepted standard that has been in use for centuries.

10   Generic CADD 5.0 Inside & Out

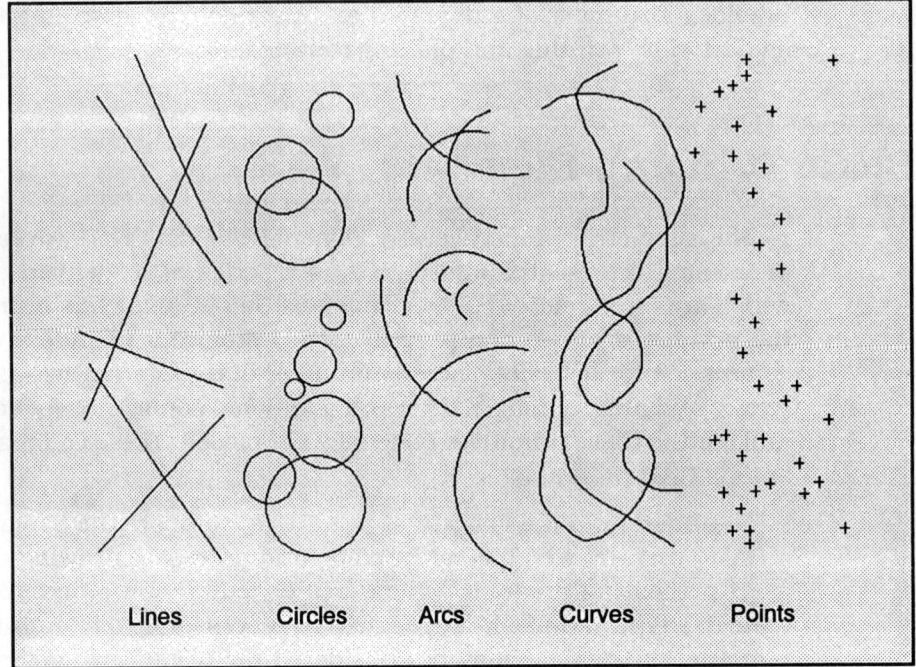

FIGURE 1-4 Typical CAD primitives

The writer conquers the 26-character limitation of the alphabet by combining these characters into words and then combining these words into sentences, poems, novels, and software user manuals. In a similar way, the CAD drafter combines various geometric primitives to form more complex shapes and to describe objects, and then places these objects in relation to one another, creating everything from garage sale signs to circuit board diagrams, to building details, to conceptual layouts for space stations.

Grouping Primitives

In addition to providing an assortment of primitives, CAD programs typically provide a number of ways to organize them. At the most basic level, primitives are used to draw "things." These things must then be given identities, so that they can be referenced, replicated, and manipulated as objects.

Drawing Files

Although CAD programs identify these objects in a variety of ways, almost all CAD programs store a certain amount of drawing information as a *drawing file*. This is similar to the way in which a word processor stores a certain amount of text information as a document file. Working within the computer's operating system, which separates information into files stored on disk, this is a logical way to organize text information at the most basic level. Likewise, one drawing—a readily identifiable group of drawn elements—can also be placed into a file that is a nameable, storable, retrievable quantity of computer data.

Definable Objects

At the next "higher" level, small portions of the drawing are often called *symbols*, *components*, or *blocks*, depending on the CAD program you are using. These consist of a number of primitives that have been placed in such a way as to describe one object, usually an object that appears more than once in the drawing.

These objects can often be replicated within the drawing by referring to their name or number. They can also generally be placed in the drawing at other scales and orientations than those at which they were originally created. In some cases, they can be redefined after they have been placed in the drawing, allowing global editing commands to make changes throughout a drawing.

The rules that govern the use of defined objects vary among CAD programs. Some programs allow *nested definitions*, in which defined objects contain the definitions of others, and some programs do not. Some even allow a *recursive definition*, which is a definition that contains a definition of itself. Generic CADD 5.0 allows both methods. Still other programs provide a specific type of definition and set of rules for each nesting level. For instance, drawings might be made of parts which are, in turn, composed of symbols, which are composed of the most basic elements, the program's specific primitives.

The storage of these defined objects is another area in which CAD programs vary. Some store the definitions within the drawing file; others store them in separate definition files. In some cases, these definition files are treated exactly as if they were drawing files, allowing any drawing to be treated as a defined object with another file. Generic CADD 5.0 allows a number of combinations of these storage schemes, depending on your needs, as explained in Chapter 8.

Associated Entities

Often, certain elements in a drawing do not create a specific object but instead share some other common characteristic. Most CAD programs provide an organizational device called a *layer*, a *level*, or an *overlay* that allows you to group entities. A layer is often visualized as a transparent sheet on which certain entities have been drawn. In CAD, this device provides a means of identifying certain entities that have something in common.

The characteristic that is shared by a group of entities varies depending on the application. A circuit board designer, for example, might group together all items that are to be etched in copper and separate into another group the items that are to be silkscreened onto the board. An architect might put a basic floor plan on one layer and place the wiring, plumbing, and heating systems onto separate layers.

Display and editing control are often associated with these groupings. The CAD user can usually choose to display certain groups of information while excluding others. In addition, the user sometimes has control over which layers can be edited and which are "display only." Generic CADD 5.0 provides both display and editing control over layers.

The interaction between drawing files, definable objects, and related groups of information is one feature that defines the "personality" of a particular CAD program. The simple but effective way in which Generic CADD 5.0 deals with these relationships is a major reason for the program's popularity and usefulness.

Hardware Independence

The storage of definitions (rather than images) means that CAD programs are essentially hardware-independent; that is, neither the program nor the data is bound to specific hardware configurations. Any graphics card can represent a line of specific length or a circle of a given diameter. The same is true for printers and plotters.

Hardware Support

In practice, the devices to be used with the CAD program (graphics card, printer, and so on) must be supported by that CAD program. The CAD program must contain or have access to instructions that make it compatible with your particular hardware devices. Currently, major CAD vendors such as Generic Software are making this part of their programs accessible to third-party developers and equipment manufacturers so that their programs can work with the latest technology on the market.

Resolution

Even though CAD programs are theoretically hardware-independent, the capability of the particular display or output device does determine the displayed resolution at any given time. Even when the defined data contains a great deal of information, the CAD program cannot create any more dots on the screen or paper than the hardware allows. Figure 1-5 shows a simple drawing displayed at different resolutions on different display devices.

Data Transferability

Device independence means that drawings created on one system can often be transferred to another without losing important information or

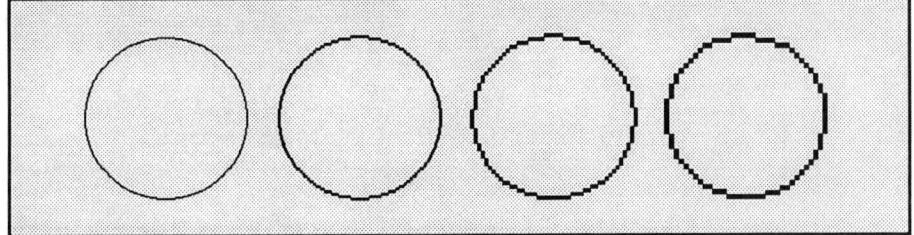

The same circle on several different display devices

degrading data. Because the information stored by a CAD program is essentially geometric, not graphic, transfers can also be made between higher- and lower-resolution systems, systems with or without color, and even among machines that run on different operating systems.

Although no standard in the CAD world is as widely accepted as ASCII is in the text-oriented community, numerous CAD-specific data transfer formats have gained wide acceptance in a variety of disciplines in which CAD is used frequently. Among these are IGES, the Initial Graphics Exchange Standard, and DXF, a drawing exchange format developed and promoted by AutoDesk, Inc. Generic CADD data files can be exchanged with other CAD software through either of these popular formats.

CAD as a Drawing Medium

Once you have a general understanding of CAD's capabilities as a computer program, you can begin to understand CAD's advantages as a drawing tool. CAD is a surprisingly flexible drawing medium. Like every medium, CAD has certain physical limitations within which the artist or drafter works. The artistry lies in the user's ability to transcend the medium by blending personal expression with the inherent characteristics of the medium.

Figures 1-6 through 1-9 show several different types of CAD drawings, ranging from technically oriented drawings, which use real world scale and exact dimensions, to more purely creative uses of CAD. The more

A CAD drawing of a minivan

FIGURE 1-7 A CAD elevation of a house (courtesy of WORKSHOP 3D Design Studio)

experimental drawings vary in their approach to scale, as they are not typical representations of reality.

As a tool for technical drawing, CAD offers precision, pure geometry, and subtlety of detail and technique. When considered as works of art or craftsmanship, CAD drawings differ from drawings done in other mediums in that they have several distinct physical forms. Created with

FIGURE 1-8 Architectural detail drawn on a CAD program (courtesy of WORKSHOP 3D Design Studio)

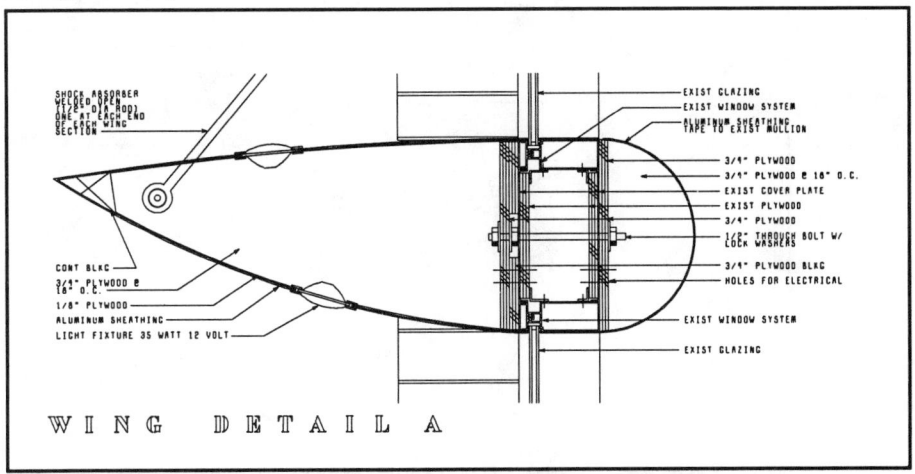

FIGURE 1-9 A creative CAD drawing (courtesy of Del Saul)

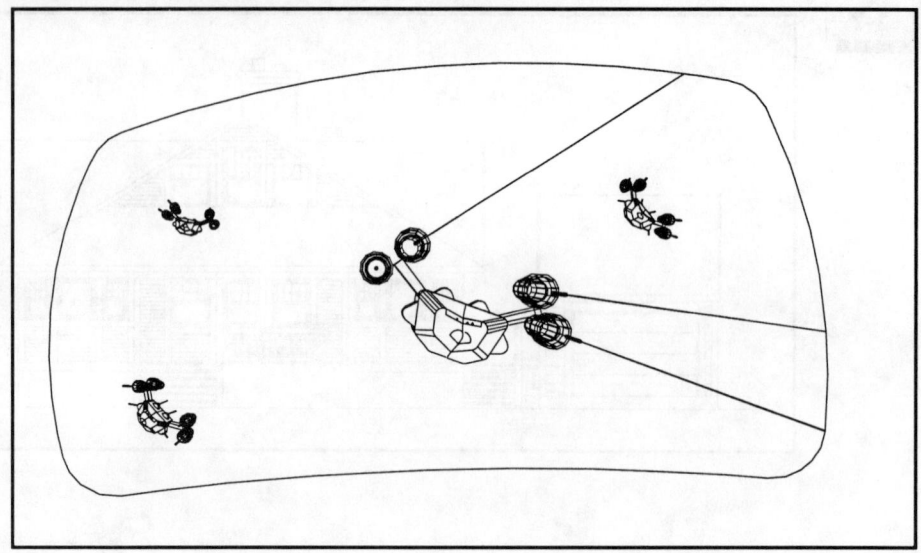

FIGURE 1-10 CAD used to create fold-up art (courtesy of Del Saul)

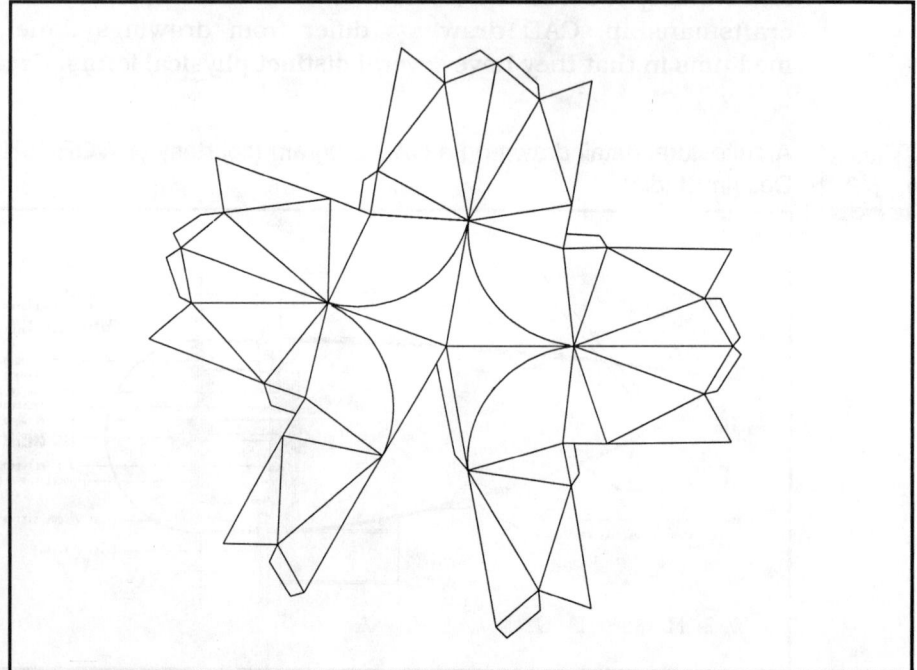

FIGURE 1-11 Photo of finished piece folded from a CAD drawing (courtesy of Del Saul)

drawing and editing commands, the CAD drawing first appears on the computer screen as an electronic image. In another form, the CAD drawing appears as hard copy printed on a mechanical device such as a printer or a plotter. A third and intermediate manifestation of the CAD drawing is in the form of a disk file, which has no visible attributes at all. Because you can think of any of these as the actual drawing, CAD offers a virtually infinite number of opportunities for artistic manipulation of the physical drawing process.

Figure 1-10 shows another example of a multiple-process artistic investigation with CAD—the design of a folded object. Figure 1-11 shows the finished product, a hybrid object that was first created electronically using the automated drawing capabilities of a CAD program, then plotted on paper, and finally folded by the human hand. As the capabilities of CAD become available to a wide audience through inexpensive, easy-to-use programs like Generic CADD, inventive and artistic applications will continue to develop.

As you can see from this brief overview, Computer Aided Design is both a valuable electronic drawing tool and a creative artistic medium. In the following chapters, you will learn how to harness the versatility and efficiency of Generic CADD 5.0 to accomplish your specific drawing tasks.

CHAPTER 2

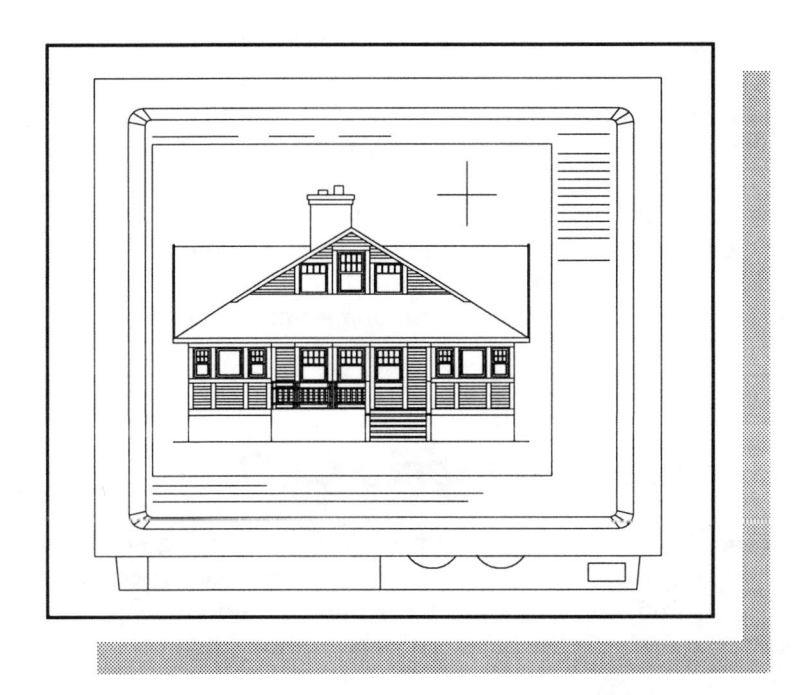

The Generic Approach

This chapter first focuses on how Generic CADD specifically approaches the general issues discussed in Chapter 1, "The Essence of CAD." Then, the chapter introduces Generic CADD's user interface, including the basic screens that you will encounter and the structure of Generic CADD's menus and commands.

History

Generic CADD was introduced in 1985 as a low-cost alternative to the CAD software available for PCs at that time. Since that introduction of version 1.0, Generic Software has subscribed to the basic CAD concepts that are generally well accepted in the industry (see Chapter 1). The development of the product through versions 2.0, 3.0, Levels 1, 2, 3, and the current version 5.0 has not changed the basic direction of the program in any way. The maturation of Generic CADD has, however, added speed, more sophisticated editing commands, and expanded capabilities, such as associative dimensioning, hatching and filling, and geometric referencing (snaps and trims), among several other enhancements.

Generic CADD Versus generic CAD

Chapter 1 described CAD in general terms. The following sections refine some of these general definitions, making them more specific to Generic CADD 5.0, and introduce the terms and definitions used in Generic CADD 5.0 to describe the basic features and functions of a CAD program.

The Generic CADD Drawing Database

Generic CADD stores drawing data as a collection of primitives or entities, which are referred to as *lines*. The term applies to all basic entities, whether they are circles, arcs, curves, points, or straight lines. This book, however, generally uses the term *entity* to avoid confusion with Generic's Straight Line command. Occasionally, the term *line* is used when it helps to coordinate the discussion with Generic's own terminology in its menus and prompts.

Entities are described using a number of properties, attributes, and coordinates, which are organized according to predefined rules. Attributes, such as color, are stored for every entity, while coordinates are used to define specific geometric properties, such as the location of the center point of a circle. The use of coordinates is different for each entity type, as are properties such as roundness or straightness.

The drawing database for all versions of Generic CADD has always remained essentially downwardly compatible with all previous versions. Changes have been made from time to time, such as adding new entity types, or eliminating obsolete ones. However, it has always been possible to load drawings made with a previous version into the current release. Although Generic CADD 5.0 represents the most significant change in the database so far, with the addition of environment data, associative dimensions, text attributes, and other enhancements, it is still possible to load drawings made with earlier versions and to save drawings in the Level 3 format. This downward compatibility allows you to load your old drawing files into the new program, and gives third-party vendors some time to catch up with the new database. Figures 2-1 through 2-5 show drawings created with Generic CADD versions 1.0 through 5.0.

Hardware Support

As part of a true CAD system, the Generic CADD 5.0 drawing database is device-independent; that is, the same information is stored no matter which type of system you make your drawings on. A Generic CADD drawing made on a high-resolution color system can be displayed and edited on a lower-resolution monochrome system without losing any information, and vice versa. Even monochrome systems can create drawings using color as an attribute of the entities for later color printing or display on a color system. These colors, of course, cannot be displayed on a monochrome monitor.

To take advantage of this device independence, Generic CADD 5.0 utilizes a device "driver" system. Essentially, this means that the parts of the program that communicate with external devices are separate from the rest of the program. When you install and configure Generic CADD

22 Generic CADD 5.0 Inside & Out

FIGURE 2-1 A drawing made with Generic CADD 1.0

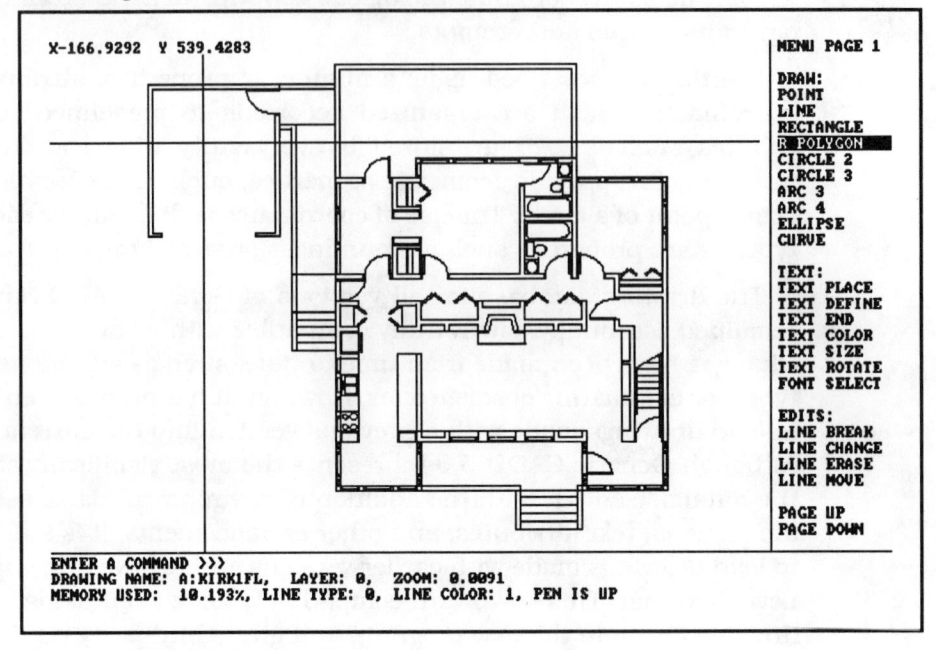

FIGURE 2-2 The same drawing in Generic CADD 2.0

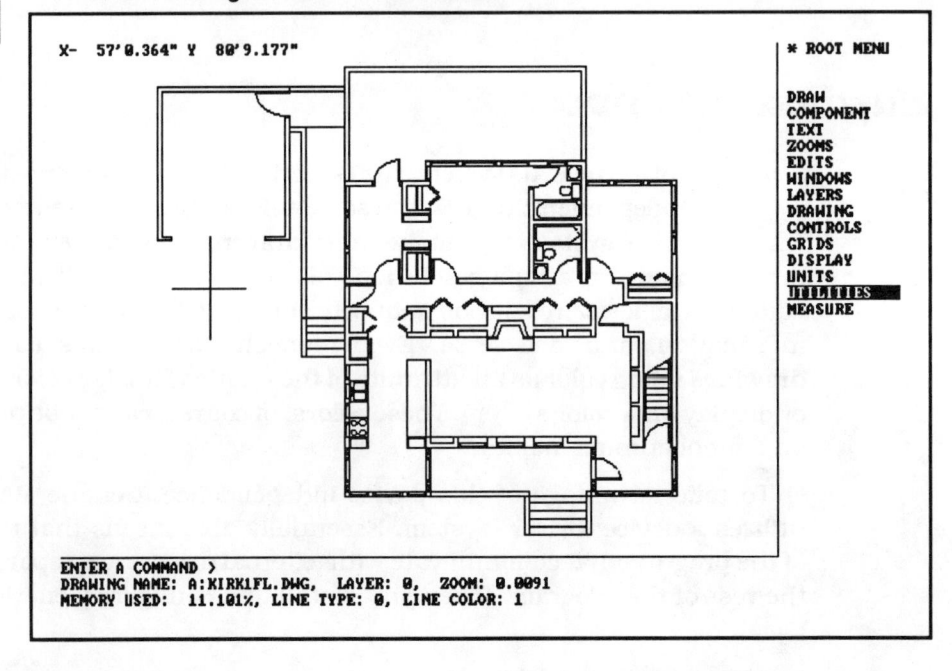

Chapter 2: The Generic Approach

FIGURE 2-3 The same drawing in Generic CADD 3.0

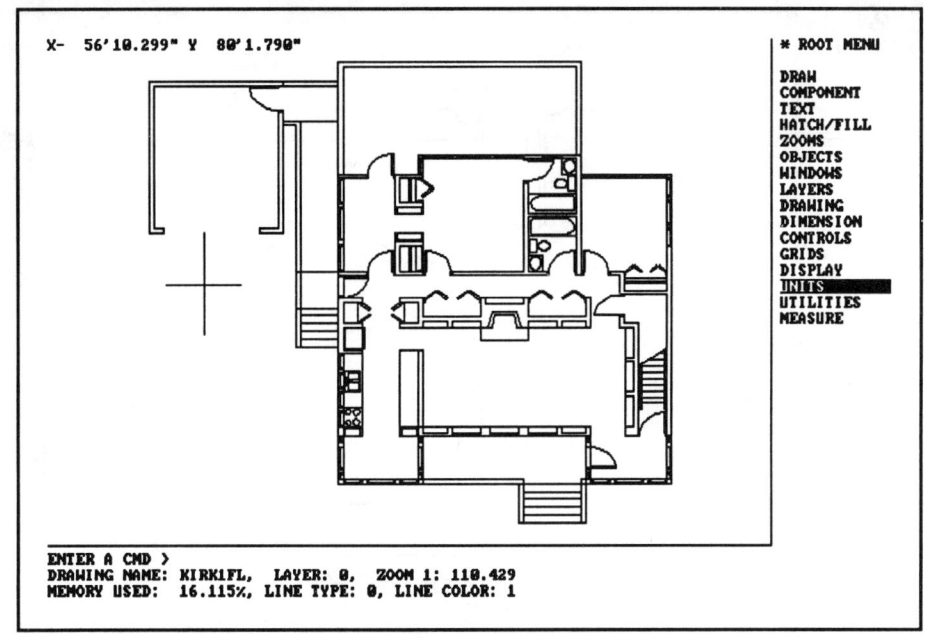

FIGURE 2-4 The same drawing in Generic CADD Level 3

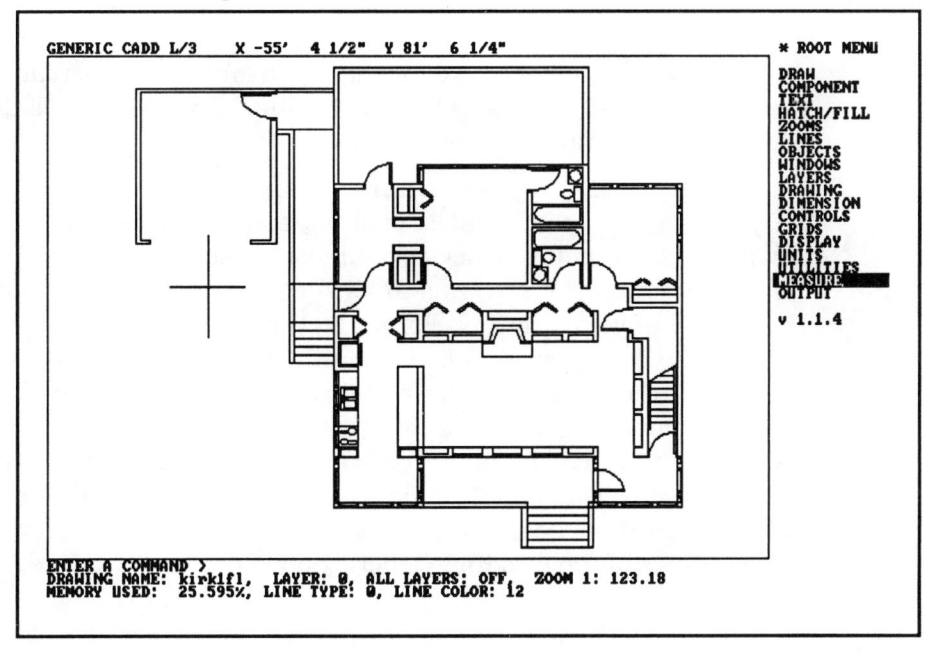

FIGURE 2-5 The same drawing in Generic CADD 5.0

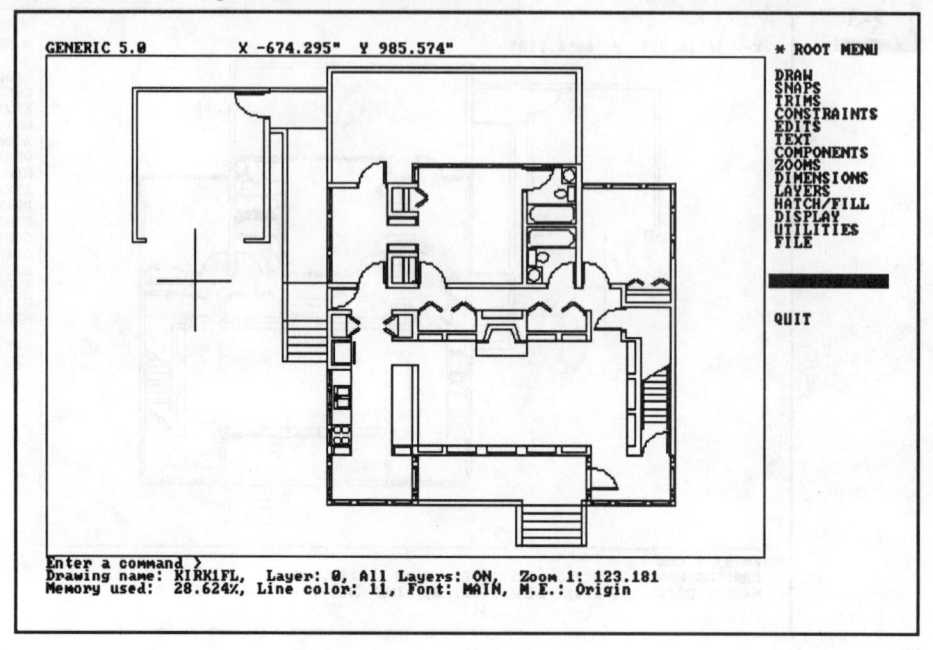

5.0, you select the drivers you want to use for your particular computer setup. Figure 2-6 illustrates the relationship between Generic CADD, the device drivers, and the external devices.

Generic CADD 5.0 uses drivers for three different external devices: (1) the graphics card, which controls display of the drawing on the monitor; (2) the pointing device or mouse, which controls the movement of the cursor on the screen; and (3) the printer or plotter, which prints hard copy of your drawing. Formerly, the program code for controlling all of these devices was embedded in the main Generic CADD program, and the driver merely provided certain parameters. In Generic CADD 5.0, however, much of the code for running both the video card and the pointing device have been moved from the main Generic CADD program to the drivers. This modification saves space in the main program and allows individual board manufacturers and third-party developers to write drivers for boards that Generic Software has not tested.

FIGURE 2-6 The relationship between Generic CADD 5.0, the drivers, and the external devices

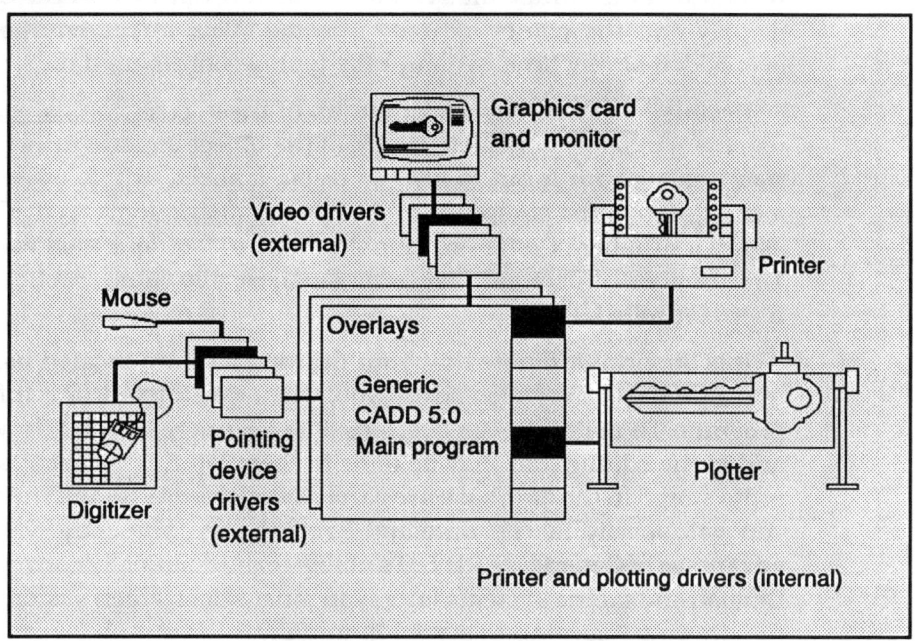

Coordinates

Generic CADD stores all numeric data as X and Y coordinates, relative to an origin, which is considered to be 0,0. This process allows every object in the drawing to be accurately located and sized in relation to every other object.

When you are placing a point (the endpoint of a line, the center of a circle, and so on), its coordinates can be typed manually by specifying an X and Y value. These values can be the actual X and Y values of the point relative to the origin, or they can be relative to a selected basepoint, or the last point entered.

Coordinates can also be specified by pointing to a location on the screen. Generic CADD displays the current coordinates of the cursor on the screen. This coordinate display, like manual entry of coordinates, is relative to the origin or to another point that you have selected.

Movement of the cursor can be adjusted to any increment or level of resolution or accuracy that you like, which is reflected in the coordinate display and the points actually selected. This incrementation can be overridden at any time by manually typing coordinate data.

Because you can choose the units of these coordinates, you should use them to specify the actual size of the object you are drawing, rather than scaling your input to fit the screen, a sheet, or any other arbitrary format—that's the computer's job. Several metric formats are available, as are a number of different combinations of foot and inch coordinates. The number of decimal places or smallest allowable fraction are also user-controlled.

It is important to note that your drawing files are created using a unit of a specified size, selected by you when you install or configure the program. To maintain the best possible accuracy in your drawing files, and in the editing that may be done to them later, it is essential that the units stored in the database are carefully selected to match the units that you will specify in the drawing. Even though you may wish to take advantage of Generic CADD 5.0's ability to automatically convert between English and metric systems later, you must select which system you want the drawing information stored in initially.

Hard Copy Output

Generic CADD 5.0 provides both printer and plotter support. Many different devices are supported, using the driver system discussed under the earlier section, "Hardware Support." Generic's printing and plotting routines allow you to fit any drawing to any sized sheet automatically or to define a specific printing or plotting scale. Drawings can be rotated 90 degrees with respect to the paper, and any portion of the drawing can be printed. Drawings may be printed in sections if they are too big to fit on one sheet of paper.

Printing and plotting are proportionately accurate, whether the drawing is scaled automatically or according to a specified scale factor. Various levels of resolution are available for most supported printers, allowing the user to select the most appropriate tradeoff between quality and speed. Plotter support allows the use of multiple pens, even on single-pen plotters, selective plotting of individual layers, and plotting to a file, for manipulation by other software at a later time.

Simple Entities

As you have seen, Generic CADD's basic building block is the line or entity. Every item in the drawing is an entity of some kind. Primitives of the type discussed in Chapter 1 are called *simple entities*, while defined groups of objects are called *complex entities*.

Simple entities in all versions of Generic CADD include the Point, Line, Circle, Arc, Ellipse, and Curve. Level 3 added the Bezier Curve to this list. Earlier versions (1.0 and 2.0) supported two other simple entities, the Rectangle and the Regular Polygon. Generic CADD 3.0 converted these Rectangle and Polygon entities to Lines when a drawing was loaded, while subsequent products discard them. As noted previously, the current version, 5.0, adds a number of new complex entity types, including associative dimensions, text attributes, and text strings.

Every simple entity in Generic CADD is defined by a certain number of definition points or *construction points*. Even though numerous methods may be used to create a particular entity type, the definition of that type of entity is always stored in the same way. A Line, for instance, is always defined by the location of its endpoints, as X and Y coordinates relative to the origin. As noted in Chapter 1, this information is enough to re-create the line on the screen or on the plotter or to determine its length, angle, and horizontal and vertical displacements.

A Circle is defined by two points: its center and one point on its perimeter. An Arc is defined by three points: its two endpoints and any point on the Arc in between. A Point requires only one definition point: the location of the Point itself. An Ellipse requires four points: the endpoints of the two axes of the Ellipse. A Curve can be defined by any number of points that form it, but at least three are required. The Bezier Curve uses four definition points: the two endpoints of the curve and two "control points" that determine its direction and curvature. (The obsolete entities, Rectangle and Regular Polygon, stored, respectively, the four corners of the Rectangle and the center and any vertex of the Regular Polygon. The number of points on the Polygon was also stored, but as an

FIGURE 2-7 Simple entities and their definition points

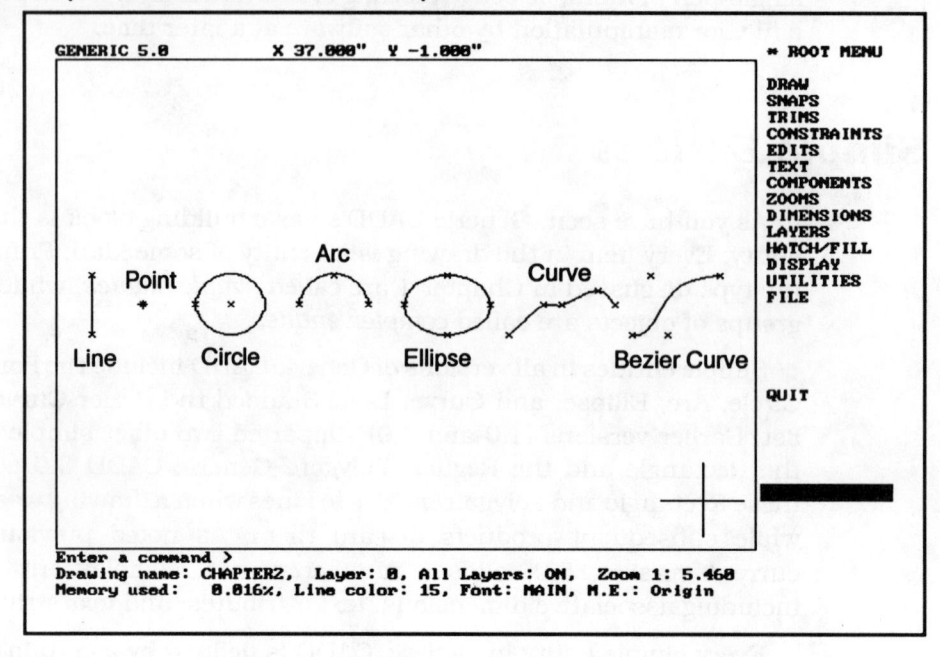

integer rather than as a coordinate.) Figure 2-7 shows the simple entity types and the definition points that are used to describe them.

Everything in the drawing, including the definitions of complex entities, is made from these simple entities. The process of drawing, as you will see, consists of placing these simple entities into the drawing with certain commands and then manipulating them with others.

Complex Entities

As described in Chapter 1, a CAD program generally includes methods for defining and placing certain objects or figures that are composed of other, simpler objects. Generic CADD currently provides several such complex entities, listed next.

- *Components* are groups of entities that can be collected, given a name, and placed into a drawing at any scale or rotation.
- *Characters* are similar to Components but are stored in different files called "Fonts" and behave in special ways due to their particular requirements as part of Generic CADD's Text functions.
- *Text Strings* are groups of characters placed together on a single line.
- *Attributes* are groups of text characters that fit a user-defined format, are attached to components, and can be extracted to provide information to other programs.
- *Associative Dimensions* are groups of lines, arrows, and text that form a drawing dimension. These are kept together as a single entity so that they can be automatically updated when the time comes.
- *Hatches* are composed of a number of simple entities that form an enclosed area, into which a specified pattern of Lines is inserted.
- *Fills* are similar to Hatches but, as their name implies, they are filled with a solid pattern rather than a pattern of Lines.

See Figure 2-8 for examples of complex entities. Note that complex entities do not have construction points but instead often have a single "reference point."

Some Generic CADD 5.0 commands produce more than one simple entity at a time, but do not produce a defined object or a combination of simple and complex entities. These combinations are called "multiple entities" to differentiate them from complex entities.

Layers

CAD programs generally provide a method for keeping track of objects that might be related in some way. Generic CADD 5.0 provides the "layer" concept for this purpose.

You can understand the concept of layers by imagining each layer as a piece of very thin, very transparent tracing paper, each laid over the next. Generic CADD 5.0 offers 256 layers, which can be referred to by number or assigned names. Any number of these layers can be viewed simultaneously, or individual layers can be turned off or *hidden*, as if

FIGURE 2-8 Complex entities and their reference points

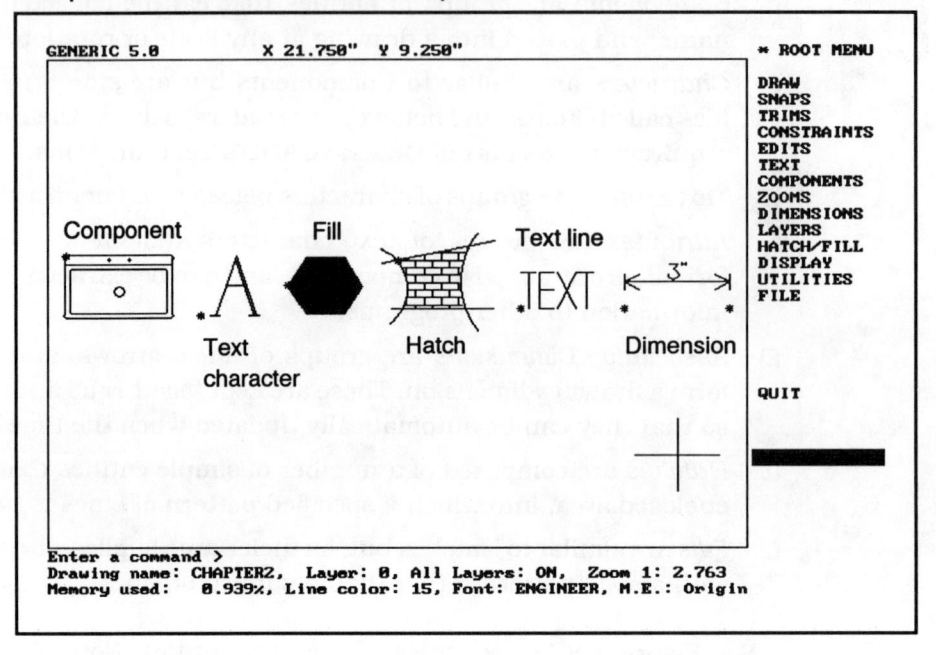

particular sheets were removed from the stack. Figure 2-9 shows a sample Generic CADD drawing composed of several layers. Figure 2-10 shows the same drawing with a single layer (layer 1) turned on. Figure 2-11 shows the same drawing again, with all layers turned on except layer 1. Layers, as you can see, provide a great deal of display flexibility.

Another way of picturing layers is simply as a characteristic of each entity. Each entity in the drawing, simple or complex, is located on a layer, or has that layer number as an attribute. In fact, this is close to the way that layer information is actually stored in the drawing database.

Both ways of thinking about layers can be useful, depending on the application. Generic CADD does not stipulate how layers are to be used;

Chapter 2: The Generic Approach 31

FIGURE 2-9 A sample drawing (courtesy of WORKSHOP 3D Design Studio)

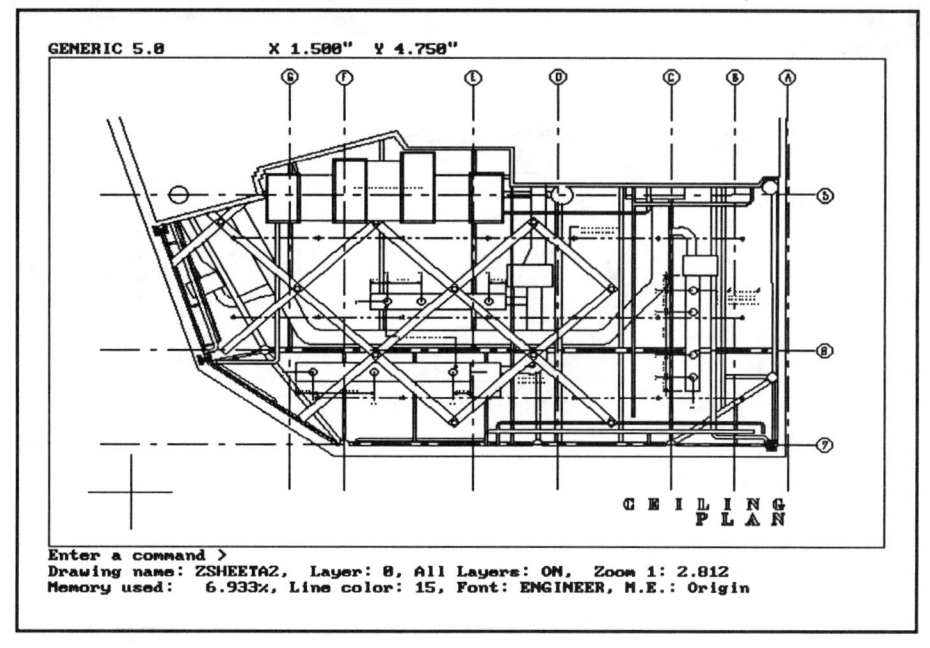

FIGURE 2-10 The same sample drawing with only layer 1 turned on

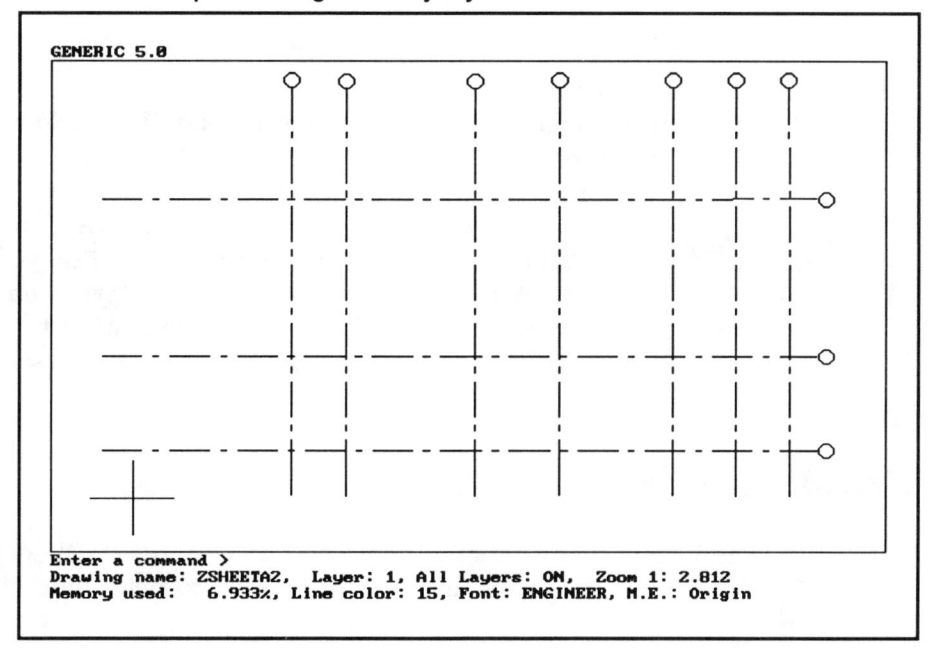

FIGURE 2-11 The same sample drawing with layer 1 turned off

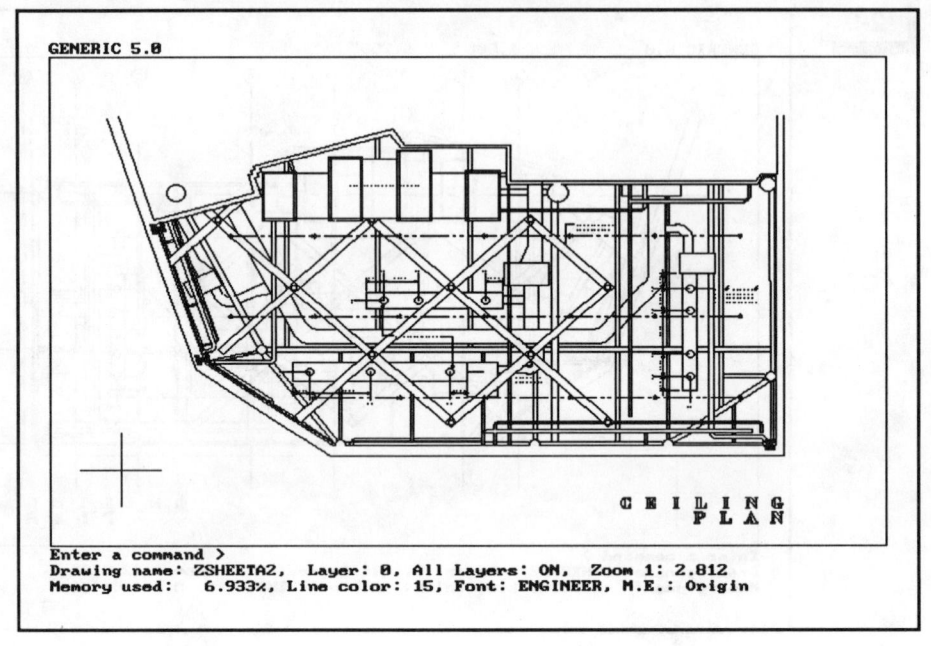

that is up to you. You will explore several ways of using layers in later chapters.

All layers in Generic CADD are either displayed or hidden, that is, visible or invisible. One layer is considered the "current" layer, and all new entities are created on this layer. Editing can be done on the current layer, or on any visible layer. Different colors are often used on different layers to distinguish them. If you are using a color monitor, you can see which entities are on each layer without turning layers on and off. Color-coding of layers can also be useful when you want to plot some layers with one pen and some with another.

Drawing Files

The largest organizational structure for Generic CADD data is the drawing file itself. Again, it is up to the user to determine how much information goes into a single drawing file, but "one drawing, one file" is common practice.

Each drawing file contains the definitions and placements of all of the complex entities and all of the simple entities. The definitions of repeatable complex entities are stored only once in each file, even though it might be placed in the drawing several times. As a result, the use of components, where appropriate, can save drawing file space.

Drawing file space is valuable and worth conserving. Smaller files take up less space on your disk, load and save faster, and allow Generic CADD to run faster for many tasks. For certain applications you may want to break up a sheet of drawings into several drawing files; this strategy will let you run Generic CADD faster and more efficiently.

Generic CADD 5.0 uses standard DOS filenames, with the extension .DWG for drawing files. This means that you can use up to eight characters (not including the extension) for a filename. Drawing files are stored in directories, which can be organized any way you like. Other extensions used by Generic CADD are

.CMP for component files
.FNT for font files
.HCH for hatch files
.MNU for menu files
.TXT for batch files
.ATB for attribute files
.CSV for comma-delimited files
.WK1 for Lotus format files
.GX2 for screen image files

Modeling Reality

Generic CADD 5.0 is ideally suited for simulations of real world objects. Simple entities are adequate to describe almost any physical object, and these entities can then be combined to define repeatable components that represent actual parts of an object or symbols used to describe an object; these complex entities and symbols can then be inserted by name at any scale or rotation. Layers can be used to organize your drawing data to simulate the real object or to impose a strictly imaginary hierarchy, as you see fit.

The Look and Feel of Generic CADD

Several aspects of Generic CADD 5.0 contribute to the overall look and feel of the program, including the organization and operation of the screen, the way that text menus and the cursor are implemented, and the methods for giving instructions to the program. These facets of Generic CADD are investigated in the remainder of this chapter.

The Generic CADD Screen

If you have not yet installed and configured Generic CADD 5.0 as described in the Generic CADD manual, do so now. (If you are having trouble, see Chapter 3, "Preliminary Considerations," of this book for help.) Go to the directory where you have installed Generic CADD, type **CADD**, and press ENTER.

The first screen that appears is the copyright and configuration screen (see Figure 2-12). This screen shows you which version of Generic CADD you have loaded, which device drivers have been selected, how much memory you have available for your drawing, and the Generic Software copyright notice. To move on to the next screen, press ENTER. Note that when you first typed **CADD** at the DOS prompt, you could have pressed ENTER twice, which would take you past this screen automatically.

You now arrive at the main Generic CADD 5.0 screen, which should look similar to the one shown in Figure 2-13. (There may be some variation in the size of the text and the proportion of the screen due to the graphics card in your computer.) This screen is displayed most of the time while you are running Generic CADD. Let's examine this screen in detail, so that you always know where to find important information as you draw with Generic CADD. If you do not see this screen, you have probably configured your graphics card improperly. You must either return to Generic's CONFIG program and select a different graphics card or adjust hardware or software switches on your graphics card. See the

Chapter 2: The Generic Approach   35

FIGURE 2-12 The copyright and configuration screen

```
              ****** Generic CADD ******
                     Version 5.0

    Configured for:

        IBM Video Graphics Array (VGA), 640 x 480 - 16 colors

        LOGITECH - MOUSE.COM LOADED

        H.P. 7475A PLOTTER

          RAM Memory available for drawing data:   1064k
           Virtual memory reserved on hard disk:   Disabled. Memory Error.
          Total memory available to CADD drawing:  1064k

        Use of an authorized copy of this software beyond this point
        constitutes your acceptance of the accompanying license agreement.
        Copyright(c) 1985,90 by Generic Software,Inc. All rights reserved.


          ******  Press <RET> to begin - <ESC> to quit  ******
```

FIGURE 2-13 The main Generic CADD screen

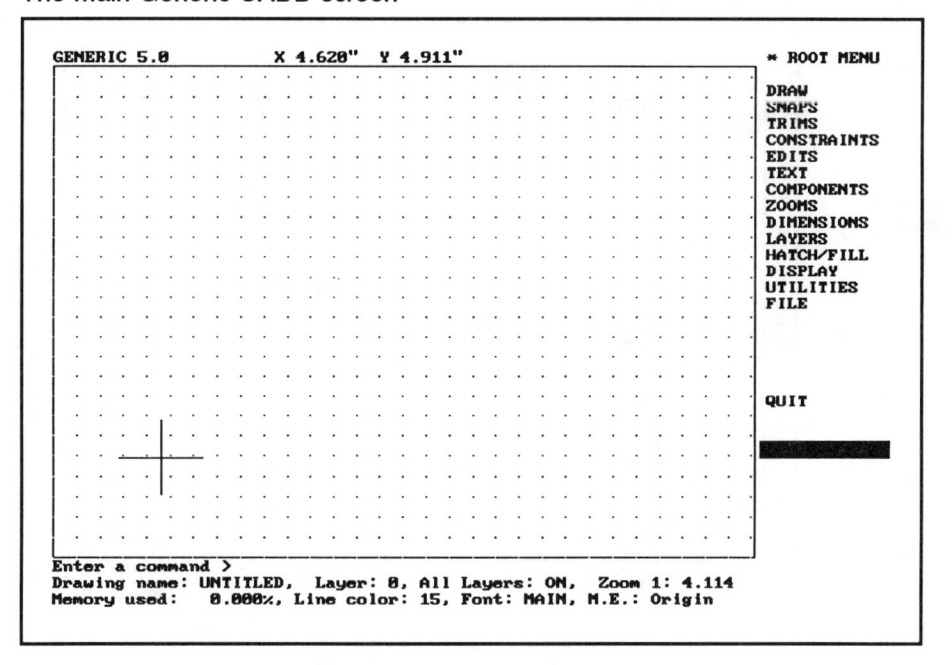

```
GENERIC 5.0         X 4.620"  Y 4.911"              * ROOT MENU
                                                    DRAW
                                                    SNAPS
                                                    TRIMS
                                                    CONSTRAINTS
                                                    EDITS
                                                    TEXT
                                                    COMPONENTS
                                                    ZOOMS
                                                    DIMENSIONS
                                                    LAYERS
                                                    HATCH/FILL
                                                    DISPLAY
                                                    UTILITIES
                                                    FILE




                                                    QUIT



         +



Enter a command >
Drawing name: UNTITLED,  Layer: 0, All Layers: ON,  Zoom 1: 4.114
Memory used:    0.000%, Line color: 15, Font: MAIN, M.E.: Origin
```

instructions that came with your card to make sure that it is set up properly.

Drawing Area

By far the largest area on the screen is the *drawing area* (now blank except for the drawing cursor and possibly a grid of dots), as shown in Figure 2-14 (more about the grid shortly). Let's take a look at the cursor. When you move the pointing device (mouse, rollerball, digitizer, or the like), the cursor moves around the drawing area. Move the pointing device to the right, and the cursor moves to the right; move the pointing device forward (away from you), and the cursor moves up the screen, and so on. Notice that you cannot move the drawing cursor beyond the boundaries of the current drawing area. Keep in mind that as the drawing area is only a viewport to your drawing, the drawing might actually be larger than the portion currently shown on the screen. In order to move the cursor to another part of the drawing, you must change the location or

FIGURE 2-14 The drawing area

size of viewport by using one of the Zoom commands. More about these commands later.

Coordinate Area

At the top of the screen is the *coordinate area*—a single line of text that starts in the upper-left corner of the screen and begins with the name of the program. As shown in Figure 2-15, you should see the words "GENERIC 5.0." Following this, you may see more text in the form of X and Y coordinates. These coordinates indicate the location of the drawing cursor. Depending on your Generic CADD configuration, you may see: *Absolute coordinates* (the distance the cursor is to the right (X) and above (Y) the lower-left corner (origin) of the drawing; *Relative coordinates*, the distance from the cursor to the last point entered (if no point has been entered, they will be relative to the origin): *Polar coordinates*, shown as a distance and angle; or no coordinates at all—they may be turned off and not visible. All that's really important now is to know where to find them.

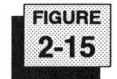

FIGURE 2-15 The coordinate area

GENERIC 5.0   X 2.761" Y 2.689"

and to notice that they change as you move the drawing cursor around the drawing area.

Prompt Area

At the bottom of the screen, there is space for three lines of text. This space is the *prompt area*, also called the *message area*, and is shown in Figure 2-16. This is where Generic CADD asks (prompts) you for information and where your typed responses will appear. Similarly, Generic CADD uses this area to display information that you request. Again, depending on the settings of your defaults, the information in the prompt area may vary, but at the very least you should see the current prompt, which reads "Enter a command >". This prompt tells you that Generic CADD is waiting for instructions.

Video Menu Area

Along the right side of the screen is the *video menu*, as illustrated in Figure 2-17. This area lists commands that you can select with the pointing device. Notice that a highlighted bar moves up and down the menu as you move the pointing device forward and back. This bar is called the *menu cursor*, and it moves simultaneously with the movement of the drawing cursor (though it does not move from side to side). Like the drawing cursor, its movement is restricted to its own area of the screen.

Two Cursors Are Better Than One

If you are unfamiliar with Generic CADD 5.0, you may wonder how two cursors can be active on the screen at the same time. The drawing cursor, which looks like cross hairs, is used for pointing in the drawing area, and the menu cursor is used for selecting items from the video menu—but how can they be used simultaneously?

When the program asks you for the location of a point, you will probably use the drawing cursor to point to a location on the screen; when you see the prompt "Enter a command >" you generally use the menu cursor to select it. However, you may want to use a menu item to do something like turning on a grid before specifying the point. There are

Chapter 2: The Generic Approach

FIGURE 2-16 The prompt area

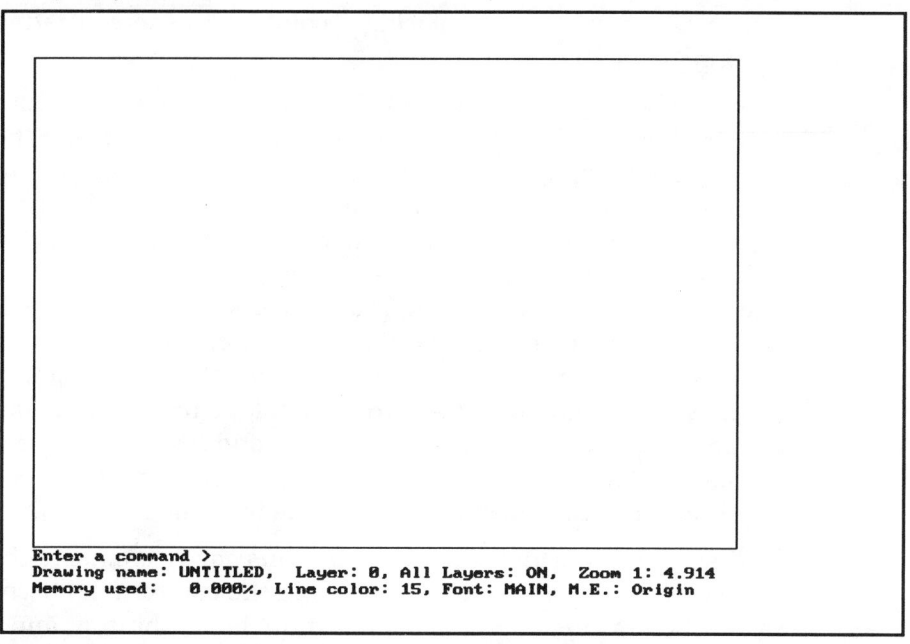

```
Enter a command >
Drawing name: UNTITLED, Layer: 0, All Layers: ON, Zoom 1: 4.914
Memory used:    0.000%, Line color: 15, Font: MAIN, M.E.: Origin
```

FIGURE 2-17 The menu area

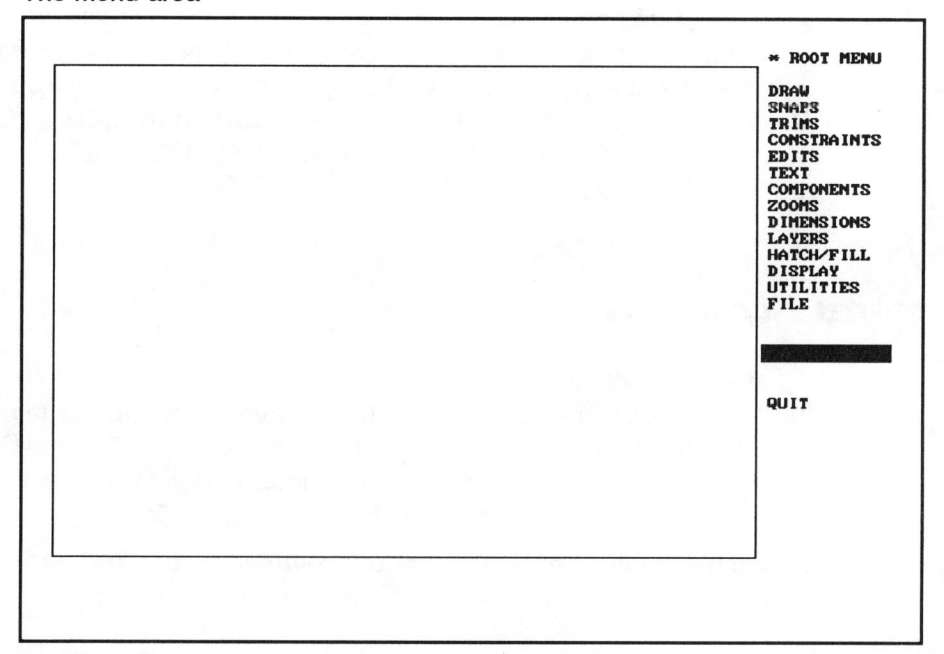

```
* ROOT MENU

DRAW
SNAPS
TRIMS
CONSTRAINTS
EDITS
TEXT
COMPONENTS
ZOOMS
DIMENSIONS
LAYERS
HATCH/FILL
DISPLAY
UTILITIES
FILE




QUIT
```

also times when you will be asked to "Enter a command >" and you will start a Line command by placing a point on the screen rather than by selecting a menu item.

So you need quick access to both cursors almost all the time. It is easy to keep track of which cursor you want to use. First, ignore the one that you are not using. If you want to select a point on the screen, for example, don't worry about the menu cursor; its location is irrelevant. Similarly, if you are selecting a menu item, use only the menu cursor and pay no attention to the location of the drawing cursor. Second, if you are selecting a point on the screen, press the first button (the one farthest to the left) on your pointing device. If you are selecting a menu item, press the second button. (On a two-button mouse this is the right button; on a three-button mouse this is the middle button. On a multibutton digitizer puck, it is the button with the second-lowest number.) If you are not using a mouse or digitizer, press the ENTER key to select points on the screen and the HOME key to select menu items.

When you consider these two buttons for a moment, the graphic connection between the two cursors and the two buttons becomes quite clear. The drawing cursor is activated by the left button, and the menu cursor is activated by the right button. See Figure 2-18 for a diagram of how this works. This cursor control scheme is extremely efficient. Most CAD programs make you move your cursor into the menu area before you can use it to select menu items, and all of the pull-down menu schemes require you to move to the top of the screen before you can pull down a menu. This simple cursor control feature contributes significantly to the ease and fluidity with which Generic CADD 5.0 can be handled by the practiced user.

Menu Structure

At the top of the video menu are the words "ROOT MENU," which indicate that the menu is hierarchical. In fact, selecting any item on this ROOT menu takes you to a submenu, where you will find a list of menu items, including "ROOT MENU" at the bottom. Selecting this item takes you back to the ROOT menu (see Figure 2-19).

Each submenu contains a group of commands that are related in some way. The name of the submenu provides a clue to the type of commands

Chapter 2: The Generic Approach

FIGURE 2-18 How the pointing device controls two cursors at the same time

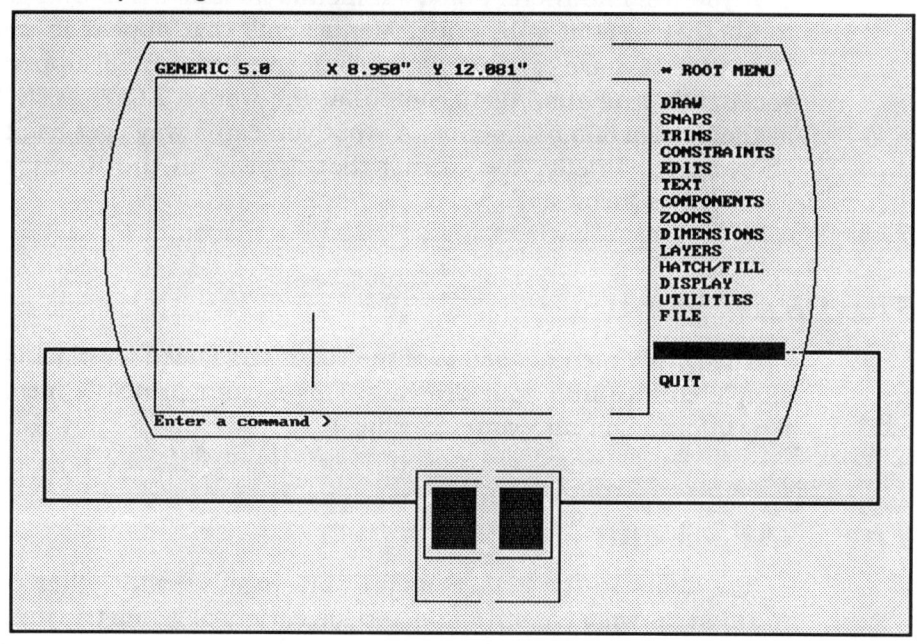

```
GENERIC 5.0      X 8.950"   Y 12.081"        ~ ROOT MENU
                                              DRAW
                                              SNAPS
                                              TRIMS
                                              CONSTRAINTS
                                              EDITS
                                              TEXT
                                              COMPONENTS
                                              ZOOMS
                                              DIMENSIONS
                                              LAYERS
                                              HATCH/FILL
                                              DISPLAY
                                              UTILITIES
                                              FILE


                                              QUIT
Enter a command >
```

FIGURE 2-19 The Generic CADD menu structure

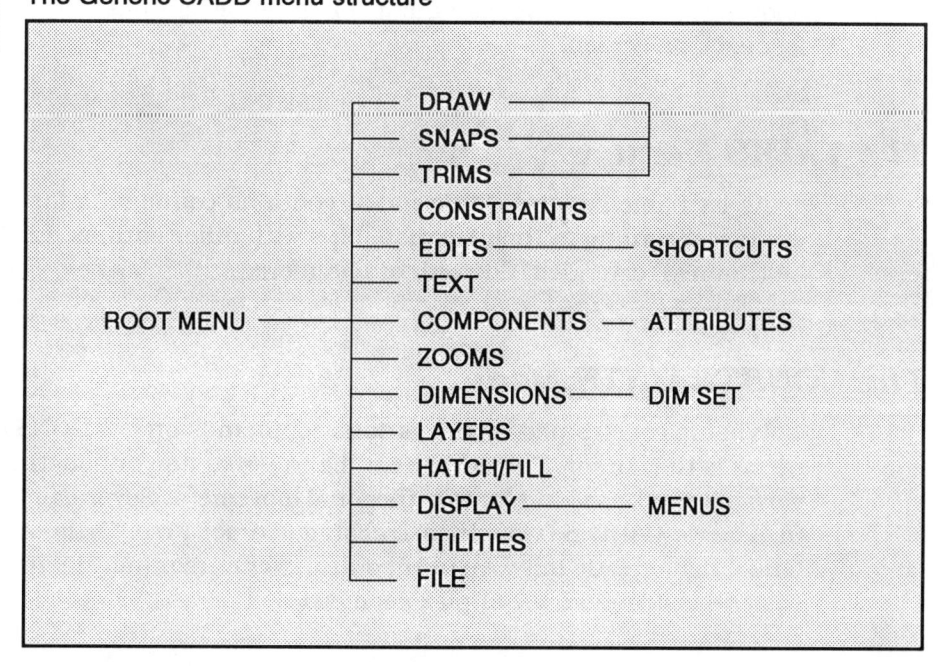

```
                        ┌── DRAW ──────────────
                        ├── SNAPS ─────────────
                        ├── TRIMS ─────────────
                        ├── CONSTRAINTS
                        ├── EDITS ──────── SHORTCUTS
                        ├── TEXT
        ROOT MENU ──────┼── COMPONENTS ── ATTRIBUTES
                        ├── ZOOMS
                        ├── DIMENSIONS ── DIM SET
                        ├── LAYERS
                        ├── HATCH/FILL
                        ├── DISPLAY ───── MENUS
                        ├── UTILITIES
                        └── FILE
```

that you will find there. Some submenus include items that give access to another level of submenus. Menu items that appear in upper- and lowercase text are commands, while menu items in all uppercase take you to other menus. Again, note that the words "ROOT MENU" appear at the bottom of most menus, so that you can always get back to where you started. Briefly, the menus that appear on the ROOT menu are arranged as follows.

The DRAW Menu

The DRAW menu consists of the commands used for placing all of the simple entities into your drawing. This is your principle means to add new information into your drawing.

The SNAPS Menu

The items on the SNAPS menu work together with other commands to aid in drawing construction. A wide variety of geometric functions are available, including midpoints, centers, parallels, perpendiculars, tangents, and so on. Generic CADD 5.0 improves on previous versions by allowing trimming and extending of multiple entities and enhanced feedback on screen.

The TRIMS Menu

As its name suggests, this menu contains commands for adjusting entities according to their relationships with other entities. Entities can be trimmed, extended, filletted, or chamfered.

The CONSTRAINTS Menu

What is constrained by the various commands on the CONSTRAINTS menu is the cursor. The cursor can be free-roaming or constrained to a variable sized grid, and/or to orthogonal movement. Several new features in Generic CADD 5.0, such as Tracking, Cursor Free, Ortho Angle, and Grid Origin greatly improve user control over cursor movement, allowing easier construction of complex geometries.

The EDITS Menu

All of the general-purpose editing commands are found on the EDITS menu. These commands allow the selection of multiple entities, using a variety of techniques, before the editing actually takes place. This menu also provides access to the editing SHORTCUTS menu, which gives streamlined editing commands for dealing with specific selection methods.

The TEXT Menu

Text placement and editing commands are found on the TEXT menu. These are divided into three groups, commands dealing specifically with Text Lines, those dealing with Text Characters, and finally the parameters that control both.

The COMPONENTS Menu

The COMPONENTS menu contains commands for creating and working with Components, the primary Generic CADD means of defining objects for replication. It also includes access to the ATTRIBUTES menu, which allows you to attach meaningful data to these objects.

The ZOOMS Menu

The commands on this menu control how much of the drawing is shown on the screen at any particular time. It includes commands for zooming in and out, fitting the whole drawing onto the screen, and other Zoom commands.

The DIMENSIONS Menu

The DIMENSIONS menu includes commands for placing dimensions into a drawing. The characteristics of these dimensions are controlled by a group of commands called the Dimension Settings on the DIM SET menu, accessed from the DIMENSIONS menu.

The LAYERS Menu

There are two different types of commands on the LAYERS menu. In the first group are "layer management" commands, which select the current layer, allow you to hide and display layers, and determine whether editing takes place on all layers or just the current layer. The second group of commands on this menu are editing "shortcuts," abbreviated versions of the most often-used editing commands streamlined for use specifically with layers.

The HATCH / FILL Menu

This menu includes commands for hatching and filling enclosed areas, and for setting the various parameters that control the operation of the various Hatch and Fill commands.

The DISPLAY Menu

Many of the characteristics of the video display menu can be found on this menu. These include toggling on and off the display of the various types of points, the format of coordinates, and the operation of several visualization aids. The first three items on this menu, on the other hand, control the entity creation parameters Line Color, Line Type, and Line Width. In previous versions of Generic CADD these parameters were on the LINES or the OBJECTS menu. This menu also provides access to the MENUS menu, for working with the video menu and an optional digitizer menu.

The UTILITIES Menu

On this menu, the Manual Entry commands (M E on the menu) control how manually typed coordinates are interpreted. The remaining commands are a grab bag of commands that don't seem to fit on any other menu. If you can't find the command you're looking for, look here.

The FILE Menu

The items on the FILE menu deal with saving your drawing to disk, retrieving files from disk, printing or plotting the drawing, and other functions related to disk access. The QUIT command for exiting Generic CADD 5.0 is found on this menu as well.

Two-Character Commands

In addition to the video menu, Generic CADD provides a second means of selecting commands—the keyboard. Every Generic CADD command can be activated by a simple two-character code. These codes can be used in place of or in combination with the video menu.

The two-character codes are, for the most part, mnemonic. One-word commands usually use two letters of the word, often the first two, such as LI for Line and PO for Point. Two-word commands often use the initials of the two words, such as ZA for Zoom All and DL for Drawing Load. A complete list of the two-character codes is shown in Appendix B. This list also classifies the commands into a number of types, which may help you to understand when each can or should be used.

Standard Abbreviations

To avoid confusion, Generic CADD uses certain characters to mean the same thing in different commands. The position of these characters (first or second keystroke) is also relatively consistent for certain types of commands.

First Character

In many cases, there is a direct relationship between the first character of the two-character command and the submenu on which the command is found. For example, all of the Zoom commands start with the letter Z.

As noted above, the abbreviation for Zoom All is ZA. Zoom In is ZI, Zoom Out is ZO, and so on. The only exception is the code for Pan, which is PA (because ZP is already used for Zoom Previous). Pan is a borderline Zoom command anyway, because it moves sideways instead of in and out.

All Component command codes begin with *C*, except for Component Snaps, which is GC. Again, the exception is little different in function from the rest because it could be considered a Control command (it controls whether or not construction points inside placed components can be accessed by other commands). The letters GC come from Generic's original working name for the command, Ghost Components. Explode Layer, XY, is considered a Layer command.

Similarly, the TEXT commands begin with the letter *T*, with the exception of the Font Select command. True to form, the exception in this case is quite different from the rest of the Text commands, and has its own distinct initials, FS. The other exception, Load ASCII, LA, is considered a Load shortcut.

Shortcuts dealing with OBJECTS begin with *O*, except for Move Point, which is abbreviated MP. Window shortcuts begin with *W*, and the Layer commands start with *Y*. Similarly, most of the Snap commands begin with *S*, and all three Manual Entry commands begin with *M*. Finally, the commands governing the display of various types of Points all start with the letter *P*.

Second Character

The second character is often used to distinguish among the commands of a certain family that share a common first character. Many of these second-character codes share common traits.

The letter *G* in the second position, for example, signifies a Change command. The letters *H* and *F* in this position stand for Hatch and Fill, respectively.

The actions of the editing shortcut commands are somewhat standardized by letter as well. Move is indicated by an *M* as the second character, and Copy is signified by a *C* in the second position. The letter *Z* always relates to Size or Scale, while *X* usually indicates Erase when found in this position, although there are some exceptions: Text Delete, for example, is TD, and the letter *X* is used by the dimensioning command as well.

Third Character

Many two-character commands bring up a prompt that asks you to enter a third character. This third character may allow you to select between several options, or, as is often the case, it may allow you to specify additional parameters before initiating the command. Many of the editing commands allow you to edit by a process called *selection* as you will see in the next section and in more detail in Chapter 10, "Advanced Drawing and Editing Techniques." This process involves pressing additional keys after the command has been initiated to specify how you want to *select* the entities. These keys are always standardized as *W* for Window, *O* for Object, *Y* for Layer, *D* for the whole Drawing, *L* for the Last Selection, and *F* for Filtered. Other commands use their own specified third-letter options, and you will be prompted for them.

Editing Shortcuts

A particular group of editing commands, including Move, Copy, and Erase, form an interesting pattern in this alphabet soup, called the *editing shortcuts*. They have a logical construction that makes them very easy to remember, so they will most likely be the two-character codes you learn first. This is fortunate because they are typically the most-used commands.

Nouns and Verbs

Within this structure, there are four different ways of selecting what you want to edit: Object, Window, Layer, or the whole Drawing. In the two-character code format, each of these is represented by a first-position character, standing for a *noun*: *O* for Object, *W* for Window, *Y* for Layer, and *D* for Drawing. A number of different actions, or *verbs*, can be combined with these nouns to create a command. These include *E* or *X* for Erase, *M* for Move, *C* for Copy, *R* for Rotate, *Z* for Scale, *I* for Mirror, and two nonediting actions, *L* for Load, and *S* for Save.

Combinations

From these four nouns and eight verbs, you can theoretically construct 32 different commands. Not all of the combinations are valid commands, but a majority of them are. See Table 2-1 for a complete matrix of the possibilities. This noun-verb construction of the editing commands

TABLE 2-1 Generic CADD Editing Shortcut Commands

Verbs \ Nouns	Chars	Object O	Window W	Layer Y	Drawing D
Erase	E X	OE	WE	YX	DX
Break	B	OB			
Copy	C	OC	WC		
Move	M	OM	WM		DO[a]
Mirror	I		WI		
Change	G	OG	WG	YG	DG
Rotate	R		WR	YR	DR
Re-Scale	Z		WZ	YZ	DZ
Load[b]	L			YL	DL
Save[b]	S			YS	DS

Notes: [a] The Drawing Re-Origin (DO) command performs the same function as would a Drawing Move

[b] Load and Save are not editing commands, but this table still applies

means that you don't have to memorize the codes but can, in most cases, create them extemporaneously by knowing what you want to edit and how you want to edit it.

How Shall I Command Thee? Let Me Count the Ways...

The two-character codes are really the heart of Generic's command structure, even though they appear to be quite separate from the video menu. In fact, when you select an item from the video menu, Generic CADD simply types the corresponding two-character code for you. Actually, commands can be issued in a number of ways.

Two-Character Commands

The two-character codes cannot be changed by the user. They have been, for the most part, consistent among various releases of Generic CADD, with some exceptions. Turn to Appendix B for a complete list of commands and two-character codes.

Prompt Line Options

As noted previously, you will often be prompted for an additional parameter or option after issuing a two-character command or selecting an item from the menu. These options can be selected in two ways. One character in each word or option will be highlighted. You can simply type this character on the keyboard. Alternately, you can use the pointing device to move a small block cursor to the option that you wish to select and press the first button on the pointing device. Note that the cursor does not have to be on the highlighted letter, but may be anywhere on the desired option or word. The ENTER key may also be emulated in many of these instances by pointing to and selecting with the first button the ENTER symbol (a bent arrow pointing left), which appears at the end of the prompt line. Finally, for many YES or NO questions, you will be given the option of pressing the first or second buttons on the pointing device as an alternative to typing a letter.

Video Menu

The video menu is really just a list of words that appear on the screen, with each word followed by a two-character command that is typed automatically when you select that word. This list is in an ASCII file, called CADDS.MNU or HELPS.MNU. This file can be rearranged if you like, and the words that appear on the menu can be changed. More than one command can be issued by a single selection from the menu and can be combined with user input. For example, the CONSTRAINTS menu, which allows you to select typical grid sizes, can be used to type more than one command. These commands are followed by a number which sets the grid size. See the user manual and Chapter 15 of this book for more information on the video menu.

Digitizer Menu

For users who have a digitizer, the tablet can be set up to issue commands in much the same way as the video menu. As a digitizer has no display, a grid of rectangles is defined on the tablet, and each rectangle is assigned a line of text, with a format similar to that of video menus. Several different gridded areas can be assigned simultaneously on the same tablet, and each can be activated independently. See the user manual, as well as Chapters 14 and 15 of this book for more information.

Function Keys

Using the Macro Assign command, multiple-command macros can be assigned to each of the function keys as well as to their SHIFT, ALT, and CTRL combinations. This can be an effective way to gain quick access to some of your most-used commands.

Pointing Device Buttons

Users who have a pointing device with more than two buttons can use the Macro Assign command to assign a macro command to each button beyond the first two. The third button of a three-button mouse is initially assigned the NP (Nearest Point) function.

Batch Files

ASCII files full of Generic CADD two-character commands, intermixed with pauses for user input can be created and loaded into any Generic CADD drawing and executed at any time. These commands can be used for automating certain procedures that occur regularly or for programming other software to produce batch files as output, allowing a method for Generic CADD drawings to be generated by nongraphic software. For more information see the user manual and Chapter 17 of this book.

Together with Chapter 1, this chapter gives you a good idea of what Generic CADD 5.0 does and how it compares conceptually with other drawing software that you may have used. You should now be able to recognize the various items on the Generic CADD screen and the various Generic CADD menus and commands.

CHAPTER 3

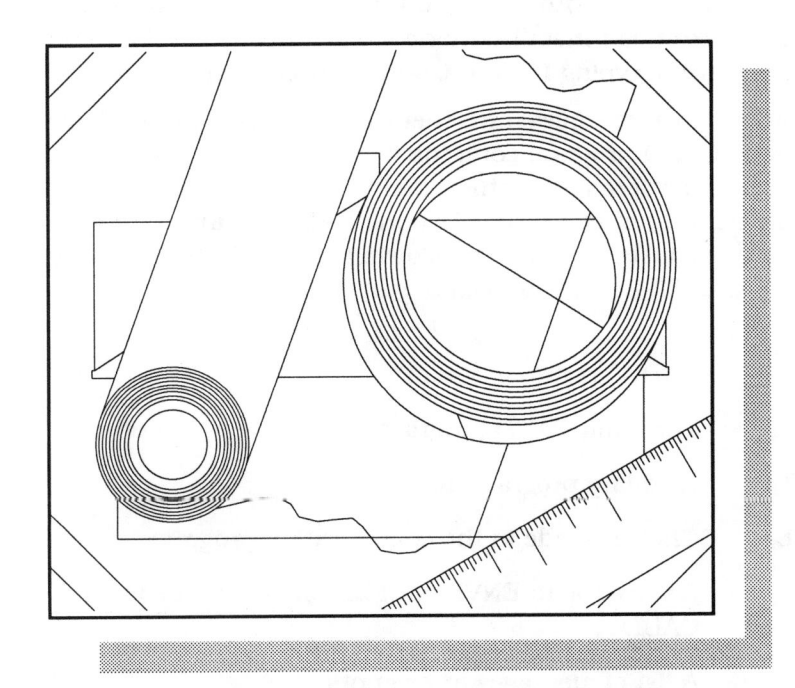

Preliminary Considerations

*B*efore you begin drawing, you still have several decisions to make: how you will set up the hardware and software; where your drawings are going to be stored; what type of unit system you are going to be using; how much area you are going to need for your drawing; and others.

Installing Generic CADD 5.0

Generic CADD 5.0 comes with a program that installs Generic CADD on your computer. You can install Generic CADD by putting the main program disk in drive A, typing **INSTALL**, and pressing ENTER.

The installation program copies the Generic CADD files onto your hard disk. The Generic CADD program contains a number of files, including files for fonts, hatch patterns, and other auxiliary files. If you are trying to minimize the amount of space that Generic CADD occupies on your disk after you have installed it, the following list includes the very minimum number of files that you need to run Generic CADD:

CADD.EXE	CADD startup program
GCADD.EXE	The main CADD program
GCADD.OVR	Auxiliary program file
CONFIG5.FIL	Choices made in the configuration program
CADD5.MNU	A video menu ENVIRON.FIL. Choices made inside CADD
MESSAGE	A list of messages or prompts
*.VGD	The video driver that you have selected
*.TPR	The printer driver that you have selected

Additionally, the following files are required to set up Generic CADD, or change the configuration:

Chapter 3: Preliminary Considerations

CONFIG.EXE	The configuration program
POINTERS.TDG	The pointer drivers
POINTERS.EXE	Pointer reference file
PLOTTERS.TPL	The plotter drivers
PLOTTERS.EXE	Plotter reference file
MESSAGE2	A list of messages or prompts for CONFIG.EXE
*.IPD	Pointing device drivers
*.TPR	Printer drivers
*.VGD	Video drivers
LGVIDEO.TVD	A list of image save video drivers
LGVIDEO.EXE	Large video drivers
SMVIDEO.TVD	A list of small video drivers
SMVIDEO.EXE	Small video drivers

The following files are required to take advantage of certain features of Generic CADD:

*.HCH	Hatch patterns
*.FNT	Font files; may be in any directory
MACROCMD.FIL	Text file containing macros assigned to function keys and pointer buttons

Finally, these files are created as you use Generic CADD:

*.WK1	Attributes in Lotus format
*.DWG	Drawing files

*.CMP	Component files
*.TXT	Batch files
*.GX2	Image files
*.ATB	Attributes
*.CSV	Attributes in ASCII comma-separated values
*.DPF	Plot files
*.PRF	Print files
*.DEV	PostScript device files
*.EPS	PostScript files for Ventura, PageMaker, and so on

Setting Up CADD to Run on Your Computer

When you install Generic CADD, all of the files are automatically placed in several directories on your hard disk. Note that running from floppy disks requires a 1.2 MB 5 1/4-inch drive or a 720K 3 1/2-inch drive to keep all of these files available at one time and must be installed manually.

Certain files are stored in subdirectories below the Generic CADD directory. There are six types of files that can be stored separately from the main program: fonts (.FNT), hatches (.HCH), menus (.MNU), batch files (.TXT), components (.CMP), and drawings (.DWG). CADD can find these files through the "default file paths," which can be set from within CADD.

Suppose, for example, that your Generic CADD 5.0 program files are in a directory called CADD5. You might want to keep your font files in a subdirectory called .FNT, your components in .CMP, and your drawings in .DWG. To do this, you need to create these three directories, place the files where they belong, and configure Generic CADD to look in the right directories for these files. You can either let the installation program create the directories for you, or you can do it yourself.

Creating Subdirectories

To create the directories, at the DOS prompt type **CD \CADD5** and press ENTER (use the name of your Generic CADD directory). When you see the DOS prompt again, type

MD DWG and press ENTER (creates a subdirectory called .DWG)

MD CMP and press ENTER (creates a subdirectory called .CMP)

MD FNT and press ENTER (creates a subdirectory called .FNT)

These commands create the subdirectories within the current directory (CADD5) that you will use to store the individual files. Subdirectories for Hatch (.HCH), Batch (.TXT), and Menu (.MNU) files can be created in the same way. Remember, these subdirectories may already exist if you used the INSTALL program.

Copying Files

If you have already installed Generic CADD without subdirectories, all of the font files will be in the main Generic CADD directory. If you wish to keep them separate, as suggested above, stay in the Generic CADD directory and type **COPY ∗.FNT FNT** and press ENTER. When all of the fonts have been copied to the FNT subdirectory, you may wish to delete them from the main directory.

If you have already made some drawings with Generic CADD, you probably saved them in the main Generic CADD directory. It is good practice to keep these files separate as well. To separate them from the program and copy them into their own directory, type **COPY ∗.DWG DWG** and press ENTER.

Any drawings that you have created, or that may have come as sample drawings on the Generic CADD distribution disks, are now copied into the .DWG subdirectory. To eliminate the duplicates in the current directory, you may wish to delete them after verifying the copy.

Similarly, to move any components that you may have made into their own directory, type **COPY ∗.CMP CMP** and press ENTER. Delete the components in the current directory if you wish.

These maneuvers should clear the main Generic CADD directory of any extraneous files that are not needed to run the program. Though the program will run satisfactorily even with these extra files, separating these files creates a cleaner environment for troubleshooting if something goes wrong. Again, all of this can be avoided by using the INSTALL program properly.

Configuration Options

The important configuration options are a Video Graphics Card, Pointing Device, and Drawing Unit. The printer and/or plotter are selected from within Generic CADD, and the memory variables are set automatically. The CONFIGURATION menu is shown in Figure 3-1.

If you haven't tried some of the options that might work with your system, don't be afraid to experiment. If you have an EGA clone, for instance, try the VESA drivers. Your card might work at a higher resolution than you think. Several pointing device drivers work with the

FIGURE 3-1 The Generic CADD 5.0 configuration screen

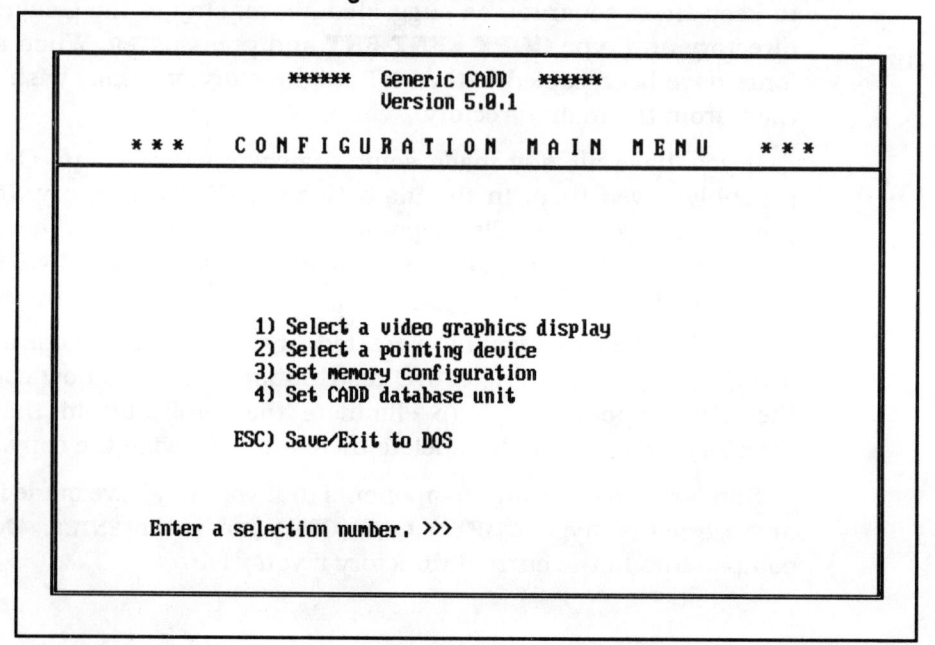

```
            ****** Generic CADD ******
                    Version 5.0.1

      ***    CONFIGURATION  MAIN  MENU    ***




                1) Select a video graphics display
                2) Select a pointing device
                3) Set memory configuration
                4) Set CADD database unit

             ESC) Save/Exit to DOS



        Enter a selection number. >>>
```

Logitech mouse, and the MOUSE.COM drivers let you set the sensitivity. If you are having trouble with your mouse, try unplugging it from the computer and then plugging it back in again. Your mouse might have a memory that gets programmed by the driver and can't forget what you tell it until you turn off the power.

Starting Generic CADD 5.0

As you discovered in Chapter 2, "The Generic Approach," Generic CADD is not a program in which you work your way through various menu screens. For the most part, the program looks the same the entire time you are running it. Of course, there are a few exceptions, such as the copyright and configuration screen that appears when you first start up and the inquiry screens that are available for looking up files.

Loading a Drawing

Starting Generic CADD and loading a drawing file are almost identical processes. You cannot really start Generic CADD without specifying a new or existing drawing file. If you don't, CADD assumes that you are working on a drawing called UNTITLED.DWG.

As a shortcut, you can simply follow the word CADD with the name of the drawing file that you want to load. For example, typing **CADD BOOKCASE** loads Generic CADD and brings up the drawing called BOOKCASE.DWG. You don't have to type .DWG because Generic CADD can only load files that have the extension .DWG, so it is therefore assumed.

If the file BOOKCASE does not exist, Generic CADD will simply start a new drawing with this name.

Loading from Other than the Default Directory

Since Generic CADD uses a "default directory" to look for drawing files, it sometimes cannot find the drawing that you are trying to load. This may happen when you want to load a drawing from a disk, or any time your drawing is located on a drive or directory that is not on the default drawing path. In these instances, you will need to type the full pathname of the drawing file that you are trying to load. For example, typing **A:CHAIR** is the proper way to identify a drawing that is called CHAIR.DWG on the A drive, and **\CADD5\HOUSE\PLAN1** is the required pathname for a drawing called PLAN1.DWG that is in the subdirectory HOUSE under the CADD5 directory, when DWG is the default drawing path.

Another way to go about loading these files is to change the default drawing path (from inside Generic CADD 5.0) before attempting to load these drawings. Changing default drawing paths can save a lot of needless typing if you frequently work on drawings from the same directory. For more information on default paths, see Chapter 15 "Customizing Generic CADD 5.0."

Beginning a New Drawing

Even when you start from scratch with a blank screen, you may specify a *filename*—the name of the file in which the drawing will be stored if you elect to keep it. Filenames can be up to eight characters and must not include any spaces, or certain other characters, such as * or ?. An underscore is a good substitute for a space if you really need one. Think of a name that has significance to your drawing. If nothing else comes to mind, type **TRY1**, so that you can distinguish it from your next one, which you might call TRY2, and so on.

Notice that if you try to start a new drawing using the same filename as an existing one, the existing drawing is simply called up instead. You must erase the existing file either before starting the drawing or when it is loaded by Generic CADD.

First Things First

You probably want to start drawing right away, which is natural, but you still have a few more tasks; doing these tasks before you start will make drawing a lot easier later.

Many of the topics that we cover in this section are configurable options, which can be set permanently once you know how you want them set when you start a drawing.

Selecting a Unit System

The unit system controls how coordinates are displayed at the top of the screen, as well as how they are interpreted when you type them as dimensions in response to Generic CADD prompts for information. The CONFIG program determines what kind of units will be stored in the database, but you may want to use a different system for display and your own input.

Two primary unit systems are available, and several variations within these. The Units (UN) command is a "parameter setting" (see Appendix B for a complete list of all the commands and an explanation of how they might be divided into types). A *parameter* is a variable value that controls how other commands work. In the case of the Units command, selecting a specific option sets the parameter to a specific value or setting. These parameter settings are distinct from *toggles*, which turn something on when you select them the first time, and then turn it off when you select them again. These parameter settings might be considered "one-way toggles," or "mode" settings; that is, they only switch on, and they stay on unless you select contradictory settings. If you select M, for example, you are choosing millimeters as your unit system. If you select M again, you are still working in millimeters. If you select I, you are switching to inches. As many times as you select I, you can never return to millimeters unless you select M. When we come to the discussion of toggles in the next chapter, you'll understand the importance of these rules.

For your primary unit system, you can choose one of the following options from the Units command:

Meters	(S)
Centimeters	(C)
Millimeters	(M)
Feet	(T)

Feet/Inches   (F)

Inches   (I)

Position the menu cursor over the word Units on the DISPLAY menu and press the second pointing device button. Then move the menu cursor over the option that you wish to select and press the first button. An alternative method is to type the two-character command code on the keyboard (you do not need to press ENTER) and the letter for the option that you want.

If you do not choose a unit system, whichever system is configured will be used by default. If you have never configured for any particular unit system, you will use whatever parameter was configured on the factory-release disk, probably Inches. To follow along with the examples in this chapter, select Inches for your unit system now.

It is important to notice that you can change unit systems whenever you like, and that changing your units does not change the size of your drawing or the scale of your objects in any way. Objects are always drawn at real size, and stored in the database using the default units, even though the units that you use to measure or describe them may change. It is not a problem, then, to create your drawing using Feet and Inches, and later change to one of the metric formats for dimensioning; this is one of Generic CADD's convenient features.

You can also control the level of accuracy of the units. If you use a unit system that involves inches, you can choose to display fractional parts of an inch as fractions or as decimals. The command Numeric Format controls these parameter settings.

To change any of the parameters governing the display of coordinates, select the Num Format command from the DISPLAY menu or type **NF** on the keyboard. You will be presented with a list of options in the prompt area. Each of these can be selected either with the prompt cursor and the first button on the pointing device or by typing an appropriate letter, which will be highlighted on the menu. Some of the options will vary depending on the setting of other parameters. When you are done making changes to the Numeric Format, press ENTER to exit the command. Note that the format specified here is used by the Dimension and Measure commands as well as by the coordinate display.

Angular

This option controls the way that partial angles are displayed. The choices are Degrees, to a number of places specified by the Decimal Value option of this command, and DEG:MIN:SEC, in which Degrees, Minutes, and Seconds are shown, to integer values only. As a toggle, each time that you select it from the prompt or type its letter, **A**, it reverses its status.

Linear

This option controls whether partial units of distances and lengths are displayed in fractional or decimal formats, and only applies to unit formats Feet, Inches, and Feet/Inches. All metric formats are always displayed in decimal format.

As a toggle, this option switches back and forth between Decimal and Fractions every time that you pick it from the prompt or type its letter, **L**. Also, the prompt option following this one on the menu changes depending on the setting of this parameter. If Linear format is set to Fractions, the next option will be Fractional Value, so that you can specify the smallest fraction that you want to display. If this option is set to Decimal, the following option will be Decimal Value, so that you can specify how many digits you wish to display beyond the decimal point.

Fractional Value

This option sets the smallest fraction that will be displayed as a partial unit in Feet, Inches, and Feet/Inches formats. When you select it from the prompt or press **F**, you will be asked to specify a new value. The number that you type will become the smallest allowable denominator for fractional displays, and must be a power of 2, from 2 to 64. For example, if you type 16, the smallest allowable fraction will be 1/16th of a unit. These make the most sense in Inches and Feet/Inches formats.

> *Note* Keep in mind that this is a Display parameter, and does not in any way constrain actual drawing data to any limit that you might set here. In fact, setting Fraction Value too low may result in misleading displays that make you think that your data is more accurate than it is.

To limit the actual data itself, always draw with Snap to Grid turned on.

Decimal Value

This option sets the number of places after the decimal point that will be displayed. This parameter always applies to metric units and angles measured in degrees, and also applies to Feet, Inches, and Feet/Inches when Linear is set to Decimal.

When you select this option from the prompt or type **D** during a Numeric Format command, you will be prompted for a new Decimal Precision. Allowable values are between 0 and 6. The number that you specify will be the number of places to the right of the decimal point that will be displayed, even if they are zeros. Note that this option is always available by typing **D** after initiating an NF command, even if it is not shown in the prompt. Even when Units is set to Inches, and Linear is Fractions, this parameter still controls the display of angles measured in degrees, for example, so you might still need to set it. The DV command from previous versions is still available as well.

Leading Zeros

This option controls the use of zeros on the left side of the decimal point, in the case of decimal displays, and the display of zero feet or inches in fractional displays. As with the other options in this group, you activate it by selecting it from the prompt or by typing its letter, in this case, **Z**. The current value is always shown in the Numeric Format prompt.

The following are examples of values that might be displayed with Leading Zeros turned on and off:

Leading Zeros On	Leading Zeros Off
0.1456m	.1456m
0' 10 1/2"	10 1/2"
0 1/16"	1/16"
0' 0 1/2"	1/2"
10.0000mm	10.0000mm

There is no change in the last example, as this option only deals with Leading Zeros, not Trailing Zeros. To get rid of the extra zeros in the last example, change the Decimal Value to zero.

Show Units

Another Numeric Format toggle, Show Units, simply determines whether or not the unit designator is used in the display or not. It is toggled on or off by choosing it from the prompt or by typing the letter **S** on the keyboard. The following are examples of values that might be displayed with Show Units turned on and off:

Show Units On	**Show Units Off**
0.114300m	0.114300
-1 3/4"	-1 3/4
1.75'	1.75
3/16'	3/16
1' 6"	1' 6"

Note once again that there is no change in the final example. This time, it's because when you use the Feet/Inches format, the units always show up to avoid confusion. Otherwise, what would be the difference between the display of one inch and one foot if Leading Zeros was turned off? Without the inch and foot marks, they would display the same thing. So, you can't turn off the display of units in Feet/Inches format. Notice also that the next to the last example is a little bizarre, in that you don't usually think of feet as being divided into sixteenths. This is the mixture of Feet format with Fraction display mentioned earlier. If you've got this kind of an application, fine; otherwise, avoid this combination. It is bound to confuse.

Defining the Drawing Space

Next on the agenda is the question of how much drawing space you need. This is in some ways a meaningless question, because Generic

CADD can handle both very large and very small numbers; you can draw objects almost any size. In addition, Generic CADD has built-in features to adjust both the display and the printed image to the objects in the drawing.

However, you might be a bit uneasy about looking at a blank screen and wondering how much space is represented there. Keep in mind that once you have drawn an object of a certain size, the amount of space on the screen will become clear, by comparison to the object that you have drawn. But where do you start?

Generic CADD uses a concept called "limits" to determine the size of the drawing area. The idea of limits is to make drawing more convenient, and does not impose any special constraints on the use of Generic CADD. You are free to draw outside the limits, if you like, with no penalty or undue hardship. Defining the limits of the drawing area is like creating an imaginary dotted line around a certain amount of space, and saying, "This is about how much room I need for this drawing." The limits are defined by two numbers—the height and the width—and can be changed as often as you like.

In some ways, setting the limits for your drawing is like choosing the paper size when you are drawing by hand. This comparison is somewhat strained, however, and can often be misleading. The limits are measured in the units of the objects that you are drawing, not in the scaled units of the final output. In other words, your limits can be measured in hundredths or even thousandths of feet, while the piece of paper on which the drawing is printed might be only 24" x 36". Also, the paper analogy implies that the limits are more restrictive than they actually are. When drawing by hand, if you run off the edge of the paper, you end up drawing on the desk. With Generic CADD, drawing outside the limits has no similar repercussions.

A good rule of thumb for setting limits is to make them a little larger (perhaps 25 to 50 percent larger) than the object in the drawing. If you are going to draw a typical office workstation, for example, with a desk, chair, and work table, you might set the limits at 12' x 12', allowing plenty of work space. You would do this by selecting Limits from the UTILITIES menu or by typing **LS** on the keyboard. Generic CADD will show the defaults for the height and width and ask you for new values. When asked for each, type **12'** and press ENTER. Notice that if you just typed **12** and pressed ENTER, your input would be interpreted as 12 inches, because Inches is our currently selected unit system, so you must add the foot mark ('). Also note that the lower-left corner of the limits is assumed to be located at the origin, 0,0, and that your values become not only the height and width of the limits, but the upper limits of the coordinates as well.

Adjusting the Display

While we have set the drawing limits as 12 feet x 12 feet, the screen has not changed. Generic CADD now knows your drawing limits but hasn't been asked to do anything about it.

The commands that control how much of the drawing is displayed on the screen are the Zoom commands. You will learn these in detail later, once you have a drawing on the screen, but for now one command is particularly useful—the Zoom Limits (ZL) command. This command adjusts the display so that the Limits you have set with the previous command are shown on the screen.

You can execute this command by selecting Limits from the ZOOM menu or by typing **ZL** on the keyboard. Apart from a flash of the display—which may happen so quickly that you don't see it—the screen shows no apparent change, even though, in fact, it has changed. If you move the drawing cursor around now and look at the coordinate area, you'll notice that the Y coordinate ranges between 0 at the bottom of the screen and 12' 0" at the top of the screen (approximately). If you do not see these coordinates, type **DC** on the keyboard, or select Coordinates from the DISPLAY menu, and then press **A** to activate Absolute Coordinates.

You might wonder why the X coordinates are not constrained by the same range. The reason is that your monitor probably has greater width than height. Generic CADD simply adds the "leftover" space on the right side of the screen to the drawing area.

You now know that the height shown on the screen represents 12 feet, and the width a little more than 12 feet. Now you need only do a few more things before you start drawing.

Turning on the Grid

Generic CADD 5.0 provides a grid that is similar to the graph paper often used when drawing by hand. The grid allows you to visualize the size of a unit more easily, and can be used to provide a certain level of accuracy.

To try this feature, type **GS** or select Grid Size from the CONSTRAINTS menu. You are shown the current (default) grid size and asked to specify a new one. Type **12** (for 12 inches) or **1'**, press ENTER twice, and you will see a grid displayed on the screen, in which the dots are 12 inches apart in both the horizontal (X) and vertical (Y) directions. You now have an additional visual cue to use when making your drawing. The screen should be divided into 12 spaces vertically and about 15 spaces horizontally, depending on the proportional resolution of your video card and monitor. Whenever you change the grid size, the grid is automatically turned on, whether it was on before you changed the size or not. Figure 3-2 shows the Generic CADD screen with the 12-inch grid.

If you like, you can show the grid spacing on the screen, rather than typing the value. When asked for the new Grid Size, type **D** (for Distance) on the keyboard instead of typing a number. You will be asked to place two points. The distance between the two points will be measured and used as the new X Grid Size. Set the Y Grid Size in the same way, or by typing a number, or by simply pressing ENTER to make it the same as the X Grid Size. If you want to know what the Grid Size has been set to, simply use the same command again, from the menu, the keyboard, or by pressing the SPACEBAR. You will be asked for the new Grid Size and shown the default, which will be the value that you have just shown on the screen. If you are just checking, press either ESC or ENTER.

You can use this same technique with many of the commands that ask for a size or distance. If you are unsure, try typing **D** on the keyboard. If nothing happens, you cannot show a distance but must type a value instead.

Using the Grid

The grid can be used simply as a visual device, or it can be used to control the actual points that are input with the pointing device. Move the drawing cursor around the screen, and you will see that the grid is just like a transparent overlay: It has no effect on cursor movement or the coordinates that appear at the top of the screen. However, if you type **SG** or select Snap to Grid from the CONSTRAINTS menu, you'll see that the movement of the cursor is now tied to the grid, as shown in Figure 3-3. Each time you move the cursor, it jumps to the next grid point. The coordinate display at the top of the screen reflects this condition: both X and Y are shown in even inches with no fractions.

If you type **SG** or select Snap to Grid again, cursor movement is "freed" from the grid, and the coordinates again begin to show all of the inches and fractions of inches between grid points. The Snap to Grid (SG) command is, as we can see, a toggle: Selecting it once creates one condition; selecting it again creates the opposite condition. Many of the toggles turn something on or off. Snap to Grid is an example of this type of toggle. If Snap to Grid is on, selecting the command will turn it off. If it is off, selecting Snap to Grid will turn it on.

FIGURE 3-2 The grid appears as dots on the screen

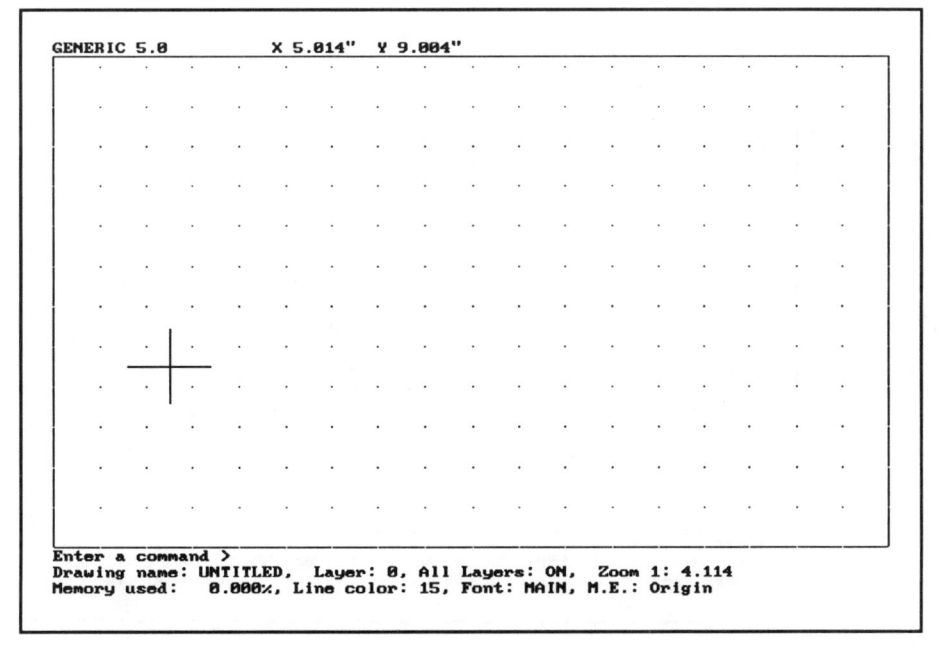

For now, turn Snap to Grid on so you can see how it is used. Change the grid size to 6 (select Grid Size or type **GS**, type **6**, and press ENTER twice). The cursor now jumps six inches in both horizontal and vertical directions. The grid then, together with Snap to Grid, can be used to control the level of accuracy of cursor movement and entry of point data. Snap to Grid continues to work even if the grid itself is not displayed, which you can verify by selecting Grid On/Off or by typing **GR** from the CONSTRAINTS menu.

You may think that Snap to Grid is an option that you turn on only when you need it. On the contrary, to preserve the precision of your drawing (and CADD drawings are always precise, whether they are accurate or not), you should leave Snap to Grid turned on most of the time, and turned off only when it gets in the way. Chances are, if the point you want to select is not on the grid, the spacing of the grid is just too large. Rather than turning off Snap to Grid, make the grid size smaller. The CONSTRAINTS menu contains a number of commonly used grid sizes that can be selected directly from the menu. If you use other

FIGURE 3-3 With Snap to Grid turned on, the cursor "sticks" to the grid

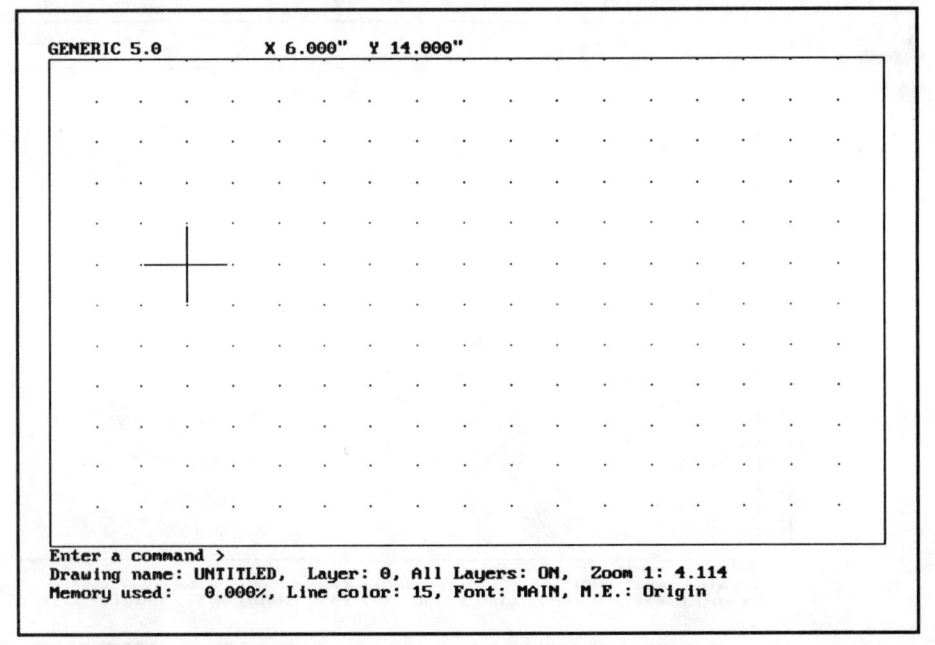

grid sizes frequently, these can be added to the menu (see Appendix A of the Generic CADD manual and Chapter 14 of this book for instructions).

Setting the Current Drawing Parameters

Numerous commands set parameters that determine the attributes of new entities placed into the drawing. For example, if the current line color is 2, all new entities drawn will be color 2. The current line color is set by the Line Color command, which is selected from the DISPLAY menu or by typing the two-character code **LK**.

Other similar parameter-setting commands include the Line Type (LT) and Line Width (LW) commands, also listed on the DISPLAY menu. Each of these commands sets attributes that are picked up by all new entities created. Each of these commands also activates a special display in the video menu area that shows examples of these attributes that you can select. See Figures 3-4 and 3-5 for illustrations of the Line Type and Line Width menus. Again, your display might be slightly different, depending on your graphics card. If you are configured for a color system, the Line Color command will also bring up a similar special menu display. None of these special menu displays will be shown if the video menu is currently turned off.

You may set any of these three parameters by choosing from the examples shown using the menu cursor and the second pointing device button, or you may type a number and press ENTER. The range of allowable values for these parameters is shown in the prompt area at the bottom of the screen. For Line Color, values from 0 to 255 are available, no matter how many colors can actually be generated by your graphics card. If you have, for example, 16 colors, colors 0 through 15 will be as shown on the Line Color menu, and these same 16 colors repeat for numbers 16 to 31, 32 to 47, and so on.

Line Types vary from 0 to 255 as well, and the first 10 (0 to 9) are shown on the special video menu display when you select the command. However, these Line Types do not repeat in the same way as the colors. Line Types 0 to 9 always look the same, no matter how much you zoom in or out or at what scale you print or plot your drawing. These might be considered "hardware" line types, that is, the length of the dashes is tied to the display or printed output rather than the real size of the drawing.

The Line Type menu

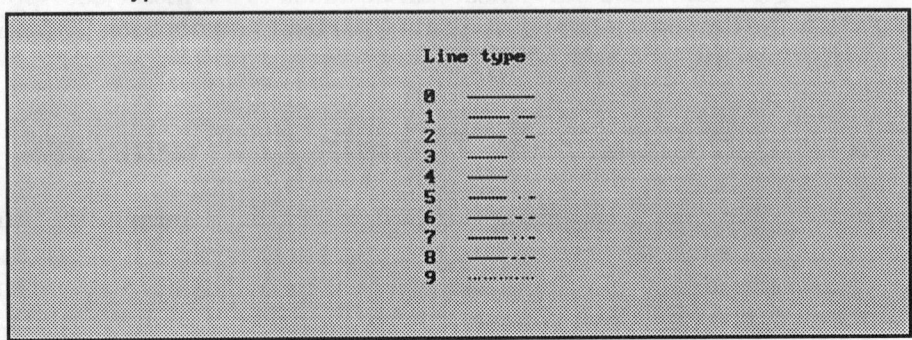

FIGURE 3-4

Line Types 10 to 19, on the other hand, can be scaled to the objects that you are drawing. The distance from the start of one dash to the start of the next dash is controlled by the Line Scale (LZ) command, also listed on the LINES menu. The default value for Line Scale is 1, or one dash per inch, unless you change the Line Scale.

When you change the Line Scale, the space between the dashes in Line Types 10 to 19 changes as well. A Line Scale of 2 means one dash every two inches. More complex Line Types, such as number 17 (which looks like number 7, but is scalable), may be composed of more than one size of dash. In these cases, the entire pattern of dashes repeats according to

The Line Width menu

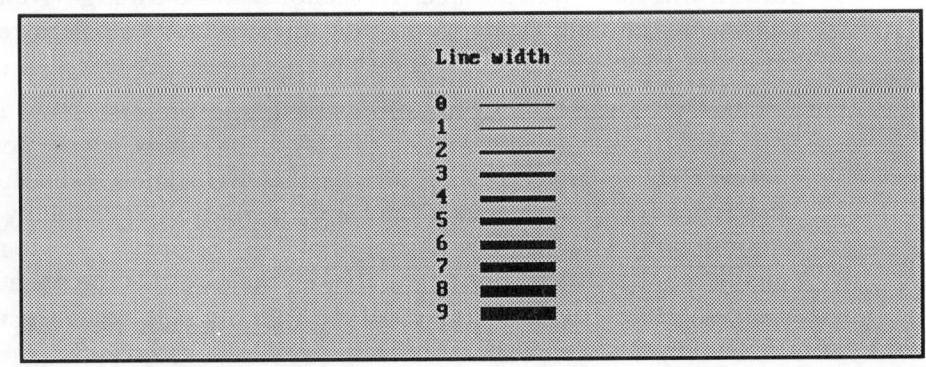

FIGURE 3-5

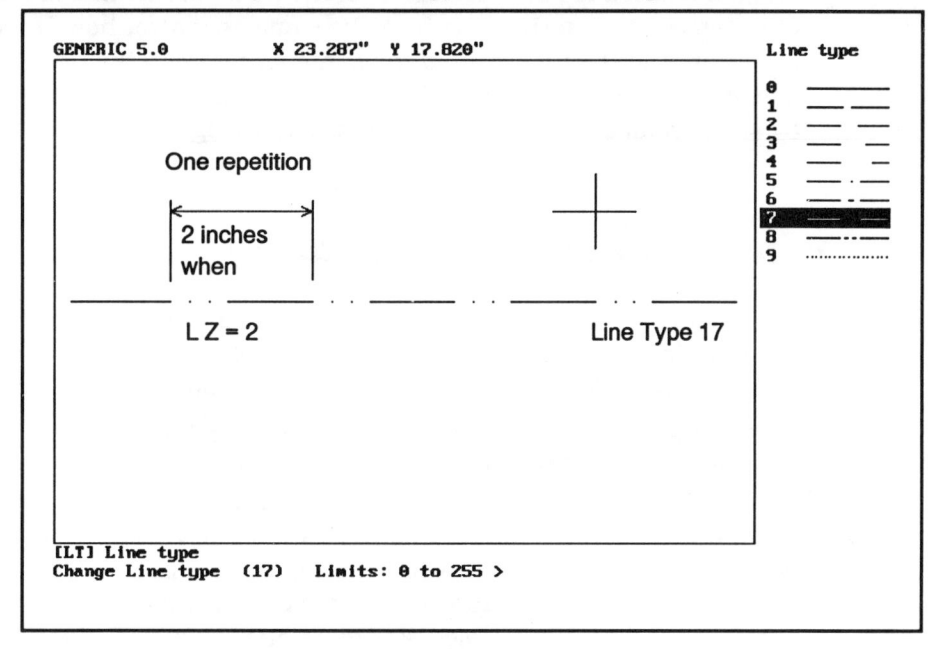

FIGURE 3-6 One repetition of any scaled Line Type is one unit long

the module specified by the Line Scale. With the Line Scale set at 2 and Line Type at 17, one long dash and two short ones would appear every two inches, as shown in Figure 3-6.

You may want to use lines that have the same pattern at different scales. Line Types 20 to 255 are provided for this purpose. Line Types 20 to 29 are the same as 10 to 19, but twice as long, while Line Types 30 to 39 are three times as long. In other words, with a line scale of 1, the dash interval within a line of Line Type 22 will be 2 units, while the interval for Line Type 32 will be 3 units. If the Line Scale is changed to 2, the line will consist of one dash every four inches in Line Type 22 and one dash every six inches in a line of type 32. Lines that use types 0 to 9 will not be affected by the Line Scale.

Fortunately, Line Width is not nearly as complex because only the ten options shown on the screen are available. However, the actual width does vary with your display or output device because the width of the line is measured in dots. On the screen, this means pixels, while on the printer it translates to print elements (pins). On a plotter, each incremental Line Width adds another stroke of the pen. Line Widths are similar to Line Types 0 to 9 in that they look the same no matter how far you zoom in or out, and they are plotted the same no matter which plot scale you use. A Line Width of 3 translates to three strokes of the plotter pen, side by side, no matter what the scale of the drawing.

Choosing the Layer for Drawing

Just as you set the Line Color, Line Type, and Line Width before you draw anything, you also select the layer on which you want to draw. The default is layer 0, but you have another 255 from which to choose.

To draw on any layer other than 0, use the Current Layer (or Layer Current) command from the LAYERS menu, or type **YC** on the keyboard. Generic CADD indicates the current layer and asks you to type the new current layer. Type a number between 0 and 255 and press ENTER. Any new entities that you create will then appear on this layer. You may also select from the list that appears in the video menu by using the second button on the pointing device. For more on this special video menu, see Chapter 16.

The current layer has one quality that the other current drawing parameters don't have: Editing can be limited to this layer as well. Generic CADD allows you to edit either on the current layer only, or on all visible layers, using the All Layers command (AL) from the LAYERS menu. All Layers is a true toggle—each time you select it, it reverses its status, from Edit All Layers Off to Edit All Layers On and back again.

Coordinate Display Modes

The coordinates at the top of the screen, as you have seen, are in the format specified by the current unit system and Numeric Format. You can also control where they are measured from, and how they are measured.

The Coordinates command on the DISPLAY menu controls the coordinate display mode. This command can also be activated by typing **DC** on the keyboard. A number of options in the prompt line accompany this command, which can be selected either with the first button on the pointing device or by pressing the letter highlighted in the prompt.

The first of these options, also called Coordinates, controls whether coordinates are displayed in X,Y format or Polar format. X,Y format gives you a horizontal and a vertical component, while Polar supplies a distance and an angle. Each may be useful under different circumstances. The character for this toggle is C. Note, that as with each of these options, the current status is shown in the prompt.

The remaining three options determine where the coordinates, X,Y or Polar, are measured from. Each is toggled by selecting it from the prompt or by pressing its letter, **A** for Absolute Coordinates, **R** for Relative Coordinates, or **B** for Basepoint Coordinates. Note that only one of these can be active at one time, so if you turn any of the three on, it turns the other two off. If you turn them all off, no coordinates will be displayed.

The effect of all four of these options is immediate. The coordinates are updated even before you leave the command, so you can make sure you've got the one you want. Relative Coordinates are identified by a small triangle in the coordinate area, Basepoint Coordinates by a small diamond, and Absolute Coordinates have no symbol, being the closest thing to actual database coordinates. For more information on coordinates, see Chapter 6, "Drawing Aids and Controls." For now, set your coordinates to X,Y and Absolute, then press ENTER to exit the command.

You will find that different types of coordinates have different uses, and you may want to change back and forth between these types fairly frequently. Whichever you use most often, especially at the beginning of a drawing session, can be configured to be in effect automatically every time you load Generic CADD. As you begin to draw, you'll need to be aware of which coordinate display is currently on. The Delta Coordinates are marked with small triangles (resembling the Greek letter delta) in front of the X and Y at the top of the screen.

Manual Entry of Coordinates

Just as the display of coordinates can be set relative to the origin or the last point, so can the keyboard or manual entry of coordinates.

You can type Absolute Coordinates of points by selecting the M E Origin command on the UTILITIES menu, or by typing **MO** on the keyboard. This is the default mode for manual entry of coordinate data. Whenever you type a set of X and Y coordinates, it is assumed that you mean them to be measured from the origin, 0,0.

Many times, however, it is much more convenient to type the distance from the last point entered (because you happen to know it), rather than figuring out how far it is from the origin. This mode of manual entry can be selected with the M E Relative command on the UTILITIES menu, or by typing **MR** on the keyboard. Now, whenever you type coordinate data, your X and Y values are assumed to be measured from the last point entered. This method is appropriate for situations when you know the length of a line or the distance that you want to move or copy something. If you are just starting your drawing and there is no last point, the first point specified in this mode will be relative to the origin, 0,0.

One more manual entry mode is available. Sometimes you may want to measure entities from a particular point in the drawing, other than the origin. You can place the basepoint at this location (with the Set Basepoint (BP) command on the UTILITIES menu), and then select M E Basepnt from the UTILITIES menu, or type **MB** on the keyboard. All subsequent manual entry will use this basepoint as its reference.

All Manual Entry commands are one-way toggles, or, in other words, parameter-setting commands. Each one forces all manual entry to be in its own mode, no matter which mode was previously active. There is no state in which all modes are off, as there is no way to turn off a particular manual entry mode other than selecting a different one.

Once again, each mode has a variety of uses, and you will use these commands frequently as you draw and edit. When you start your first line, M E Origin works well because there is no last point from which to measure. As you develop the drawing, M E Relative and M E Basepnt become more valuable, although M E Origin may still be used. M E Relative is particularly useful with the editing commands, such as Move and Copy. For now, leave manual entry set to Origin.

There is an undocumented method for manual entry that may be helpful in certain instances. It works the same way no matter which manual entry mode you are in, although it acts most like Relative mode.

Insiders at Generic Software call it "Direct Distance" manual entry, and it works almost any time that you are asked for a point.

Direct Distance is employed simply by moving the cursor from any point previously specified in the direction of the next point that you want. Once the cursor is located at the new point, type a number (let's use 3) and press ENTER. No need to press a pointing device button. The new point will be located 3 units away from the last point (or whichever number you typed), in the direction you moved the cursor. This method works best when Ortho Mode is turned on, so that you can be sure of the angle between the last point and the cursor, when dimensional accuracy is important but angular accuracy is not.

While we have not yet actually discussed drawing, the information in this chapter, together with the preceding conceptual material in the first two chapters, has laid the groundwork for the real task at hand. Many of the commands introduced in this chapter will come to be among those you will most commonly use. In subsequent chapters, we will expand on the ideas discussed here, utilizing them to quickly get started with a variety of drawing tasks. As you will see, Generic CADD 5.0 offers a number of other drawing aids, which will be introduced as the complexity of the drawing examples increases.

CHAPTER 4

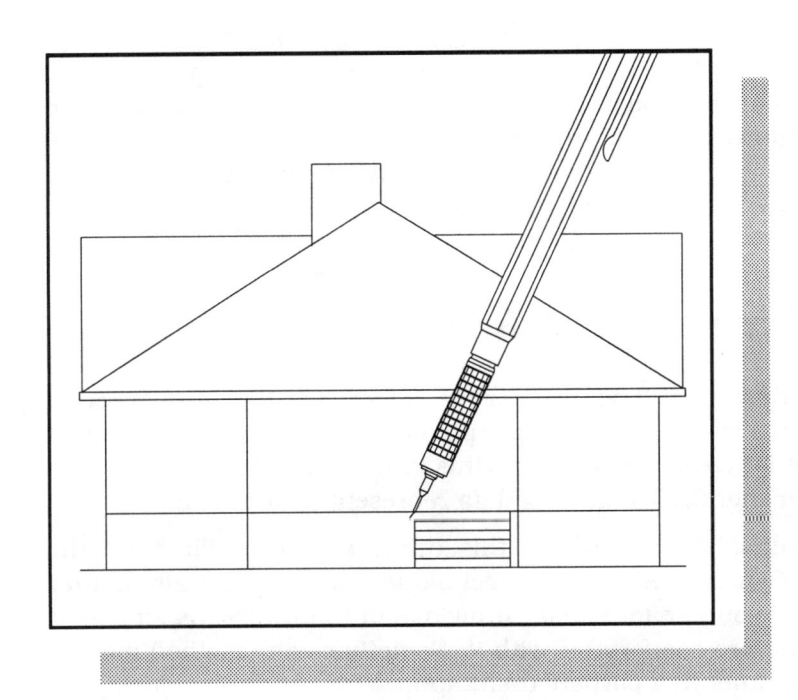

Basic Drawing Tasks

This chapter introduces Generic CADD's entity drawing commands and a number of basic drawing techniques through several simple drawing examples. If you do these examples on your computer, you will better learn the commands and also end up with some simple drawing files for use in later chapters. You will also be able to try some of the parameters and drawing aids that were discussed in previous chapters, as well as a few new ones.

If you are following along with Generic CADD, just pick up where you left off in the last chapter. If you are starting from scratch, call up CADD and start a new drawing, select Inches for your units, set your Limits at 12' x 12', and turn on a 12" grid. Make sure that Snap to Grid is on by typing **SG**. If you get the message "Snap to Grid is OFF," type **SG** again. If you get "Snap to Grid is ON," make sure that you have Absolute Coordinates on too. If you are uncertain, select Coordinates from the DISPLAY menu or type **DC**. At the prompt, type **A** for Absolute. It won't matter whether it is already on; this will make sure that it is.

Your First Drawing: A Room

Your first drawing will be the floor plan of an eight-by-ten-foot room, as shown in Figure 4-1. Drawing floor plans may not be exactly what you have in mind for Generic CADD, but this kind of practical example acts as a reminder that CADD drawing data represents real information.

Several methods are used for this drawing task to illustrate the flexibility of Generic CADD input techniques. It doesn't really matter which method you use for similar drawings in the future, as long as it works and you are comfortable with it. Sometimes one method may be faster than another in a particular situation.

Drawing a Rectangle

The simplest way to draw a rectangle is with the Rectangle command. From the ROOT menu, go to the DRAW menu by positioning the menu cursor over the word "DRAW" and pressing the second button on the

FIGURE 4-1 The first drawing: an eight-by-ten-foot room

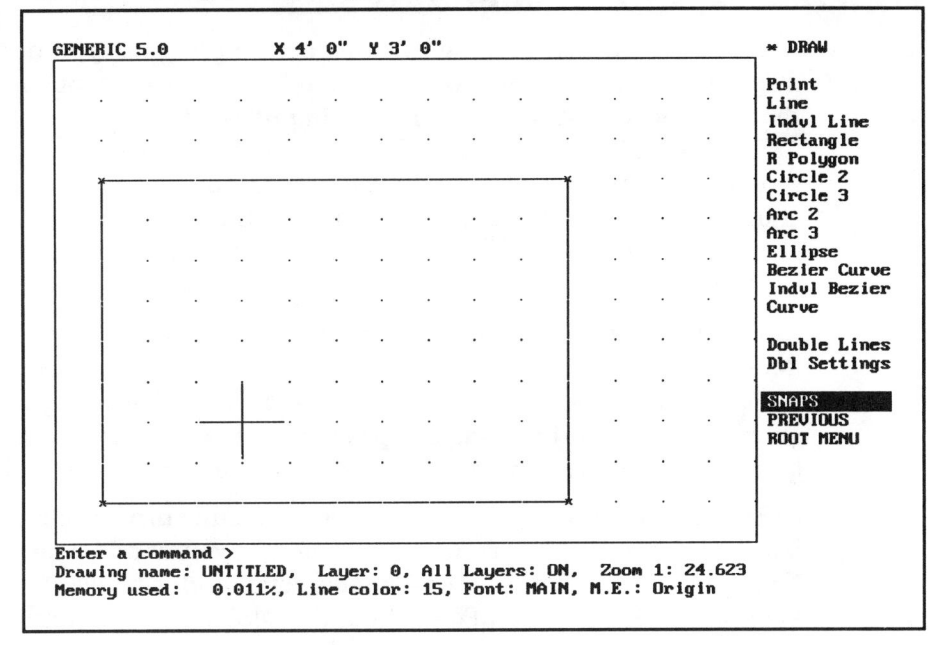

```
GENERIC 5.0          X 4' 0"   Y 3' 0"                    * DRAW
                                                          Point
                                                          Line
                                                          Indvl Line
                                                          Rectangle
                                                          R Polygon
                                                          Circle 2
                                                          Circle 3
                                                          Arc 2
                                                          Arc 3
                                                          Ellipse
                                                          Bezier Curve
                                                          Indvl Bezier
                                                          Curve

                                                          Double Lines
                                                          Dbl Settings

                                                          SNAPS
                                                          PREVIOUS
                                                          ROOT MENU

Enter a command >
Drawing name: UNTITLED, Layer: 0, All Layers: ON, Zoom 1: 24.623
Memory used:    0.011%, Line color: 15, Font: MAIN, M.E.: Origin
```

pointing device. From the DRAW menu, select the Rectangle command, using the same technique.

Notice that moving from the ROOT menu to the DRAW menu causes no change in the prompt area, but selecting Rectangle brings up a series of prompts. The first prompt asks you to enter the first corner of the rectangle.

The First Corner

As discussed, there are a number of ways to enter points. In this case, specify the first corner by moving the drawing cursor to the lower-left corner of the screen (it really doesn't matter where you start as long as you leave enough space to draw the eight-by-ten-foot room). When the cursor is in the right place, say one grid point up from the bottom and two or three in from the left, press the first pointing device button.

Preferences for Drawing Aids

As Generic CADD is a highly configurable program, you might see a number of things at this point. A small "x" may appear at the location that you have just selected. If this happens, it is because you have Construction Points turned on; if not, Construction Points is off. Construction points, which let you see the points that you have already chosen, can be very useful for visualizing the object you are drawing. However, they are optional. You may prefer other visualizing devices, and you can customize Generic CADD to fit your preferences.

You might see a rectangle that changes size as you move the cursor. (Move the cursor around to see if this is the case.) Like construction points, this "rubber band" rectangle aids in visualizing as you draw. If such a rubber band rectangle appears on the screen, you have Rubberbanding turned on; if no such line is displayed, Rubberbanding is off.

To change the way that Generic CADD is currently handling rubberbanding, you must first cancel the Rectangle command by pressing ESC. You do not need to cancel the Rectangle command to toggle Construction Points. Simply select Con.Points from the DISPLAY menu or type **PC** and continue the command. To toggle Rubberbanding on or off, select Rubberband from the same DISPLAY menu, or type **RB**.

In order to see what you are drawing, it is usually a good idea to have one of these commands turned on. If you have a relatively fast computer (286 or 386) or a math coprocessor, rubberbanding is a great help for most drawing tasks. If you have a slow computer (8086 or 8088) or no math coprocessor, rubberbanding can be slow. If this is the case, use construction points instead. It is easier to work with the examples in this book if they are both turned on. Later, as you do more drawings, you will learn which method works best for you.

If you have interrupted the Rectangle command to change Rubberbanding, select it again from the DRAW menu or type **RE** on the keyboard and place your first point again, near the lower left corner of the screen.

The Opposite Corner

Now you are ready to select the second point—the upper-right corner of the Rectangle. Because you intend to draw a room of specified dimensions, eight by ten feet, you need to be precise about the location of the second point. The second point should be exactly ten feet to the right and eight feet above the first point.

Counting grid points as you move the cursor would, of course, work just fine. In fact, when you are only moving a few grid points, and the grid is composed of a round number of dots, such as 12, this can be the best way. However, Generic CADD provides several other means that are not as tedious as counting grid dots.

Using Coordinates

One of these methods is provided by the coordinates, which show the location of the cursor. When Absolute Coordinates are turned on, they change by one foot every time you move the cursor one grid point in any direction. If you note the location of your first point, you can simply add ten feet in the X direction (to the right) and eight feet in the Y direction (toward the top of the screen), and move the cursor until these values appear.

You *can* improve on this technique. If you type **DC**, select Relative from the prompt, and press ENTER, you will activate Relative Coordinates, which refers to the last point selected. For this example, that is exactly the information you need to select the second corner of the rectangle accurately. Now, you can move the cursor until the X coordinate reads "10' " and the Y coordinate reads "8'," as you can see in Figure 4-2.

When you have the cursor in the right place, press the first pointing device button to select the point. Your rectangle will be drawn, the prompt will read "Enter a command >", and the cursor will float freely from dot to dot with no rubber band. Notice that you do not have to interrupt the Rectangle command to change the coordinate display. The Coordinates command is a "transparent" toggle, meaning that you can use it anytime, even in the middle of another command. Rubberband (RB), on the other hand, is not transparent: the prompt "Enter a command >" must be displayed in order to use it.

Drawing Another Rectangle

For the next task, let's assume that you want to place an exterior wall six inches around the outside of the room to represent wall thickness, as

FIGURE 4-2 Finishing the Rectangle using Delta Coordinates

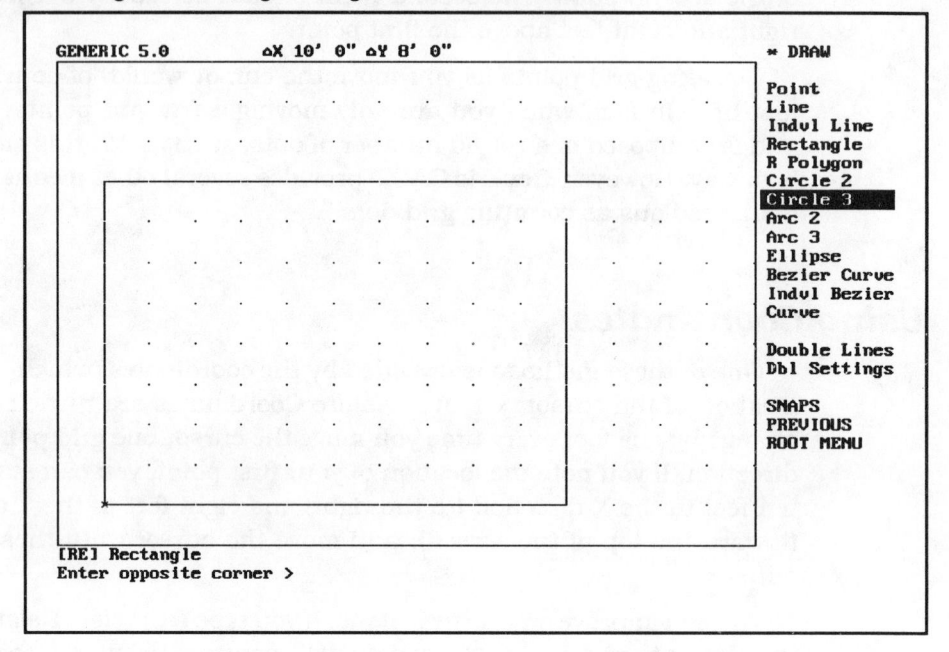

```
GENERIC 5.0        ΔX 10' 0"  ΔY 8' 0"                    * DRAW

                                                          Point
                                                          Line
                                                          Indvl Line
                                                          Rectangle
                                                          R Polygon
                                                          Circle 2
                                                          Circle 3
                                                          Arc 2
                                                          Arc 3
                                                          Ellipse
                                                          Bezier Curve
                                                          Indvl Bezier
                                                          Curve

                                                          Double Lines
                                                          Dbl Settings

                                                          SNAPS
                                                          PREVIOUS
                                                          ROOT MENU

[RE] Rectangle
Enter opposite corner >
```

shown in Figure 4-3. Because the grid spacing is too big (12 inches), you may be tempted to turn Snap to Grid off in order to draw off the grid. Resist this impulse! Instead, change the Grid to six inches and leave Snap to Grid turned on. Use the Grid Size command from the GRIDS menu, or type **GS**. Then, go back to the DRAW menu and select the Rectangle command, or type **RE**. Show the first point of the outside wall by going to one corner of the existing rectangle, moving toward the outside by one grid point in each direction, and then pressing the first pointing device button. (Even though you started in the lower-left corner to draw the room, you can start with any corner for the exterior wall.) Notice that all of the grid points might not be represented by visible dots, depending on your graphics card, but that you are still able to snap to these invisible grid points.

Move the cursor until it is one grid point outside the opposite corner, and press the first pointing device button to select the point. Note that the coordinates show X to be 11 feet and Y to be 9 feet, until the point is

FIGURE 4-3 The room with six-inch-thick walls

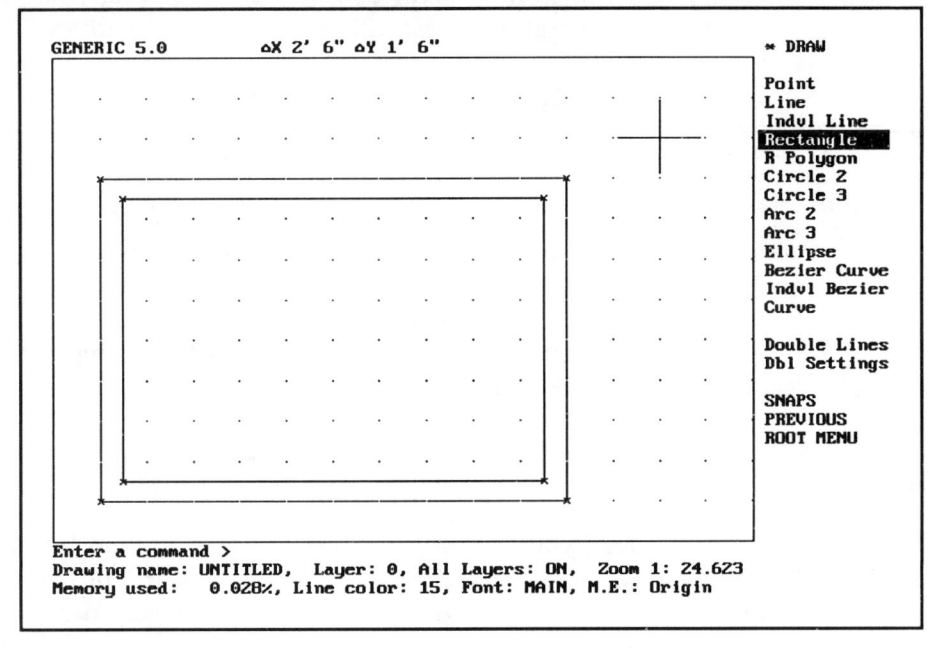

selected. Once you select the second corner of the rectangle, it becomes the last point selected, and the coordinates change to 0,0.

Erasing the Drawing

Let's try another method of drawing an eight-by-ten-foot box. First, erase what you've drawn so far. The fastest, most powerful erasing command is Drawing Erase, which removes all entities from the current drawing. However, it does leave the Grid Size, the Limits, and all of the toggles as currently set, so that even though your drawing is erased, you don't have to start completely from scratch. Select Erase from the DRAW menu, or type **DX** on the keyboard. Since this command is not reversible, Generic CADD asks you if you are sure that you want to do this. To go ahead, type **Y**. (If you had selected the Erase command by mistake, you would now have a chance to cancel it by typing **N**.) After you type **Y**, the screen and the current drawing will be cleared of all entities.

Using Lines

The second way to create the eight-by-ten-foot room is with the Line command. With the Line command, you draw each side of the box, starting in one corner and working your way around until you get back to the same point. Notice that the Drawing Erase command did not clear the 6-inch grid from the screen. Before you start drawing lines, change the Grid Size (GS) back to 12 inches.

The First Line

To start a line, you can either use the Line command by selecting it from the DRAW menu or by typing **LI** on the keyboard, or you can select a starting point of the line. Whenever the "Enter a command >" prompt is displayed and you select a point, Generic CADD assumes that you are initiating a Line command. Therefore, using the Line command itself is optional, although under certain conditions you might prefer to use the command instead of selecting points, as you will see later. So, either execute the command or choose a point. If you use the Line command or type **LI**, you are asked for the starting point of the line. Pick a point near the lower-left corner of the screen, just as you did when you were using the Rectangle command. If Construction Points is turned on, you will see a small "x" appear at the location you selected; if Rubberbanding is on, a rubber band line will stretch from this first point to the current cursor location. If you use LI, Rubberbanding is on automatically. Move the cursor to the right, watching the coordinates at the top of the screen. When the X coordinate reads 10' (and the Y coordinate reads 0'), select the second point. The first side of the box and a new rubber band line appear, as shown in Figure 4-4.

Continuing Around

Now, even though the prompt reads "Enter a command >," you can continue selecting points to draw the rest of the box. Move the cursor

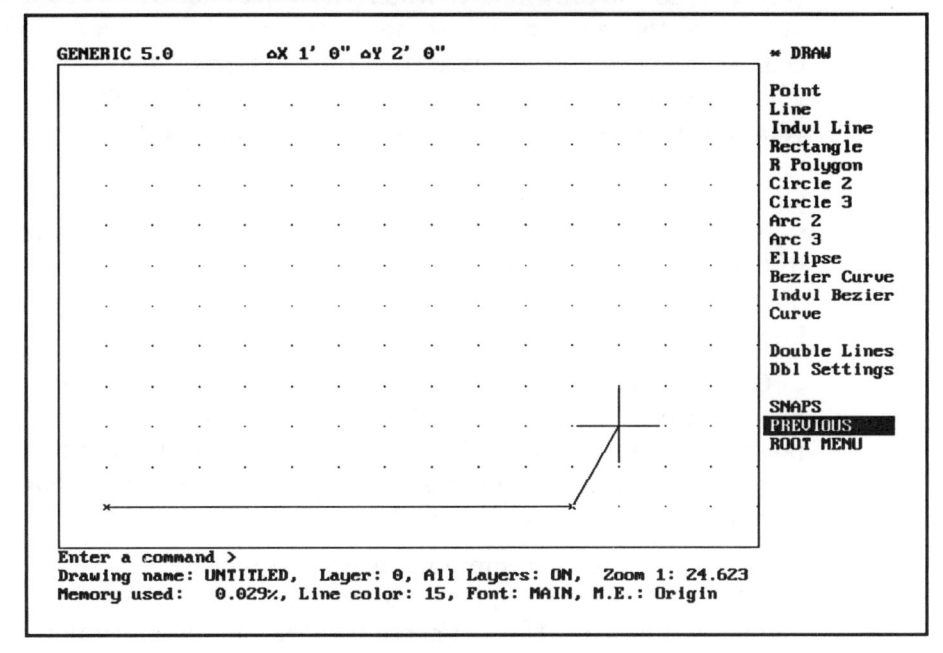

FIGURE 4-4 One side of the room drawn with the Line command

```
GENERIC 5.0          ΔX 1' 0"  ΔY 2' 0"                    ** DRAW

                                                           Point
                                                           Line
                                                           Indvl Line
                                                           Rectangle
                                                           R Polygon
                                                           Circle 2
                                                           Circle 3
                                                           Arc 2
                                                           Arc 3
                                                           Ellipse
                                                           Bezier Curve
                                                           Indvl Bezier
                                                           Curve

                                                           Double Lines
                                                           Dbl Settings

                                                           SNAPS
                                                           PREVIOUS
                                                           ROOT MENU


Enter a command >
Drawing name: UNTITLED,  Layer: 0, All Layers: ON,  Zoom 1: 24.623
Memory used:    0.029%, Line color: 15, Font: MAIN, M.E.: Origin
```

until Y is 8', making sure that this time X stays at 0'. Select this point. Continuing on, move the cursor to the left until X reads -10'. Notice that the coordinate is negative because you are moving to the left instead of to the right. For X (horizontal) movement, positive is to the right and negative is to the left. For Y (vertical) movement, up (toward the top of the screen) is positive and down (toward the bottom of the screen) is negative.

More Drawing Aids

Before you select the fourth point, the upper-left corner of the box, you might want to add one more helpful command to your arsenal, Snap Ortho or Ortho Mode. Select this command from the Controls menu, or type **OR** on the keyboard. You don't have to interrupt the Line command, as this is another transparent toggle that can be used whenever you want. When Ortho Mode is on, you can only move directly to the right or left, or straight up or down. This means that one of the coordinates will always stay at 0', so you only have to watch the other one. When you are moving directly to the left, as you are now, for example, you can ignore the Y coordinate, because it stays at 0'. The advantage of this command is that you can retain your accuracy without having to be quite as careful, so you can draw faster. If you hold down the CTRL key while moving the cursor, the status of the Ortho toggle is temporarily reversed. This allows you to draw diagonal lines while Ortho is on and orthogonal lines while it is off, without actually issuing the command. As soon as you release the CTRL key, Ortho returns to its proper status. This method is great for oddball lines, or when you are drawing both orthogonal and diagonal lines within a single command.

Go ahead and select the fourth point, and then continue on to the beginning point at the lower-left corner. After you have selected this final point, press ESC to end the Line command. If you have been using Rubberbanding, the rubber band line disappears when you end the Line command. The box is now complete.

Notice that the Line command is not as quick for this simple figure as the Rectangle command, as it requires that you place all four corners, instead of just two. The Line command is, however, significantly more flexible. With the Line command you can create a box, for example, with a two-foot-square notch cut out of one corner or any other shape that you want. As you will see later when you begin to edit your drawings, using the Rectangle command or drawing four lines individually produces exactly the same result. Remember, the Generic CADD primitives do not include a simple entity called a Rectangle. The Rectangle command is really just a quick way of drawing this simple shape when you do not need anything more complex.

Typing the Dimensions

One last method for drawing a box requires typing the coordinates of points rather than selecting them on the screen. This method can be used with either the Line or Rectangle command, but for illustration purposes, continue with the Line command.

Manual entry requires that you select a point of reference. Generic CADD offers the options Origin, Basepoint, or the last point entered (Relative). In this case, Relative Coordinates are the most useful. Notice

Chapter 4: Basic Drawing Tasks

that Relative Manual Entry and Relative Coordinates are each activated by their own commands. Just because you have Relative Coordinates on the screen doesn't mean that the coordinates you type will be interpreted in the same way. To select Relative mode for manual entry, select M E Relative from the UTILITIES menu or type **MR** on the keyboard.

Describing a Box with Coordinates

To practice this method, let's draw the same outer box six inches outside the one that you have on the screen now. Since you won't be showing points on the screen, you don't need to change the grid. Start an implicit Line command either by typing the coordinates of the first point, by using a Line command selected from the DRAW menu, or by typing **LI**. Since the last point that you entered was the lower-left corner of the existing box, you can specify your first point by typing **-6,-6** and pressing ENTER. This indicates a point six inches to the left and six inches below the last point placed. To place the next point, moving horizontally to the right, type **11',0** and press ENTER, indicating 11 feet to the right and zero feet vertically. Don't forget the foot mark ('), or you'll only move 11 inches. The coordinates of the next point are **0,9'**, and then **-11',0** (remember, negative numbers indicate movement to the left), and finally **0,-9'** (down nine feet) to get back to your starting point. After selecting this last point, press ESC to end the Line command.

Notice that manual entry can be used to specify exact lengths of lines, or exact cursor movements, regardless of the current grid and regardless of the setting of Ortho. By it's nature, manual entry is more accurate than pointing on the screen, and so it overrides any toggles or drawing aids that you have set to help with cursor movement and point selection.

Saving the Drawing

If you want to edit this drawing later, you must save it. This process sends the drawing from the computer's temporary memory, where it is now, to a file on a hard or floppy disk. If you don't save your drawing before you end Generic CADD or turn off the computer, you will have to start from scratch the next time you want to work on it.

One of the easiest ways of saving the drawing is by selecting the Quit command from the FILE menu, or by typing **QU** on the keyboard. Although the Quit command has a number of different functions, one of the most important options of the Quit command is the option to Save the drawing.

When you issue the Quit command, you are asked if you want to save the drawing. For the purpose of this example, type **Y**. The filename of the drawing is shown, together with the default drawing path where the file will be saved. If the path and the filename are correct, you can just press ENTER. If you want to make a change, type the new drawing name (don't include the extension .DWG) and press ENTER. In fact, you can save this drawing in a new file called ROOM by typing **ROOM** now. (If you want to save the drawing somewhere other than in the default path, type the new pathname, including the drawing name without the .DWG extension, and press ENTER.) The drawing will be saved on disk. If the file already exists, you will be asked if you want to Overwrite or Rename the existing file.

Overwrite or Rename?

At this point you have three options: (1) You can type **O** to Overwrite, which will replace the old file with the new one. (2) You can type **R** to Rename the old file. The old file will be renamed with the same name, except for the extension, which will be changed to .BAK (for backup). This allows you to have two versions of the drawing on the disk at the same time: the current version, which will have the extension .DWG, and an older version (as it was before the current drawing session) with the extension .BAK. (3) You can press ESC and start the process over again with a different filename altogether.

Quit or Continue?

After the file is saved, you will be asked if you want to quit or continue. If you type **Q**, you automatically exit to DOS. From here, if you want to work on another drawing, you must start up Generic CADD again by typing **CADD** and pressing ENTER or by typing **CADD** and the filename and pressing ENTER. If you type **C**, you can continue working on your drawing just as you were before.

You should quit this drawing now so that you can start a new one. Even if you are not finished with the drawing, it is a good idea to save it after ending a specific task, in case you need to retrieve the file from disk.

Your Second Drawing: A Musical Staff

In the previous example of the room, you were able to use a continuous series of lines because the basic box could be drawn without stopping. This is rather like drawing a figure without lifting the pencil from the paper. You will, of course, want to draw more complex objects.

In the next example, you will draw a series of parallel lines that represent a musical staff, as shown in Figure 4-5, to illustrate the repeated use of the Line command in a noncontinuous mode. At the DOS prompt, start up CADD and the new drawing by typing **CADD MUSIC** and pressing ENTER.

The Drawing Setup

Whenever you start a new drawing, you need to ask yourself the same questions: What units will I use? How much space do I need? What size grid is appropriate? Do I want to use settings other than the default line color, type, width, or layer?

For units, select Inches from the Units command on the DISPLAY menu, or type **UN**, followed by **I**, and press ENTER. For drawing space, set the Limits (by choosing the command from the UTILITIES menu or by typing **LS** on the keyboard) to 6 inches high by 9 inches wide. Don't forget to Zoom Limits (choose Limits from the ZOOMS menu, or type **ZL**) after setting the limits. Set your Grid Size, from the CONSTRAINTS menu or **GS** on the keyboard, to 1/8 inch. (You can type either **1/8** or **.125** and press ENTER twice; it doesn't matter which.) Turn on Snap to Grid, also on the CONSTRAINTS menu, or type **SG** on the keyboard. When you select the command, note whether it goes on or off. If it turns off, select it again to turn it on. Turn on Relative Coordinates by selecting Coor-

FIGURE 4-5 The second drawing: a musical staff

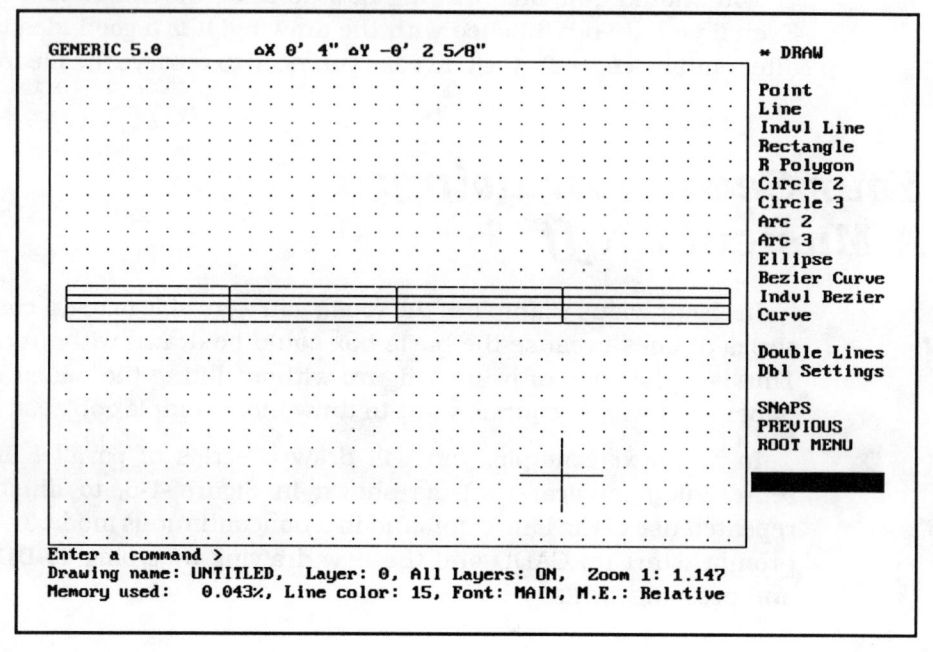

dinates from the DISPLAY menu and selecting Relative or by typing **DC**, then **R**, and pressing ENTER. All of the default drawing attributes (color, type, width, and layer) are fine the way they are.

The First Line

You can start the staff the same way you did the box in the previous drawing. Pick the Line command from the DRAW menu or type **LI** on the keyboard. When asked for the first point, select a point near the upper-left corner of the screen, a few grid dots down from the top and in from the left. Move the cursor eight inches to the right (watch the coordinates), and select the second point. If you have trouble moving the cursor in a straight horizontal line because the grid is relatively small, select Ortho Mode from the CONSTRAINTS menu or type **OR**.

Repeating the Line Command

To draw the next line, you need to stop the previous Line command and start a new one. You could use the same technique that you used for the box drawing—pressing ESC and starting a new line with another Line command—but there is a faster way. Most Generic CADD commands can be repeated by pressing SPACEBAR (the long horizontal bar at the bottom of the keyboard). If you have just drawn one line using the Line command, you can start a new one simply by pressing SPACEBAR. The rubber band line, if you are using Rubberbanding, will end, and you will get a prompt asking you for the first point of the line.

With this method, complete the four remaining horizontal lines of the musical staff. Place two points, each of which is one grid point (visible or invisible) below the starting points and endpoints of the last line drawn, and press SPACEBAR. Do the same three more times. When you have finished the last line, press ESC instead of SPACEBAR, so that you don't get another Line command. You should end up with five eight-inch lines, 1/8 inch apart. Notice that this technique does not work if you start the first line by simply picking a point instead of using the Line command, because there will be no Line command to repeat. Instead, whatever command you issued before starting the line will be repeated.

Also note that toggles that are used during another command cannot be repeated with the SPACEBAR. This means that even if you use a toggle command while doing a line, when you press SPACEBAR it will either be the Line command or no command at all that will be repeated rather than the toggle.

Distance Between Lines

So far, you have been using Relative Coordinates to show the actual length of lines as you draw. These coordinates can also be used to determine the distance between lines as well. Select another Line command by pressing SPACEBAR. Note that you can repeat the Line command even though you ended it with ESC. Draw the first vertical line at the far left end of the musical staff. It will be 1/2 inch long. Notice that as you choose the second point, the Relative Coordinates return to 0,0.

To draw the next vertical line, press SPACEBAR again and move the cursor to the right, noticing that the coordinates show how far the cursor has moved from the end of the last line. Move exactly two inches to the right, and draw the second line. Press SPACEBAR again, and draw three more lines the same way. Then press ESC to end the last Line command.

Notice that if you drew your first line with an upstroke (second point above the first), your second line will be drawn with a downstroke, the third up, fourth down, and so on. If you started with a downstroke, the order is reversed. This is a good technique for drawing a series of lines when you know the horizontal or vertical distances between their endpoints.

Save the Drawing

To save this drawing for later use, select Quit from the FILE menu, or type **QU** on the keyboard. Type **Y** when asked if you want to save the drawing, press ENTER when shown the default drawing name (MUSIC.DWG), and then type **Q** when asked if you want to Quit or Continue. After some time, you will become very familiar with this series of keystrokes.

Your Third Drawing: A Key

The third drawing, the key shown in Figure 4-6, is more complex. You should feel comfortable with the Line command by this time, so the examples will use it freely from now on. Also, you should now know how to select a unit system, set the Limits and the Grid Size, and how to turn on and off Relative Coordinates, Snap to Grid, and Ortho Mode. (Review previous chapters if you're unsure.)

Starting Out

Start the key by typing **CADD KEY** and pressing ENTER at the DOS prompt. It can be drawn using Inches and Fractions, with Fraction Value set to 1/16 as the units in a drawing space (Limits) of 3 inches high by

FIGURE 4-6 The third drawing: a key

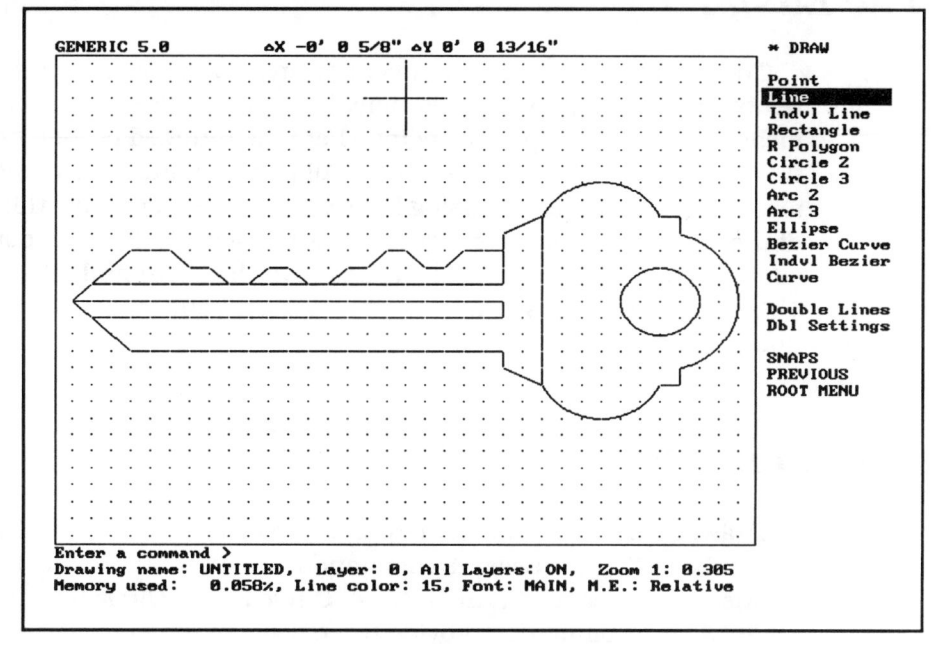

[Screenshot of Generic 5.0 CAD program showing a key drawing with DRAW menu on the right listing: Point, Line, Indvl Line, Rectangle, R Polygon, Circle 2, Circle 3, Arc 2, Arc 3, Ellipse, Bezier Curve, Indvl Bezier Curve, Double Lines, Dbl Settings, SNAPS, PREVIOUS, ROOT MENU]

4 inches wide (don't forget to Zoom Limits). The Grid Size should be set for 1/16 inch, and Snap to Grid should be on.

A good way to start a complex drawing is with a *reference line.* This key happens to have a center line that passes through both the tip of the key and the center of the hole at the other end. The exact length of this key is 2 1/8 inches. So the first entity to draw is this horizontal line. Start on the left of the screen, using manual entry in the Relative mode (M E Relative on the UTILITIES menu or **MR** on the keyboard) to select the second point, which should be typed as **2 1/8,0** or **2.125,0**. (Note that the X coordinate would be negative if you had started on the right.)

A vertical reference line will also come in handy. Use another Line command to draw this line starting at -7/16,7/16 (relative to the last point placed on the right end of the line) and going down to 0,-7/8. This line will help you to construct the head of the key later. (You could also use Tracking, discussed in Chapter 10, "Advanced Drawing and Editing Techniques," to draw the head without a reference line.)

The Easy Part

The left side of the key is made entirely from lines and should be relatively easy to draw by this time. This portion is 1 1/2 inches long, measured from the tip to the point where the rounded portion begins. At this point, the key is 5/8 inch wide. All points required to draw the key are on a grid snap point. Using Figure 4-7 as a guide, draw this portion of the key. If you compare Figure 4-6 with Figure 4-7, you'll notice that you need to draw a horizontal line on top of the horizontal reference line. This line will be obscured on your screen, but you should draw it nonetheless.

The Round Parts

Drawing the rest of the key requires two new entity types, a Circle and a number of Arcs. Several commands are used to create these two entities: you'll see Arc 2, Arc 3, Arc 4, Circle 2, and Circle 3 on the DRAW menu. These commands provide three ways of drawing an arc and two methods for circles. For the key drawing, you can use the Arc 3 and Circle 2 commands and explore the others later.

Three-Point Arcs

The name "Arc 3" means that you are going to draw an arc by specifying three points: the two endpoints and a third point located somewhere on the arc. Generic CADD defines the term *arc* as a circle segment, that is, part of a circle with the same centerpoint as the circle. As all points on the arc are an equal distance from that center, a unique arc can be drawn for any three such points. All Arcs in Generic CADD, regardless of the command used to create them, are stored in this three-point format.

Drawing Arcs

To draw a three-point arc, select the command Arc 3 from the DRAW menu or type **A3** on the keyboard. The arc and circle two-character codes are particularly easy to remember. As shown in Figure 4-8, note that the second point of each arc is located exactly on the end of one of your

Chapter 4: Basic Drawing Tasks

FIGURE 4-7 A portion of the key, drawn entirely with Lines

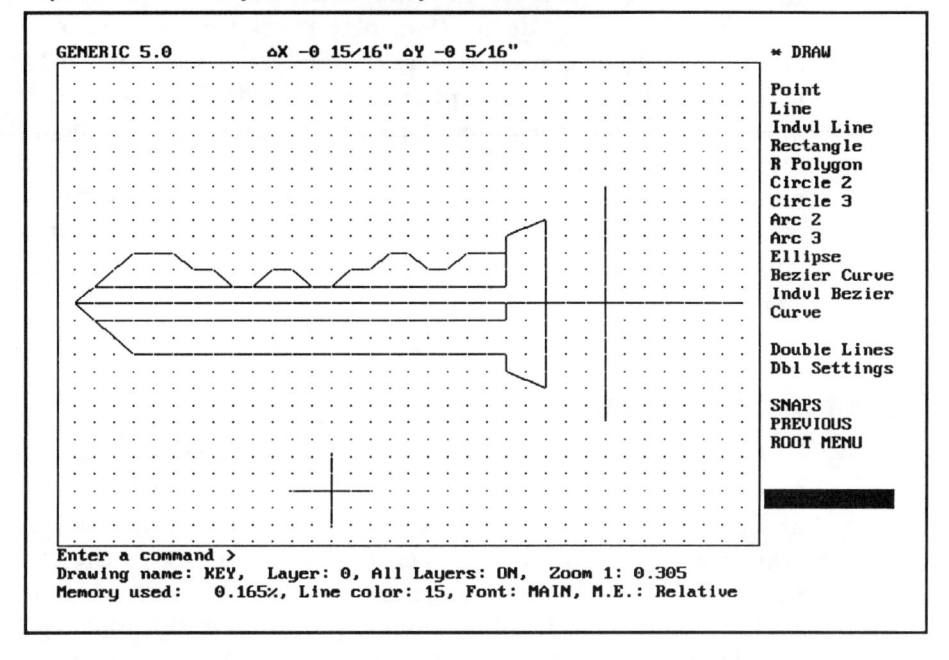

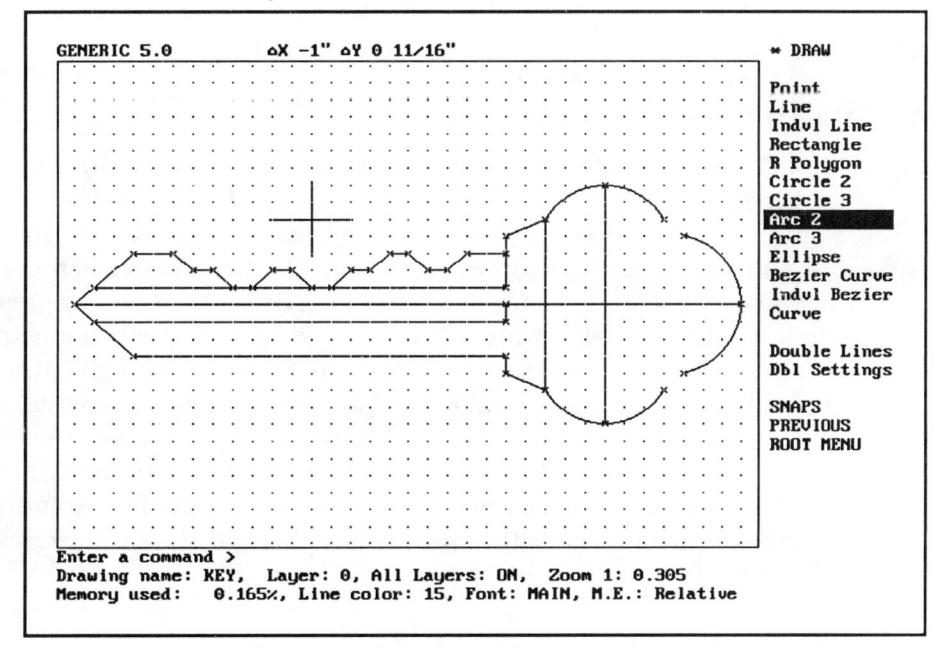

FIGURE 4-8 Arcs added to the key, with Construction Points on

reference lines. With this in mind, draw the three arcs that appear on the head of the key. The locations of the first and last points for each arc should be easy to locate on the grid. After you select the Arc 3 command, you are prompted for each point in turn. With Snap to Grid turned on, move the cursor to the proper location and press the first pointing device button. If you place any of the points in the wrong place, simply press ESC and issue the Arc 3 command again. When you have completed each of the first two arcs, press SPACEBAR to get another Arc 3 command. When you have finished with the arcs, draw the four short lines that connect them at the corners.

Two-Point Circles

Again, the name of this command, Circle 2, provides a significant clue to its operation. The two points required are the center point of the circle and any point on the circle itself. This is a good command to use when you know the location of the center and the radius of the circle, as the distance between the two points is the radius. After showing or specifying the first point, use Relative mode for manual entry, and type a second coordinate that has the length of the radius as X and zero as Y. All Generic CADD circles are stored using the center and one point, regardless of the command that is used to create them.

Drawing Circles

The key drawing contains one circle, which you can draw by selecting Circle 2 from the DRAW menu or by typing **C2** on the keyboard. You will be asked for the center point. Position the cursor, using Figure 4-6 as a guide. Note that the center point is on the horizontal reference line, so you can locate it by counting grid points. Select the point by pressing the first pointing device button. You will next be prompted for a point on the circle. Move the cursor to the desired point, again using Figure 4-6 as a guide, noticing that the radius will be displayed as one coordinate of the Relative Coordinate display if you move either vertically or horizontally. In addition, if Rubberbanding is turned on, a rubber band circle helps you to visualize the circle as you draw it. Press the first pointing device button once you have the cursor properly located, and the circle will be drawn.

A Less Powerful Erase Command

Now that the key is complete, you need to erase your reference lines. Obviously, the Drawing Erase command that you used earlier is too wide-ranging for this task, so something simpler is needed. A number of editing commands work on only one entity or object at a time.

To erase a single line, select Object Erase from the SHORTCUTS menu (located via the EDITS menu) or type **OE** on the keyboard. A prompt asks you to select the object to be erased. Position the drawing cursor near the lines that you want to erase, preferably near the middle of the line and not near another entity. The important criterion is that the object you want to erase is the closest object to the cursor. When you press the first pointing device button, the object nearest to the cursor will be erased. To erase another object, press SPACEBAR to repeat the command, and select this line in the same way. When you are finished erasing, you may want to do a Redraw (RD) to clean up the screen.

Oops!

If you make a mistake and erase the wrong entity, use the Unerase command from the EDITS menu, or type **UE** on the keyboard, to reverse the action of the Erase command. The Unerase command returns to the screen whatever was erased in the last Erase command. In this case, since the Object Erase command erases only one entity at a time, the Unerase command brings back only one object when it is chosen. If you are using a command that erases more than one object at a time, the Unerase command brings back the same number of objects. The Unerase command has certain limitations, which will be investigated later. Among other things, it cannot reverse the action of a Drawing Erase command. Generic CADD 5.0 includes two additional commands, Undo (OO) and Redo (UU) to help reverse the actions of commands that have gone awry. (See Chapter 10 for information on these.)

Save and Exit to DOS

Once the reference lines have been erased, save the drawing by selecting Quit from the FILE menu or typing **QU** on the keyboard. Type

Y and press ENTER, and then type **Q** to save the drawing under the default name (the one you used to start the drawing) and exit to DOS. If you have previously saved the drawing, you will be asked if you want to Rename or Overwrite it. In this case, type the letter **O** to update the file.

Your Fourth Drawing: A Star

With this drawing, you will get a chance to use two more commands, Regular Polygon and Snap to Nearest Point. By combining Generic CADD's ability to create a figure with any number of equal sides and its ability to snap new points exactly onto the location of points already in the drawing, you will find it quite easy to draw a star-shaped figure, as shown in Figure 4-9.

FIGURE 4-9

The fourth drawing: a star

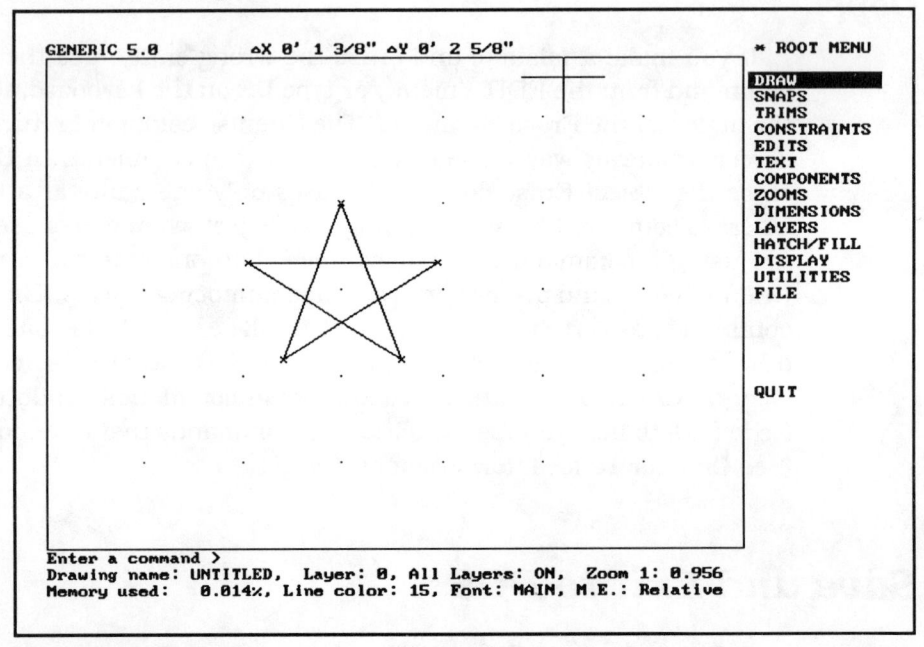

The Drawing Setup

Begin a new drawing called STAR, by typing **CADD STAR** at the DOS prompt and starting Generic CADD in the usual way. The star is going to be two inches high, so use Inches for your Units, and set your Limits to 5 inches high by 7 inches wide. Follow the setting of the limits, as usual, with a Zoom All. Set your Grid to 1 inch by 1 inch, and turn on Relative Coordinates and Snap to Grid. The choice of Rubberbanding and/or Construction Points is up to you.

A Five-Sided Figure

The easiest way to draw a star is to use Generic CADD's ability to create a figure with any number of sides, in this case, five. You can then use this five-sided figure as a construction aid to draw the star.

Select the Regular Polygon command from the DRAW menu or type **RP** on the keyboard. When you are asked for the number of sides of the polygon, type **5** and press ENTER. Next, type **C** for Center construction, and select a point right in the middle of the screen. When you are asked for a corner of the polygon—one of the five vertices of the polygon and also the top point of the star—move the cursor up one inch to the next grid point, select that point, and the regular polygon appears, as shown in Figure 4-10. Note that the method of construction can be selected by picking it from the prompt with the pointing device, or by simply pressing ENTER if the correct method is already bracketed in the prompt because it was the last method used.

Like the Rectangle command, the Regular Polygon command is really a drawing aid that helps you to draw a specific type of figure using lines. There is no such primitive entity as a "regular polygon." In this case, you have just placed five lines into the drawing, and will be able to take advantage of the fact that each line has its own endpoints as you draw the star.

FIGURE 4-10 A five-sided regular polygon

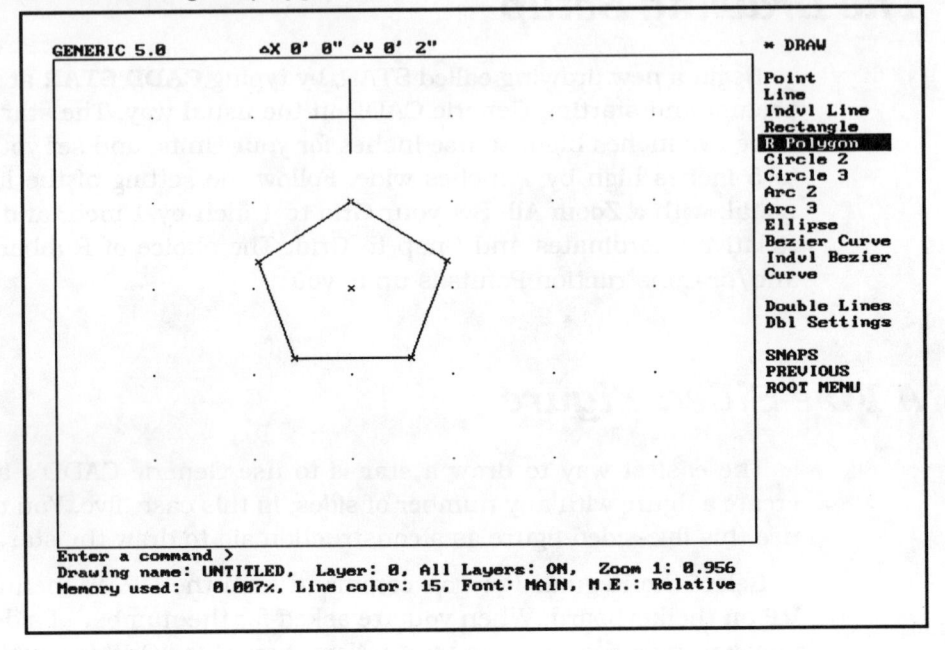

```
GENERIC 5.0        ΔX 0' 0"  ΔY 0' 2"              * DRAW

                                                   Point
                                                   Line
                        +                          Indvl Line
                                                   Rectangle
                                                   R Polygon
                                                   Circle 2
                                                   Circle 3
                                                   Arc 2
                                                   Arc 3
                      _____                       Ellipse
                     /      \                      Bezier Curve
                    /        \                     Indvl Bezier
                   /     x    \                    Curve
                   \          /
                    \        /                     Double Lines
                     _____/                      Dbl Settings

                                                   SNAPS
                                                   PREVIOUS
                                                   ROOT MENU

Enter a command >
Drawing name: UNTITLED,  Layer: 0, All Layers: ON,  Zoom 1: 0.956
Memory used:   0.007%, Line color: 15, Font: MAIN, M.E.: Relative
```

Snapping to an Existing Endpoint

The Snap to Nearest Point (NP) command is unusual in that it does not appear on any menu and does not display prompts when you use it. You will find, however, that you will probably use this command more than any other, with the possible exception of the automatic Line command. If you have a three-button mouse, the Snap to Nearest Point command is on the third button of the mouse. Whenever you press the third button, you get an NP command. If you have not changed the configuration of the pointing device buttons using the Macro Assign command, your mouse or other pointing device should be set up to use the third button in this way.

Because no prompts are associated with the Snap to Nearest Point command, you must position the drawing cursor before issuing the command. Since you will be snapping to the nearest point, you no longer need to snap to the grid. In fact, if Snap to Grid is on, you will have trouble getting near enough to the points that you want to snap to. Turn off Snap to Grid by selecting it from the Grids menu or by typing **SG** on the keyboard.

Start an implicit Line command by positioning the cursor near the top of the five-sided figure on the screen and pressing the third button on the pointing device or typing **NP**. You should try to be within 1/4 inch or so from the point that you are trying to select. What really matters is that the desired point is closer to the cursor than any other point. For this reason, selecting a cursor location slightly above the top of the figure ensures that the top point will be selected.

Do not use the first pointing device button to select the point. When using the NP command, pressing the third button or typing **NP** on the keyboard replaces the normal point selection process. As soon as you issue the NP command, the cursor jumps to the nearest point, and places a construction point or connects a rubber band if you have turned on either of these features.

Continuing with the NP Command

Now that you have started the Line command, cross to one of the opposite sides of the figure on the screen and select another corner with the NP command: Use the third button on the pointing device or type **NP**. The first Line will be placed. Continue adding more lines by criss-crossing the figure and snapping from corner to corner of the five-sided figure. When you have drawn five lines and have returned to the starting point, press ESC to end the automatic Line command. Your drawing should now resemble Figure 4-11.

Erasing the Construction Lines

Erase the construction lines of the original five-sided figure by using the Object Erase command from the SHORTCUTS menu, or by typing **OE** on the keyboard. The command asks you to select an object to erase. Position the cursor near one of the original five lines, and press the first button on the pointing device. Just make sure the line that you want to erase is closest to the cursor before you press the button.

FIGURE 4-11 The star drawn by snapping to the existing points

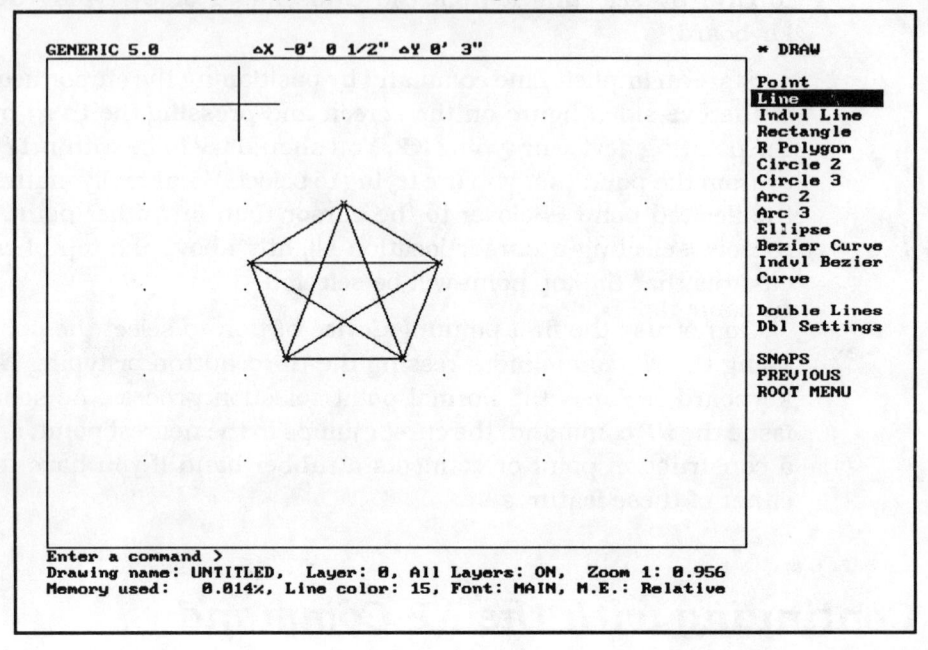

To erase another Line, issue another Object Erase command by pressing the SPACEBAR and then selecting the Line. Continue this process until all five construction lines have been removed.

Save and Exit

To save the drawing, select Quit from the FILE menu or Type **QU**. Type **Y** to indicate that you want to save the drawing, and press ENTER to verify the filename, STAR.DWG. When asked if you want to Quit or Continue, type **Q**.

Adding to Your First Drawing: A Bathroom

For this drawing task, you will return to a previously saved drawing and change it. You will use the eight-by-ten-foot room, which is stored in the drawing file ROOM.DWG. You will turn this room into a bathroom by adding a number of typical bathroom fixtures as shown in Figure 4-12, and learn some new Draw commands and another Zoom command at the same time.

To return to the ROOM drawing, type **CADD ROOM** at the DOS prompt. The drawing will be loaded automatically. Alternatively, you could just type **CADD** at the DOS prompt, and load the drawing with the Drawing Load (DL) or the Load (LO,D) command. Some operating systems do not recognize the drawing name after the CADD command, so you may need to load the drawing even if you type it at the DOS prompt. (For more information on loading drawings, see Chapter 12, "File Storage and Retrieval.")

Reviewing the Room

Notice that when Generic CADD loads an existing drawing, it automatically does a Zoom All, so that the entire drawing is shown on the screen. In addition, you should notice that all of the toggles and settings are saved with the drawing file. The Units, Limits, and Grid Size settings, together with the Snap to Grid, Ortho Mode, Rubberbanding, Construction Points, and Coordinates toggles, always start out the way that they were set the last time you worked on the drawing.

Getting Ready to Draw

Before you start drawing again, set Units to Feet/Inches. Don't worry about the Limits, because you won't be drawing anything beyond the area that is already displayed on the screen. Set Grid Size to 6 by 6 inches.

FIGURE 4-12 The ROOM drawing with bathroom fixtures added

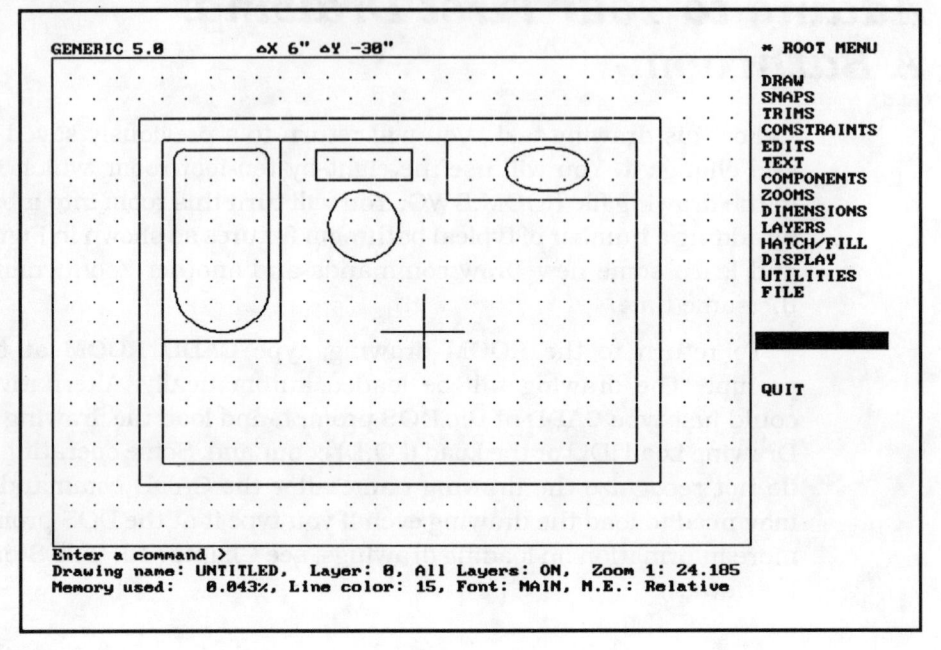

Turn on Snap to Grid, Ortho Mode, and Delta Coordinates, and set Construction Points and Rubberbanding to your own preferences.

Adding Lines and Rectangles

Using the Line and Rectangle commands add the counter top, the back of the toilet, and the tub surround. Figure 4-13 will serve as a guide. The counter top and the tub surround should be drawn first, as they fit onto the six inch grid. Make the counter 1 1/2 feet deep by 4 feet wide using two Lines, and the tub 2 1/2 feet wide by 5 feet long with another two Lines. To draw the back of the toilet, reduce the Grid Size (GS) to 3 x 3 inches, and then use a Rectangle to create it. The three-inch grid allows you to place the back of the toilet three inches from the wall. Make the Rectangle 24 inches wide by 9 inches deep.

FIGURE 4-13 Lines and Rectangles provide the basic layout

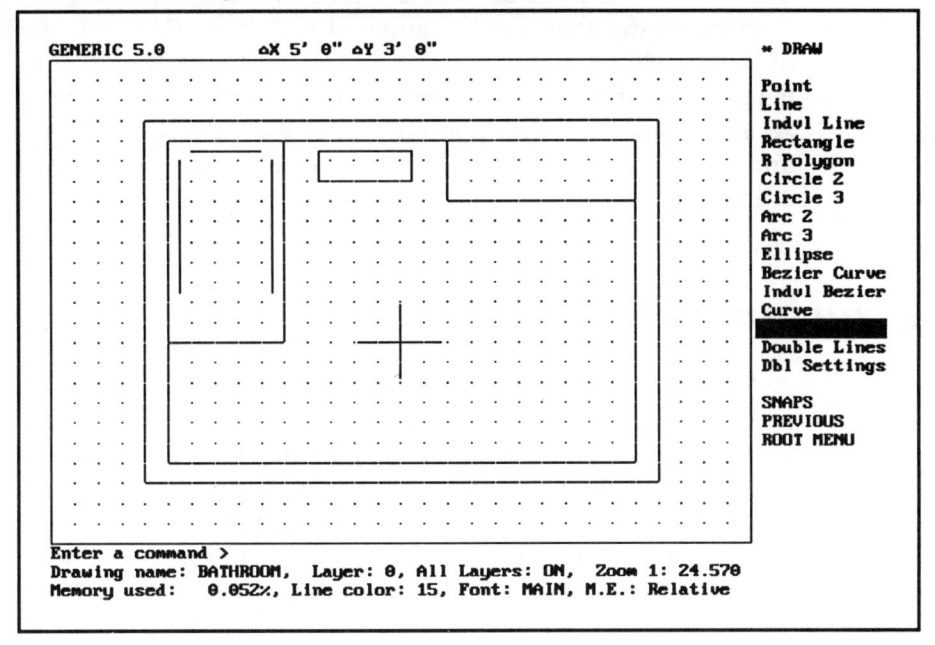

```
GENERIC 5.0          ΔX 5' 0"  ΔY 3' 0"                    * DRAW
                                                           Point
                                                           Line
                                                           Indvl Line
                                                           Rectangle
                                                           R Polygon
                                                           Circle 2
                                                           Circle 3
                                                           Arc 2
                                                           Arc 3
                                                           Ellipse
                                                           Bezier Curve
                                                           Indvl Bezier
                                                           Curve

                                                           Double Lines
                                                           Dbl Settings

                                                           SNAPS
                                                           PREVIOUS
                                                           ROOT MENU

Enter a command >
Drawing name: BATHROOM,  Layer: 0, All Layers: ON,  Zoom 1: 24.570
Memory used:    0.052%, Line color: 15, Font: MAIN, M.E.: Relative
```

Zooming in Closer

You will be using an ellipse to complete the toilet, on a 1 1/2-inch grid. When you set the Grid Size (GS) to 1.5 by 1.5, you might notice that it is a little difficult to position the cursor accurately. Snap to Grid works well when the grid is large, but when it is small, it can be hard to tell how far you are moving, and the cursor tends to jump around.

The solution to this problem is to zoom in closer on the area that you want to work on, so that 1 1/2 inches appears larger on the screen. Once you do this, cursor movement will be back to normal.

To zoom in closer to a specific area, select In from the ZOOMS menu, or type **ZI** on the keyboard. Generic CADD asks you to indicate the new center of the screen. Use the drawing cursor and the first pointing device button to select a point about where the middle of the toilet will be drawn, a little below the back, which you have already drawn. As soon as you select this point, the display will be adjusted, and objects will appear exactly twice as large as they did a moment ago. To fit this part of the drawing on the screen at the larger size, Generic CADD must drop some of the drawing around the edges. Don't worry, this part of the drawing isn't lost, it just isn't displayed at the moment. Each time you use the Zoom In command, the apparent size of objects on the screen is doubled, and the display is recentered around an area that you select. As you will see later, Zoom Out (ZO) has exactly the opposite effect.

Drawing an Ellipse

An ellipse is defined by the locations of the endpoints of one axis and half the length of the other axis. It is important to notice the distinction between *location* and *length*. The first two points position the location of the ellipse, while the third point merely specifies its width, which is the length of the second axis. Therefore, the ellipse actually passes through the first two points, but it might not pass through the third.

The Major Axis

To draw an ellipse, select the Ellipse command from the DRAW menu or type **EP**. Generic CADD asks you for the first endpoint of the major axis, usually defined as the longer axis. In Generic CADD, however, the major axis can be the longer or shorter one, depending on which is placed first. It is also considered major because the ellipse actually passes through its endpoints.

Position the first endpoint carefully, 1 1/2 inches or one grid point below the back of the toilet, centered below the back. For the other endpoint, move the drawing cursor straight down until the Y coordinate reads -21.

The Minor Axis

As discussed, the point that you pick for the minor axis is simply used to specify the width of the ellipse. The perpendicular distance between this point and the major axis is calculated, and the ellipse drawn. To help visualize this width, the axis is rubberbanded. Construction points should not be placed too far away from the ellipse itself, as they can cause trouble later if you forget where you put them.

For the width of the minor axis, visualize an imaginary ellipse where you think you want it, and place the point about nine inches from the center. Again, don't worry too much if the point is not placed exactly in the right location; it is important, however, that it be about 9 inches from the major axis.

True or Construction Ellipse?

The Ellipse command is capable of producing two different types of primitives: a single ellipse, defined by the four points that you just specified, or four arcs that are fit into the same ellipse shape, each defined by three points, just like any other arc.

Once you have located the four points required to construct the ellipse, you are asked if you want a True or a Construction Ellipse. Typing **T** produces the single ellipse entity, while typing **C** creates four arcs. You will find that the two different types, True and Construction, have different uses. If the ellipse can stand alone (you will not have to edit it later or use it to edit other entities) the single entity is best, as it uses less space in the database. The four arcs are required if you want to edit the ellipse, break it into segments, or trim other entities to it. The difference will become clear when you begin editing your drawings. In this case, choose a True Ellipse by typing **T** or selecting it from the prompt, as you will not be editing it.

Another Ellipse: The Sink

Use the Zoom All (ZA) command to return to the full drawing, and then Zoom In (ZI) on the area around the bathroom sink, and draw another ellipse. Use the 1 1/2-inch grid and Figure 4-14 as a guide. This time, after you have selected the four points, specify a True Ellipse, as you will not need to do any more work on this one. Zoom All when you are done, and then Zoom In on the bathtub area.

FIGURE 4-14 Ellipses added with Construction Points on

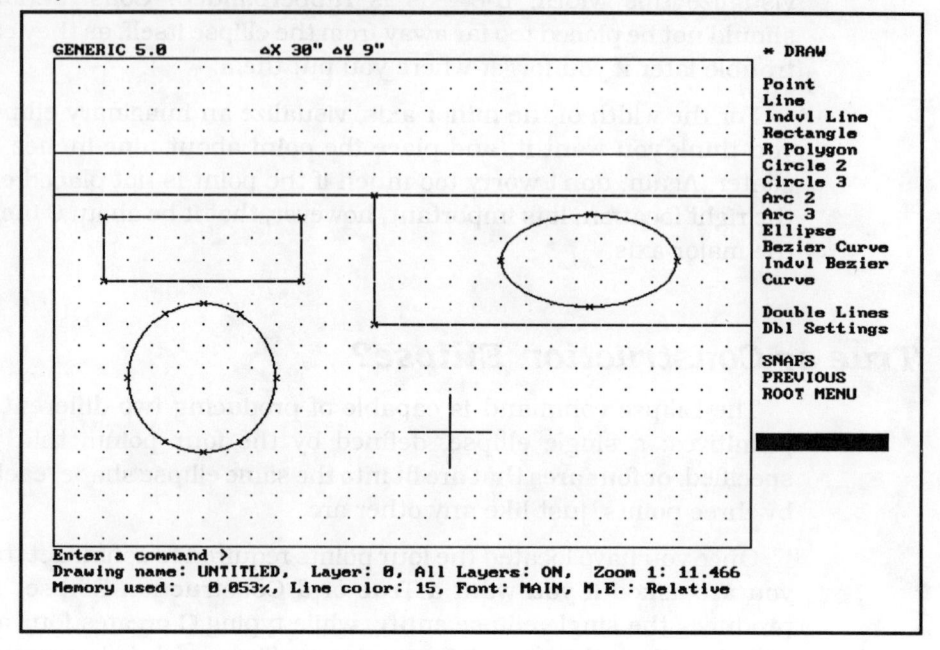

More Arcs

To round the corners of the bathtub, you should use arcs. Remember, you must place three points to define an arc with the Arc 3 command. For the large arc at the foot of the tub, you can use a three-point arc, because you can place the two endpoints and a point on the arc fairly easily. For the smaller arcs at the two corners of the tub, the point between the two endpoints is not so easy to locate. For these arcs, you have two more commands, Arc 2 and Arc 4, both of which allow you to construct an arc, rather than placing one with three points.

The Arc 4 Command

As you might expect, the Arc 4 command requires four points: (1) the centerpoint of the arc, (2) one endpoint, (3) a point indicating the direction of the arc from the endpoint, and (4) the final endpoint.

Of these four points, only the second point (one of the endpoints) is necessarily on the arc. The center is not on the arc by definition. The third point, which specifies the direction, might be on the arc, but only if you are really lucky, and the final point, which specifies the second endpoint, might also be on the arc, especially if Snap to Grid is turned on and the point is on the grid. On the other hand, because the centerpoint is already located, and the radius has been determined by the location of the first point, the last point doesn't have to be on the arc. An imaginary line is projected between the center of the arc and the last point you select, and the arc is cut along this line.

This command is activated by typing **A4** on the keyboard; you won't find it on the menu. Try it out on the upper-left corner of the bathtub. You might even Zoom In (ZI) a little closer if you desire. How far you need to zoom is determined by personal preference and the resolution of your graphics card. With higher-resolution hardware, you don't have to zoom as much.

After you select the command, you are asked for the center point of the arc. Starting with the arc on the left corner, select a point directly below the end of the horizontal line, and directly to the right of the vertical line. When you are asked for the first endpoint, select the left end of the existing horizontal line. When asked for the midpoint, select a point that is located approximately on the arc that you are creating, somewhat to the left of the point you just selected. You need not be too precise with this last point, as it is only used to tell Generic CADD which direction you want to go from the previous point. You might want to temporarily turn Snap to Grid off by typing **SG**. After you have selected the (approximate) midpoint, turn SG back on again. Finally, select the top of the vertical line for the other endpoint. See Figure 4-15 for the locations of all four points.

Constructing a four-point arc

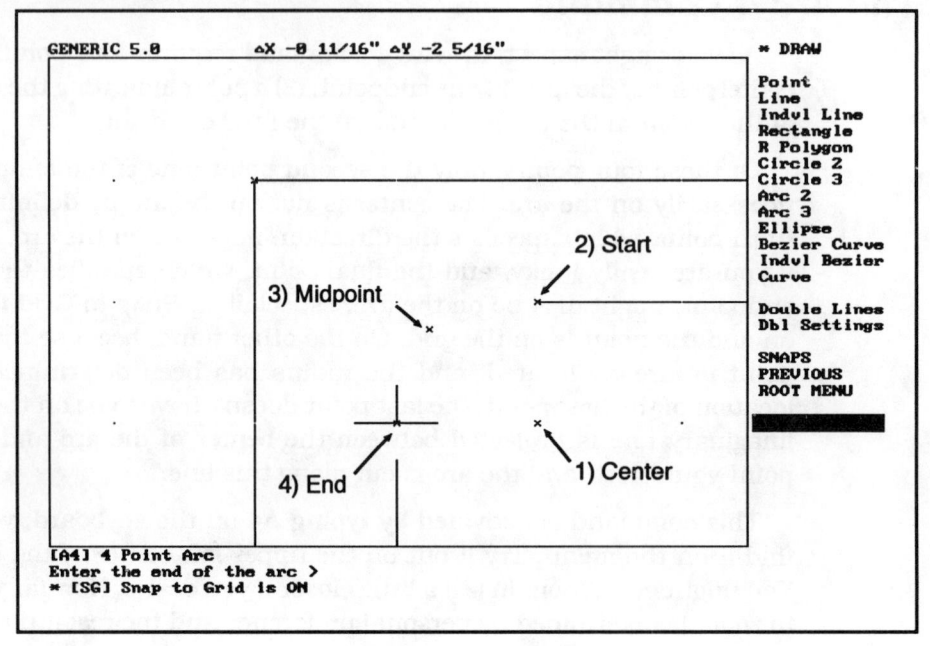

Figure 4-15

The arc will be drawn after you indicate the last point. If you have turned on Construction Points, you might notice an extra point or two appear as the arc is drawn. These are due to the fact that even though you specified this arc using four points, it is defined and stored by Generic CADD using three points on the arc, just like an Arc 3. All arcs created by Generic CADD are stored in this same format.

The Arc 2 Command

The Arc 2 command is quite similar to Arc 4. The name may lead you to assume that this arc is created by selecting only two points, but three are required. (Arc 2 was chosen to fit into this naming convention because Arc 3 and Arc 4 already existed, and because Arc 2 is simpler in many ways than the other two.)

Use the Arc 2 command to draw the upper-right corner of the bathtub. First, Zoom Out (ZO) and then Zoom In (ZI) to move this corner to the

Chapter 4: Basic Drawing Tasks

center of the screen. Then select the Arc 2 command from the DRAW menu or type **A2** on the keyboard.

Specify the center and the first endpoint in the same way that you did with the Arc 4 command. After specifying these two points, turn off Snap to Grid by typing **SG**. You will immediately see why Arc 2 is called a "rubber arc." As you move the cursor clockwise around the centerpoint, the arc will be "rubberbanded" in that direction as shown in Figure 4-16. When you move the other way, the rubber arc follows. Instead of turning Snap to Grid back on, use the Snap to Nearest Point command to select the final endpoint. Drag the arc to approximately where you want it and type **NP** on the keyboard, or press the third button on the pointing device, if you have three buttons. The arc will be drawn.

One Last Arc: Your Choice

To complete this drawing, draw the final arc at the foot of the bathtub. Zoom Out (ZO) until you can see this area, and then Zoom In (ZI) on it.

FIGURE 4-16 Constructing a two-point rubber arc

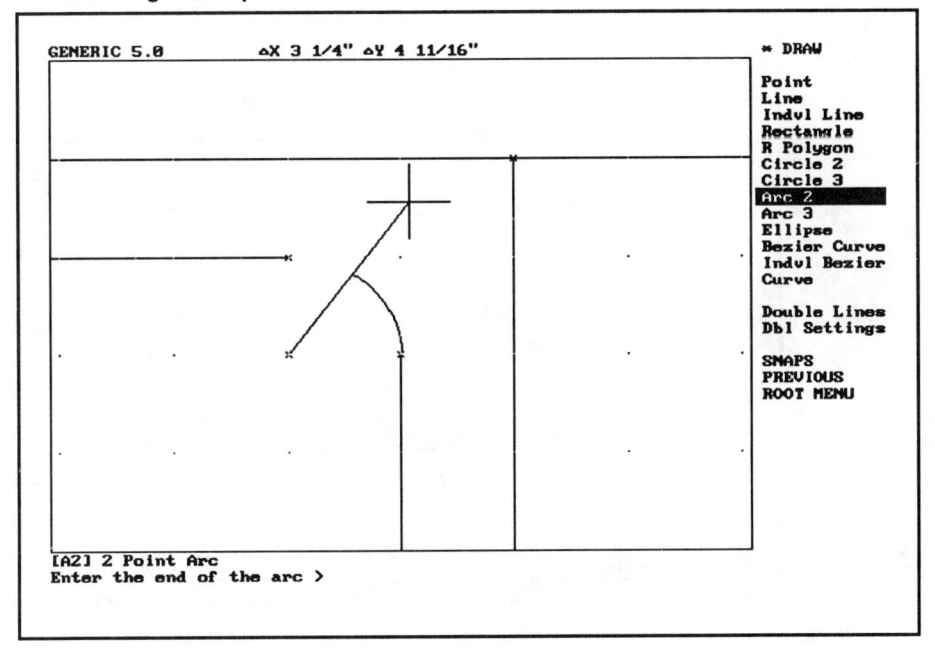

Place the arc using any of the three commands. (Be sure to turn Snap to Grid back on before you start.) When you have finished, Zoom All (ZA) to examine your work, and then save the drawing by using the Quit (QU) command.

Your Fifth Drawing: A Site Plan

The last example in this chapter, the site plan shown in Figure 4-17, is more ambitious than the drawings you have made so far. The 50-by-100-foot site includes a sidewalk, house, driveway, walk, patio, swimming pool, and some trees. This drawing illustrates several new Draw commands and a few new drawing techniques and reinforces the fact that you can easily draw objects that are much larger than the drawing screen.

FIGURE 4-17 The site plan drawing

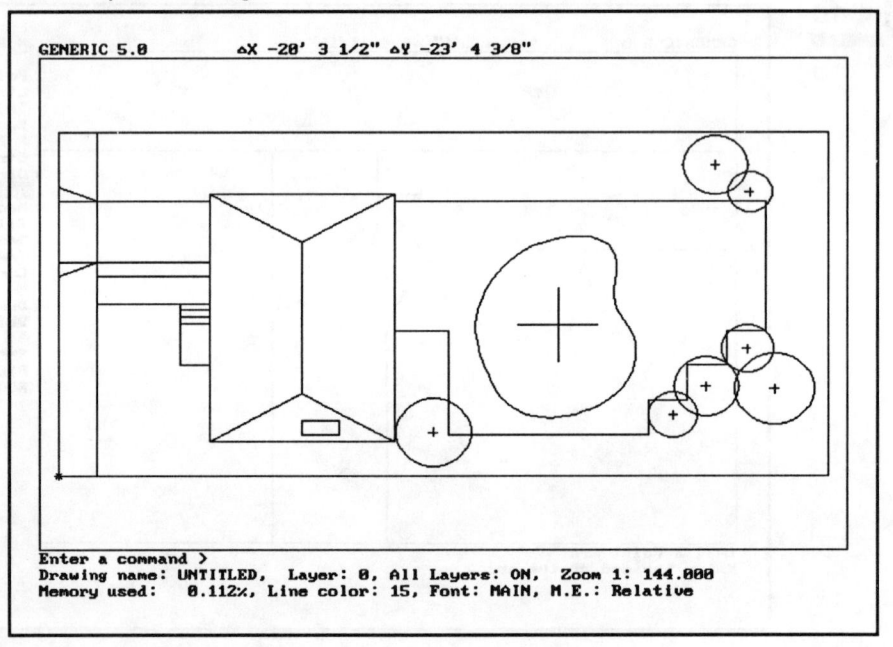

Starting Up

To start this drawing, type **CADD SITEPLAN** at the DOS prompt. When you get Generic CADD running, set your Units to Feet, your Limits to 60' high by 120' wide, and your Grid Size to 10 feet by 10 feet. Also turn on Snap to Grid, Absolute Coordinates rather than Relative, and Ortho Mode. Construction Points and Rubberbanding should be turned on for illustrative purposes.

The Reference Point Command

One more drawing aid will be useful as you start this drawing—Ref. Points from the DISPLAY menu, or **PR** on the keyboard. This command toggles the display of reference points on or off. If the message in the prompt area tells you that it is turned off when you give the command, issue it again to turn it back on. Reference points have several uses, but one in particular will help with this drawing. When Reference Points is on, a reference point is displayed at the origin, 0,0.

Note It is a good idea to start all of your drawings at the origin, so that if you ever want to combine drawings, you have a common reference.

Drawing the Lines and Rectangles

As with the key example, it is often easiest to start a drawing with the basic entities, Lines and Rectangles, that set up the overall configuration and then add the other entities that fill out the detail.

Start this drawing with a Rectangle (RE), which will represent the boundary of the site. For the first point, move the cursor to the reference point at the origin. (It may be just barely peeking out of the lower-left corner of the screen.) When the cursor is at this point, Absolute Coordinates at the top of the screen should read exactly 0,0. It should be easy to move to this point with a ten-foot grid turned on. Once you have the cursor located, select the point with the first pointing device button and drag the other corner of the rectangle to 100',50'. In this case, because you started at the origin, the Absolute Coordinates give you the actual size of the rectangle.

After you select these points, change the Grid Size (GS) to 5 feet by 5 feet and place a Line for the sidewalk, which is exactly 5 feet in from the left side of the site boundary. You can see how easy it is to be accurate by adjusting the Grid Size to your current needs. Next, change the Grid Size to 1 foot, and draw the house, 15 feet from the sidewalk and 5 feet from the lower site boundary.

Use ESC to Reset the Coordinates

Whenever you want to draw one object (the house) a certain distance from another object (the sidewalk), the Relative Coordinates command can be useful. Select Relative from the Coordinates command on the DISPLAY menu or type **DC R** and press ENTER. Your coordinates will now be measured from the last point entered instead of from the origin. But what if the point that you want to measure from (in this case, the lower end of the sidewalk line) is not the last point that you entered?

In this situation, the Relative Coordinates must be reset so that the point you want to measure from is, in fact, the last point entered. Do this simply by moving the drawing cursor to the point that you want to reference from and typing **NP** or pressing the third pointing device button. This point is selected, the coordinates are reset to 0,0, and a rubber band line is attached to this point, as Generic CADD thinks that you want to start drawing a line. Since you don't, press ESC. The point that you just selected is now the last point entered, and the coordinates will be measured from there.

The Rest of the Lines and Rectangles

Now you should be able to construct the house 15 feet from the sidewalk and 5 feet from the site boundary. Use the Rectangle (RE) command, positioning the cursor at 15',5', as displayed by the Relative Coordinates for the first point, and then at 24',36', the dimensions of the house.

Using the same technique, draw the driveway, which is 9 feet wide; the walk, 4 feet wide and 2 feet away from the driveway; and the patio, which extends 48 feet from the back of the house. The notches in the corner of the patio are 5 feet on a side. Any other dimensions you can make up. Change the Grid Size according to your needs, and use ESC to reset the coordinates if that becomes necessary. When you are finished, your drawing should resemble Figure 4-18.

A Curved Pool

The next task is to construct the curved pool. Before starting, Zoom In (ZI) to get a little closer. When you are ready to draw, use the Curve command by selecting it from the DRAW menu, or by typing **CV** on the keyboard. Messages in the prompt area explain how the Curve command works. At the bottom of the screen you will read: "Enter a point on the curve >." You must specify a series of points through which the curve is to be constructed. Above this message is the message "Enter a [PU] to complete curve >." This means that when you are finished selecting points, you must type **PU** (Pen Up) to draw the curve. An alternate method of "entering a [PU]" is to select a blank line from the video menu. As soon as you do either, the curve will be drawn.

FIGURE 4-18   The site plan Lines and Rectangles

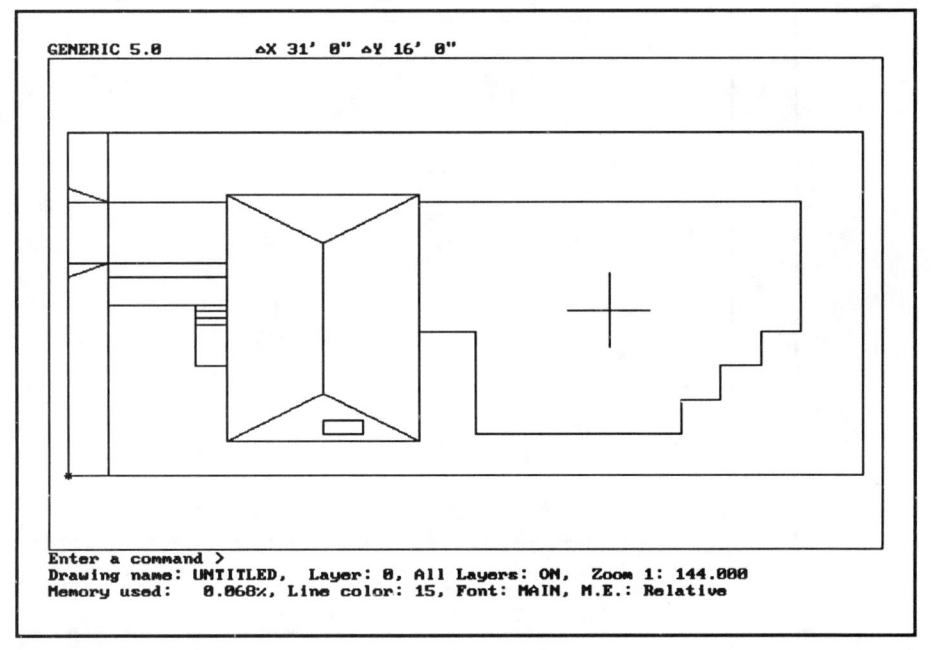

Because the pool is a free-form object, which doesn't necessarily pass through the grid points, you might want to turn off Snap to Grid before you begin selecting points. Starting with the second point, each time you indicate a new point, a temporary line is placed between the two points to help you visualize the curve. See Figure 4-19 for an example of what the curve should look like as you are drawing it. If you want to cancel the command after a number of points have been selected, press ESC.

When you are ready to close the kidney-shaped figure, use the Nearest Point snap to choose the same point that you started with by typing **NP** or pressing the third button on the pointing device. Once you have returned to the first point, type **PU** or move the menu cursor to a blank line and press the second button on the pointing device. The temporary lines will be removed, and the curve will be drawn.

Notice that because the last point was snapped onto the first point, the curve passes smoothly through this point in the same way it goes through the others, as if it was one seamless loop. If these points were not quite in the same place, you might get a slight "dent" in the pool at

FIGURE 4-19

Constructing the curve

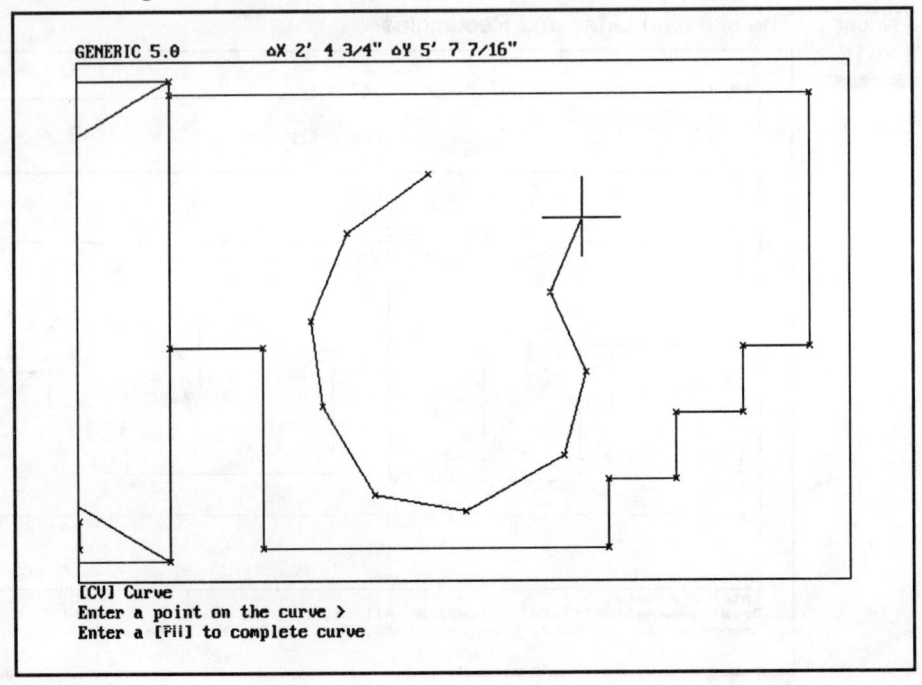

this point. Whether you want a continuous loop depends on what you are trying to draw.

One last note about the Curves command: you must specify at least three points before issuing Pen Up, or Generic CADD will not be able to construct a curve. If you want a short curve, place your points closer together. When you are done with the pool, Zoom All (ZA) to see the entire drawing.

Three-Point Circles

The trees in this drawing could be drawn with two-point circles, but you can use these trees to experiment with the other circle command, Circle 3. Like a three-point arc, these circles are constructed using three points. In this case, the first and last points are not endpoints, of course, and the second point has no special significance. The three points can be given in any order, as only one circle can be defined that passes through any three specified points. Any one of the three points can be thought of as being between the other two.

As you specify each point, a construction point appears. When you select the last point, a construction point appears not only at the cursor location, but at the center of the circle as well, because all circles, no matter how they are created, are actually defined by the location of the center and one point on the circle. When you use a three-point circle, the center and the first point that you specify are the ones that are actually stored. You can verify this with the Redraw command from the ZOOMS menu, or by typing **RD** on the keyboard. When you issue this command, the screen will be redrawn, with the construction points shown at the actual definition points of the circles rather than at the locations that you used to create the circles. Compare Figure 4-20, shown with the construction points in the locations where they are placed, with Figure 4-21, showing the actual locations of the definition points.

Use Figure 4-20 as a guide for placing your three-point circles. You might try Circle 2 (C2) to review the difference between the two commands.

120 Generic CADD 5.0 Inside & Out

FIGURE 4-20 The site plan with three-point circles for trees

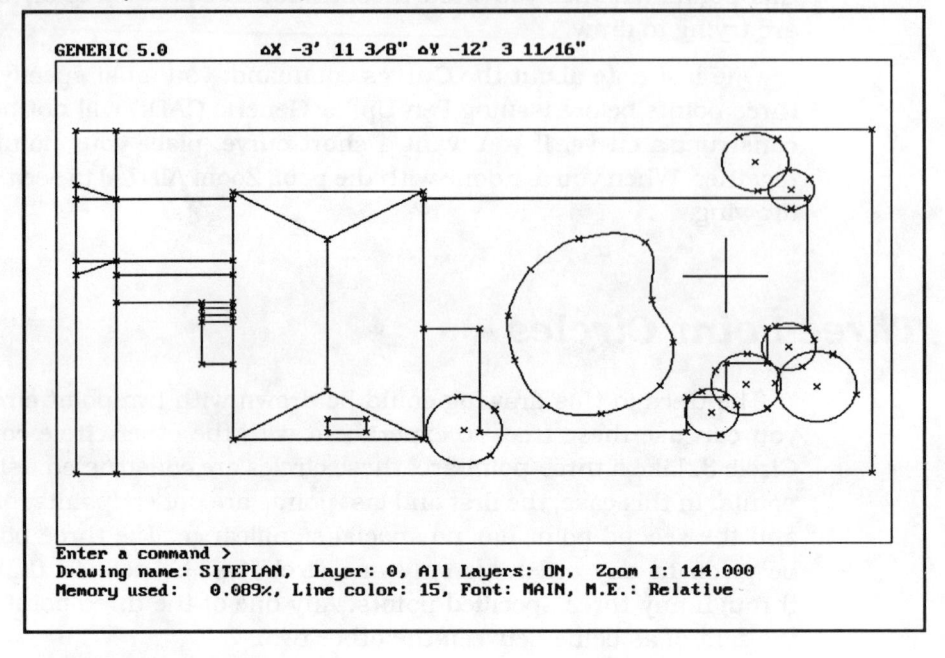

FIGURE 4-21 The actual definition points

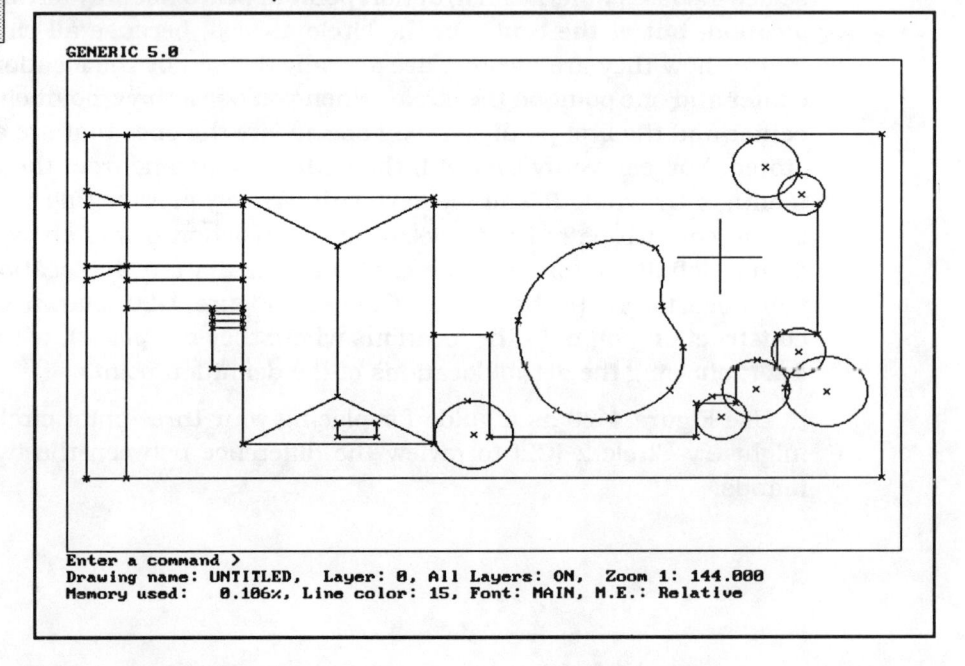

Standard Points

Another Generic CADD primitive called a *standard point* can be used to mark the locations of the trunks of these trees. These are useful if you want to mark a location visibly, and have it show up when you print or plot your drawing. Standard points can be printed, while construction points and reference points cannot.

To draw a standard point, select Point from the DRAW menu or type **PO** on the keyboard. Move the cursor to where you want to put the point, and press the first pointing device button. In the case of the trees in your drawing, you can place these Points exactly onto the centers by using the Nearest Point snap instead of the first button. When the cursor is near the center of a circle, type **NP** or press the third button on the pointing device. This will snap the point exactly where you want it. To draw another standard point, simply press SPACEBAR, and then move the cursor and snap onto the center of another circle. Continue until you have placed points in the center of every tree, and your drawing will be complete.

Display Without Construction Points

To see what your drawing really looks like, turn off Construction Points (PC) and Reference Points (PR), and execute the Redraw (RD) command. You will notice that a command on the DISPLAY menu also controls the display of Standard Points. If you turn off the display of Standard Points, they will not show up on the screen and they will not be printed either. Finally, save the drawing and exit to DOS by using the Quit (QU) command.

Through the examples provided in this chapter, you have tried out all of the basic Draw commands, including Point (PO), Line (LI) or implicit by picking points, Arc 2 (A2), Arc 3 (A3), Arc 4 (A4), Circle 2 (C2), Circle 3 (C3), Rectangle (RE), Regular Polygon (RP), Ellipse (True and Construction) (EP), and Curve (CV). The only Draw command you have not tried, Bezier, will be explored in Chapter 10.

Also, you have used some of the Zoom commands, Zoom Limits (ZL), Zoom All (ZA), Zoom In (ZI), and Zoom Out (ZO). In addition, you have used many of the drawing aids, such as Grid (GR), Grid Size (GS), Snap to Grid (SG), Ortho Mode (OR), and Snap to Nearest Point (NP or third pointing device button).

You have seen how to use Absolute and Relative Coordinates, including how to reset the Relative Coordinates with ESC, and how to use manual entry of coordinates to type actual dimensions rather than showing points on the screen. You have used the Drawing Erase (DX) command to erase the entire drawing, and the Object Erase (OE) command to erase one entity at a time. You have repeated commands using the SPACEBAR, and have used construction lines and temporary entities to construct more complex objects.

You have created and saved several drawings, and in one case called up a previously saved drawing and added more information to it. You have saved the files ROOM.DWG, MUSIC.DWG, KEY.DWG, STAR.DWG, and SITEPLAN.DWG on your disk, and will return to some of these files in later chapters. All told, you have come a long way toward becoming a productive user of Generic CADD 5.0.

CHAPTER 5

Basic Editing Tasks

This chapter provides a counterpoint to Chapter 4, "Basic Drawing Tasks," which covered the creation of new drawings and the addition of new entities into the drawing database. This chapter, in contrast, examines the editing commands.

For the most part, you will use existing drawings to experiment with these commands. However, you will see that the editing commands are also an integral part of the drawing process and that editing need not be reserved for "fixing mistakes." In fact, in many cases you will find that the editing commands as well as the drawing commands can be used to create a brand new drawing.

Editing Command Organization

Unlike the entity-creating commands, which are primarily on the DRAW menu, the entity-editing commands are located on two menus, EDITS and SHORTCUTS.

There are two distinct formats for the Generic CADD 5.0 editing commands. These are the noun-verb combinations discussed earlier, and the newer multiple-selection editing commands found on the EDITS menu.

Many of the techniques used in the shortcuts, which are located on the SHORTCUTS menu, are combined in the multiple-selection commands, also called the "master" editing commands, so these shortcut methods are discussed first.

Methods of Selection

The four shortcut methods, Object, Window, Layer, and Drawing, represent four quick ways of selecting objects. As explained in Chapter 2, "The Generic Approach," when combined with the actual objects that are selected, these four methods can be thought of as nouns—for instance, "this *object*," "the entities in this *window*," "*layer* four," and "the whole *drawing*." Each method makes its specific entity selections in a different way. In the headings below, the two letters in parentheses show the format for the accompanying editing command. The lowercase *x* is replaced with the letter representing the actual function of the editing command.

The Object Method (Ox)

All of the Object editing commands first ask you to select the object that you want to edit. This is usually done by pointing to it with the drawing cursor and pressing the first button on the pointing device. The object closest to the cursor will be selected for editing. Although each Object command affects only one entity at a time (the words "object" and "entity" are interchangeable in this context), you can always select the command again by pressing SPACEBAR and selecting another entity to edit.

The two-character commands for most of the Object commands start with the letter *O*. The second letter indicates the type of editing operation you want to perform on the selected object.

The Window Method (Wx)

The Window editing commands affect all of the objects that are selected by placing a window. When you select any of these commands, you are prompted to "Place a window." To do this, move the drawing cursor to one corner of the area in which the objects that you wish to edit are located, and press the first pointing device button. A rubber band rectangle will appear attached to the cursor. Stretch this cursor around the entities that you want to edit, and press the first button again once you surround them. If your first point proves to be in the wrong place and you can't get the window around the objects, press ESC to cancel the command and start over.

For an entity to be considered inside a window, all of the definition points of the entity must be inside the window. If the centerpoint of a circle, for instance, is inside the window, but the point on the circle is outside, the circle will not be selected. If a line passes through the window, but either endpoint is outside the window, the line will not be selected, and so on. In regard to complex entities that have no construction or definition point but only one reference point each, only the reference point need be included in the window for the entire complex object (such as a text character) to be selected.

The Window shortcut editing commands start with the letter *W* and end with a letter representing the type of editing to be done: Window Erase (WE), Window Copy (WC), and so on.

The Layer Method (Yx)

In the drawings you have made so far, all of the entities have been created on a single layer, called layer 0 (zero). The number of the layer is stored as part of that entity's data. Every entity that you have created so far includes this information. As you move on to more complex drawings, you may want to keep different types of information on different layers. You will have a chance to try layers in some of the examples to come. The simplest way to visualize a layer is to imagine a transparent overlay that contains certain entities. Up to 256 of these overlays can be combined in a single drawing file. If you store entities on different layers, the editing commands on the LAYERS menu can be used to edit selective data on a chosen layer.

When selected, each of the Layer editing commands asks you for the number of the layer you want to edit. You reply by typing a number (0 to 255) and pressing ENTER. The command then continues with its specific editing function.

The two-character Layer commands all start with the letter *Y*, including the editing commands and the commands for selecting, displaying, and hiding layers as well. The only exceptions are the All Layers Edit (AL) toggle, in which a three-letter command was shortened to the two-character format by dropping the last character, and All Layers Snap (SY), which appears on the SNAPS menu, and therefore starts with an *S*, but includes the *Y* as its second letter.

The command All Layers Edit toggles between two different modes of on-screen editing. When All Layers Edit is on, you can use any editing command to edit any entity that is visible on the screen. When All Layers Edit is off, you can only edit the entities that are on the current layer. Even with All Layers Edit turned off, you can still *use* any of the editing commands; they just won't work on entities that are not on the current layer.

As a further refinement, the toggle All Layers Snap, located on the SNAPS menu or by typing **SY** on the keyboard, controls whether or not you can snap onto entities that are not on the current layer when All

Layers Edit is off. If All Layers Snap is on, you can use entities on layers other than the current layer for reference, trim to them, and so on. When All Layers Snap is off, these layers are ignored by any command that attempts to find an entity. When All Layers Edit is on, the status of All Layers Snap is ignored, and you can snap or reference any visible entity.

The current layer is selected with the Layer Current (YC) command. You have a chance to try the layer selection and display commands in Chapter 6, "Drawing Aids and Controls."

The Drawing Method (Dx)

The Drawing editing commands edit every entity in the drawing. They are, of course, the most powerful editing commands, but at the same time they are the least discriminating.

The Drawing two-character commands—not only the editing commands, but also a number of other commands that perform operations on the drawing as a whole, such as Drawing Save (DS) and Drawing Plot (DP)—start with the letter *D*.

Combined Methods

Most of the commands on the EDITS menu, as well as a number of other commands throughout Generic CADD 5.0, make use of the combined-selection method.

With all commands of this type, the first prompt after issuing the command simply asks you to Select Objects. This prompt lends yet another name to this technique, Selection editing.

Four of the already familiar shortcut methods—Object, Window, Layer, and Drawing—are options offered at this prompt. These are activated by pressing the letter representing the method, which is highlighted in the prompt, or by selecting the word in the prompt with the first button on the mouse. Each time you pick one of these selection methods, you are then prompted to select an object, place a window, or choose a layer. The drawing method requires no additional input.

The primary difference between the selection commands and the shortcuts is that after you have made your selection, you get the Select

Objects prompt and the list of selection methods back again, rather than moving along to the edit itself.

With the selection edits, you can continue selecting entities (using any of the methods) until you have all that you want selected before you proceed with the rest of the command. If you have selected too many, they can also be deselected using any of the selection methods. You deselect by holding down the CTRL key while typing the method's letter or selecting it from the prompt with the mouse. You can repeat the processes of selection and deselection as many times as you like before continuing on with the rest of the command.

Once you are satisfied that all the entities, and only the entities that you want, are selected, press ENTER, and the command will continue on to the next prompt. (Additional selection methods will be discussed in Chapter 10, "Advanced Drawing and Editing Techniques.")

Editing Functions

Just as the various objects and entities to be edited can be thought of as nouns, the editing functions can be thought of as verbs. They are found in several different menus and represent certain operations or actions that are performed on or with the selected entities.

In general, a command that appears on more than one menu works in more or less the same way on each. When you select Object Erase (OE), for example, as you did in Chapter 4, you are asked to select an object. Once you have selected it, it is erased. If you select Window Erase (WE), you are asked to place a window. Once you place the window, the objects within it are erased. When you select Layer Erase (YX), you are asked to choose a layer. After typing the number of the layer and pressing ENTER, the selected layer is erased. When you execute Drawing Erase (DX), the entire drawing is erased. The main difference in these four commands lies in how the entities are selected.

Certain basic editing functions are illustrated in this chapter, and numerous others are covered in Chapter 9, "Multiple Entities." Again, the lowercase *x* in the two-character code represents the selection type, as it did in the previous sections.

The Erase Function (ER, xE, or xX)

You have already seen this function in action. Once the entities have been selected by object, window, layer, drawing, or multiple selection, these entities are erased, that is, removed from the display. In the case of all but the Drawing Erase command, they are not actually removed from the computer's memory, but marked as erased, so that Generic CADD knows not to display or save them any longer. Because they are not actually removed from memory, they can be rescued with the Unerase (UE) command. Any number of entities that have been erased with the Erase function can be resurrected with the Unerase command. If you erased one object, Unerase will retrieve the last object erased. If you erased an entire layer before that, the next Unerase command would revive that layer, and so on. You can continue using Unerase to reverse the effects of Erase commands until no more entities that are marked as erased remain in the database. The Unerase command does not work after a Drawing Erase (DX) command, as this command clears drawing memory rather than marking all of the objects as erased. If you use Undo (OO) instead of Unerase, the Erase can be re-created with the Redo (UU) command. See Chapter 10.

The Copy Function (CO or xC)

This function, which can be used on single objects, many objects within a window, or with multiple selection, makes exact copies of entities in your drawing. Of course, you must first specify which entity or entities you want to copy. This is done either by pointing to an object in the case of an Object Copy command, by placing a window in the case of a Window Copy command, or by any technique with Copy.

After the selection has been made, you are asked for a reference point—usually some point on the object or set of objects that you want to copy. Then, you are asked for a new reference point or offset—the location where you want the copy to appear. As you will see, the first reference point does not have to be on the objects that you are trying to copy. What really matters is the distance between the first and second points, or the "offset." The object(s) will be copied at a location equal to the distance between the two points. If the first point *is* actually on the object(s), it can help to visualize where the copy is going to end up.

If Manual Entry is set to Relative (MR) mode, the new reference point or offset can be typed in coordinate form. In this case, it doesn't matter where you put the first reference point. Because the coordinates of the second point are relative to the last point specified, they will equal the offset. If you want to copy, for example, two inches to the right and six inches up, you can enter anything for the first reference point (just press the first mouse button), and then type **2,6** for the second reference point.

Once the offset has been shown or typed, you will be asked how many copies you want to make. Type a number and press ENTER. If you simply press ENTER without typing a number, you will get one copy. The number of copies does not include the original. Each copy is copied from the last copy, so that if you copy one object two times, you end up with three objects, all equally spaced. The first copy is made at the specified distance from the first, and then the second copy is made at the specified distance from the first copy.

If you are making several copies of a complex part of the drawing, and none of these copies will need to be edited, you might consider defining and using a Component instead, to conserve drawing memory and file space. See Chapter 8, "Complex Entities," and your Generic CADD 5.0 Reference Manual.

The Move Function (MV or xM)

Like the Copy function, the Move function includes Object and Window shortcuts in addition to the Move command itself. The two-character shortcut commands end with the letter *M*. You select the object if you are using Object Move, place a window if you are using Window Move, or use any standard technique with Move. Then, you show a reference point and a new reference point or offset. These points have exactly the same meaning as in the Copy function: you want to move from somewhere to somewhere else.

As with the Copy function, the two reference points do not have to be located on, or even near, the object(s) being moved. Again, what really matters is the distance between the two points, and you can use manual entry to indicate the exact distance that you want to move the object(s).

The Stretch Command (SS)   This is a special version of the Move function that allows some objects to simply be moved while others are "stretched." Users of previous versions of Generic CADD will recognize this as the "Straight Line Stretch" option of the Window Move command augmented and separated into its own command.

There is only one version of this command, no shortcuts. In fact, it requires a sort of double selection, as you shall see. When first activated from the EDITS menu or by typing **SS** on the keyboard, a selection prompt appears. You must use multiple selection to select both the entities to be moved and those to be stretched. Type a letter for each selection method that you want to use, then use it. Use all the Windows and Objects you want (these will be the most useful), then press ENTER once you've selected them all.

Now comes the second selection. You will automatically be asked to place a Window around the points that you want to move. At this time, you can capture both whole and partial entities. If you get the whole thing, it will be moved. If you get only some of its points, it will be stretched. What is really going on here is a whole bunch of Move Point commands. Rather than moving the entities themselves, you're moving their definition points. So, if you only move some of the points, things tend to stretch. Of course, they can be squashed too. The key to expert use of this command lies in the first selection, where the groundwork is laid. If you're trying to edit around other things, be sure to get only those entities you actually want to move or stretch. On the other hand, if nothing is really in the way, and the second selection pretty well defines it, you might as well select everything in sight the first time out. A little practice with this one, and you'll get the hang of it.

The Rotate Function (RO or xR)

Both Window and the entire Drawing can be rotated with shortcuts, while any combination of entities may be rotated with multiple selection. The Window Rotate command first asks you to place a window. Next, all commands ask for an *axis point*—the point around which the selected items will be rotated. (You might imagine the drawing or the window as a pinwheel and the axis point as the pin in the center.) Then, you are asked for the *rotation angle*. This angle is measured in degrees, counter-clockwise. For example, 90 degrees will tip a straight up-and-down drawing on its side, 180 degrees will turn it upside down, and 360 degrees will have no net effect.

You can also elect to show the angle on the screen rather than typing it if you like. When asked for the angle, you may type **A** or **V** to show the angle in two different ways. If you type **A** (for Angle), you will be asked to show two points. The angle between these points will be measured, and will be entered as the rotation angle. The angle between the points is measured assuming that horizontal is zero. That is, if you pick the second point directly to the right of the first, you will specify a zero rotation; if the second point is directly above the first, you will get 90 degrees, and so on.

If you type **V** (for Vertex) instead, you will be asked for three points, the first of which is considered the *vertex* of an angle. The second point specifies an endpoint of an imaginary line projected from the vertex, while the third point specifies an endpoint of another imaginary line, projected from the same vertex. The vertex is the intersection point of these two lines. The angle between the lines is measured and used as the rotation angle.

This same technique can be used with most commands that ask you to specify an angle. If you are unsure, type **V** or **A**. If nothing happens, you must type the angle rather than showing it on the screen.

If you like, the axis point may be selected by snapping onto an existing definition point using Snap to Nearest Point (type **NP** or select the third pointing device button). Angles do not have to be in full degrees, and negative angles will produce clockwise rotations.

The Scale Function (xZ)

As with the Rotate function, you can issue Scale commands as either a Window or Drawing shortcut, or use multiple selection with the Scale function. After selecting entities, the Scale function asks for something similar to an axis point, called a *reference point.* When selected entities are rescaled (changed in size), the location of some point has to remain stationary, and all other points are repositioned in relation to this stationary reference point. For a growing child, the reference point is the floor. The reference point for an icicle that is being scaled because of an accumulation of frozen water or warmer weather is the roof edge from which it hangs.

Drawing Scale assumes that the reference point is at the origin, 0,0. In all cases, you must then specify the X and Y scale factors. The entities

Chapter 5: Basic Editing Tasks

selected can be scaled both horizontally and vertically. A scale factor of 1 indicates no change, 2 means twice as large, and .5 means half the current size. Generic CADD assumes that you want to scale the entities at the same scale factors for X and Y unless you type a different number in each case. You will notice that after you type the X scale factor, the default value for Y will be the same as X, and you can just press ENTER.

You should be aware that certain primitives do not scale well in two directions, namely circles and arcs. No matter what you do to a circle, it is still defined by a centerpoint and a point on the circle. When you scale it, it gets smaller or larger, but it does not squash. The same is true for arcs, which are really just partial circles and follow the same rules. How a circle responds to a two-direction scale depends on the location of the point on the circle. It will act differently if the point is above the centerpoint than it will if the point is to the left or right. Circles and Arcs within Components will squash properly unless the Component is exploded into individual entities, in which case Circles and Arcs become round again.

The basic rule for scaling (and rotating and moving too) is that definition points are actually affected by the command, and that the objects themselves retain their basic geometric properties no matter what you do to them. There is no way to make a Line that is not straight or a Circle that is not round.

The Mirror Commands (MI or WI)

Generic CADD's Mirror commands make a mirror image copy of the selected objects, as shown in Figure 5-1. As you can see, much drawing time can be saved when you need a reverse image of part or all of your drawing.

To make the mirrored copy, Generic CADD must know where the imaginary mirror is located, and in which direction you want to reflect the image. You can start by selecting entities using multiple selection (MI) or by using the Window shortcut (WI). After selecting the entities, you will be asked to locate the mirror, and then show the direction. The mirror can be located anywhere, including within the selected window. It is even possible to place a mirror right on top of the object. Sometimes this is desirable, but more often it is not. Usually, you will want to put

FIGURE 5-1 Mirroring a portion of a drawing

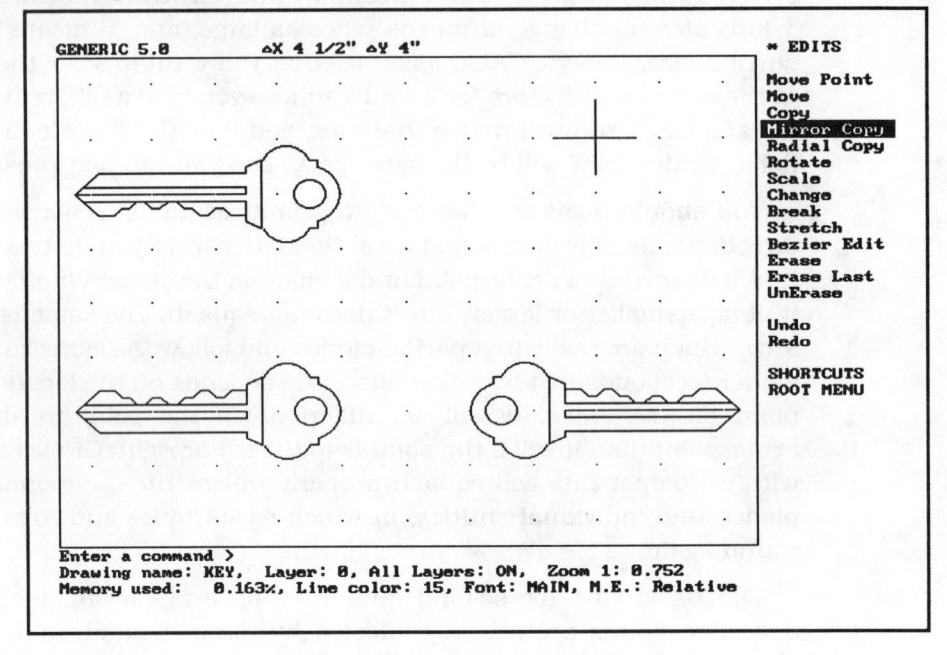

your mirror to the right, left, above, or below the entities that you have selected, and reflect them in the same direction. Diagonal reflections are also possible.

The Move Point Command (MP)

This command generally works on one entity at a time. However, if you Snap to shared endpoints, it will edit as many entities as it finds at that location. Like the Object editing shortcuts, the Move Point command first asks which object you want to edit. In this case, you are going to move one of the definition points of a simple object, or the reference point of a complex object. Point to the object that you want to edit.

Next, select the point that you want to move. Obviously, the point must be one of the definition points of the entity that you have selected in the previous step. It helps if you have Construction Points turned on, so that you can see where the definition points are located. If you are trying to move the reference point of a complex object, it helps to have Reference

Points turned on. If you need to change the status of either of these, use the appropriate toggle (PC or PR), do a Redraw (RD), and continue the Move Point (MP) command.

Finally, indicate the new location of the point that you are moving. If you have Rubberbanding turned on, Lines, Arcs, and Circles will rubberband as you move the cursor, to show what the edited entity will look like. When you pick the point, the entity is redrawn. Like many others, this command can be repeated by pressing the SPACEBAR. If two or more entities share a common point, this point may be moved on all entities simultaneously. When asked to select the object, type **NP** or use the third pointing device button to select the desired point. All entities that share that point will be selected. When asked for a point, select the same point again. Specify the new location in the usual fashion. All entities will be rubberbanded to show the effect of the relocated point.

Note that for entity selection, you normally have to select a point on the object in order for that object to be selected. This means that the centerpoint of a circle cannot be snapped onto to select the object. You must snap to the perimeter. If you wish to simultaneously move the centerpoint of several concentric circles, this can be a problem. A solution is to snap a Standard Point to the center of the circles. Then when you use the Move Point command, there is something there to locate. When the point is found, the center of the circles is found as well, and all the points are moved. When you are done, simply erase the Standard Point with an Erase Last (EL).

The Break Command (OB)

You can break only one entity at a time also, so this command is like an Object shortcut. As with Object commands, you first select the entity that you want to break. You can break Lines, Circles, Arcs, and Curves. You cannot break True Ellipses (although you can break Construction Ellipses, which are really made of Arcs), Bezier Curves, or Standard Points.

After you have selected the entity to be broken, specify the first breakpoint and the second breakpoint. The gap will be rubberbanded between these two points. With Arcs and Lines, the gap will be created between the two points, no matter what order you place them in. With Circles, clockwise and counterclockwise cursor movements are detected and used to determine which part to take out. The gap will be rubber-banded for visual reference.

If either of the selected breakpoints is beyond the end of a Line or Arc, you will get some unusual results. The gap will appear between the first breakpoint and the endpoint, and then a new segment of the Line or Arc will appear from the endpoint to the second breakpoint. See Figure 5-2 for examples of Lines, Arcs, and Circles broken in the normal fashion and in this nonstandard way.

The Change Function (CG or xG)

Appearing as a selection command and in several shortcut variations, the Change function allows you to change the line type, line width, line color, and layer of selected entities. The four shortcut commands operate somewhat differently from the master Change command. Each of these

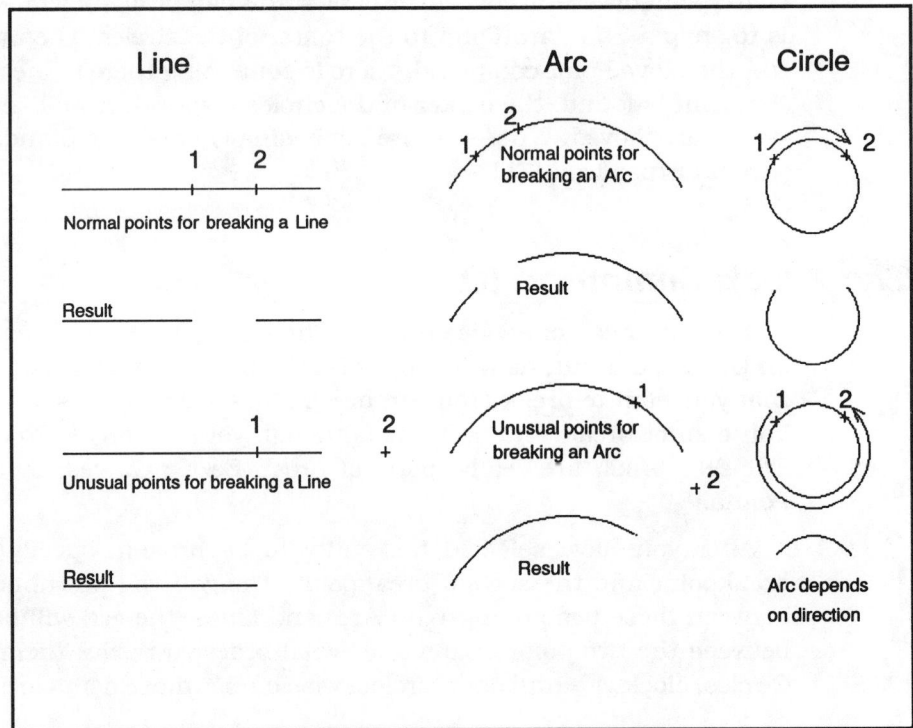

FIGURE 5-2 Examples of breaking entities: Lines, Arcs, and Circles

four shortcuts, Object, Window, Layer, and Drawing, first makes the selection in its normal way, then proceeds on to a single prompt where the changes are made. From here you can select an option from the prompt or type a letter to change the layer (Y), color (C), line type (T), or line width (W) of all of the entities selected by the shortcut method. If all of the entities selected share a common value for any of these, it will be shown in the prompt, next to the option. Otherwise, the parentheses will be empty.

For each option that you select, you will be asked to specify a new value. For Layer, you may select from the Layer List if the video menu is active. You can change as many of these parameters as you like, then press ENTER to accept the changes. If you change your mind and decide not to change anything, you can press ESC to cancel the command, as noted in the prompt. If you make any changes, the selected entities will be redrawn to reflect this. If entities disappear from the screen, you have probably changed them either to color 0 (the same as the background) or onto a hidden layer.

The Change function itself allows much more flexibility in the selection of entities through the Filter option. While this selection method is discussed in more detail in Chapter 10, it should be said here that users of previous versions of CADD who are wondering where to specify the entity parameters—type, color, layer, and so on—of the entities to be changed will find these in the Filter method. The main difference is that the entities must be selected by some combination of the first four traditional methods as well. The Filter option further refines the selection process rather than selecting anything on its own. See Chapter 10 for more information on this.

Like the other Change commands, this one ends by asking for the new values to which all of the selected entities will be changed. A final ENTER confirms the specifications, and the selected entities are redrawn to reflect the change.

Two-Character Commands

The two-character codes for each of the editing shortcuts are formed by combining the character of the selection type with the character that represents the editing function. Some of these combinations do not make sense and therefore do not work. Others are simply not active at this time. Most of the editing functions exist as multiple-selection commands as well, with their own mnemonic two-character commands.

Editing Example: ROOM

You can try several editing commands on the existing drawing ROOM. Call up this drawing either by typing **CADD ROOM** at the DOS prompt, or by typing **CADD** at the DOS prompt and loading the file ROOM with a Drawing Load (DL) command. If the file is loaded with CADD, the display will automatically be set at Zoom All, otherwise type **ZA** after loading the drawing.

Changing the Shape

Assume that you want to change the width of the bathroom from eight feet to six feet. First, change the Grid Size (GS) to 12 (inches), and turn on Snap to Grid (SG) and Relative Coordinates (DC,R). You might want to Zoom Out (ZO) to get a little more space around the edge of the room, which is probably crowding the edges of the screen.

To change the width of the room, use the Stretch (SS) command. Type **D** to select the entire drawing, then press ENTER and place the window around the lower wall of the bathroom as shown in Figure 5-3.

For a reference point, select one corner of the room. For the new reference point, move the cursor two feet upwards, until the Y coordinate reads 2' or 24". The X coordinate should stay at 0. If you are having trouble keeping the X coordinate at 0, turn on Ortho Mode by typing **OR**. After showing the new reference point, the two lower horizontal lines will be moved, and the four vertical lines will be shortened as required. Your drawing will look approximately like Figure 5-4.

You can also type coordinates to move this wall if you like. This time, make the length of the room six inches shorter. First, turn on Manual Entry Relative (MR) so that you can type the exact distance that you want to move the wall. Then, issue the Stretch (SS) command, and type **D** to select everything. Then press ENTER and place a vertical window around the right wall, as shown in Figure 5-5. It doesn't matter which point you

Chapter 5: Basic Editing Tasks 139

FIGURE 5-3 The second window used to move the bathroom wall

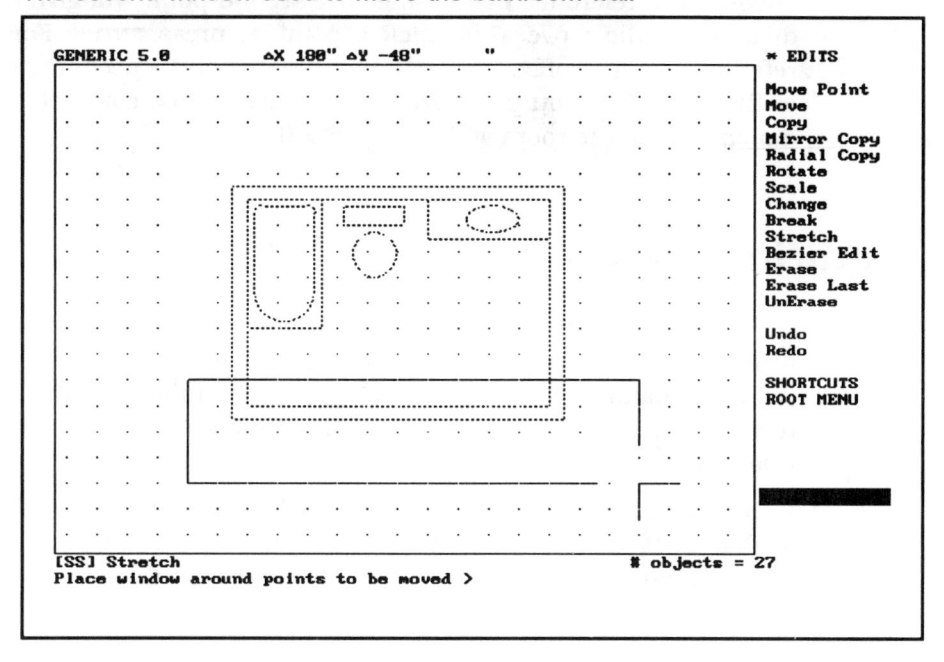

FIGURE 5-4 The six-foot-wide bathroom after stretching

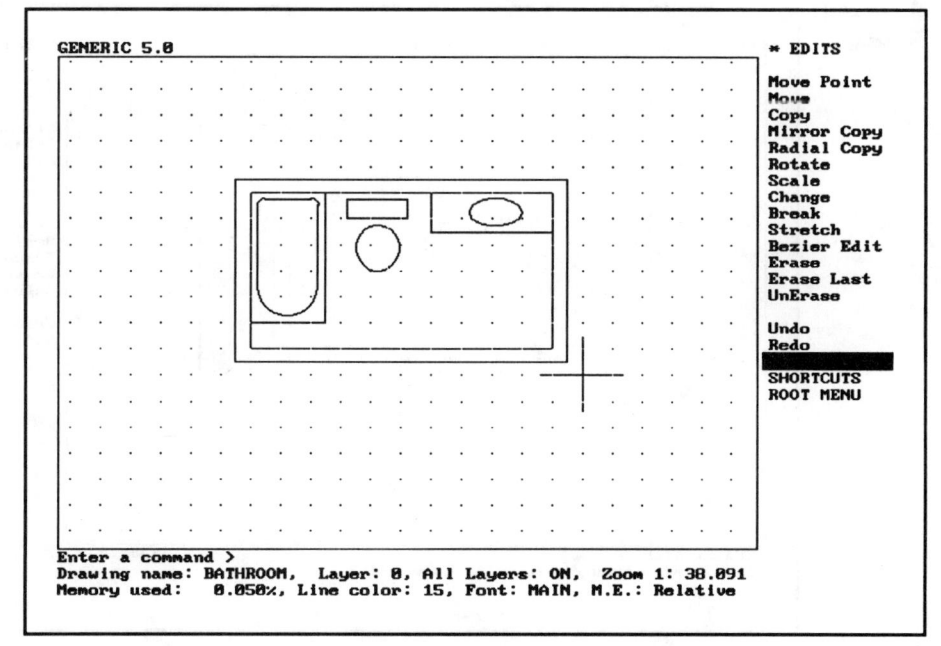

choose for a reference point, since the second point will give the actual distance of the move. Just pick a point or press ENTER. For the new reference point or offset, type the coordinates **-6,0**, specifying six inches to the left. When you press ENTER, the move will be completed, and the dimensions of the room will now be 6' x 9'6".

Rotating the Fixtures

For this exercise, suppose that you want to move the toilet to the right wall. First, you must turn the toilet on its side with the Window Rotate (WR) command. If you place the axis point carefully, you should be able to rotate the toilet to the middle of the room and then move it against this wall.

Select Win Rotate from the SHORTCUTS menu or type **WR** on the keyboard. Place a window around the toilet. You will probably need to turn off Snap to Grid (SG) temporarily to make sure that you don't include

FIGURE 5-5 Placing a window to move another bathroom wall

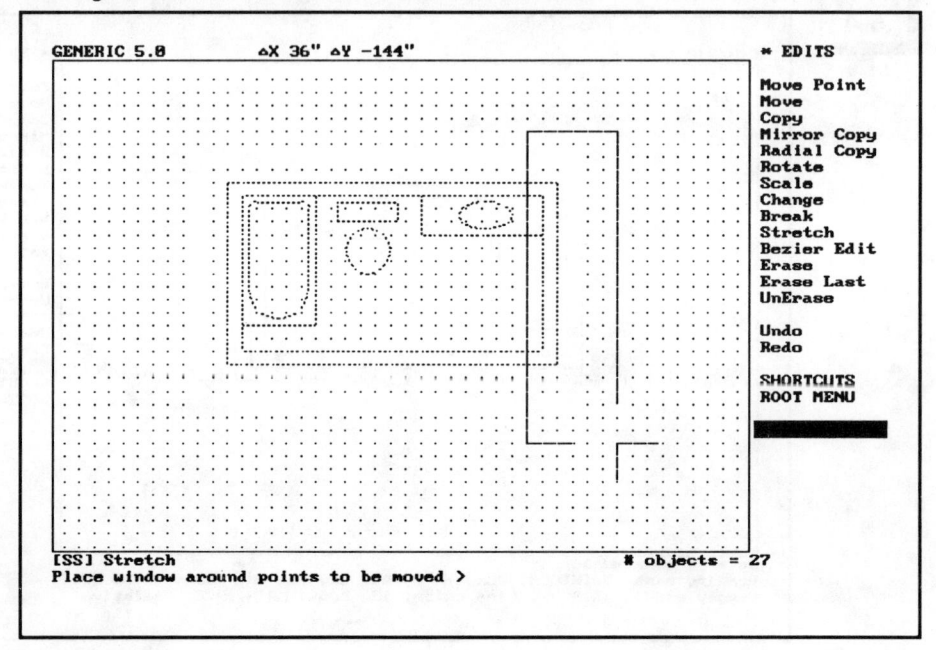

Chapter 5: Basic Editing Tasks　　　　　　　　　　　　　　　141

FIGURE 5-6　The selected entities and the axis point used to rotate the toilet

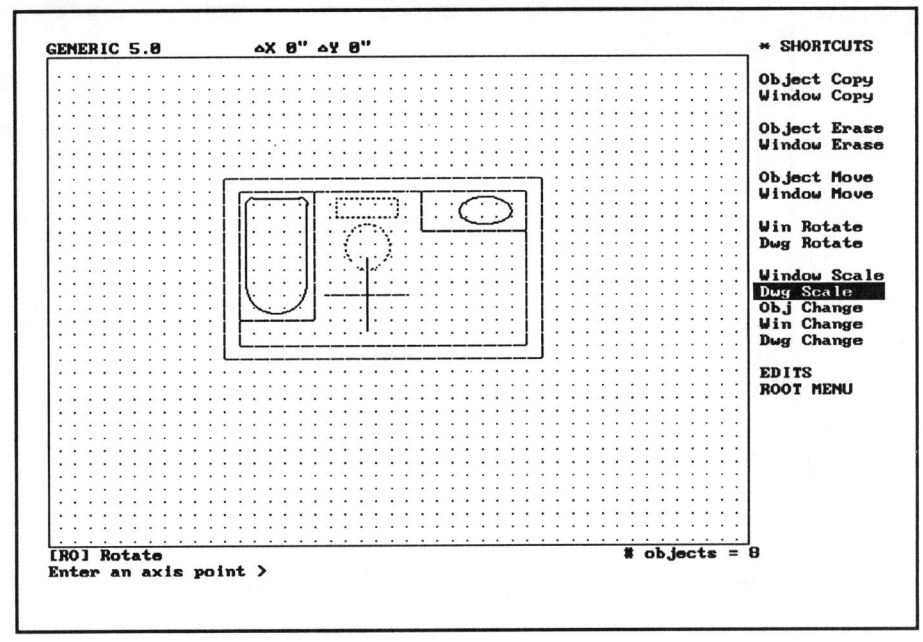

any other objects by mistake. After you have placed the window, turn Snap to Grid (SG) back on.

　　For an axis point, select a point directly below the toilet, exactly four feet into the room. In other words, with the grid set to 12 inches, and the room 6 feet wide, pick a point four feet (four grid points) from the top interior wall, as shown in Figure 5-6. For a rotation angle, type **-90** (for 90 degrees clockwise) and press ENTER. The toilet will be turned on its side, and will end up in the middle of the room, between the wall and the sink. You now need to use the Window Move (WM) or Move (MV) command to slide it into position against the right wall as shown in Figure 5-7. Again, you may need to turn off Snap to Grid (SG) temporarily to place the window. You may also need to reduce the Grid Size (GS) or use manual entry to move the toilet on a smaller module than 12 inches.

FIGURE 5-7 The bathroom with the toilet rotated and moved

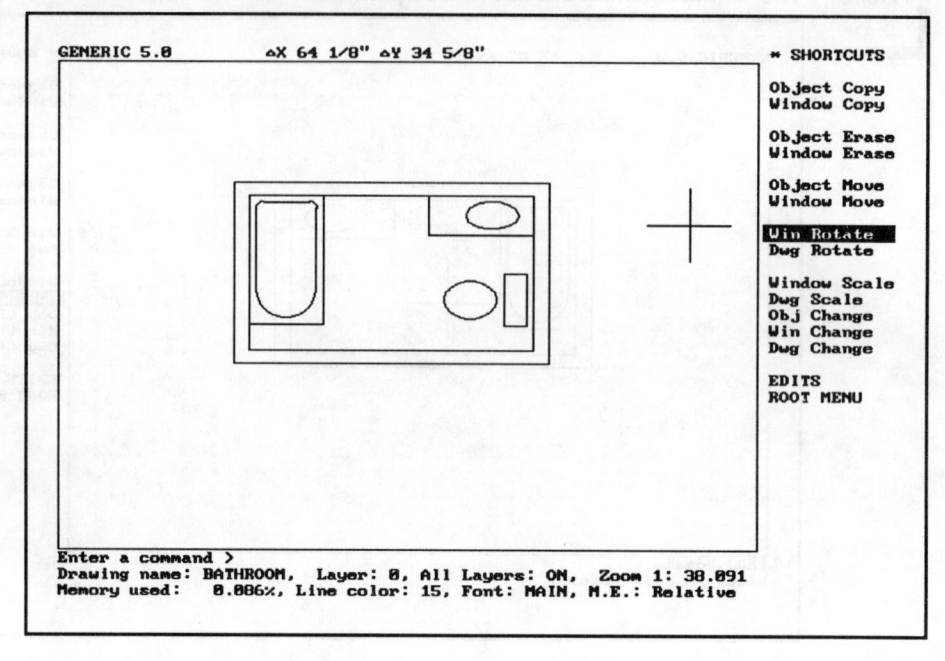

Reversing the Plan

To experiment with the Mirror (MI) command, imagine that you want to reverse the bathroom plan. You want the bathtub on the right wall instead of the left, and the toilet and sink on the left wall instead of the right.

After selecting the command, type **W** and put a window around the entire bathroom, including the six-inch exterior wall. For a mirror location, select a point just outside the window to the right of the bathroom and a point directly below this. For a direction, choose a point a little further to the right (essentially, you are telling Generic CADD to "put it right here"). The mirror image of the bathroom will be created next to the present one. The new bathroom may be partially off the screen. If so, use the Zoom All (ZA) command to see the whole drawing, which will now include the two bathrooms. Erase the original bathroom by using

FIGURE 5-8 The mirrored bathroom plan

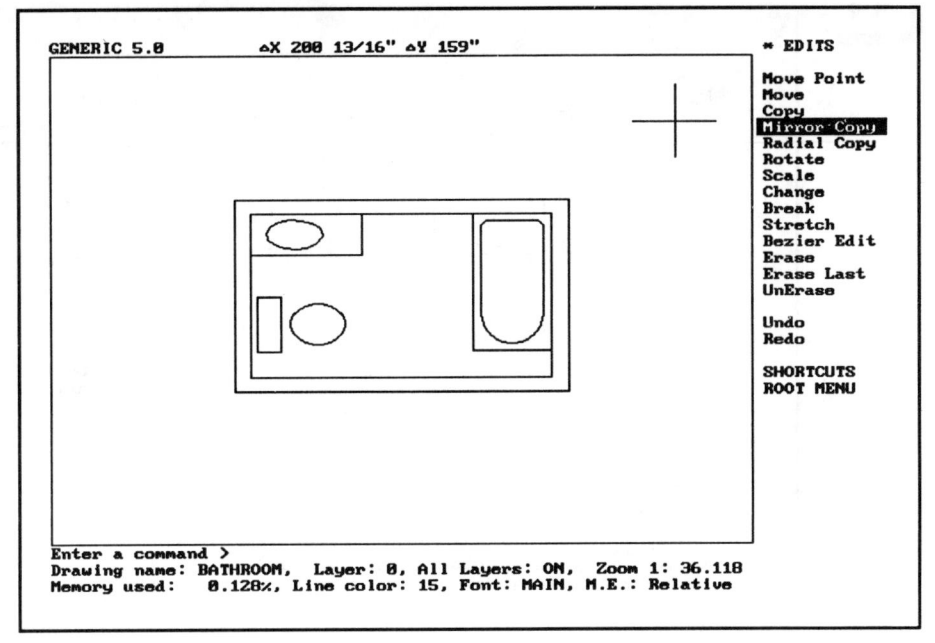

the Window Erase (WE) command. Place a window around the original bathroom. As soon as you select the second corner of the window, all entities inside the window will be erased. Use Zoom All (ZA) again to readjust the display to the new drawing contents. Your drawing should now look much like the one shown in Figure 5-8.

Cutting a Doorway

To put a doorway into this room, you will need to break some of the existing lines (walls). Set your Grid Size (GS) to 6 inches before you start, and make sure that Snap to Grid (SG) is turned on.

Select Break from the EDITS menu or type **OB** on the keyboard. You will be asked for an object to break. Select one of the two horizontal lines at the bottom of the drawing. For the first breakpoint, select a point

FIGURE 5-9 A doorway created by breaking and adding lines

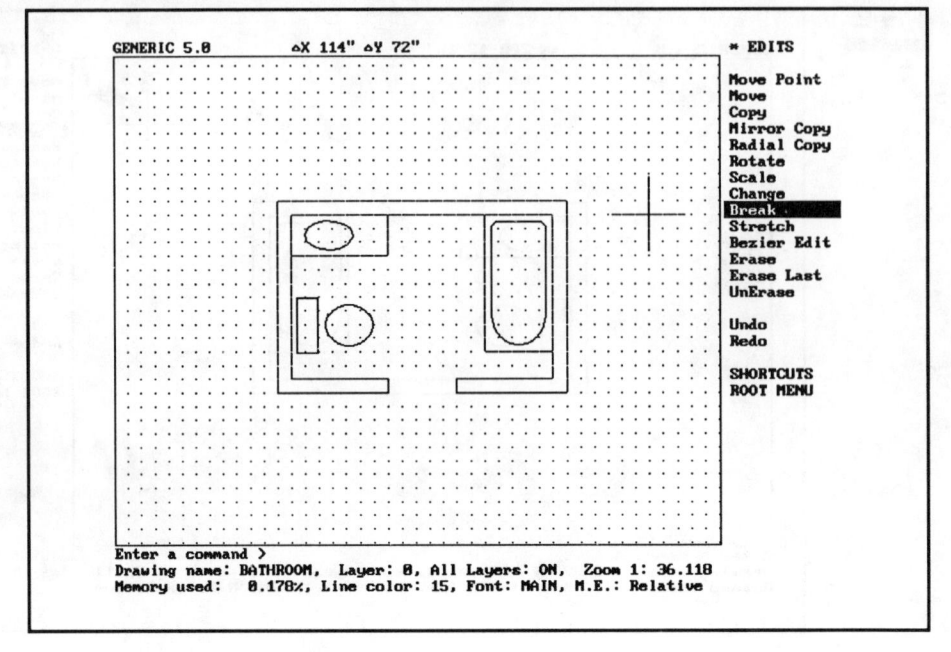

somewhere on this line where you want to start the doorway. Use Figure 5-9 as a guide. For the next breakpoint, move the cursor to the right or left until the X coordinate reads 2'6", negative or positive. The Y coordinate should remain at 0. When you select this point, the line will be broken. Note that this is not really a line with a hole in it, but two lines, separated by 2 feet 6 inches of space. Each line has its own endpoints and its own definition in the database. Break the other horizontal line in the same way. Issue another Break command by pressing the SPACEBAR and then choose points that are directly in line with the new endpoints of the lines above.

To finish off the doorway, simply snap onto one of these new endpoints with a Snap to Nearest Point (type **NP** or use the third pointing device button) to start an implicit Line command. Snap onto the opposite side of the wall by typing another **NP**, and then press ESC to end the command.

Repeat this process on the other wall end. Your drawing will now approximate the one shown in Figure 5-9.

Adding Another Sink

Assume now that you want to add another bowl to the sink fixture. You will first need to make the room longer. Use the Stretch (SS) command and the Window method to place a window around the left wall, and stretch the straight lines. Pick your second reference point two feet to the left of the first one, and the room will be longer.

A shortcut command not found on any menu, Stretch Window (SW), performs the same function as Stretch in simple cases, but does not require the first selection window.

To create another sink, you can use the Object Copy command because the sink is only one entity, a True Ellipse. If the sink were more than one entity (such as a Construction Ellipse, which is really four Arcs), you would need to use Window Copy or the master Copy command. Note that you can always use Window Copy, even if copying only one object.

Before you start, make sure that Grid Size (GS) is set to 3 inches. Select Object Copy from the SHORTCUTS menu or type **OC** on the keyboard. Select a point on the sink. For the reference points, select a point on one end of the sink, and for the second point select a new point to the right or left of where the second sink would go. It may require a little practice to get a feeling for how to select these two reference points. For the number of copies, just press ENTER for one copy. If the second sink doesn't end up exactly where you want it, use the Object Move (OM) command, which works almost exactly the same way as the Object Copy command, except that you do not specify a number of copies at the end, and the object to be moved is erased when the new one is created. You may have to move both sinks to get the spacing right.

If you want to experiment more with this drawing, go ahead. When you are done, save it into the same file, ROOM, with the Quit command. When asked if you want to Overwrite or Rename, type **O** to overwrite the old file.

Editing While Drawing: MUSIC Revisited

As noted previously, the editing commands are not just for fixing mistakes or changing your mind; they can be just as useful when you are creating your drawing. The musical staff example from Chapter 4 is a good illustration of how the editing commands can speed up the drawing process tremendously.

Two Lines Are Sometimes All You Need

Many drawings can be created by drawing only two lines, a vertical and a horizontal, and then copying, moving, rotating, breaking, and otherwise manipulating these two lines until you have the complete drawing. If you have a good deal of hand drawing experience, you may not recognize this as an advantage at first, but it can really contribute to your speed and efficiency.

Start a new drawing called **MUSIC2**. Set the Units to Inches (IN), the Limits (LS) to 6 by 9, and Zoom All (ZA). Specify a 1/2-inch Grid Size (GS), and turn on Snap to Grid (SG), Relative Coordinates (DC-R), Ortho Mode (OR), and Manual Entry Relative (MR).

As in the previous MUSIC drawing, start by drawing an eight-inch line from left to right. You should be able to read this dimension from the coordinate display as you draw. When you have drawn one horizontal line, press ESC and draw a vertical line, starting at the left endpoint of the existing line, and going downward one-half inch. The Y coordinate should read "-.5" as you select this point. Your drawing should resemble the one shown in Figure 5-10.

Editing the Rest of the Drawing into Existence

This time, instead of drawing the rest of the lines, you can create them with the Object Copy (OC) command. Before you do this, change the Grid

Chapter 5: Basic Editing Tasks 147

FIGURE 5-10 The first two lines of MUSIC2

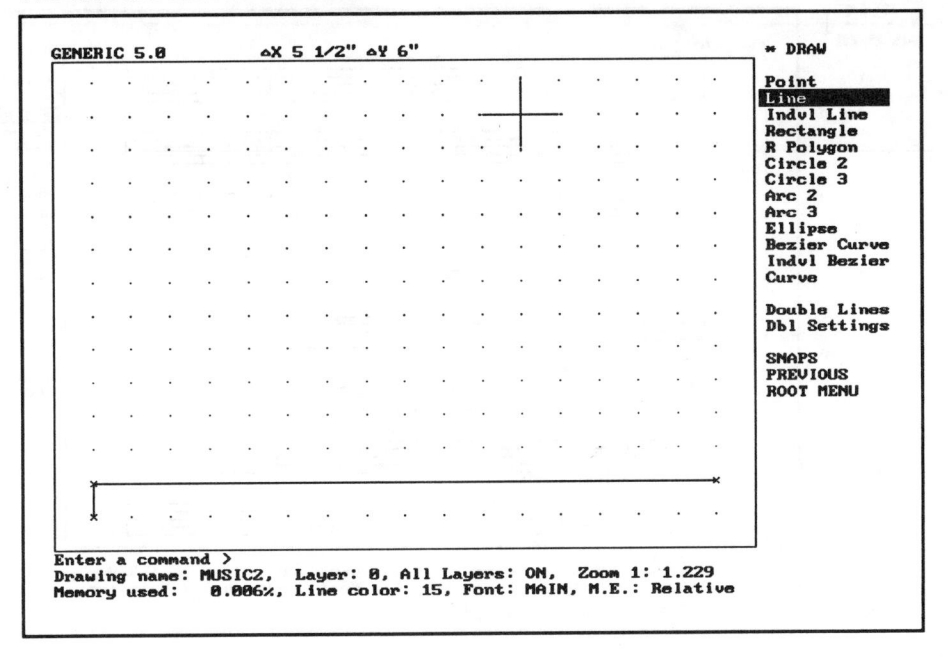

```
GENERIC 5.0          ∆X 5 1/2"  ∆Y 6"                    * DRAW
                                                         Point
                                                         Line
                                                         Indvl Line
                                                         Rectangle
                                                         R Polygon
                                                         Circle 2
                                                         Circle 3
                                                         Arc 2
                                                         Arc 3
                                                         Ellipse
                                                         Bezier Curve
                                                         Indvl Bezier
                                                         Curve

                                                         Double Lines
                                                         Dbl Settings

                                                         SNAPS
                                                         PREVIOUS
                                                         ROOT MENU

Enter a command >
Drawing name: MUSIC2,   Layer: 0, All Layers: ON,   Zoom 1: 1.229
Memory used:    0.006%, Line color: 15, Font: MAIN, M.E.: Relative
```

Size to 1/8 inch (GS). When you copy the object, select the horizontal line first, and pick the reference point on the line. For the new reference point, select a point exactly one grid point (visible or invisible) below the previous one. Specify **4** for the number of copies. You should now see all horizontal lines of the musical staff.

To replicate the vertical line, press SPACEBAR to get another Object Copy command. To select the vertical line, turn off Snap to Grid by typing **SG**. You won't need to turn it back on. After selecting the line, pick any point for a reference point. For a new reference point or offset, type **2,0** and press ENTER. For the number of copies, specify **4** again, and all of the vertical lines will be drawn.

Creating a Manuscript Page

You can quickly turn this one musical staff into an entire page of staffs with the Window Copy command. Select Window Copy from the

FIGURE 5-11 An entire music page created with the COPY function

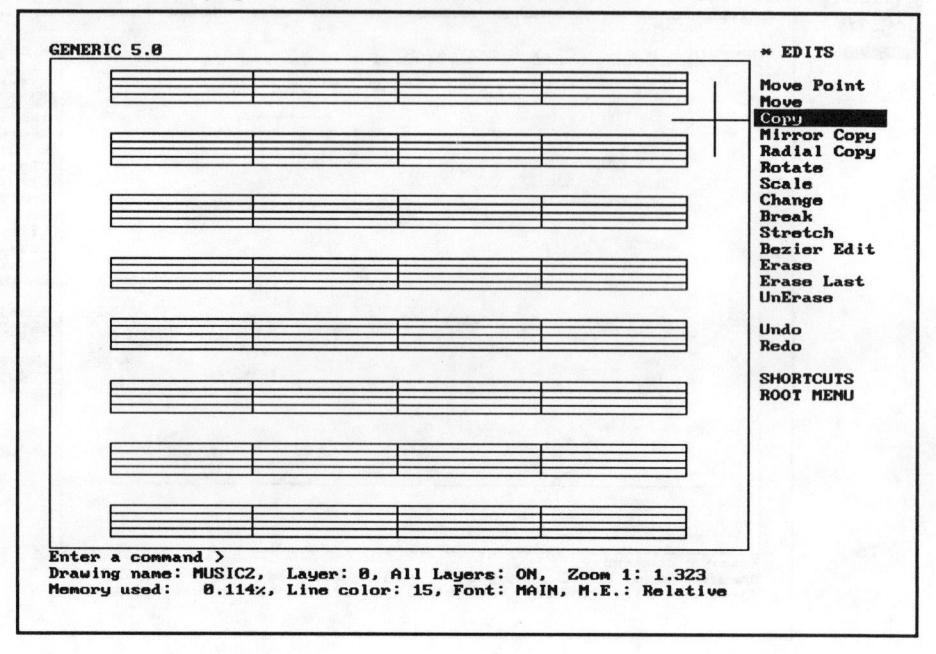

SHORTCUTS or type **WC**. Put the window around the whole drawing. Select any reference point, and type **0,1** and press ENTER for the new reference point or offset. Make 7 copies, and you'll wind up with a drawing similar to the one shown in Figure 5-11 after you Zoom All (ZA). Save the new drawing and exit to DOS with the Quit (QU) command.

This chapter has covered the structure behind the basic editing commands, including how entities are selected for editing and what each editing function does.

In the next few chapters, you will make use of many of these editing commands as you move on to more complex tasks. The remaining editing commands are addressed in Chapter 9.

CHAPTER 6

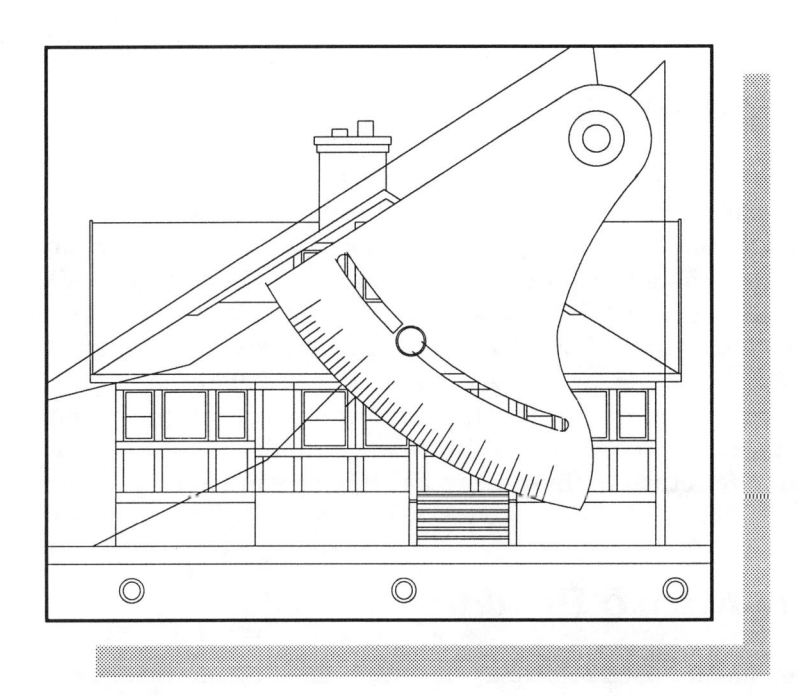

Drawing Aids and Controls

This chapter does not explore any new drawing and editing commands, but instead focuses on Generic CADD 5.0 features that can help you use the commands that you already know to draw and edit better. The commands covered in this chapter are drawing aids and controls used with the drawing and editing commands and often affect the way that these commands work; alone, however, they perform no actual work and for the most part have no direct permanent effect on the drawing database. Once you exit Generic CADD, however, some of the values that are set with these commands are stored and will reappear if you call up the same drawing file.

The Zoom Commands

The commands on the ZOOMS menu, almost all of which are represented by two-character codes that start with the letter Z, are used for adjusting the portion of the drawing that is shown on the screen. If you think of the screen as a viewport to the drawing, the Zoom commands allow you to control the way the viewport works. They let you move closer to see more detail, or move further away to see more area. They permit you to see the full drawing, or any selected portion. They also allow you to return to the portion of the drawing on which you were previously working, to store certain settings of the viewport under names of your own choice, and to return to these views as often as you like.

Displaying the Entire Drawing

Two commands are used to display the entire drawing on the screen. Their functions differ depending on your definition of "the whole drawing." Zoom All (ZA) displays every entity in the drawing; Zoom Limits (ZL) displays the area that lies between the origin and the upper-right corner of the drawing, as specified by the Limits (LS) command.

When there is no object on the screen (for example, at the beginning of a drawing session when you have just created a new file and set the Limits), these two commands have approximately the same effect, and you can use them interchangeably for the purpose of simply showing the entire drawing area on the screen before beginning to draw. If you make

Chapter 6: Drawing Aids and Controls

a new drawing and set its Limits (LS) to 10 x 10, you will see that Zoom All (ZA) and Zoom Limits (ZL) give you the same results. It helps to have a one-inch grid on the screen to see that this is true, as shown in Figure 6-1.

When you have placed entities in the drawing, however, these two commands perform two very different functions. If you draw a one-inch-square in the middle of the screen, you will quickly see the difference between these two commands. Zoom Limits continues to show the entire 10 x 10 area (plus a bit more in the horizontal direction), as illustrated in Figure 6-2. Zoom All, now that it has something specific to zoom *to*, shows only the rectangle, plus a little extra space all around. This extra space ensures that the edges of the rectangle are not covered by the border of the drawing area, and that you can place a window around this object if you decide to select it. This phenomenon is illustrated in Figure 6-3.

FIGURE 6-1 Using a one-inch grid with 10-by-10-inch limits, Zoom Limits or Zoom All gives the same results

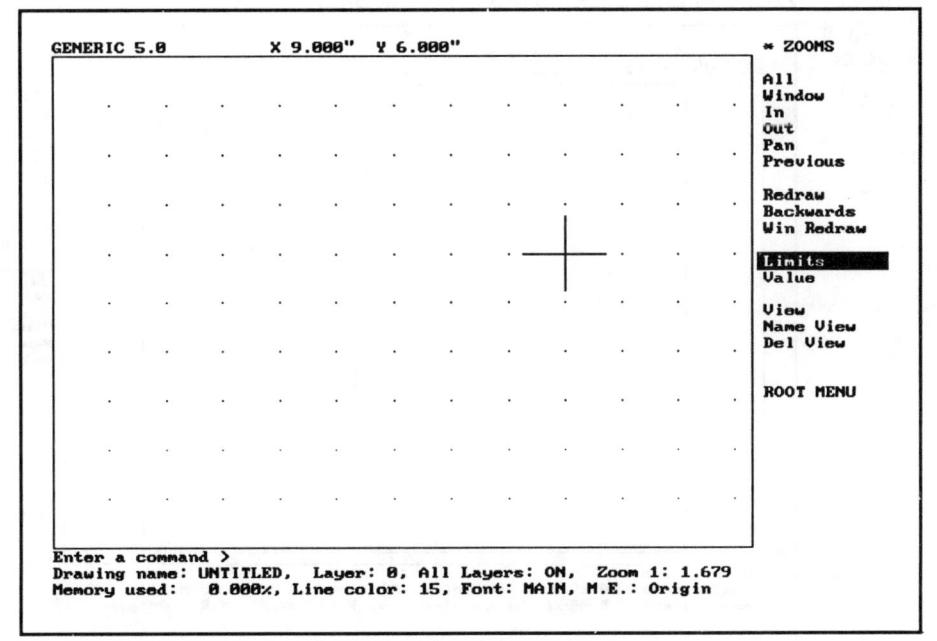

FIGURE 6-2 Zoom Limits after drawing a one-inch square

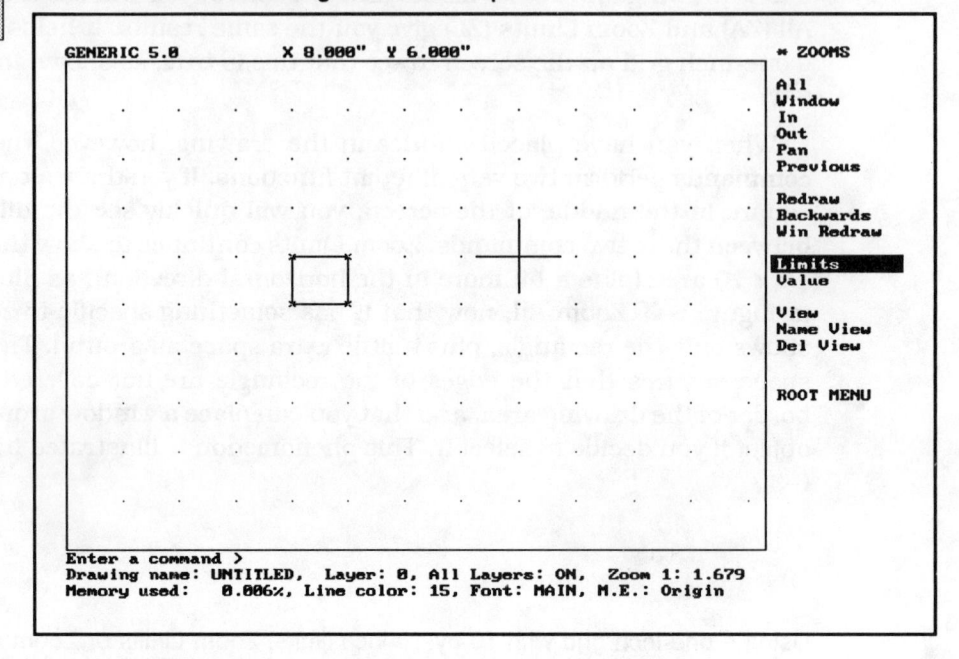

FIGURE 6-3 Zoom All after drawing a one-inch square

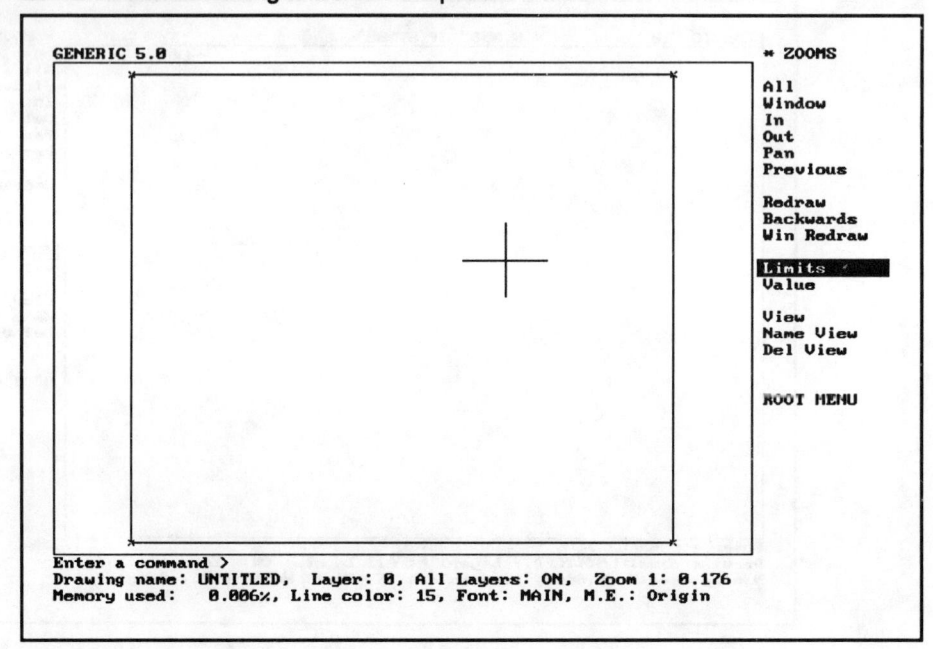

You can see, then, that the Zoom All command adjusts the display to show everything in the drawing—no more, no less—regardless of the set limits. When there is nothing in the drawing, it defaults to acting like Zoom Limits, in order to have something reasonable to do. The Zoom Limits command, on the other hand, always shows the set limits, whether the actual objects in the drawing are smaller or larger than these limits.

Generic CADD does not constrain you from drawing outside the area specified by the Limits command. The limits are simply a convenient way for you to view a known amount of area on the screen before you draw anything.

Zooming In and Out

You have used the Zoom In and Zoom Out commands in previous chapters. These two reciprocal commands display, respectively, exactly half as much and twice as much area of the drawing on the screen. When you execute Zoom In, the drawing looks larger on the screen, as if you are getting closer to it, and you may be able to see more detail. Because the drawing is enlarged, some of it may be off the edges of the screen (not lost, just not currently displayed). Zoom Out does exactly the opposite, causing the screen to react as if you have taken a step back. Every object in the drawing looks smaller, some detail may not be visible, and you should see exactly twice as much area as you could before you used Zoom Back.

Users of earlier versions of Generic CADD should note that Zoom In and Zoom Out are the new versions of the old ZOOM UP and ZOOM BACK, respectively, and work in exactly the same way as the old commands. Even the old two-character commands will work.

Call up an existing drawing, like SITEPLAN, and try these commands. When you first load it, SITEPLAN will be displayed as if you had issued Zoom All, as shown in Figure 6-4. Both Zoom In (ZI) and Zoom Out (ZO) ask you to specify a new center of the screen, which allows you to move up or back in a specific direction, rather than just focusing in on the center of the screen. Pick a point that you want to use as the middle of the screen. Figure 6-5 shows the result of a Zoom In on the SITEPLAN drawing, using a point on the roof as the center. Figure 6-6 shows the effect of a Zoom Out after a Zoom All.

FIGURE 6-4 Zoom All is automatic when you first load a drawing

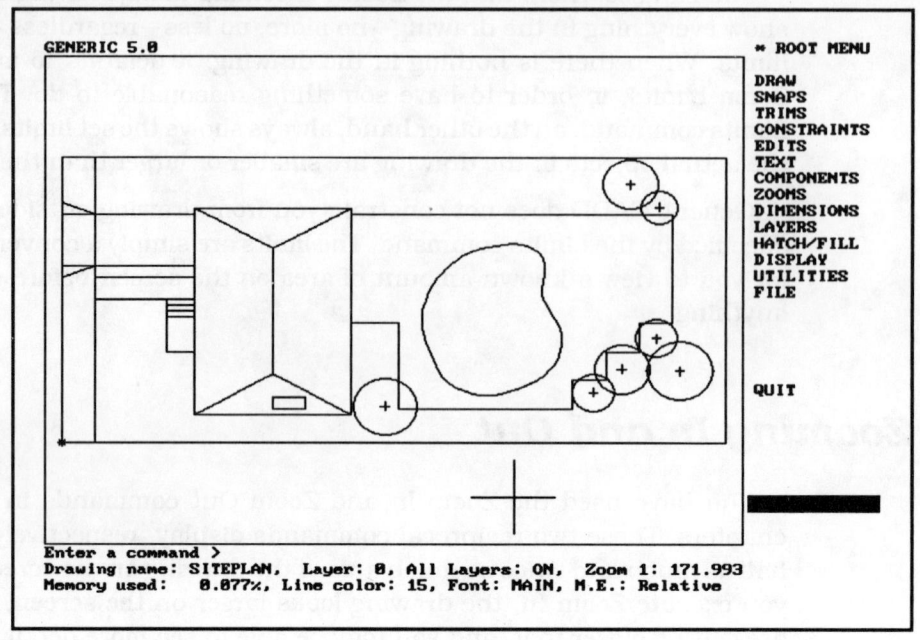

FIGURE 6-5 The display after one Zoom All and then one Zoom In

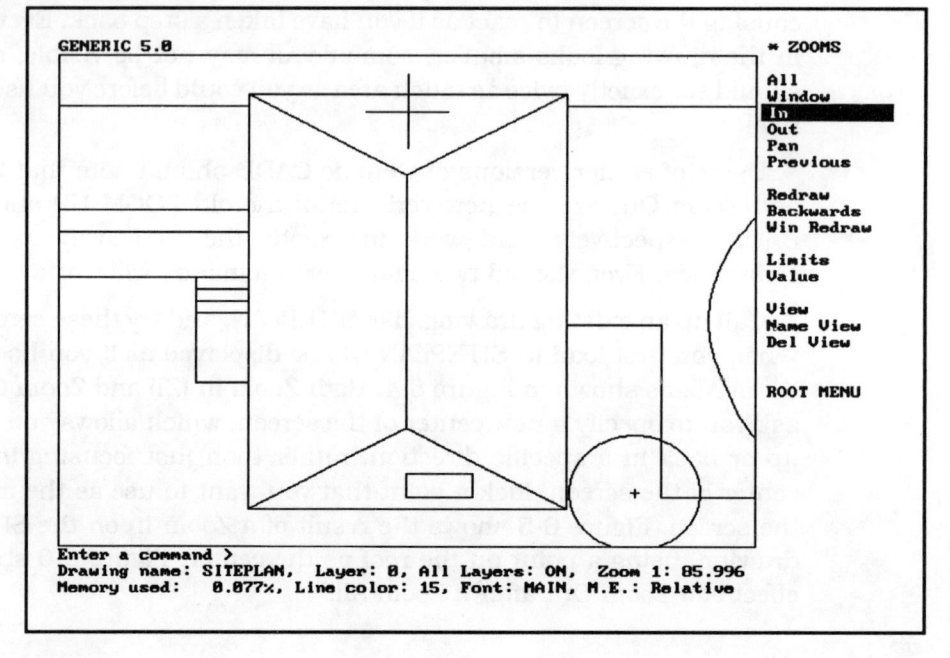

FIGURE 6-6 The display after one Zoom All and Zoom Out

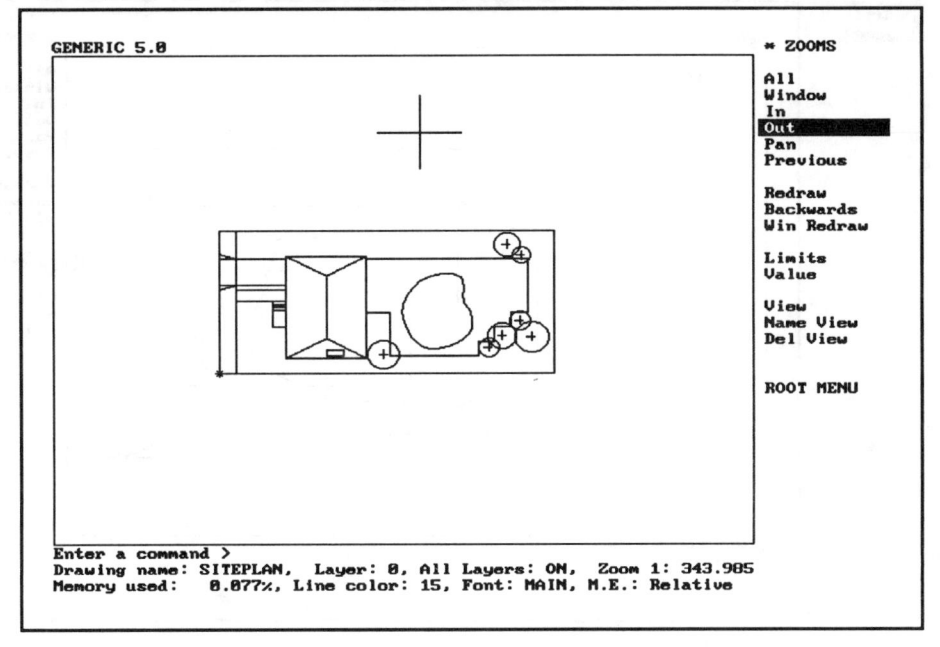

Zooming to a Specified Area

Like Zoom In, the Zoom Window command lets you zoom in on a portion of the drawing, except that the portion is selected with a window. After selecting Window from the ZOOMS menu or typing **ZW** on the keyboard, you will be asked to place a window. Put the window around the area that you want to display on the screen. Like all other windows, this window is specified by first selecting one corner with the drawing cursor, and then dragging a rubber band rectangle around the area that you want to select. If you place your first point in the wrong location, press ESC, and try the command again.

The window that you select should be about the same shape as the border around the Generic CADD display area. Figure 6-7 shows the placement of a window for Zooming into a portion of the SITEPLAN drawing. If you don't get the window the exact shape of the drawing area, Generic CADD will add a little space to the top and bottom or sides. After you have specified the window, the display will be adjusted and redrawn.

FIGURE 6-7 Placing a window for a Zoom Window

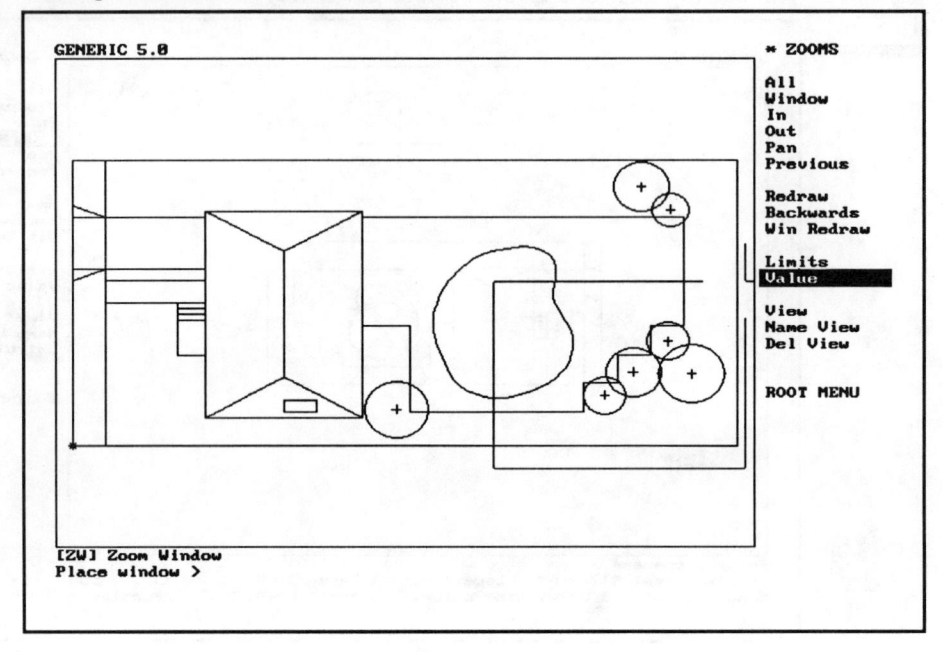

Figure 6-8 shows the display after Zooming to the window placed in Figure 6-7.

Returning to the Last Screen

The Zoom Previous (ZP) command returns to the view that you had before the last Zoom command. This command can save time and effort. For example, if you Zoom Window and then Zoom Window again, but end up with the wrong view, you can use Zoom Previous and try the Zoom Window again as opposed to issuing Zoom All and then issuing Zoom Window twice to obtain the desired view.

If you execute one Zoom Previous after another, you simply zoom back and forth between two views. Each Zoom Previous will be previous to the next, so you will end up in a loop. This is a good way to go back and forth between two views when you need to move in and out repeatedly and quickly, but can be confusing if you are not expecting it. The logic behind

Chapter 6: Drawing Aids and Controls

FIGURE 6-8 The display after the Zoom Window

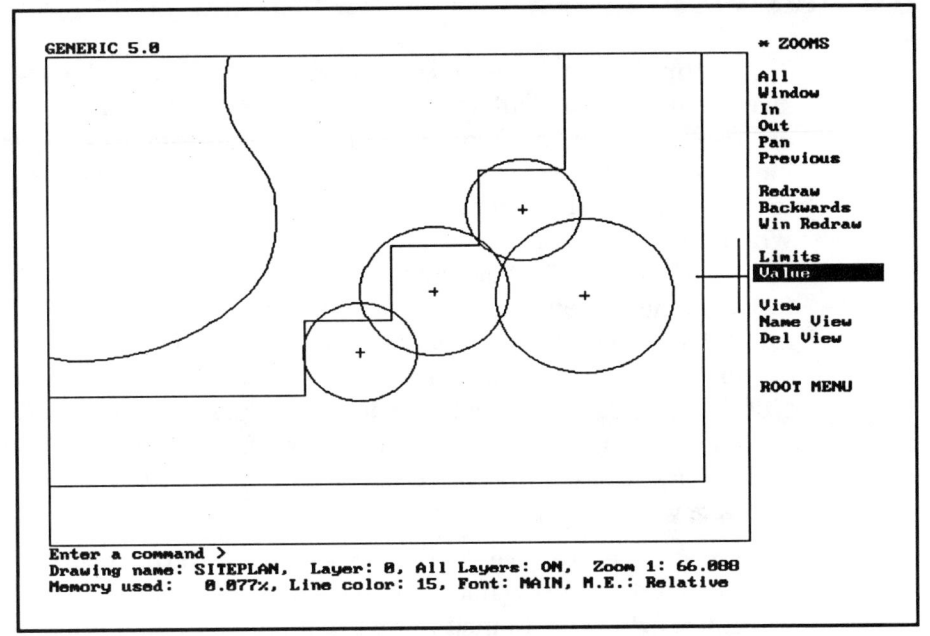

this command is that only one previous view is stored, so it is not possible to Zoom Window three times and Zoom Previous three times to get back to where you started. Instead, you will end up at the second window to which you Zoomed, as follows:

Zoom Window	(ZW)	(first window)
Zoom Window	(ZW)	(second window)
Zoom Window	(ZW)	(third window)
Zoom Previous	(ZP)	(second window)
Zoom Previous	(ZP)	(third window)
Zoom Previous	(ZP)	(second window)

As you can see, the Zoom Previous command takes its name literally. It always returns you to the view that you were looking at before the last Zoom command, even if the view is the last Zoom Previous.

Named Views

A group of commands (View, Name View, and Delete) allows users to give a name to a particular view so you can return to it later. Named views are useful for moving from one part of the drawing to another without having to Zoom All (ZA) or Zoom Out (ZO) in between. It can be very useful to give names to the various areas of the drawing that you zoom to often. Whenever you have a view that you want to name, select the Name View command or type **NV**. You will be prompted for a name, which can be up to 12 characters long. Type the name and press ENTER. To check it, Zoom All (ZA) and then Zoom In (ZI) or Zoom Window (ZW) to a different part of the drawing. Now select View from the ZOOMS menu or type **ZV** and type the same name or select it from the menu. The view that was on screen when you created the named view will be restored. Of course, you can now move easily between these two views with Zoom Previous, which will take you back and forth.

Named views are saved in the drawing file with the rest of the drawing entities, so that you do not have to Name View all over again every time you edit the drawing. Named views can build up in the database, however; you may end up with many that you don't need, or you may want to change the definition of a view stored under a particular name. In these cases, you can use the Delete View command, which is called Del View on the ZOOMS menu and is invoked with **NX** on the keyboard (Name Erase?). You will be asked to type the name of the view that you want to delete or select it from the menu. Once a named view is deleted, it is no longer saved with the drawing file, and the name can be used over again.

Notice that zooms and views only affect the way that the entities are displayed on the screen. None of these commands actually changes the size or location of any drawing entities in the database, only the way that they appear on the screen. Stored named views do not keep track of what is on the screen in that view; they only keep track of where that view is in relation to the drawing as a whole. If you change something in the interim, your view may look different when you return to it than it did when you created it. If you move entities while zoomed out to the whole drawing, you may find that there is nothing on the screen when you zoom to a particular view!

What is actually stored in the database when you create a named view is the *name* of the view and the Absolute Coordinates of the window that would be required to re-create that view with a Zoom Window. For this reason, be very careful with commands that alter the entire database. If none of your named views seems to go anywhere, you have probably Re-Origined your drawing. (See Chapter 10, "Advanced Drawing and Editing Techniques," for more information on Re-Origin.)

Getting a Scaled View

You might notice a message at the bottom of the screen from time to time that says "Zoom 1:x," where x is some number. This Zoom Factor or Zoom Value stands for the relationship between real world scale and the drawing as displayed on the monitor. If the drawing is displayed at a Zoom Value of 1, it is shown at its actual size. Although any drawing can be viewed at this Zoom Value, it only makes sense for drawings of objects that are smaller than the display screen. If you try to display a house floor plan at a Zoom Scale of 1, for example, you may see at most a line or two because the house will not fit on the screen at this Zoom Value.

When you use the other Zoom commands, Generic CADD calculates the Zoom Value automatically, which is a lot easier than doing the calculation yourself. However, if you wish to see the drawing displayed at a specific Zoom Value, you can select Value from the ZOOMS menu or type **ZM** on the keyboard. You will be asked to type a number and to select a point that will be used for the center of the screen.

You should keep in mind that even if the object can fit on the screen, and you display it at a Zoom Value of 1, the drawing that you see on the screen is not exactly what you will get when you print it at 1:1. Because the resolution of your printer or plotter is probably higher than your monitor's resolution, the printout will show more definition on circles and arcs, and there will be less visible stepping on diagonal lines, because the steps will be smaller. In general, your output will be crisper than what you see on the screen, unless you have a very high-resolution video card. Also, it is important to note that the accuracy of the Zoom Value depends on an accurately specified Screen Ratio. The Screen Ratio, specified with the RA command, requires that you measure a box that is displayed on the screen and tell CADD the dimensions, so that it can calculate the exact length of one inch on your screen.

Moving Around Without Changing Scale

The Pan (PA) command is an unusual Zoom command in that it does not adjust the apparent size of the objects on the screen; it merely changes the portion of the drawing that is displayed. This command allows you to move the viewport around on the drawing without changing the Zoom Value. After you issue this command, you simply select a new center of the screen, and the display is redrawn to reflect the newly selected center. Since the current center is, by definition, halfway from any edge of the screen, you can move up, down, right, or left a maximum of about one-half the width of the screen at one time. (If you move on the diagonal, you can go a little further than that.) The Pan command is useful when you use another Zoom command, such as Zoom In, and what you want to edit ends up just off the edge of the screen. Rather than zooming back, and then up again, you can simply pan to one side to find the objects.

On the other hand, repeated panning is not really a fast way to get from one part of the drawing to another, as the screen must be redrawn each time you pan. You can speed up the process by pressing any key to stop the screen from redrawing after the first Pan and then pressing the SPACEBAR to get another, if you know how many Pans it will take to get the object in view.

Refreshing the Screen

Though the Redraw (RD) command is on the ZOOMS menu, it is even less of a true Zoom command than Pan. The Redraw command simply refreshes the screen display to show the currently selected area on the screen, using all of the current display parameters.

This command is often used in conjunction with the Display toggles, such as Construction Points. Turning on Construction Points has no immediate effect on the display. It doesn't come into play until the next time you activate a Zoom command. The Redraw command provides a Zoom command so you can see the changes in the display parameters (such as the display of construction points), without having to go anywhere. As you will see in the next section, many toggles are not activated after switching until Redraw is used.

The Redraw command may also be used when you want to see if anything is lying underneath an erased object. If you draw one line on top of another, for example, and then Object Erase (OE) one of them, both will disappear, as Generic CADD removes the pixels of one line without realizing that another line sits in the same place. Situations like this are automatically corrected whenever any Zoom is executed. Once again, Redraw can be used to refresh the display quickly without moving the viewport. You will find the Redraw command to be very useful while editing. Sometimes, a window or even the cursor can interfere with editing and cause distorted screen displays. The Redraw command corrects any of these situations.

Changing the Order of Display

The last command on the ZOOMS menu, Backwards, is not an active Zoom command, but a Zoom toggle. When any other Zoom command (except Name View) is used, the entities in the drawing are redrawn on the screen, appearing (by default) in the order that they were drawn unless you have used certain editing commands, such as Object Break, that can change the order of entities. This can make an edited entity seem as if it were drawn more recently than unedited entities nearby. However, when the entities that you want to edit have just been drawn, it can be quicker to have the screen redraw from the opposite end of the database so that entities drawn most recently are displayed first. The Backwards command, chosen from the ZOOMS menu or issued by typing **BR** on the keyboard, reverses the display order of the database. After you have executed the command, when you Zoom Window (ZW) or Zoom In (ZI) to a certain area, the entities you last created are displayed first. If you don't need to see the whole drawing in order to edit it, you can press any key as soon as the screen shows enough information. This will stop the current Redraw, which happens implicitly as a part of every Zoom command (except Name View), and you can immediately start editing.

To toggle Backwards Redraw off, that is, to redraw in the normal order, simply select Backwards from the ZOOMS menu or type **BR** again. Like any other toggle, if it is on, it will be turned off; if it is off, it will be turned on. When you first start a drawing, Backwards Redraw is off.

The Display Commands

Many of the commands on the DISPLAY menu are toggles. For the most part, they control the display of the items on the screen that are not really part of your drawing. You have already used a few of these, such as Rubberbanding and Construction Points. There are no general rules regarding the two-character keystrokes that activate these commands. A few subgroups occasionally share a character, and these commands will be discussed in the text to follow.

The first three commands on the DISPLAY menu—Line Color, Line Type, and Line Width—are actually parameter settings. The fourth, Line Scale, is a true DISPLAY command.

The Line Commands

These commands set a number of entity attributes that become part of the definitions of all new entities placed into the drawing. All new entities are created on the layer currently selected and are also created in the current Line Color, using the current Line Type and the current Line Width. The two-character codes for each of these commands start with the letter *L*, for Line.

Although these commands appear on the DISPLAY menu, the first three control more than just the display. The values specified by Line Color, Line Type, and Line Width control the information actually stored in the database for every entity. In previous versions of Generic CADD, these commands were listed on the LINES menu.

Even though these commands establish the initial Line Color, Line Type, and Line Width of new entities, these properties can be changed with any of the Change commands. Note that these commands control the properties of all new entities created, not just Straight Lines. In

Generic CADD, when you see the word "Line" in the prompt or on the menu, it often applies to all simple entities.

The Line Color Command

The color of all new entities created is controlled by the Line Color command on the DISPLAY menu, or by typing **LC** or **LK** on the keyboard. When you select this command, you will be shown the current Line Color, and asked to select a new one. This can be done by typing a number between 0 and 255, or by selecting a color from the color bars shown in the video menu area (assuming that the video menu is active and more than two colors are available). If your video card displays less than 256 colors, the same colors repeat over and over again. On a 16-color system, for example, colors 0, 16, 32, and so on are all the same.

If you're working on a monochrome system, only two colors are available—the background color and a contrasting color. Generic CADD recognizes the background color as color 0 (zero), and the contrasting color as color 1. On some monochrome systems, notably Hercules-compatible graphics cards and the Toshiba 3100, entities always appear in color 1 no matter what color you select. On other monochrome systems, such as CGA compatibles, entities drawn using color 0 are displayed in the same color as the background, that is to say, they do not show up at all. If Display Construction Points is turned on, you will see construction points, as the entities actually exist, even though you can't see them.

The Line Width Command

The initial width of all new entities is controlled by the Line Width command on the DISPLAY menu, or by typing **LW** on the keyboard. If the video menu is active, a menu of examples numbered 0 through 10 will be shown. You can either select from the menu using the second pointing device button, or type a number and press ENTER.

The units of line width are measured in whatever increment is available on the device used to display, print, or plot the drawing. On the video screen, each unit represents one pixel, or dot, no matter how far you Zoom In or Zoom Out. On the printer, the units are also one dot, so the actual thickness of the lines depends on the resolution of your printer.

On a plotter, each unit represents one pen width. The width of the pen is controlled by a variable within the plotting command, rather than being the physical width of the pen, which Generic CADD doesn't know.

Line Width, therefore, is not an absolute measurement. It always depends on the resolution of the display or output device, and the scale at which the drawing is displayed, printed, or plotted. Line Widths 2 through 10 are most useful for emphasizing certain entities. Line Widths 0 and 1 are both defined as being one unit wide, in order to avoid objects with Line Width zero not showing up. Figure 6-9 shows a drawing that has been created using three different Line Widths, 0, 2, and 4.

The Line Type Command

The initial type of all new entities created in the drawing is controlled by the Line Type command on the DISPLAY menu, or by typing **LT** on the keyboard. Line Type can be selected from a special video menu display if the video menu is turned on, or by typing a number from 0 to 255. Line Types 1 through 9 are scaled to the output device, while the length of the

FIGURE 6-9 A drawing that uses a variety of Line Widths

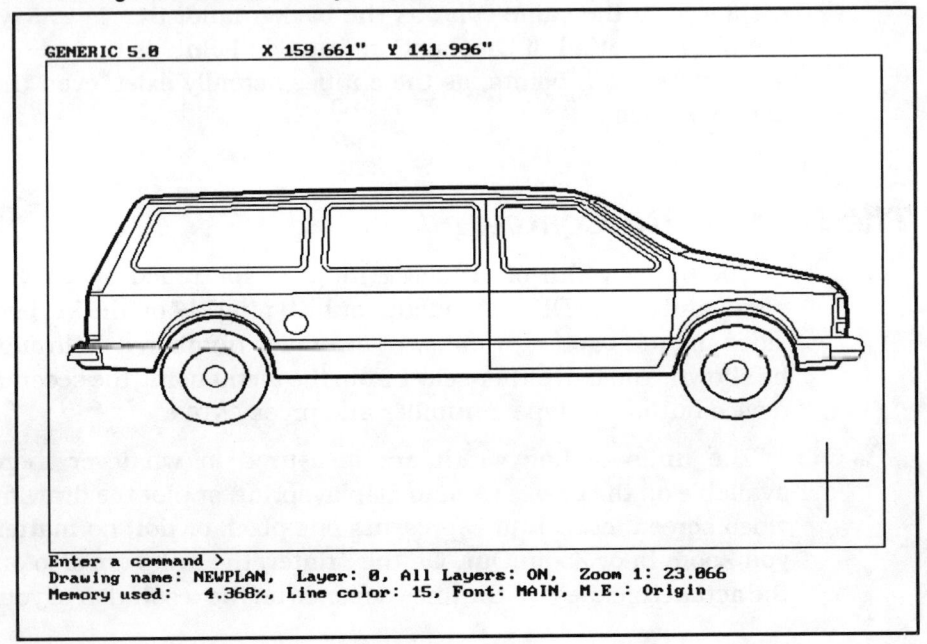

dashes that make up types 11 through 255 are controlled by the Line Scale command. These are broken into groups of ten, which are arranged in the same dash patterns as types 1 through 9, but at increasing scale factors. The dashes in types 21 through 29 are twice as long as in 11 through 19, while the dashes in types 31 through 39 are three times as long, and so on. Any Line Type value evenly divisible by 10 (0, 10, 20, 30, and so on) represents continuous lines. Figure 6-10 shows a drawing composed of a variety of Line Types. (For a complete discussion of Line Types, see Chapter 3, "Preliminary Considerations.")

The Line Scale Command

The Line Scale command on the DISPLAY menu or the two-character keyboard command **LZ** controls the length of the dash patterns in the scalable Line Types 10 through 255. The value of the Line Scale variable specifies the actual length of one repetition of any of Line Types 11 through 19. (For a complete discussion of Line Scale, see Chapter 3.)

FIGURE 6-10 A drawing that uses a variety of Line Types (courtesy of Izzie Lewis)

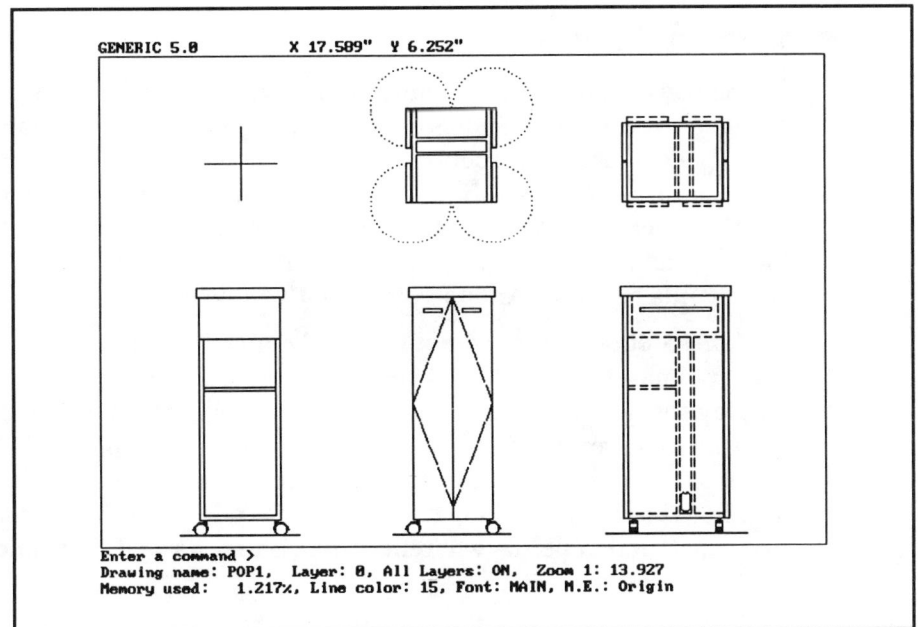

Unlike the other Line commands, Line Scale does not set a parameter that becomes imbedded as part of the definition of the entities created. Instead, it specifies an overall variable that affects *all* entities in the drawing, the next time that they are displayed. It may seem to apply only to new entities until you execute a Redraw or any other Zoom command.

Display of Points

The display of Generic CADD's three types of points is controlled by three toggles on the DISPLAY menu. Each of the two-character codes for these commands starts with the letter *P*, for Points, and ends with the first letter of the type of point. These Display toggles only affect the visibility of the points, not their function. Even when Construction Points is turned off, for example, you can still snap onto them with Snap to Nearest Point if you know where they are. Certain construction points are easy to identify, such as the endpoints of lines, while others, such as the points on a curve, are difficult to identify without displaying them. The diagram in Figure 6-11 includes all three types of points, with all three turned off.

Construction Points

Display of construction points is toggled on and off by the Con. Points toggle on the DISPLAY menu, or by typing **PC** on the keyboard. When this toggle is on, construction points are shown at the definition points of all entities, such as the endpoints of lines, and the center and one point on a circle. They also appear when marking the offset on Copy and Move commands, and are used by many of the other Draw and Edit commands to show various points that you select.

Construction points do not magically appear or disappear as soon as this command is given. This command, as well as the rest of the point display toggles, enables or disables the display of points starting from the time that you toggle it. Construction points will appear or disappear the next time you do a Zoom or any other command that causes the screen to be redrawn. Also, all Draw commands and Edit commands that use construction points will reflect the change as well. The quickest way

FIGURE 6-11 A sample drawing with all points turned off

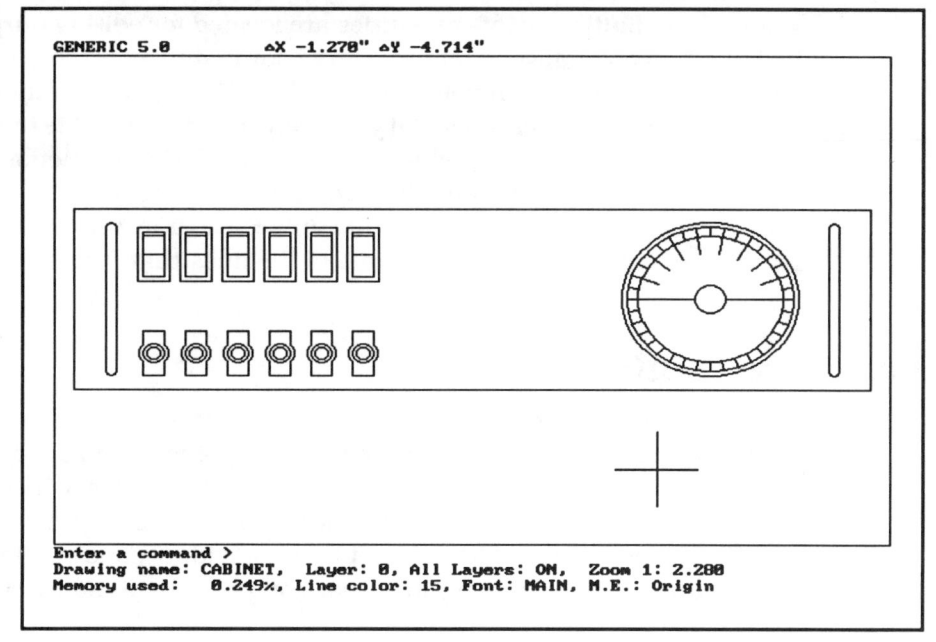

to see the results of the Con. Points toggle without changing anything else in the drawing or on the screen is to issue a Redraw (RD) command.

Construction points do not plot or print, and are saved with the drawing only to the extent that every definition point of every entity in the drawing is represented by a construction point when the toggle is turned on. The status of this toggle is saved with the drawing file, and can be configured to a default value with the Environment (EN) command. The size of construction points is scaled to the screen, not to your drawing, so that they always appear to be the same size (a few pixels in each direction) no matter how far you Zoom in on them. Construction points are always displayed in white on color systems, or in whatever color your monochrome system uses.

The principle function of construction points is to provide visual feedback when you are drawing new entities or editing old ones. For example, it is helpful to see where you put the first point on an arc when you try to place the second one. It helps to see the initial reference point of a Move or Copy command marked on the screen when you try to select the new reference point. You can also use construction points to see where the definition points of entities are located for editing purposes. It is difficult to do a Move Point on a curve, for instance, when you are not sure where the definition points are located. When placing windows, the only points on simple entities that you really have to get inside the window are the definition points, which are marked by construction points. Figure 6-12 shows the same diagram shown in Figure 6-11, but with Construction Points turned on. You can see them at the corners of the large boxes, indicating the endpoints of the lines that form the boxes.

Reference Points

Display of reference points is controlled by this toggle, found on the DISPLAY menu as Ref. Points, or toggled by typing **PR** on the keyboard. Reference points are the origin points for complex entities, which include Components, Text Characters, Hatches, Fills, Associative Dimensions, and Text Lines. These entities do not have individual construction points to accompany the simple entities that compose them, so the reference

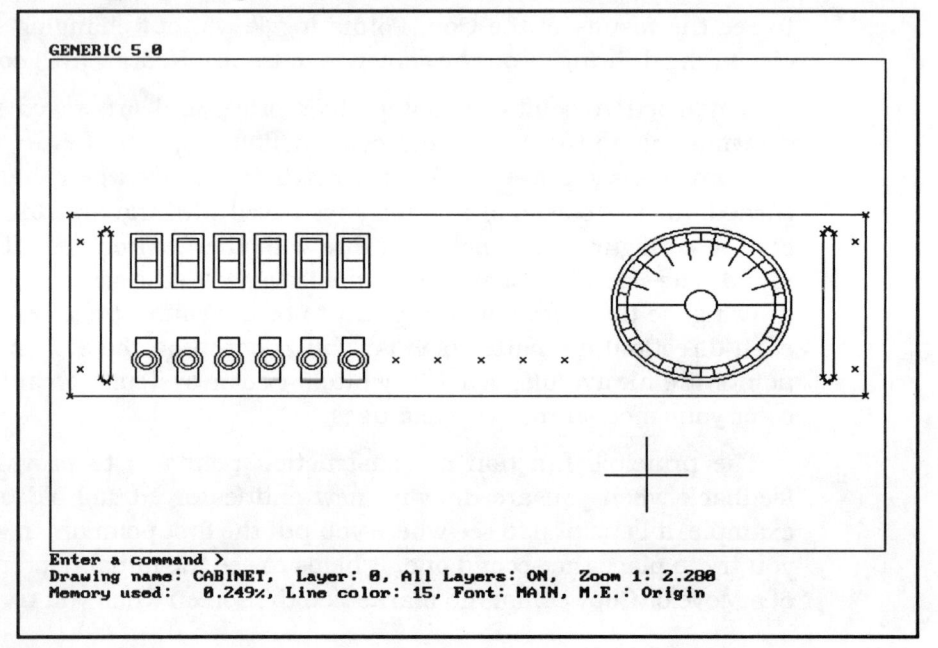

FIGURE 6-12 The sample drawing with Construction Points turned on

point is the only point that you can display. It becomes a sort of "handle" for the complex entity, which can be selected for the Move Point and other commands. It is also the point that determines whether a complex entity is inside a window: if the reference point is within the window, the entire entity is within the window as well.

Like construction points, reference points do not automatically appear as soon as you toggle on their display, nor do they ever print or plot. They *will* appear on all new complex entities and on existing ones whenever the screen is redrawn. Their primary purpose is for editing, so it makes no difference whether or not they are displayed.

One reference point is always located at 0,0, to help you see where the origin is, especially when you first start a drawing. This reference point cannot be removed, but as with all other reference points, its display is controlled by the Reference Points toggle. For reasons of visibility, the reference points of text characters are never displayed, even when the toggle is on. The reference points of text characters are in the lower-left corner of the letter; you should be able to locate them easily enough by snapping onto them with the Snap to Nearest Point (NP) command, or with the third pointing device button.

The status of this toggle is saved with the drawing file, and can be made the default with the Environment (EN) command. Like construction points, reference points are scaled to the screen rather than to your drawing, so that they always seem the same size, no matter how far you zoom in on them, and they are always white or your monochrome color. Figure 6-13 shows the diagram drawing with Reference Points turned on, in addition to the construction points already on. You can see the reference points at the insertion points of the various symbols on the diagram, which have been drawn using predefined components. Note that the components do not have construction points.

Standard Points

This command, represented by the abbreviation Std. Points on the DISPLAY menu and typed **PS** on the keyboard, toggles on and off the display of points that you place in the drawing with the Point command on the DRAW menu.

As is the case with the other types of points, standard points do not appear or disappear when you select the toggle; they appear when the

FIGURE 6-13 The sample drawing with Reference Points turned on

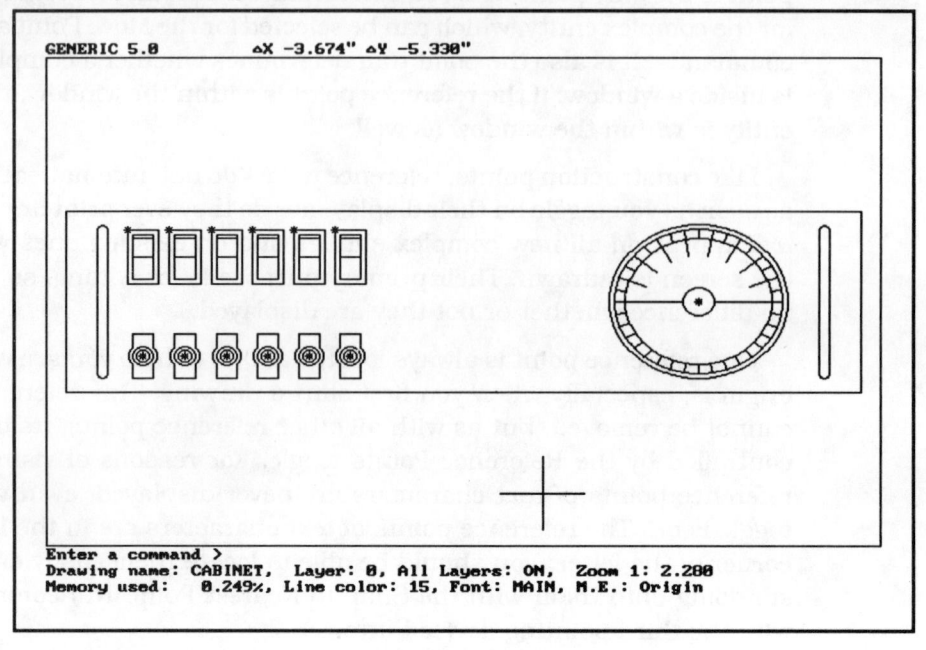

screen is redrawn or when you use the Point command. Points are always the same size, but have their own colors, which are determined by the current Line Color when the point is originally placed, or by the color to which it is changed by using any of the Change commands. Standard points *will be* printed or plotted if they are currently displayed. Figure 6-14 shows the diagram drawing with Standard Points turned on. Compare this to the previous two figures. The points in this drawing are part of the components, so the construction points, which would normally be at the center of each point, do not appear.

The only time that you will find standard points that you didn't put into the drawing yourself is when the Fast Text toggle is turned on. The effect of this command is that text is replaced, for display purposes, with standard points. This causes the screen to regenerate much more quickly, and you can still tell where the text is, even though you can't read it. However, if Display Standard Points (PS) is turned off, you won't see anything at all where your text is supposed to be. If you turn Fast

Chapter 6: Drawing Aids and Controls

FIGURE 6-14 The sample drawing with Standard Points turned on

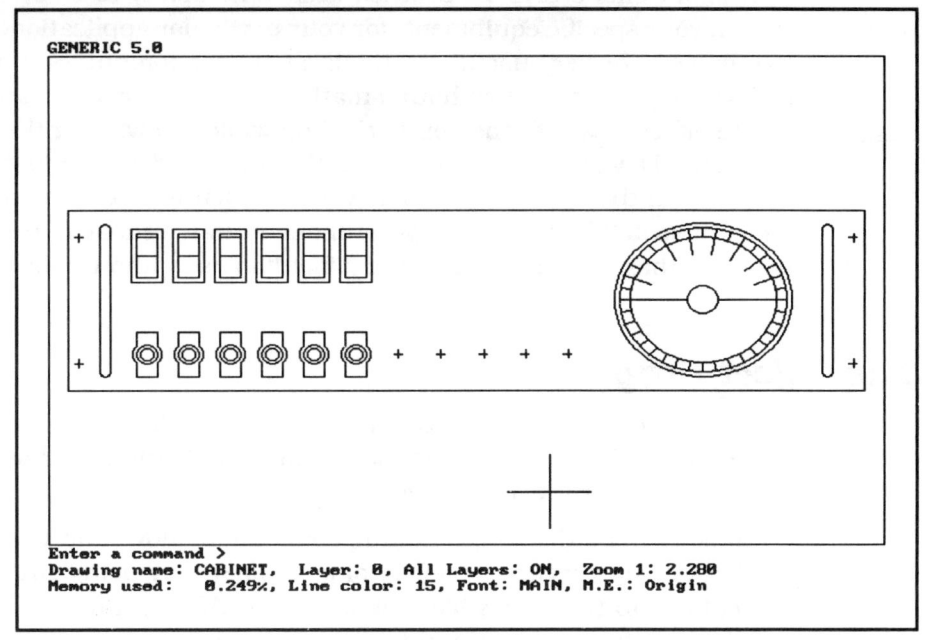

Text on and your text disappears, type **PS** to turn on Standard Points, and then Redraw (RD) the screen. Don't worry if this isn't clear right now; there will be more about Fast Text in Chapter 8, "Complex Entities."

Rubberbanding

As you have seen in previous chapters, Rubberbanding is toggled on and off by selecting the Rubberband command on the DISPLAY menu, or by typing **RB** on the keyboard. Some commands incorporate rubberbanding automatically regardless of the status of the toggle. You have seen rubberbanding at work in the drawing of lines (LI), two-point circles (C2), and rubber arcs (A2). You may have also experimented with it when you used the Move Point command on lines, arcs, circles, and curves.

Rubberbanding displays the entity as it is being drawn during certain Draw and Object commands. At any given time, it shows you what the entity will look like if you select the point where the cursor is located.

One of Generic CADD's best features is its ability to be optimized to run on your specific equipment, for your particular application. Rubberbanding can be very useful, particularly on fast computers. If you have a slow computer or one without a math coprocessor, rubberbanding can create difficulties with the point selection while you wait for the object to redraw and try to press the button on the pointing device at just the right moment. In these cases, you may want to turn Rubberbanding off and use Construction Points as your main visual feedback. Be advised, however, that some commands are difficult to use without rubberbanding.

The Object Drag Command

The Object Drag command is not really an Object command, as the name might imply, but an operational toggle. (Drag may have been a simpler name for this command.)

Some Generic CADD 5.0 editing commands, Move and Copy in particular, let you preview the effect of a command by using Drag to move the entities to their possible new locations. After entities are selected, either by a shortcut or a multiple-selection technique, and a reference point is selected, a *drag image* is created to help you test the new location. This test image is a ghosted version of the selected entities, with every other pixel missing so that you can see through it. Your original reference point is indicated by a tiny screen cursor about the size of a Standard Point.

To enable or disable the Object Drag command, select it from the DISPLAY menu or type **OD** on the keyboard. As a toggle, it will be turned off if it is currently on, and on if it is already off.

Drag is useful for general editing purposes, but you might want to turn it off when moving or copying large portions of a drawing to avoid the time required to create the drag image.

The Highlighting Command

Like Object Drag, Highlighting is a visualization aid. This command is a toggle that controls whether or not you want Highlighting.

When Highlighting is on, every time you select entities with any technique, shortcut or multiple-selection, the objects selected are highlighted. (Technically, every other pixel currently used to display the entity is turned off, so the effect is more of a lowlighting.) Highlighting lets you see which entities have been selected so far. If and when entities are deselected, and when you are done making your selection, the turned off pixels are turned back on.

To toggle Highlighting on or off, select it from the DISPLAY menu or type **HI** on the keyboard. Its current status will be reversed, from on to off or off to on.

As with Object Drag, if you plan to edit large portions of the drawing, you might want to turn Highlighting off to avoid having to later figure out which pixels to turn off and on.

Display of Coordinates

As you have seen, three different modes of coordinate display are possible (four, if you count no coordinates at all).

Coordinates display the location of the cursor in relation to some point. The coordinates may be (1) Absolute, that is, measured from the origin, 0,0; (2) Relative (also known as Delta), in which case they are measured from the last point entered; or (3) Polar (explanation follows).

Coordinates are displayed as X and Y values, which indicate the horizontal distance (X) and vertical distance (Y) from the point of reference. Positive X values mean "to the right," while negative X values indicate "to the left." For Y values, positive is toward the top of the screen or drawing, and negative is toward the bottom. Relative Coordinates are differentiated by the small triangle (Greek letter *delta*) that appears in front of the X and Y. Relative Coordinates are used when it is more important to know the distances between points rather than their X and Y coordinates.

Polar Coordinates show both distance and direction from the last point entered. The direction is measured in degrees above a horizontal line passing through the last point. Therefore, a point directly to the right of the last point entered would be at zero degrees, a point directly above would be at 90 degrees, and a point directly to the left would be at 180 degrees.

Because these commands are all toggles, if all coordinate display is turned off, there will be no coordinates at all. Turning off the coordinate display when you don't need it can make the drawing cursor move more smoothly, especially on slower machines.

It is worth noting that coordinate display is actually triggered by movement of the drawing cursor. Occasionally, you will not see any coordinates after a Zoom or some other command that causes the screen to redraw, even when you have Relative or Absolute Coordinates turned on. This is because you have not moved the cursor since the redraw. If you move the pointing device a little, the coordinates will appear. This is particularly likely to occur when you have Snap to Grid (SG) turned on with a large Grid Size (GS).

Absolute Coordinates

The display of Absolute Coordinates is toggled on and off by choosing the Absolute option of the Coordinates command on the DISPLAY menu, or by typing **DC** followed by **A** and ENTER on the keyboard. Absolute Coordinates track and display the location of the cursor using the currently selected unit system, as specified by the commands on the Units menu. The number of decimal places is controlled by the Decimal Value option of the Numeric Display command, and the smallest fraction displayed when using fractions is controlled by the Fraction Value (FV) option. These are also found on the DISPLAY menu.

When Absolute Coordinates are displayed, the numbers at the top of the screen will be labeled X and Y. These values represent the actual horizontal and vertical distances between the cursor and the origin, 0,0. These values are rounded to the decimal or fractional value that you have indicated, and can be affected by pixel resolution of your graphics card. If you are at a Zoom All (ZA) in the SITEPLAN drawing, for example, your cursor will probably jump a few inches at a time, even without having Snap to Grid (SG) turned on. These large jumps are simply due to the fact that there are no locations in between for the cursor to stop at. If you Zoom In (ZI) a few times, or Zoom Window (ZW) to a smaller area of the drawing, your cursor will move in smaller and smaller increments. When you zoom way in to a Zoom Value (ZM) of one, your cursor will display every last bit of resolution that you have allowed with the Units commands. Don't forget, you can always override the cursor position with manual entry if you need to specify a dimension to the nearest 1/8 inch when zoomed out further.

Relative Coordinates

The display of Relative (or Delta) Coordinates is toggled with the Relative option of the Coordinates command on the DISPLAY menu or the two-character code **DC** followed by **R** and ENTER. Relative Coordinates track and display the location of the cursor relative to the last point selected. As with Absolute Coordinates, the format and precision of these coordinates is controlled by the Numeric Display (NF) commands, and how far you are zoomed in to the drawing.

It should be noted that Absolute and Relative Coordinates cannot be turned on at the same time. While it is true that you can turn on Relative Coordinates, and then turn on Absolute Coordinates, you will not get Relative Coordinates back when you turn off Absolute Coordinates. Turning on a second mode of coordinate display turns off the first mode automatically, so that they will not be displayed on top of one another. Anytime you turn off either system of coordinates, you end up with no coordinates at all until you turn one of them back on again.

Remember that the "last point entered" does not have to be an endpoint of a line, construction point, or definition point. You can simply select a point on the screen, using Snap to Nearest Point (NP) if you like, and then press ESC to cancel the implicit Line command that will start as a result. This point is now the last point entered, even though the Line command was canceled. When executing a Move or a Copy command, the first reference point that you select becomes the last point entered when you are selecting the new reference point, so that you can see how far you are moving or copying the object. When you issue the Object Erase or Object Change command, the point that you use to select the object becomes the last point entered. Almost any point selected on the screen becomes the last point entered and causes Relative Coordinates to be reset to 0,0.

Polar Coordinates

Polar Coordinates are toggled with the Coordinates option of the Coordinates command on the DISPLAY menu or **DC** followed by **C** and ENTER on the keyboard. Polar Coordinates display the distance from the cursor to the appropriate reference point, and also the angle between these two points, measured counterclockwise from an imaginary horizontal line passing through the last point. They can be useful if you want to draw a line of a particular length, or copy or move an object in a direction that is not strictly horizontal or vertical. Like the other coordinate displays, the format and accuracy of Polar Coordinates is controlled by the Numeric Display (NF) commands and how much drawing space is represented on the screen at the time. Polar Coordinates may be either absolute or relative.

Cursor and Screen Text Display

One command, Screen Display (DI), controls the display of the drawing cursor and the screen text. This command is designed to adapt to your personal preferences and also has some functional uses.

The Cursor Size Option

The size of the drawing cursor (in pixels or dots) is determined by the Cursor Size option of the Screen Display command on the DISPLAY menu; the option is also activated by typing **DI**, then **Z** (for siZe), or just **CU** (for CUrsor). The default size is 32. The smallest cursor available is 1 pixel. You can specify zero. Instead of no cursor at all, with this selection you get a cursor that goes to all four edges of the drawing screen, as shown in Figure 6-15. This type of cursor can be very useful for checking to see if objects are aligned correctly from one side of the screen to the other, especially if you are using a small grid. However, you still might want to use the grid; just because objects *appear* to be aligned on the screen does not mean that they really are. The screen-size cursor should be used only as a tool for checking alignment when it is difficult to follow the grid dots all the way across the screen.

All other cursors contain almost the specified number of pixels on each of the four arms of the cursor. The left and top arms have the specified

FIGURE 6-15 The cursor with Cursor Size set at zero

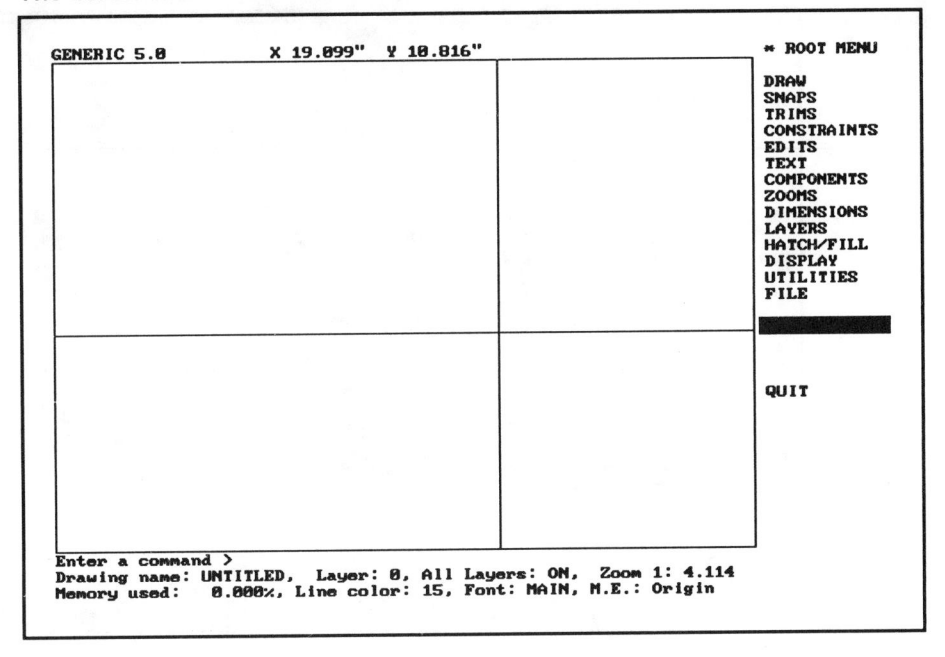

```
GENERIC 5.0        X 19.099"  Y 10.816"              * ROOT MENU

                                                     DRAW
                                                     SNAPS
                                                     TRIMS
                                                     CONSTRAINTS
                                                     EDITS
                                                     TEXT
                                                     COMPONENTS
                                                     ZOOMS
                                                     DIMENSIONS
                                                     LAYERS
                                                     HATCH/FILL
                                                     DISPLAY
                                                     UTILITIES
                                                     FILE


                                                     QUIT




Enter a command >
Drawing name: UNTITLED,  Layer: 0, All Layers: ON,  Zoom 1: 4.114
Memory used:   0.000%, Line color: 15, Font: MAIN, M.E.: Origin
```

number, but the right and bottom arms have one less than the specified number. The missing pixel is actually the one in the middle of the cursor, which is blank, so that the cursor is slightly off-balance to the top-left. You will notice this only when you have a very small cursor. If you try a Cursor Size of one, you will see two dots, one for the top arm and one for the left. The actual center of the cursor, where your points are actually selected, is the blank pixel between these two dots to the lower right. See Figure 6-16 for an enlarged view of several small cursors.

The Cursor Color Option

You can also customize cursor color with the Cursor Color option of the Screen Display command on the DISPLAY menu, or by typing **DI**, then **C** and pressing ENTER on the keyboard.

When you select this option, if the video menu is on and more than two colors are available, you will get the special video menu color selection bars (see Chapter 3, "Preliminary Considerations," for a discussion of

178   Generic CADD 5.0 Inside & Out

FIGURE 6-16 The enlarged view of different-sized cursors

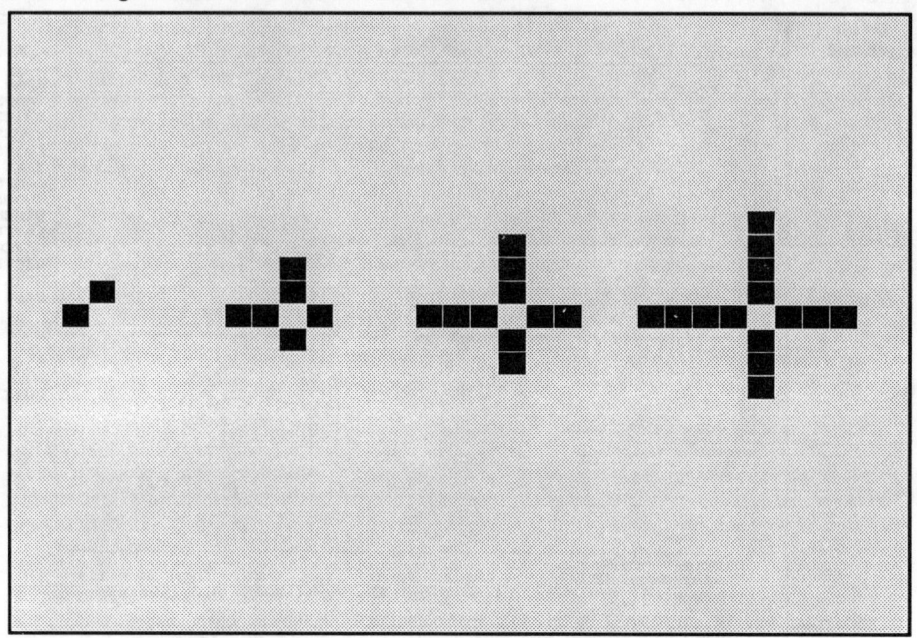

these bars in relation to Line Color). You can either select from this menu, using the second pointing device button, or type a number. If the menu is off or if you are working on a monochrome system, the color bars will not appear, so you must type a number. The current color will be shown in the prompt. If you decide not to change it, just press ENTER. You can configure the initial cursor color with the EN command. If you find one you particularly like, you can configure the initial cursor color with the EN command.

This option also controls the color of the box around the drawing area. Both the cursor and the box change color immediately upon your selection of a new color. You won't need to do a Redraw to see the effects of the change.

With the Cursor Color option, you can also eliminate the cursor altogether. You might want to do this to save an image with no box, or use some other screen-grabbing software for importing into other programs. If you select a color 0 (zero), the cursor and the box around the drawing area both disappear. This even works on some monochrome systems; on others, the box vanishes, but the cursor remains. In this case, the closest you can get to getting rid of the cursor is to change the Cursor Size to one.

The Display Color Option

This option, activated by choosing the Display Color option of the Screen Display command on the DISPLAY menu or by typing **DI**, then **D** and pressing ENTER on the keyboard, controls the color of the text in the menu area, the prompt area, and the coordinate area. It also controls the color of the grid dots. It can be selected from menu color bars or by typing a number. As with the Cursor Color option, it can be set to zero to get rid of the items whose color it controls. Unfortunately, this last function is not available with certain monochrome configurations, where all colors, even color 0 (zero), are defined as simply being in contrast to the background.

On most systems, the best way to display a Generic CADD drawing on the screen all by itself, just as it will be printed on a sheet of paper, is to set Cursor Color to zero, set Display Color to zero, and issue the Zoom All (ZA) command. This is the biggest, cleanest drawing-only display you can get. You may find this display difficult to draw in and edit, but it may serve other purposes. Figure 6-17 shows the SITEPLAN drawing displayed in a manner that is ideal for on-screen presentations and capturing screen images.

The Fast Redraw Command

How fast your drawing is regenerated on the video screen is determined by many factors: the speed of your computer, whether or not you have a math coprocessor, the complexity of your drawing, and other factors. Certain entities are somewhat self-optimizing. Circles, for instance, are drawn more crudely the smaller they get. It doesn't matter how accurately they're calculated if there are only a few pixels available to display them.

Text and components both turn into dots at some threshold zoom factor, and the internal complexity is ignored. The threshold depends upon the resolution of your graphics device. This explains why you sometimes seem to have more characters when zoomed out than when zoomed in. When text is small enough to be shown as dots, even spaces

FIGURE 6-17 The display when the Cursor Color and Display Color are set to zero with Zoom All issued

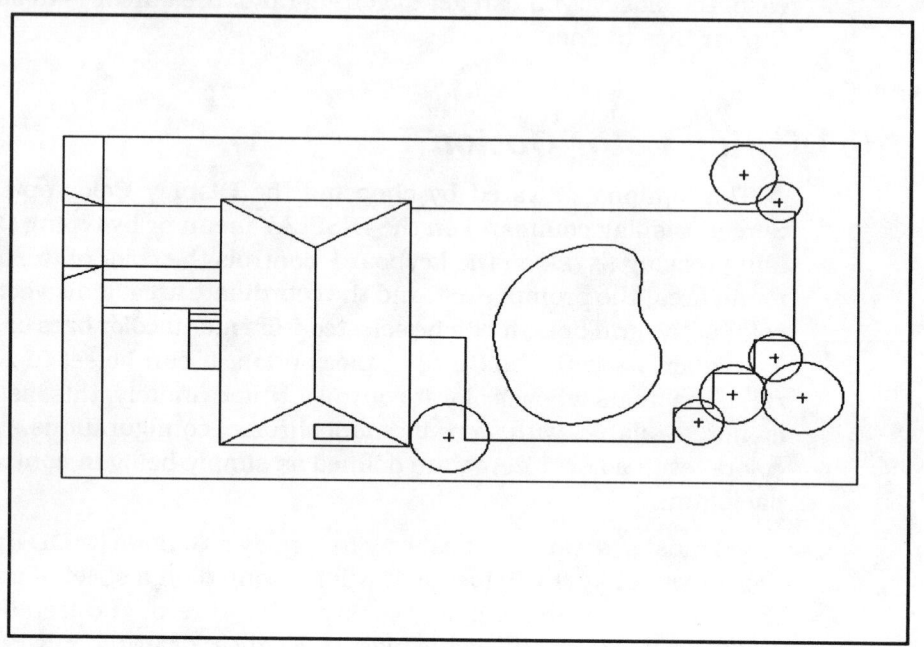

are displayed this way. The actual character definition is not checked to see if there is anything in it or not.

Similarly, a multicolored component, usually displayed using the colors of the individual entities within when you zoom out enough, changes to a single pixel displayed in the Line Color that was active when the component was placed. Once again, to optimize redraw time, the actual component definition is ignored below some threshold of visibility.

There are a number of additional ways of speeding up the regeneration of the drawing on the screen that can be toggled on and off by the user. These are all connected to the Fast Redraw (FA) command on the DISPLAY menu. Each involves a trade-off of speed over accuracy, visibility, or some other factor. The nature of your drawing determines how much each of these will speed up regeneration, and whether the trade-off is worth it. Each of these is also related to the display of specific entity types, so your choice of which, if any, to use should be based on what's slowing down the redraw in the first place. Fast Text, for example, a real time-saver if you have lots of text in your drawing, won't help at all if you don't have any.

To activate or deactivate any of these options, select it from the Fast Redraw prompt or type the associated character on the keyboard. You can switch as many of these as you like before pressing ENTER to end the Fast Redraw command.

Note With the exception of Fast Arcs, all of these display toggles affect printed and plotted output as well as the video display. Arcs and Circles are always printed or plotted at the maximum resolution available on the selected mode of the output device.

Fast Text When Fast Text is active, all Text Characters are represented on the display by Standard Points, and Text Lines are shown as Straight Lines, indicating where text is placed. As mentioned previously, Fast Text makes one of the most noticeable improvements in redraw speed, especially when your fonts are complicated and/or you have a lot of text in your drawing. The obvious compromise is that you can't read the text. Often, however, it is sufficient to simply know where the text is, and that it does, in fact, exist. You may not always need to know what it says. If you do need to know, you can either turn Fast Text back off and Redraw the screen, or you can use the View Fast Text command on the UTILITIES menu (TV on the keyboard) to temporarily make text visible without a full redraw. This command will ask you to place a window around the text that you wish to view, and will then display it. You can tell where it is, of course, by the Points or Line. If you wish to view Text Lines, be sure to get the beginning of the line. Capture the whole Text Line in the window if you're not sure where the beginning is.

To toggle Fast Text on or off, type the letter **T** after activating the Fast Redraw command. The status of the toggle will be shown in parentheses following its name in the prompt.

Since the idea is to speed up redraws, this toggle will not issue a redundant redraw just so you can see the effect. You will see it on the next Zoom, Pan, or other command that regenerates the display.

Fast Arcs Arcs and circles are always drawn with many short straight line segments. You usually don't see them, because Generic CADD figures out how many it will take so that you won't. The higher the resolution of your screen, and the bigger the arc or circle on it, the more sides Generic CADD will draw to keep up the illusion of perfectly rounded circles and arcs.

You can speed up the display of circles and arcs by activating the Fast Arcs option of the Fast Redraw command. When this toggle is active, another option appears in the prompt for Fast Redraw, which allows you to specify the actual number of line segments that will be used to display circles and arcs. Fast Arcs is toggled on or off by typing **A** after activating the Fast Redraw command, or by selecting it from the Fast Redraw prompt. As with Fast Text, this toggle will not cause an immediate change in the display, but will be in effect the next time the screen is redrawn.

Arc Sides When Fast Arcs is active, the Arc Sides option will appear on the Fast Redraw prompt, followed by the current setting. This parameter is limited to values between 3 and 12. Three sides is the minimum required to create a figure, and more than twelve fixed sides would slow down small circles, causing you to lose any benefit. To change the number of sides, type **S** or pick Arc Sides after issuing the Fast Redraw command. Type a number and press ENTER.

Remember This option will not be available unless Fast Arcs is turned on.

Disable LW and LT This toggle allows you to disable the display of Line Weight and Line Type. When this toggle is turned on, all entities are displayed using Line Type 0 (zero) and Line Width 0 (zero). When this toggle is off, Line Type and Line Width are displayed according to the actual values present as part of the definition of each entity. To operate this toggle, type **D** or pick Disable LW & LT from the prompt line after issuing the Fast Redraw command. Remember that the syntax for this option is phrased in the negative. If it is off, Line Type and Line Width are displayed; if it is on, they are not.

Fill Display The display of fills can be toggled on and off with the Fill Display option of the Fast Redraw command, represented by the letter *F*. When Fill Display is on, Fills are displayed. When it is off, they are not.

Fills that are not displayed are *not* like hidden layers. It is important to realize that even though fills are not displayed, they are still there. Invisible fills can be moved, copied, erased, and otherwise edited just as if they were visible.

The two-character keyboard command DF may also be used to turn the display of fills on and off.

Hatch Display   The display of hatches may also be turned on and off, with the Hatch Display option of Fast Redraw, signified by the letter *H*. When this toggle is turned off, hatches are not displayed. Hatches are displayed normally when this toggle is on. As with fills, invisible hatches can be edited exactly as if they were visible, so be careful. There is also a shortcut two-character command left over from previous versions, DH.

Layer Update   This option controls the automatic updating of layers when Layer Display and Hide are used. Layer update is toggled on and off by pressing the letter *L* or selecting Layer update from the Fast prompt.

When Layer update is on, the effect of selecting a layer number or name in the Layer Hide and Layer Display commands is immediate. Layers are hidden or displayed as they are selected. When Layer update is off, the updating of the screen is delayed until after you have specified as many layers as you want to Hide or Display, which occur only when you exit the command.

In order to save redraw time, it is useful to turn this toggle off when you are planning to display or hide several layers frequently.

Making More Room on the Screen

You can maximize the amount of display space for your drawing by eliminating the video menu. Although this means that you will have to use two-character commands to run Generic CADD, many users find they can learn these commands fairly quickly.

Display of the video menu is toggled with the Display Menu command on the DISPLAY menu, or by typing **VM** on the keyboard. The menu vanishes, and the box around the edge of the drawing screen expands so that this area is now available for drawing, as shown in Figure 6-18. If you are zoomed in to a portion of the drawing, the area that was covered by the video menu will be blank at first, but you can remedy this situation by issuing the Redraw (RD) command from the ZOOMS menu.

To turn the video menu back on, simply select the command or type **VM** again. The box around the drawing area returns to its normal size, and the menu reappears. A portion of the drawing display will no longer be visible, of course, but nothing in the drawing has actually been lost—it is just hidden "under" the video menu. Whenever you turn on the video menu, it always starts with the ROOT menu, rather than the menu that you had on the screen when you turned it off.

You can see the advantage of a larger screen when you examine the diagram drawing. Compare Figure 6-19, which shows the same drawing with no video menu at a Zoom All, with 6-18, before the new larger area was utilized. With the video menu off, you get a little more detail, and do not have to Zoom In quite as much, because the objects have a little better resolution. This technique will have a greater impact on more complicated drawings because there will be more detail to view and you will need to zoom more. If the drawing was more vertically oriented, turning off the video menu would not make as much difference, because all of the gain in drawing space is in the horizontal direction.

Note There is no way to gain more space in the vertical direction. When you turn off the coordinates, the drawing area does not expand; the coordinates just do not appear. The same is true with the three lines below the drawing area. The drawing area is not expandable into this space.

The Layers Commands

The commands on the LAYERS menu fall into two groups, those for *editing* layers and those for *managing* layers. The Layer editing commands were explained in Chapter 5, "Basic Editing Tasks." This section will concentrate on the Layer management commands. Once you have a drawing with a few layers in it, you can try some of the editing commands.

It is often a good idea to set up a standard system of layers, so that you always know where to find certain types of information. If you use Dimensioning, you can use a special command to specify the layer for creating these dimensions. Drawings can be plotted a layer at a time if you like, layers can be saved in a drawing file, and entire drawings can be inserted onto a specified layer in your current drawing.

Layers are one of the more powerful data-organizing devices in Generic CADD 5.0, particularly for determining exactly what information should

Chapter 6: Drawing Aids and Controls 185

FIGURE 6-18 The display when the video menu is first turned off

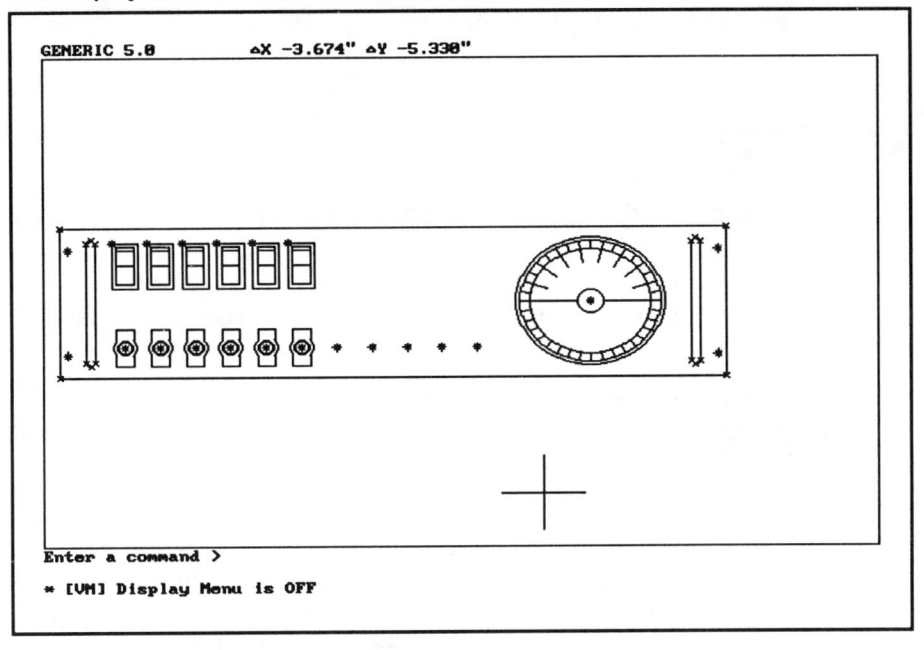

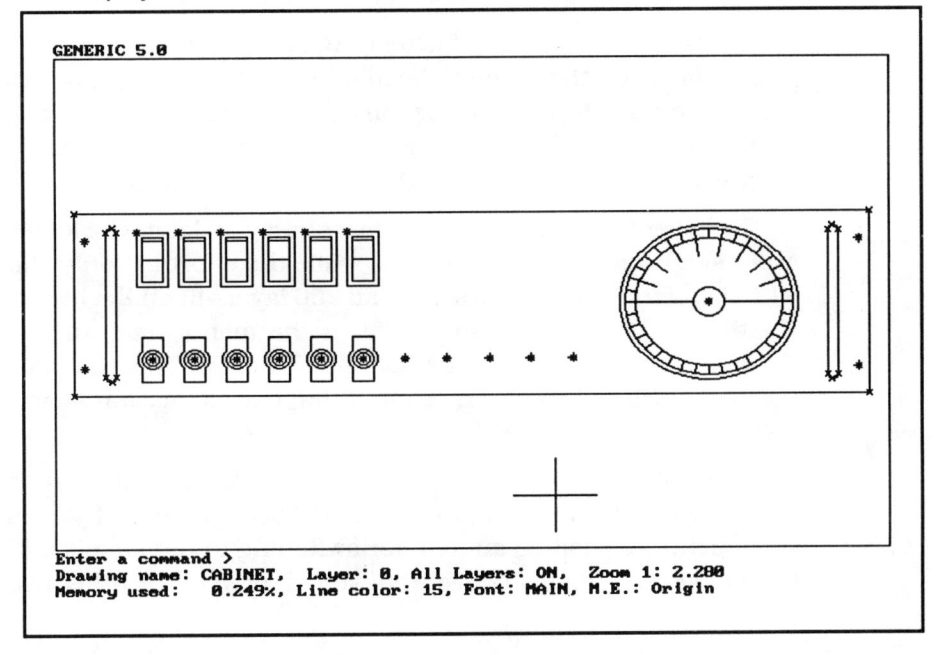

FIGURE 6-19 The display without a video menu after a Zoom All

be displayed on the screen at a given time. Most Layer commands start with the letter Y (the middle letter in the word laYer).

The Layer List

Many of the Layer commands bring up a list of layers on the video menu if the video menu is currently active. This list provides information about the status of the layers in your drawing and also allows you to specify layers by simply picking them from the menu just like any other menu item.

The layers are listed in numerical order, starting with zero. If you have assigned names to any of your layers, these will be shown instead of the number. However, a layer does not lose its number when you name it, so they always stay in the same order.

Several informative items appear on the layer list next to each layer number or name. A small dot appears next to each visible layer. Since it is quite possible for a layer to have nothing on it, you may prefer to think of the absence of a dot as representing a hidden layer, rather than each dot representing a layer in use. There is a slight logical problem with trying to imagine layers that don't yet exist as being visible or invisible.

Layers that do exist, by virtue of the fact that they have at least one entity placed on them, are indicated by a small triangle, or delta, in the column to the left. Finally, the current layer is indicated by the letter *c* in the dot column. This leaves no room for the dot, but since the current layer can't be hidden anyway, the dot would be redundant.

The Layer List comes in two forms, short and long. The long list shows every single one of the 256 layers, while the short list only shows those with data on them. Of course, not all 256 layers fit on the list at one time. If either list is longer than will fit in the menu area, an item labeled "More . . ." will appear at the bottom of the list. This item takes you to the next page of layers. The same thing can be accomplished with the PGDN key on the keyboard.

If the long list is currently shown, there will be an item at the bottom of the menu for switching to the short list. Similarly, if you are on the short list, there will be an item for switching to the long list. Whichever list you select remains active until you change to the other list.

Whenever you are prompted to select a layer, you may choose it from this list, just like any other menu item.

The Current Layer Command

To take full advantage of the management capabilities of layers, you should assign each entity in the drawing to a specific layer. So far, all of the examples in this book have used only one layer—layer 0 (zero). All new entities are created on the current layer, and layer 0 (zero) is the default for all new drawings. To create entities on other layers, the current layer must be changed with the Current Layer command on the LAYERS menu, or by typing **YC** on the keyboard.

When you use this command, you are shown the current layer and asked to specify the new current layer. Allowable values are from 0 to 255, which means you can have up to 256 layers in your drawing. Type a number or name and press ENTER or select a layer from the Layer List on the menu. From this point on, until you change the current layer, all entities created will be placed on this new current layer. Note that the current layer is shown on the Status Line, so that you always know which layer you are working on. The ability to specify a Current Layer can also make your editing a little easier.

Editing on the Current Layer

In previous editing examples, whenever you chose an entity with an Object command or selected entities with a Window command, all entities on the screen were available because they were all located on one layer, which also happened to be the current layer, layer 0 (zero).

Layers, however, can be used to refine the selection process. You have a choice of selecting from all entities visible on the screen or only those entities residing on the current layer.

To change from editing only the current layer to editing all layers, use the All Layers Edit command, shown as All Layers on the LAYERS menu, and abbreviated AL for the keyboard command. This toggle switches the layer editing mode back and forth between Current-Only and All Layers. Whenever you use this command, a message in the prompt area will

FIGURE 6-20 A drawing made with several layers (courtesy of Mobile Office Vehicle Engineering)

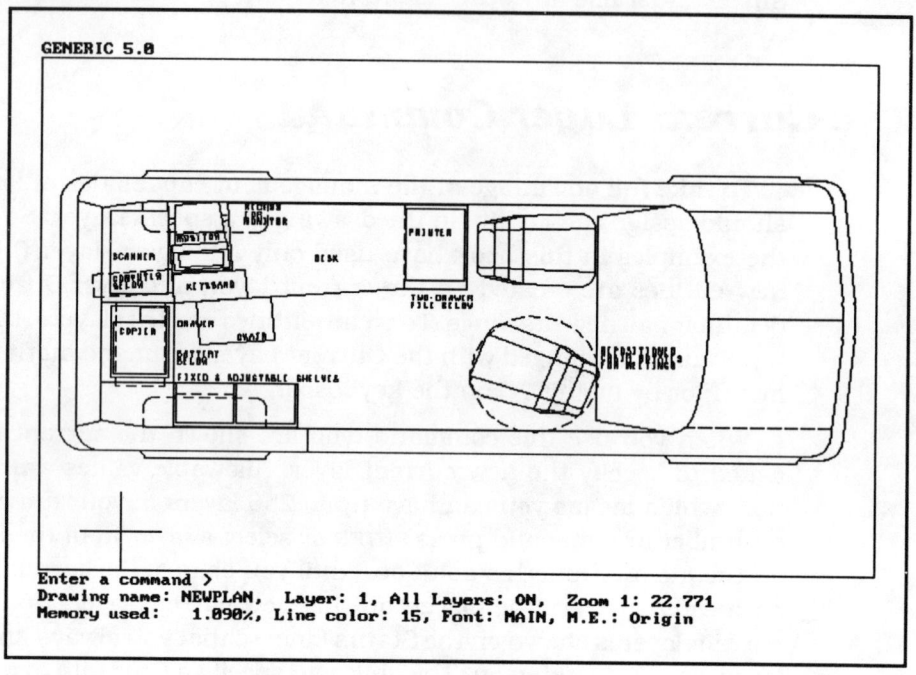

inform you of the new status of the Edit All Layers toggle. If it was previously on, the message will state "Edit all layers OFF," meaning that you can only edit on the current layer now. If it was already off, you will get the message "Edit all layers ON," meaning that you can now edit all entities visible on the screen. If you have Status Line turned on, the status of the Edit All Layers toggle is shown whenever the Status Line is displayed.

Figures 6-20 through 6-22 illustrate the difference between editing with the Edit All Layers toggle on and off. Figure 6-20 shows a drawing that has been constructed on several layers. The basic drawing is on one layer, the text is on another, the dimension lines on another, and so on. Figure 6-21 shows what happens with a Window Erase when the layer that contains the text is the Current Layer and Edit All Layers is off. Only the text is erased, even though many other entities are in the window. Figure 6-22 shows the same command with approximately the same window, but with Edit All Layers turned on. All entities visible on the

Chapter 6: Drawing Aids and Controls 189

FIGURE 6-21 A Window Erase with All Layers Edit turned off erases only the ghosted entities

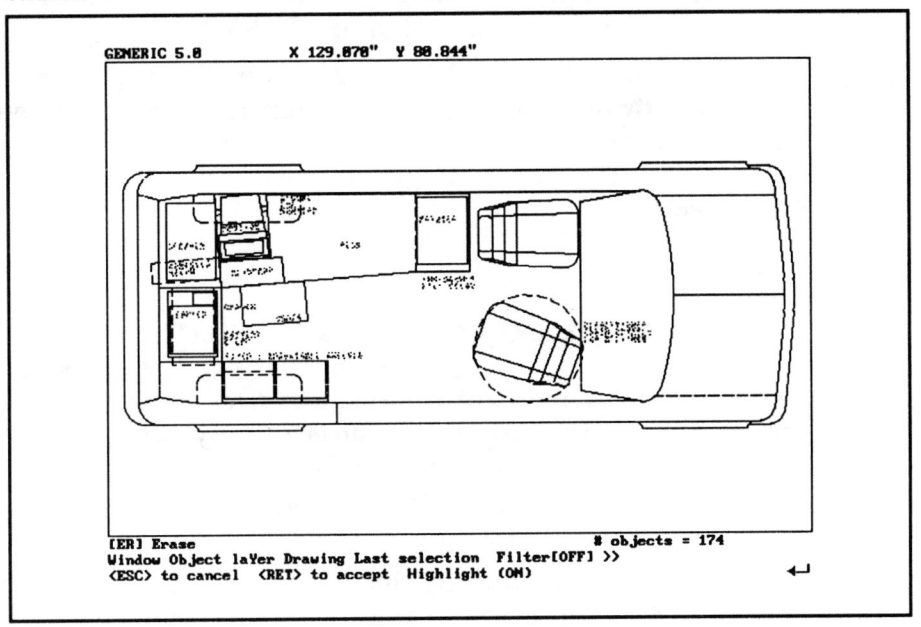

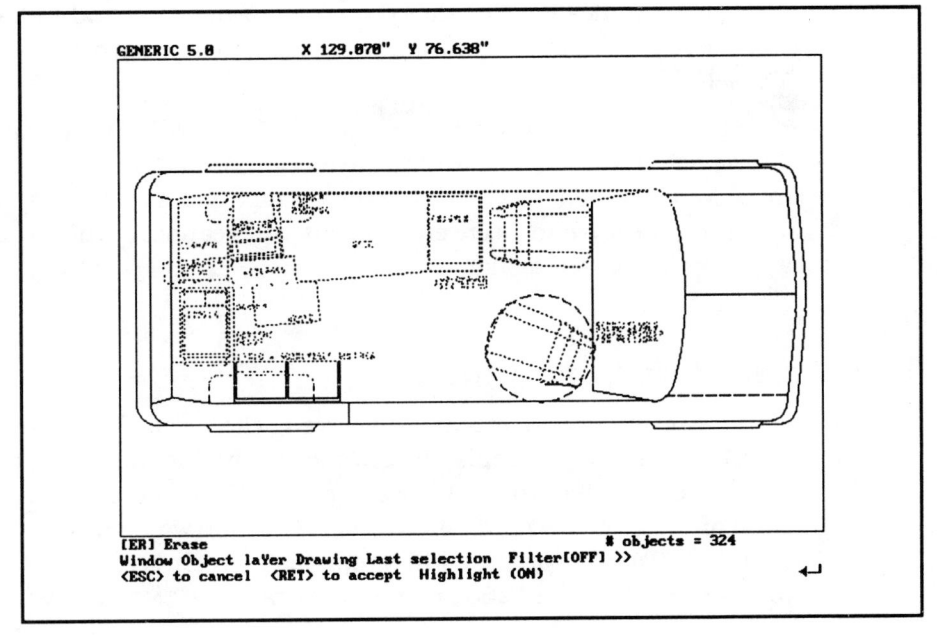

FIGURE 6-22 A Window Erase with All Layers Edit turned on

screen that are defined entirely within the window are erased. A few lines passing through the window are not erased, because one or the other or both of their endpoints are not in the window.

No matter what the status of the All Layers Edit toggle, layers that are not currently displayed cannot be edited with the Object and Window editing commands. If you want to use objects to reference layers other than the current layer (but not edit them), turn All Layers Edit off and All Layers Snap (SY) on.

Selecting Which Layers to Display

One of the advantages of using more than one layer is having the choice to make all of the entities on a certain layer or layers temporarily invisible. This process is called *hiding* layers. One reason for hiding layers is to temporarily get rid of information that has no bearing on the task at hand or is obscuring the entities that you want to edit.

Layers can be used to try different variations on a portion of your drawing. Then you can incorporate one of them into the final drawing by using one of the Change commands to move certain entities onto your final layers, and the Layer Erase command to get rid of the extras. Construction lines can be placed on their own layer, and hidden when it's time to print. You might even designate one layer strictly for notes to yourself.

Entities on hidden layers cannot be edited with Object or Window editing commands. The Current Layer cannot be hidden. Entities that are moved to a hidden layer using the Change command vanish from the screen as if they had been erased, but will reappear when the hidden layers are displayed again.

The Layer Hide Command

Because all 256 layers are displayed when you first start Generic CADD, if you want to display layers selectively, the first thing to do is to hide the one(s) that you don't want to see. This is done with the Hide command on the LAYERS menu, or with the two-character keyboard command **YH**. The prompt will simply ask which layer to hide. Type a number between 0 and 255 or a name, followed by ENTER, or select a layer from the Layer List. Any entities on the selected layer will immediately be removed from the screen. If you want to hide more than one layer, select another. Repeat this process until you have specified all of the layers to be hidden, and then press ENTER.

If you want to hide all the layers (except for the Current Layer), type **256** when prompted for which layer to hide.

The Layer Display Command

If you have hidden one or more layers and you want to see them again, use the Display command on the LAYERS menu, or type **YD** on the keyboard. If you are not sure which layers are currently displayed, look on the Layer List that is displayed when you use this command. Each visible layer will have a dot next to its name or number. When you first start Generic CADD, all layers are displayed, so there won't be any hidden layers unless you have previously used the Hide command.

When you use the Layer Display (YD) command, you will get a prompt asking you to select the layer that you want to display. Type a number or a name, and then press ENTER or select a layer from the Layer List. As with Layer Hide, selecting the layer does not automatically trigger a redraw of the selected layer. Type **256**, or select All from the menu to display all layers. You can specify more than one layer to display. When you have finished specifying layers, press ENTER.

The Layer Name Command

In Generic CADD 5.0, you may assign names to any layer that you wish. As noted previously, assigning a name to a layer does not eliminate its number. Named layers still show up in numerical, not alphabetical, order on the Layer List, and may be referred to by either number or name.

To name a layer, select the Name command from the LAYER menu or type **YN** on the keyboard. You will be asked to select a layer, which you can do either by typing a number or an existing layer name, or by selecting a layer from the Layer List. If the selected layer does not already have a name, you will be prompted for a name. Layer names can be up to eight characters in length. When you have typed the layer name, press ENTER. You may use the BACKSPACE key to delete characters if you make a mistake. If the name that you type is already in use for another layer, the name will not be accepted. Otherwise, the newly defined layer name will appear on the Layer List in the future, in place of the number. From now until you change it, you can specify this layer by typing either the number or the name, or by picking the name from the Layer List in the menu area.

If the layer that you select already has a name, you will first get a prompt asking whether you want to Rename, Un-Name, or Escape. If you type **R** for Rename, you will simply be prompted for a layer name in the manner described previously. If you type **U**, for Un-Name, the layer will revert back to using its number on the Layer List, and typing the name will no longer allow you to identify the layer. If you type **E** for Escape, you will exit the command without changing the existing layer name.

Learning the material in this chapter should give you much greater control over your drawings and how they are displayed on the screen. Your drawing and editing should now be easier, more efficient, and more accurate. In addition, you should be able to organize the information in your drawings more efficiently and access that information for editing and for use in future drawings.

CHAPTER 7

Information and Inquiries

This chapter focuses on the information that Generic CADD 5.0 can provide about your drawing as you work on it. This information ranges from the status of certain toggles and drawing parameters to real data that can be calculated from the entities you have created. Several commands provide these different types of information. One of these appears on the DISPLAY menu and two are listed on the UTILITIES menu.

The Status Lines

The simplest form of on-screen feedback available while running Generic CADD 5.0, beyond the coordinates (see Chapter 6, "Drawing Aids and Controls"), is the Status Lines—the two lines of text that appear below the "Enter a command >" prompt if the Status Line toggle is on (see Figure 7-1). Information provided on the first Status Line includes the name of the drawing on which you are working, the current layer, the status of the All Layers toggle (discussed later in this chapter), and the current zoom value. The second Status Line shows the percentage of available memory used by the drawing and the current Line Color, Font, and Manual Entry mode.

The Status Lines are only displayed while the "Enter a command >" prompt is on the screen—that is, when you are not performing a command operation. The rest of the time the prompt area is used for command prompts. The Status Line area is regenerated at the end of every command. If the current command causes change in any information shown in the Status Line, it is reflected there immediately upon exiting the command.

To toggle the display of the Status Lines on or off, use the Screen Dsply command on the DISPLAY menu, also activated by typing **DI** on the

FIGURE 7-1   The Status Lines

```
Enter a command >
Drawing name: UNTITLED,  Layer: 0, All Layers: ON,   Zoom 1: 4.114
Memory used:    0.000%, Line color: 15, Font: MAIN, M.E.: Origin
```

keyboard. Select the Status Line option by choosing it with the first button on the pointing device or by typing **S** on the keyboard. The display status of the Status Lines will be shown in parentheses after the prompt. Press ENTER or select the Enter symbol at the far right end of the prompt to return to the "Enter a command >" prompt. The new display status will be used upon your return.

In some situations the Status Line is not shown, even when you are not executing a command, such as after invoking a toggle command. After a toggle, Generic CADD flashes a message, such as "Snap to Grid is ON," which stays on the screen until the next command is issued. These messages are provided because sometimes you don't remember if a toggle is on or off, so you issue the command just to find out. If you get a message that you don't like, issue it again to return to the desired status.

Another time that you might not see the Status Line is when you have a small grid size (relative to the area currently shown on the screen). Generic CADD refuses to put the dots so close together that your drawing is difficult to see, so it leaves out some of them. You might get a message such as "Only every 4th-X 4th-Y grid point shown" when you execute a redraw, indicating that for each visible grid dot, there are three invisible ones between. You will see this clearly if you turn on Snap to Grid.

Anytime that both the "Enter a command >" prompt and a message causes the disappearance of the Status Lines, you can clear the message by pressing ESC. As soon as the message is cleared, the Status Lines appear.

More Information: The Screen Flip Command

More information is available to users of Generic CADD 5.0 with the Screen Flip command on the UTILITIES menu. The two-character command code is SF.

Generic CADD 5.0 users may be interested to learn that the Screen Flip command actually generates a text screen, rather than a graphics screen like the rest of the program. This screen provides a place to run memory-resident software that requires a text screen in order to be activated. In Level 3, the Screen Flip (called FLIP SCREEN in previous releases) was on a graphics screen like the rest of the program.

In 5.0, the Screen Flip command offers options that provide information requiring more than the three lines at the bottom of the screen. Select an option by pressing the number alongside it (see Figure 7-2).

Display Drawing Status

This option provides some of the same information shown on the Status Lines (the drawing name and the layer), plus the number of points, entities, and definitions in the drawing. The memory usage is described in actual bytes instead of a percentage, and many more of the current drawing parameters are shown in addition to the Line Type and Line Color that you get on the Status Line. The status of some of the more important toggles is shown, as are the locations of the basepoint, database unit, display unit, disk space, and disk usage data. Figure 7-3 shows the status screen for the SITEPLAN drawing.

FIGURE 7-2 The Screen Flip menu

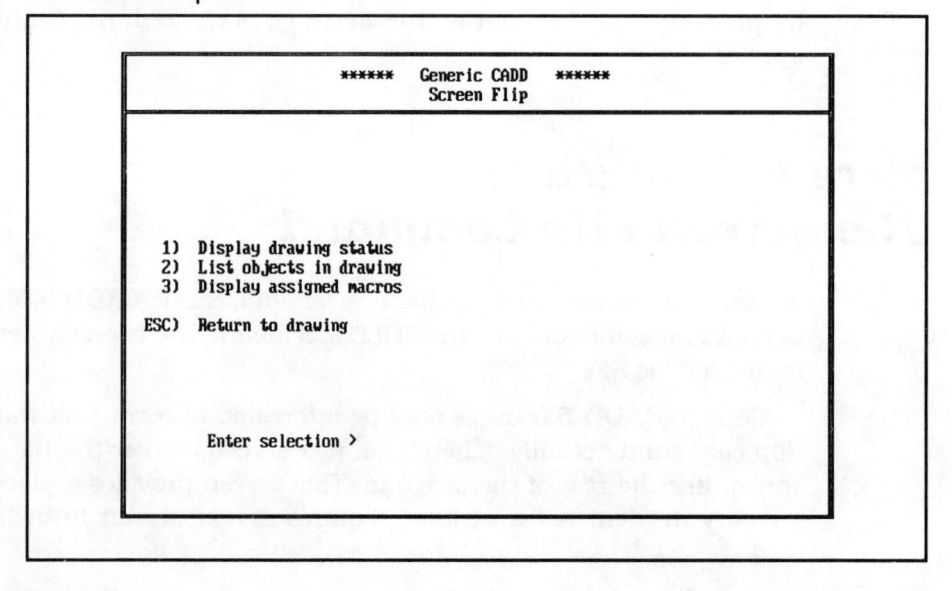

```
               ****** Generic CADD ******
                      Screen Flip




         1) Display drawing status
         2) List objects in drawing
         3) Display assigned macros

    ESC) Return to drawing





         Enter selection >
```

Even though the prompt at the bottom of the screen tells you to press RETURN to exit the screen, you will be returned to the Screen Flip menu if you press any key.

List Objects in Drawing

This option gives you a list of entities in the current drawing file. The type of entity is shown, along with its Line Type, Width, Color, and Layer.

When you first select this option, you will get a prompt asking whether you want to list entities in the current View, the whole Drawing, or just items currently Selected. The first two options are self-explanatory, and Selection List is discussed in Chapter 10, "Advanced Drawing and Editing Techniques." Type **V**, **D**, or **S** to indicate the type of list that you want. The pointing device won't help here. Figure 7-4 shows the List Objects display screen.

The list that you get is numbered according to each entity's current location in the database. Note that although the list is always sequential, it is never consecutive, because the actual locations of the definition points are not listed here, but take up space just the same. There will be

FIGURE 7-3 The Drawing Status screen

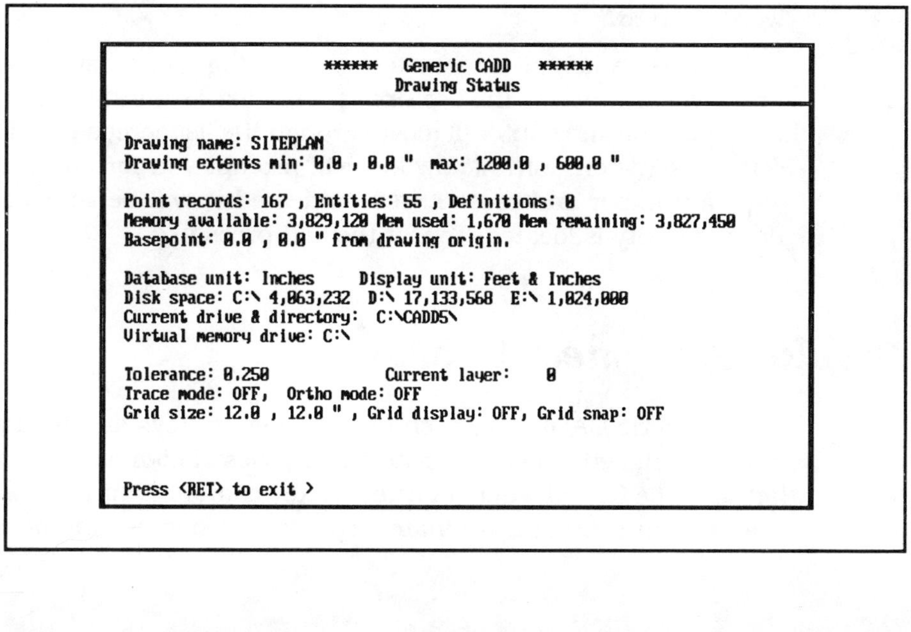

```
****** Generic CADD ******
            Drawing Status

Drawing name: SITEPLAN
Drawing extents min: 0.0 , 0.0 "  max: 1200.0 , 600.0 "

Point records: 167 , Entities: 55 , Definitions: 0
Memory available: 3,829,120 Mem used: 1,670 Mem remaining: 3,827,450
Basepoint: 0.0 , 0.0 " from drawing origin.

Database unit: Inches     Display unit: Feet & Inches
Disk space: C:\ 4,063,232  D:\ 17,133,568  E:\ 1,024,000
Current drive & directory:  C:\CADD5\
Virtual memory drive: C:\

Tolerance: 0.250          Current layer:    0
Trace mode: OFF,  Ortho mode: OFF
Grid size: 12.0 , 12.0 " , Grid display: OFF, Grid snap: OFF



Press <RET> to exit >
```

FIGURE 7-4 The List Objects display screen

```
                    ******  Generic CADD  ******
                             List Objects

    Item   Description    Type    Width    Color    Layer

    1      line           0       0        12       0
    4      line           0       0        12       0
    7      line           0       0        12       0
    10     line           0       0        12       0
    13     circle         0       0        12       0
    16     line           0       0        12       0
    19     line           0       0        12       0
    22     arc            0       0        12       0
    26     curve          0       0        12       0
    36     curve          0       0        12       0
    46     curve          0       0        12       0
    56     curve          0       0        12       0
    66     curve          0       0        10       101
    82     curve          0       0        10       101
    93     curve          0       0        10       101

    <PgDn> Next pg  <PgUp> Previous pg  <-> Goto  <Home/End>  -  <ESC> exit
```

one missing number after a Point, two after a Line or a Circle, three after an Arc, and so on.

Following the entity number is the type of entity, and the entity's Line Type, Line Width, Color, and Layer. If the entity has been erased and the database has not been packed, it will show up on the list followed by the word "Erased."

If the list is long, it may be navigated using a number of cursor keys. HOME will take you to the beginning of the list, while END will take you to the end. PGUP and PGDN will move through the list screen by screen, while a LEFT ARROW or RIGHT ARROW key will prompt you for an item number. Type a number and press ENTER, and the list will be scrolled until the desired entity is located. To exit the list, press ESC.

Display Assigned Macros

In Generic CADD 5.0, each of the function keys and mouse buttons can be assigned a macro. A *macro* is a series of commands that you can set up to be issued when a button or key combination is pressed. These macros can contain coordinates, component names, and other data as well as commands. They provide a mechanism for programming Generic CADD to perform certain repeatable functions automatically. For more information on writing macros, see Chapter 16.

This option allows you to view and edit the macros assigned to each key or button. In addition to the function keys themselves, macros can be assigned to combinations of several other keys—SHIFT, CTRL, ALT and the function keys—for a total of either 40 function key macros on 10 function keys or 48 macros on 12 function keys depending on your keyboard.

The first screen that you see when you select this option will list each function key along with the macro assigned to it. If you wish to view the SHIFT, CTRL, or ALT key combinations, type the letter highlighted in the prompt area. The macros assigned to the pointing device buttons can be displayed by typing **P**. To get back to the plain function keys, type **F**. These letters are also highlighted in the prompt area.

You can edit the macros from this screen as well. Simply type the key or key combination that you wish to edit or assign. The macro will be displayed for editing in the prompt at the bottom of the screen. You can BACKSPACE over macro text, use the cursor keys to move into it, and type new text over or into existing commands. Initially, you will be in Insert mode, but you can toggle this off and on by pressing INS on the keyboard. DEL works here as well. When you are done, press ENTER to return to the list.

Return to Drawing

This last option simply restores the main Generic CADD screen so that you can continue working on your drawing.

The Measure Command

The Measure command on the UTILITIES menu provides access to information concerning the numeric data and geometric properties of the drawing. The information available includes distances, areas, and angles. These are accessed from options on the Measure prompt.

The Distance Option

The Distance option of the Measure command, represented by **ME** followed by **D** on the keyboard, lets you obtain the distance between any two points, or the cumulative distance between a number of points.

When you select this option, you are asked to specify the starting point. If you want to measure the distance between the endpoints of two lines, for example, you can use the Snap to Nearest Point command to locate the first endpoint by using the third button on the pointing device or by typing **NP** when you have positioned the cursor near the point that you want to select. You can use the same method to choose the second point. Once you have selected two points, the distance between these points is shown in the prompt area. Figure 7-5 shows the results of measuring the top line in the SITEPLAN drawing. When have finished the Measure command, press ESC, type **PU** (for Pen Up), or choose a blank menu line with the second pointing device button to return to the "Enter a command >" prompt.

If you want to know the cumulative distance between a number of points, simply select more points. As you select each point, the cumulative distance will be shown. When you specify the last point, you will see

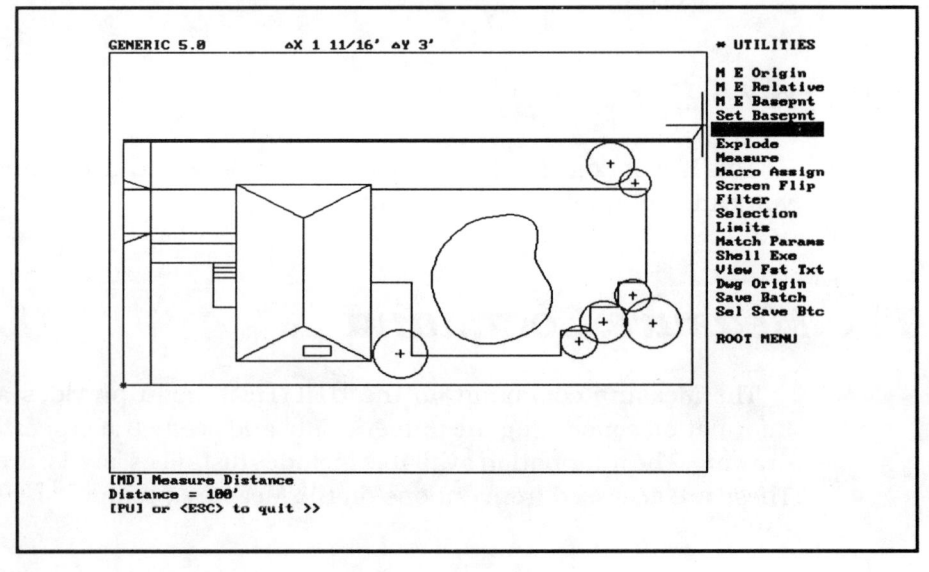

FIGURE 7-5 Measuring the distance between the corners of the property

the total distance. You must press ESC, type **PU**, or select a blank menu line with the pointing device to stop entering points and return to the "Enter a command >" prompt. If you forget to do this, your next command may not work properly.

The Area Option

The Area option of the Measure command is activated by typing the keyboard command **ME** followed by **A**. It measures area in any unit system you happen to be using. If the display units are inches, you will get square inches; if you are using feet, your area measurements will be in square feet. Similarly, the metric unit systems can provide square meters, centimeters, or millimeters.

When you activate the Area option, you will be asked to select points. You simply pick points at each corner of the shape as if you were drawing lines around the perimeter until you get back to the beginning point. When you press ESC, the area will be shown. You can use the Snap to Nearest Point command while picking points, to get a more accurate area measurement. Figure 7-6 shows the result of measuring the area of the roof of the house in the SITEPLAN drawing.

The area that you are trying to measure must be closed. In other words, you must return to the starting point before pressing ESC. If you do not, Generic CADD assumes that the boundary of the area that you are trying to measure is a straight line between the last point entered back to the beginning point.

An undocumented feature of the Area option allows you to measure more than one area in the same command and get a cumulative total. You can do this by typing **PU** instead of pressing ESC when you return to the beginning point of the first area. You will remain in the Area option, but the calculation of the area will be temporarily suspended. Move the cursor to a corner of the next area to be measured and begin choosing points again. When you return to the starting point of the second area, press ESC. The area shown will be the combined area of the two figures. This technique can be extended to combine as many figures as you like into one area calculation.

Users of early versions of Generic CADD will be interested to note that if you went around a figure clockwise, you got a positive number for the

FIGURE 7-6 Measuring the area of a roof

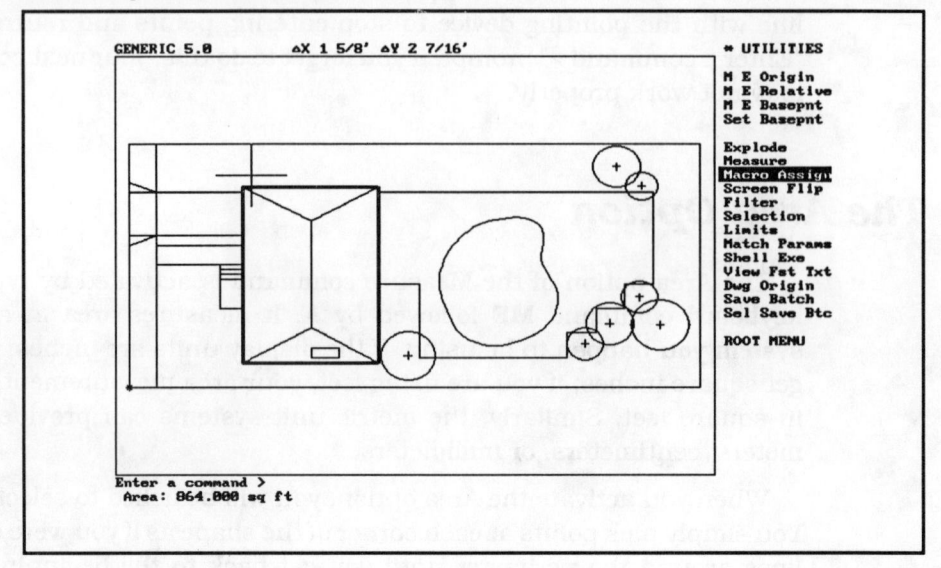

area, and if you went around counterclockwise, you got a negative result. On certain versions, if you combine this technique with the method of combining multiple areas, you can calculate the area of a shape that has a hole in it. First, go clockwise around the entire figure, type **PU**, and then go counterclockwise around the hole. The result will be the area of the first shape minus the area of the second shape. Some versions with positive and negative area calculations do not allow multiple areas, and the Levels products and the current version 5.0 always calculate only positive areas.

The Angle Options

The Angle options of the Measure command, activated by typing **ME** followed by **2** or **3**, provide a display of the angle between two selected points or lines. The angle is displayed in the currently selected unit system for angles.

When you select the 2-point angle option, you are asked to select two points. As with all of the Measure options, these can be selected as free-floating points, snapped onto existing points, or specified by manual entry. After you select the second point, the angle is shown in the prompt area. Figure 7-7 illustrates the 2-point option used on the wall of the house in a modified version of the SITEPLAN drawing. The convention for angle displays is that a horizontal line from left to right is considered to be zero, and angles are measured counterclockwise from the following position: straight up from bottom to top is 90 degrees; horizontal right to left is 180 degrees; straight down is 270 degrees. In this command, there are no negative angles. The angle between any two points is always calculated as a positive angle between zero and 360 degrees.

The 3-point angle option calculates the angle between two lines. As with the 2-point angle option, this angle is always measured in a counterclockwise direction. However, rather than being measured from a fixed horizontal, the angle of the second line is measured relative to the first. When you select this option you will be asked for a basepoint and two additional points. The basepoint must be the point of intersection between the two lines. If the two points do not share a common endpoint, this basepoint may be established by using the Snap Intersection command before selecting the point. The next two points should be on the two lines that form the angle you are trying to measure. Snap to the endpoints with the NP (Nearest Point) command, or press the third button

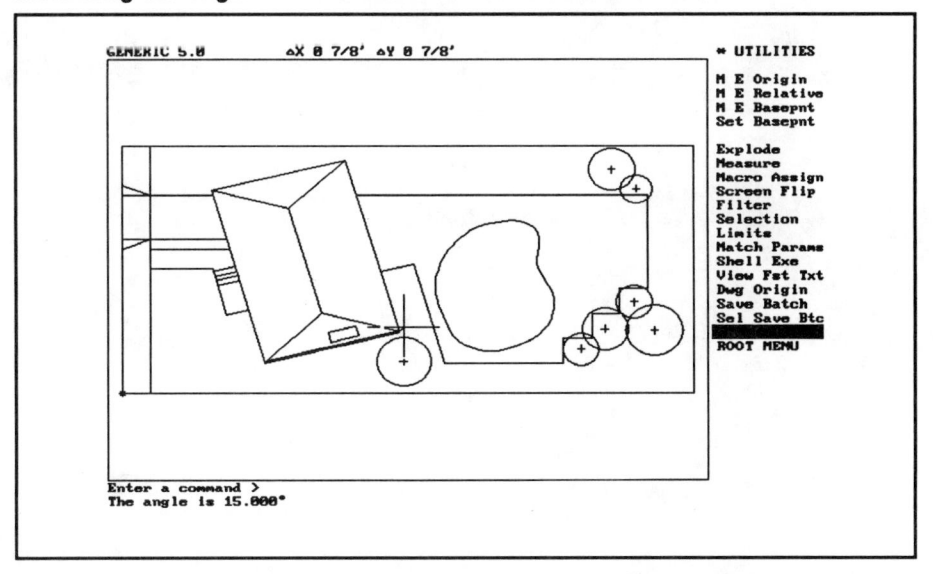

FIGURE 7-7 Measuring the angle of the SITEPLAN house after it is rotated

on the pointing device. Remember, the angle will be measured counterclockwise in the order in which you pick the points.

Note Because you are not actually selecting the lines themselves, but only their endpoints, the two lines do not actually have to exist in the drawing. You can find the angle between any three points. Just remember that the first point given should be the base or inside corner of the angle.

As you have seen in this chapter, Generic CADD 5.0 keeps track of the information that you put into the drawing, but can also provide additional information. As a graphic model of reality that contains accurate data, a Generic CADD drawing can be used as a tool both to store existing information and to extrapolate additional information as you need it.

CHAPTER 8

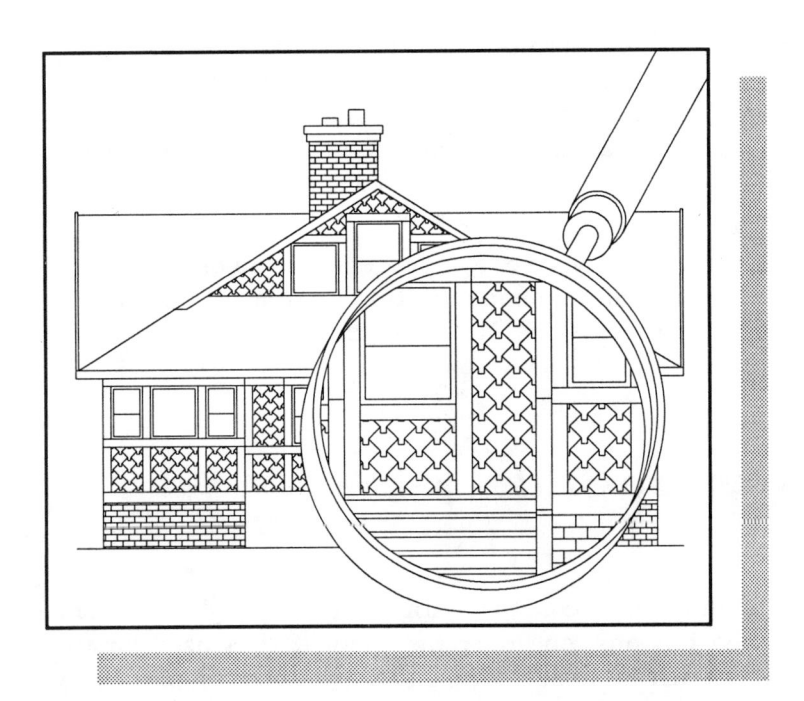

Complex Entities

Until now, you have created and edited only simple entities. These simple entities, Points, Lines, Circles, Arcs, Ellipses, and Curves, are the basic building blocks from which all drawings in Generic CADD 5.0 are created. In this chapter you will see how simple entities can be combined to create complex entities.

What Are Complex Entities?

Complex entities are composed of one or more other entities, usually simple entities, though complex entities can also be created from other complex entities already in the drawing. In some cases, you define complex entities; in other cases, you may use predefined complex entities, such as Text Characters. Still other complex entities, such as Hatches and Fills, are created automatically by Generic CADD.

Generic CADD has seven types of complex entities, all of which have certain features in common: Components, Text Characters, Text Lines, Attributes, Associative Dimensions, Hatches, and Fills.

Complex Entities Are Still Just Entities

Like a simple entity, each complex entity can be thought of as one distinct item. Each has only one reference point that is used for the editing commands, such as Erase, Move, and Copy. Each complex entity is described in the database by the location of its reference point, the number of the layer on which it is located, its color, and so on. Each entity is placed with a single command that asks for points, just like the simple-entity Draw commands. When you request a list of the items in the current window from the Screen Flip (SF) command, each complex entity appears as one line item. The individual entities that make up a complex entity are not normally selectable, for editing or other purposes. However, there are some exceptions to this general rule, as you will see.

Complex Entities Are Defined Once

One of the obvious advantages of a complex entity is that once you've drawn it, you never have to draw it again. This aspect is usually the most useful for Components and Text Characters. Another less apparent advantage is that each complex entity is defined once and then *placed* each time it appears. The main benefit of this feature is its space-saving capability. Compare the effect on the database of drawing a figure composed of 20 Lines and then copying it three times, to defining a complex entity and placing it four times. In the first case, you end up with a total of 80 entities (20 originals and 60 copies), each occupying space in memory and eventually on a disk. In the second instance, you have a total of 24 entities—the 20 original entities, plus one additional entity each time the complex entity is placed. (The second example actually contains 26 entities if you include the beginning and ending of the definition.) In reality, while complex entities take up a little more space than simple entities, they certainly do not take up the space of 80 simple entities. You never really see these extra entities, but they do take up space in the database. In this example, if the simple entities were all Lines, these two drawings would take up 2410 bytes and 910 bytes, respectively, plus about 645 bytes each for the storage of environmental variables, which illustrates the space-saving advantage of complex entities.

Even copying a complex entity does not cause the definition to be repeated in the computer memory or the disk file. The *placement* of the complex entity is copied, not the definition itself.

Placement Parameters

Each of the complex entity types has its own set of *placement parameters*—values or conditions that are set before placing the complex entity. These placement parameters greatly speed up the placement of complex entities, because you do not have to select them every time you place an entity. These placement parameters are comparable to the simple entity placement parameters—Line Color, Line Type, Line Width, and Current Layer. In fact, Current Layer is used by complex entities as well.

Components have two parameters that are set before a component is placed: (1) scale, which allows you to place the predefined component in a size different from the original size, and (2) rotation, which lets you turn a complex entity on any angle. These parameters rule all components that you place until the parameters are changed. When you change these parameters, only new component placements are affected. Once a component is placed, the parameters become part of that particular complex entity placement and can only be changed with the editing commands.

Text Characters have several parameters, including size and rotation, that are similar to the component parameter's scale and rotation. Text uses "size" instead of "scale" because characters are defined to be one unit tall. For example, when scaled by a factor of two, a Text Character will actually be two units tall. This is not necessarily true with components, which can be defined at any size. Text Character placement parameters also include color, aspect ratio (ratio of width to height), slant, font, and spacing. While components are placed by typing or selecting their name and showing a location, Text Characters are selected by combining the currently selected font and the characters that you type when you place the text. Several fonts are provided with Generic CADD.

Hatch placement parameters include the name of the Hatch that you are using, the rotation, scale, and color. Fill placements require only the rotation, scale, and color parameters, as there is only one type of fill: solid. Otherwise, Hatches and Fills are placed in a very similar manner, by selecting the objects to be hatched or filled.

Attributes and Associative Dimensions, the most complicated of the complex entities, are controlled by a number of special placement parameters. The parameters for *attributes*, specially formatted blocks of variable text associated with component placements, include many of the text placement parameters plus a Display option, auto placement option, and the opportunity to edit the text during component placement.

Associative Dimensions are controlled by a plethora of parameters, from simple ones such as Color, Layer, Text Font, and Size to more specialized options such as Arrow Type and Location, Text Placement Settings, Proximity and Offset control, and so on. Various placement Modes are also available, including options for Single, Partitioned, and Cumulative Dimensions, and direction options for creating Horizontal, Vertical, and Angled Dimensions, either Aligned with objects in the drawing or at a specified angle. Attributes are discussed later in this chapter and in Chapter 17, while Dimensions, Associative and otherwise, are covered in Chapter 11, "Dimensioning."

Predefined Versus "On the Fly" Complex Entities

Complex entities can be divided into three distinct groups. One group includes Components and Text Characters; the commands for these entities are found on the COMPONENTS menu and TEXT menu, respectively. Hatches and Fills, the second group, are located together on one menu, HATCH/FILL. The third group includes Attributes, appearing on the ATTRIBUTES menu, accessed through the COMPONENTS menu, and Dimensions, located on the DIMENSIONS menu.

The first group (Components and Text Characters) may be called *predefined complex entities,* meaning that someone must draw the complex entity before it can be placed. In the case of Components, you can draw your own or purchase components in the form of *symbols libraries* from Generic Software or third-party developers. Each Component in a drawing has a unique name assigned to it when it is created. In the case of Text Characters, several fonts are included with Generic CADD, and others are available from Generic Software and third-party developers. Each font generally includes the upper- and lowercase alphabet, numerals, and punctuation marks. The name of a particular Text Character is a combination of the font and the character itself. You can also create your own fonts with Generic CADD or with software available from Generic and third parties.

The second group (Hatches and Fills) is defined *on the fly,* that is, instead of predefining a particular hatched or filled area and then placing it, the area to be hatched or filled is selected each time you use the Hatch or Fill command. A specific hatched or filled area has no particular name that you can use to place another of the same description. Generally, a hatched or filled area is a unique condition. If you need to place the same hatched or filled figure repeatedly, you can make a component that includes the hatched or filled area, or you can copy a hatched or filled area already existing in the drawing.

Attributes and Dimensions are hybrids of these two types because they are defined partly in advance and partly during placement. Although predefined, each instance may be different.

As you will see in the following sections, the seven types of complex entities differ in other ways, depending on their intended uses.

Components

The use of components is Generic CADD's primary method for creating repeating objects or symbols and placing them into your drawing. Components may be repeated within one drawing or throughout several drawings. Components are what people typically mean when they say, "With CAD, once you've drawn something you never have to draw it again."

Components are made by first drawing the object, and then defining it as a component. This process consists of giving the component a name and a reference point, and selecting the objects that make up the component. Commands dealing specifically with components are found on the COMPONENTS menu. All but one of these commands use a two-character command code that starts with the letter C. The one exception uses C for its second letter.

Creating a Component

To create a component, start up Generic CADD and create a new drawing called DINNER. Set units to Inches, Limits to 18 inches x 24 inches, and Grid to 1/2 inch x 1/2 inch. The other toggles may be set to your own preferences. Use any color(s) that you like.

Draw the Object

First, draw the place setting shown in Figure 8-1. Use the Draw and Edit commands that you already know, and make the grid smaller or turn on the Snap to Grid command (SG) as necessary. The plate shown in the figure is 11 inches in diameter, but you need not copy the drawing

FIGURE 8-1 A drawing of a place setting

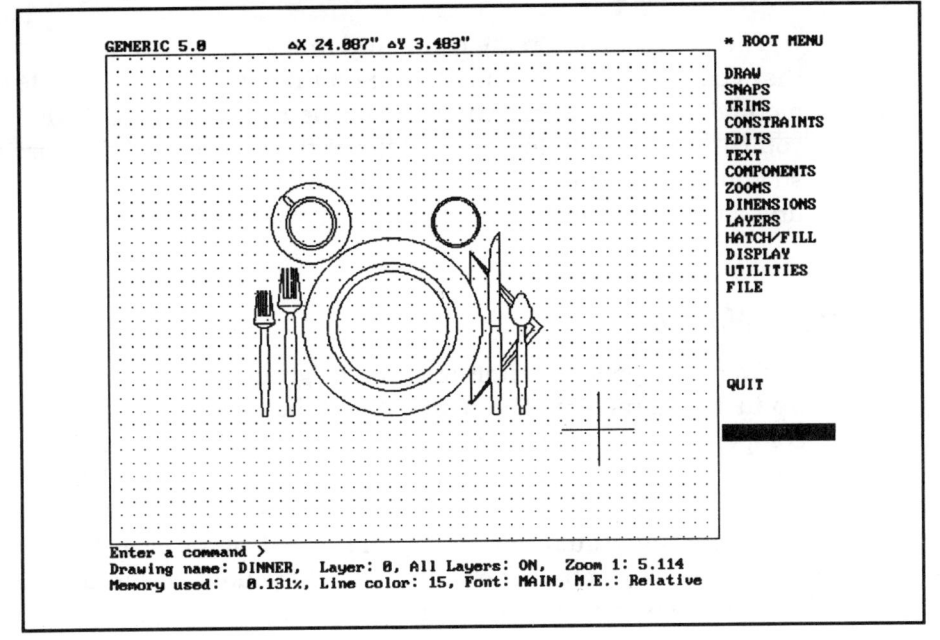

precisely. If you want, draw your own silverware and dishes instead of the ones in the example.

When making a drawing that will become a component, you can use any commands that you need; there are no restrictions on what can or cannot be part of a component. In fact, you can return to previous drawings and select either the whole drawing or portions of it to become part of or an entire component, no matter which commands were used to create it.

Once you have completed the drawing, use the Create command on the COMPONENTS menu or type **CC** on the keyboard to turn it into a component. This command actually defines a component with a specified name and insertion point that looks exactly like the drawing that you have just made. In fact, the entities that you have just drawn remain unchanged and stay as individual entities in the database, unless you replace them with the component itself when you have finished creating it. When you use the Component Create command, you are asked to perform four tasks, as explained in the following sections.

Select the Entities

The Component Create command first asks you to select the objects that compose the component. You do this by using any of the selection methods you've learned thus far. In the case of your DINNER drawing, you can place a window around the entire drawing. Make sure that you surround the entire drawing, as shown in Figure 8-2. If you place your first window corner incorrectly, press ESC and try it again.

Assign a Name

Every component definition must be given a name, which can include up to 12 characters. The name should be descriptive. If you use many components, you may need to invent some sort of naming system that allows you to keep track of your components easily. Consider using a system that includes only eight characters—the maximum allowed by the operating system for saving individual files—even though Generic CADD allows 12 characters internally. (If you choose to use 12, the last four characters won't show when you view the files in DOS.)

FIGURE 8-2 Placing a window to define a component named "PLACESET"

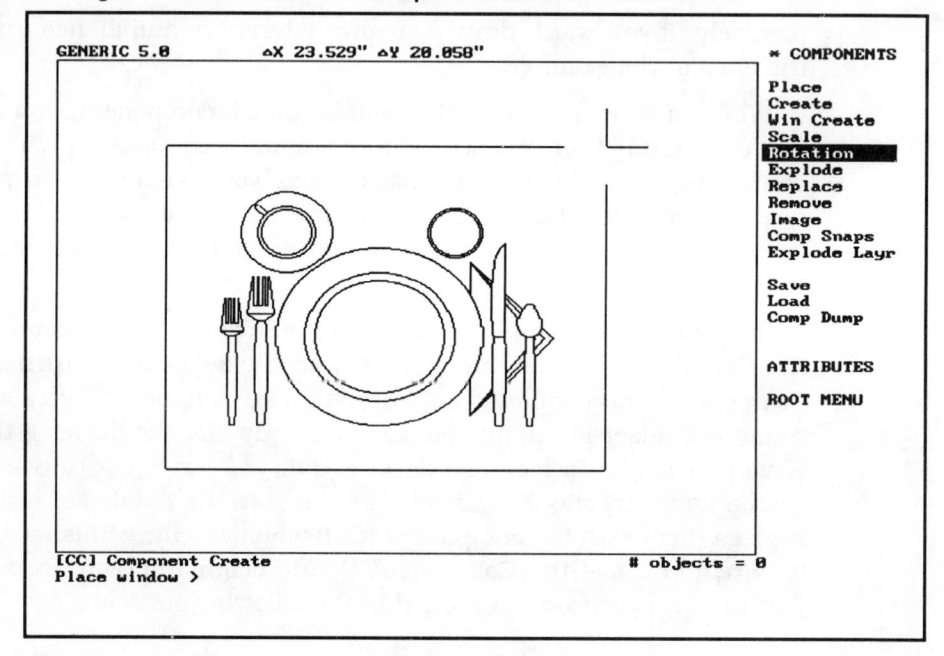

Component names cannot include spaces, commas, periods, or several other punctuation marks. Dashes and underlines are allowed both in Generic CADD component names and DOS filenames, but you should stay away from asterisks and question marks to avoid confusion when you want to save your components to disk. For the current drawing, type the name **PLACESET**, and press ENTER. This name works as both a component name and a disk filename, and lets you easily identify the component in the future.

Select a Reference Point

Later, when you are ready to place a copy of this component into the drawing, you will need to specify where you want to put it. This will be done by selecting the *reference point* of the component. If you choose a reference point near the lower-right corner of the drawing, the component will always appear to the upper right of the point you select (assuming that you place it with a rotation of zero). If you pick a reference point in the center, the component will always be drawn around this point.

Sometimes you might want to pick a point that is not on the component itself, but in a location that will be easier to select when you decide to place the component. In the case of PLACESET, for example, it might be wise to place the reference point just below the bottom of the plate. This way, whenever you use PLACESET, you can choose a point on the edge of the table, and the component will always be placed the same distance from the edge. Figure 8-3 shows the selection of a reference point in this location.

Placing the Component

The last prompt that you will encounter while creating a component asks whether you want to stop now or complete the command. Completing it will replace the individual entities that you used to create the component with a placement of the component itself. To leave the individual entities in the database as they are, simply press ENTER.

Note The prompt, here and elsewhere, often calls the ENTER key RET or RETURN. This is old typewriter terminology. Don't be alarmed if there is no RETURN key on your PC keyboard. Use ENTER.

FIGURE 8-3 Selecting a reference point for PLACESET

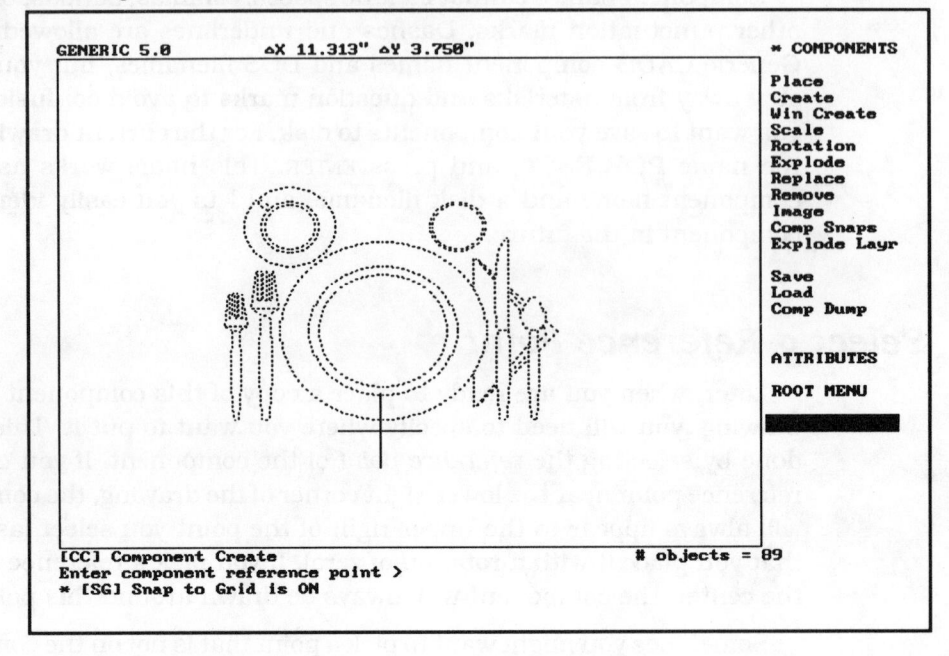

```
GENERIC 5.0        ΔX 11.313"  ΔY 3.750"           * COMPONENTS

                                                    Place
                                                    Create
                                                    Win Create
                                                    Scale
                                                    Rotation
                                                    Explode
                                                    Replace
                                                    Remove
                                                    Image
                                                    Comp Snaps
                                                    Explode Layr

                                                    Save
                                                    Load
                                                    Comp Dump

                                                    ATTRIBUTES
                                                    ROOT MENU


[CC] Component Create                              # objects = 89
Enter component reference point >
* [SG] Snap to Grid is ON
```

If you want to replace the entities with a component placement, type **R** or select the Replace option from the prompt. This is a new feature of Generic CADD 5.0, and it's usually a pretty good idea. This option makes sure that there is at least one instance of your component placed in the drawing so that it doesn't get purged when the drawing is saved. On the other hand, if you are using some of the same entities to create several different components, you might not want them turned into placements just yet. If you don't want them turned into placements, simply press ENTER.

If you have defined any attributes. there will be a third option at this last prompt, asking if you want to attach any of these predefined attributes to this component definition. If you respond to this option by typing **A** or selecting it from the prompt, you will get an Attribute List in the menu area. After choosing one or more attributes, you again have the opportunity to either stop or replace the entities by placing the component. For more information on attributes, see Chapter 17.

What Really Happened?

If you have created the component successfully, you will see no message, just the "Enter a command >" prompt and the Status Lines if Status Lines (SL) is turned on. If you made a mistake, however, you will see a prompt such as "Component already exists." Remember, each component in the drawing must have a unique name. You may use the same name for different components in separate drawings, but watch out for potential conflicts if you plan to move components around between drawings.

When you created the PLACESET component, the entities that you surrounded with the window were copied into another area of memory, where they were combined with the name of the component and the location of the reference point to form a *definition* for this component. If you pressed ENTER to end the command, these entities occur twice in the drawing—once in their original form on the screen, and once in the computer memory as part of the component definition.

Note It is very important to remember that if you never *place* the component into the drawing, the definition is removed when the drawing is saved as a file. Generic CADD only saves definitions of components that are *actually used* in the drawing. This is a very convenient way of making sure that old components no longer in use don't clog up memory or disk space. However, this process can lead to big trouble if you are not aware of it. If you want to make sure that the component that you have just created will be saved, make sure that you either *place* one in the drawing or *save* the component individually as a component file. If you used the Replace option at the end of the command, you have automatically placed the component once already. See the section entitled "Placing Your First Component" later in this chapter.

The first clue that your component actually exists comes from the Component List, accessible from the Place command on the COMPONENTS menu. When you select this command, you get a list of components that are currently defined in the drawing. These components were already in the drawing when you loaded it, have been defined since you started the drawing session, or have been loaded specifically for use in this drawing.

If more components exist than will fit in the menu area, you can select the "More..." item at the bottom of the menu or press the PGUP and PGDN keys on the keyboard to move through the list of component names. As you will see, the Component List can be used for placing components, as well as checking to see which components are in the drawing. You can use the "Look on disk" item on the menu to look in the default component path for components that you might want to place, as well.

Setting the Table

To make use of the PLACESET component, draw a table on which you can place these dishes and silverware. Before drawing the table, erase the drawing that was used to create the component definition with the Window Erase (WE) command. You no longer need this drawing because it is now stored in memory as a component definition. Do not use the Drawing Erase (DX) command, as it erases not only what you see on the screen but also the area of memory where the definitions are stored.

Figure 8-4 shows a drawing of a table that might be used to place the new component. Your table need not be an exact duplicate of the one shown; just make sure that it is large enough for at least several place settings to fit on it.

Placing Your First Component

There are two different ways to place a component into the drawing. The first is with the Place command from the COMPONENTS menu or by typing **CP** on the keyboard. This command asks you to specify the component and then to specify the location where you want to place the component. You may use the Component List to select the name of the component from the video menu instead of typing it. Pick a component name from the Component List on the video menu by using the second button on the pointing device.

Next, you are prompted to place the component reference point. If Object Drag is turned on, a ghosted image of the component is dragged along with your cursor to aid in placing the component, as shown in Figure 8-5. This ghosted image helps you to see the size of your component

Chapter 8: Complex Entities

FIGURE 8-4 A simple table ready to be set

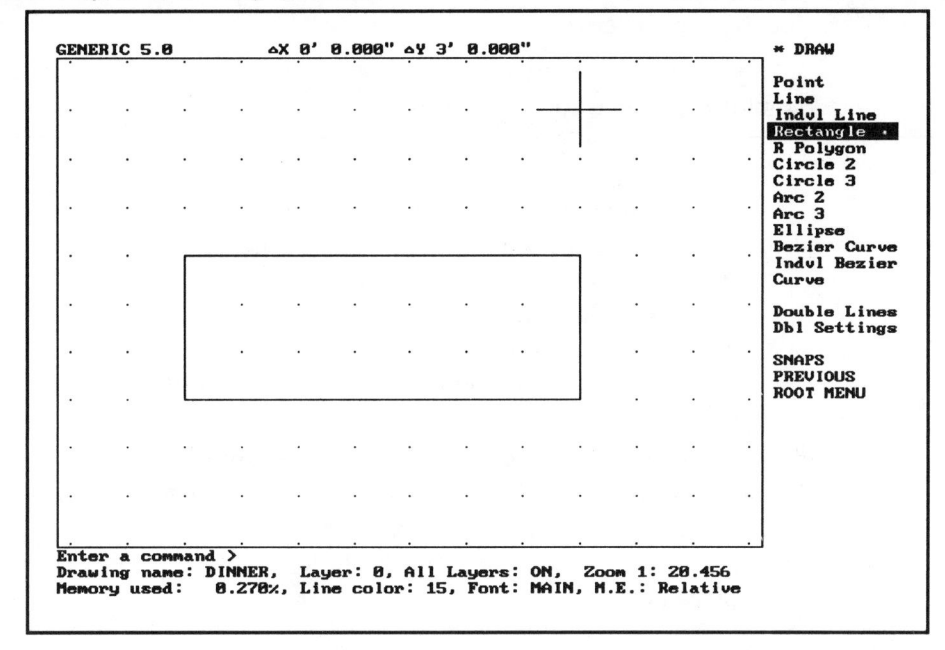

FIGURE 8-5 Dragging PLACESET into place

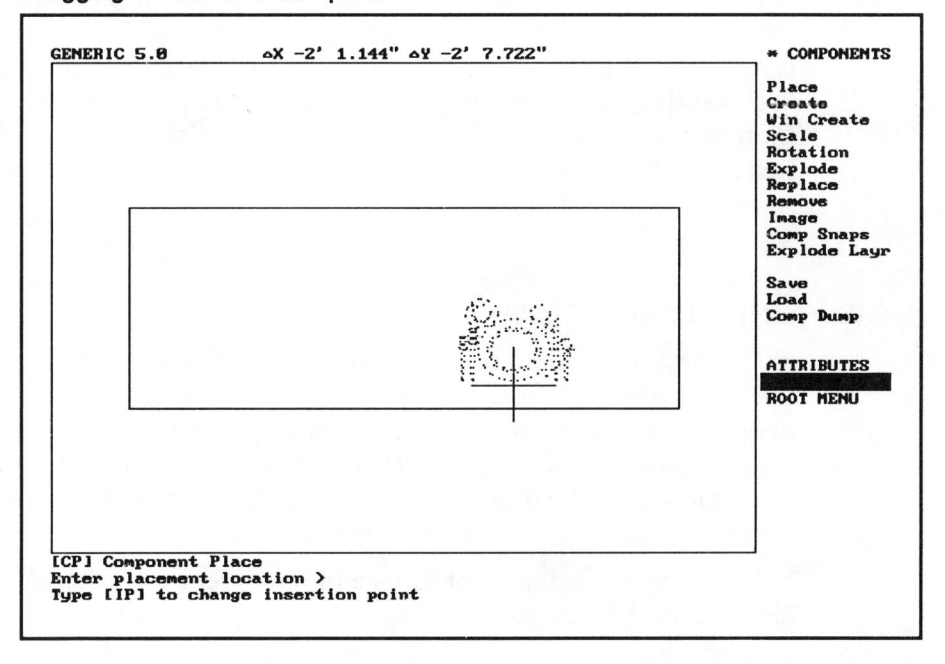

and the direction it is facing. The reference point is represented by the location of the cursor.

If you do not see the ghosted image of the component as you are trying to place it, check the following items.

1. Make sure that Object Drag (OD) is turned on. This toggle enables and disables the dragging of images. Select Object Drag from the DISPLAY menu or type **OD** on the keyboard. You will get a message that tells you whether you have just turned it on or off. Make sure that it is on and try placing the component again. (For very complicated components, the ghosted image is often more trouble than it is worth, and in these cases you might want to turn Object Drag off.)

2. Be certain that the component is not larger than the screen. If it is larger, you may need to Zoom Out (ZO) a few times until there is enough room for your component. (This should not happen with PLACESET, because if the table fits on the screen, so should the place setting.)

In the case of PLACESET, drag the component to a location at the edge of the table, as shown in Figure 8-6. Note that because of the location of the reference point, you can select a point on the table edge to place the component. When you get the component where you want it, press the first pointing device button to place it. It should appear in full lines rather than as a ghosted image as soon as you select the location. If Display Reference Points is turned on, a reference point will appear at the reference point of the components.

Changing the Rotation

The first component is placed in exactly the same size and facing in the same direction as when you first drew it because the component placement parameters, Scale (CZ) and Rotation (CR), were set at their default values of 1 and 0, respectively. A Scale of 1 means you are using the same size as the original, which is fine for now, because you want all of your place settings to be the same size.

If you want a component to face in a different direction (in this case facing toward the bottom of the screen), you must change the Component

Chapter 8: Complex Entities 219

FIGURE 8-6 The first PLACESET placed on the table

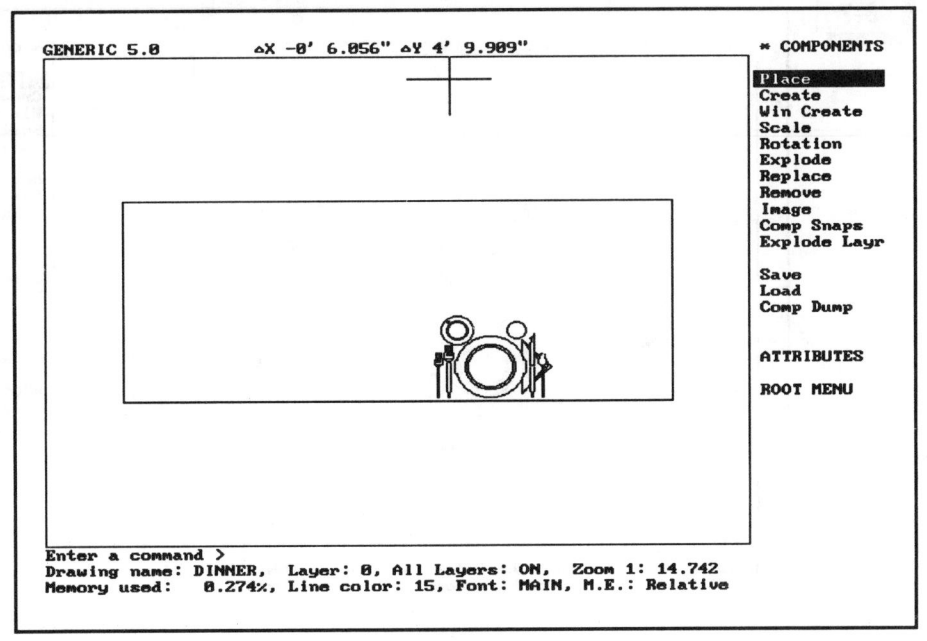

```
GENERIC 5.0         ΔX -0' 6.056"  ΔY 4' 9.909"              * COMPONENTS
                                                             Place
                                                             Create
                                                             Win Create
                                                             Scale
                                                             Rotation
                                                             Explode
                                                             Replace
                                                             Remove
                                                             Image
                                                             Comp Snaps
                                                             Explode Layr

                                                             Save
                                                             Load
                                                             Comp Dump

                                                             ATTRIBUTES
                                                             ROOT MENU

Enter a command >
Drawing name: DINNER,  Layer: 0, All Layers: ON,  Zoom 1: 14.742
Memory used:    0.274%, Line color: 15, Font: MAIN, M.E.: Relative
```

Rotation before or during the placement of the component. This is done by selecting the Rotation command on the COMPONENTS menu, or by typing **CR** on the keyboard. When you select this command, you are asked to type a number. To position a PLACESET on the right end of the table, select a rotation of 90 degrees by typing **90**. This rotation will apply to all components placed until you either change the Component Rotation command or define a new component.

After changing the rotation, use the Component Place command to place another PLACESET component. As you drag it on the screen, notice that it is dragged in its rotated position. This way you can tell before you place it whether you rotated it in the right direction or not. If not, simply type **CR** before putting it down, change the rotation, and place it again. After placing the rotated component at the end of the table, continue placing components until you have set the entire table, changing the rotation whenever necessary, according to Figure 8-7. You can get very accurate component placements if the Grid Size (GS) is set to the right

FIGURE 8-7 The fully set table

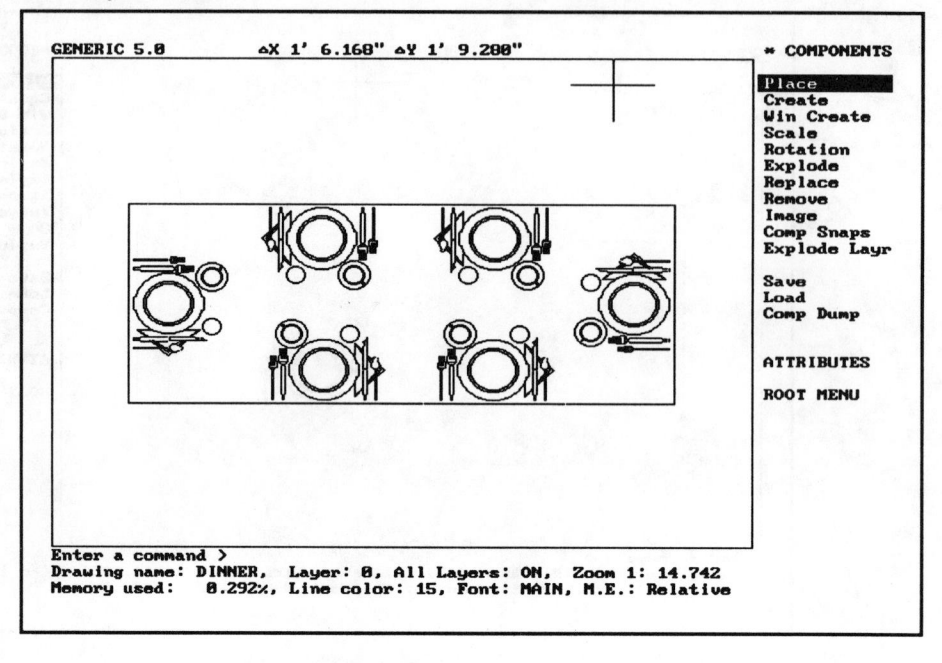

value and you use Snap to Grid (SG). For the fully set table shown in the sample drawing, a Grid Size of 3 was used.

The allowable values for a rotation are shown in the prompt. Components can be rotated in either positive (counterclockwise) or negative (clockwise) direction, up to 360 degrees either way. A rotation of -90 is 1/4 turn clockwise and yields the same result as a 3/4 turn counterclockwise, or 270 degrees. If you type a number outside of the allowable range, you will not be allowed to continue. Illegal values will be accepted, but will be converted to an equivalent within the allowable range. Note that rotation can be specified in partial degrees, such as 12.5 or -5.75, as well as whole numbers. If you start a Component Place command and find that the rotation is wrong, just type **CR** and adjust the rotation. The preview image that you are dragging will be updated to reflect the change.

Changing the Size

Like Rotation, the Scale parameter is set before or during a component placement, and remains in effect for all components placed until the scale is changed or a new component is defined. The Component Scale command actually consists of two separate parameters that control the horizontal or X scale and the vertical or Y scale of components that are placed into a drawing.

If you want to place a smaller version of the PLACESET component, you need to change the Component Scale parameters. To see how this works, select Scale from the COMPONENTS menu. You are first asked for the X scale factor. Values larger than 1 create component placements larger than their original size; values smaller than 1 create smaller component placements.

To place components at half their original size, select a value of .5, and press ENTER. Next, you are asked for the Y scale factor, and the X scale factor that you just specified is shown as the default. (Generic CADD assumes that in most cases you want to enlarge or reduce your components equally in X and Y directions, so it gives you the value of X for the Y default.) To accept this default condition, simply press ENTER. If you want to scale your components differently in Y than in X, type another value before pressing ENTER. For now, just press ENTER without typing a second value.

All values are allowable for scale factors, including negative numbers. A setting of -1 for X and 1 for Y, for example, produces a mirror-image place setting, with all objects in the component on the opposite side from where they are currently. This is an easy way to produce a large number of variations from a single component by combining scale and rotation parameters.

After you have set the new smaller scale factors, place another PLACESET to see the result. The ghosted image that appears as you drag the component into place should be smaller than before, because the ghosted image always reflects the current Scale and Rotation settings. Figure 8-8 shows an extra PLACESET inserted at the smaller size. Again, note that this command may be used in the middle of a Component Place command if you forgot to use it first.

FIGURE 8-8 A half-sized PLACESET added to the table

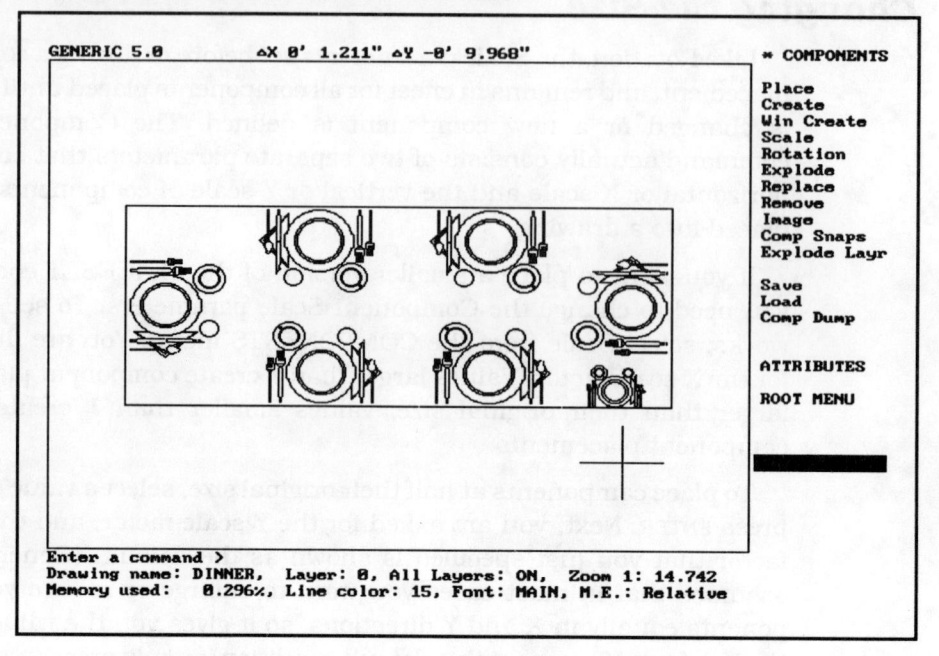

It is important to understand that only the component *placements* are being rotated and scaled as they are placed. Although the current values for Component Rotation and Component Scale are stored as part of the component placement entity in the database, no change whatsoever is made to the *original component definition*. The original component is still exactly the same size and facing in the same direction as when you first drew it. This common reference is required to maintain the integrity and accuracy of the drawing. You can always get a component *exactly* like the one that you first drew by setting both X and Y scale to 1 and Rotation to 0.

Real Objects Versus Symbols

The place setting that you have drawn can be considered a *real* object, because it is a true scale representation of a real object. Later, you will be able to choose to print or plot it at any scale. Some objects that appear in drawings, however, do not represent real objects. These objects can be considered *symbols*. These include descriptive text or notes, drawing symbols such as North arrows, detail bugs, grid bubbles, dimension lines, and so on.

How big are these symbols, really? Most of the time, we think of the size of these symbols in relation to the paper on which they will be printed. With CAD, however, we must consider the size of these symbols relative to the real world objects with which they coexist. For example, if you want to include in your drawing a letter to refer to a particular note or detail, you might think of drawing a 1/2-inch diameter circle with a 1/8-inch high letter in the middle of it. However, if you are drawing a house plan, and printing it at 1/4" = 1', a 1/2-inch circle will show up as little more than a dot. Conversely, if you are drawing an electrical circuit diagram to be printed at several times actual size, the 1/2-inch circle might be larger than the entire drawing.

One way to overcome this problem is to think of the symbols as part of the "real" object that you are drawing. In the house plan example, think of the circle as if it were painted on the floor, with a two-foot diameter. When the drawing is printed, this two-foot diameter circle will be scaled down to a very visible 1/2 inch. In the circuit drawing the circle might be drawn with a 1/8-inch diameter if the drawing is to be printed at four times its actual size.

The scale factors for the placement of components (and, as you will see later in this chapter, text) must be adjusted differently for symbols than for real objects. The general rule is to use actual dimensions for real objects, and to scale text or drawing symbology. This will become more obvious as you begin to work with text in the section following this next one on components.

One Component, One Entity, One Reference Point

If you try to use any of the editing commands on a component, you will notice that the component is treated as one object. In PLACESET, for instance, you cannot erase a single plate without also erasing the silverware and other items in the component. The whole component placement is considered one entity. As noted previously, the only point that you need to capture for any form of selection is the component's reference point. This makes components easy to work with when you need to select the entire object. You need not select every object when you want to move, copy, or otherwise edit a component.

Exploding a Component

Sometimes, however, you may need to work with the individual entities that make up the component. Perhaps you need to replace the dinner knife on one of the guest's place settings with a steak knife. In this case, you need to edit a single component placement, but leave the others the same. You can select the Explode command from the COMPONENTS menu or type **CE** on the keyboard to replace any component placement with the entities that compose it.

When you select this command, a prompt asks you to point to the reference point of the component that you want to explode. When you select this point, the component is replaced with entities that can be edited individually. That particular component now acts exactly as if you drew it from scratch, without the Component Place command. In fact, from the point of view of Generic CADD, the component that you have just exploded is no longer a component placement. The placement entity is removed from the database and replaced with simple entities, which means that any commands that work specifically on components will no longer work on this part of the drawing. If the component contains other components, which is possible, the second level of components cannot be exploded unless you use the Explode command on it as well.

Destination Layer

When you explode components you also need to keep in mind their layers. The component placement is on the layer that is current when you place the component. However, the simple entities inside the component definition are located on the layers that *were* active when *they* were created. When the component is unexploded, the entire component is considered to be on one layer.

When a component is exploded, the entities can end up in one of three places, depending on the status of the Explode Destination Layer parameter, identified as Explode Layr on the COMPONENTS menu or reached by typing **XY** on the keyboard. The command brings up a prompt with three options on it: Original, Current, and Placement. One of these, the current setting, will be in parentheses. In some ways, you might think of this parameter as a three-way toggle. When you pick one of these from the prompt with the first button on the pointing device or type its letter, **O**, **C**, and **P**, respectively, it switches to the selected mode. One, and only one, of these three is active at any one time.

If Explode Destination Layer is set to Original when a component is exploded, the individual entities return to the layers where they originated. If you explode a component and it vanishes from the screen, you are probably experiencing this phenomenon. Suppose that you define a component on layer 1, and then place it on layer 2. Meanwhile, you turn off layer 1 with Layer Hide (YH). You will still see the component on layer 2 as long as it is actually a component. If you explode it, it will return to layer 1, which is turned off, and the component will disappear. If you turn layer 1 back on with Layer Display (YD), you will see the entities again.

Alternatively, all of the entities in the exploding component can be routed to a single layer via the Current and Placement options. If Explode Destination Layer is set to Current when the component is exploded, all of the entities will end up on the current layer. Since the current layer cannot be hidden, these entities will always remain visible. The Placement mode causes the entities in a component that is exploded to end up on the layer on which the component was originally placed. This layer may or may not be currently visible, so the entities have some chance of disappearing from sight. Note that under all three settings, the entities in fragmented components retain their original Line Color, Line Type, and Line Width. It is only the destination layer that is in question here.

Placing Exploded Components

Most of the time, you will want components to be stored in the database as components, to save space and allow global component editing. However, if you find that you are placing components and then exploding them consistently, you may want to place them already exploded. This can be done using the Image toggle on the COMPONENTS menu, by typing the two-character code **CI** on the keyboard.

When Component Image is turned on, all components will be inserted in the drawing as if they had been exploded. In this mode, components are really just a quick way to copy entities in convenient groups. The inserted entities are not a component placement at all, but are in fact made up of copies of the simple entities that make up the original component definition. You can still use different scales and rotations, subject to the same limitations as true components.

Keep in mind that, as with components that you explode, components placed with Image turned on are not treated as components at all by Generic CADD, and any editing command must now deal with each entity individually. If there are components inside the component definition, they will still be placed as true components.

A Circle Is a Circle, and an Arc Is an Arc

You may be surprised if you try to explode a PLACESET component that has been placed with different X and Y scale factors. Values of 2 for X and 1 for Y, for example, do produce a component that is twice as wide (but still the same height) as when you first drew it, but this may not be the case if you explode it.

Because entities are always defined by their basic geometric properties and a number of definition points, their shapes always remain the same. When you explode a component made of Lines, for instance, it does not matter how you have "pushed" or "pulled" on it; the Lines remain the same basic shape. If you stretch a square, it becomes a rectangle. If you rotate it, it becomes a diamond. In either case, the Lines themselves stay the same shape; they just get longer, shorter, or rotate.

It is also the case that if you stretch a Circle, you appear to get an ellipse. However, you will see that if you explode a PLACESET with a scale factor of 2 for X and 1 for Y, this will not remain true: The Circles that represent the plate, saucer, and glass may get larger, or they may not; some may even get larger and some may stay the same size. Regardless, they always will return to *round*—the basic geometric property of a Circle.

When you stretch or squash a CADD drawing or component, what you are really doing is pushing the definition points closer together or farther apart, and then reconstructing the drawing. Under these rules, you cannot make an Ellipse out of a Circle no matter how hard you try. It only looks that way while it is part of the Component Placement. If you had drawn the plate using a series of Curves, so that many definition points were located around the perimeter, you *could* stretch it, because as the points were pulled apart the shape of the Curve would change. That is the basic geometric nature of a Curve. In fact, this is such an important distinction that Generic Software sells a program as part of its utilities package for changing Circles and Arcs to Curves in case this is a problem for you.

But why do some Circles become larger and others stay the same size when the scale factor is 2 for X and 1 for Y? This has to do with the location of the definition point on the perimeter of the circle. If this definition point is to the right or left of the center, the point will be moved farther from the center and the circle will expand when the component is placed. If the point is directly above or below the center, however, the circle will stay exactly the same size, as the distance between the center and the point on the circle will stay the same. Points not directly above, below, right, or left of center will cause proportionate expansion of the circle when the component is placed with these scale factors.

The same basic facts are true for Arcs. Because Arcs are really circle segments, they do not change their shape to become ellipse segments when a stretched or squashed component is exploded. How their size changes depends on the location of their definition points. Because Construction Ellipses are made of Arcs facing in four different directions, they will be subject to somewhat bizarre distortions if they are part of exploded components that are placed with unequal X and Y scale factors.

Manipulating Component Definitions

As noted earlier, component placements can be edited as individual entities with any selection method, or they can be edited with the Window method if the component's reference point is captured in a window. Component placements are also subject to the Layer method, which acts on the layers on which they are placed. The definitions themselves, however, are not affected by these commands. Several commands on the COMPONENTS menu deal specifically with component definitions, one at a time or globally.

Replacing One Definition with Another

One of the advantages of components is that their definitions can be swapped, allowing you to make global changes in your drawing to update it with new information or to try different ideas. Figure 8-9 shows the

FIGURE 8-9 The table with chairs added

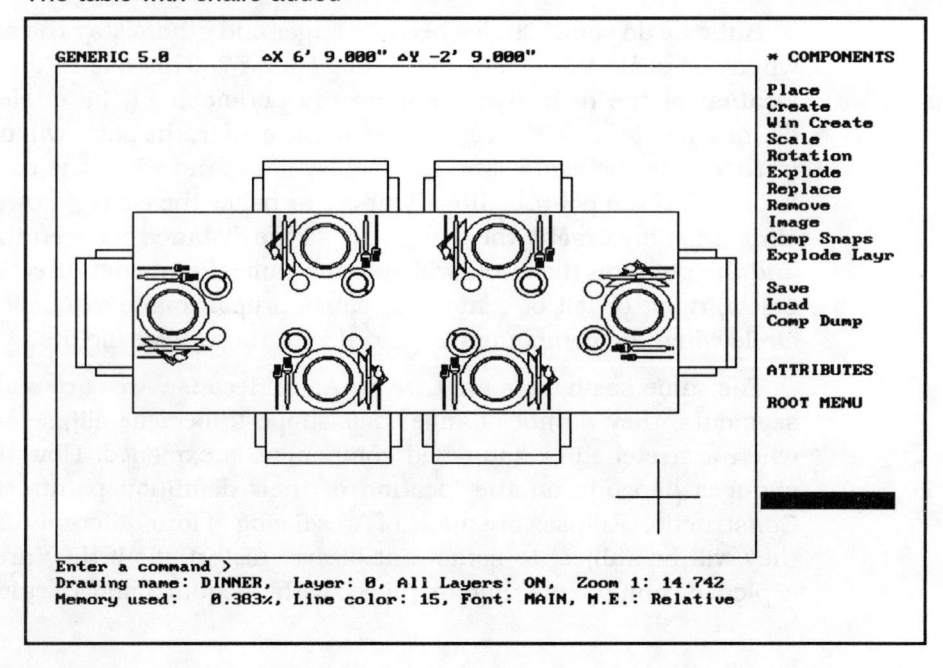

Creating a new component, CHAIR2

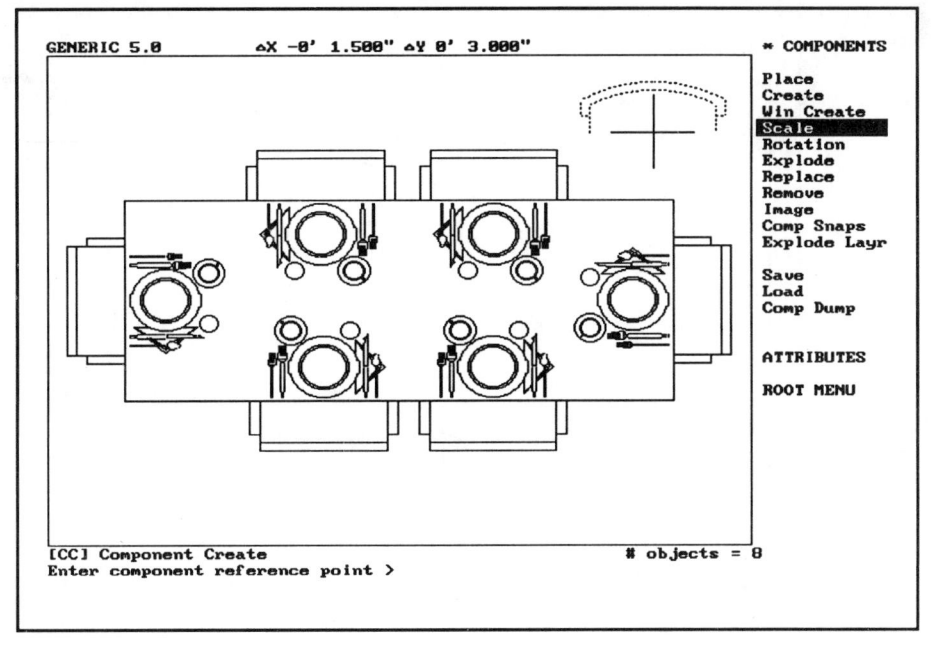

FIGURE 8-10

```
GENERIC 5.0      ΔX -0' 1.500"  ΔY 0' 3.000"              * COMPONENTS
                                                           Place
                                                           Create
                                                           Win Create
                                                           Scale
                                                           Rotation
                                                           Explode
                                                           Replace
                                                           Remove
                                                           Image
                                                           Comp Snaps
                                                           Explode Layr

                                                           Save
                                                           Load
                                                           Comp Dump

                                                           ATTRIBUTES

                                                           ROOT MENU

[CC] Component Create                      # objects = 0
Enter component reference point >
```

PLACESET table with six chairs that were added by creating a component called "CHAIR" placed at four different rotations. Suppose that you decide to use a different style chair. You can create a new component, as shown in Figure 8-10. This new component can be created in a number of steps. First, place a CHAIR at a scale of 1,1 and a rotation of 0 and explode it. (It is easiest if you place it on the Grid so that you can locate the former reference point.) Then, edit the exploded chair to form the new round-back design. Once the new drawing is ready, use Component Create (CC) again to create a new component called CHAIR2. Make sure that you select the same reference point that you did when you made CHAIR. Finally, once the new component has been created, erase the temporary drawing of the new chair.

To swap chairs, use the Replace command on the COMPONENTS menu or type **CN** on the keyboard. You are prompted for the name of the component that you want replaced, CHAIR, and the name of the replacing component, CHAIR2. When you have supplied this information, press

FIGURE 8-11 The table with new chairs

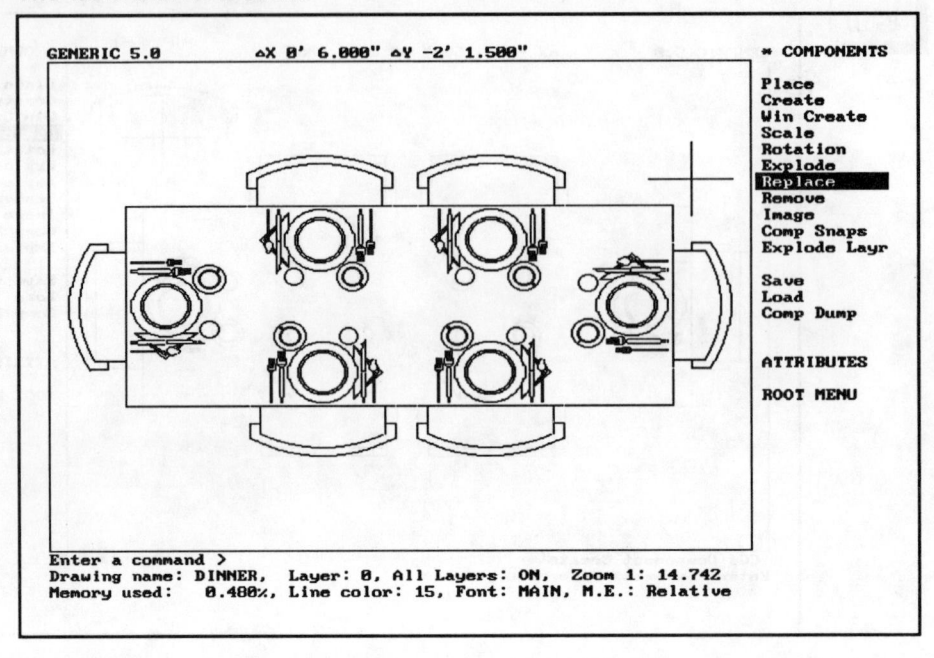

ENTER, and CHAIR will be replaced with CHAIR2 in every placement. Note that you have the option of replacing only selected placements (instead of all of them) by typing **S** at the end of this command instead of ENTER. Rotation and scale will remain the same. Figure 8-11 shows the set table with the new chairs.

The exploded components are not replaced, because, as discussed previously, these are no longer really components. The same is true for components that have been placed with Component Image turned on. You can substitute the original chairs with another Component Replace (CN), specifying CHAIR2 as the component to replace and CHAIR as the replacing component.

Eliminating Components

Occasionally, you may need to remove components from the database. If you Create a component and never Place it, the definition will be lost. With your DINNER drawing, if you were to save the drawing after replacing CHAIR with CHAIR2 and then quit, the definition of CHAIR would be eliminated.

If you want to remove a component definition from the drawing without quitting, either to remove an unused component from the Component List or to erase all of the placements of a certain component, you may use the Remove command from the COMPONENTS menu, or type **CX** on the keyboard. When you select this command, you are asked for a component name. Both the component definition and all placements (if any) of the specified component are eliminated from the drawing. A warning prompt makes you verify that you really want to do this.

If you want to remove a component from the current drawing but still wish to be able to use it in another drawing, use the Component Save (CS) or Component Dump (CD) command to create a component file on a disk before using the Component Remove command (see Chapter 12, "File Storage and Retrieval").

Snapping onto Internal Definition Points

Component placements have only one definition point, which is the reference point of the component. Therefore, the Snap to Nearest Point command normally can snap to only one point. The rest of the definition points are "hidden" in the definition. However, the Comp Snaps command, located on the COMPONENTS menu or accessed by typing **GC** on the keyboard, allows you to snap onto the definition points of the entities that make up the component definition.

The Comp Snaps command is a toggle, so it is either on or off. You don't have to select it every time you want to snap onto internal definition points. The abbreviation GC stands for "Ghost Components," meaning that the component placement acts as if it were made of individual entities *only for the purpose of snapping.* In every other respect, components still act like components whether Comp Snaps is on or not.

Comp Snaps is a global command, affecting *all* components and all snap commands. This means that if you have a lot of complicated components in your drawing, snapping will be slowed down noticeably. If you are not trying to snap to definition points in components, you should leave GC turned off and turn it on only when you need it. Comp Snaps works with the rest of the snaps discussed in Chapter 10, "Advanced Drawing and Editing Techniques," as well as with Snap to Nearest Point.

Text

In many ways, Text Characters are very similar to Components. A number of placement parameters are set before you place the text, and a Place command actually inserts the text into the drawing. Each Text Character is a separate complex entity made up of simple entities that cannot be altered by normal editing commands. In addition, groups of text characters can form another complex entity called a Text Line.

There are more placement parameters for text than for Components, and unlike Components, many of these parameters will probably need to be changed before placing text. Text Characters can be exploded, but cannot be replaced one for another globally. Numerous special editing commands work only on text, giving you a great deal of control over the text in your drawing. Most of the two-character Text commands start with the letter *T*.

Selecting the Type Style

The first parameter you will want to set is FONT. Generic CADD 5.0 comes with several fonts, which are listed in the back of the manual. Additional fonts are also available from Generic Software and from third-party vendors. In addition, you can create your own.

You can select and load a font with the Font Select command on the TEXT menu, or by typing **FS**, then **T**, on the keyboard. When you choose

Font Select, Generic CADD displays a menu of fonts from the default Font directory from which you can choose. You can also type the name of a font. If the font exists, it will be loaded. If you never use the Font Select command, the default font will be loaded the first time you place a character. Later in this chapter, you will place some text on the DINNER drawing, so select the font you want now.

If the font cannot be found, you are asked if this is a new font. Usually, the font is found unless you are trying to create your own font. If the font exists, but cannot be found, you may need to change the font PATH. This can be done with the FP command, or **P3**.

After you have placed text using the current font, you may select and load another font and place characters using the new font. Note that loading several fonts in succession reduces the amount of space available in memory for your drawing. It is best not to load too many fonts in a single drawing session. If you do, however, they can be unloaded with the Definition Unload (DU) command discussed in Chapter 10.

Setting the Spacing

Several parameters involving the spacing of text characters are controlled by a single multi-option command, Text Spacing, identified as Spacing on the TEXT menu and typed **TS** on the keyboard. This brings up a number of parameter options, with current values for each shown in parentheses after each option. These are changed individually by selecting them from the prompt or typing their two-letter designator on the keyboard. Most require values, one offers three options, and one is a toggle.

Between Character

This parameter sets, as a percentage of the text height (specified as Text Size), the amount of space between characters when proportional Text Lines are used. This space is measured from the end of one character to the start of the next. In all other modes, text character spacing is measured from the reference point of one character to the next, and is calculated as the Text Size multiplied by the Text Aspect (a width modifier, described a little later). Any integer value may be specified.

Negative numbers will produce text in which the characters are in reverse order.

Between Lines

This parameter controls the distance from one line of text to the next, measured from baseline to baseline. You can think of it as how far down the cursor moves when you press ENTER. Of course, if the Text Rotation is not zero, the cursor may not move down but perpendicular to the text direction. Like the Between Character parameter, it is specified as a percentage of text height. All integer values are valid. Zero will produce no space, and text lines will appear one on top of the next. Negative values cause the cursor to move up at the end of a line, with the same rules regarding Text Rotation in force. Between Lines spacing applies to all modes of text placement, both Lines and Chars, proportional and monospaced text.

Proportional

The third option in the Text Spacing prompt is a toggle that controls whether Text Lines utilizes proportional spacing or not. When this toggle is off, the distance from the reference point of one character to the next is always the same, calculated as described earlier, according to the product of Text Size and Aspect. This is often referred to as monospaced text, and has been the only mechanism available for spacing text in Generic CADD until 5.0 was released.

When Proportional is on, characters in Text Lines are spaced according to their individual widths. The constant here is the spaces between characters, specified via the Between Character option discussed previously. The Proportional parameter applies only to Text Lines, as Text Character placements are always monospaced.

Slant

You can create an italic typeface from any font by using the Slant option. The Text Slant is specified in degrees, and causes the characters to lean to the left or the right. Values between -45 and +45 degrees are

Chapter 8: Complex Entities 235

valid, with negative values causing a lean to the left and positive values a lean to the right. The slant factor is applied to the characters before the Text Aspect, so that if Aspect is less than one, the slant will appear to be less than what you have specified. Keep in mind that the characters are slanted first, and then widened or narrowed. Conversely, if the Text Aspect is greater than one, the final slant will end up as more than the specified value. For the DINNER drawing example, try setting the Slant at various degrees until you like the way it looks.

Aspect

The width of the Text characters is proportional to the height by default. If you want to make your characters narrower or wider, you can select the Aspect option. The value of the Aspect is a multiplier of the Text Size. For instance, an Aspect of 0.5 produces text that is half as wide as it is tall. An Aspect of 2 produces text that is twice as wide as it is tall.

Although Aspect controls the width of text, it does it only by association with the Text Size. The value of the Aspect should not be thought of as the real width of the text, unless the Text Size is one. Any integer values are allowable, although reasonable values are usually between 0.5 and 2, unless you want some very unusual-looking characters. For the first test, leave Aspect set at the default of 1.

Justification

This parameter, which controls only Text Lines, controls how Text Lines are placed with respect to the "starting point" used to place the text. The three available options, Left, Center, and Right, actually make this placement point into the starting point, centerpoint, and endpoint, respectively.

By controlling the location of the Text Line, this parameter also controls the alignment of multiple Text Lines. Left produces multiple Text Lines aligned on the left, Right produces Text Lines aligned on the right, and Center produces Text Lines centered one over the next, as you might expect. In this case, the current value is shown in square brackets at the end of the prompt. As soon as you pick an option or type its letter, you are returned to the Text Spacing prompt. When you are done changing as many of these parameters as you like, as many times as you like, press ENTER or ESC to end the prompt.

Setting the Text Color

Unlike simple entities, complex entities do not use the current line color. Components use the colors of the entities that make up the definition. Text uses a parameter called Text Color, selected by Color on the TEXT menu or by typing **TC** on the keyboard. If the video menu is on and you have more than one color option, you will see a special menu of color bars from which you can choose. Either use this menu or type a number between 0 and 255. The colors shown on the video menu repeat depending on your video card. All new text that you place will use this color, although it can be changed later with any of the Change editing commands.

Setting the Text Size

The height of text is controlled by the Size command on the TEXT menu, or by typing **TZ** on the keyboard. The default value is one unit. Type a value representing the actual height of a typical uppercase letter.

Unless you are designing a sign, text is usually considered symbols, which means that you probably have some idea of how large you want it to be in the final print. If you are planning to print the drawing full size, you can use the actual height of the finished text for the Text Size. If the drawing will be printed at other than 1 to 1, you should size your text accordingly. For example, if you are working on a floor plan that will be printed at 1/4" = 1', text that you want to print at 1/4" high should be placed with a Text Size of one foot or 12 inches. Text that you want to print at 1/8" should be placed at 6 inches, and so on.

To add text to the back of your chairs in your DINNER drawing, try setting the Text Size to 2.5 inches for now. You may want to change it after you have tried placing some text.

Setting the Rotation

The default value for Text Rotation is zero, which means that text will be placed along a horizontal line running from left to right, just like a typewriter. If you want to create text on some other angle (from top to bottom for instance), you can use the Rotation command on the TEXT menu or type **TR** on the keyboard. Allowable values range from 360 to -360. As with component rotations, values such as -90 and 270 have the same effect. A value of 90 produces text that runs up the screen from bottom to top, while -90 or 270 yields text running downward. For the DINNER drawing, start with the Text Rotation at the default value of zero to place the text horizontally on the first chair, and change it as required.

Placing the Text

Generic CADD 5.0 provides two distinctly different techniques for placing text into your drawings. These are represented on the video menu by the first two groups of commands. The final group of commands on the TEXT menu contains the parameter-setting commands discussed previously, which apply, except where noted, to both placement methods.

The first group of commands is associated with Text Lines. A Text Line is a group of characters typed in a single command, and treated by Generic CADD as a single entity. The three commands specifically dealing with Text Lines include Line Place (TL), for creating the Text Lines in the first place, Text Change (TG), for changing the parameters of Text Lines already placed, and Text Edit (TE), for editing the content of Text Lines. Note that in some of the prompts, Text Lines are referred to as Text Strings. Text Lines are limited in length to 128 characters, including any spaces and/or punctuation.

The second group of commands deals with Text Characters. These characters are individual entities. Each one has its own reference point, and stores its own Layer, Color, Line Type, Line Width, and even Font information. The first of these commands is Char Place, which places these text entities into the drawing. You can place as many of these as you like with a single command, using BACKSPACE to erase them when you make a mistake and ENTER to move down to the next line. As noted, most of the Text Parameters apply to Text Characters as well as to Text Strings. Also in this group are three commands for editing Text Characters: Insert, Delete, and Replace. These commands are intended primarily for working with groups of Text Characters that form words, sentences, or other structures.

The most fundamental difference between Text Lines and Text Characters lies in how much text each considers to be a single entity. With Text Lines, all of the text placed until you press ENTER is considered a single entity, while with Text Characters, each character is an individual entity. The various advantages of each method stem from this difference. Text Lines take up less space in the database, can be edited an entire line at a time on the prompt line, and are subject to after-the-fact adjustment of some of the placement parameters, specifically Font, Justification, and Between Character spacing. They also "stick together" when you move and copy them. Text Lines are a new feature of Generic CADD 5.0.

Text Characters have their advantages, as well. With Text Characters you have more control over individual character placement. When manually spacing text to fit into a grid, rotating individual characters around a curve, or using other applications that require access to the Size, Color, Placement, Rotation, or any other parameter affecting individual characters, Text Characters work quite well. In the examples that follow, you may use whichever method you prefer.

After setting all the placement parameters, you can place text with either the Place command from the TEXT menu or by typing **TP** or **TL** on the keyboard. For a test, try placing some names on the chairs in the DINNER drawing.

Before you start typing, both Place commands ask you to select the starting point. Note that for other than Left-Justified text, this is really the Reference Point. Select a point on the screen, as shown in Figure 8-12. Because you should allow enough room for the text to appear, select a point at least one inch (the current Text Size) away from the table. After the starting point has been selected, a new type of cursor, the text cursor, will appear and you can start typing. For Text Chars, this cursor is an underscore; for Text Lines, it is a box.

Begin by typing the word **MOM**. Each character appears in the preset font, color, size, aspect, rotation, and slant, at the location of the text

Chapter 8: Complex Entities

FIGURE 8-12 Selecting a text starting point

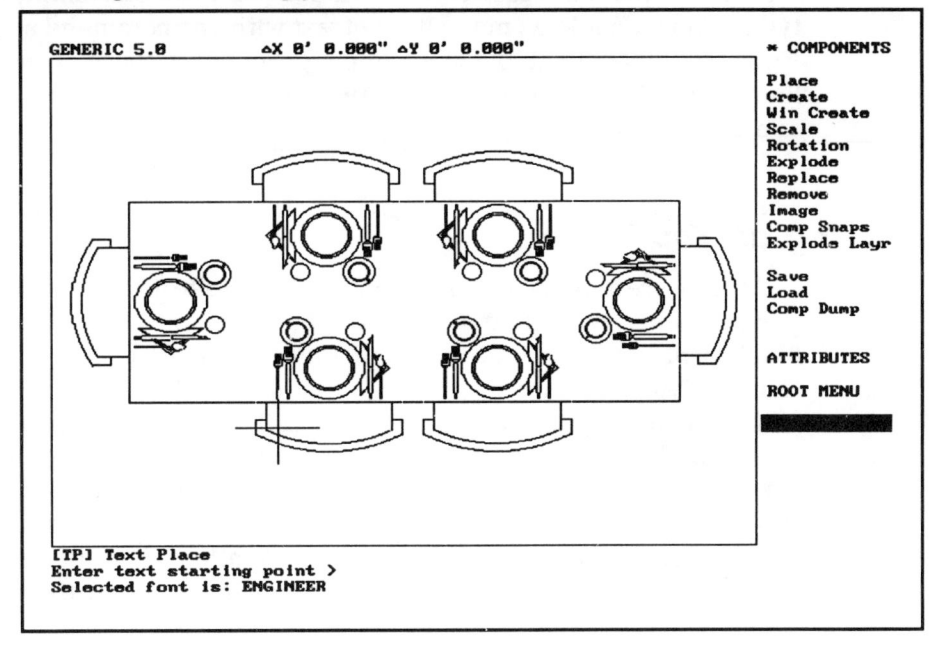

cursor, as you type it, if you are using Text Char. With Text Lines, the text appears at the prompt line, and the box on the screen grows to show you how much room is taken up by the text. If you type an incorrect character, press BACKSPACE to remove it, and then type the correct character. When you get to the end of the text that you want to place, press ESC to end the Char Place command or press ENTER, then ESC, to end the Line Place command. To place more text in another location, use another Text Place command, and repeat the same procedure. To place some of the names on the rest of the chairs, you will need to change the Text Rotation and Aspect before placing the text. Figure 8-13 shows text placed at different rotations and different aspects around the table.

More than One Line of Text

It is possible to type more than one line of text with a single Place command. Simply press ENTER at the end of a line of text, and the text cursor will move down one line and back to a point directly below the reference point of the previous line. At this point you can simply continue typing. You can add as many lines of text with one command as you like. If you would like to skip a line, simply press ENTER twice at the end of a line of text. Note that this technique works equally well for Text Chars and Text Lines.

Editing as You Type

As you are typing, you may notice a mistake that you made on a previous line. With Text Chars, rather than waiting until you have finished placing text and using an Edit command to insert new text, Generic CADD 5.0 allows you to do a limited amount of text editing as you go. Simply press the UP ARROW key on the numeric keypad or cursor control pad, and the text cursor will move up one line of text. The RIGHT ARROW, LEFT ARROW, and DOWN ARROW keys work in much the same way. Position your text cursor to the right of the error, and press BACKSPACE. The offending character will be removed. Another character is removed each time you press BACKSPACE. Once you have made the necessary

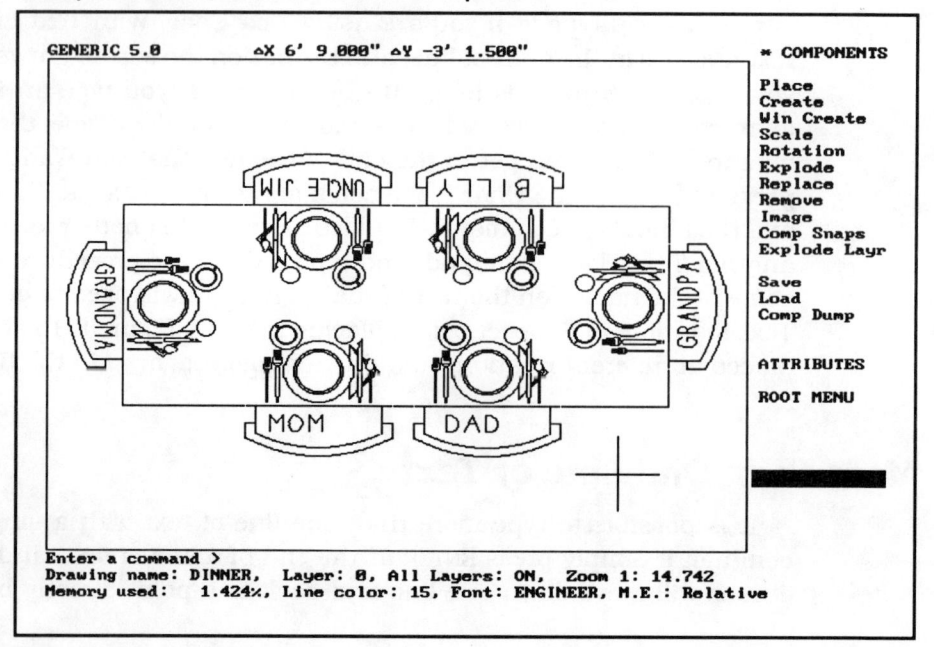

FIGURE 8-13 Text placed at various rotations and aspects

deletion, simply type the new text into the space you have just cleared. If the error requires that you add characters to the line, you may have to move to the end of the line and BACKSPACE to the point of the error. When you have finished editing, use the arrow keys to return the cursor to the point where you left off typing and continue until you are done. When your last line of text is complete, press ESC. Remember that this technique applies only to Text Chars, not Text Lines. To edit Text Lines, use the Text Edit command, discussed in the next section.

Editing Text That Is Already Placed

Periodically, you will need to correct or change text that has already been placed, when you are no longer in the Place command. Several commands allow you to replace, insert, and delete characters within Text Char placements, or edit entire Text Line placements. While Generic CADD 5.0 would hardly pass for a word processor, these editing commands do provide a great deal of control over the text in your drawings.

To replace one or more characters of existing Text, use the Replace command on the TEXT menu, or type **TX** on the keyboard. You are asked to select the character to be replaced. Place the cursor near the lower-left corner of the character and use the Snap to Nearest Point option by typing **NP** on the keyboard or pressing the third button on the pointing device. Once the character has been selected, you can type a character to replace the existing one. You can replace a number of characters this way. Press ESC when you have finished. If you replace all the characters on a line, the command will be ended automatically.

Another useful editing method, particularly when you want to add text to an existing line, is the Char Place command. When asked for the starting point, snap onto the last character in the line. Press the RIGHT ARROW key once to move one space to the right of the last character, and then BACKSPACE until you have deleted all the characters you want to replace. Now you can type as many new characters as you want without exiting the command.

To insert a single character between two existing characters, use the Insert command on the TEXT menu, or type **TI** on the keyboard. When you select a location, preferably by snapping onto an existing character, all characters to the right (including the character selected) move one space to the right. You are then asked to insert the character. If you wish to insert more than one character, repeat the command by pressing SPACEBAR.

To delete a single character in the middle of a line of existing text, use the Delete command from the TEXT menu, or type **TD** on the keyboard. Select a character by snapping onto it, and it will be removed. All characters on the same line to the right of the removed character slide one character to the left to fill the gap. To delete more than one character, simply repeat the command by pressing SPACEBAR, and pick another character to be deleted.

Note In order to use any of the techniques for inserting or replacing text characters, the same font must be active as was used when the text was originally placed. Characters can only be inserted, replaced, or placed in the currently selected font.

Text Lines are edited by calling a line of text back to the prompt line with the Text Edit command, with Edit on the TEXT menu or by typing **TE** on the keyboard. When you issue this command, you are asked to pick a Text Line to edit. Simply use the cursor to point to the Text Line that you want to edit and select it with the first button on the pointing device. When selected, it will be surrounded with a box, much like the box used to indicate its size when it was first created. In addition, the text itself will appear on the second line of the prompt lines with a text cursor following it. The following keys may be used to edit the text string at this point:

BACKSPACE deletes text to the left of the cursor, in the style often referred to as a *destructive backspace.* BACKSPACE can be used to wipe out the current text before typing in new text.

LEFT and RIGHT ARROWS move the text cursor back and forth within the text string without changing text.

DEL deletes the character at the current cursor location.

INS toggles the Insert mode on and off. When on, typing at the cursor in the middle of a Text Line causes the text to the right of the cursor to be pushed to the right, allowing characters to be inserted. When off, new characters may be typed over old ones. Insert mode starts out on, as the default.

ENTER ends the Text Edit command, causing the original text to be replaced with the newly edited version. Prior to pressing ENTER, the box around the text is adjusted to show the effect of the change that you are making.

ESC aborts the command, leaving the Text Line unchanged.

First mouse button allows you to move the Text Placement during Text Edit.

Large Amounts of Text

If you need to place large amounts of text into your Generic CADD drawings, you might want to take advantage of spelling checkers, style analyzers, dictionaries, or other writing aids. You might want to use spreadsheets or database information on a schedule or chart. In this case, you will need to load the information from a file instead of typing it in Generic CADD.

You do this by using ASCII files. ASCII files are simple files containing no extraneous codes—that is, margin, font, tab, or other codes often placed in a file by your word processor or other software for its own use. Most programs can create an ASCII file from your normal data via one of several means. In some cases, you may find an obvious Save as ASCII File option somewhere in your file-saving function or menu. Other programs use a printing option such as Print to a File to create ASCII files. Still other software may require a special conversion program. ASCII files might be known by your software as STRIPPED, PLAIN TEXT, or NON-DOCUMENT files.

To be loaded into Generic CADD 5.0, your ASCII file must have a filename that includes the extension .DOC. If your application cannot apply this extension, use the DOS RENAME command to accomplish the task. Suppose that you have created an ASCII file called MYTEXT.TXT. At the DOS prompt, type **REN MYTEXT.TXT MYTEXT.DOC** and press ENTER. The file may now be imported into Generic CADD 5.0 as text. Suppose that you created such a file, and now want to put it into your drawing. There are several simple steps to take. First, set all the normal Text parameters. Select a Font, set the Rotation, the Color, and the various spacing options. Next, set the path for ASCII files to where your ASCII file is located. Use File Paths on the FILE menu or type **FP** on the keyboard, then select the Misc option or type **I**. Type the path where the ASCII file can be found. Include the disk drive letter and directory name.

Finally, use the Load ASCII command on either the TEXT or FILE menu or type **LA** on the keyboard.

A prompt asking for the name of the ASCII file to be loaded will come up, as well as a file selection list, if the video menu is active. Select a file either by typing its name or selecting it from the list. The text will be read from the file, and converted to Text Lines in Generic CADD, in exactly the same order and with the same line breaks as it had in the original file. When this has been done, a box showing the size of the block of text being added to the drawing will be displayed, and you will be asked to specify a location. You can either drag the box around and place it with the pointing device, or you may type the desired coordinates of the lower-left corner of the box on the keyboard, using any form of manual entry. Once a location has been selected using either method, the Text Lines will be placed.

FIGURE 8-14 The drawing redrawn with Fast Text turned on

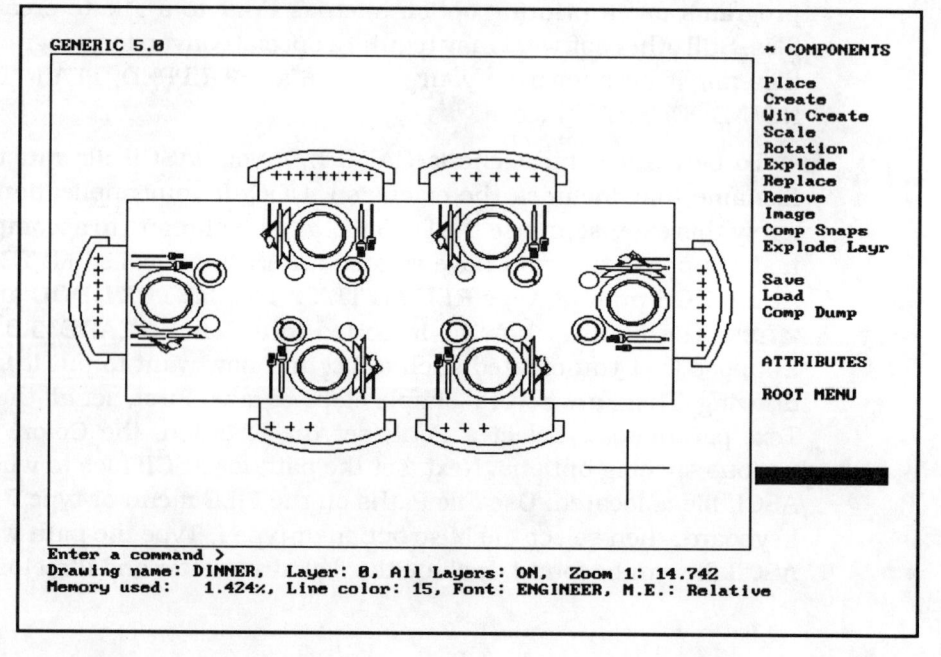

Chapter 8: Complex Entities

Controlling Text Display

Text characters, relatively complicated entities, tend to display slowly on the screen, especially if there are many of them. If you use a great deal of text in your drawings, you may wish to speed up the display when you don't need to read the text. This is accomplished by using the Fast Text command, a toggle on the TEXT menu that can also be activated by typing **FA**, then **T** or **TF**, on the keyboard. When Fast Text is off, the default condition, text displays normally, as you have seen. When Fast Text is turned on, text is replaced with Standard Points, one for each character, as shown in Figure 8-14. As the main purpose of the command is to save time, text is not redrawn immediately when you select it. Instead, the new status of Fast Text is considered the next time that the screen is redrawn when you use any of the Zoom commands. If the text disappears entirely, it is probably because Display Standard Points (PS) is turned off. If you turn it on and execute Redraw (RD), you should see the text as points. If more points seem to be displayed than the text characters they are supposed to represent, remember that spaces are also considered text characters; although they simply appear as blank spaces

FIGURE 8-15 Using Text View to "peek" at some text

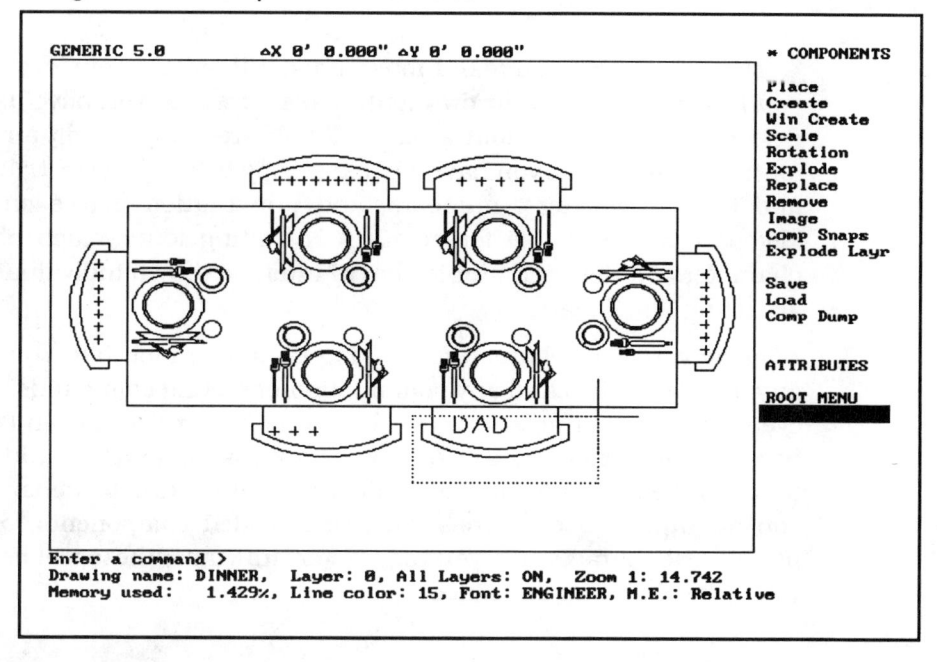

when Fast Text is off, they show up as standard points when Fast Text is on.

When you need to "peek" at a particular passage of text but do not want to turn on all the text, you can issue the Text View command on the TEXT menu, or type **TV** on the keyboard. When you select this command, you are asked to place a window. Put the window around the standard points that represent the text that you want to see. The characters within the window will become visible again, as shown in Figure 8-15. This is a temporary condition, and the characters will revert to standard points on the next screen redraw.

Although text can be edited with the Insert, Replace, and Delete commands while Fast Text is on, the display will not act properly, even if you use Text View first. If you want to edit text, it is best to turn off Fast Text first and then Redraw (RD) the screen. The Text Place command always places visible text, even when Fast Text is on, so placing text in this manner presents no display problems because Fast Text is turned off automatically. After all, in many cases the only time that you actually need to see the text is while you are placing it.

Creating Your Own Fonts

The Win Create command may be used to create your own fonts. If you intend to create your own font, make sure that you have used Font Select to give the new font a name. If you are going to edit an existing font, make sure that you have a backup copy before you start. All upper- and lowercase letters, numbers, and punctuation marks on the PC keyboard are available for creating or editing fonts. Each of the 94 characters on the computer keyboard must be drawn individually if you are using Win Create.

Draw your new characters, making them one inch tall. You can use any simple entities and any combination of editing commands. You can even copy one character to a new location on your drawing and edit it to become another character. You can draw your characters and preview them on the screen before you make them into actual text characters. If you attempt to use hatches, fills, unexploded components, or actual placed text characters in your character drawings, these will be ignored when the character is defined.

Chapter 8: Complex Entities

After you have drawn characters that you want to add to the font, use the Text command on the Windows menu, or type **WT** on the keyboard. You will be asked to place a window. Put a window around the drawing of the text character that you are defining, making sure that you get the entire character in the window. Once you have specified the window, you will be asked which character you want to define. If you are working on an uppercase letter, be sure to press SHIFT. If the character is already defined, you will be asked if you want to redefine it.

Finally, you will be asked for the lower-left corner of the character. This point will become the insertion point or reference point for the character. Figure 8-16 illustrates the use of the Window Text command.

When creating text characters using this method, be sure that the base height of the characters is 1 inch. If you plan to use monospaced text, your characters should not be more than 1 inch wide. In fact, they should be a little narrower, so that there will be space between characters. Characters created in this way can have descenders or ascenders, as long as you make sure to capture these in the window, and place the lower-left

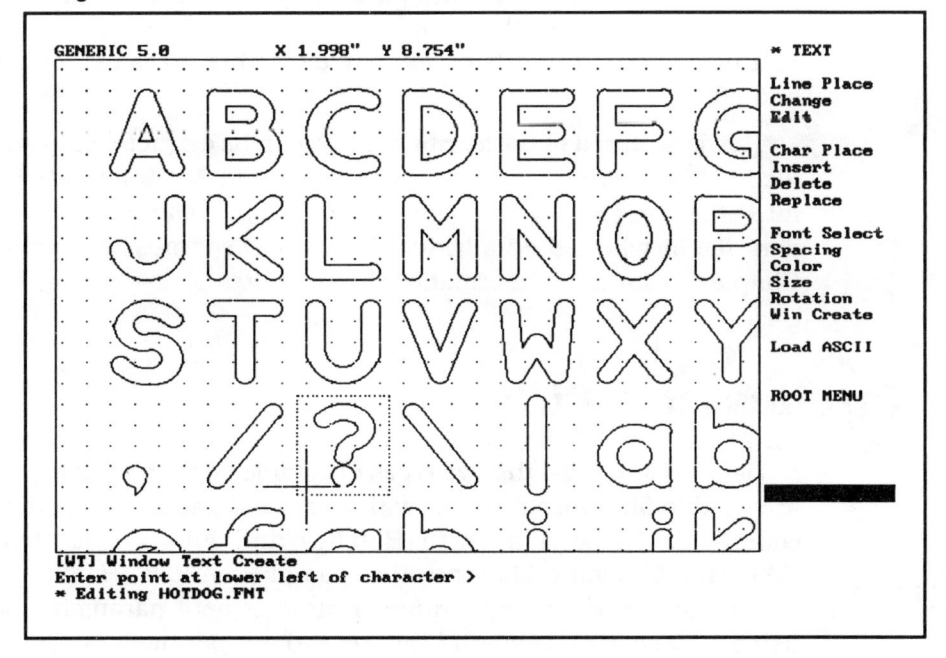

FIGURE 8-16 Using the Window Text command to define a character

corner at the correct point. Don't forget to make a space by windowing a blank portion of the screen.

Attributes

Attributes are a special type of text that differs from other text, in that the information contained in attributes can be considered real data, rather than just drawings of characters. Like components, attributes are first defined and then placed. Unlike components, each placement of an attribute is unique. Each placement contains data in the same predefined format, but the data itself is unique to the individual placement.

Once it is defined, an attribute is placed by attaching it to one or more component definitions. It is then placed automatically each time the associated component is placed. Each attribute definition has a unique name, a number of user-defined fields, each with its own name, and default values for each field. Attribute definitions may be saved on disk for use in other drawings.

When a component with an attribute definition attached to it is placed, you are prompted for the data for each field with the name of the field, unless you have set it for Default/Auto Placement in the Attributes Settings screen. The attributes may be visible, invisible, or toggled on and off.

The data stored in the attribute fields can be extracted into an external file in either Lotus .WK1 or comma-separated ASCII formats for import into other programs. (A *comma-separated*, or *comma-delimited*, file is a data file in which the individual fields are separated by commas.) See Chapter 17 for more information on attributes.

Hatches and Fills

Hatches and Fills, the two types of complex entities created on the fly, are used to fill a specified area with a selected pattern or solid color. The commands for working with Hatches and Fills are located on the HATCH/FILL menu. Like the other complex entities, Hatches and Fills are created by specifying a number of placement parameters and then using a placement command that uses these parameters.

The commands that create Hatches and Fills are so similar that fills might be thought of as a special case of hatches. The pattern used for hatching is selected from a number of patterns, while the pattern for fills is simply a solid color. Rotation and Scale, two placement parameters used for Hatches, do not make sense with fills; you cannot discern the angle or the scale of a solid area of color.

Placement Parameters

Both Hatches and Fills have a Color placement parameter: for hatches it is the Color (C) option of the Hatch Settings (HS) command; for fills it is Fill Color (FL or FK). Notice that all of the hatch two-character codes either start or end with *H*, and the fill codes start or end with *F*. The remaining character is the same for both sets of commands where identical or similar functions are concerned. Both color commands bring up color bars on the video menu if the video menu is active. Colors are numbered from 0 to 255, and work just like any other color-setting commands.

As mentioned above, Hatches have a number of additional parameters. Hatch Settings on the HATCH/FILL menu, or typing **HS** on the keyboard, results in a prompt for all of these parameters. Each hatch pattern, represented by a file on your disk with the extension .HCH, is illustrated in the back of the Generic CADD manual. The hatch files must be in the default Hatch directory.

To select the hatch pattern from the Hatch List, select the Pattern option from the prompt or type **P**. The available files will be shown. If the first menu only shows a partial list, you can see the rest by selecting "More..." from the first list. Once you select a hatch pattern, you will return to the Hatch Settings prompt.

The other parameters that differentiate Hatch from Fill, Rotation and Scale, apply to the hatch pattern definitions as they are shown in the Generic CADD manual. Rotation (option R) allows hatches to be placed at an angle other than the angle at which they were originally created. If you specify 0, which is the default, hatches will appear at the same angle shown in the back of the manual. Allowable rotations are between -360 and +360 degrees, and work the same way as Component and Text rotations. A Hatch Rotation of 90, for instance, turns a hatch pattern on its side.

Hatch Scale (option S) changes the distance between the lines that compose the hatch pattern. Although many of the hatch patterns are defined with one unit of space between lines, this is not true in all cases. Therefore, Hatch Scale does not translate into Hatch Size. The Scale is a factor that is applied to the size at which the hatch was originally created. These vary, and while in some cases the illustrations in the Generic CADD manual are printed at a Hatch Scale of 1, others are not, so you will have to experiment a little to determine the spacing of the original definition. A scale factor of 0.5 produces hatches with twice as many lines, and a scale factor of 2 makes the lines twice as far apart.

Hatches may also be created with or without boundaries. This choice is made through the Boundary toggle (the B option). Finally, the display of hatches can be controlled from within the Hatch Settings command via the D option.

Placing Hatches and Fills

The commands for placing Hatch and Fill entities are functionally identical. There are four ways to place each entity type—Window, Object, Fitted, and Boundary. The Hatch command codes are WH, OH, FH, and BH, while the Fill codes are WF, OF, FF, and BF. Each of these Hatch and Fill placement methods has its own rules.

Window Hatch and Fill

In order to use a Window Hatch (WH) or Window Fill (WF), the area *must* be enclosed by simple entities that connect end to end, as in Rectangle (RE), for example. A tic-tac-toe figure is a good example of a figure that you *cannot* hatch or fill with a window. Figure 8-17 shows an example of a figure that can be hatched or filled with a Window.

Window Fill works on all simple entities, while Window Hatch works on all but Curves. Even though component placements cannot be hatched or filled, a Hatch or Fill may be part of a component definition,

Chapter 8: Complex Entities   251

and the entities that make up a component placement may be hatched or filled if the component is exploded.

A Window Hatch or Fill will attempt to use *all* of the valid entities that it finds in the window. This can lead to bizarre results if areas are not enclosed at all or are ambiguously defined. Figure 8-18 shows a group of lines that will fill or hatch in an unpredictable fashion. Figure 8-19 shows what happens if you attempt a Window Fill on this group of lines. On the other hand, the fact that Window Hatch and Fill commands try to hatch all entities in a window creates opportunities to fill or hatch some pretty unusual shapes with enclosed entities inside each other, and other unusual configurations. Figure 8-20 shows a complex drawing with several enclosed areas inside each other that has been hatched at a fairly small scale. As you can see, the Hatch and Fill entities *start* when one boundary is encountered, and *stop* when they find another.

FIGURE 8-17 An area that can be easily hatched or filled with a Window

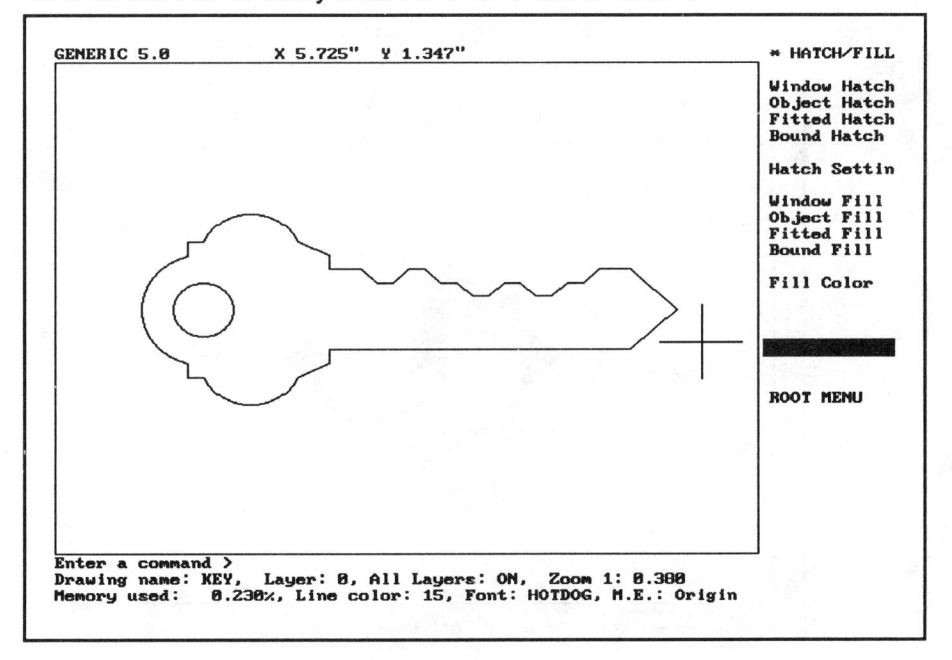

252   Generic CADD 5.0 Inside & Out

FIGURE 8-18   A drawing that defines ambiguous areas

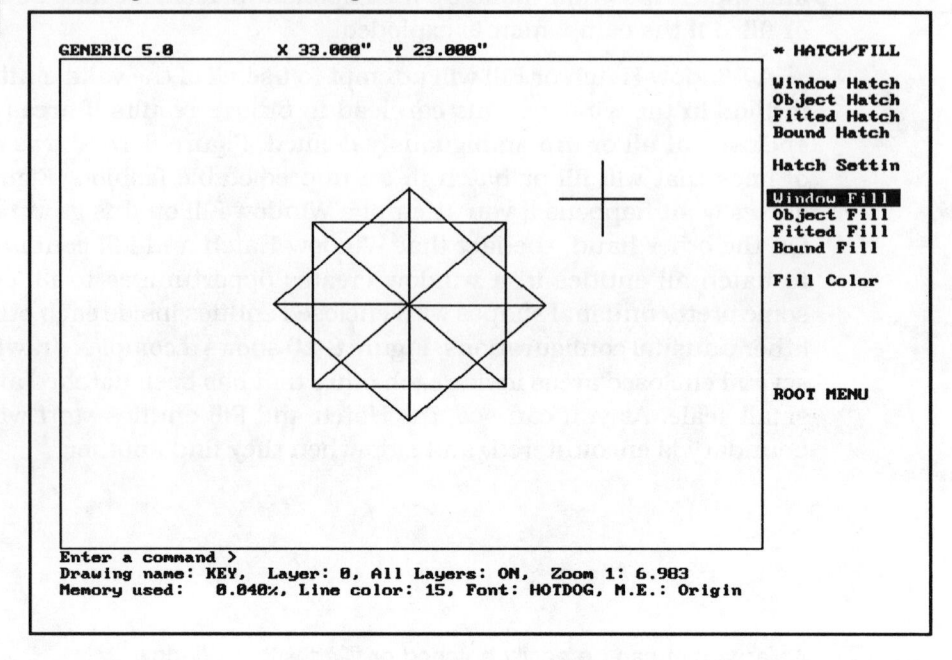

FIGURE 8-19   An unsuccessful attempt at filling ambiguous areas

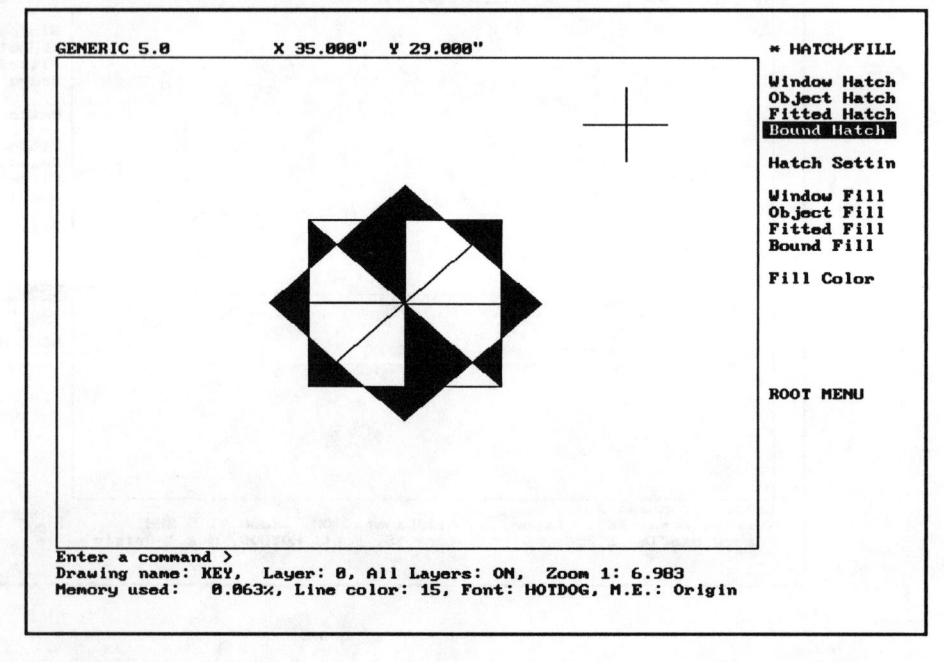

Object Hatch and Fill

The Object Hatch (OH) and Object Fill (OF) commands also require completely enclosed areas, but you are not constrained by a window. This technique requires a little more work on your part, but you can be much more selective about what you are hatching.

When you use either the Object Hatch or Object Fill command, you are asked to select the objects to hatch. Select the objects that define the enclosed area in any order; the same entity types that work for the Window methods will work here. Objects that are not selected will be ignored as if they were not there. Figure 8-21 shows the same drawing as Figure 8-20 hatched with Object Hatch, where only the perimeter was selected.

FIGURE 8-20 A complex drawing with nested areas, hatched with Window Hatch

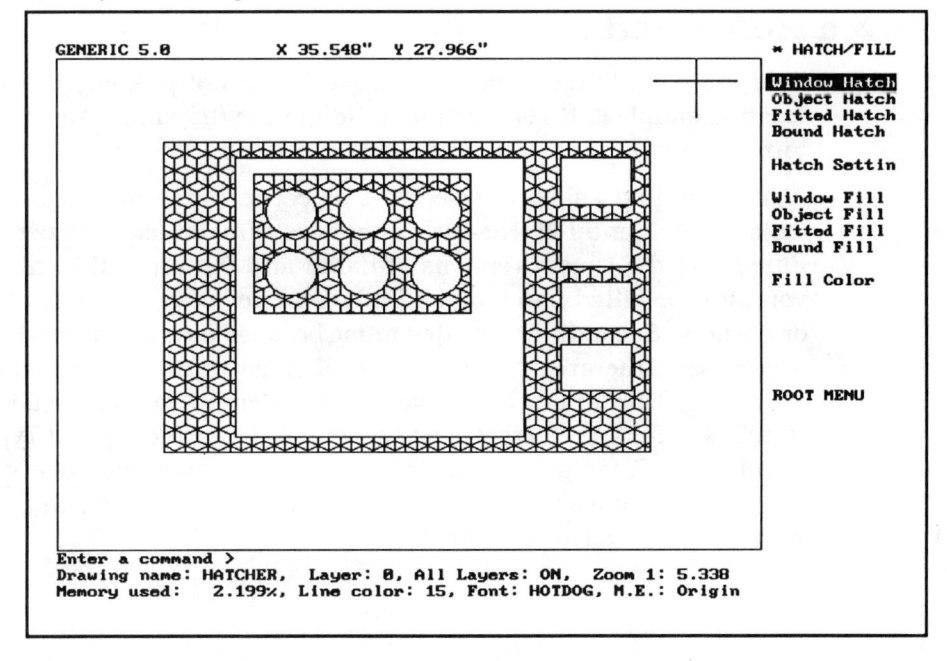

FIGURE 8-21 Hatching only the outer boundaries of the same drawing with Object Hatch

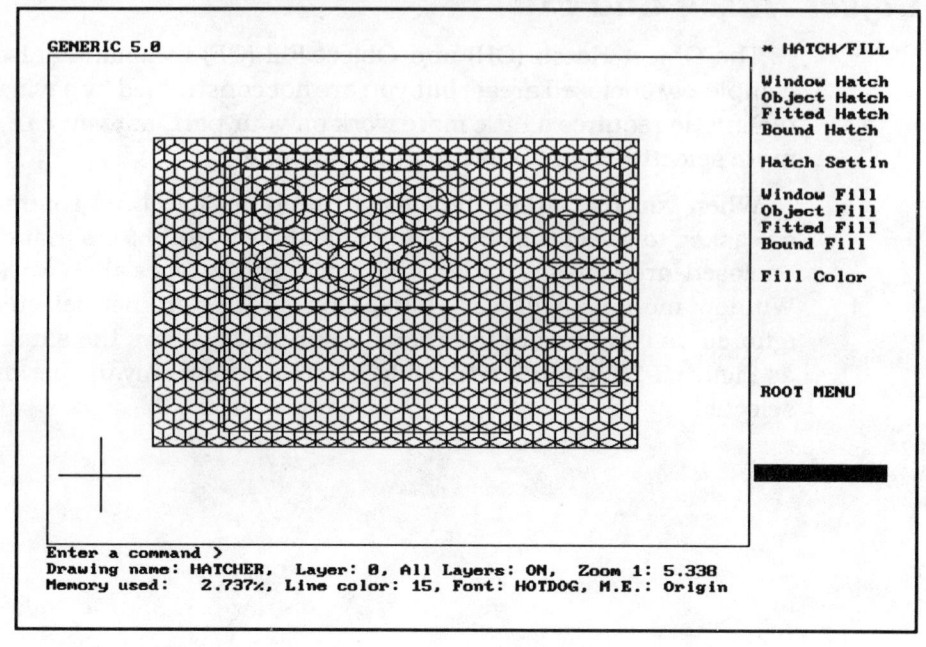

Fitted Hatch and Fitted Fill

If you want to hatch or fill an area that is not properly described by existing simple entities, such as a tic-tac-toe drawing, you can use the Fitted Hatch (FH) or the Fitted Fill (FF) command.

You are first asked to select the object to hatch or fill, just as with Object Hatch and Fill. However, there are three differences between the Fitted and the Object versions of hatch and fill. First, the entities that you pick for Fitted hatching and filling do not have to meet at the ends or corners. Second, the entities must be picked in order, working your way around the area to be hatched or filled until you get back to the beginning. Third, Ellipses, Curves, and Beziers cannot be used for Fitted Hatches or Fills. (Beziers will be covered in the next chapter.) Type **PU** or select a blank menu item to issue a Pen Up command when you have finished selecting entities; a new boundary will be created, and then the area will be hatched or filled.

You cannot hatch or fill areas within other areas ("islands") with the Fitted commands because each entity must intersect the next entity. Fitted Hatch and Fill commands require at least three entities to work.

Boundary Hatch and Boundary Fill

One final method exists for hatching or filling areas that have not yet been described. These are called Boundary methods, because you create the Hatch or Fill by drawing its boundary.

Using Boundary Hatch (BH) or Boundary Fill (BF) is very much like drawing continuous Lines. You simply enter one point after another, moving in any direction. As you move, these points are connected by a boundary line, to help you visualize the area that you are describing. When you get back to the starting point, issue a Pen Up command by typing **PU** or by selecting a blank menu item. If you do not return to your starting point before issuing the Pen Up, the boundary will be completed anyway—a line will automatically connect your first and last points. This is a perfectly valid method of completing the boundary. Once again, if you make a mistake, you may eliminate your last point entry by pressing CTRL and BACKSPACE together. This technique works for Object, Fitted, and Boundary methods.

Once the boundary has been created, the Hatch or Fill will be created, using all of the currently active parameters, just as with any of the other methods. Note that because of the method for describing the boundary, all edges of the Hatch or Fill will be straight lines.

Hatching and Filling Complicated Areas

Because the Window Hatch (WH) and Window Fill (WF) commands allow you to select many entities with one window, as opposed to tracing around entities trying to make sure that you cover all of them, you should use these commands if at all possible.

The easiest way to ensure that you can use the Window Hatch and Fill commands on complicated areas is to draw the boundary entities on a separate layer from the layers containing the entities that you do not want to hatch or fill. Even if you have already drawn the complicated area, it can be easier and more useful for future editing to Change (OG, WG, YG, DG, or CG) the boundary entities onto their own layer, make that layer the current layer with the Layer Current (YC) command, turn off Edit All Layers (AL), and then proceed to hatch or fill the area with a Window.

Hatching the Bathroom Floor

The ROOM drawing that you created in Chapter 4, "Basic Drawing Tasks," and edited in Chapter 5, "Basic Editing Tasks," is a good example of a reasonably complex area that would often require hatching. Suppose that you want to install 6-inch tiles on the floor. Before deciding which technique to use, you should analyze several factors. First, at least two islands should not be hatched—the rectangle (four lines) and construc-

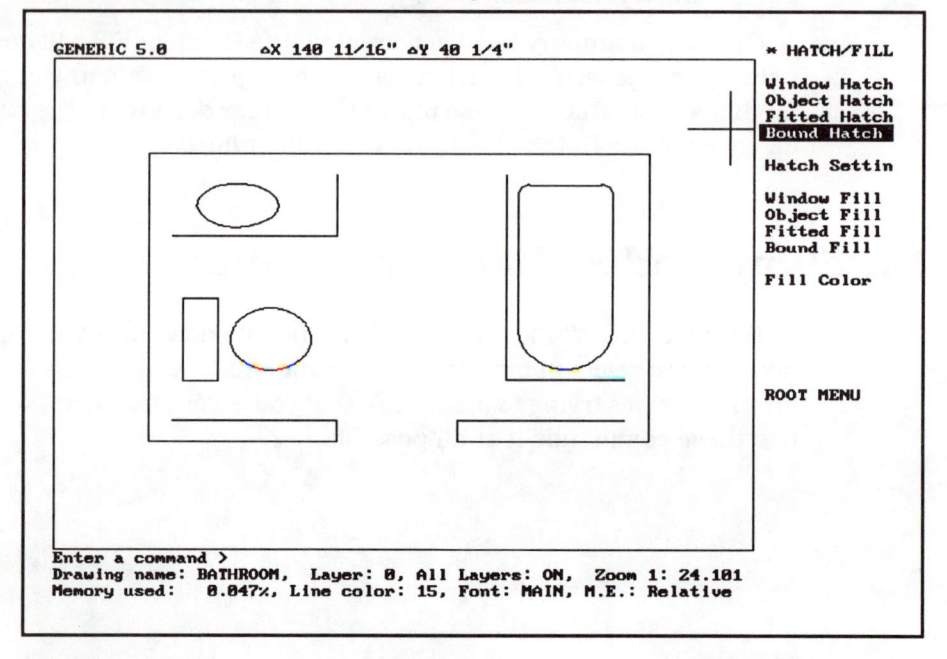

FIGURE 8-22 The bathroom drawing with the too-long lines removed

tion ellipse (four arcs) that define the toilet. This means that the floor cannot be hatched with the Fitted Hatch command, as islands are not allowed.

Second, the corners of the room are not accurately defined by lines that meet at their endpoints. Specifically, the places where the bathtub surround and the countertop hit the perimeter wall are a problem. These conditions cannot be properly hatched with Object Hatch, which requires an accurately defined area. In addition, the doorway needs to be closed in order to define a hatchable area. Third, the entire drawing has been made on one layer, layer 0 (zero), which prohibits the use of the Window Hatch command, because too many objects will be enclosed in the hatching area; in other words, the hatch will not go around the objects that you want it to miss.

These three factors indicate that the drawing must be changed in some way before it can be hatched. The most significant problems are the ill-defined corners and the open door. If these problems are corrected, you can use Object Hatch. The simplest way to correct this situation is to erase the three lines that make up the inside left, right, and top interior walls, and replace these with shorter line segments. After erasing these two lines, which are shown in Figure 8-22, set the Grid Size (GS) to 6 x 6 inches, turn on Snap to Grid (SG), and draw the new lines, starting in the lower-left corner, placing points at the lower-left edge of the counter, the upper-left corner of the room, the upper-right corner of the counter, the upper-left corner of the tub, the upper-right corner of the room, the lower-right corner of the tub, and finally, the lower-right corner of the room. You have now replaced the original three long lines with seven shorter ones. Finally, draw a line across the inside of the doorway to form an edge for the tile. Now that a defined area exists, you can use Object Hatch (OH) to hatch this area.

1. Select the NET hatch from the Hatch List, and then set the Hatch Scale (HS,S) to 6. This produces a six-inch grid, because the NET pattern was originally defined with lines one inch apart.
2. To make sure that the tile pattern runs parallel to the walls, check to make sure that the Hatch Rotation (HS,R) is set at 0.
3. When you use Object Hatch (OH), start at one wall and work your way around the room, choosing only those entities that form the border of the floor. When you have gone around the room selecting every line segment on the perimeter, pick all of the entities that make

up the toilet, making sure that you get all four lines of the rectangle and all four arcs of the construction ellipse. If you make a mistake and pick the wrong entity, press CTRL and BACKSPACE together to remove it and try again.

4. Once you've selected all of the entities, type **PU** or pick a blank line from the video menu to issue a Pen Up command. If you've selected every line segment correctly, the floor should resemble the one shown in Figure 8-23.

Instead of selecting so many different entities and risking missing one or two (in which case you must erase the hatch with Erase Last (EL) and start over), you could use the easier Window Hatch command. To use Window Hatch, it would be best if the hatchable entities were all on a separate layer. To try this technique, erase the hatch with Erase Last (EL), and then Redraw (RD). Make sure that Edit All Layers is on for now.

FIGURE 8-23 The bathroom floor successfully hatched with the Object Hatch command

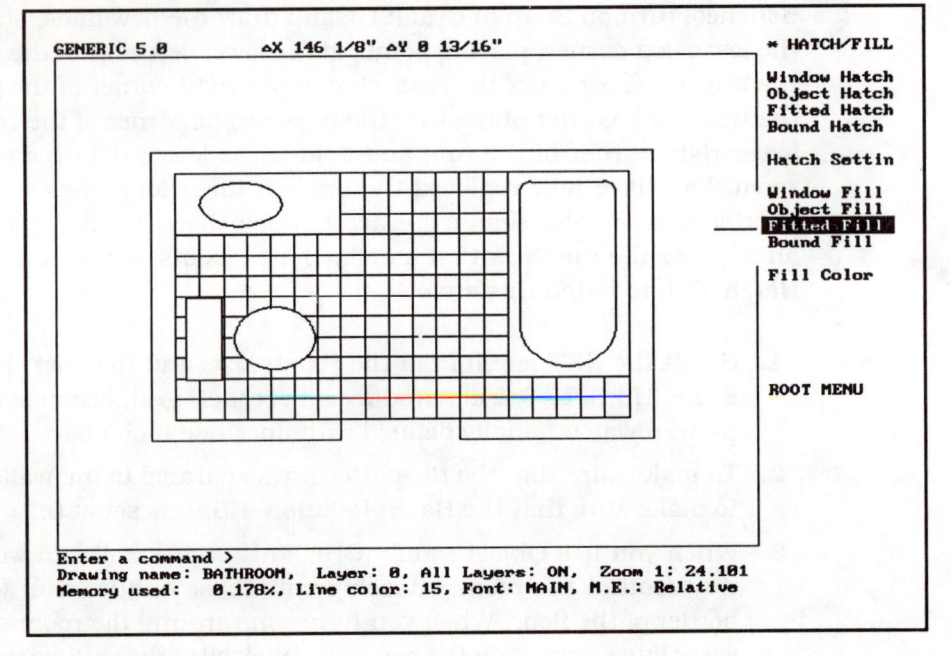

Chapter 8: Complex Entities 259

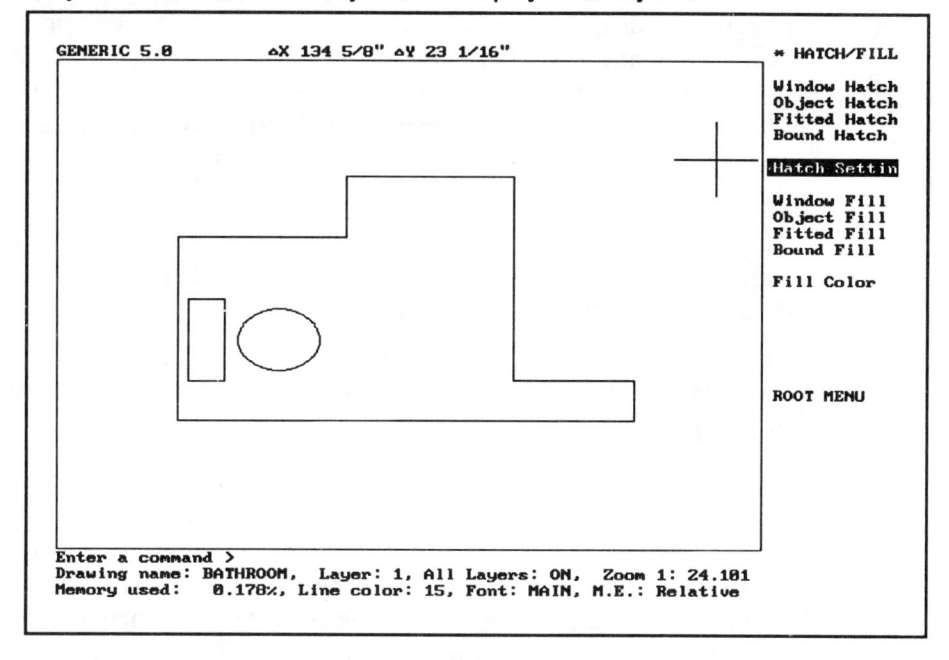

FIGURE 8-24 Only the hatchable boundary entities displayed on layer 1

```
GENERIC 5.0        ΔX 134 5/8"  ΔY 23 1/16"              * HATCH/FILL

                                                          Window Hatch
                                                          Object Hatch
                                                          Fitted Hatch
                                                          Bound Hatch

                                                          Hatch Settin

                                                          Window Fill
                                                          Object Fill
                                                          Fitted Fill
                                                          Bound Fill

                                                          Fill Color



                                                          ROOT MENU




Enter a command >
Drawing name: BATHROOM,   Layer: 1, All Layers: ON,  Zoom 1: 24.101
Memory used:    0.178%, Line color: 15, Font: MAIN, M.E.: Relative
```

The easiest way to get these entities onto their own layer is with the Window Change (WG) command. Place a window around everything but the very outside wall. Your window should go right down the middle of the wall on all four sides. Don't worry that you are selecting too many objects. It's easier to put a few back with another window than to change each entity individually with the Object Change command. After you have placed the window, type **Y** for layer; then type **1** (or the number of any unused layer) and press ENTER. Press ENTER again to end the command. At this point, make layer 1 the active layer with a Layer Current (YC) command, and turn off the display of layer 0 (zero) with the Layer Hide (YH) command. Only the items that you changed to layer 1 should be visible. Use the Window Change (WG) and Object Change (OG) commands to put the rest of the entities that you don't want to use for hatch boundaries back onto layer 0 (zero). Each should vanish as you change it, because layer 0 (zero) is hidden. After a few commands, only the hatchable boundaries should remain (see Figure 8-24). Once you have this on the screen, use the Window Hatch command to hatch this area.

One big advantage of this technique is that you can try different patterns, scales, and rotations easily, without reselecting the same entities over and over. You can easily Erase Last (EL) to change a few parameters, and do another Window Hatch. Once you have the correct hatch, turn the rest of the drawing back on with a Layer Display (YD), entering a value of 256 to see the entire drawing or select All from the menu.

If you want to change the pattern later, simply go back to this layer, turn Edit All Layers off, erase the existing hatch pattern (by putting a Window Erase window around its reference points), and hatch again.

If the available hatch patterns are not what you need, you can create others with a text editor. Hatch patterns are also available from third-party developers.

In this chapter, you have seen how to combine existing entities to form components, how to place text into your drawing using any of a number of different fonts, and how to Hatch and Fill portions of your drawing. You have seen that all of these complex entities are placed by first setting a number of specific placement parameters, and then using a placement command to put the complex entity into the drawing. Complex entities should be used in place of repetitive simple entities whenever possible: they provide a number of sophisticated features and techniques and save space in the database at the same time.

CHAPTER 9

Multiple Entities

A number of entity placement commands fall between the simple entities (Line, Arc, Circle, and so on) and the complex entities (Component, Text, Hatch, and Fill). Each of these commands places into the drawing a number of simple entities simultaneously. Three of these commands were covered in Chapter 4, "Basic Drawing Tasks": the Rectangle, Regular Polygon, and Construction Ellipse commands. Rectangle and Regular Polygon create multiple Lines, while Construction Ellipse creates four Arcs. In this chapter, you will be introduced to a few other commands that create more than one entity at the same time.

Early versions of Generic CADD, specifically 2.0 and earlier, included the simple entities Rectangle, Regular Polygon, and True Ellipse, but no Construction Ellipse. Rectangles and Regular Polygons are no longer used in Generic CADD. Version 3.0 automatically converted Rectangles and Regular Polygons to multiple straight lines when they were encountered, but the current version does not. If you want to call up these older drawing files in Generic CADD 5.0, you will need to either first call them up and save them in 3.0, or update the files using *File Diagnostics*, available from WORKSHOP 3D Software, a third-party vendor of utilities for Generic Software.

Bezier Curves

Generic CADD provides two ways of constructing a curve between a given set of points, the Curve (CV) command (see Chapter 4) and the Bezier Curve (BV) command. The Curve command creates one continuous *spline curve* through as many points as you select. The whole curve is one long entity, with a variable number of points. The Bezier Curve command creates individual *Bezier Curves*, one between the first two points, another between the second and third, and so on.

The entities created by the Bezier Curve command are quite different than those created by the Curve command. While the Curve command attempts to create as smooth a curve as possible through a variable number of points, a rather loosely defined task, each individual Bezier created by the Bezier Curve command is much more specifically defined. Although you only specify the endpoints of each, a single Bezier Curve is actually defined by four points—two endpoints and two *control points*. The locations of the control points are calculated automatically by Generic CADD, but can be changed later if you wish. (See Chapter 10,

"Advanced Drawing and Editing Techniques," for a discussion on editing Bezier Curves.) Bezier Curves are often used when you are not sure what shape you want because they are so easy to edit. The Curve command is more useful when you are not likely to do much editing because Curves are much easier to place initially than Bezier Curves. Bezier Curves take on the current Line parameters of Color (LK), Width (LW), and Line Type (LT) as part of their definition. Like all entities, Bezier Curves are created on the current layer.

Figure 9-1 shows a single Bezier (though when you use the Bezier Curve command, you actually create a number of these entities). Notice that at each end, the Bezier is tangent to an imaginary line between the control point and the endpoint of the Bezier. This is how the curvature of the Bezier is determined.

Figure 9-2 shows two Beziers, created with a single Bezier Curve command. Notice that not only does each Bezier remain tangent to the imaginary line between control point and endpoint, but that the imagi-

FIGURE 9-1 A single Bezier Curve

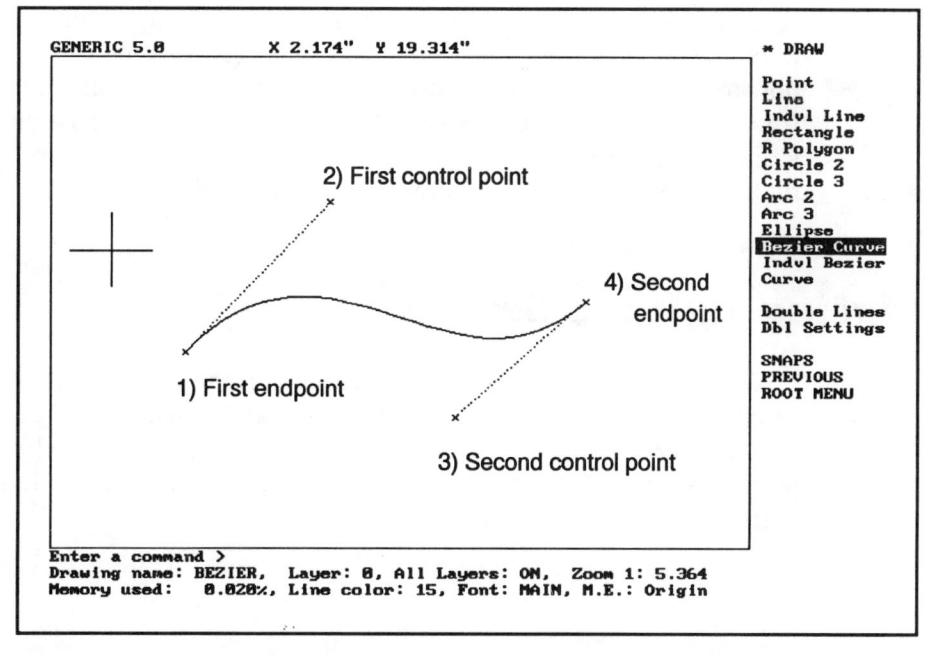

FIGURE 9-2 The relationship between two continuous Bezier Curves

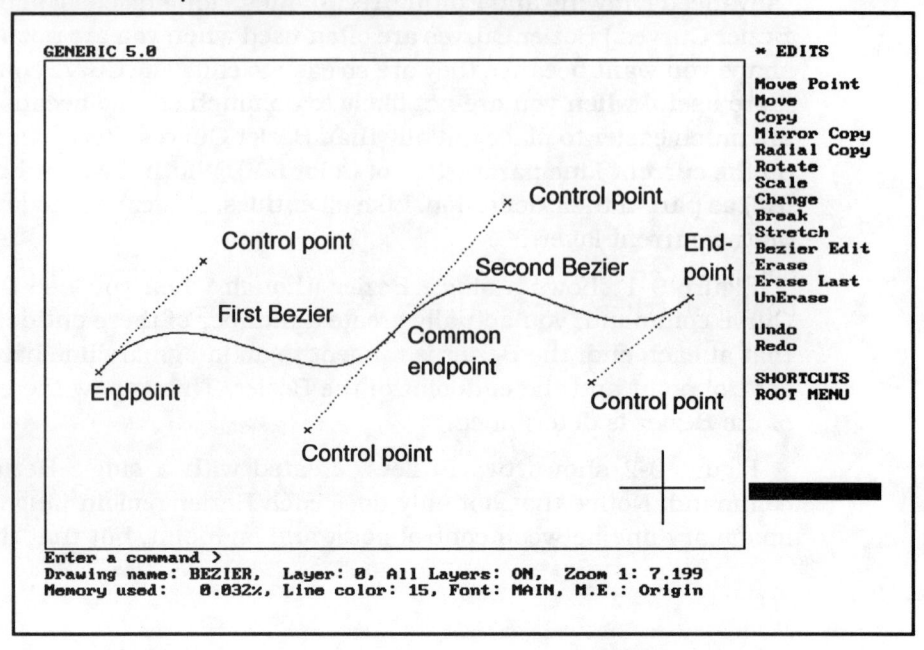

nary line between the second control point of the first Bezier and the first control point of the second Bezier passes through their shared endpoint. Because each Bezier is tangent to this imaginary line, the two Beziers flow together with no break in between, as if they were one curve. Again, this condition is established by the creation of multiple Beziers with a single Bezier Curve command. You need not line up the control points to make the curve smooth; it happens automatically.

Placing Multiple Beziers

To place Bezier Curves, use the Bezier command on the DRAW menu, or type **BV** on the keyboard. The prompts and placement of points work in a similar way to the Curve command. When you are finished placing points, you type **PU** or pick a blank line from the video menu to issue the Pen Up command.

The screen display for the Bezier Curve command is quite different from that for the Curve command. Instead of placing temporary straight lines between curve points, the Bezier Curve command displays the individual Bezier entities as soon as it has enough information. Since Beziers that meet end-to-end influence each other, Generic CADD cannot actually calculate and draw the first Bezier until you have defined the endpoints of the second. This means that the first Bezier actually appears when you have placed the third point. Each subsequent point provides enough information to create another segment. When you get to the last point and type **PU** or pick a blank menu item, the last Bezier is placed.

The first control point of the first Bezier and the second control point of the last Bezier are arbitrarily placed by Generic CADD, using an internal algorithm. If you type **PU** after only two points, you produce only one Bezier. Since this is both the first and the last Bezier placed, there are no tangent Beziers to control the starting and ending directions. Both the first and second control points are arbitrarily placed by Generic CADD. You will be able to predict these locations after you have used the Bezier Curve command a few times.

Placing Single Beziers

At times you may want to place only one Bezier, but want to have more control over its shape than you do when you use the Bezier Curve command with only two points. Indvl Bezier (command code BW), intended specifically for placing a single Bezier, lets you place not only the endpoints but the control points as well. The letter W does not stand for anything; it just happens to be the next letter in the alphabet after V, which is used for the multiple Bezier Curve command.

When you use the BW command, you are asked for four points in order: (1) the first endpoint, (2) the first control point, (3) the second control point, and (4) the second endpoint. By examining Figure 9-1 you can see how these four points define the single Bezier Curve. You do not have to type **PU** at the end because a single Bezier is always defined by these four points. After you have placed the four points, the Bezier will be drawn.

Editing Bezier Curves

As noted previously, one of the primary advantages of Bezier Curves is the ease with which they can be edited. The definition of a Bezier Curve includes two control points, which can be used to create the specific shapes that you are trying to draw.

Using Move Point (MP) with Bezier Curves

When you use the Move Point (MP) command, you are asked to select an entity. If the entity that you select is a Bezier Curve, placed either with a single or a multiple Bezier command, dashed lines will appear between each endpoint and the control point that controls that end of the Bezier. When you select the point to be moved, you can specify either end of the dashed line. The Bezier will be stretched in various directions as you move the selected point. When you actually place the point, the Bezier will be redrawn.

If you use Move Point to move the control point of a single Bezier in the middle of a string of Beziers, you will probably create a corner where the Beziers are not tangent to one another.

Maintaining Tangent Bezier Curves

To keep all continuous Bezier curves tangent to one another, you can use the Bezier Edit (BE) command. This command works just like Move Point, except that you have to select *two* Bezier Curves before selecting the point that you want to move. If you try to select any other type of entity, the command will not work.

Once you have selected the two Beziers that you want to edit, dashed lines will be displayed at each end of both Beziers, as with Move Point, and you will be asked to select a point to be edited. At the point where the two Beziers meet, two of the dashed lines may appear to be one straight line, but they are not. Choose one of the two control points at the end of one of the dashed lines that connect to the point where the two Beziers meet. As you move this point, *both* control points move to maintain the straight line between them. Both Bezier Curves will be rubberbanded as you move the point. The tangential relationship be-

FIGURE 9-3 Using the Bezier Edit command to move two control points

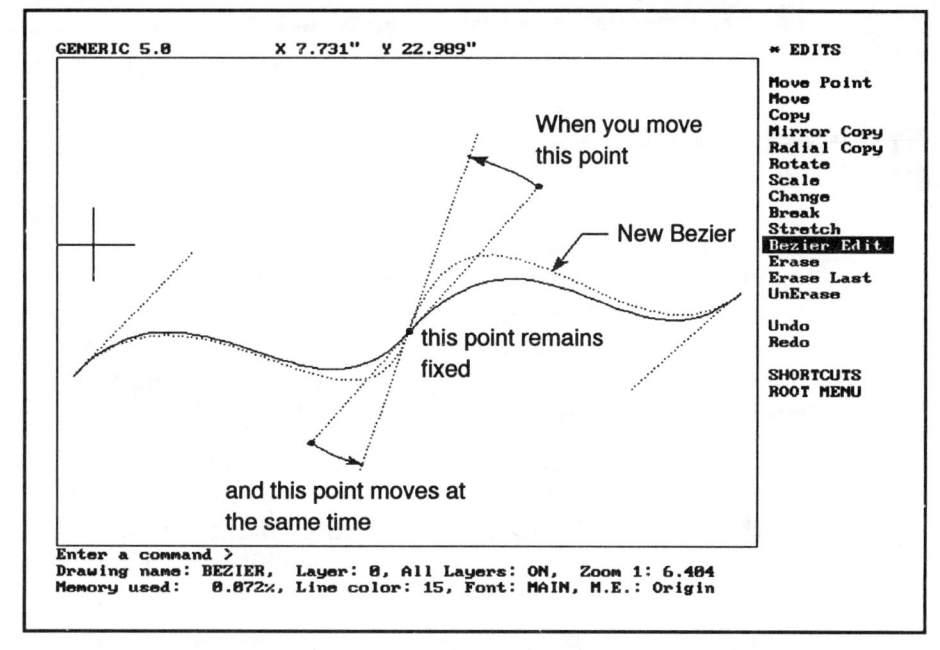

tween the two Beziers will be preserved. Figure 9-3 illustrates how moving one point changes both Beziers.

Although the Bezier Edit command is intended for editing two Beziers that share a common endpoint, you can also select two Beziers that do not touch. Even if the two Beziers are not tangent when you start, they will be when you are done. If you first use the Bezier Edit command on two noncontinuous Beziers and then Move them together, the connection between them will be perfectly smooth.

Smart Lines

Generic CADD 5.0 provides a number of additional multiple entity placement commands. Like the Bezier Curve command, these commands place more than one simple or complex entity with a single command. These commands act more like complex entity commands than the

Bezier Curve command, as they use placement parameters and placement commands, so one could call them Smart Lines.

Filleted Lines

You might say that the Line command creates multiple entities, because you do not have to pick another Line command to draw additional line segments. You can just keep selecting points, and more lines will be drawn until you select another command or press ESC. The multiple lines created automatically by the Line command meet exactly at the corners, because the second point of one line becomes the first point of the next line.

This function can be altered using the Autofillet command on the TRIMS menu, available from the DRAW or SNAPS menu, or by typing **AF** on the keyboard. This mode of drawing lines works with another command, Fillet Radius (FR or RF), which establishes the radius of an arc to be inserted at each new intersection as the lines are drawn.

Once the Fillet Radius command is set and Autofillet is activated, you use the Line command just as before, with one difference. To end the command, you must press ESC or type **PU**. You won't notice any difference on the first line segment, but as soon as you place the second, an arc will be inserted tangent to the first and second lines, and the lines will be trimmed, as shown in Figure 9-4. Step A shows two lines and a circle of the specified fillet radius. Step B shows how the circle is placed tangent to the two lines. Steps C and D show how lines are trimmed at the tangent points, and the circle is trimmed to an arc to meet the endpoints of the lines exactly.

All the Lines and Arcs you have created take on the current Line parameters—Color, Type, Width, and the Current Layer. If the angle between the lines or the length of the lines makes the insertion of a tangent arc impossible, you will get a simple trimmed intersection instead of a filleted corner. As a toggle, Autofillet is turned off the same way that it was turned on, by typing **AF** or by selecting Autofillet from the TRIMS menu.

If Autofillet is on and the Fillet Radius command is set to 0, no arcs will appear between lines; in this case, you must press ESC or type **PU** to

Chapter 9: Multiple Entities 269

FIGURE 9-4 How two lines are filleted

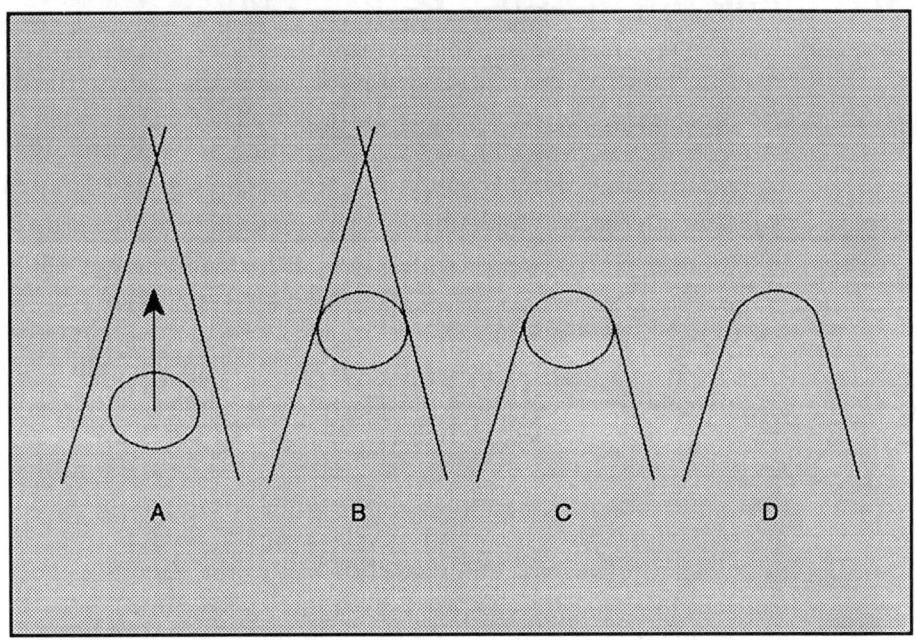

A   B   C   D

exit the Line command. It is usually better to turn off Autofillet when you do not want it instead of setting the Fillet Radius command to 0. The Fillet Radius command can be used without Autofillet turned on, as you will see in Chapter 10.

Double Lines

The Double Lines command creates two lines at the same time. When you use the Double Lines command, you actually place two separate entities into the database for every pair of endpoints that you select. When using this command, you place two points, just as in drawing a normal line, but the two lines that are created are actually placed offset from an imaginary line between these two points, by distances specified by the Double Width parameter.

Specifying the Distance Between Lines

First, you need to set the two Double Width values that indicate the distance between the double lines—or, more accurately, the offsets from the imaginary line. The idea is quite simple: If you specify "1" for each value, the two lines will be two inches apart, each one inch from the imaginary center line. If you make one of the values 0, one of the lines will connect the two endpoints.

The only tricky part is which side of the imaginary line each line is drawn on. The rule is this: If you consider every line to be drawn from left to right, the first line always appears *above* the imaginary line if the Double Width value is positive, and the second line will appear below. Negative values reverse the placement of the lines. Not every line in the drawing goes from left to right, of course, so you have to pretend that they do. In other words, if the second point is actually to the left of the first point, the first line will appear below these points, and the second above. If you turned the monitor upside down, the line *would* go from left to right, and the first line *would* be above the second. Another way to think of it is that if you consider all lines drawn from left to right to be going clockwise around some imaginary center, the first line is always placed to the *outside,* and the second line to the *inside,* as shown in Figure 9-5.

This conceptualization assumes that the values for Double Width are both positive. If the Double Width values are negative, simply reverse the line placements.

The Double Width command exists as a separate two-character command or as part of the Del Settings command on the DRAW menu. It can be activated by typing **TH** on the keyboard. (TH stands for THickness or widTH; take your pick.) When you select it, you are shown the current values and asked to specify new values. Type a number and press ENTER to set a new value for each, or simply press ENTER to leave the value as it is. Alternately, select Dbl Settings or type **DB**, then select each offset (**L** for Left, **R** for Right) individually.

Drawing Double Lines

Once you have set the Double Width variables, you are ready to draw Double Lines. Select Double Lines from the DRAW menu, or type **L2** on

FIGURE 9-5 How the first and second double lines are created

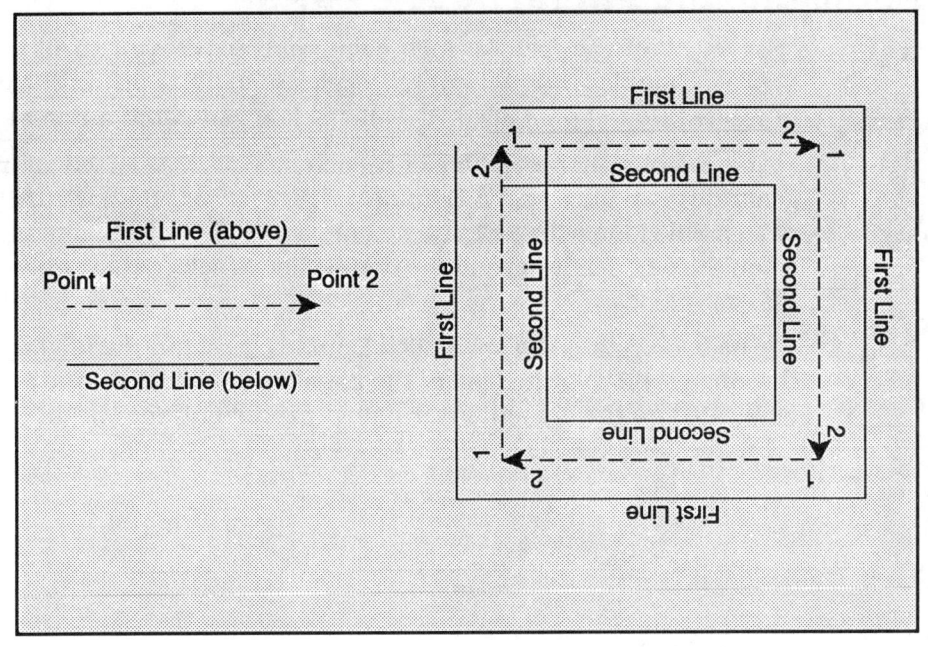

the keyboard. Just as in drawing a Straight Line, you are asked to specify endpoints. However, unlike the Line command, Double Lines does not return to the "Enter a command >" prompt immediately after you select the second point; you can keep picking points after the first two. The intersections between subsequent pairs of double lines are automatically adjusted as each new set of double lines is added, shortening or lengthening each side as required. When you have finished placing double lines, press ESC, type **PU**, or select a blank line from the video menu.

Each line created using the Double Lines command is an individual entity. The two sides of the double line have no built-in relationship. In the database, these entities behave exactly as if you had drawn one line and then the other, with two separate line commands. The Color, Width, and Type of these Lines are controlled by the current settings of the variables on the DISPLAY menu.

Automatically Filling Double Lines

A toggle of the Dbl Settings command allows you to fill the space between Double Lines. When this toggle, Solid (S), is on, an enclosed area is created that can be filled. The fill itself is generated automatically.

Instead of a simple double line, each new point selected after the first generates two lines and a Boundary Fill. Figure 9-6 shows the creation of a Double Line with Solid turned on. The Fill entity is actually created when the *next* point beyond the double line is selected, or when you type **PU** or press ESC.

The lines created by solid filled Double Lines and the fill itself take on the current fill color instead of the usual line color. All of the entities will be located on the current layer using the current line width.

FIGURE 9-6 The Line entities created by the Double Lines command with the Solid Fill command turned on

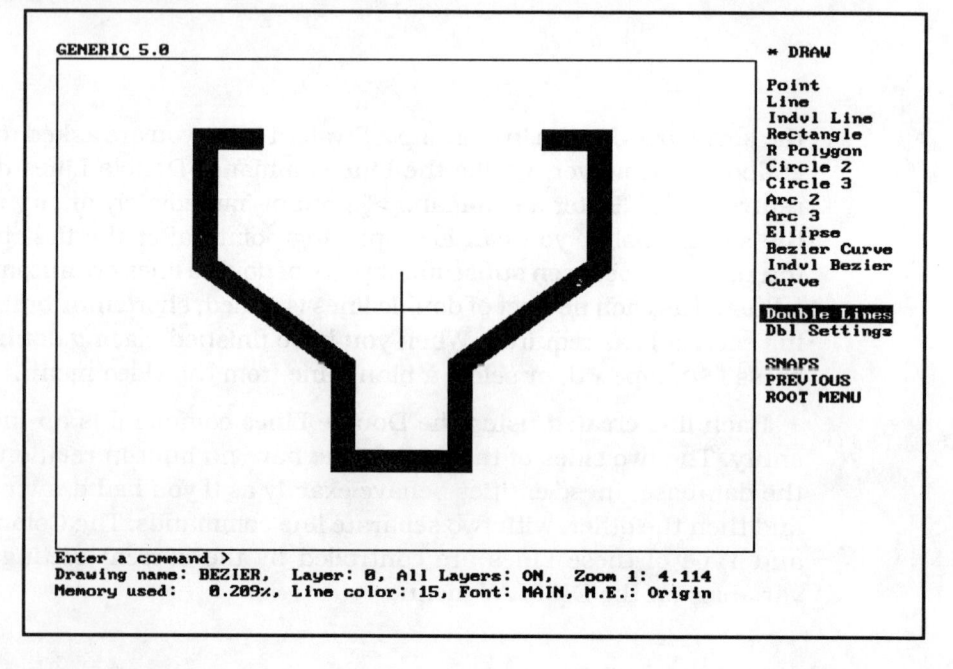

Chapter 9: Multiple Entities 273

Double Filleted Lines

If Autofilleting (AF) is on when you use the Double Line (L2) command, both lines will be filleted. The inside corner will use the specified Fillet Radius command (RF), and the outside radius will be adjusted to remain parallel. Autofilleting and Fillet Radius can also be turned on and off from within the Dbl Settings command, with the A and F options. If Solid is on, the areas bounded by the two arcs and the perpendicular connectors between the parallel lines will be filled as well. All entities will be in the current fill color, on the current layer. The Lines and Arcs will use the current line width. See Figure 9-7 for an example of a drawing made with filleted double lines.

Double Line Tips

A standard way of using double lines is to set one of the Double Width values to 0, usually the second one. One of the lines will then have as its endpoints the points that you specify when you place the Double Line.

FIGURE 9-7 Double filleted lines

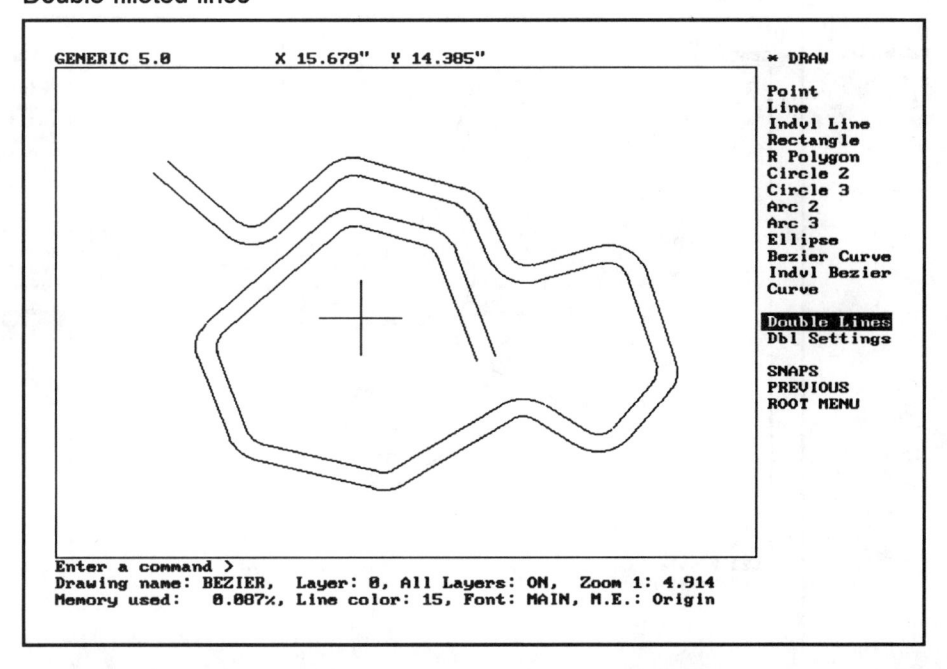

The other side of the double line will be offset by the distance specified. This allows you to snap one side of the double line exactly onto either the grid or existing points in the drawing.

Double lines can also be used for offsetting a pair of lines from an existing object. This can be done by specifying one positive and one negative value for the Double Width. Suppose that you want to draw a six-inch-thick wall ten feet above an existing wall. You could set your Double Width values to 10'6" and -10'0". If you then draw a double line by using Snap to Nearest Point on both ends of an existing wall, the first line will be drawn 10'6" above the existing wall. The second line will be drawn -10'0" below, or 10'0" above, the existing wall. As a result, you end up with one line 10' above and one line 10'6" above the existing wall, which creates a six-inch wall ten feet above the existing wall. Figure 9-8 shows how you can create a double line five feet from an existing figure by tracing around the figure with Double Width set at 5'6" and -5'0".

FIGURE 9-8 Offsetting a double line with a negative and positive value

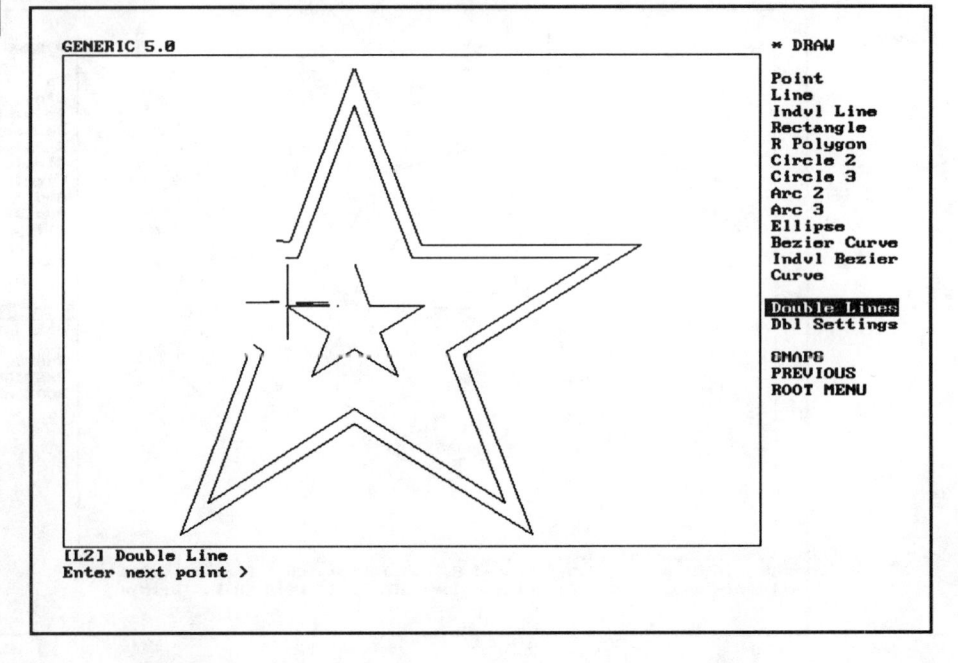

In this chapter, you have seen that the number of entities actually created by the Draw command varies. Some commands create a single simple entity, while others create either multiple simple entities or a combination of several simple and complex entities. The entities that are created by a given command are sometimes controlled by other mode- or parameter-setting commands.

It should be clear that there is not necessarily a direct relationship between the commands and the entities in all cases. Many of the commands that create multiple entities can be thought of more as "macro" or complex commands, aiding in the creation of simple shapes. As you will see in Chapter 15, you can invent your own menu items that act very much like these multiple-entity commands in order to create shapes that are not included with Generic CADD.

CHAPTER 10

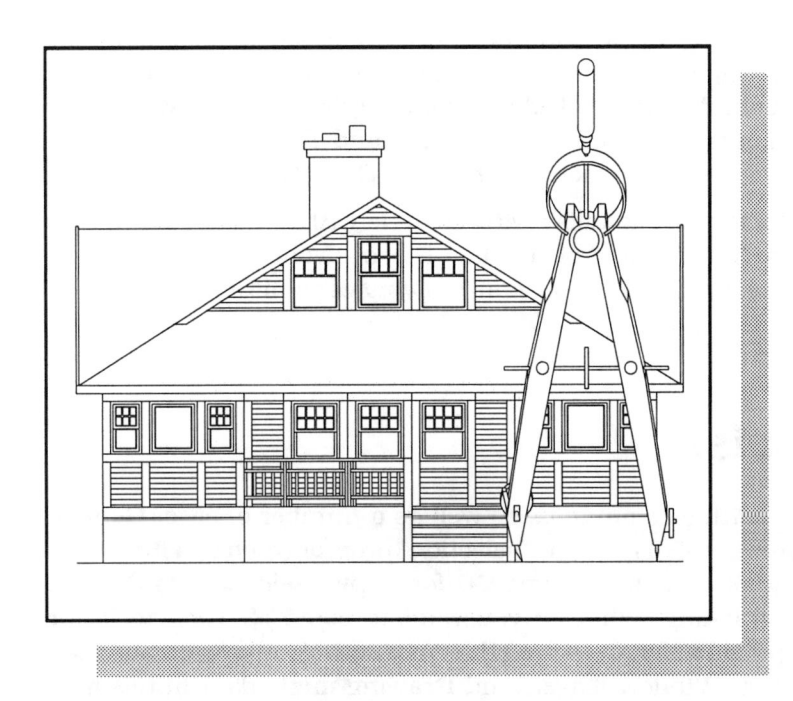

Advanced Drawing and Editing Techniques

In previous chapters, you learned several of the basic editing functions, together with four basic selection methods. The methods—Object, Window, Layer, and Drawing—can be combined with the functions—Erase, Move, Copy, Rotate, Change, and Scale—in two ways. The first is with Shortcuts. The Shortcuts, compatible with previous versions of Generic CADD, are a fast way of using commands such as Window Erase (WE), Object Change (OG), Drawing Rotate (DR), and so on. The second way is with the Master or Selection editing commands on the EDITS menu, new to Generic CADD 5.0, which provide even more powerful tools for manipulating your CADD drawings.

In addition, there are a number of editing-enhancement tools for working with particular entities, in specific situations, or in an unusual way, to make both drawing and editing commands more powerful. Many of these commands are found on the SNAPS and TRIMS menus, accessible either from the ROOT menu or from the DRAW and EDITS menus.

As you become more familiar with Generic CADD 5.0, you will find that editing is an integral part of drawing. These advanced, more powerful editing tools will greatly increase your drawing capabilities.

Selection Revisited

Most of the editing commands, as well as a number of other Generic CADD 5.0 commands, display the "selection" prompt when you first issue them. For example, when you type **CO** for Copy, "selection" is Generic CADD's way of asking "What do you want to copy?" Several tools, or methods, are provided for answering this question. You have already read about the Object, Window, Layer, and Drawing methods. Entities may be selected using any of these methods by simply typing the entity's letter or selecting it from the prompt, then using the appropriate method: pointing to an object, placing a window, or specifying a layer. (The drawing method requires no further input.) Each time you complete one of these methods, the selection prompt returns; you may continue using any method to select entities until you press ENTER. (Pressing the SPACEBAR repeats the same selection method.) Entities may be deselected as well, by holding down the CTRL key while choosing the method. Several more methods give you both more finesse and quicker access to the entities that you wish to select.

The Last Selection Method

Whenever you use the selection prompt to select entities, those entities remain available for automatic reselection with the Last Selection method. Instead of using more Object, Window, or other methods, simply initiate the command that you wish to perform and type **L** or choose Last Selection from the prompt. The same entities selected the last time you used Generic CADD will be selected again.

Suppose, for example, that you want to Scale and Move several entities. Start with the Scale (SZ) command, use whichever methods are required to select the entities, then specify the reference point and scale factors. The entities are now scaled. To move them, issue a Move (MV), and use Last Selection to select the entities. A reference point and new location are now all that you need.

A Special Command: Selection

Selection (SE) exists specifically for selecting entities without editing them. The Selection command is simply the selection prompt that you get with the editing commands, and you use it in exactly the same way. You select and deselect objects using any of the available methods, including Last Selection and Filter (discussed in the next section of this chapter).

While it may not be obvious at first, there are a number of reasons for this command to exist. Among these is the fact that during selection, the selected entities are counted. In the first line of the prompt, toward the right side of the screen, a message indicating "# objects =", is followed by a number. As entities are selected, this number increases accordingly. Selection, then, can be a convenient way to count entities. This technique will become even more useful when combined with Filtering.

A second use for the Selection command is to inquire about entities. The Screen Flip (SF) "List Objects in Drawing" function includes three options: View, Drawing, and Selected List. Selected List applies to entities selected the last time a selection prompt was used. This command gives you access to a selection prompt without editing anything, thus providing you with a means of selecting entities specifically for the purpose of listing them with this function.

Finally, it may be easier to separate the process of selection from the process of editing so that you can use other commands in between. For example, you might want to select some entities with Selection, draw a Line, Standard Point, or other entity, and then Move the selected entities (use Last Selection) using the new entities for reference. The entities added since the selection was used will not be a part of the selection list.

The creation of the Selection command from the editing commands themselves is a move toward a more sophisticated command structure. With Generic CADD 5.0, Generic Software has moved a step closer to a language-like interface, in which individual commands represent more discrete functions. These very specific commands can then be combined in numerous ways to perform unique and complex tasks.

The Filter Method

One further refinement of selection is provided as a part of every selection prompt, just like the Selection command. This is the Filter method, know in command form as Entity Filter (EF). It allows entities to be selected according to their characteristics rather than their location. Filtering might be thought of as a preselection technique rather than as another selection method, because the entities must be selected with another method before they are actually entered into the Selection List.

The characteristics by which entities can be filtered include Entity Type (Point, Line, Circle, Arc, and so on), Layer, Color, Line Type, and Line Width. These can be combined to create very specific descriptions, such as "Circles on Layer 5, Color 7, Line Type 12, Line Width 2," or less discrete specifications like "anything in Color 2." Any of the characteristics by which entities may be filtered can be set to ALL, which disables filtering by that characteristic. Selection without any filtering gives you the same results as setting all characteristics to ALL.

When the Filter function is invoked, either from the Selection prompt or from the Entity Filter (EF) command, the first prompt asks for an entity type by listing all of the possibilities. Each Entity Type includes a highlighted letter for a keyboard (or macro) entry. A message at the right side of the prompt normally indicates "Filter = OFF" unless you have prefiltered some entities and not used them. Type a letter or select an entity type from the prompt. If you don't care about entity type, select

ALL or type **A**. The message at the right will verify your selection. You may reselect an entity type if you change your mind or make a mistake. Press ENTER when your selection is as you want it. Note that you can filter either one entity type or all of them with a single command but you cannot filter for two or three of them this way. You cannot filter for all Circles and Arcs, for instance.

After you have selected an entity type, another prompt asks for Layer, Color, Line Type, and Line Width characteristics. You specify each of these by typing the appropriate letter (highlighted in the prompt) or selecting an option from the prompt, then specifying a value. If the video menu is active, each of these will activate a selection menu. All of these will default to ALL, unless you have changed them in a previous filtering operation. Selecting the ALL option from this prompt will return all four options to the ALL default. You can set as many or as few of these options as you like, and can reselect any that you have already set if you change your mind or make a mistake. If you decide not to proceed with the filtering, press ESC; otherwise, press ENTER when you are done specifying the characteristics to be filtered.

Once the filter has been set, it is considered to be on, and all further selection, *until after an editing operation has taken place,* will be subject to the limitations of the filter. When you use the Window method, for example, only those entities in the window that meet the specifications of the filter will be selected. There is no such thing as defiltering by combining CTRL with setting the filter. You can select all entities that meet the filtering criteria by using the Drawing selection method after setting the filter specifications.

While filtering is available as a part of every selection prompt, and can therefore be used with any editing function, it is particularly useful with the Change function, which changes the Layer, Color, Line Type, and Line Width characteristics of selected entities. When used with filtering, the Change commands become true Search and Replace functions, allowing you to change all red circles to blue, and the like.

Filtering the Shortcuts

Because the Entity Filter (EF) command is so readily available, the filter function is easily accessible even with the editing shortcuts. First, the filter is specified with the Entity Filter, and then the shortcut is used.

When you use Entity Filter this way, note that the filter always turns itself off after every editing function. If you set the filter, and then use Window Erase (WE), only the items in the window that meet the filter specifications will be erased. If you do *another* Window Erase, all entities in the window will be erased (assuming All Layers Edit is on) even if you place exactly the same window. The filter is ignored the second time because it was automatically turned off after the first Window Erase. Any of the editing shortcuts can make use of filtering in this way.

Turning the Filter On and Off

A filter that has been turned off by an editing command (such as Window Erase used in the previous section) may be turned back on simply by selecting the Filter option from the Filter prompt of any selection command or the Entity Filter (EF) command itself. In many instances, this is faster than respecifying the same filter again. This technique allows you to use several editing commands with the same filter. Set it the first time, then simply turn it on as the first action in each subsequent edit. Although you will not usually need to turn it off (remember, it is automatically turned off after each command), you *can* turn it off with the Filter option on the Filter prompt, which is a toggle.

Filtering by Comparison

All filtering characteristics can be set automatically by using the Like option of the Filter prompt. You select this option by choosing it from the prompt or by pressing the = key on the keyboard. You are then prompted to select an object. The Entity Type, Layer, Color, Line Type, and Line Width of this object are taken as the filter specification. Note that only the Entity Type is shown on the first prompt, and you must still press ENTER to move on to the second prompt, where the other four characteristics will be prespecified to those of the selected object. Press ENTER to complete filter specification, or change any of the characteristics that you wish.

As with the stand-alone Selection command, the availability of Filtering as an independent function seems to indicate that Generic Software is working toward developing a language-oriented command structure. These commands will offer even more power when a new macro and programming language becomes available.

The Like (=) Function

As with the filtering example just discussed, many parameter specifications throughout Generic CADD 5.0 may be specified by using the Like function. If there is an entity on the screen that currently exhibits the characteristic that you want to set, you can select the entity to derive that characteristic rather than typing the value yourself.

Suppose, for example, that you want to set the current Line Color to the same color as a line that you drew earlier. Instead of remembering and typing the same number again, simply press the = key when prompted for the color number by either the Line Color (LK) or Color Setting-Line (CS, L) command. When prompted, point to the object whose color you want to borrow. The current Line Color will be set to the extracted value. Almost every drawing parameter can be set in this way, including Text Size, Hatch Rotation, Component Scale, and the Dimensioning variables, just to name a few examples.

Like Everything!

Multiple parameters can be set simultaneously with the Match Parameters (MH) command. This command will set as many parameters as can be derived from any entity that you select. The actual parameters that will be set will vary from entity to entity, but since every entity has Layer, Color, Line Type, and Line Width parameters, at least these will be set. If you Match a Component, Component Scales and Rotation will be set as well. With Text, the Font, Size, Spacing parameters, Rotation, and so on will be derived. Be careful when using Match to set parameters, as the entity that you select may contain more parameters than you realize.

Multiple Color Selection

While most of the color parameters have their own specific commands, a single command is also provided for setting all of the entity colors simultaneously. The Color Settings (CS) command, identified as Color on the DISPLAY menu, provides access to the Line Color (LK or LC), Text Color (TC), Dimension and Attribute colors, and the Hatch (HK or HC) and Fill (FK or FC) colors. Each is selected by a highlighted letter or from the prompt, and can be set by typing a value or selecting from the menu.

Note Display Color and Cursor Color must be set with their own commands, DK and CK, respectively, or with the Display and Cursor options of the Display (DI) command.

Damage Control

Sometimes editing or drawing commands go awry. Maybe you forgot that All Layers Edit was on, and you copied too many entities. Or maybe you typed **WE** when you meant to type **WH**. One of the most entertaining and devastating errors you can make is Stretching a portion of your drawing by specifying what you intend as Manual Entry Relative Coordinates and finding out by the results that Manual Entry was set to Origin instead. Talk about major unintentional design changes!

Several commands are available to deal with this type of situation. Some of these are old standbys and others are new to Generic CADD 5.0. These commands should alleviate any fear you might have about trying other commands. Even if a command does not do exactly what you expected, you can always switch things back to the way they were—instantly.

Remember There is no substitute for saving your drawing often. Even the commands you're about to learn won't help in the event of the mythical power failure software companies always warn you about, or the more inevitable fatal system crash. The command is DS on the keyboard, and if you assigned a name when you started CADD and/or loaded the drawing, you can just press ENTER to use the same name. The Rename option in fact provides one more level of security, in case of hardware problems with the original file or indigestion by the software.

I Didn't Mean To—The Undo Command

There is an item at the bottom of the EDITS menu that really doesn't belong there—at least it doesn't belong *just* there. The Undo command (along with the Redo command, discussed next) works with any entity creating or editing command, and would be at home on the DRAW, TRIMS, TEXT, COMPONENTS, DIMENSIONS, and HATCH/FILL menus. You can even Undo naming a layer, so it would also come in handy on the LAYERS menu!

The keyboard characters typed for Undo, OO, make the purpose of the Undo command clear—as in Oh-Oh, better try that again. The Undo command is designed to deal with those situations in which the command, for whatever reason, didn't do what you thought (or hoped) it would. While the actions of almost every command can be undone manually, Undo makes reversing an action a lot easier.

In fact, Undo goes somewhat further than just fixing up the last errant command. Because you can Undo 25 commands in succession (or back to the last point at which the database was packed—more on packed data shortly), Undo allows you to try out experimental drawing and editing combinations, and then Undo them if they don't work. You can try moving a line here and a circle there, rotating this a bit, and rescaling that. Not happy with the result? Change it back by typing **OO** with as many SPACEBAR taps (SPACEBAR repeats the OO function) as you need to get back to where you started, and try something else.

Users of Generic 3D (also known as Generic 3D Drafting) will recognize the command as one of their favorites. It was first introduced with Generic 3D to deal with the added complexity of drawing in three dimensions. Because 3D is a design tool, it had to give designers the ability to experiment. The effects of some drawing and editing commands are harder to visualize in 3D, so a better safety net was required. Undo worked so well that it was brought into this release of CADD, and enhanced with its new partner, Redo.

Yes, I Did Mean To—The Redo Command

Because Undo undoes one command after another, in succession, you can't Undo an Undo. You can, however, Redo an Undo. Redo is available for those situations in which you Undo more than you wanted to, or when you have second thoughts and think maybe it *was* right the way that you had it.

The two-character command for Redo, UU, isn't quite as memorable as OO. While OO enjoys the distinction of being the only two-character command that is a meaningful pronounceable word (as well as an abbreviation for Oops), UU can be remembered as standing for Un-Undo. The fact that it is the only other double-identical vowel command gives it perhaps a little more distinction.

What Have I Undone?

Almost any command that makes an addition or change to the database can be Undone and Redone. However, the previous condition must exist in memory for the Undo to work. Generic CADD 5.0 keeps track of changes to the database during your drawing session, so you can Undo and Redo up to the start of a drawing session, with these exceptions:

- *You cannot Undo changes made in a previous drawing session.* When a drawing is loaded from disk, all changes made after the load can be undone, but if you try to go any further than that, the drawing will be unloaded.

- *You cannot Undo a Drawing Erase (DX) command.* The drawing memory is cleared when this command is executed, including the information about changes to the database. The only way to reverse a Drawing Erase is to load the drawing again, assuming that you saved it.

- *You cannot Undo past the point at which a Pack Data (PD) command was executed.* Pack Data is used specifically to release the memory area where erased entities and database changes are stored. This provides more memory for new entities, but sacrifices the ability to Undo, Unerase, and Redo. As a Definition Unload (DU) command automatically issues a Pack Data, you cannot Undo beyond the point at which a DU was done either. The same is true for any other command or macro that issues a Pack Data.

- *While a Drawing Origin (DO) command changes the database, it cannot be Undone.* A prompt-area message warns you of this fact when the command is issued. This command changes not only the coordinates of every single definition point of every entity in the database, but the point of reference for all new entities as well. Such a fundamental change cannot be reversed by a simple OO. If you need to be able to put the Origin back to a specific place, put an entity marker such as a Standard Point there, so that you can Snap onto it later with another DO command.

- *Redo must follow Undo before any other changes in the database occur.* While you can Undo almost anything, the only thing that you can Redo is an Undo. And you can Redo lots of them, *if* they were executed sequentially without other database changes in between. You can go back and forth, Undo, Undo, Undo, Redo, Redo, Redo, Undo, Undo, Undo, with no problem. But throw in a single Object Erase command and the game's over. Sure, you can Undo it, and Redo it too, but you can't Redo an Undo that happened before the edit.

More About the Pack Data Command

If you work on your Generic CADD drawing for a long time in one drawing session, more and more of your computer's available memory will fill up. Much of this, of course, is due to the additional entities that you are creating and placing into the drawing. However, even if you just move things around, change their properties, and erase as many things as you draw, your memory gets used up.

All of the erased entities and database changes that you make as you go are still floating around out there; you can Unerase and Undo them should the need arise. It takes memory to keep track of these, so the longer you work the more memory you use. The Pack Data (PD) command provides a quick method for retrieving this memory for other uses, specifically the storage of new drawing entities, or the loading of larger files from disk.

When you save your drawings, the erased entities and a history of database changes are not stored with it, so the number of changes that you make to the drawing does not impact its final file size (unless you add more entities than you erase or vice-versa). Similarly, when you load a file from disk, only the entities that survived the last save are loaded. A file loaded from disk never brings with it erased entities or database change information.

Both the Drawing Erase (DX) and Definition Unload (DU) commands perform automatic Pack Data functions, in addition to their other memory-releasing tasks.

Definitions

Most of Generic CADD 5.0's complex entities use definitions stored in the database and in memory. When you create a component, for example, the definition of your component is stored once, and then used whenever the component is placed. This saves space in memory and on the disk, because the entities that make up the component don't have to be stored several times. The only information stored at the placement is the name, location, basic entity parameters such as Layer and Color, and parameters specific to component placements, such as Rotation and Scale.

As long as there is at least one placement of a complex entity in the drawing, the definition of that entity will be saved along with the drawing file. If there are no instances of the entity, its definition is not saved. This is true for Components, Text Characters, Hatches, Fills, and Attributes. Associative Dimensions all conform to a set definition that is part of the program and never saved with the drawing file. The parameter settings for all of these, on the other hand, are always saved as part of the drawing environment, which is saved with every Generic CADD 5.0 drawing file.

Hatches are implemented as defined entities because of the amount of space that they take up in the database, and so that they are *protected* from being edited accidentally. Once an area has been hatched, a definition for the hatch is created and stored in the drawing file; the hatch that you see is actually a one-time placement of this definition. This way, if you ever copy or move the hatch, every entity doesn't have to be re-created in the new location. The definition stays the same and the location simply changes, or additional locations are added. This greatly improves both speed and memory usages in cases where hatches are copied, with little disadvantage where they are used only once. In fact, the advantage of this scheme for single-placement hatches is that they don't get accidentally moved or partially erased. Acting as a placement of a definition, the hatch always hangs together. Fills operate in much the same manner, because, technically, they are implemented somewhat as simplified hatches.

Attribute definitions are discussed in detail in Chapter 17, "Communicating with Other Programs." Simply note here that they are defined by the user, and like components, may or may not ever actually be used in the final drawing.

Eliminating Ghosts in the Attic with the Definition Unload Command

With the separation of the definitions from the placements of Components, Text, Hatches, Fills, and Attributes, it should be clear that from time to time you will end up with unused definitions floating around clogging up your computer's memory. When you save the drawing and end the Generic CADD session, of course, these unused definitions are expelled from memory, and will not be in your way the next time you begin to draw. But there are less drastic means than exiting CADD for exorcising these unwanted guests to retrieve that memory.

Pack Data's not quite strong enough for the task, although it's good for cleaning up erased entities and database change history, as discussed previously. Using Drawing Erase is a lot like throwing the baby out with the bath water: the definitions will be gone, and you'll have plenty of free memory, but no drawing (unless you saved it on disk).

Definition Unload (DU) on the FILE menu is the command for the job. It includes options for unloading (removing from memory) only a specific type of definition, Text, Component, Hatch, Fill, or Attribute, or All unused definitions regardless of type.

Text definitions rank among the worst offenders for loitering in your drawing space. When you select and use a font, all of the definitions for all of the characters are loaded, even though you might only need a few. Previous versions of Generic CADD automatically unloaded all current character definitions whenever a new font was loaded. In 5.0 they hang around until you make them leave. This can be desirable behavior if you have plenty of memory and want to be able to switch back and forth among several fonts at will. If you need the space, though, unloading unused character definitions is a good place to start.

When you select an option from the prompt or type its letter, all unused definitions of the specified type are immediately removed, the database is packed, and the command is ended. To remove definitions of another type, you must reselect the command (you can press the SPACEBAR), and select another option. Of course, selecting ALL the first time circumvents this, but may remove more than you need.

Additional Editing Functions

Previous chapters have discussed the basic editing functions, Erase, Move, Copy, Change, Stretch, Rotate, and Scale. These are found on the EDITS and the SHORTCUTS menus. Several more complex editing functions exist, scattered among the various menus wherever they fit in.

Copying Around a Circle

The Radial Copy (RC) command on the EDITS menu copies objects in a circular pattern. As with the rest of the editing commands, entities may be selected by any of the selection methods, including Last Selection and Filtering (discussed earlier in this chapter). Additional information required by the command includes the centerpoint around which to make the copies, the portion of a circle (from 0 to 360 degrees) around which you want to copy the selected objects, and the total number of copies that you want, including the original.

Setting a Round Table

Try using Radial Copy on one of the place settings in the DINNER drawing (see Chapter 8, "Complex Entities"). To start, call up that drawing and Zoom Out (ZO). Place a PLACESET component using Component Place (CP), putting it into a blank area to the left or right of the table, and then Zoom In (ZI) on the area around the new place setting. For a screen center, pick a point above the PLACESET that you have just placed. Your screen should resemble the one shown in Figure 10-1.

Select Radial Copy from the EDITS menu or type **RC** on the keyboard. Select the Window option from the prompt or type **W**. Place a Window around the PLACESET component, keeping in mind that you need only enclose its reference point within the window to select it. Press ENTER to end selection and continue the command. Next, place the axis point directly above the PLACESET, a few feet away, as shown in Figure 10-2.

FIGURE 10-1 One PLACESET component ready to be radially copied

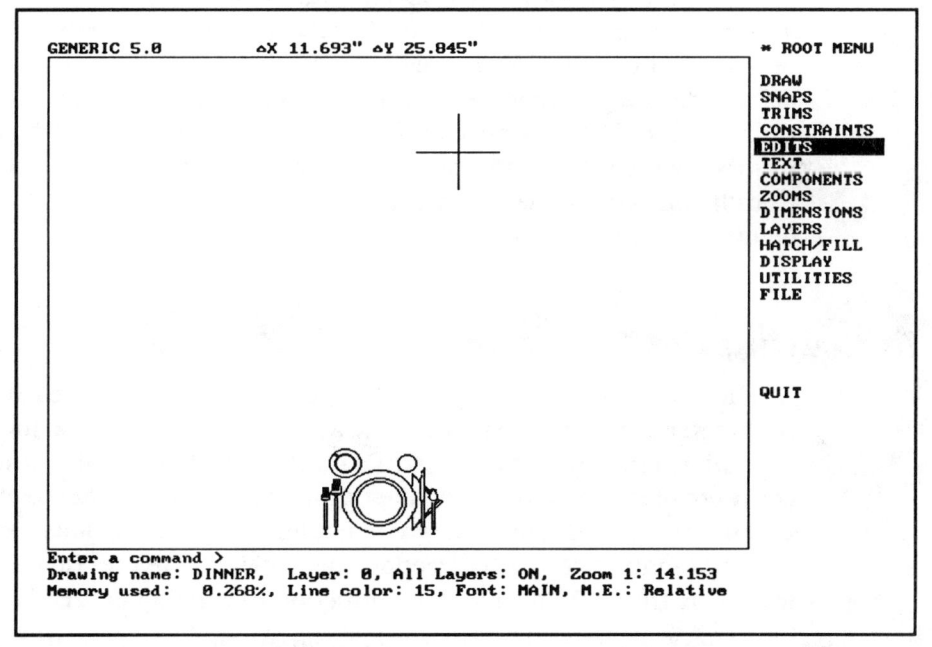

When asked for the number of degrees to span, type **360**, for a full circle. Finally, type **6** for the total number of copies, including the original. The Radial Copy command will be executed, resulting in a drawing much like Figure 10-3.

Total Items Versus Number of Copies

Notice that the number specified works differently in the Radial Copy command than in the other Copy commands. In Copy, Window Copy, and other Copy commands, you specify the number of copies that you want, not including the original. This means that if you have one object and you make one copy, you end up with two objects. This makes perfect sense when copying in a straight line, and specifying the distance between copies by a displacement, or two points. However, in the Radial Copy command, you specify the *total* number of objects, including the original. Therefore, you need to specify at least two objects in order for the command to work at all.

Although this procedure may sound awkward at first, it is much more convenient in practice when working with objects copied around a circle. When specifying four objects, for instance, you are probably thinking of one facing in each of four direction, up, down, left, and right. Selecting six objects, as you have seen, places them 60 degrees apart. In general, the number that you specify for degrees of a circle is divided by the number of items to obtain the angle between copies. This is more intuitive than if you had to specify, say, seven copies when what you want is an octagonal configuration.

Indicating the Direction

The direction of the copying is specified by the degrees of a circle parameter. The protocol is the same as the standard method for measuring all angles in Generic CADD 5.0. Positive angles indicate a counterclockwise direction, while negative angles translate to clockwise. If you are copying around a whole circle, as in the previous example, it does not matter in which direction the copies are made. However, if you want less than 360 degrees, the direction of copying is very important.

To see the effect of the copying direction, place another PLACESET in a blank part of the drawing at a 30-degree Component Rotation (CR).

Chapter 10: Advanced Drawing and Editing Techniques 293

FIGURE 10-2 Placing an axis point for the Radial Copy command

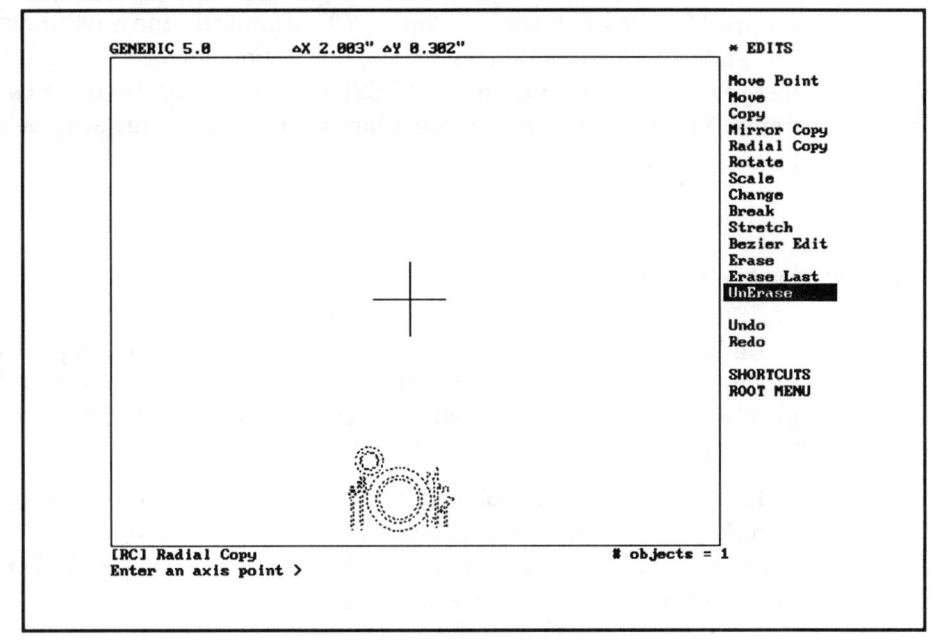

FIGURE 10-3 Six PLACESET components after the Radial Copy

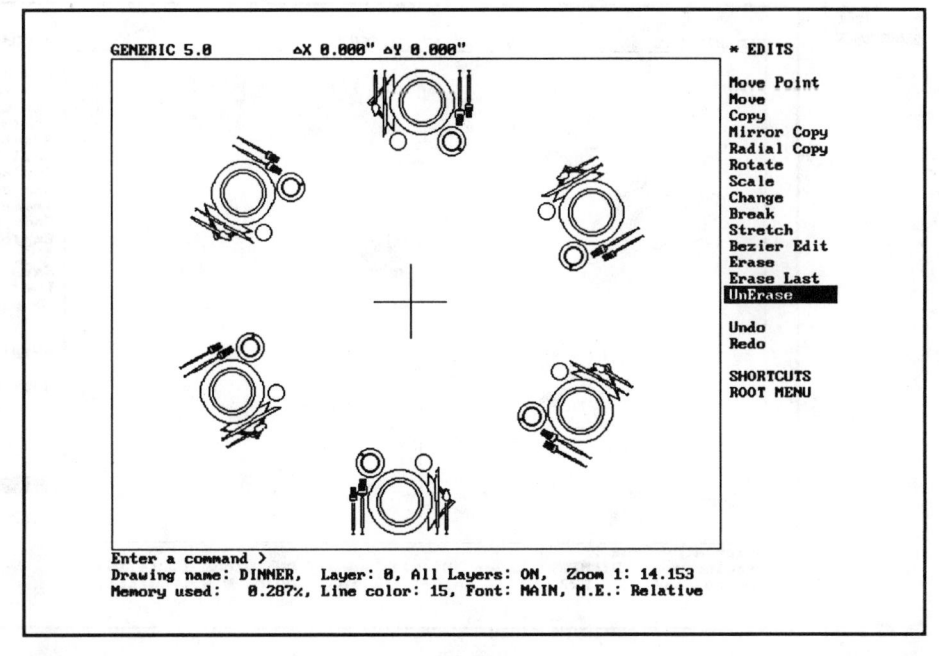

Zoom or Pan until the PLACESET is to the left side of the screen as in Figure 10-4. Issue a Radial Copy (RC) command, use a window to select the PLACESET, press ENTER to move on, then select an axis point a few feet to the lower right of the PLACESET, and specify -60 degrees and four items. You should see the four placesettings along an arc, as shown in Figure 10-5.

A Variety of Effects

Radial Copy can also be used to copy an object on top of itself, by placing the axis point in the center, or near the center, of a simple object, as opposed to at some distance away from the object. Figure 10-6 illustrates some of the possibilities.

Radial Copy can also place text along the periphery of arcs and circles. Simply place a single Text Character (TP), use the Radial Copy command to replicate it, then edit the copies with the Text Replace (TX) command. They will retain their placement and rotation.

FIGURE 10-4 One PLACESET component ready for another Radial Copy

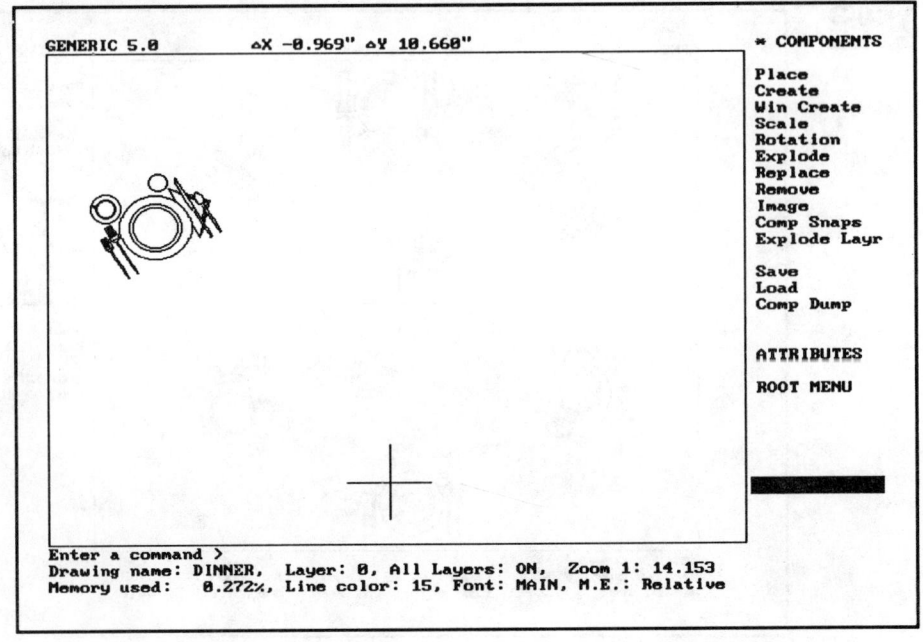

Chapter 10: Advanced Drawing and Editing Techniques 295

FIGURE 10-5 Four PLACESET components radially copied along an arc

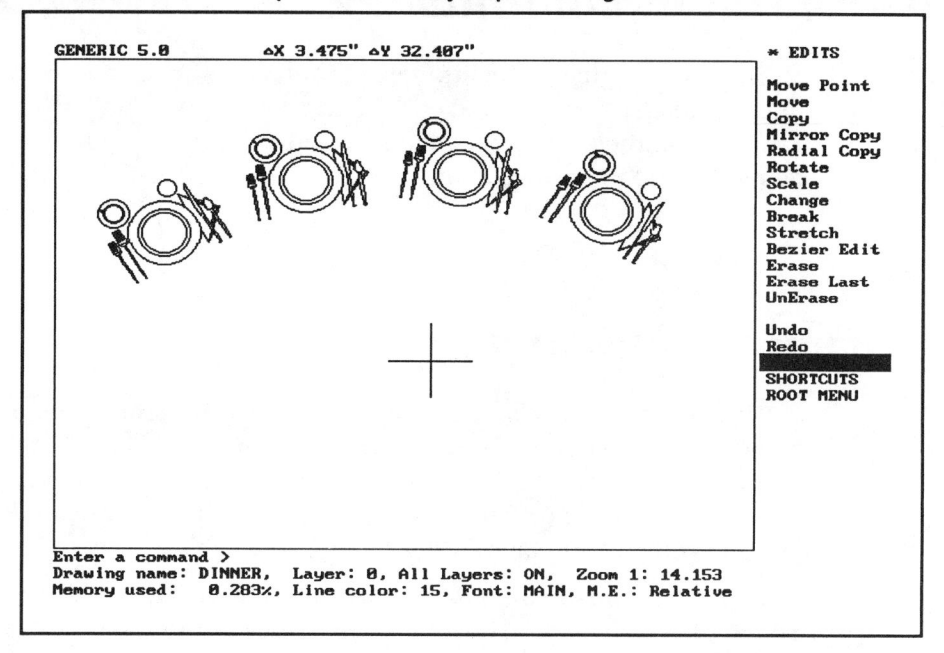

FIGURE 10-6 A variety of effects produced with the Radial Copy command

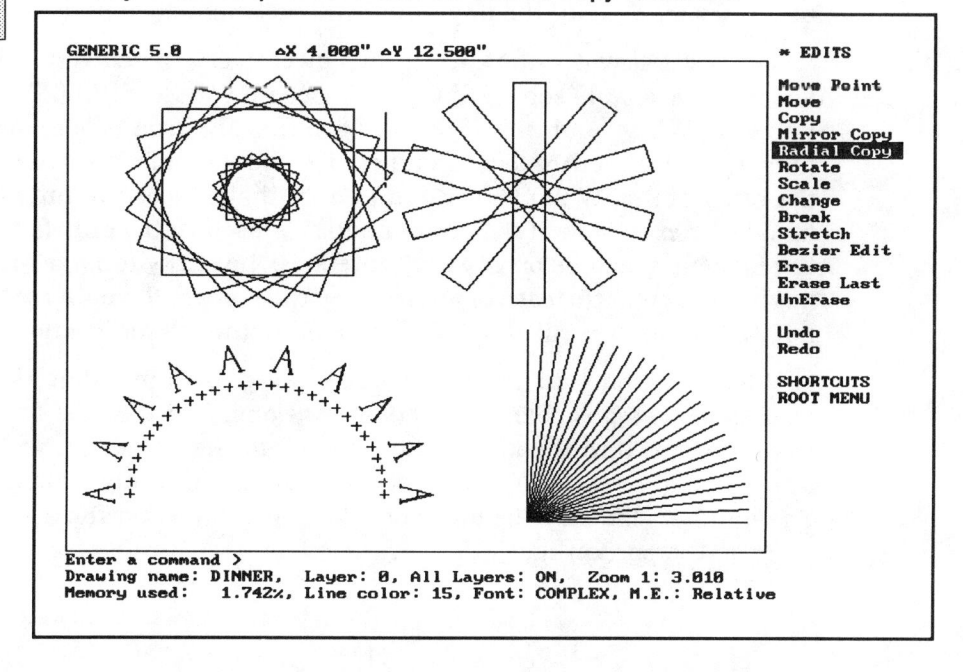

The Trim Commands

Yet another group of editing commands can be found on the TRIMS menu. Not all of the selected entities are actually modified with all of the Trim commands. These commands edit or modify existing entities depending upon their relationships to other entities.

Trimming Lines and Arcs

The first command on the TRIMS menu is the Trim command itself, typed **RM** (for tRiM) on the keyboard. Lines and Arcs can be trimmed to other Lines and Arcs, or to Circles. Trimming essentially means shortening, or removing a portion of a Line or Arc that currently extends beyond another intersecting Line, Arc, or Circle.

To trim a Line or Arc, select Trim from the TRIMS menu or type **RM**. You are asked to choose the object that you want to trim. Make sure that the point that you use to select it is on the side of the entity that you want to keep. Next you are asked for the entity to trim to. Select this boundary entity, and the first entity will be trimmed back to meet it.

The point at which the two entities meet is calculated very precisely, not to the available screen resolution. Even if you Zoom In (ZI) or Zoom Window (ZW) several times, you will see that the trim is very accurate. In fact, the Line or Arc to be trimmed does not actually have to intersect the other entity. When you trim an entity that it does not intersect, an imaginary extension of the second entity is used to trim the first one. If the imaginary extension does not intersect the entity to be trimmed, as might happen in the case of an Arc or parallel lines, the entity will either not be trimmed or will simply be trimmed to the cursor location.

When trimming to Arcs or Circles, keep in mind that there are sometimes two possible intersection locations, and that the first entity will be trimmed to the intersection closest to the point that you use to select it. Figure 10-7 illustrates some examples of trimming conditions. The numbers indicate the order of selecting points, and the dotted lines indicate the portion that will be trimmed off.

Extending Lines and Arcs

The opposite of the Trim command is the Extend command, also found on the TRIMS menu, and activated by typing **XT** (for eXTend) on the keyboard. As its name implies, the Extend command stretches or extends one entity to meet another. Lines and Arcs can be extended to meet Lines, Arcs, or Circles.

You can use the Extend command whenever you have a Line or an Arc that does not quite meet another Line, Arc, or Circle. Select Extend from the TRIMS menu or type **XT**, and you will be asked to select the entity you want to extend. After you select the entity, you are asked which entity you want to extend to. Once you select this second entity, the first entity will be extended.

As with the Trim command, you can use the Extend command to extend a Line or Arc to an imaginary extension of the boundary entity. If the entity to be extended does not meet either the actual boundary entity

FIGURE 10-7 Examples of trimming conditions

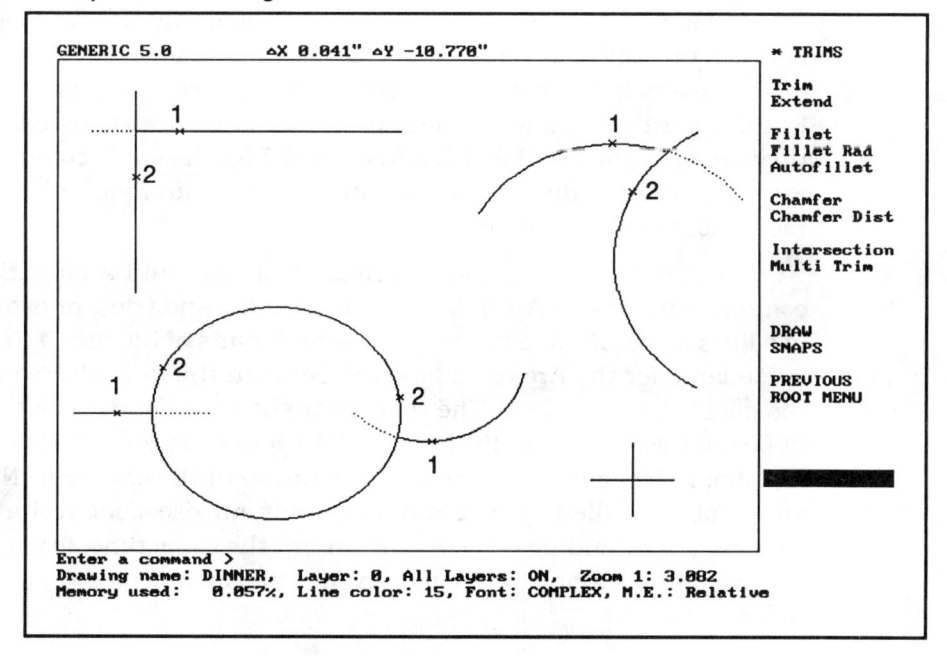

or its imaginary extension, the entity will either not be trimmed or will be trimmed arbitrarily to the cursor location.

When you are working only with Lines, Trim and Extend are pretty much interchangeable. Trim will automatically extend a Line if necessary, and Extend will return the favor and perform a Trim. This is very convenient for editing, as you can Trim or Extend Lines by issuing either command, selecting two entities, pressing the SPACEBAR, selecting two more entities, and so on. Note that if several lines need to be trimmed to the same boundary entity, you can use the Multi-Trim command discussed later in this chapter.

If Arcs or Circles are involved, either as the entity to be trimmed or extended or as the boundary entity, you have to be more precise about using the proper command, as there is likely to be more than one intersection point possible between the entities. Trim will always cut off part of the entity selected, and Extend will always add to it in these cases.

Manually Filleting Lines and Arcs

Two Lines can be trimmed simultaneously, or an Arc can be inserted between two Lines or two Arcs with the Fillet command. Arcs are inserted in a manner similar to the Auto-Fillet command (see Chapter 9, "Multiple Entities"), except that it is done after the Lines are drawn instead of while they are being drawn. Fillet Radius (FR or RF), the same command that establishes the radius of the arc inserted by Auto-Fillet, also sets the radius for the Fillet command.

When used on two Lines, two Arcs, or an Arc and a Line, the Fillet command inserts an Arc of the specified radius and trims or extends the two lines as required to meet the exact endpoints of the Arc. If the radius is too large for the Arc to be inserted between the two selected entities, the fillet will not be done. The radius cannot, by definition, be too small. In fact, if the radius specified by the Fillet Radius is zero, the two entities are simply trimmed or extended as required until they meet. No Arc is added at all. Filleting with radius zero is an excellent technique for trimming or extending two Lines or Arcs at the same time, to each other. Parallel lines cannot be filleted, even with an arc of the appropriate radius.

The Color, Line Type, and Line Width of the inserted Arc are derived from the second entity selected. In other words, if you fillet a blue line to a red line, you will get a red arc inserted. In addition, the first line will turn red to match. When you have finished the fillet, all three entities will be the same Color, Line Type, and Line Width. This means that if the two entities are different in any of these attributes, it matters which entity you select first. The original entities retain their layers, while the newly inserted Arc takes on the current layer.

To fillet two Lines, two Arcs, or a Line to an Arc, first set the radius using the Fillet Radius (FR or RF) command. Then select Fillet from the TRIMS menu or type **FL** on the keyboard. You are asked to select one entity and then the other. As soon as both entities have been selected, the fillet will occur.

Chamfering Lines

The Chamfer command on the TRIMS menu, typed **CH** on the keyboard, is similar in many ways to the Fillet command. Instead of inserting an Arc, the Chamfer command inserts a Line near the intersection of two selected Lines. Arcs cannot be chamfered. Chamfer works with a control variable, similar to Fillet Radius, called *Chamfer Distances.* This command, shortened to Chamfer Dist on the TRIMS menu and typed **CA** on the keyboard, sets the distances from the intersection at which the endpoints of the new line will be placed. Two values need to be supplied: one for the endpoint on the first line selected, and one for the endpoint on the second line.

Figure 10-8 shows the relationship between the two lines, their intersection point, and the Chamfer Distances. As with the Fillet command, the two lines are trimmed or extended as required to meet the endpoints of the new line exactly. Note that the Chamfer Distances are measured from the intersection of the two lines selected, not from their original endpoints. The Color, Line Type, and Line Width of all three entities are absorbed from the second Line selected, just as with Fillet. If either of the values specified by the Chamfer Distances is zero, the Chamfer command will act just like a fillet with radius zero.

How a Line is inserted by the Chamfer command

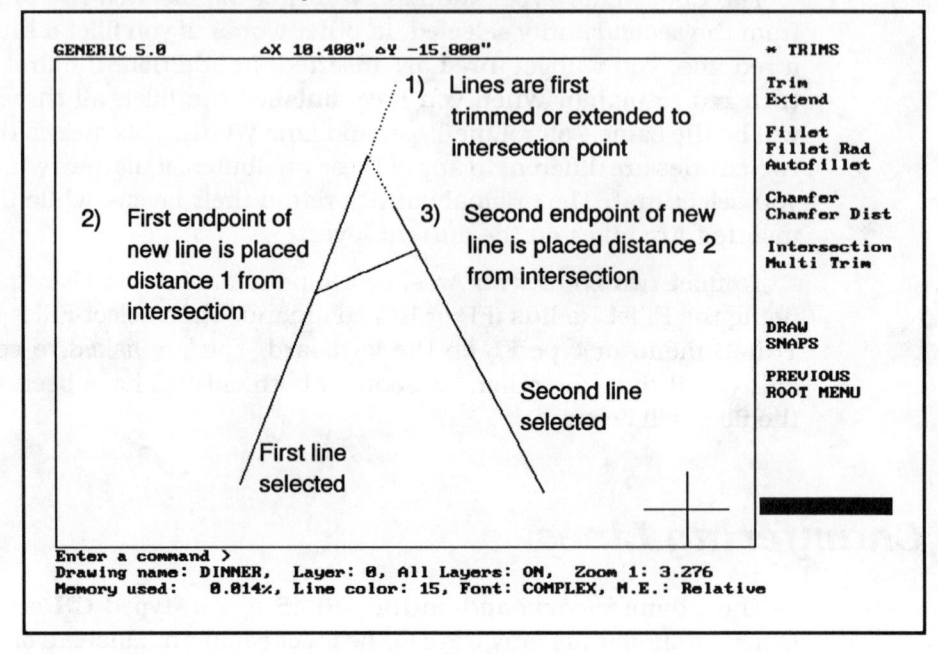

FIGURE 10-8

Filleting Four Lines at the Same Time

A more powerful trimming command for intersections of two sets of parallel lines is available as Intersection Trim, also located on the TRIMS menu, and typed **IT**. (The old two-character command **KT** for Korner Trim still works here as well.) Figure 10-9 shows three examples of the type of condition that this command was meant for. These three sets of lines could have been created at any time with the Line command, or with Double Line (L2), as long as each is a separate entity and not part of a component or hatch pattern. The Lines do not have to intersect at exactly right angles, nor do the individual pairs need to be exactly parallel. As long as one pair extends beyond the other pair so that there are true intersections between every set of lines, this command can be used.

To use Intersection Trim, select it from the TRIMS menu or type **IT** or **KT** on the keyboard. You will be asked to select a point inside the intersection, as shown in Figure 10-10. The second prompt asks you to enter a point outside the corner, which allows you to select a number of

Chapter 10: Advanced Drawing and Editing Techniques 301

FIGURE 10-9 Three intersecting sets of parallel lines

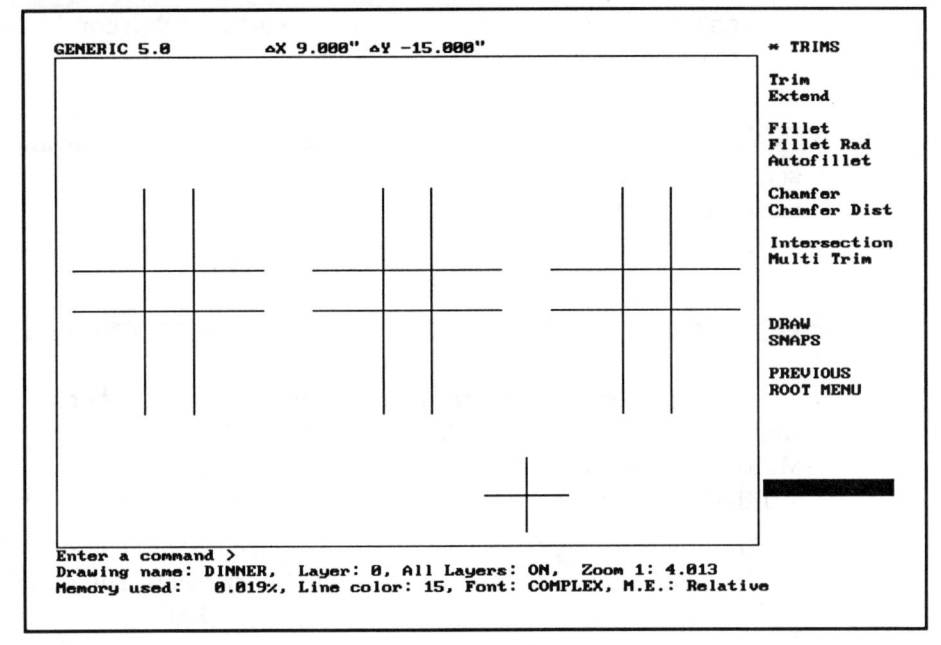

possible variations on the results of this command, three of which follow. (Rubberbanding is implemented to show the effect of each of these choices as you move the cursor.)

1. If you pick a second point inside the intersection, all four lines are broken and trimmed, as shown on the extreme left of Figure 10-11. The Layer, Colors, Line Type, and Line Width of all four lines are preserved.

2. If you choose a point outside the intersection between two perpendicular lines, as shown in Figure 10-12, the lines are trimmed so that the opposite corner remains. The selected point should be located within the corner established by the perpendicular lines, not beyond the length of either.

3. If you select a point outside the intersection but between two of the parallel lines, that set of lines will be trimmed off, and the remaining lines will form a "T" figure, as shown in the far-right drawing in Figure 10-13. Again, if your second point is beyond the endpoint of

either line, the command will probably not work properly. This is one reason that you must have a true intersection condition in order to use this command.

Again, note that the effect of your choice of points is previewed on the screen as you move the cursor around, so that you can select your point correctly, as there are nine possibilities in all.

The Buzz Saw—The Multi-Trim Command

One more very powerful trim, on the top of the wish list of many veteran Generic CADD users, has been incorporated into Generic CADD 5.0. Multi-Trim is located on the TRIMS menu and typed **MT** on the keyboard. Multi-Trim trims a number of lines to a single Line, Arc, or Circle.

Multi-Trim incorporates a selection prompt, so you can use whichever method you want to select the entities to be trimmed. You can select any

FIGURE 10-10 Picking the first point inside the intersection

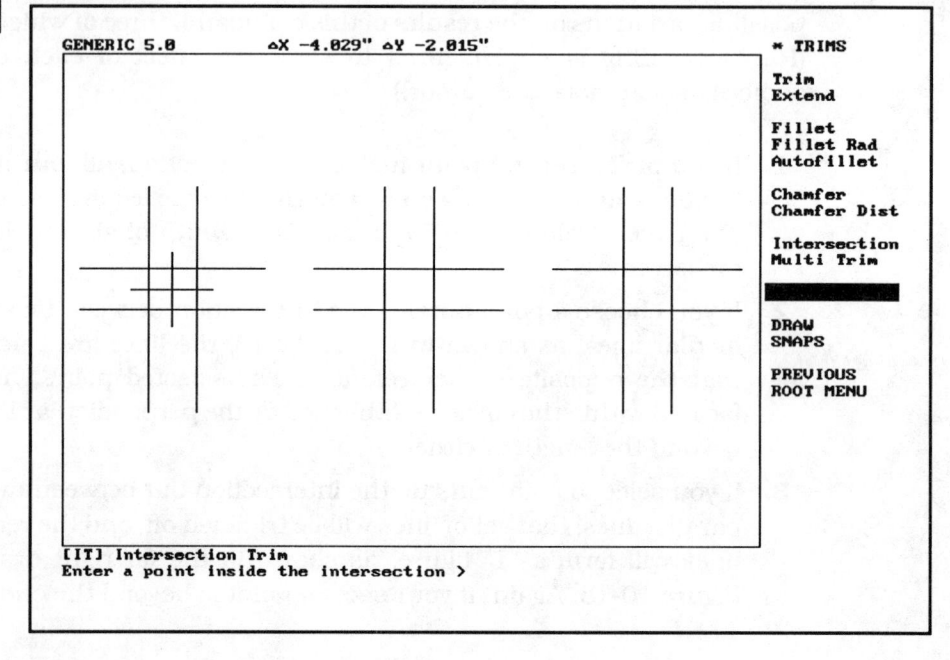

FIGURE 10-11 A four-way trimmed intersection

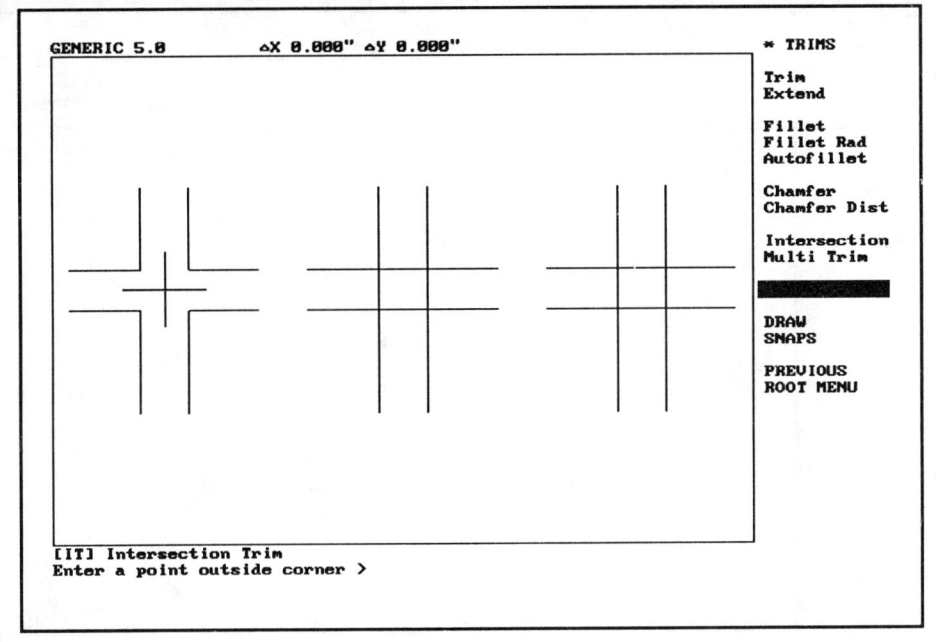

FIGURE 10-12 Picking a point to create a corner intersection

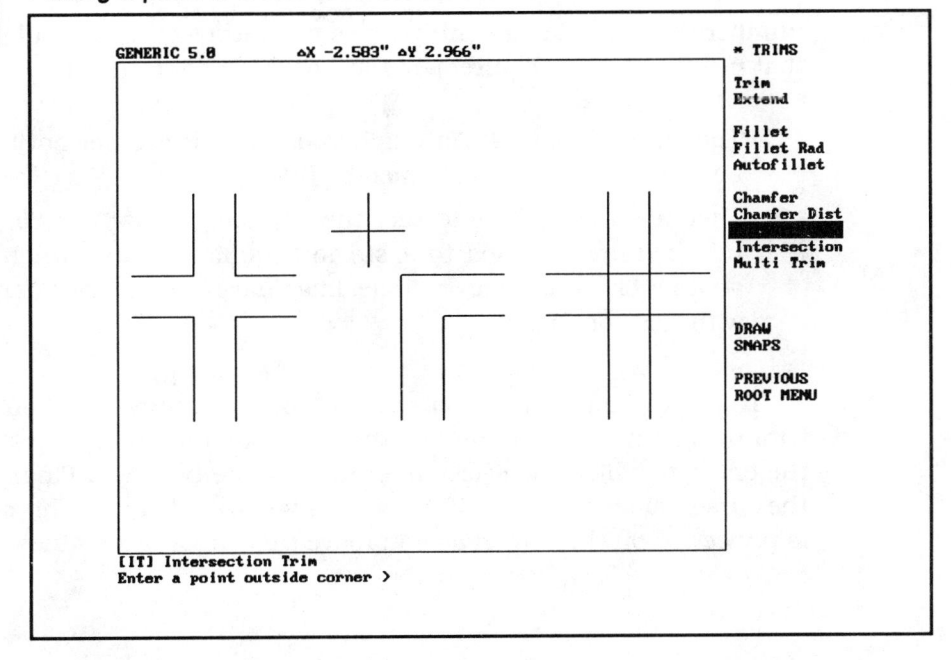

FIGURE 10-13 Picking a point to create a "T" intersection

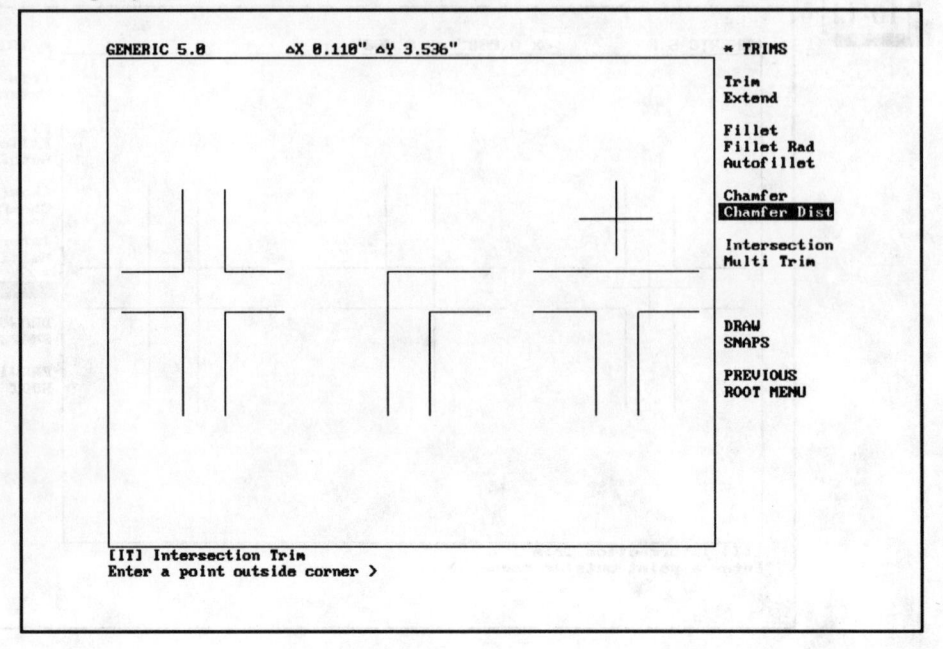

number that you like; all entity types can be selected, but only entities that meet these two requirements will actually be trimmed:

1. They must be Lines. Although you can select other entities, only Lines will actually be trimmed by this command.
2. They must actually intersect the trimming entity. All Lines to be trimmed are trimmed to a single trimming entity, which can be another Line or an Arc or Circle. Imaginary intersections don't count with this command.

To use the command, first select all of the entities that you wish to trim using any selection method that you like, then press ENTER. Select the entity to which the selected entities will be trimmed. Finally, using the cursor, choose the side of the entities you want to keep. This selection is previewed on the screen as you move the cursor. All entities must be

Chapter 10: Advanced Drawing and Editing Techniques 305

trimmed to the same side of the Line or Arc selected, or in the case of a Circle, to the inside or the outside. When the rubberbanding preview shows the side that you want, press the first button on the pointing device or ENTER on the keyboard.

Figures 10-14 and 10-15 illustrate the capabilities of this command. The leftmost drawing in each figure shows the entities before trimming, and the two possible trim conditions, selectable with the cursor, are shown to the right. The entities in Figure 10-15 were selected by putting a window around everything. The Circle could be deselected with CTRL-O, but it won't be trimmed anyway, since it's not a Line. As you can see, this command can save a lot of time over individual Trim commands. It can even incorporate an Object Break command when a Line passes all the way through a Circle, to find intersections automatically.

FIGURE 10-14 Before, and the two possibilities after, a Multi-Trim

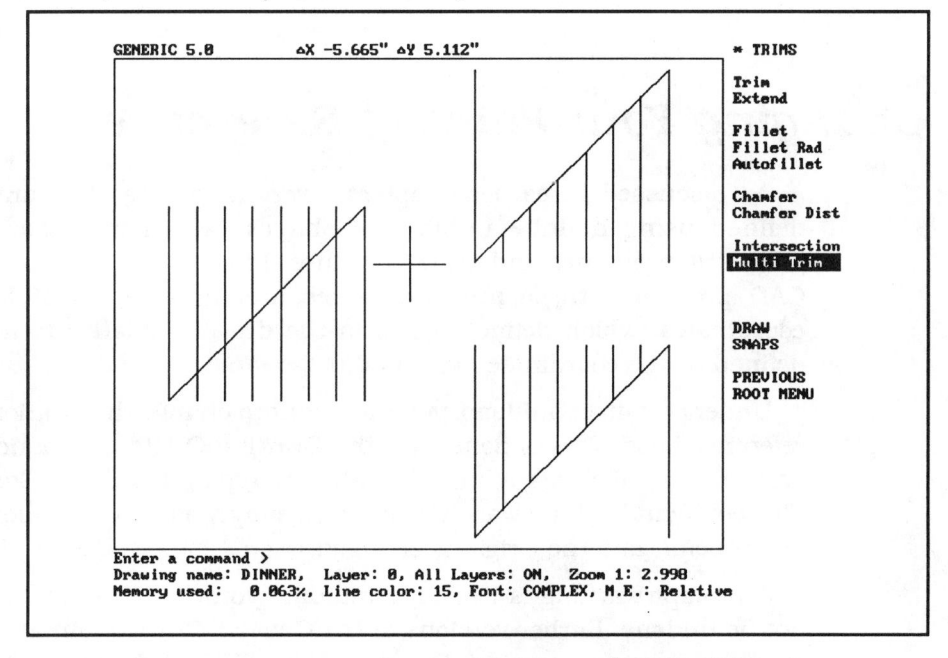

FIGURE 10-15 Another Multi-Trim

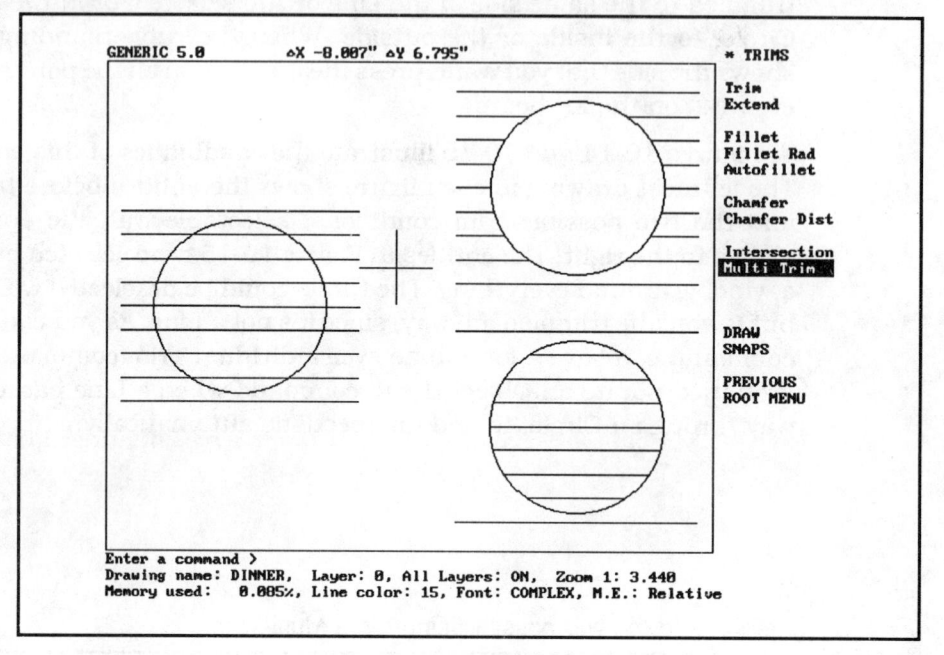

Changing Your Point of Reference

As discussed in earlier chapters, everything in a CAD drawing is defined using a finite number of shapes, which are described by geometric properties and numeric values. In Generic CADD, as in most CAD programs, these numeric values are in the form of X and Y coordinates, which define objects in the drawing relative to an origin defined by the coordinate location 0,0.

Under certain conditions, you may want to change the location of this reference base. This is done with the Drawing Origin command, found on the UTILITIES menu, and activated by typing **DO** on the keyboard. This command, after a warning message, simply asks you to select a new origin point, and the Origin is changed.

A prompt warning is issued, reminding you that this command can not be undone. Earlier versions of the Generic CADD manual included an even stronger warning: DO NOT USE THIS COMMAND. This was meant to keep you out of trouble. Changing the Origin does not confuse Generic CADD or the computer in any way, but could confuse you.

When you use Drawing Origin on a drawing, not only do the X and Y coordinates of every point on every entity in the drawing change, but so do the Grid, Named Views, and just about everything else. Two forms of Manual Entry, Origin and Basepoint, will respond differently after a Drawing Origin command than before. The coordinates of the Basepoint, of course, are relative to the Origin.

Uses of the Origin

On the other hand, this command can come in handy. Plotting and Printing both reference the Origin as the default lower-left corner for the sheet. The lower-left corner of the Limits is at the Origin, so the location of the Origin has an effect on the way the Zoom Limits command works. Often the Basepoint can be used as a temporary origin; however, sometimes moving the Origin is the best way. When one drawing is loaded into another, or into Generic 3D Drafting, the Origin is used as a reference point. The Third Dimension, an add-on utility to create perspective drawings from Generic CADD drawing files, requires that you use the Drawing Origin command on the drawing to establish a focal point for the perspective. Once you have completed a drawing, moving the Origin for any of these purposes has very little impact on the drawing.

Think of It As Moving the Entire Drawing

The Drawing Origin command can be thought of as a replacement for a shortcut command that doesn't exist. (If it did, it would be called Drawing Move.) If there were such a command, you would simply be asked for a reference point and a new location. With the Drawing Origin command, the reference point is assumed to be the current origin, 0,0, and you specify only the new location. Of course, the new location of the Origin is specified in terms of the coordinate system and the mode of Manual Entry that is active when you issue the command.

To use the Drawing Origin command, select it from the UTILITIES menu or type **DO** on the keyboard. When you are asked for the new origin, either select a point on the screen or type the coordinates of the desired point. If you are typing coordinates, make sure you know which manual entry mode you are using. (It doesn't hurt to reselect MO, MR, or MB again, as all of the Manual Entry commands are one-way toggles that always go on when you select them.)

The Drawing Origin command will change all of the definition points of every entity in the drawing to reflect the new origin and automatically perform a Zoom All. This automatic Zoom All acts as a visual cue that you have significantly adjusted the drawing, and alerts you that you are at a fresh starting point.

If you want to be able to put the Origin back where it was, put an entity, such as a Standard Point, at the original location before using the Drawing Origin command. This way, you can use another Origin command and snap back onto the reference entity when you are ready.

Making Use of Existing Geometric Properties

One of the big advantages of CAD over hand drawing and other types of programs is its ability to not only remember data that you have input, but to extrapolate additional information from this data. This is true with geometric properties as well as with numeric data.

You have already had the opportunity to use the Snap to Nearest Point function, which allows you to snap to an existing definition point of an object. This command lets you specify the exact endpoint of any line on the screen whenever Generic CADD asks you to specify a point. You simply position the cursor and type **NP** or press the third button on the pointing device. Other definition points that can be found with the **NP** snap include the center of a Circle, the endpoints of an Arc, the axis points of an Ellipse, the definition points of a Curve, the control and endpoints of a Bezier Curve, the placement location of Text Characters and Text Lines, and the reference points of Components.

In addition, you have seen how the various Trim commands use existing entities as boundaries or references for the editing of other entities. The Snap commands discussed in the following sections take this idea one step further, giving you access to real geometric properties, eliminating much of the tedious construction work associated with hand drawing, while at the same time allowing much greater precision.

The Snap Commands

The commands on the SNAPS menu modify the actions of many other commands to make them more accurate. For this reason, the SNAPS menu is accessible from the DRAW and EDITS menus, as well as from the ROOT menu.

Like the Snap to Nearest Point (NP) command, the Snap commands help you to locate points whenever you are asked for them. Each provides a specific geometric function, as demonstrated by the examples on the following pages. The two-character codes for the Snap commands start with the letter S, followed by a letter indicating the type of snap.

Another Nearest Point

As you may have noticed, the Snap to Nearest Point command is unlike any other Generic CADD command, in that it must be selected while you are positioning the cursor. This means that it cannot be selected from the video menu, which also requires that you position the cursor. While this makes Snap to Nearest Point extremely easy to use in most cases, it is somewhat inconsistent with the rest of the Snap commands, which follow Generic CADD's syntax more closely. The normal sequence is to select the command first, then select the point or points requested.

On the SNAPS menu, a command is provided that does the same thing as Snap to Nearest Point, but in a form closer to the normal command format. Snap Close (Close on the video menu), typed on the keyboard or in macros as **SC**, brings up a prompt that asks you to select the point that you want to snap close to. After selecting the command, respond to this prompt by positioning the cursor near the definition point that you want to snap onto, then use the first button on the pointing device to select the point. Just like Snap to Nearest Point, any construction point on any entity can be found by the Snap Close command.

The only difference between these two commands (NP and SC) is in the way that they are activated. The result is the same. Snap Close is done in three steps: selecting the command, positioning the cursor, and picking the point. Nearest Point requires only two steps: positioning the cursor and typing **NP** or pressing the third button on the pointing device. The second step simultaneously selects the command and the point.

How Close Is Close Enough?

These two snaps can find a point anywhere on the screen. If you draw a line in one corner of the screen, and then start another line and use Snap to Nearest Point, you will always snap onto one of the endpoints, even if it is on the other side of the screen. The rest of the snaps, however, are not quite so generous. The specific location that you are trying to snap to, or at least the entities used to find this location, must be within a certain distance of the center of the cursor when you select the points on the screen. This distance is specified using the Tolerance command, located on the SNAPS menu or activated by typing **TO** on the keyboard. The factory default is 0.25 (1/4 inch), but this can be changed any time, and is saved as part of the drawing environment.

When you use the Tolerance command, you are asked to type a value. It is important to note that tolerance is measured on your video screen, not in the units of the drawing. This means that if tolerance is set to 0.25, your cursor must be within 1/4 inch of the entity or condition that you are looking for. This rule may be difficult to remember at first, because it is entirely different from all other size or scale specifications in Generic CADD 5.0 (specifications are normally in the scale of the drawing). It makes sense, though, because if tolerance were measured to scale, it would be ruled by the current Zoom. You would have to pick your points closer to where you wanted them when you were zoomed out, and would not need to be so precise when you were zoomed in closer. This would defeat the purpose of the tolerance, which is to remain fixed no matter how large or small your drawing is displayed on the screen.

Tolerance also controls how close the cursor must be to an object in order to select it with the Object editing method. With the Move Point command, for example, tolerance controls how close you have to be not only to select the object, but to select one of the definition points to move as well.

Snap to Anything in Sight

Sometimes you are not looking for any specific geometric point on an object, but just any point at all. You may simply want to make sure that the line you are drawing actually touches another line. Selecting Object from the SNAPS menu or typing **SO** before selecting the point assures this.

Simply select the Snap Object or type **SO** whenever you are selecting a point that merely needs to touch another object. When asked which object you want to snap to, position the cursor and press the first button on the pointing device. The cursor will jump to the nearest object within the distance specified by the tolerance. It jumps in a straight line to the closest possible point on the object, so it is still important where you position the cursor.

Snap Object, like many of the other snaps, overrides Ortho Mode and Snap to Grid. Be careful when you use Snap Object and the rest of the Snap commands with these drawing controls, as you may not get the point that you want. It is quite possible to draw lines that are not aligned with the current Ortho angle by using Snap Object or Snap Close even when Ortho is active.

Locating a Midpoint

The Midpoint Snap command can be used to find the midpoint of a Line, Arc, or Circle. The midpoint of a Line is a point, as you would guess, half the length of the line from either end. The midpoint of an Arc is similarly defined as being halfway around from either endpoint. The midpoint of a Circle is arbitrarily defined, somewhat less intuitively, as a point 180 degrees (half the circle) from a starting point at 0 degrees. In the standard Generic way, 0 degrees is defined as the point on the right side of the Circle, horizontally orthogonal to the center, otherwise known as the Eastern vertex, or 3 o'clock. The midpoint is therefore at the Western vertex, or 9 o'clock.

You can use the Midpoint Snap anytime that you are prompted for a point. Simply select Midpoint from the SNAPS menu or type **SM** on the keyboard. You will be asked to select the object for which you want to locate the midpoint. Remember, midpoints are only defined for Lines, Arcs, and Circles. If you pick a Curve or a Bezier, the entity will not be found, and your point will not be selected. If you select a true Ellipse, type entity will be found, but as midpoint is not defined for ellipses, the point will simply be located at the cursor position.

The Midpoint Snap can be especially handy when used with some of the editing commands. For example, Figure 10-16 shows the placement of a circle in the exact center of a rectangle. This can be done with one Circle command, and then a Move command that uses Midpoint Snap

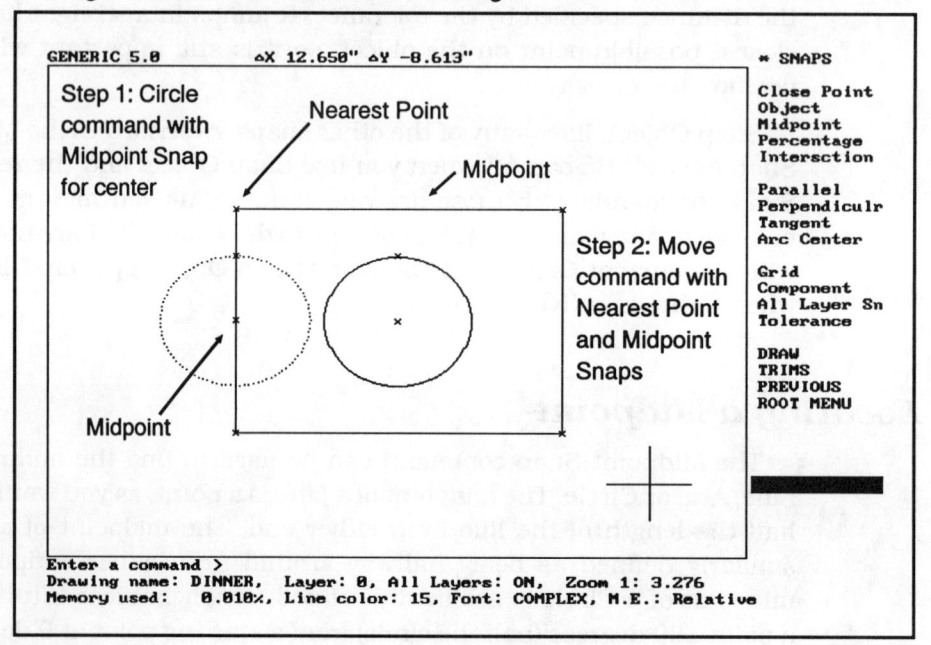

FIGURE 10-16 Placing a Circle in the center of a Rectangle

as the second point of a displacement. This operation can be simplified even further, eliminating the Move by using Tracking and Cursor Free, discussed at the end of this chapter.

Somewhere Down the Line...

An extension of the idea of the Midpoint Snap is the Percentage Snap, which allows you to snap to a specified percentage of the distance along an entity. Since this command also works on Lines, Arcs, and Circles in the same way, using the Midpoint Snap is really just like using the Percentage Snap command with the percentage set to 50 percent.

Like all of these Snap commands, Percentage Snap can be selected from the SNAPS menu anytime you are asked to select a point. It can also be activated by typing **SR** on the keyboard. Like the Midpoint Snap, a prompt asks you to select the object that you want to snap to. Pick a point nearer to the end of the Line or Arc that you want the percentage to be measured from. With Circles, it doesn't matter where you select the point, as the percentage will be measured from the 3 o'clock position counterclockwise. After selecting this object, you are prompted for the percentage along the object. Type a number between 0 and 100 and press ENTER. The percentage used last will be shown as the default, and can be reselected by simply pressing ENTER.

If you specify 0 percent, your point will be selected at the endpoint of the Line or Arc nearest the point you picked, or at the 3 o'clock position on a Circle. If you select 100 percent, the other endpoint of a Line or Arc or the same 3 o'clock position on the Circle will be identified.

Finding an Intersection

The Intersection Snap command can find the intersection point between any combination of Lines, Arcs, and Circles. The types of intersections that can be located are shown in Figure 10-17. These include intersections between a Line and another Line, a Line and an Arc, a Line and a Circle, an Arc and another Arc, an Arc and a Circle, and between two Circles. You can also find intersections with Rectangles, Regular Polygons, and Construction Ellipses, because they are actually made from Lines and Arcs. Intersections with Curves, Beziers, and True Ellipses cannot be found.

FIGURE 10-17 Various intersection conditions

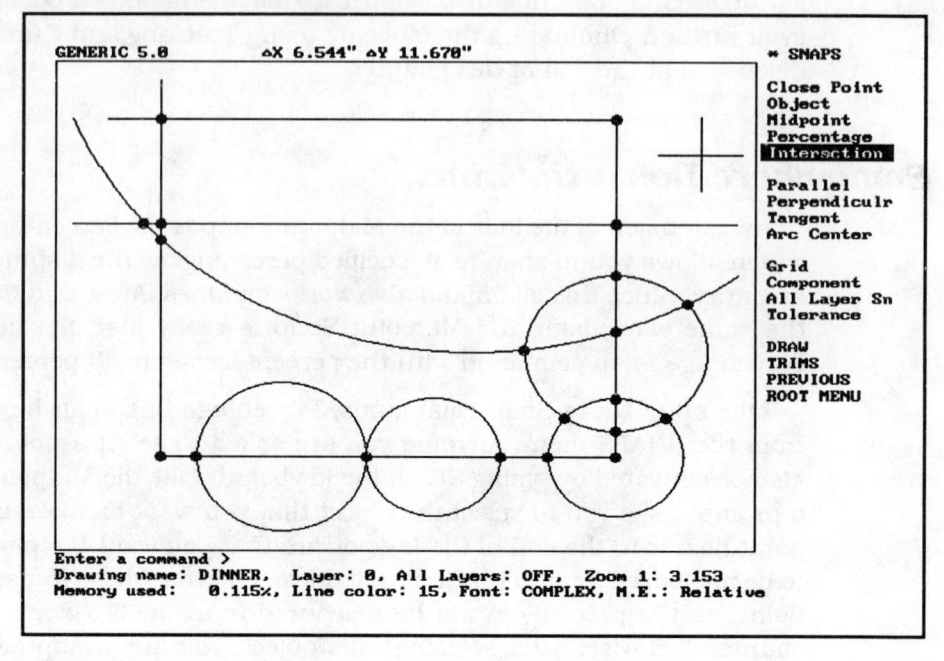

An intersection is defined as the point where two entities cross. Therefore, there is an intersection defined even if one entity is just touching another entity, and where two entities simply share a common endpoint. Of course, these particular conditions could also be located with a Nearest Point or Snap Close command, if you are sure that it is the endpoint that you want. As with all of the rest of the Snap commands, this command can be selected from the SNAPS menu anytime you are trying to place a point, whether you are executing a Draw or Edit command or even placing a Window for selection. This and other Snap commands can be used not only to locate definition points of entities, but as the beginning or ending point for displacements in commands such as Move and Copy.

Snapping Parallel to a Line, Arc, or Circle

CADD is tailor-made for certain geometric constructions, such as creating a Line or Arc parallel to an existing Line, Circle, or Arc. Generic CADD offers two different ways to use this Snap command, depending upon your circumstances.

Snap Parallel may be used only in connection with the commands that create Lines, Circles, and Arcs, but may be used in various ways within these commands. To try these, make a drawing similar to that in Figure 10-18. Your drawing should include a number of Lines, Circles, and Arcs.

With the Line command, Snap Parallel may be used when you are selecting either the first point or the second point, and will respond differently in either case. If you select Parallel from the SNAPS menu or

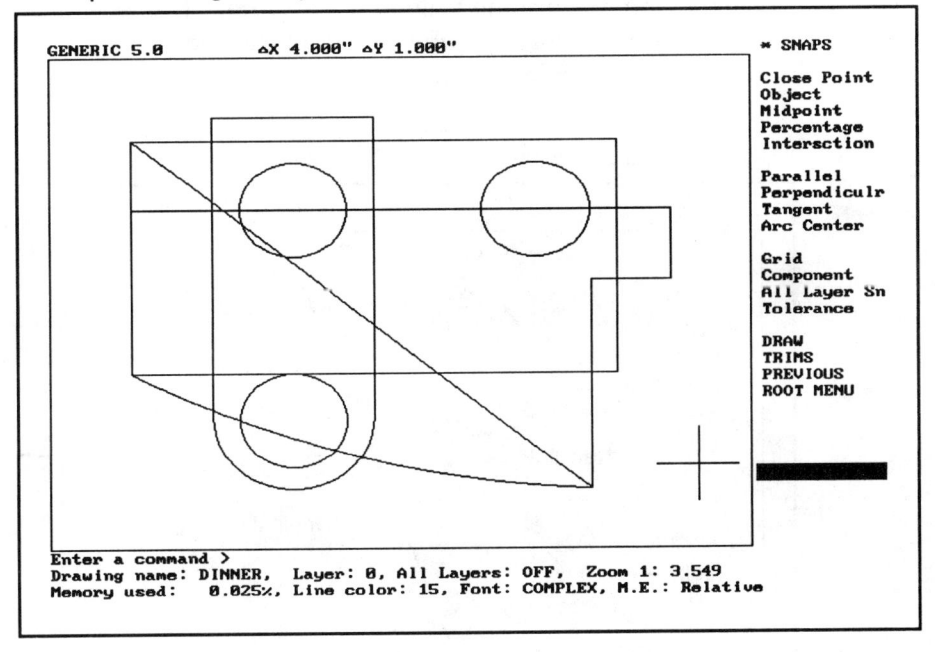

FIGURE 10-18 A sample drawing for experimenting with Snaps

type **SL** when you are asked for the starting point of a Line, you will be asked to select the line that you want to draw parallel to. Next, you will be asked to specify an *offset distance,* which determines how far away from the original line the parallel line will be placed. Type a number and press ENTER. You are then asked to place the first point and the second point. The new line will be constructed parallel to the selected line as shown in Figure 10-19, on the side of the original line where you place the first point after specifying the offset. Note that the default offset is shown at the offset prompt, and can be reselected simply by pressing ENTER.

You may also issue the Snap Parallel command after placing the first point on the line. Again, you will be asked to select the line that you want to Snap Parallel to, and prompted for an offset. The point that you have already selected will be adjusted to the offset specified, and you will be prompted for the second point. If the Line ends up on the wrong side of the reference Line, specify a negative offset. Users of Level 3 or other previous Generic products should note that this is a change in the operation of Snap Parallel when used on the second point.

FIGURE 10-19

How endpoints are derived for parallel lines

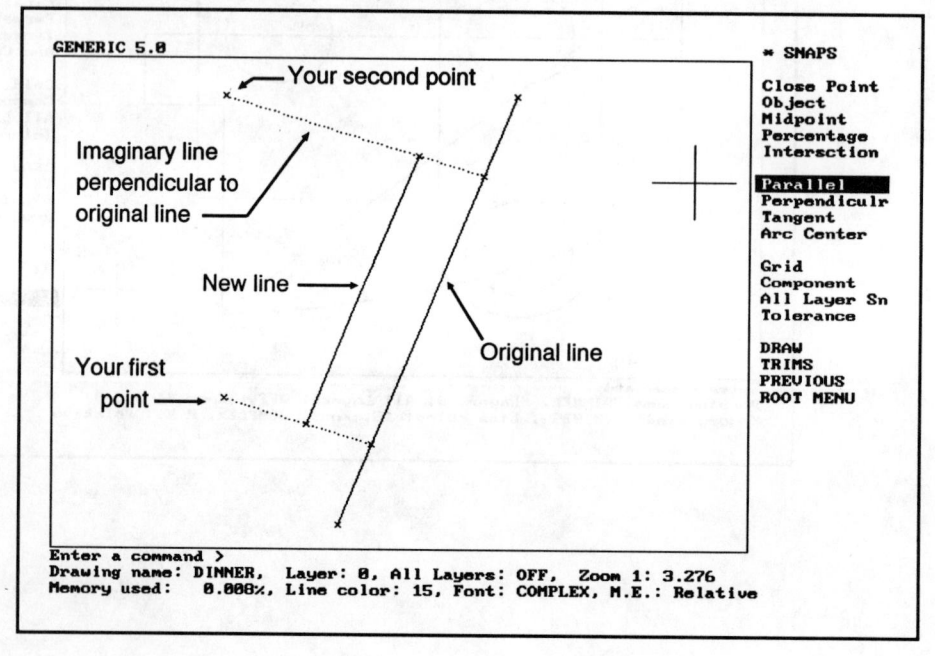

When drawing lines, you can only Snap Parallel to another Line. Although you will be allowed to select an Arc or Circle, the result will be arbitrary, because there is no standard geometric meaning for a Line parallel to an Arc or a Circle. You may find some uses for these unorthodox specifications, but they were not intended.

You can snap one Arc parallel to another using the first method described earlier with the Arc 3 (A3) command. You must issue the Snap Parallel command before placing any of the points of the Arc. To create an Arc parallel to another Arc, select Arc 3 from the DRAW menu or type **A3** on the keyboard. When asked for the first endpoint, select Parallel from the SNAPS menu or type **SL**. You will be asked to select an object to Snap Parallel to and to specify an offset distance. Finally, you can select which side (inside or outside) of the original Arc the new Arc should be on, using the cursor. The prompt here may not be correct in some copies of Generic CADD 5.0, but previewing the Arc back and forth on either side of the original Arc as you move the cursor should help you choose.

A Circle may be snapped parallel to another Circle or to an Arc, creating concentric circles. Use the Circle 2 (C2) or Circle 3 (C3) command and issue the Snap Parallel (SL) command as soon as you are asked for the first point. Specify the entity to Snap Parallel to and an offset. As in other offset prompts, if the default, left over from the last time you used Snap Parallel, is what you want, simply press ENTER to respecify it. As with Arcs, a final prompt, sometimes erroneously phrased, allows you to select a location for the new Circle inside or outside the old one.

Note While you can create a Circle parallel to an existing Arc, if you try to create an Arc by snapping parallel to an existing Circle, you will get another Circle.

Snapping Perpendicular to a Line, Circle, or Arc

Another geometric construction simplified by Generic CADD is a Line that meets another entity at a 90-degree angle. A Line may be snapped perpendicular to another Line, a Circle, or an Arc. While a Line cannot really meet a Circle or an Arc at 90 degrees unless the radius of the Circle or Arc is infinite, a line perpendicular to a Circle or Arc is defined in Generic CADD 5.0 as one that, if extended, would pass through the center of the Circle or Arc. Figure 10-20 shows several Lines snapped perpen-

FIGURE 10-20 Several Lines snapped perpendicular to a Circle

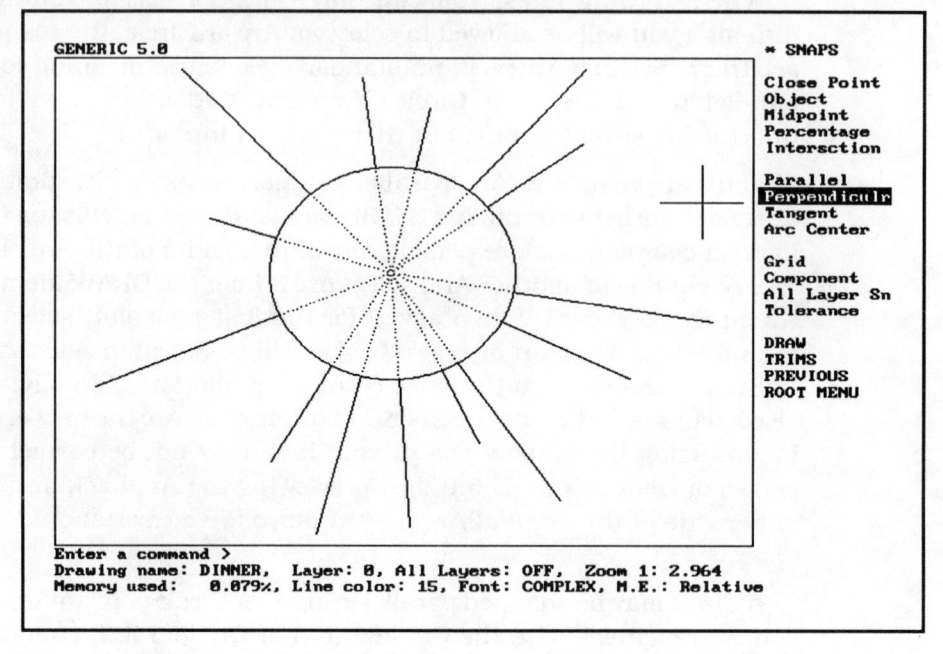

dicular to a Circle. The dotted lines indicate imaginary extensions of the Lines, which all meet at the center of the Circle.

The Snap Perpendicular command, typed **SP** on the keyboard, can be used before selecting either the first or the second endpoint of a line. If you select Snap Perpendicular before placing the first point, you will be asked for the entity to snap to, then for the first point. Pick the entity and any point. The location of the point that you pick is all but ignored. The Line command simply requires a certain number of points (two), so you have to pick something. A point on the entity selected is located as close to where you pick the first point as possible, so the point that you select has some impact on how the command operates. However, when you are asked for the second point, you are free to move the line about, using rubberbanding, and the first point is continuously adjusted as you move the cursor so that the rubber band line is always perpendicular to the entity that you have selected.

In fact, you can move the cursor from one side of a Line to the other, from the outside of a Circle to the inside, and the rubber band preview line will follow. When you pick the second point, the Line will be drawn.

If you position a first point, and then issue a Snap Perpendicular command, you will simply be asked for the entity that you want to Snap Perpendicular to. When this entity is chosen, a line will be constructed from the first point to the selected entity. Note that the line does not have to actually touch a selected Arc or Circle, as imaginary perpendicular intersections can be found. If you attempt to use Snap Perpendicular on anything other than Lines, Arcs, or Circles, the results will be unpredictable, as no geometric model for these conditions exists.

Snapping Tangent to an Arc or Circle

Yet another Snap command provides an automated method for performing one of the more difficult geometric constructions in hand drawing: a Line tangent to an Arc or a Circle. The Snap Tangent (ST) command provides this function for Lines only, tangent to one or two Circles, Arcs, or a Circle and an Arc.

If tangency is a new concept for you, it might help to think of the Circle or Arc as being tangent to the Line rather than the other way around. For example, a billiard ball sitting on a table is *tangent* to the surface of the table, as it touches at only one point. A beach ball floating in the water, on the other hand, is not tangent to the surface of the water, because part of the ball is below the water line.

The Tangent command on the SNAPS menu allows you to construct a Line tangent to a selected Arc or Circle at either or both ends. Start with the Line command, and use Snap Tangent for either or both endpoints. If you use Snap Tangent with the first point, you will be asked for the object to snap tangent to, and then for the first point. As with Snap Perpendicular, this first point is used only for a starting point for rubberbanding. Next, you will be asked for the second point. As you select the second point, the Line will be rubberbanded tangent to the selected object.

You will probably notice that the initial rubber band line spins off in a counterclockwise direction. As you move around the Circle or Arc that you have snapped onto, the direction does not change. To change to clockwise (or to change back, if you have already switched), move your cursor through the selected entity, rather than around it.

If you use Snap Tangent for the second endpoint of a Line, it will immediately be snapped tangent to the side of the Circle or Arc nearest the point used to select the entity. If the first point is a tangent point as well, it will be adjusted to suit. Note that you cannot reliably use the Snap Tangent command to create new Arcs or Circles, even though the command may appear to work. In many cases, when you use Snap Tangent, the command that you are using will change to a Line command; Generic CADD assumes that if you want to Snap Tangent, you must be trying to draw a Line. Figure 10-21 shows several Lines snapped tangent to a number of Circles.

Snapping to the Center of an Arc or Circle

The last geometric Snap command on the SNAPS menu is the Arc Center snap, which will snap to the geometric center of Arcs and Circles.

FIGURE 10-21 Lines snapped tangent to several Circles

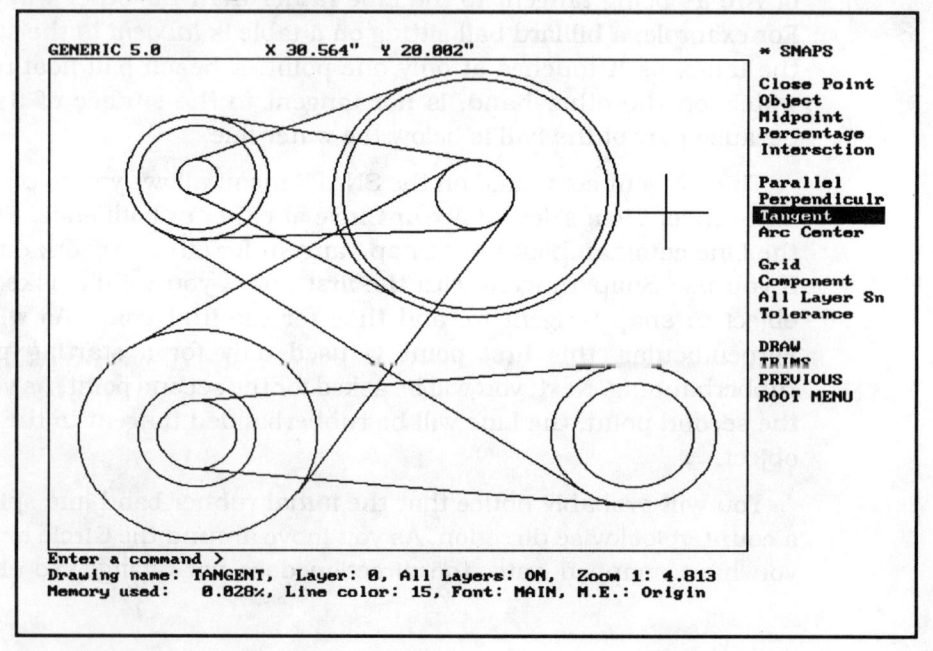

Actually, the center of a Circle can be located by a number of other Snap commands, because the center is one of the definition points of a Circle. However, it may sometimes be more convenient to locate the center by selecting a point on the Circle—since there is no definition point at the center of an Arc, Snap Arc Center can come in handy.

Unlike the previous geometric Snap commands, which only work on certain entity types, Snap Arc Center can be used anytime you are asked for a point. Select Arc Center from the SNAPS menu or type **SN** on the keyboard. You are then asked to select the object that you want to snap to the center of, and the location of the point is calculated and located. You must pick a point on the Arc or Circle itself, not out in the middle where you think the center might be. The centerpoint is calculated, rather than found. For an Arc, it does not even exist until you use this command. If you select an object that does not have a center (anything other than a Circle or Arc), the point will simply not be located, and you will have to reissue the command if you want to try again.

Eligible Entities

The ability to use the Snap commands on entities is subject to the status of two toggles. The first of these is the All Layers Edit toggle, located on the LAYERS menu and typed **AL** on the keyboard. If this toggle is on, you can snap onto any entity visible on the screen with any of the Snap commands, just as you can edit any entity on the screen.

If All Layers Edit is off, the ability to snap to entities not on the current layer becomes subject to the second toggle, All Layers Snap, located on the SNAPS menu, and typed **SY** on the keyboard. If this toggle is on, you can snap to anything visible on the screen. If this toggle is off (and All Layers Edit is off), you can snap only to entities on the current layer.

All Layers Snap is a feature new to Generic CADD 5.0, and the combination of these two commands provides you with much more finesse in dealing with the editing of entities on specific layers, using other entities for reference. When snapping to entities in a crowded portion of the drawing, make sure that you are aware of the status of these two toggles. In some cases it may help to turn layers off with the Layer Hide (YH) command.

Cursor Control

Two more snap-related features have been introduced with Generic CADD 5.0. Actually, these commands have migrated over from Generic 3D Drafting, where they were developed to deal with the complexity of three dimensions. After seeing them at work there, it became obvious that they would be of use in CADD as well. These two features, Tracking and Cursor Free, give you more flexibility in the use of the cursor to locate points in combination with the Geometric Snaps, Snap Ortho, and, optionally, Snap Grid, to find points that may be geometrically related to entities in the drawing, but not actually on them. All of the commands that you will need to deal with these features are located on the CONSTRAINTS menu.

Tracking—Starting in the Right Place

Earlier in this chapter, the use of the Snap Midpoint command was demonstrated in Figure 10-16. In this example, a Circle was drawn at the midpoint of one side of a Rectangle, then moved to the center of the Rectangle by way of a Move command, using Snap Midpoint again in the displacement. While this works perfectly well, Tracking makes it possible to draw the Circle in the right place the first time around, eliminating the need for the Move.

New Cursor Freedom

Often, tracking works best with the Cursor Free command turned on, so let's start there. Normally, when Ortho Mode is on (OR on the keyboard), the cursor is constrained to movement in two directions, nominally horizontal and vertical. You can move back and forth, or up and down. Rotating the Ortho Angle changes the definitions of horizontal and vertical, but the cursor is still constrained, just the same. Cursor Free cuts the cursor loose from the Ortho directions, so that it is free to move around the screen and snap onto any point.

So why not just turn Ortho off? Cursor Free allows the Line that you are drawing or the displacement that you are specifying to take advantage of Ortho Mode while the cursor itself is free to move about. It's easier to see this than to explain it, so try this.

Draw a Line at an arbitrary angle on the screen. Don't worry about size for now. Next, turn on Ortho Mode by selecting it from the CONSTRAINTS menu or typing **OR** on the keyboard. Turn on Cursor Free by typing **CF** or selecting it from the CONSTRAINTS menu. Now draw a line starting near the lower-left corner of the screen. As you move the cursor to the right, you will see that it will be rubberbanded on a horizontal line as you would expect. Note, however, that as you move the cursor up and down, it does not stick to the rubber band line. It moves about freely. Use the Nearest Point Snap (position the cursor and type **NP** or press the third button on the pointing device) to snap onto the rightmost endpoint of the original angled line. To stop the Line and see what you've got, press ESC.

You will see that the Line has been terminated immediately below the selected point. If you were to draw an imaginary vertical line from the end of the angled line down to your new line, it would pass through the new endpoint. Cursor Free, therefore, does not override Ortho Mode; it simply allows you to snap to entities that may not be directly on the Ortho path. The point, when located, is transferred in an orthogonal direction to the rubber band line that you have been stretching.

Back to Tracking

Tracking adds another layer of power to this whole scenario. It allows you to use existing points as references, and to move the cursor a number of times in both Ortho directions before actually selecting the desired point, utilizing Snap commands if you wish. Once again, seeing is believing, so try this. Draw a Rectangle somewhere on the screen. You're going to do that centered Circle now, without a Move.

Start the Circle with the Circle 2 (C2) command on the DRAW menu. When asked for the first point, select Tracking from the CONSTRAINTS menu or type **TK**. The first prompt will ask at which point to start tracking. Choose one of the corners of the rectangle (the endpoint of one of the lines that makes up the rectangle, actually) with an **NP** or third button snap. The next prompt will remind you that you are tracking—not drawing Lines—and tell you that you can stop tracking (when ready) by typing **PU**. As you move the cursor, you will notice that it is moving in the Ortho directions, whether you have Ortho Mode on or not. Tracking incorporates Ortho automatically.

Move to the right or left to make sure that your rubber band line has started in this direction. Now, select Midpoint from the SNAPS menu or type **SM** on the keyboard. When asked to select an object, pick either the top or bottom Line of the rectangle. You will snap to it, and get another rubber band line that moves in orthogonal directions from the newly selected point. You are tracking. Move up or down to make sure that your rubber band line is off to a good start. You must get it started manually by moving the cursor in the right direction. Now issue another Snap Midpoint command and choose either the right or left side of the rectangle. The point out in the middle of the rectangle will be found, and rubberbanding will be restarted at this point, as shown in Figure 10-22.

To end tracking and select this latest point as the center of your Circle, type **PU** on the keyboard or select a blank item from the video menu, which issues an automatic **PU**. Tracking will be ended and your Circle command will pick up where it left off. The center is now at the exact center of the rectangle, as it has been snapped to the midpoint of both a

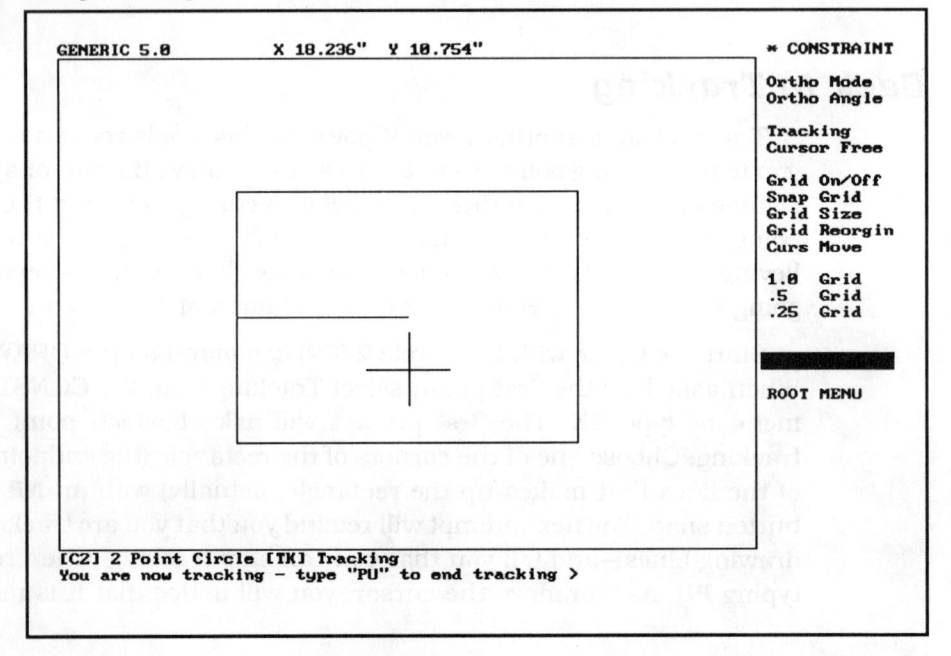

FIGURE 10-22 Using Tracking to locate the center of a Circle

horizontal and a vertical side. Select the second point of the circle to move it wherever you want it.

Note that Tracking works well with Snap to Grid turned on, so you can move specific distances without snapping to existing objects. It also works with Manual Entry set to Relative mode (MR). An undocumented variant of Manual Entry works especially well with Tracking.

Once you have started the rubber band line by moving the cursor, the direction is established, so you don't really need true X and Y coordinates. A distance will do. Simply move the cursor in the direction you want to go while tracking and type the distance on the keyboard. Press ENTER. Your tracking will be restarted at the specified distance in the direction shown. This can be repeated as many times as you like until you type PU. If you use negative numbers, tracking will move in the direction opposite your actual cursor movement.

Tracking from the Last Point

An additional Tracking option is shown at the first prompt, while you are selecting your starting point. Rather than picking a point on the screen, you can type the letter **L** on the keyboard, and tracking will start from the last point entered. This might be the second endpoint of the last Line that you drew, a point on a Circle, or the second point of a displacement if you have just done a Move or a Copy. Any point, not including corners of windows that you have specified last, will be used.

Tracking and Cursor Free are powerful new features of Generic CADD 5.0 that become even more useful when used together or in conjunction with other Snap commands.

This chapter completes the coverage of all of the basic and advanced general-purpose Generic CADD 5.0 drawing and editing commands. The additional features discussed in this chapter, such as the Snap, Trim, and Tracking commands, greatly enhance your ability to create accurate drawings quickly and to edit these drawings efficiently and accurately. Many of these commands are especially useful for otherwise difficult or time-consuming geometric constructions. With the commands in this chapter, you can begin to harness the power of Generic CADD 5.0.

CHAPTER 11

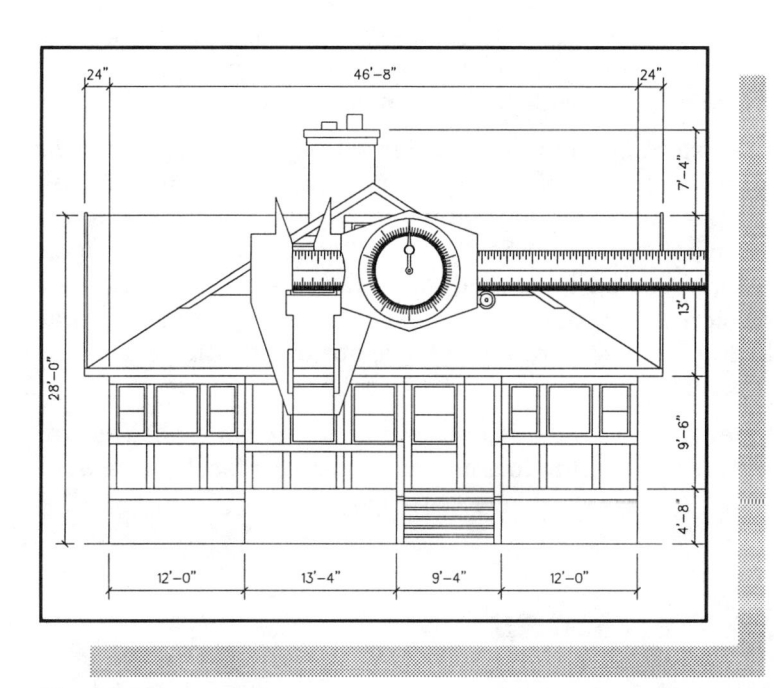

Dimensioning

Generic CADD 5.0 features greatly expanded and improved dimensioning capabilities. These features are fairly self-contained, and in many ways seem like a separate program inside Generic CADD 5.0. However, the dimensioning commands and features also follow many Generic CADD standards, and are similar to some of the commands previously discussed.

Dimensioning has many things in common with the other complex entity commands, as discussed in Chapter 8, "Complex Entities." A number of parameter-setting commands determine the way that dimensions are placed, much like text placement parameters control the placement of text and the component placement parameters control the placement of components. As with text and components, these parameters may be changed while the dimension is being placed.

Like text, dimensioning has its own color-setting command, its own font command, and more. In fact, almost everything about dimensioning is controlled by a parameter-setting command. So many parameters can be set that they have their own menu, instead of being on the same menu with the dimensions. The parameters that are usually set as a default or set once in a session are on their own menu, while the parameters that are set often during dimension placement are out front with the Dimension Placement commands.

The SNAPS menu commands discussed in the previous chapter are usually used with dimensioning to snap onto existing objects, to assure accuracy.

Associative Dimensions

The Generic CADD 5.0 Dimension commands produce entities known as Associative Dimensions. *Associative Dimensions* are single entities, with definitions and real data stored in them. They are very much like flexible components with attributes preattached. In this case, the attribute carries information regarding the length, angle, radius, or diameter described by the dimension. What makes them associative is that this data changes when the dimension is edited, either by a Stretch or a Move Point command, or even by a Scale command. These Associative Dimensions are very powerful, but they're also pretty complicated.

Chapter 11: Dimensioning

> **Note** The word *Associative* has replaced the term *Automatic* in discussion of dimensions. Although highly parameterized, dimensioning is far from automatic (how can the program know what you want to dimension?), and associativity is far more important.

Understanding the Dimensioning Menu

First, let's look at the menu. The first five items on the menu form a group. The first two, Linear and Angular, are Dimension Placement commands, while the remaining three, Mode, Direction, and Proximity, are Dimension Parameters. The three parameters are included here because they control only these two commands, and will often be used interactively while dimensioning.

> **Hint** After reading Chapter 16, "Programming Generic CADD 5.0," you might want to do something to the menu to make this a little more obvious. (Perhaps you don't want the parameters to start with uppercase letters, for example.)

The next group contains four commands, the first three of which are more Dimension Placement commands, Radial, Diameter, and Leader, while the fourth is a parameter that controls only these, Shoulder Length.

Of the final group of similar-looking commands, the first two, Dim Move and Dim Change are actually Dimension Editing commands, while the third, Dim Tolerance, is another parameter.

Right before ROOT menu is an option that should be recognizable as another menu because it is uppercase, DIM SET. This item takes you to the DIMENSION SETTINGS menu, which gives access to a number of commands that control all Associative Dimensions.

Creating a Dimensioning Style

The DIM SET menu contains all of the commands necessary to define a dimensioning style. These parameters control the layer, color, and length of various parts of the dimensions, type of arrowheads used, the

Figure 11-1: A dimensioned drawing (dimension lines are not broken and text is aligned)

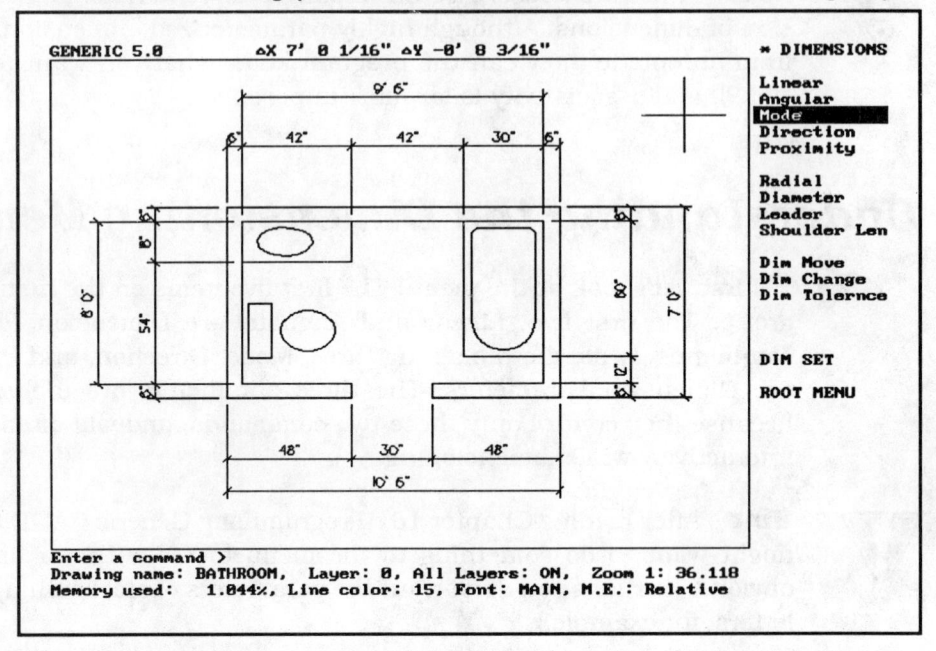

Figure 11-2: A drawing dimensioned in a different style (dimension lines are broken and text is horizontal)

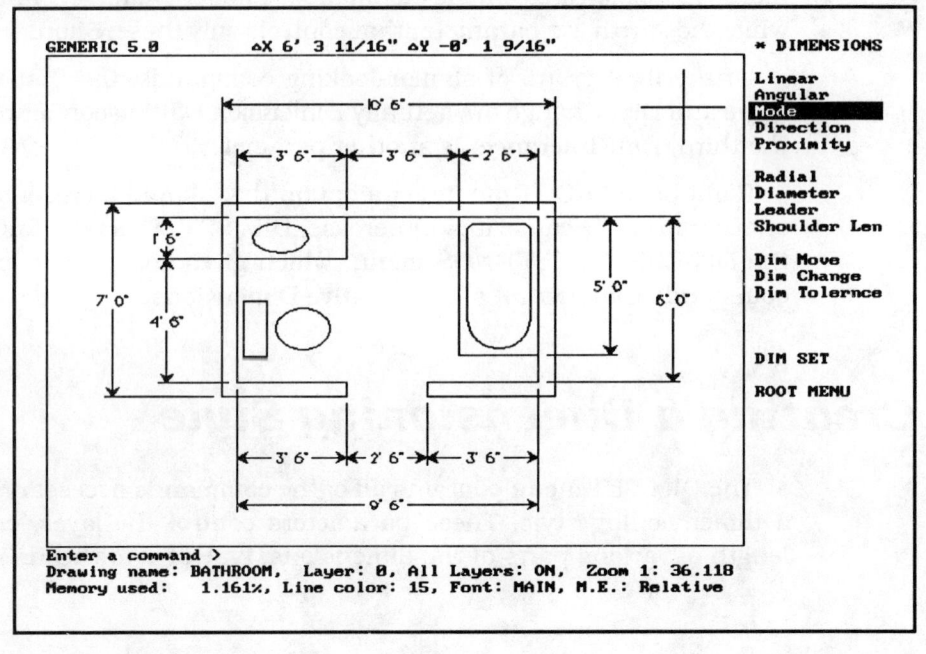

font and text parameters, and so on. Figures 11-1 and 11-2 show two typical styles of linear dimensioning.

If you always use the same style of dimensioning, you will rarely have to change these parameters more than once during a drawing to adjust for scale. Several of these parameters may be set only once, then made a permanent part of your Generic CADD 5.0 configuration by the use of the Environment (EN) command. See Chapter 15, "Customizing Generic CADD 5.0," for more information on the Environment command and customizing Generic CADD 5.0.

Each dimensioning parameter command controls one particular aspect of dimensioning. Although they are listed on the video menu pretty much according to frequency of use, they are examined in this chapter in more or less reversed order, which more closely approximates how you might use them to create your own dimensioning style.

Layer and Color

The Dim Color item on the DIM SET menu provides access to the Color Setting (CS) command, and automatically selects the Dimension (D) option. All dimension entities created with any of the Dimensioning commands will be drawn in this color. As usual, if the video menu is active, you may select from the color bars displayed.

The Dim Layer item on the DIM SET menu activates the Dimension Layer (UY) command. (Several of the two-character Dimension commands start with U, and the Y stands for laYer.) All dimension entities created with any of the Dimensioning commands will be placed on this layer. As usual, if the video menu is active you may select from the menu.

Note You can put dimensions on layers other than the current layer with the Dimension Layer command. You can place dimensions on one layer while snapping exclusively to entities on the current layer with the All Layers Edit and All Layers Snap commands turned off. This may become confusing if you place a dimension and then try to edit it, however, so you may want to set the dimension layer to be the same as the current layer if you don't need this capability, or just remember to turn on All Layers Edit (AL) before trying to edit a dimension that you just placed.

Dimensioning Text

Three commands control the appearance of the dimension text. The first of these, the Font Select (FS) command, automatically selects the Dimension (D) option. If the video menu is active, you may select from it, or use the File Selector. See Chapter 12, "File Storage and Retrieval," if you are having any trouble.

After the font is selected, it is automatically loaded, if it has not been loaded already. Just as with any font, the font that you want to use must be on a disk in some disk drive or on your hard disk, and the path for locating fonts should be set with the FP command, option F. (Again, for more information, see Chapter 12.) Note that you may have several fonts loaded for different purposes, including Text, Attributes, and Dimensions. All text created as a part of any dimensioning entity will be in the selected font.

The second of these three commands, the Text Size (TZ) command, controls the dimensioning Text Size and automatically selects the Dimension (D) option. This controls the height of all text used in dimensioning entities. Note that because there is no dimensioning Text Aspect command, this command controls the width of your text as well. The third text command on the DIM SET menu, Dim Text, controls a number of additional parameters related to your dimensioning text. This command can be typed as **DT** on the keyboard or selected from the DIM SET menu. The various options within the Dim Text prompt control the parameters covered next.

Placement

This parameter is a toggle that controls whether dimension lines are broken for text or not. In Figure 11-1 the dimension lines are not broken, while in Figure 11-2 they are. The style shown in Figure 11-1 is called *above line*, which really means that, if possible, the dimension line will not be broken, and the text will be moved out of the way. In the case of horizontal dimension lines, the text will be moved up, so that it is above the line. In other cases, the text will be moved in other directions. However, if you imagine rotating the drawing so that the dimension line is horizontal, the text would be placed above it.

The second style, shown in Figure 11-2, is called *in line*—the dimension line is broken and the text inserted in the break. Note that in some cases, such as when you want your text to always be horizontal, the dimension line may be broken in either case.

Direction

This parameter is another toggle, this time controlling the direction of dimension text. The two options are Horizontal and Aligned. When Horizontal is selected, all text created as part of any dimensioning entity will be drawn horizontally, or at a zero rotation angle, regardless of the direction of the dimension itself. When Aligned is selected, the text will be rotated to align with the dimension. Again, Figures 11-1 and 11-2 provide examples of the two different states of this toggle. In Figure 11-1, dimension text is aligned with the dimensions, while it is always horizontal in Figure 11-2.

Refer now to Figure 11-3, which illustrates the parts of a typical dimension discussed in the next sections.

Centered

Another toggle, the Centered parameter, controls whether or not dimension text is automatically centered in the dimension line. If it is on, text is centered while you preview the dimension, and its location is not affected by the location of your cursor. If Centered is off, the location of the text is rubberbanded during placement to allow you to select the location with your cursor. The text in all of the dimensions in Figures 11-1, 11-2, and 11-3 is centered.

In-Line Offset

When the dimension text is inserted into the dimension line, a certain amount of space is left at each end of the text, between the text itself and the point where the dimension line starts up again. The size of this gap is set by the In-Line Offset parameter, which is changed by selecting it from the Dim Text prompt or by typing **I** at the same prompt, typing a number, and pressing ENTER. The new value will be used for all new dimensions created. The In-Line Offset is shown in Figure 11-3. The In-Line Offset is not used, of course, if the dimension text does not break the dimension line.

Above Offset

When the dimension text is above the dimension line (as opposed to in-line), a certain amount of space exists between the dimension line itself and the text. The Above Offset parameter, as illustrated in Figure 11-3, sets the size of this space. To change it, select Above Offset from the Dim Text prompt or type **A** at the same prompt. Next, type a number and press ENTER. The new value will be used for all new dimensions in which the dimension text is above the dimension line. This variable has no effect when the text breaks the dimension line (in-line text).

FIGURE 11-3 The parts of a dimension

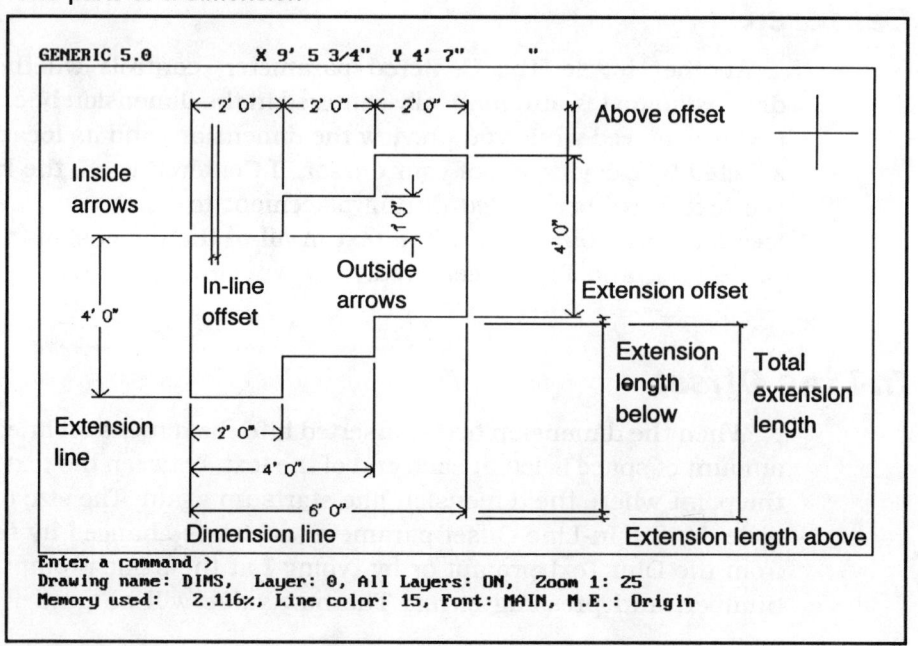

Tolerance

Tolerances in the dimension text show the range of allowable values that a dimension may have. For instance, a rough door opening might be dimensioned as 3' 0" with a 1/2" tolerance in either direction. The Tolerance option has four basic selections, some of which also require values: None, Min/Max, Stacked Variance, and Fixed Variance. The four options give you four separate ways to show tolerances, which is especially helpful to the various disciplines that need to use different formats for tolerances.

To start the selection, choose Tolerance from the Dim Text prompt or type **T** at the same prompt. A new prompt will be provided to let you select among the four options. These same Tolerance options can also be set by selecting Dim Tolerance from the DIMENSIONS menu or by typing **UT** on the keyboard.

None

The first of these options, None, does exactly what you would expect. No Tolerances are generated, and you get only one number in the dimension text, the dimension itself, in the currently Active Unit (UN) system, displayed in the currently active Numeric Format (NF). To specify no tolerances, select None from the Tolerance prompt or type **N** at the same prompt.

Min/Max

The second Dim Text Tolerance option is Min/Max. This option creates two texts whenever you create a dimension. One text shows the highest value possible and the other shows the least value allowable. The highest value is stacked on top of the lesser value when a dimension is created. The amount by which these texts are greater and less than the actual dimension is controlled by two parameters requested when you select this option from the Tolerance prompt or type **M** at the same prompt. These are the Lower Tolerance and the Upper Tolerance parameters. For each, specify a value that will be subtracted or added, respectively, from the actual dimension. Finally, you will be prompted for the number of decimal places for the text, to be used for angular dimensions and for linear dimensions if the Numeric Format is set to Decimal rather than Fraction when the dimensions are placed. See Figure 11-4 for an example of Min/Max tolerances.

Stacked Variance

The third Dim Text Tolerance option is called Stacked Variance. This option shows the actual dimension, and adds the amount of the lower and upper values as separate figures stacked after the dimension text, rather than actually adding and subtracting them for you as Min/Max does. The dimension in Figure 11-4 is 4'0". The upper value on top shows that the highest possible dimension is 2" above 4, or 4' 2". (Remember that Min/Max does the math for you while Stacked Variance just gives you the amount that you can add to or subtract from the dimension.) As with Min/Max, you will be prompted for both a Lower and Upper Tolerance value, and asked to supply the number of decimal places. If any of these values are already set, simply press ENTER to move to the next prompt. Note that these values are shared with Min/Max, so they may already be set if you have set them for Min/Max.

Fixed Variance

The final option of the Dim Text Tolerance prompt is called Fixed Variance, which simply means that the Upper and Lower Tolerances are the same, so they need only be shown once in the dimension text, labeled as "plus or minus." Only one tolerance value will be requested, along with the decimal precision. These values are shared with Min/Max and Stacked Variance, so they may already be set. Simply press ENTER to move past any parameter that you don't need to change. See Figure 11-4 for an example of Fixed Variance.

Arrows and Other Line Terminators

Moving up the DIM SET menu, you next find the Arrow (AR) command. The Arrow command leads to a prompt containing four variables that control the nature of arrowheads and other optional dimension line terminators.

Chapter 11: Dimensioning

FIGURE 11-4 Dimension Tolerance styles

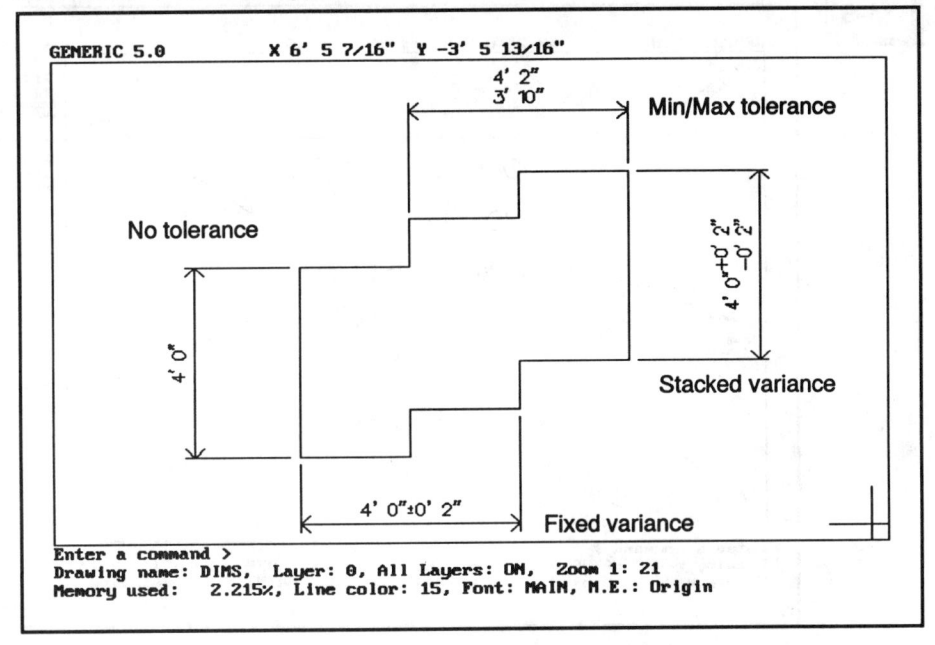

Note Users of previous versions of Generic CADD should note that, like much of dimensioning, arrowheads are specified in a significantly different way than before.

Arrow Type

The first option of the Arrow command, selected from the prompt or by typing **A** at the prompt, determines the basic shape of the arrowhead. See Figure 11-5 for illustrations of all seven of these basic types. As usual, you can select the type that you want from the menu, or press the highlighted letter corresponding to the one that you want.

Briefly, these types fall into three catagories, normal, circles, and slashes. Starting with the last, slashes are simply a diagonal line at the end of the dimension line, in a style often preferred by architects. Both the angle and length of this diagonal line are controlled by the other options within the Arrow command. Circles are either open or filled, and their size is controlled by another of these variables. Finally, normal

FIGURE 11-5 The seven different arrow types

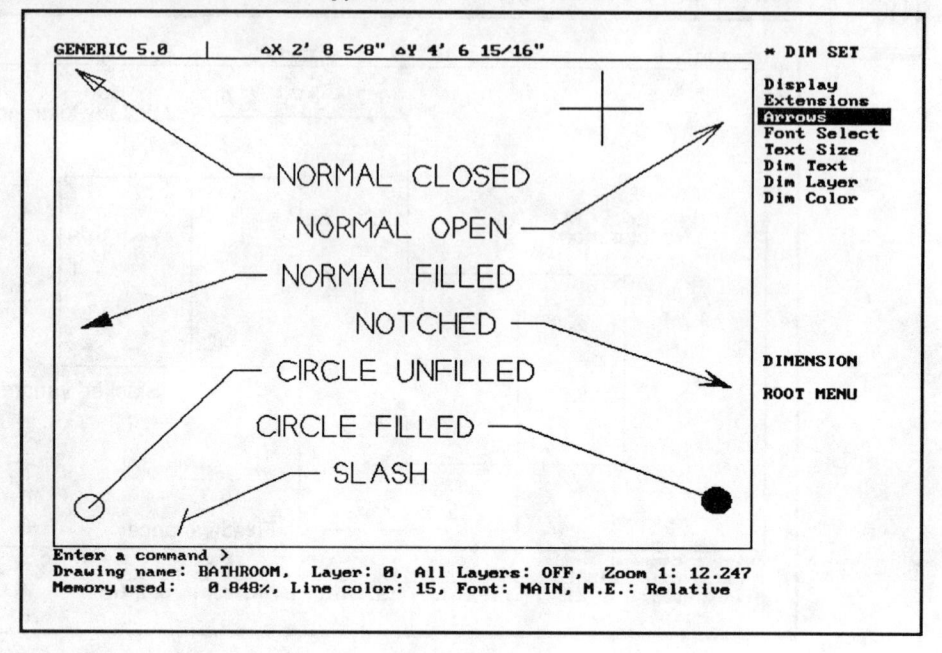

arrows end with arrowheads. These come in four varieties: open, which are simply two angled lines, one on either side of the dimension line; closed normal arrows, which add a third line that connects the two angled lines at their non-pointed end; filled normal arrows, which have this triangular zone filled; and notched arrows, which are filled, but the back side is pushed in toward the point, creating nontriangular, more traditional arrowheads.

Angle

The next Arrow option, Angle (A on the keyboard), sets the angle of normal and slash arrows. Circle arrowheads ignore this setting, as you might expect. For normal arrowheads, the angle will be measured from the dimension line, in whichever direction is appropriate for an arrowhead. Smaller angles create thinner arrowheads. Although the prompt allows values from -360 to 360 degrees, anything outside the range of -45 to 45 degrees will be treated as 45 degrees for normal arrows, and the minus sign is ignored.

For slashes, however, angles are always measured counterclockwise from the dimension line, and the minus sign makes a difference, as do values outside the 45-degree range. This allows infinite control over the direction and angle of slash arrowheads.

Length

The length, or size, of the various arrow types is controlled by the next variable on the Arrow prompt, Length (L). Arrow size was formerly controlled, in previous versions, by the Dimension Text Size command. Arrow size now has its own parameter. Normal arrows are measured along the angle of the arrow, from the point to the end of a side. Slashes are measured from one end to the other, so that the distance from the intersection with the dimension is exactly halfway in the slash line. Circles are specified by their diameter, so their radius is half the value you assign to length.

Location

The final value on the Arrows prompt selects the location (O) of the arrowhead. (Actually, in most cases, it has more to do with the location of the dimension line—the arrowheads just follow.) In the cases of circle and slash arrowheads, this parameter does not change the appearance of the heads, only of the line. While most dimensions may be done with the dimension line located Inside the extension lines (refer back to Figure 11-3 to see this), you may occasionally need to toggle them to the Outside with this command. See Figure 11-3 again for examples of Inside and Outside Arrow Locations. It is important to note that like the rest of the dimension parameters, the status of this toggle can be changed for a specific dimension after it has been placed if it turns out to require special handling due to local circumstances.

Extension Lines

Another multi-part parameter controls extension lines. These are the lines that extend from the object that you want to dimension to the dimension line, which is the line with the text on it. Extension lines are sometimes known as *witness lines*. See Figure 11-3 for the location of extension lines.

The four parameters inside the Extension (XS) command include an Offset distance, two lengths called Length Above and Length Below, and a toggle called Stretch.

Extension Offset

You may not want the extension lines to actually touch the object you are dimensioning. Graphic clarity usually mandates leaving some space around the dimensioned object. The amount of space between the object and the extension lines is controlled by the Offset variable of the Extension command. This can be activated by typing **O** or selecting Offset at the prompt. A value of zero produces extension lines that touch the object. Positive values leave a space of the specified size, while negative values create extension lines that cross into the object being dimensioned (these should be avoided unless you have unusual circumstances requiring this technique). The Extension Offset is labeled in Figure 11-3.

Extension Lengths

The two length variables, Length Above and Length Below, determine the default length of the extension lines. These are the A and B options in the Extensions prompt. As shown in Figure 11-4, the two together control the total length. Length Below controls the distance from the dimension line to the start of the extension line, where it is offset from the object, and Length Above controls the length of the portion from the dimension line outward, away from the object being dimensioned.

The names Above and Below are used rather loosely here, as if all dimensions were drawn horizontally across the top of an object. Above is really outside, or away from, the object while Below is inside, or toward, the object, no matter which side of an object the dimension is placed on.

Note that the outside value (Above) is always used, while the inside value (Below) may or may not be used, depending on the setting of other parameters, including Stretch, discussed next. Positive values yield the most conventional results, while negative values may be supplied to create an unusual dimensioning style.

Extension Stretch

The Stretch toggle, activated by typing **S** or selecting it at the Extension prompt, controls how seriously the Offset and Below Length variables are taken by the dimensioning commands. If Stretch is off, the value for the Below portion of extension lines will be used, and the Offset may be adjusted as required, as shown in Figure 11-6. In this example, several dimensions have been created using Partitioned Mode, discussed later. All of the extension lines are the same length, as specified by the Extension Length variables, because they have not been allowed to stretch. Note, however, that the Offset is used only on the first one, and then abandoned in favor of keeping the lengths the same.

Figure 11-7 shows the effect of turning Extension Stretch on. In this case, the extension lines are stretched, and the Offset is observed more rigorously. Again, the extension lines for the first dimension are important, as they establish the location of the dimension line. The location of the dimension line is established on this first dimension, and then maintained as more dimensions are added.

Note that if the two points specified for the first dimension are not the same distance from the dimension line, the Below Length will be used on the shorter of the two and the second will be stretched. Whether Stretch is on or off, the Below Length is used as a minimum for this first dimension.

Note also that the Proximity Fixed toggle, discussed later in this chapter, may override the Extension Length Below even on the first dimension.

Dimension Display Variables

Working up the video menu, the first item on the DIM SET menu controls the Display of various parts of your dimensions. It can be

FIGURE 11-6 Dimension Stretch turned off

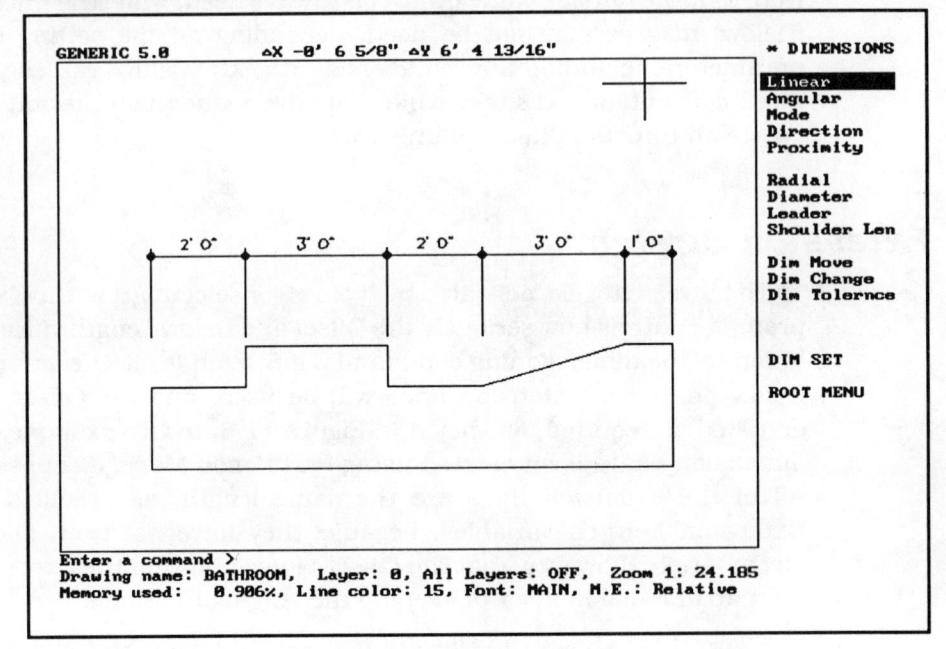

FIGURE 11-7 Dimension Stretch turned on

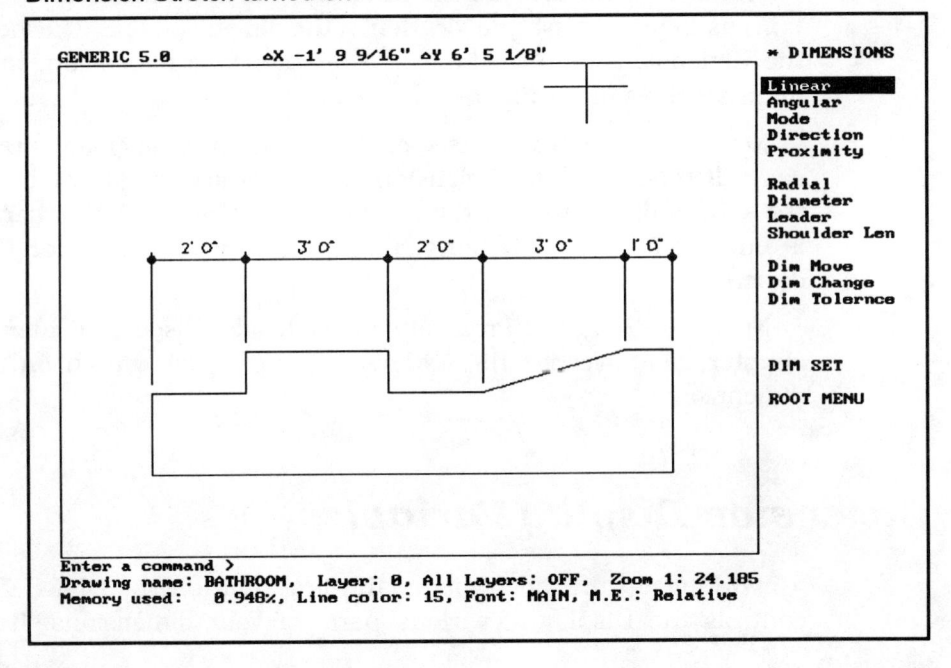

Chapter 11: Dimensioning

activated by typing **DD** on the keyboard, and controls six individual toggles, all of which toggle the display of one part of a dimension on or off. Note that like all parameters, these control the display of entities yet to be placed into the drawing, not those already created. To change the display attributes of dimensions already placed, use the Dimension Change (UG) command. The effect of these variables is demonstrated in Figure 11-8. The dimensions were created in a clockwise direction.

Left and Right Arrows

The Left and Right Arrow options, L and R in the prompt, respectively, control the display of the arrows at either end of your dimension lines. These are really only at the left and right of a "standard" horizontal linear dimension drawn from left to right. In all other cases, you can think of these as First and Second, rather than Right and Left. For example, in horizontal linear dimensions drawn from right to left rather than left to right, the so-called "Right" arrow will be on the left and the "Left" one on

FIGURE 11-8 Various parts of a dimension turned off

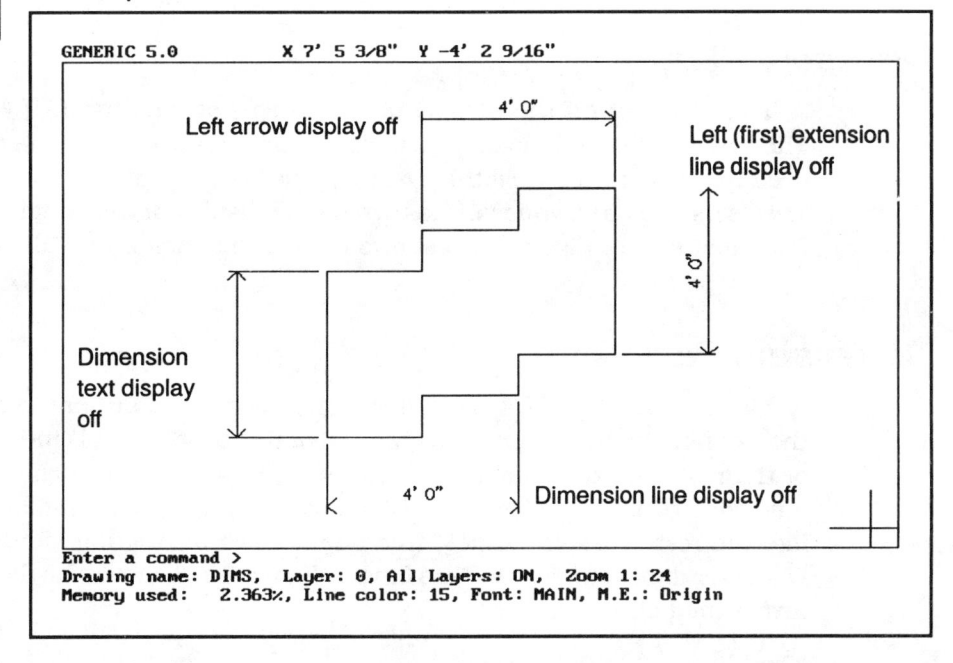

the right. First and Second makes more sense. Figure 11-8 shows the left arrow turned off.

In any case, dimensions created while Left (first) or Right (second) are toggled off will not display the corresponding arrowheads. This can be useful in special circumstances where you don't want one or both arrowheads for some reason. As with all of these toggles, keep in mind that they control only the display of the arrowheads, not their existence. Should you want to see these arrowheads later, you will not have to create them; you just turn their display on with the Dimension Change (UG) command. When asked for the part of the dimension to change, point to the place where the arrow would be if it was visible.

Left and Right Extension Lines

First and Second, instead of Left and Right, works here too. Again, these can be toggled on and off with the E and X options in the Display prompt. (If you've got a good mnemonic device for these, send it to me. I'll be darned if I can come up with one.) These come in handy when you are dimensioning from an object to a grid line, or between objects. Figure 11-8 shows the left extension line turned off.

Dimension Line

You can turn off the display of the dimension line itself, if you like. The arrowheads, extension lines, and dimension text will still show up, of course, unless you turn them off too. This is the D option in the prompt. This is useful when you want to turn off the display of the dimension line for some reason. Figure 11-8 shows the left dimension line turned off.

Dimension Text

Finally, the display of the dimension text may be suppressed, using the T option on the prompt. Like the rest of these toggles, it is independent of the rest, and dimensions created while this toggle is turned off can have their text restored with the Dimension Change (UG) command. Also, like the rest of these toggles, this one applies to Angular, Radial, and Diameter dimensions as well as Linear. Figure 11-8 shows the dimension text turned off.

Linear and Angular Dimension Parameters

As noted previously, the three parameters grouped with Linear and Angular dimensions on the DIMENSIONS menu apply only to these two types of dimensions. They make an interesting group. The first one, Mode, is not transparent and cannot be changed while you are placing dimensions. The middle one, Direction, applies only to linear dimensions. Finally, the last one, Proximity, is a toggle.

Proximity Fixed Toggle

In keeping with the rest of the discussion regarding parameters, let's start with the last one, Proximity. This toggle controls whether the location of the dimension line is calculated automatically or specified during placement. If it is on, Proximity is said to be *Fixed*, meaning that the distance between the object (or the point that you use to place your dimension) and the dimension line is based on the Extension Length Below and the Offset. When you are asked for the dimension location during placement, you will only be specifying which side of the object you want it on, not the exact location. If Proximity Fixed is off, you will be asked for the actual location of the dimension line during placement. This parameter applies to both Linear and Angular dimensions. If you start a dimension and reach a point where you are asked for the location and realize that you need to change this toggle, you can go ahead and do it without leaving the command you are in.

Dimension Direction

The Dimension Direction parameter applies only to Linear dimensions. Its four possible settings determine whether your dimension line will be Aligned at the angle between the points that you use to place the dimension, or forced to Horizontal, Vertical, or some other Angle.

Between any two points, three possible dimensions can be dimensioned: the actual shortest distance between the two points, which would be measured at the angle between the points; the horizontal distance; and the vertical distance. All of these are illustrated in Figure 11-9. Of course, if you pick an arbitrary angle to measure, you can generate as many dimensions as you like.

The distance you are actually dimensioning when you pick two points is determined by the Dimension Direction (UD) command. You are presented with the four choices already mentioned: Aligned (shortest distance), Horizontal, Vertical, and at an arbitrary Angle. Select one of these by picking it from the prompt or typing the highlighted letter. If you choose the arbitrary Angle, you will be prompted for the angle. This command will be used often, even if almost everything in your drawing is rectangular, as you move back and forth between Horizontal and Vertical. For very simple drawings, you may not need to change too often if you set Direction to Aligned. If you start a dimension and then realize that you have specified the wrong Direction, you can use this command without exiting the Dimension command.

FIGURE 11-9 Various dimension directions

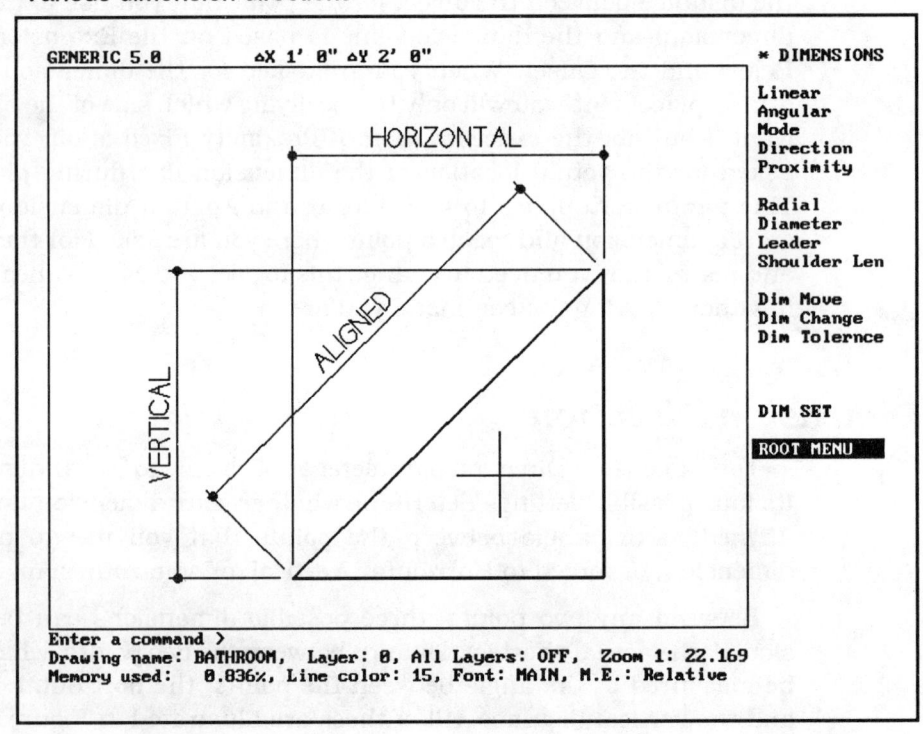

Dimension Mode

Finally, the command that *must* be set before you start a dimension is the Mode command. This three-way parameter controls how dimensions after the first one are created when using dimensioning to create multiple dimensions. No matter what the setting of this parameter, the first dimension is always created in the same way. Mode only applies to subsequent dimensions within the same command.

The three options that appear when you select Dimension Mode (UM) are Single, Partitioned, and Cumulative. The current mode is enclosed in parentheses, and is changed by selecting a new mode from the prompt or typing the highlighted character.

Single Dimension Mode   The Single option of the Mode prompt simply specifies that every dimension will be placed with its own command. After you have selected the points, placed the dimension, and verified, changed, and/or added to the text, the dimension is placed and you are returned to the "Enter a command >" prompt. To create another dimension, select the command again by choosing it from the menu, typing its two-character command, or by pressing the SPACEBAR to repeat the last command.

Partitioned Mode   If you select Partitioned Mode, you will create dimensions end on end until you press ESC to stop. The first dimension is created as usual. However, from there on, you will only be asked for the second point for each new dimension, as the second point of the previous dimension becomes the first point for the new dimension. All dimension lines connect one to the next as shown in Figure 11-10. This mode is used to create a *string* of dimensions. Note that if you press ESC to end the string, you will be asked for a new first point the next time that you use a Dimension command.

Cumulative Mode   As with Partitioned Mode, Cumulative Mode allows you to produce more than one dimension with the same command. In this case, however, it is the first point of the dimensions that is shared, so that the first point of the first dimension is the first point of each subsequent dimension, and you are asked only for the second points, as before. Each new dimension line is spaced from the previous one by a distance equal to the total of both Extension Lengths. The extension lines

FIGURE 11-10 Partitioned Mode dimensioning

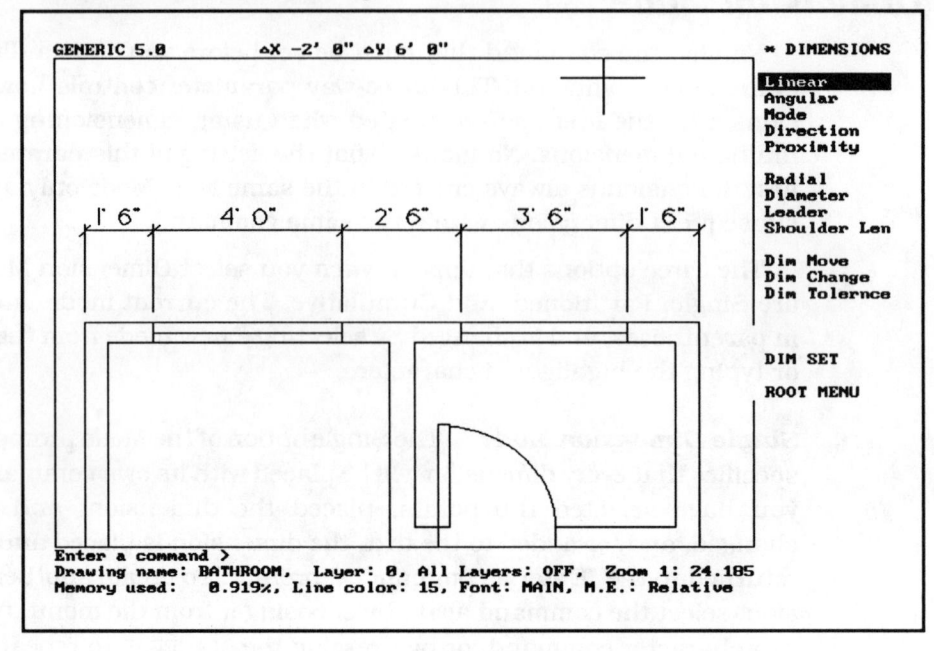

themselves stack up end on end. For an example of Cumulative Mode dimensioning, see Figure 11-11.

Leader Shoulder Length

The parameter at the bottom of the next group on the menu applies only to leaders, discussed briefly here and in more depth later in this chapter. It appears as Shoulder Len on the menu, and is called Leader Shoulder Size in the prompt, even though it applies to Radial and Diameter dimensions as well. Shoulder Length is activated by the two-character command LL.

A leader, as you shall see, is made up of an arrowhead, two lines, and a text string. Working from the arrowhead (usually located at the object that you want to use the leader to point to) out to the text, the first line is rubberbanded during placement. It looks just like a Line, except that there's an arrowhead on one end (which continuously updates its angle

FIGURE 11-11 Cumulative Mode dimensioning

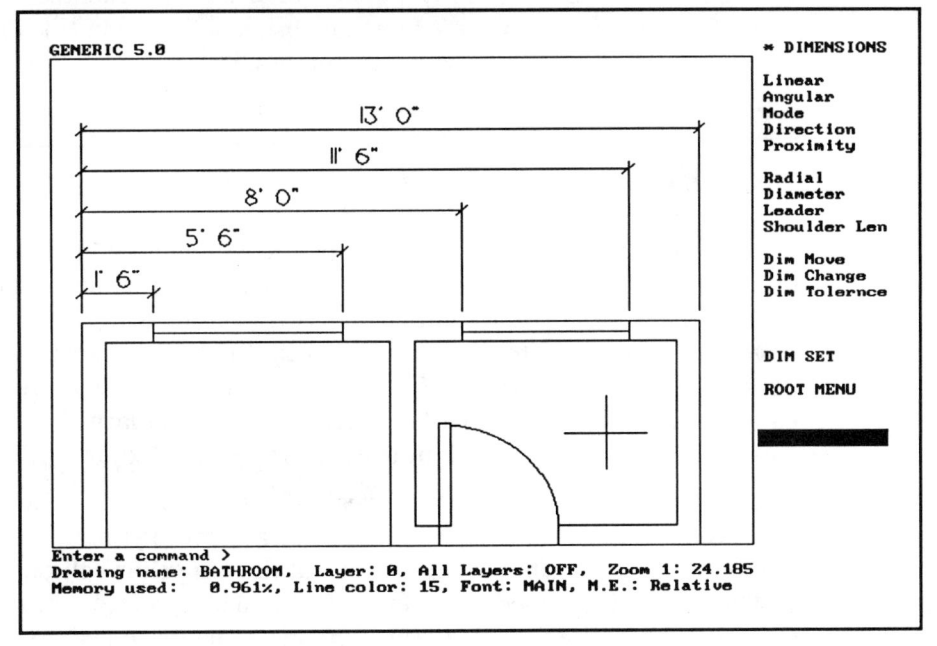

as you rubberband), the line bends to become horizontal at the other end, and a text string is appended to it. It's the length of this horizontal bend that is controlled by Shoulder Length. The type of arrowhead is controlled within the Arrow command, and the text string is supplied during placement, using text parameters from the DIM SET menu. More on Leaders later in this chapter.

Trying Out Possibilities with the Dimension Change Command

With so many variables to set, it is quite possible that you will not achieve the correct result on the first few tries. You may need to try putting various combinations of these parameters together until you find a style that you like. Use the ROOM plan, for example, or another existing drawing. Once your work is close to what you want, you can use the Dimension Change (UG) command to fine-tune some sample dimensions. Just don't forget to set the actual parameters to match what you find you like. Dimension Change only applies to the one dimension that you actually change! Dimension Change is discussed later in this chapter in the section "Editing Dimension Parameters."

Notes on Dimension Scale

Dimensions fall into the category of CADD items defined as symbols (see Chapter 8). As with all symbols, the size of dimensions on the printed sheet is more important than their size in the drawing. However, you have to put them into the drawing next to the objects that you are dimensioning, so the issue of scale arises. As with other symbols, the values that specify size must be adjusted, usually enlarged, so that they can be scaled back down when the drawing is printed or plotted.

You do this by multiplying the desired values by a scale factor that is the inverse of the scale factor to be applied at printing time. For instance, if you are dimensioning an architectural drawing that will be plotted at 1/4"=1', the actual scale factor is 1/48 of real size, or 1:48. Therefore, all of the values for the dimensioning variables must be scaled up by a factor or 48. To get a 1/8" Extension Offset, for instance, you must use a value of 6" (1/8 x 48). When the drawing is printed, 6" represented at the scale of 1/4"=1' will appear as 1/8" on the page.

Once you have established a style with the various parameters, the variables should be saved as part of the Environment with the EN command. If you print most of your drawings at a certain scale, you may want to include the values for your variables at that scale. If you use many different scales, you might instead set the values for their printed sizes, or at 1:1, to remind yourself to adjust these values for the scale of each drawing before starting to dimension. If you like, the scalable values could be stored in either Batch files or menu items. See Chapters 15 and 16 for more information on the Environment and other forms of customization that make the storage of this information easier.

Placing Dimensions

Setting the parameters is the hard part. Once you've done that, the Dimension Placement commands themselves are quite simple. You've used Linear dimensions as the primary example in most of the explanations given earlier, so they will be especially easy. Angular, Radial, and Diameter dimensions will require only marginally more experimentation.

Linear Dimensions

These are a snap. The only trick is to make sure that you've got both Dimension Mode and Dimension Direction set the way that you want. You may end up changing these frequently between placements of Linear dimensions. Units (UN) and Numeric Format (NF) should be checked too, since these will come to bear on your dimension text. Once these are all set, simply select Linear from the DIMENSIONS menu or type **LX** on the keyboard. Select the two points that you want to dimension between. It's best to snap onto some existing endpoints to maintain the accuracy of your dimensions.

After selecting your two points, you will be asked for the location of the dimension and the text. The order may vary according to the Mode. When location is requested, the dimension will be previewed on the screen in a rubberbanding style, so that you can place it visually. Remember, what you are actually selecting when you specify the location depends on the status of the Stretch toggle within the Extension command.

When the text is specified, Generic CADD 5.0 will generate a text string that describes the distance between the two points, using the current direction, in the currently operative Units and Numeric Format. This text will be displayed in a prompt, and presented to you for editing.

Note that on the editing line, the # symbol stands for the generated text. If you add to this by typing more at the prompt, the dimension text will contain the generated text followed by your text. You may wish to add a space. If you wish to *replace* the dimension text, simply use BACKSPACE to wipe out the # symbol and type your text. The generated text can be added to or replaced only. It cannot be edited, because it is based on actual data. If you later move one of the endpoints of the dimension, this generated text will be updated.

If you are in Partitioned or Cumulative Mode, the Linear dimension command will ask only for second points and text. First points will not be required, as they are based on the preceding dimension, and the location of the dimension line will be based on the location of the first one. To end the command if you are in either of these modes, press ESC.

Angular Dimensions

Angular dimensions are almost as easy as Linear dimensions. Figure 11-12 shows some of the many possibilities of Angular dimensioning. Use the two-character command AX or select Angular from the menu. You will need a point at the intersection of the angle to snap onto. If such a point doesn't exist, you might want to put a Standard Point (PO) there for this purpose. This must be done before you start the command.

You will be asked for three points for an Angular dimension, the center point (at the apex of the angle), and a point on each of the objects that you want to dimension the angle between. The prompt calls these points on the first and next radius, but don't be intimidated. Simply use any snap (third button or NP works well) to select these objects. If there isn't

FIGURE 11-12 A number of Angular dimensions

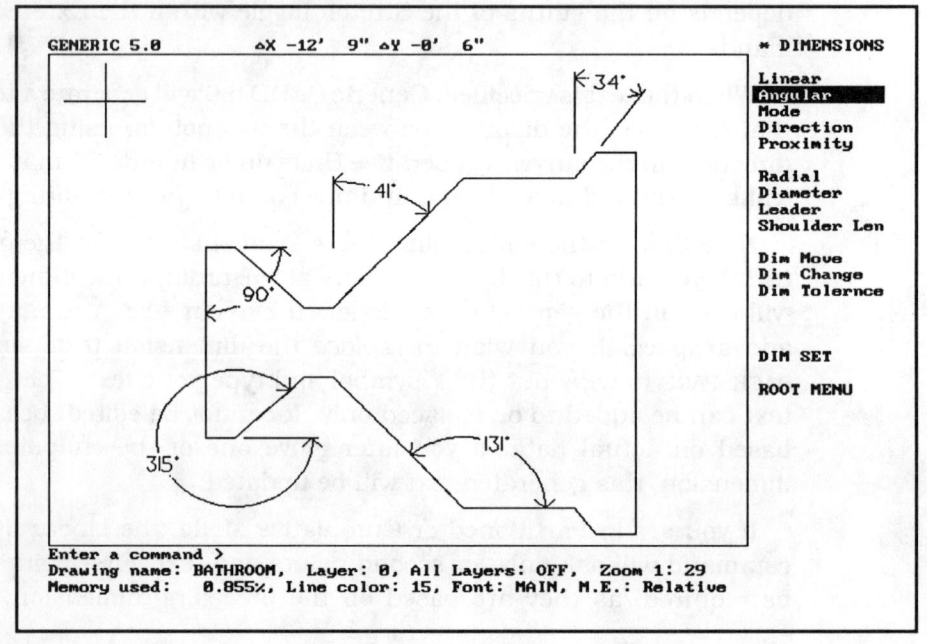

Chapter 11: Dimensioning

any other convenient point around, use the Closest Point (SC) command to pick the object. *Don't eyeball it!* Figure 11-13 shows the points required to create an Angular dimension. As with Linear dimensions, you will be asked for the location and the text, which are specified in the same way. Again, the order of these may vary. Since Mode applies here, you can continue on with second points and text if you are in Partitioned or Cumulative Mode until you press ESC.

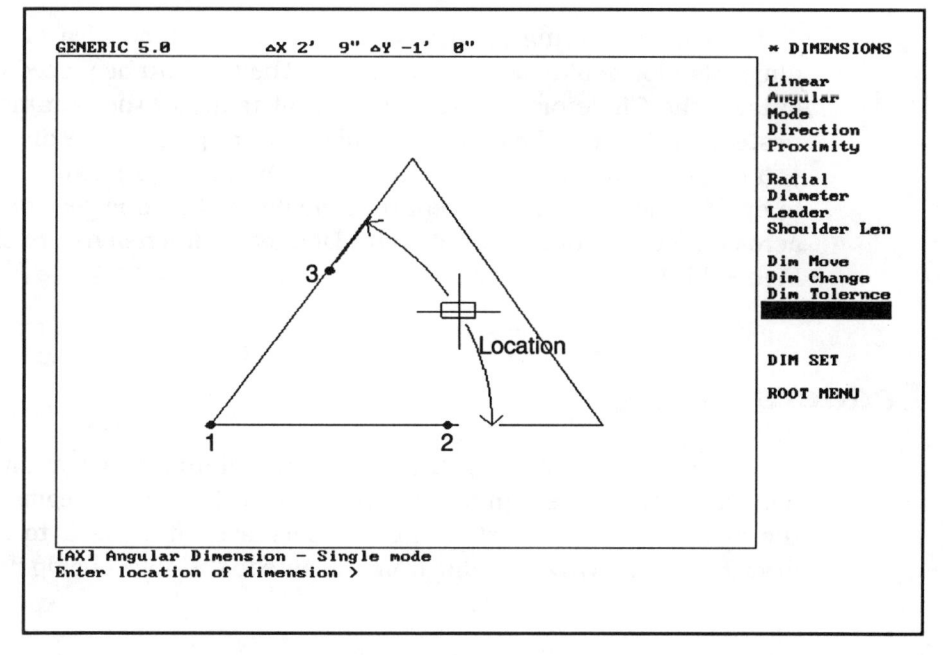

Radial and Diameter Dimensions

To dimension the radius of a Circle or Arc, use the Radial command in the second group of dimension commands, or type **RX** on the keyboard. You will be asked to specify only the object to be dimensioned, the text, and the location of the dimension. All appropriate parameters, such as the Arrow and Text parameters, come into play. Shoulder Length is used if Dim Text Direction is set to Horizontal.

FIGURE 11-13 The points required to create an Angular dimension

FIGURE 11-14 Radial and Diameter dimensions

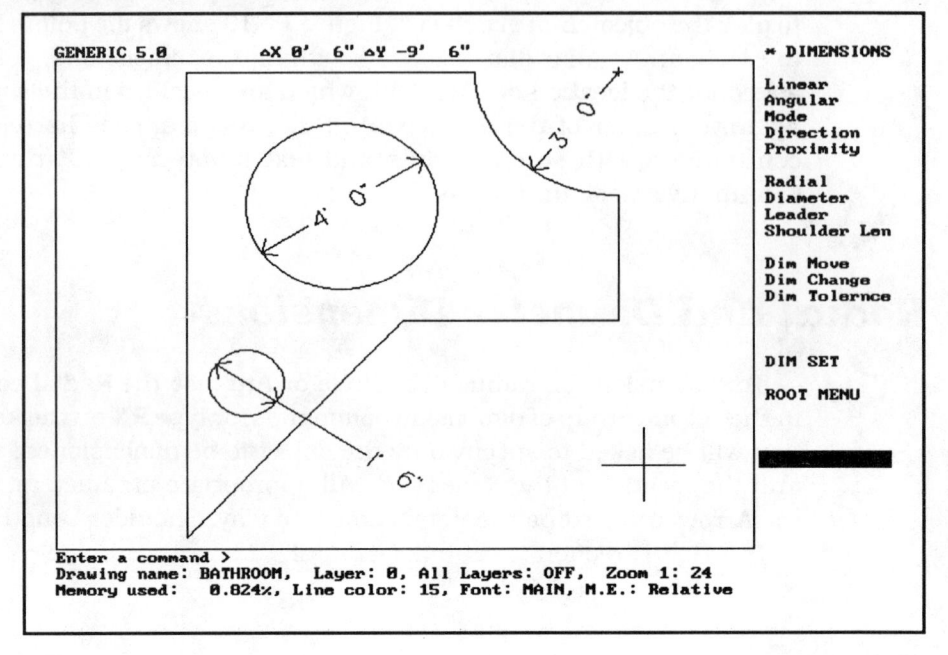

The rubberbanding preview gives you a very good idea of what the dimension looks like before you place it. The text can be placed inside or outside the Circle or Arc. Remember that many of the parameters are nested, so they can be changed while you are placing the dimension if you don't like what you are getting. The Diameter (IX) command works in exactly the same way, except that the dimension line goes all the way across the Circle or Arc. Radial and Diameter dimensions are shown in Figure 11-14.

Leaders

As discussed previously, Leaders consist of an arrowhead, a rubber-banded straight line terminating in a bended horizontal segment called the shoulder, and a text string. Leaders are often used to annotate drawings, with arrows leading from the note to the object being described, as shown in Figure 11-15.

Chapter 11: Dimensioning

FIGURE 11-15 A drawing with leaders

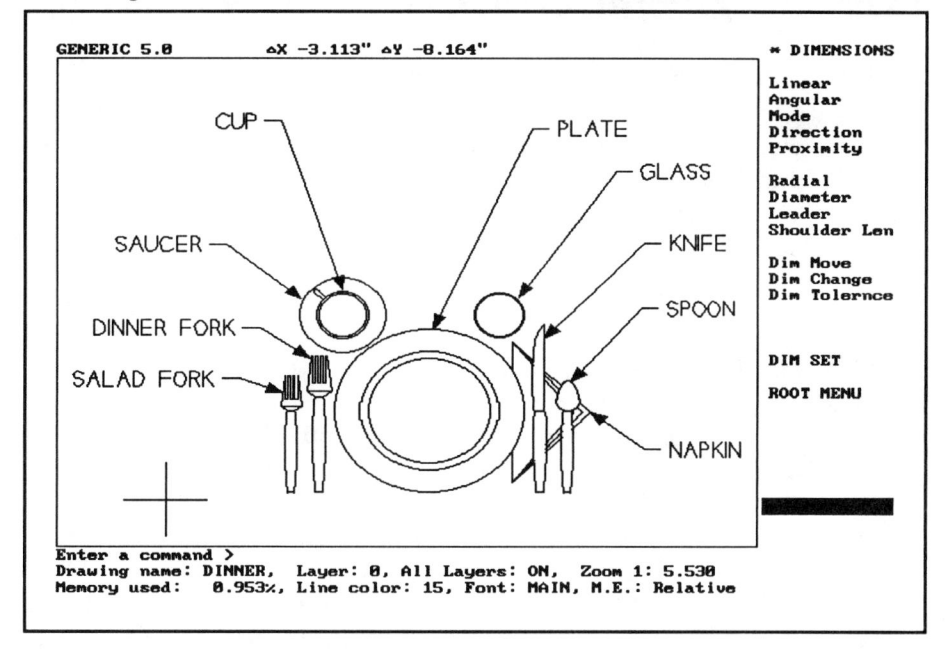

When you want to draw a leader, select Leader from the DIMENSIONS menu or type **LE** on the keyboard. You will first be asked for the Text. Type your text, using the BACKSPACE key if you make an error. The cursor keys and INS and DEL work here too. Press ENTER when you are done with the text. The text will all appear on a single line.

Next, you will be asked for the Starting Point. This is the arrowhead end, or a point on the object that you want the arrow to be pointing to. You can snap if you like.

Next is the terminal point. This is really the text end of the leader. To be absolutely accurate, the point that you select is actually the bend point, where the shoulder is connected. You will see the text previewed in the rubberbanding as a box as you drag this point around.

Finally, select the shoulder direction, which determines which side of the line the text ends up on. While Leaders cannot be edited with Dimension Change, you can use Dimension Move to correct errant Leaders in case you goof or change your mind later.

Editing Dimensions

Two editing commands exist specifically for the purpose of editing Associative dimensions. Note that neither of these will work on dimensions that have been exploded, as these become simply lines, arcs, text, and fills that are not subject to the parameters that govern dimensions. The following parameters and the definition points of Associative Dimensions may be edited.

Editing Dimension Parameters

Every Associative Dimension is considered a placed instance of a dimension of its type, just like a placed Component or a Text String or Character. The parameters that are active when the dimension is placed, along with the points used to place the dimension, are stored in the database at the placement locations. These parameters, therefore, can be edited to change the way that each dimension looks. This is done with the Dimension Change (UG) command in the last group on the DIMENSIONS menu.

When you use the Dimension Change command, notice that you are not asked simply to specify the dimension that you want to change, but to point to the specific part of the dimension that you want to change. This could be the Arrowhead, the Dimension Line, the Dimension Text, or one of the Extension Lines. Each of these is controlled by different parameters, so the parameters presented for editing will be different depending on which part of the dimension you choose. If you point to an arrowhead, for instance, you will access the Arrow parameters, which can be set just like you set the Arrow command. Similarly, the prompts for each part of the dimension are customized to provide access to all of the parameters that control that particular part. The number of parameters that you can edit depends on which part of the dimension you select. If you select the Dimension Text, a complex prompt including an Edit option for editing the text, access to both the Units and Numeric Format of the text is provided. You can use this command to edit almost any parameter controlling any dimension. Leaders are the only dimension entity that cannot be edited in this way.

Moving Dimensions

The Dimension Move (UV) command is used to change the location of the dimension line for Linear and Angular dimensioning, and the bend point for Radial, Diameter, and Leader dimensions. In all cases, the entire dimension is re-previewed when it is selected. This allows you to change the angle of the Radial, Diameter, and Leader dimensions. In the case of leaders, you will also be asked for a new shoulder direction. Shoulders for Radial and Diameter dimensions are placed automatically during the preview. After issuing the command, simply pick the dimension line that you want to move, and place the new point based on the rubberbanding preview on the screen.

Updating Dimensions

Many of the normal editing commands work on dimensions as well. The important thing to keep in mind about editing dimensions is that they are controlled by two or more definition points. In the case of Linear dimensions, these are the first two points used to place the dimension. With Angular dimensions, the center point is included. For Radial and Diameter dimensions, these definition points are the center point of the entity and a point on the entity. For Circles, the definition points of the circle are used, so editing works well. For Arcs, the middle point of the arc is used together with a calculated center. If you move one of the endpoints, the dimension will no longer be valid. Expect erratic behavior when editing Radial and Diameter dimensions attached to arcs.

Normally, the dimensions will be edited at the same time as the entities to which they have been snapped. When you use a Move Point command, for example, if you snap onto the point, all definition points located there will be moved. This includes dimensions. The Stretch Editing command moves dimension definition points located within the final selection window; however, you must select the dimension entity itself in the first part of the command by capturing all of its definition points in a window. When stretching, don't be too picky with the initial selection. Get everything in sight!

Associative Dimensioning is one of the very powerful features introduced with Generic CADD 5.0; it makes dimensioning and annotating drawings much easier than ever before. Note, however, that despite the moniker Associative, these dimensions are in no way tied permanently to the entities that you are dimensioning. If the dimensioning layer is turned off while you edit the drawing, for instance, you will see when you turn it back on that the dimensions have not simply updated themselves to reflect the new conditions. It is the fact that the definition points for the dimensions are snapped onto other entities in the drawing, and can therefore be edited at the same time as other entities with the Move Point and Stretch editing commands, that makes them seem to behave associatively. With this is mind, you should be able to create dimensions that you can update along with your drawing without much effort.

CHAPTER 12

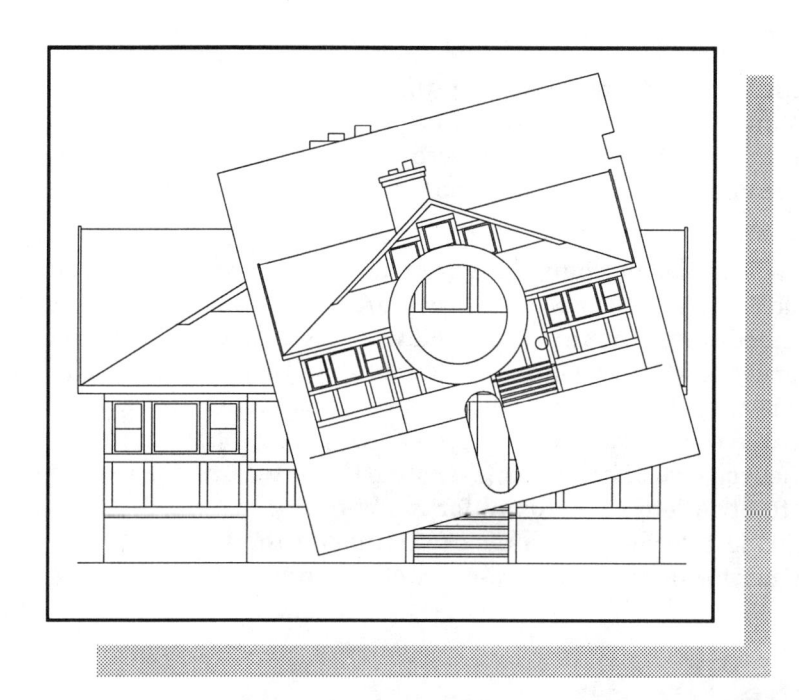

File Storage and Retrieval

One of the most important functions of any computer program is to store and retrieve information. This information is stored on disks in files. Because Generic CADD 5.0 stores several different kinds of information, it uses several different types of files.

On MS-DOS systems, filenames can be up to eight characters, and may be followed by a period and three additional characters, called the *filename extension*. As discussed in Chapter 3, "Preliminary Considerations," Generic CADD, like many modern application programs, uses these three characters to identify the type of information stored in the file.

Drawings are stored in files with the extension .DWG, components with the extension .CMP, and fonts with the extension .FNT. A number of additional file extensions are used, as you shall see later in this chapter. The program itself uses files with a variety of different extensions. For more information on manipulating files on your computer, see Chapter 3.

There are a number of commands that deal with the storage and retrieval of information in files. Many of these are in the FILE menu, while others are located on the menu associated with the type of information being saved or retrieved, and share the first letter of their two-character command code with the other commands on that menu. In general, Generic CADD 5.0 uses the term "LOAD" as part of the name for commands that retrieve information (assigning the letter *L* as the second character of the two-letter command for many of these), and the term "SAVE" for saving information on disk (often using the letter *S* as the second character for many other two-character commands).

Default Paths

Whenever you load or save a file, Generic CADD 5.0 needs to know where you want to find or put that file. In MS-DOS terminology, the location on disk where you want to store a file is known as the *path*. You can set up default paths for the location of drawing files, component files, font files, batch files, hatch files, menu files, other programs that you might need access to, and miscellaneous files. Although the various loading and saving commands can locate your files anywhere, it is easier and faster if you tell them in advance where to look.

There are two different styles of commands available for setting your default paths. The File Paths command offers a prompt menu giving the various file paths that you might want to set; individual shortcut commands, inherited from the previous version of Generic CADD, allow you to change the drawing, component, and font paths individually.

The File Paths Command

To change any or all of the paths from a multiple-selection prompt, select File Paths from the FILE menu or type **FP** on the keyboard. A list of the various paths that you can set will be shown. You can select from these by choosing from the prompt with the prompt cursor and the first button on the pointing device or by pressing the highlighted letter on the keyboard.

The first six on the list are six different paths for files with six corresponding extensions. The Dwg option, for example, sets the path where Generic CADD 5.0 will look for drawing files, which always use the extension .DWG. Similarly, the Cmp (component) option sets the path for files with the .CMP extension, and Fnt (font) sets the path for .FNT files. The Batch option is for .TXT files, the Hatch option is for .HCH files, and the Menu option is for .MNU files.

The seventh item on the list, Shell, is where you can locate additional programs that you might need while using Generic CADD 5.0. For more information about using the Shell capabilities of Generic CADD 5.0, see Chapter 17, "Communicating with Other Programs." The last path option, mIsc, identifies the path for any other files that Generic CADD 5.0 might need to create or use while running. These include image (.GX2) files, Printer and Pointing device drivers (.TPR and .IPD), and ASCII files that you might want to import as text, as well as other miscellaneous files.

When you select any of these, you will be prompted with the current path, which you may either edit or retype. BACKSPACE, the cursor keys, INS, and DEL can all be used here. If you start by typing a disk drive designator, such as A:, B:, C:, and so on, the current path will be removed as soon as you type the colon. You can do this instead of backspacing over a long existing path. After editing the old path or typing a new one, press ENTER to return to the File Paths prompt. Note that if you do not include a backslash (\) at the end of your path specification, it will be added for you, as a backslash is required to separate the pathname from the filename of the actual file that you will be loading or saving using this path.

When you have set all of the paths that you wish to, press ENTER to end the File Paths command or select it from the prompt. Like many other settings, these paths are saved with the drawing file, so you don't need to set them up for every drawing session. Each path should include the disk drive designator and directory where you want to keep the specified type of file. If the disk is the same as the disk where Generic CADD 5.0 files are stored, you don't really have to include it, but it is good practice.

The Individual Path Commands

For compatibility with earlier versions, and as a convenient shortcut to some of the more often-changed paths, three individual commands are provided for specifying the drawing, component, and font paths. These are designated P1, P2, and P3, respectively, and don't appear on any menus.

The Drawing Path Command

Drawing files are stored in the default drawing path. These files are typically saved when you quit Generic CADD and loaded when you first start Generic CADD. In addition to the entities in your drawing, most of the current parameter settings are stored in your drawing files as well.

To change the default drawing path, you can use the Dwg option of the File Paths command discussed previously, or type **P1** on the keyboard with the same result. You are shown the name of the current path, and given the opportunity to edit it. If you simply press ENTER, you will keep the path shown. If you BACKSPACE the path out, leaving it blank, Generic CADD will look for drawing files in your Generic CADD directory (no path). As a rule you won't want to do this. It may work at first when you don't have many drawing files, but once you have more than just a few, it makes more sense to keep them in their own subdirectory and give them their own path. When you install Generic CADD 5.0, a subdirectory for drawings is set up automatically, and the default drawing path set to this. You may want to further divide drawing files by job, drawing type, or some other organizing scheme.

The drawing path will be used by all commands that load or save drawing files, including such commands as Quit (QU), Load Drawing (DL), Layer Load and Save (YL and YS), and others.

The Component Path Command

Component files contain individual components that can be loaded and used in your drawings. These components may be of your own creation, they may be purchased from Generic Software or third-party sources, or they might come from your consultants, clients, colleagues, or friends. In any case, Generic CADD 5.0 expects to find them in the default component path, which can be set individually by typing the command code, **P2**.

The component path is declared in the same way as the drawing path, with the same results if you simply press ENTER instead of typing a pathname or if you delete the path entirely. It is possible to store your components in the same directory as your program files, but you will probably want to put them in their own subdirectory. The installation program creates a subdirectory called CMP for this purpose and initializes the component path accordingly. Some of the commands that use the component path are Component Place (CP), Save Component (SA,C), Component Load (CL or LO,C), and Component Dump (CD). For more information on components, see Chapter 6, "Drawing Aids and Controls."

The Font Path Command

Fonts are stored in the default font path, each font in its own file with the extension .FNT. When you use any type of text, you must have a currently active font, loaded from the current font path. Several fonts come with Generic CADD 5.0, and additional fonts are available from Generic Software and third-party developers. You can also make up your own font, either within Generic CADD, or with a pair of font-making utilities available from either Generic Software as part of their UTILITIES package or from WORKSHOP 3D Design Studio as a stand-alone utility.

The font path is specified exactly like all other paths, and a directory in which supplied fonts are stored is set up upon installation. This becomes the initial default setting for the font path. The font path is used by the Font Select command, which selects the fonts for various uses.

Storing Information

Generic CADD 5.0 provides a wide range of methods for saving information. Not only can various types of information be saved in a variety of file formats, but the same type of information can often be saved through a number of different commands. The Save (SA) commands provide generalized access via a prompt menu to a number of different types of files, while most file types also have their own load and save commands, located on various menus.

Saving Drawing Files

Drawing files are the most common and most important files that you save and load when working with Generic CADD 5.0. Everything that Generic CADD knows about the drawing is saved in a drawing file: the location of every entity, the definition of every component, and the settings of all of the parameters. All geometric relationships are preserved, and all numeric data is accurately recorded. Several commands are available for the storage of drawing files.

The Quit Command

You may wish to save your drawing file at other times as well, but you will almost always want to save it when you exit Generic CADD. Whenever you issue a Quit (QU) command, you are asked if you want to save your drawing file. A default name (including the drawing path, if any) is suggested, based on the name that you used to load the drawing. If you started Generic CADD without loading a drawing, the name UNTITLED will be suggested. This is more a warning than a serious suggestion. If you simply press ENTER, the drawing will be saved using the suggested name. However, in most cases you'll give the file a different name by either editing the name suggested or typing a new one. If you simply start typing a name, the suggested name will be removed back as far as the end of the pathname. If you instead first press the BACKSPACE or the left arrow cursor, you can then edit the name shown. If at any time you type a disk drive designator such as A: or B: (including a colon), the path will be replaced as well. After typing a new name or editing the old one, press ENTER.

Once you have selected a filename, Generic CADD checks to see if the file already exists on the disk, in the path specified. If it does not, the file is immediately saved under your filename. If a file by the specified name already exists, you will be warned that the file exists and asked if you want to "Rename" or "Overwrite" the existing file. If you elect to overwrite the file (by typing **O**), the new drawing will simply replace it. If you select the rename option (by typing **R**), Generic CADD renames the original file using the same eight-character filename, with the extension .BAK. The new drawing file is then saved, using the same name with the extension .DWG. This option allows you to keep backup files that are previous versions of your current drawing files.

Finally, after the drawing has been saved, you are asked if you want to Quit or Continue. If you type **Q** to Quit, you are returned to DOS; if you type **C** to continue, you return to the "Enter a command >" prompt where you may continue your Generic CADD drawing session. If you type **E**, an option not shown on the prompt, you will be given the opportunity to save the current toggle settings and parameters as the default Environment. For more on the Environment, see Chapter 16, "Programming Generic CADD 5.0."

If for any reason Generic CADD cannot save your file, a brief message in the prompt area informs you that the file has not been saved. Possible reasons for this might be a path that does not exist (the pathname may have a typo) or a full or damaged disk. Generic CADD does not refuse to save a file simply because you use more than eight characters in a filename. Instead, it simply chops off the extra characters and saves the file using the first eight characters you typed as the filename.

The Drawing Save Command

The Drawing Save command is a shortcut left over from previous versions of Generic CADD. While not listed on any menu, it provides a quick two-character method (DS) for saving your drawing file in the middle of a drawing session. This command operates in much the same manner as Quit, with two exceptions: (1) It does not ask you if you want to save the drawing, as that is its only purpose, and (2) it does not ask you if you want to quit or continue at the end of the command, but instead simply returns you to the "Enter a command >" prompt as soon as it has saved the drawing.

The Drawing Save command is a particularly easy command to use for simply saving your drawing file once in a while. Assuming that you have already named the drawing properly while loading it, you can simply type **DS**, then press ENTER to accept the suggested pathname and filename. Saving your drawing on a regular basis is highly recommended, and this is a good quick way to do it. Of course, you can edit both filenames and pathnames at the prompt if you wish.

The Save Command

A more generalized approach to the same task is available with Generic CADD 5.0 that was not available with earlier releases. The Save command on the FILE menu (SA on the keyboard) allows you to save a variety of different file types. Drawing is the first option in the prompt, along with Component, Batch file, Attribute, Level 3 file, and perhaps Image, depending upon your graphics card and options selected during installation. Selecting Drawing from this prompt or typing **D** produces the same result as using the Drawing Save command.

Level 3 file is a special option for saving drawing files in a format compatible with Generic CADD Level 3, the previous release of Generic CADD. These files are different from 5.0 drawing files in a number of ways. Most importantly, they do not include the parameter settings or any entities not recognized by Level 3, such as Associative Dimensions, Text Lines, and Attributes. These entities are exploded into entities recognizable by Level 3. In addition to providing compatibility with Level 3, these files are compatible with Generic 3D Drafting versions 1.0 and 1.1, AutoConvert version 4.0, and Generic and third-party utilities developed for the Level 3 file format. Later versions of Generic Software products than those mentioned should not require Level 3 drawing files for compatibility.

Note Loading Level 3 format drawing files into Generic CADD 5.0 is done in the normal way and doesn't require any special command or option.

The Selection Save Command

In some cases you may want to save only a portion of your drawing. Sel Save Dwg on the FILE menu, or **SV** on the keyboard, allows you to use any of the entity selection methods, including Filter and Last Selection as well as the more typical Object, Window, Layer, and Drawing. After issuing this command, you can use any method to select the entities that you want to save into a drawing file. Remember that you can hold down CTRL while selecting a method to activate deselection in case you select too many or the wrong ones. You can zoom while selecting, if you like. When you are done selecting entities, press ENTER, and the command will continue, prompting with a suggested filename, which you can then edit in the usual fashion.

The Layer Save Command

The Save option on the LAYERS menu will issue the SV command followed by a Y option. However, there is another command called Layer Save, which is a shortcut for saving a single layer, held over from previous releases of Generic CADD. Typed **YS**, this command simply asks you to select a layer, and then proceeds immediately to the suggested name. The name suggested will be LAYER followed by three digits representing the layer number. As usual, you can edit this filename before pressing ENTER to actually save the file.

The Window Save Command

Users of previous versions will probably be surprised when typing **WS** gets no response. In Generic CADD 5.0, the Window Save function is handled by Selection Save, SV above, using the Window (W) option. You could make this into a macro if you like. See Chapter 16 if you want to learn how to do this.

Saving Component Files

When you first create a component, it resides only within the drawing file in which it was created. In this form, it cannot be used unless this drawing file is loaded. In order to make a component accessible to other drawing files, the component must be in a file by itself. Component files are slightly different from drawing files, and are designated by the extension .CMP for this reason. Although you cannot directly call up a component file as if it were a drawing file, you can use a component that is saved in its own file while another drawing file is loaded. Generic CADD 5.0 includes two commands for saving components into files: the Save command and the Component Dump command.

The Save Command

Individual components within a drawing can be saved to disk files with the Component option of the Save (SA) command. This command can be accessed from the FILE or COMPONENTS menus. If you select it from the COMPONENTS menu, the Component option is selected automatically. If you type **SA** or select it from the FILE menu, select the Component option from the prompt or type **C**.

This command asks you to select the component that you want to save, either by typing it or selecting it from the menu, then proposes a filename, made up of the current default Component path and the first eight characters of the name of the component itself. As usual, this proposed filename can be edited. You do not need to add or include the extension .CMP, as this will be added automatically when the file is saved.

Note that when you later load the component into another drawing file, you will be required to use the component name, rather than the filename, to place the component. If possible, it is a good idea to use the same name for both the component and the file used to store it, in order to avoid confusion. It is awkward to load a component by one name, then see it appear on the menu under a different name.

Keep in mind that although component names can have up to 12 characters, DOS filenames can have only 8. Interestingly, the four characters that are chopped off when the component is saved into a file are not permanently lost. If you have a component called "ELEPHANTEARS," which contains 12 characters, Generic CADD 5.0 will save it in a file called "ELEPHANT.CMP" by default. However, when you later load the component ELEPHANT into another drawing file, it will appear on the menu as ELEPHANTEARS, and you must use this name to place the component after the initial load.

The Component Dump Command

To save all of the components in a drawing file with one command, use Comp Dump on the COMPONENTS menu or type **CD** on the keyboard. This command simply runs through all of the components currently defined in the drawing file one by one, proposing filenames for each, and saving each to a separate file in the default component directory.

When you issue this command, the first proposed filename (consisting of the component path and the name of the first component in the file) will be shown. You may edit before saving, or accept as is by simply pressing ENTER. Repeatedly pressing ENTER as the names are provided saves one component after another until they have all been saved.

When Generic CADD 5.0 finds that one of your new component filenames already exists on the disk, it asks if you want to overwrite or rename the old file. If you rename it, the extension of the original file is changed from .CMP to .BAK. Be careful: once the extension has been changed, it is difficult to distinguish component files from drawing files. (This is a good reason to keep component files in their own directory.)

Saving Batch Files

Since drawing files are stored in a format that cannot easily be accessed by other application programs not written specifically to deal with them, Generic CADD 5.0 provides an alternative ASCII format called a *Batch file*. This file format contains all of the Generic CADD commands required to re-create the drawing. This makes it possible to access the information in your drawing file with other software, including any word processor that can read ASCII files. The format and use of Batch files is covered in Chapter 16.

Three commands will save your drawing in the batch format, which uses the file extension .TXT. The Batch (B) option of the Save (SA) command saves Batch files, as does the shortcut Save Batch (SB) command on the UTILITIES menu. Finally, the Sel Save Btc command on the same menu, short for Selection Save Batch and typed **BS** on the keyboard, allows you to save a subset of the entire drawing as a Batch file using any combination of the standard selection methods. Unlike most of the Selection commands, this one doesn't start with selection. You are asked for the filename first, and then asked to select the entities.

A special file extension may be required by the software that you are using to manipulate the Batch file. If you do not wish to use the extension .TXT, you may delete it and use another. To get no extension at all, type a period at the end of the filename. Note that as with other file types, if the file already exists, you will be asked if you want to overwrite or rename the existing version. If you rename, the old Batch file becomes a .BAK file.

Saving Attributes

Like Components, Attributes created in a drawing file remain in that drawing file only unless you save them into disk files. Attributes are saved on disk in their own files, with the extension .ATB. This is done with the Attribute option of the Save command on the FILE menu, which can be accessed automatically by selecting it from the ATTRIBUTES menu instead.

Once selected, this command presents you with a menu of the Attributes currently defined in the drawing, asking you to select which one you want to save. You can select it from the menu or type a name. A filename is then suggested, using the default component path and the name of the Attribute itself. As with components, if the attribute name is more than eight characters, only the first eight will be used in the filename. You do not need to type the extension .ATB, as it will be added automatically during saving. For more information on Attributes, see Chapter 17.

Saving Image Files

Generic CADD is capable of capturing screen images on some graphics cards, if you have elected in favor of this capability during installation. Screen images are simply a record of how the dots on the screen are currently displayed. Screen images are similar to the type of file used by painting programs: no actual CADD data is saved, only pixel locations.

To save a screen image, use the Save command on the FILE menu, and select the Image option or type **I**. You are asked for an image filename. The current drawing filename, with the extension .GX2 substituted for .DWG, is suggested. You can edit this or simply accept it by pressing ENTER. Once you have entered or accepted the filename, you are asked if you want to save the full screen. If you are saving the image for reloading into Generic CADD 5.0 or perhaps 3D Drafting, type **N**, and only the drawing area, including the border, will be saved. If you are saving the image for use with Generic Paint, Present, or another image-processing program, you will probably want to type **Y** and save the entire screen. The use of image files with other software is discussed in Chapter 17.

If your video driver does not support image files, the Image option will not be present on the Save prompt. If you are using a standard video driver such as CGA, EGA, VGA, or Hercules, and the Image option is not present, it is because you are using the small video driver supplied with Generic CADD. This is selected at installation when you are asked whether or not you want the image function. The large drivers are called this because they take up more memory, leaving less space available for your drawing. If you do not use images, you should probably leave the smaller driver installed. Use CONFIG to change to a large driver.

Saving the Default Parameters with the Environment Command

When you load a drawing file, all of the parameter settings that were current when the drawing was last saved are used. Often, however, you will want to start up Generic CADD with no drawing file, and create a brand-new one. You need a place, then, to store the default parameters that will be used with new drawing files.

These are stored in a drawing file called GCADD.DWG, which is really just a drawing file with no drawing in it. Only the parameter settings are stored. This drawing file is stored in the Generic CADD directory, rather than on any drawing path, so that you will always have access to it even if you change the drawing path.

A special command, the Environment command, exists specifically for updating this file, when you want to change the default parameter settings for new files. Technically, this file *could* be created by simply starting a new drawing, setting the parameters the way that you want them, not drawing anything, and saving the drawing file to GCADD. However, you have to remember to set the path to the Generic CADD directory, or the file will be updated in the wrong directory.

The Environment command on the FILE menu is simpler and safer. When you select it or type **EN** on the keyboard, you will be asked to verify that you want to update the default environment (parameter settings). This check is provided just in case you type the command accidentally. Type **Y** and GCADD.DWG will be updated to reflect the current parameter settings. Typing **N** will cancel the command. Alternatively, the Environment may be updated with the E option of the Quit command.

Retrieving Information

Generic CADD 5.0 gives you almost as many ways to retrieve information as to store it. For each type of file, one or more commands allow you to load files, producing a variety of results.

Generic CADD 5.0 can only load files that strictly follow Generic file formats. This means that files must have been created by Generic CADD, Generic 3D Drafting, AutoConvert, or another program that produces Generic CADD files. Level 3 format drawing files can also be loaded. In the case of Batch files, image files, attribute files, component files, and other files, the format for the appropriate file type must be followed. Generic CADD 5.0 can load Level 3 Component and Font files as well as drawing files. Batch files may be created in a number of ways, even with a word processor, but they must follow Generic's format very strictly, or they will not work. Even ASCII files loaded as text are subject to certain requirements. See Chapter 8, "Complex Entities," for more information on these.

Loading Drawing Files

Drawing files can be loaded as you start Generic CADD, or they may be loaded after Generic CADD 5.0 has been started. Loading a drawing file when another is already loaded allows you to move information from one drawing into another. A variety of commands are provided for loading drawing files.

Automatic Loading

When you start CADD, you may add the name of the drawing file after the word CADD at the DOS prompt line. For example, if you type **CADD SITEPLAN** at the DOS prompt, Generic CADD will be loaded, the default directory that was active the last time you used Generic CADD will be searched for this drawing, and it will be loaded if it is found. If it is not present, a new drawing by this name will be started.

Note When you start Generic CADD 5.0 in this way, the copyright screen is not displayed. Users of earlier versions will need to kick the habit of pressing ENTER twice to skip the copyright screen when using this method. If this is done, the second ENTER will interrupt the automatic Zoom All at the beginning of the drawing session, and the drawing area will come up blank. A Redraw (RD) will show that the drawing really does exist after all, and you can let your heart settle back to its normal location.

The Drawing Load Command

The simplest command for loading drawings after a Generic CADD 5.0 session has been initiated is Drawing Load (DL). This is a shortcut from previous versions, and doesn't appear on any menu. You are simply asked for a filename, which you can choose from the menu if you like. The files on the menu will be the files in the current default drawing directory with the extension .DWG. If there are more than will fit on the screen, the word MORE will appear at the bottom of the menu (you can use this to see *more* of the list). CANCEL, also near the bottom of the menu, cancels the command, as you might expect.

If the default drawing path is a directory on a disk, and you want to load a file from a different directory, you can select the top item on the menu "..", which means moving to the parent directory of the directory you are currently viewing. You can either select files from this directory, or move to yet another directory by selecting one of the items on the menu that starts with a backslash (\). These are other directories. Selecting one of these shows you a directory of .DWG files in the selected directory rather than trying to use the directory name as a filename. If you select one of these files, it will be loaded.

If you wish to load a file from a different disk, type the disk drive designator, including the colon (:), at the prompt and press ENTER. The menu will be updated to show the drawing files available on the selected disk. You may now select a file from this list.

Once you have selected a file to be loaded, you will be asked if you want to "rename the working drawing." If you do, the current name of the drawing that you are working on is changed to the name of the file that you are loading. Nothing actually happens on the disk to rename the file at this point, however. The new name will simply be the one suggested the next time that you save the file. If you choose not to rename, the default name for saving stays the same as it was before the load was initiated.

Before the loaded drawing is placed into the current drawing, it is first loaded into memory, where the extents are calculated. A rectangle is displayed to preview the size of the drawing, and you are given the opportunity to select a location by dragging the preview rectangle and placing it, as shown in Figure 12-1. If you wish to place the origin of the loaded drawing at the origin of the current drawing, simply press ENTER instead of dragging the rectangle around.

When you load one drawing into another at any point other than the origin of the current drawing, the loaded drawing essentially goes through a Drawing Origin. All of the points in all of the entities in the loaded drawing are adjusted by an amount equal to the distance between the origins of the two drawings. When you simply press ENTER, this step is skipped. This process allows you to load two drawings into a single drawing file without having them overlap, even if both were originally created at the same place in relation to their own origins.

The component and other complex entity definitions in the loaded drawing are brought into the current drawing as well. However, if there is a conflict in definitions, as when you have different components with the same name in the two files, the definitions already in the current drawing will take precedence over those being loaded. All instances of components, for example, in the loaded drawing will appear as placements of the components by the same name in the current drawing.

Neither is the environment information from the loaded drawing brought into the current drawing. All of the current parameter settings

Chapter 12: File Storage and Retrieval

FIGURE 12-1 Loading a drawing into Generic CADD 5.0

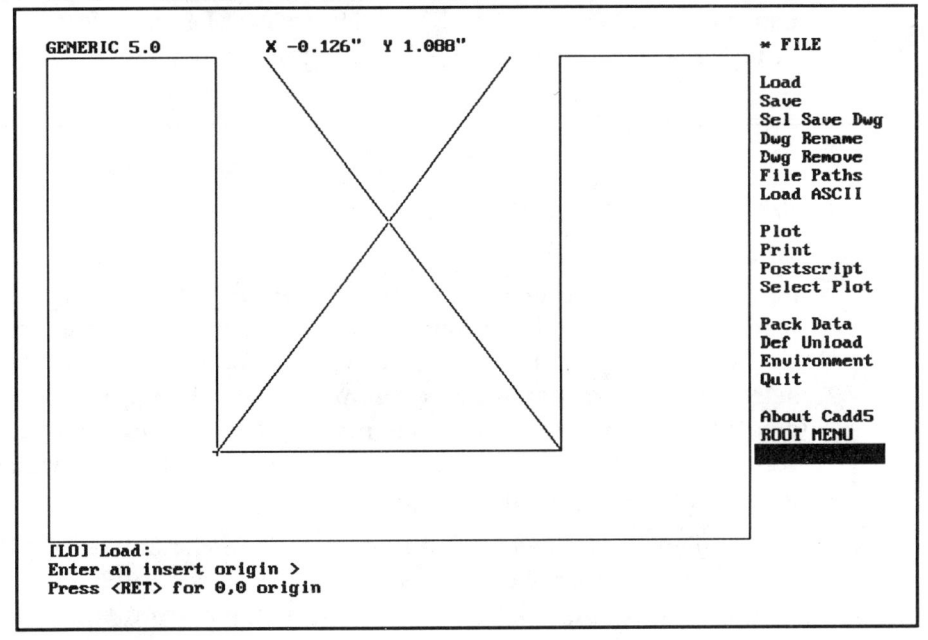

are preserved during a load, rather than changed to the new ones in the loaded file. To load the environment of a drawing file, the drawing should be loaded from the DOS prompt by typing its name after the word CADD, as in **CADD MUSIC**, to bring up the drawing MUSIC with its environment intact.

The Load Command

The Load command on the FILE menu is a general-purpose command for loading files of various types, a complement to the Save command on the same menu, discussed earlier. This command brings up a prompt-line menu of file types that can be loaded, including Drawing, which performs exactly the same function, using the same prompts and requiring the same responses as the Drawing Load command, discussed earlier. Other file types that can be loaded with this command include Component definitions, Batch files, Attributes, ASCII files as text lines, and Image files if your video driver supports them.

To load a drawing using this command, select Load from the FILE menu or type **LO** on the keyboard. Next select Drawing from the prompt or type **K**. Proceed as you did for Drawing Load.

The Layer Load Command

A special form of the Drawing Load command allows you to load an entire drawing file onto a single layer of the current drawing. The principle feature of the Layer Load command as opposed to Drawing Load is that as the drawing file is loaded, all entities loaded are relocated to one selected layer, rather than remaining on the layers where they were created. All other characteristics remain intact. This command is convenient for maintaining display control over multiple drawings placed into a single drawing file.

When you select Layer Load from the LAYERS menu or type **YL** on the keyboard, you are asked to specify a layer. This can be done using the menu or by typing a number. After specifying a layer, you are asked for the drawing name, then the location. You are not asked if you want to rename the drawing.

Note that the Layer Load command does not load a single layer from another drawing file, but rather the entire drawing onto a single layer in the current drawing. If you want to load a single layer from another drawing file, you must first go to that drawing file and use the Layer Save command to create a file with the desired layer in it, so that you can load this file into the desired drawing.

Loading Components

If you have saved components from any of your drawing files, or if you have purchased component libraries from Generic Software or third-party vendors, you can load these components into your current drawing file and place them. These component files can either be loaded before you place the components, or as you are placing them.

Automatic Component Loading

If you attempt to place a component that does not appear on the component list when you use the Component Place command, the default Component directory will be searched for the component whose name you typed, and the component will be loaded automatically if it is found. Otherwise, you will get a message that the component definition could not be found.

If you want to place a component that you have saved into the default directory, but don't remember its name, select the item "look on disk" at the bottom of the component list after issuing the Component Place command. You will get a menu of component files that are in the default component directory. As with other file lists that appear on the menu, you can move back to the parent directory by selecting the ".." item, or forward to another directory by selecting an item with a backslash (\) in front of it.

You can also type alternate disk drive designators, such as **A:**, at the prompt and press ENTER to get a menu of component files on any disk drive. Once the component has been loaded in this way, it will always appear on the Component List in the future. You can then place it without loading it again.

The Component Load Command

You may wish to preload components before placing them so that you don't have to worry about finding them while actually working on your drawing. As with components loaded during placement, they will appear on the Component List every time you use the Component Place command.

To load a component definition without placing it, use the Load command on the COMPONENTS menu or type **CL** on the keyboard. You will be shown a menu of the component files in the current default Component directory, from which you can choose. You can move around to various directories with the ".." and "\ name" options, or select a different disk, if you like. Once selected, the component file will be loaded.

Note If you try to load a component that has the same name as one that already exists in the drawing, the new definition will be ignored. Remember that although the filename is limited to eight characters, the component name itself may have as many as twelve. Also, if the component filename is different from the component name, the name that appears on the Component List in the future will be different from the name that you used to load the component. Several components may be loaded simultaneously using the Tag option of the File Selector program. See later sections in this chapter for more on the File Selector.

The Load Command

The general-purpose Load command on the FILE menu may be used to load components in the same way. Simply use the Component option or type **C** on the keyboard and proceed as you did for Component Load, discussed earlier.

Loading Batch Files

Generic CADD 5.0 has the capability to load text files containing commands and numeric data in a special format, which are interpreted as commands and point or parameter values. These files can be created either with Generic CADD, using the Save Batch or Save command Batch option, or by other software.

When you save a Batch file from Generic CADD 5.0, all of the commands and numeric input required to create that drawing are saved. If you start a new drawing and load a Batch file that has previously been saved, the drawing is created step-by-step at top speed. This produces a kind of "player piano" effect: if you barely touch the keys and wiggle your fingers very quickly, you can amaze your friends with your "proficiency" at the computer.

To load a Batch file, use either the Load command on the FILE menu, with the Batch option, typed **B**, or the Load Batch shortcut command, typed **LB** and not found on any menu. Either of these will ask for the name of the Batch file, and will present a menu for you to choose from. The video menu may be manipulated as usual for file selection. Once you have selected a Batch file, it will be executed, step by step.

Batch files can be created by other software, including a word processor. Almost any Generic CADD 5.0 command can be executed from a Batch file, so Batch files can be used to automate certain drawing tasks.

See Chapter 16, "Programming Generic CADD 5.0," for more information on using Batch files.

Loading Attributes

Attributes that have been saved to disk files can be retrieved so that they may be attached to new components in your current drawing file. For more information on the use of attributes, see Chapter 17, "Communicating with Other Programs."

To load an attribute, use the Load command on the FILE menu (LO), and select the Attribute option or type **A**. Selecting Load from the ATTRIBUTES menu simply activates the same Load command with the Attribute option already selected. A filename will be requested and a menu presented. When you select the file, the attribute is loaded, and may be used in the same way as an attribute created within the drawing.

Loading Image Files

Image files that have been saved on a disk, either from the current drawing or from another drawing, can be loaded onto the screen. To load properly, the image must have been saved using the same video driver that you are currently using, set to the same resolution, and you must be currently using one of the large drivers. For example, you cannot load an image that has been created using a Hercules monochrome card if you are currently using an EGA. Images should also *not* be saved as full screens, since only the drawing area is affected by the Load.

Image files created by Generic PAINT (part of Generic's Presentation package) must be converted with PaintConvert before they can be loaded onto the Generic CADD screen. Convert .GX2 to .GX2, even though this might seem odd. PaintConvert will know what to do. See Chapter 17 for more information on .GX2 files.

Keep in mind that when you load an image file, you are not loading any entities, only the images of those entities. If you perform a Redraw or any sort of Zoom after loading an image, the image quickly disappears. Possible uses for images are discussed in Chapters 16 and 17.

To load an image, use the Load command on the FILE menu, and select the Image option or type **I**. You will be asked for a filename and presented with a menu of possible files. Select or type a filename. If the image is found and is compatible with your current video driver, it is loaded onto the screen, temporarily obscuring the current drawing.

Note Be very careful about drawing and editing while an image is on the screen. If you use an erase command, for example, you will erase entities in the drawing, which you cannot see, rather than the image on the screen, which is visible.

The File Selector

Whenever you have a file-selection menu on the screen, you will notice that there is an item below the menu labeled "File Selector." This item provides access to a separate file selection program from which you may select and load your file or files. (The File Selector is actually a separate program that is called from inside Generic CADD, so you will have to wait a few seconds while Generic CADD 5.0 and your current drawing are put on hold and the File Selector program is called up.)

The File Selector screen is organized into three areas: an area on the left displaying your files, an area on the right displaying your disk directory tree, and an area at the bottom where command options are located. The command options may be used at any time, while one or the other of the two larger areas must be "active" to be used. Each of the two upper areas has a border around it. The one with the double line is the active area, while the inactive area is surrounded by only a single line. You can make either area active (and the other inactive) by moving your mouse cursor to that area and pressing the first button. The border lines will reflect the new status. You can also move back and forth between the two areas by pressing the TAB key on your keyboard. Note that the mouse cursor is only active if you are using a mouse driver.

The Files Area

The leftmost area displays all of the files that match the current file specification. When you first load the File Selector from a specific menu within Generic CADD, the file specification will be derived from the type of file that you are trying to load, which will determine the extension, and the default path for that file type, which will determine the disk and directory to display files from. The file specification will be shown at the top of this area.

If you have entered the File Selector from the Drawing Load command's file selection menu, for example, and your default drawing path is set to C:\CADD5\DWG, the file specification will be C:\CADD5\DWG*.DWG, and all files matching this specification will be displayed in the Files area. As this file specification is changed, the list of files in this area will be updated to match the new specification.

Selecting Files

You can use your mouse cursor to select files from the list. Simply place the cursor over the name of the file that you want to select and press the first button. Alternately, use the cursor keys, including all of the arrow keys, the PGUP and PGDN keys, and the HOME and END keys to move your cursor around. Press ENTER to select the file once the cursor is located. Note that a complete directory listing for the currently selected file appears at the bottom of the Files area, including the size of the file and the date and time that it was created.

If there are more files on the list than will fit on the screen, you can use the vertical scroll bar at the right side of the Files area to scroll through the list. Click on this scroll bar with the first mouse button to move the list up or down, or use PGUP and PGDN on the keyboard.

The Directory Tree Area

The right side of the screen displays a directory tree for the disk that you are currently looking at. The disk selected comes from the default path for the file type that you are looking for. When you first enter the File Selector from CADD, the default directory for the file type that you are loading will be selected and highlighted. You can move this block up and down through the list, thereby changing the file specification, causing the Files list to be updated with files from the selected directory.

You can move up and down the directory tree by using the UP ARROW and DOWN ARROW keys on the keyboard. Use the PGUP and PGDN keys to move a whole screen at a time, and use the mouse cursor to select a new directory name. HOME and END will move you to the top and bottom of the tree, and the scroll bar at the right side of the screen will help you move the tree up and down with the mouse.

File Selector Commands

The commands that operate the File Selector are shown at the bottom of the screen, and can be selected either by holding down the ALT key on the keyboard and pressing the highlighted letter for each command, or by selecting the command with the mouse cursor. These commands perform a variety of tasks within the File Selector.

The Help (H) Command

Selecting Help brings up a list of the various keys that work with the File Selector.

The Drive (D) Command

The Drive command allows you to select a different disk drive. If you use this command and select a new disk drive, both the Directory Tree area and the Files area will be updated to reflect the new selection.

The Filespec (F) Command

The Filespec command allows you to type your own specification for files that you want to look for. You can use this command to narrow the search to only files that start with a particular letter, or to search for files with an extension different from the default extension. This is the only way to search for files lacking one of the standard Generic CADD file extensions. Note that in most cases Generic CADD will not load files without standard extensions. However, this is a good way to look on the disk, if you simply need the information.

The Search (S) Command

The Search command causes the File Selector to search the disk for files that meet the current file specification. When you issue this command, the disk is searched from the top of the directory tree until a matching file is found. All files in the same directory with the located file that also match the specification will be displayed. If you don't see the file that you want, issue the command again to continue searching.

The Tag (T) Command

When loading Components and Attributes, the Tag command is available to allow you to select several files and load them all at the same time. After issuing this command, move to the File area and select all of the files that you want to load. As each is selected, it is "tagged" with an arrow pointing to it, so that you can tell which ones you have already selected. If you select one by mistake, simply select it again, and the tag will disappear.

The All (A) Command

The All command becomes available once you have issued the Tag command. It allows you to tag all of the files on the current Files list. Use this command even if you don't really want to select all of the files, but do want more than half of them. You can then deselect the ones that you don't want by selecting them with the mouse cursor or the cursor arrow keys and ENTER.

The Load (L) Command

Once you have selected one or more files, you may elect to Load them into Generic CADD 5.0. Presumably, that's why you're in the File Selector in the first place. When you select this command, you will be returned to CADD with the desired file in tow, and it will be automatically loaded.

The Exit (X) Command

If you can't find the file that you want, or want to return to Generic CADD without a file for any other reason, use the Exit command. A prompt will ask you if you really want to leave empty-handed. You can answer by typing either a **Y** or an **N** on the keyboard, or by selecting Yes or No from the prompt with the mouse cursor.

Utilizing the commands and techniques discussed in this chapter, you should be able to save a variety of different types of data into a number of different file types from within Generic CADD 5.0, for later use with Generic CADD, or possibly for use with other programs. (See Chapter 17 for more information on communicating with other programs.) You should also be able to load data of varying types into Generic CADD from a variety of file types, either from inside CADD, or from the DOS prompt. This allows you to either recall information previously generated with Generic CADD, or to process information from other sources using Generic CADD 5.0.

CHAPTER 13

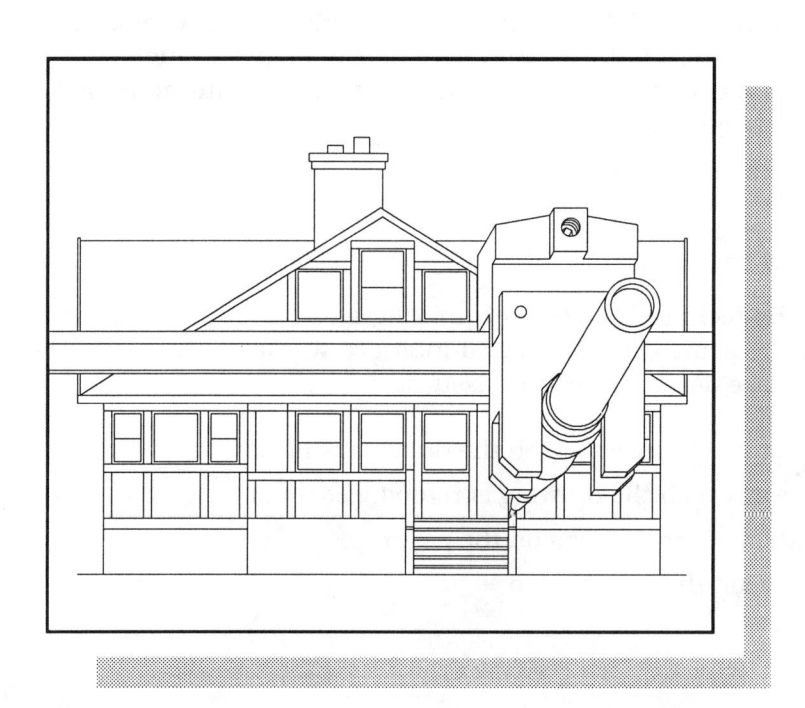

Printing Your Drawings

Until now, you have had the luxury of the expansive Generic CADD 5.0 drawing area. This imaginary space can hold objects of almost any size without reducing them or losing any detail, and it always has room to spare. When you're ready to print the drawing, however, you must deal with more constraining physical limitations.

Printing and plotting, the two most common methods for producing paper output in Generic CADD, utilize several common principles, all concerning the translation of your drawing data from an infinite electronic workspace to a finite sheet of paper.

Printing and plotting differ primarily in the technical aspects of the two different processes. Printers work with individual dots, much like a high-resolution video display; plotters use pens to draw continuous lines from one point to another.

Basic Concepts

Although the technical aspects of printing and plotting differ, they make use of the same commands and interface within Generic CADD 5.0. This interface deals with several issues:

- The size of the paper on which the drawing is placed
- The scale at which the drawing is reproduced
- The location of the drawing on the paper
- Where to send the information

Paper Size

Whether you are printing or plotting, Generic CADD 5.0 must know the space available for the drawing. Although Generic CADD calls this measure "page size," what it really means is the printable area on a sheet. If you are printing with a dot matrix printer on an individual 8 1/2" x 11" sheet, for example, it is not likely that your printer can print all the way to the edge of the paper. A more reasonable specification for "page size" would be 8" x 10", which leaves 1/4 inch on the sides, and 1/2 inch on the top and bottom. Dot matrix printers generally have the most trouble printing near the bottom of an individual sheet because the paper tends to slip out of the roller. If you use continuous feed paper, you can probably specify 8" x 10 1/2" or even 8 1/2" x 11" if you position the paper very carefully.

Plotters usually do not plot all the way to the edge of the sheet either. Your plotter probably leaves an unprintable margin all the way around the sheet, sometimes varying at the four edges. Some plotters need as much as one full inch of margin. A typical sheet size specification for a 24" x 36" sheet might be 22" x 34". You can use less than the printable area, of course, simply by specifying a smaller sheet size. This is especially useful for printers when you want the drawing to be much smaller than the physical sheet. This can be done with plotters as well. For example, you might want to plot only half a sheet and use the other half for another drawing.

If you are unsure of the allowable sheet size for your output device, you can find it in the device manual. In your plotter manual, look for the *hard clip limit*, which is the margin, and subtract these dimensions from the paper size. The easiest way to test the printable area is to create a drawing of a rectangle that is the actual size of the paper, with the lower-left corner of the rectangle at the origin. When you plot this drawing at full size, you will then be able to measure how close the drawing will actually plot to the edges of the sheet. See Figure 13-1 for an illustration of this technique.

Reducing or Enlarging the Drawing

Generic CADD 5.0 can store drawings that are very small or very large, but you will probably have to reduce or enlarge your drawing to fit it onto a piece of paper. You cannot print building floor plans at full size, for example, because no plotter is big enough and the drawing would be unmanageable anyway: you would need a room larger than the building itself to examine the drawings. At the other extreme, integrated circuit layouts plotted at full size would probably appear as a black blob on paper: the individual entities in the drawing could be smaller than a single dot on your printer or the width of the pen on your plotter.

For these reasons, you must either specify a scale or let Generic CADD choose one for you. In the printing and plotting interface, a scale is simply

FIGURE 13-1 A rectangle plotted onto a sheet of the same size

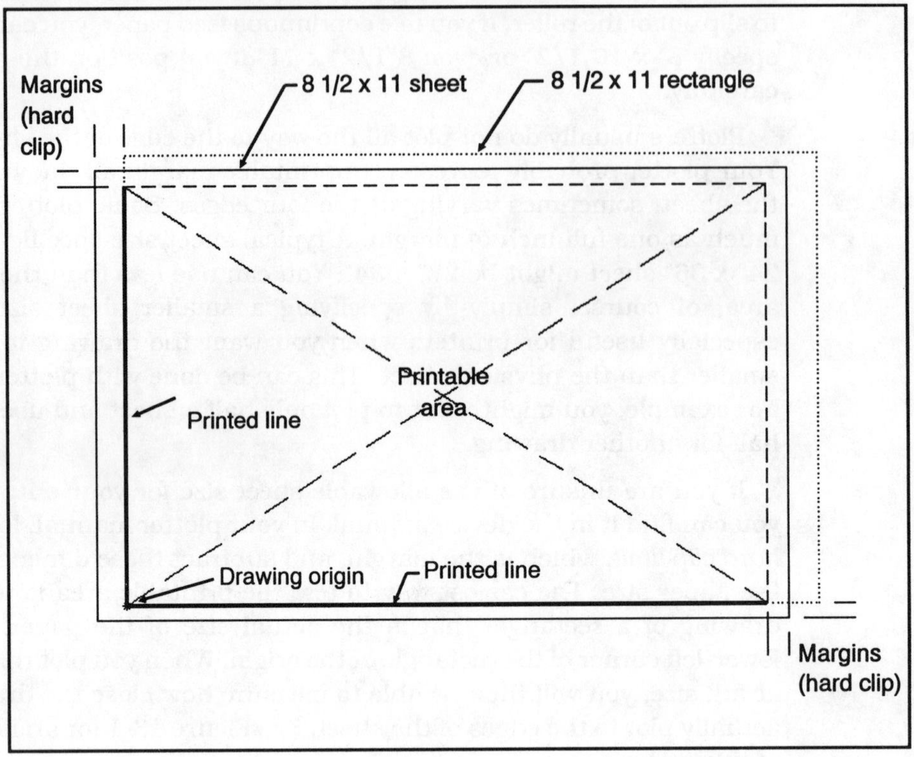
Margins
(hard
clip)
8 1/2 x 11 sheet
8 1/2 x 11 rectangle
Printable
area
Printed line
Drawing origin
Printed line
Margins
(hard clip)

a factor by which the drawing is reduced. It is specified as part of a ratio, 1:*x*, where *x* is the scale. If the scale supplied is 2, for example, the ratio of printed output to actual CADD data is 1:2, or one-half real size. Another way to think of it is that one unit on the paper represents two units in the drawing. If you want to double the size of the drawing, you would supply a scale of 0.5, meaning that one unit on the paper represents one-half of a unit in your actual drawing.

If your drawing is the right size to fit correctly onto a sheet of paper, you can specify a scale of 1. If you do not know what scale will fit, you can ask the printing or plotting program to calculate it for you. (You will learn how to do this later in this chapter.)

Telling CADD Where on the Paper to Place Drawings

Because the data in the CADD 5.0 drawing is based on an X and Y coordinates system, the drawing contains an origin where the coordinates are 0,0. To determine where on the sheet to print your drawing, CADD uses the location of this origin. If you are letting Generic CADD scale the drawing, the location of the origin is not important, because Generic CADD will calculate this point too. However, if you are specifying the scale, you must also tell Generic CADD where to place the origin.

If the origin of your drawing is at the lower-left corner and you specify a plot or print origin of 0,0, your drawing is placed in the lower-left corner of the paper. However, if the drawing origin is somewhere else, you may need to specify another origin so that the entire drawing is positioned on the paper the way you want it.

Strangely enough, Generic CADD 5.0's print or plot origin is specified in the real scale of your drawing, not the reduced size of the actual sheet of paper. Thus, if you are trying to print a 20" by 20" box on a 10" by 10" sheet of paper at a scale of 1:2 (reduced to half real size), you would have to specify a plot origin of 10,10 if the actual drawing origin was in the middle of the 20" by 20" box. At half real size, the box would be moved up 5 inches and to the right 5 inches, where it would fit exactly. Therefore, when you specify the plot origin you are actually telling Generic CADD where on the sheet, in the scale of the drawing, you want the drawing origin to be placed.

Fortunately, Generic CADD provides a visual method for positioning the drawing on the sheet—moving over the drawing a box that represents the sheet until it fits the way you want it (see the "Page Setup" section later in this chapter).

Plotting

Using these basic ideas, Generic CADD provides a single interface containing a number of alternative options, depending on your output device. Printing, Plotting, and Output to PostScript files and devices are all included in the Drawing Plot (DP) command. From the FILE menu, three separate items access this command, each with the device preselected. Plot activates the plotter, Print activates the printer, and PostScript selects output to a PostScript device or file. Since all are actually just options of the Drawing Plot command, note that the word Plot is used within this interface to refer to all three technologies.

Preparation

Before plotting, you may turn off layers that you don't want to plot, toggle on and off the display of standard points, hatches, and fills, and select Fast Text if you wish. You can also zoom in to a particular part of the drawing if you want to print only part of the drawing.

Plotting Selected Entities

An alternative plotting command, Selection Plot (PL) provides a standard selection prompt, so that you can use any of the selection methods to select the entities you want to plot. After you have selected the entities in the usual way, including using Filtering if appropriate, press ENTER to move to the Output menu from which the entities will be plotted.

Once the drawing is loaded and properly displayed, select one of the three items discussed earlier, type **DP** on the keyboard, or choose Selection Plot or type **PL** on the keyboard. You will be presented with the Output menu, from which you may specify how you want the drawing plotted.

Type of Device

The first item on the Output menu determines which technology or output format you wish to utilize, Plotting, Printing, or PostScript. The currently selected format is shown at the end of the menu item. This format is initially selected by the menu item that you choose, or defaults to the last format used if you typed a two-character command or used Selection Plot to reach this point. To change to a different format, select the "Sent to" item from this menu by typing **1**. You do not need to press

ENTER. When you select this item, you are presented with a menu of format options. Select one by typing its number, or press ESC to leave the format the way it was.

Where to Send the Data

As far as Generic CADD 5.0 is concerned, plotting is simply the act of sending information about your drawing to an output device, formatted in a manner that the output device understands, so that it can reproduce your drawing on paper. While the first item on the Output menu controls what type of information is sent, the second item determines where it is actually sent.

The information can be routed to any serial or parallel port on your computer, or to a file on disk. Typically, printers use a parallel port and plotters a serial port, but this is not always the case; you may need to change this option to reflect both your printer or plotter and the way that it is connected. PostScript information is often routed to a file, so that it can be used in conjunction with a desktop publishing program, or other software that utilizes PostScript files. This option allows you to send plotting information of any format to any of these locations.

To change the destination for the plot output, select this option by typing **2** on your keyboard. You will be presented with a menu of the possible locations to which your file can be sent. Of these items, COM1 and COM2 represent your first and second serial ports, and LPT1, LPT2, and LPT3 represent three possible parallel ports. Note that these options will show up on this menu even if your computer does not have so many ports.

For printers and plotters, the last item, Disk file, allows you to specify the name of the file where you want the information to be sent. A default name consisting of the name of the current drawing with the extension .DPF is suggested. You may either press ENTER to accept this name, or edit it first. If you have selected PostScript in item 1, there will be two items on the menu for files, one for "device files" and the other for EPS, or Encapsulated PostScript, files.

As with printer and plotter files, PostScript device files might be used to simply store information in a file for sending it to the device later. EPS files are often used to transfer information to other programs. Each suggests a filename, which can be edited if you wish. The extension .DEV is suggested for device file, while .EPS is used for EPS files.

Specifying Page Size

The default or currently selected size is shown at the end of the menu item. If you select this option, you will get a menu of standard sizes for the currently configured device. The last of these options will be for a user-selected page size. If you select this option, you are asked in turn for the length and width of the page. If you wish to leave one or both of these alone, simply press ENTER when the prompt comes up.

Next, specify the area on the paper available for printed output as discussed earlier. Length is first, then width. Generic CADD 5.0 offers default sizes based on your printer configuration. Use the actual area, not the size that the paper would be if you enlarged it to the size of the drawing. For most printers, the maximum width is 13.6 inches. You can specify greater widths, but you will probably get blank lines on your printed output. The length is limited only to the actual length of the paper; however, to save time and paper, you probably do not want to overestimate by too much or a great deal of blank space will appear at both the top and bottom of the drawing.

Options

This item provides a menu of options that are specific to the output format that you have selected. The menu that you get when you select this command depends, therefore, on whether you selected Plotter, Printer, or PostScript format in the first option on the menu.

Standard Options

A few of the items on the various Options menus appear on more than one of these menus. These work in the same way no matter which output format is currently selected.

Configure

On the Printer and Plotter Options menus, this item allows you to select a new device. A list of available drivers is shown, then options within these drivers, if any. You may be asked to specify the path where the drivers can be found. This will usually be the same as your Generic CADD 5.0 directory. Normally, this will be the default shown at the bottom of the screen, so just press ENTER.

After you have selected a new device, you will be returned to the appropriate Options menu. If you selected this item by mistake, simply press ESC to return to the Options menu.

Number of Copies

This item is standard for all three formats. When you select it, you will be asked to type a number, indicating how many copies of the drawing you want sent to the device. The minimum number is one, and the maximum is 32,767. (Not many printers hold that much paper.)

Plotter Options

A menu of both standard and plotter-specific options is presented when you select Options with the Plotter selected. The plotter-specific options follow.

Plot Hardware Arcs & Circles

Your plotter may have internal routines for plotting Arcs and Circles. These internal routines may be either more accurate or faster than Generic CADD 5.0's similar routines. On the other hand, they may not be. Check your plotter manual to see if they exist, and try them to see if they're easier for you. Selecting this item toggles the use of these internal plotter routines on and off. If the screen shows OFF, Generic CADD will create the circles and arcs itself. If it shows ON, the plotter's own routines will be used.

Pen Settings

This item provides yet another menu with options concerning the pen speed, pen width, number of pens, pen sorting, and pen changing. Any of these items may be changed by typing its corresponding number and supplying a new value if required.

Pen Speed   Check your plotter manual to see if pen speed applies to your plotter. If the speed of your plotter is adjustable, the number you supply is fed straight to the plotter. The allowable values vary from plotter to plotter.

Pen Width   Pen width is used for creating line widths and for filling solid areas. If you want solid areas to be completely filled, use a pen width that is slightly smaller than the width of the pen tip, so that each pass of the pen slightly overlaps the one before it. For faster plots, or if the composition of filled areas is not that important to you, use a larger number.

Number of Plotter Pens   The number of pens determines both whether or not pens can be automatically swapped and which pens get assigned to which colors. If the number that appears for this item is 1, you can either change pens manually or plot the entire drawing with the same pen. If the number is greater than 1, color 1 is assigned to pen 1, color 2 to pen 2, and so on, until the number of pens is exhausted, at which point the pen numbers start over while the color numbers continue. For example, if you specify four pens, colors 1 to 4 will be plotted with pens 1 to 4; color 5 will be plotted with pen 1, color 6 with pen 2, and so on.

With many plotters, you do not have to use all available pens. If you specify two pens on a one-pen plotter, for instance, manual pen-swapping is disabled, and Generic CADD simply thinks that it can use pens 1 and 2 for all plotting. Because your plotter actually has only one pen, this pen will be used for everything.

Pen Sort by Color   Pen sort by color is a toggle that determines whether entities are plotted in the order that you drew them, or color by color. If this toggle is on, entities are sorted by color, and plotted one color at a time. This is especially useful if you are using a single-pen plotter and changing pens yourself because with this option you only have to change pens once for each color.

Prompt for Pen Change   This item is a toggle that determines whether Generic CADD 5.0 pauses between colors to allow you to change pens. If you have a multi-pen plotter and can preassign the pens, or if you want to plot your entire drawing with one pen, you can turn this toggle off. If your plotter holds fewer pens than you want to use for your plot, on the other hand, you should set this toggle to on. If you want to use more than one pen with a single-pen plotter, this toggle must be turned on. If it is on, Generic CADD will stop between colors to ask you to change the pen. It is a good idea to use Pen Sort by Color if you are changing pens, so that you don't have to change them as often.

Import Plotter Command File

This option allows the plot program to import plot files. These files must be in a special format that can be understood by your plotter. These files can be created for later use by routing plotting to a file instead of to a port when plotting.

If you would like to combine an existing plot file into the plot of your current drawing, select this option, and type the name of the file, including the pathname if it is different from the Generic CADD directory. This file is sent to the plotter when you use the Start Plot option from the main Output menu before the current drawing is plotted.

The Import Plotter Command File option essentially has two uses. The first occurs when your plotter needs to be sent an initialization string before plotting actually begins. For example, your plotter may not be supported by Generic CADD 5.0 but can be made to emulate a supported plotter by putting the proper commands into an ASCII file and sending them to the plotter.

The second, more common use is for printing title blocks or borders on specific drawing sheets, but not on every drawing that you plan to plot. You can plot the title block or border once, using the File Port option. Later, when you plot your drawing, specify that this file be imported. In this way, a title block and border will be printed onto each sheet that you plot.

Printer Options

If you select Options with the Printer format selected, the menu that you will get contains only the standard options, Configure and Number of Copies. There are no printer-specific options that can or need to be set.

PostScript Options

Three PostScript-specific options are provided, in addition to the standard option, Number of Copies. These options are somewhat interdependent, as you will see.

Default Line Width

This option controls the width of lines that are sent to the PostScript device or file. As with the Line Width command inside CADD, this controls the width of all entities, not just Straight Lines. This width is measured in absolute terms, however, rather than relative terms, as in CADD. Acceptable values range from 0 to 25 points. Zero values will produce the thinnest possible line available on the device.

Grayscale for Filled Objects

For monochrome PostScript files, this option is a combination toggle and parameter setting. It can either be supplied with a value or set to Variable. If a value is supplied, all filled objects will be shaded in with a dot pattern according to the supplied value. Acceptable values range from 0 (black) to 1 (white, or no shading). The actual color of the fill is ignored.

If this setting is toggled to Variable, the dot pattern used to shade the filled entities will be adjusted according to the color of the fill.

If Color PostScript is selected, this option is disabled, because grayscales are not required. Note that setting this option while Color PostScript is selected will disable Color PostScript, as it is not possible to use both grayscales and color at the same time.

Color PostScript

This option is a toggle that determines whether or not color information will be sent to your selected PostScript destination. Note that if you turn this toggle on and send to a monochrome device, all colors in your drawing will be represented by shades of gray, not just filled objects.

Selecting the View Type

The View Type option determines whether you or Generic CADD are going to specify the scale of the print and what part of the drawing you want to print. Three alternatives are offered from a menu: "Use current view," "Fit full drawing," and "Specify scale and origin." Only the last of these options requires you to specify the scale; under the first two options, Generic CADD 5.0 supplies the scale. Note, however, that your selection here is only a starting point, and may be modified somewhat later in the Page Setup option. The three alternatives function as follows.

Use Current View

Under this option, Generic CADD 5.0 fits the current display screen to the paper as closely as possible. This means that if you have some space around the screen drawing, you will get space around the printed drawing. If you are zoomed in to a small portion of the drawing so that the lines in the drawing are chopped off at the edges of the screen, the print will turn out the same way. Figure 13-2 is an example of a drawing display that you might want to print.

In many cases, your screen is horizontal, and your paper is vertical. To deal with this situation, Generic CADD centers the image on the paper, adding extra space above and below. You have the opportunity to rotate the drawing 90 degrees to make it as large as possible on the sheet with the Page Setup option, discussed later in this chapter. If you want to avoid this adjustment, simply supply a width and length for the paper size that match as closely as possible the actual proportions of the drawing area on the screen. Figure 13-3 shows how the sample drawing would be printed using this plot type on a horizontal and a vertical sheet.

398 Generic CADD 5.0 Inside & Out

FIGURE 13-2 A sample drawing with the current display shown by the dashed rectangle

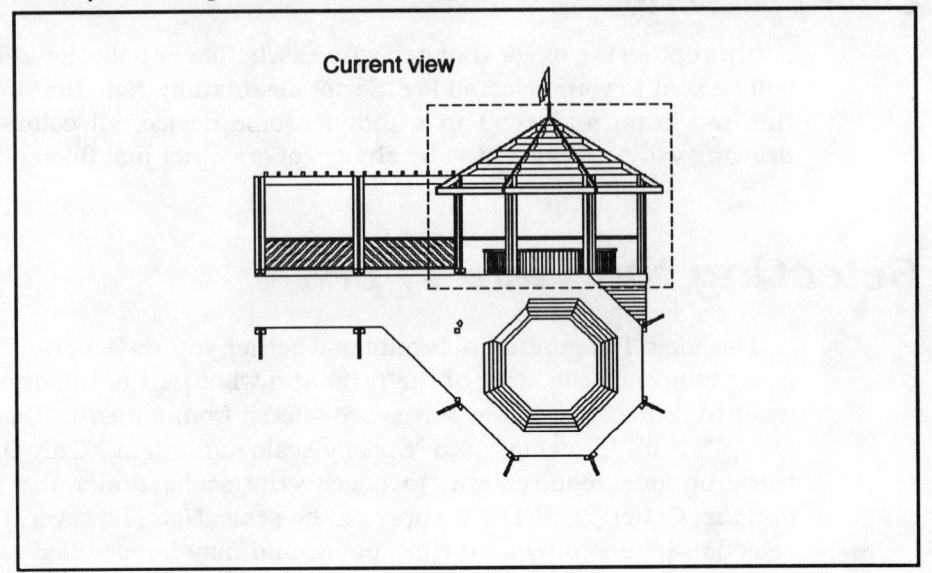

FIGURE 13-3 The Current View fitted to a) a horizontal sheet and b) a vertical sheet

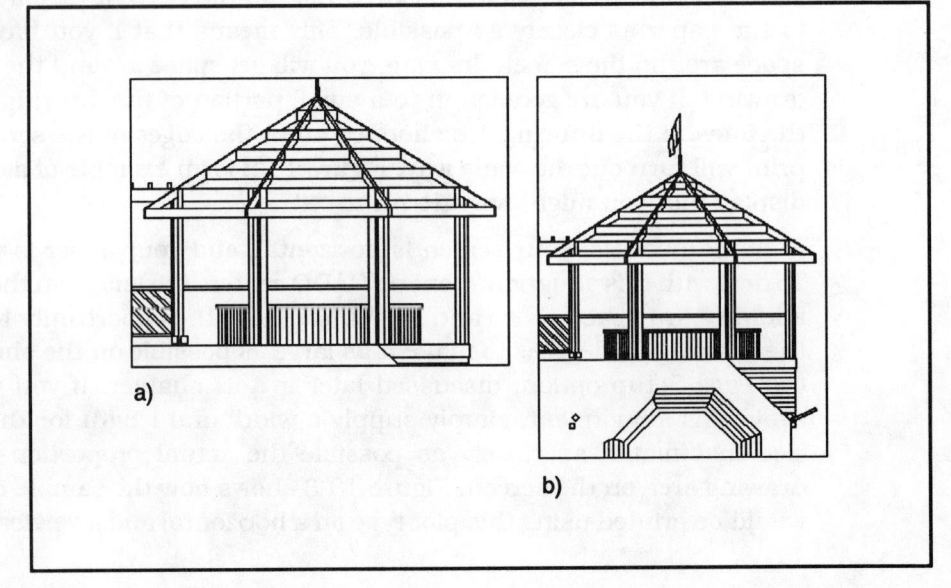

Fit Full Drawing

This plot type option asks Generic CADD to make the drawing fit the paper. The drawing is printed exactly as wide or as tall as you have specified for the sheet size. Unless the drawing is exactly the same proportion as the sheet size, some blank space is added in the direction that does not fit exactly. No further questions are asked regarding scale or origin, as these are decided by the program. Figure 13-4 shows how the sample drawing would be printed using this plot type on a horizontal and a vertical sheet.

Specify Scale and Origin

This plot type option lets you decide the scale and origin. If you select this option, you will need to supply three specifications before printing begins, using the Page Setup option on the Options menu: (1) the plot

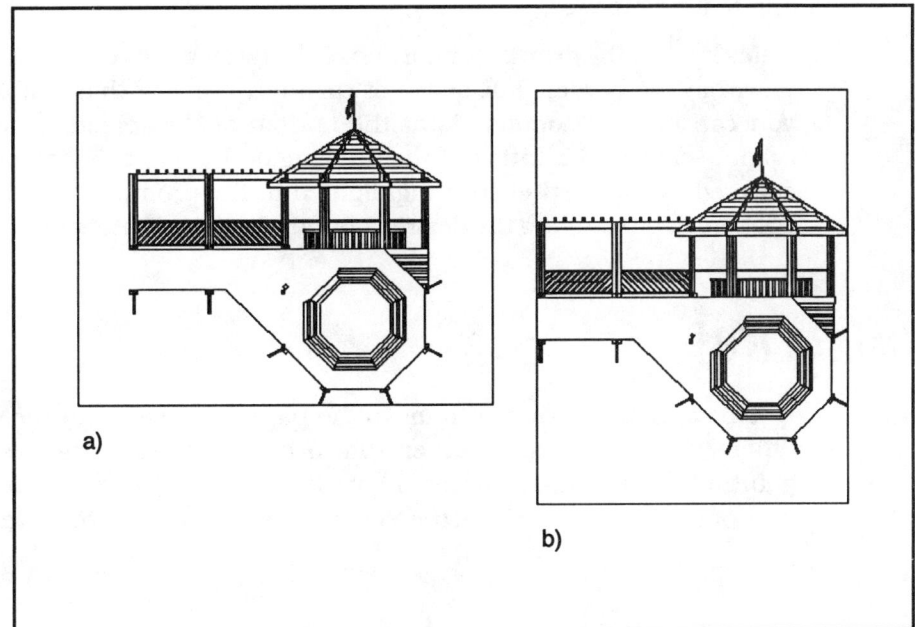

FIGURE 13-4 The Full Drawing fitted to a) a horizontal sheet and b) a vertical sheet

scale, as discussed earlier, specified as a ratio of 1 to the number that you type; (2) whether to rotate the drawing 90 degrees—if your drawing is horizontal and your sheet vertical, select Rotate during Page Setup to rotate the drawing; and (3) the location for the plot origin—this can be done either by typing coordinates or by dragging a sheet border over the drawing.

Page Setup

After selecting the plot format, destination, size, and type, you can preview the plot on the screen before sending it to the printer. This is usually a good idea, and is required if you have elected to specify the scale and origin yourself. When you select this option, you are asked if you want a Fast Redraw. Without the Fast Redraw, the drawing will be shown on the screen surrounded by a box indicating the borders of the paper. With Fast Redraw, the extents of your drawing will be indicated by a dashed rectangle. Fast Redraw is, of course, faster, but does not allow you to easily select what portion of the drawing you want to print. If you are going to print the whole drawing, Fast Redraw is usually fine. Type **Y** or **N** to make your choice known, and the preview display will be created.

Make sure the drawing or portion of the drawing that you want to print is within the border. If it does not turn out the way that you expected, you can use the commands at the bottom of the screen to adjust the origin, scale, and rotation of the drawing on the paper. Each of these is selected by typing the letter highlighted in the prompt at the bottom of the screen or selecting the desired option with the pointing device cursor.

Origin (O)

This option allows you to move the paper in relation to the drawing. When you select it, the border shown on the screen attaches to your pointing device, and you can move it wherever you want. If you are bumping into the edges of the screen, use the Zoom commands while placing the Origin. Simply type the two-character command (usually ZO for Zoom Out), for more room to properly place the border.

You can also type the coordinates of the origin if you want. If you wish to do this, you should be aware of the unusual relationship between the coordinates shown on the screen and the coordinates that you type. The coordinates shown on the screen are measured from the lower-left corner of the paper to the actual origin of the drawing. The coordinates that you type are measured in reverse, from the origin of the drawing to the lower-left corner of the paper.

In addition, while the coordinates shown on the screen are always relative to the corner of the paper, the coordinates that you type depend on the Manual Entry mode currently active. You may change the Manual Entry mode while placing the border by typing a two-character command. MR, Manual Entry Relative, will give you coordinates measured from the corner of the paper (because it is the last point entered, as far as Generic CADD 5.0 is concerned), while MO, Manual Entry Origin, will allow you to type coordinates relative to the origin of the drawing.

The key to operating within these rules is simpler than the rules themselves. Simply type your coordinates with the opposite sign from the coordinates shown. If the current origin is at 5,5, for instance, you would not get the same plot by selecting Origin and typing 5,5. You would have to type -5,-5, assuming Manual Entry Origin is set. To move the drawing one inch to the right, you would type -6,-5 for the origin, or turn on Manual Entry Relative (MR) and specify an Origin of -1,0. It's usually easier to show the border on the screen.

Scale (S)

If the drawing doesn't fit on the paper at the scale shown, you can change the scale with this option. Note that if you have elected to supply the scale yourself, the default scale will come up at 1 to 1, and you may not even see the border of the paper, especially if your drawing is very large. Simply select this item and specify a scale, as discussed previously. Remember that scale is expressed as a ratio of units on the paper to units in the drawing. 1/4"=1' becomes 1:48, for example, and you only have to specify the 48.

Rotate (R)

If the drawing would fit better onto the paper if you turn it on its side, select this option. The display will be regenerated with the drawing rotated 90 degrees. Note that after selecting this option, you may need to respecify the Scale or the Origin or both.

Fit (F)

The Fit option provides automatic scaling of the drawing to the page, no matter which View Type you started with, and may be used in place of the Scale option to get Generic CADD to figure out the largest scale that will work with the current sheet size. You may use this option even if you had originally elected to specify the scale yourself. If the drawing has been Rotated using the previous option, this option provides a good method for fitting the rotated drawing to the sheet.

Center (C)

This option provides automatic placement of the drawing on the sheet, no matter which View Type you started with, and may be used in place of the Origin option to get Generic CADD to figure out the best origin for centering the drawing, based on the current scale and rotation. You may use this option even if you had originally elected to specify the origin yourself. This is a good option to use once you have determined the appropriate scale.

Return to Accept

Once you have the drawing on the sheet the way that you want it, press ENTER or select the Enter symbol from the prompt to return to the Output menu. From there you can start the plot.

Start Plot

This option tells Generic CADD 5.0 to go ahead and begin sending information to the selected destination. What actually happens next depends upon the selected format.

With PostScript selected, the drawing is sent immediately. Several status lines at the bottom of the screen keep you up to date on what is going on. If plotting, the drawing may first be sorted by color, if you have selected this option, and then the drawing will be sent to the plotter, with the status lines displayed as it proceeds.

Printing requires first that the program examines the entire drawing file to determine how it is going to resolve the lines, circles, arcs, and so on into dots. Generic CADD cannot just print them on the paper in the order that you drew them as it does when plotting or generating the video display, because most printers only advance the paper in one direction, or accept information one line at a time. For this reason, each line, whether printed or blank, requires many, many calculations.

When you start the plot with the printer selected, an area of memory, called a *buffer*, is set aside for storing the dots that will be sent. Generic CADD 5.0 then calculates as much of the print as possible before sending it to the printer. Depending on the complexity of your drawing and the amount of memory available, your printer may pause several times during printing while this buffer is refilled as more calculations are done. If you are printing a large drawing file, you might plan to do other tasks while the drawing is being printed. Extremely large drawing files are best printed at the end of the day when you do not need the computer for other functions.

If you want to abort the plot for any reason, press ESC. The program pauses and you are given the opportunity to abort or to continue plotting. (If you need to put more ink in a pen, for example, you might press ESC and then continue plotting once you have refilled the pen.)

When the plot is done, you are returned to the Output menu, where you can change the parameters and do another plot if you like.

The streamlined interface for printing and plotting discussed in this chapter provides a high degree of flexibility in sheet size, scale, orientation, and placement of your drawing. From this single interface, prints, plots, and a variety of output file formats may be produced, customized to both your available hardware and your requirements. The optional creation of files allows you to export PostScript files, as well as printer and plotter output files to a variety of external applications.

CHAPTER 14

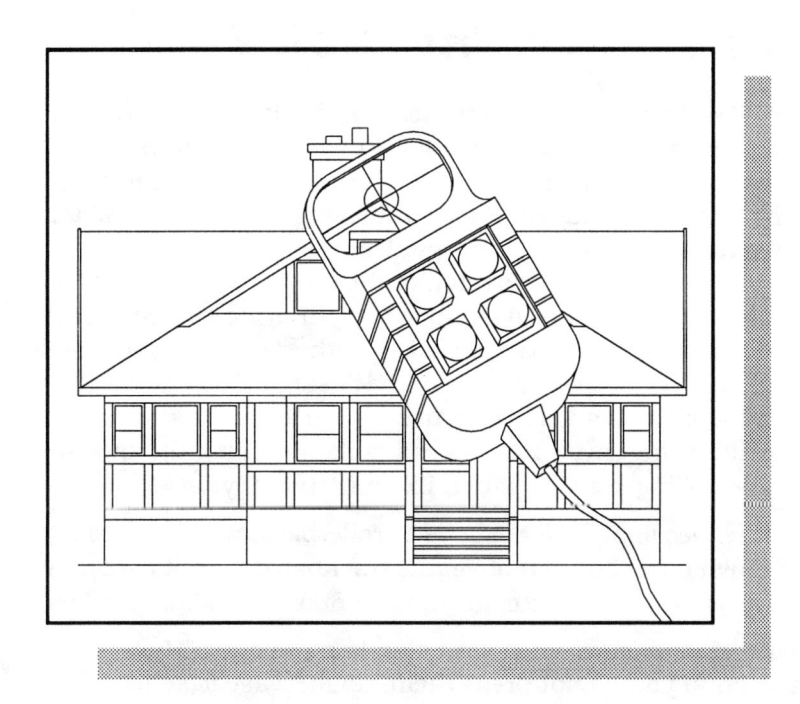

Using a Digitizer

As one of the peripheral devices that can be used with Generic CADD, the digitizer is somewhat unique. Within Generic CADD 5.0, digitizers are found on the Select a Pointing Device menu of the CONFIG program, but digitizers are different in a number of ways from the other pointing devices—mice, trackballs, and the keyboard cursor keys—because digitizers provide several functions in addition to simply pointing to areas on the screen: you will also use your digitizer to trace and to select commands.

The Digitizer as a Pointing Device

Pointing devices typically send information back to the program regarding their movement and the direction in which they move. When you move a mouse to the right, for example, a series of electrical impulses is translated by Generic CADD 5.0 into "I'm moving to the right." When you stop moving the mouse, it sends a signal saying "I'm not moving." In this way, the mouse controls the position of the cursor by telling CADD that you have moved it, and CADD responds by moving the cursor. A mouse cannot communicate to Generic CADD the fact that you have picked it up and moved it to another part of the desktop. This means that you do not need a lot of desk space to use a mouse, because you can move it further than the physical room available by rolling the mouse, picking it up, and rolling it again, much like a friction toy.

The same principles apply to trackballs or rollerballs, which are really sort of upside-down mice. Like a mouse, the trackball does not care how you move it—that is, with one long continuous motion or in short strokes.

The keyboard cursor keys send very simple messages: "Up," "Left," "Down," and so on. If you do not press them, no message is sent.

Digitizers, on the other hand, send very different information back to Generic CADD 5.0. Physically, a digitizer usually consists of a rectangular flat box called a *tablet*, which contains a grid of very closely spaced wires all connected to a central circuit. Attached to this tablet, usually by a wire, but sometimes by a radio signal, is a device that resembles a mouse or a pen, often called a *stylus*. This device is positioned over the tablet and sends a signal indicating not which direction it is moving, but where it is on the tablet. This information is sent in the form of X and Y coordinates that are related to the grid of wires inside the tablet.

There is a very straightforward relationship between the location of the *digitizer puck* (as the mouselike pointer is often called) on the tablet and the position of the cursor on the screen. It is as if you simply tipped the screen down onto the desk and can now drag the cursor around. When the puck is at the top of the tablet, the cursor is at the top of the screen; when you move the puck to the bottom of the tablet, the cursor moves to the bottom of the screen. Unlike the mouse, the puck sends a signal indicating its position. It does little good, therefore, to lift the puck in an attempt to move the cursor. As soon as the puck is lifted a half-inch or so (the active distance varies depending on the digitizer), the signal becomes too weak for Generic CADD to detect its location, and the cursor stops moving even if you continue to move the digitizer.

If you alternate between a mouse and a digitizer in Generic CADD 5.0, you will probably need to adjust mentally each time you switch: although the physical feeling of the mouse and the digitizer puck are very similar, the action on the screen is very different.

Selecting the Active Area

If you have a large digitizer, you may want to set it up to use only a small portion of the actual surface (called the active area) for screen pointing. This will save you from making sweeping arm movements across the tablet surface just to get to the other side of the screen. This can be done with the Active Area command on the MENUS menu, which is a submenu of the DISPLAY menu, or by typing **AA** on the keyboard. If Generic CADD 5.0 is not currently configured for a digitizer, this command will not work.

The active area has approximately the same proportions as the screen. After the active area has been set, the boundaries of this area become mapped to the boundaries of the screen, and locations outside this area cannot be used for pointing.

If your digitizer is attached and properly configured, you are asked to *digitize* the lower-left corner of the active area. Digitizing simply means using the digitizer puck to select a point on the digitizer. In this case, point to the lower-left corner of the area that you want to use for pointing. If your digitizer has a pen, simply position the point of the pen over this point. If you are using a puck, position the cross hairs of the puck over this point. The cross hairs are usually found on a transparent extension of the puck so that you can see a drawing or digitizer overlay placed on the digitizer. In some cases, the active area might be outlined on a sheet that you place over the digitizer. If so, select the lower-left corner of this area.

Once you have positioned the pen or puck, select the point by pressing the first button on the puck, or by pressing down on the pen. Digitizer pens have an internal button that is activated when you apply downward pressure. If you are using a digitizer pen, you should hold the pen as vertically as possible, while still maintaining a comfortable position. If you hold the pen at a slant, the point may move when you press down on it, hampering accuracy.

When selecting the point, do not worry about the location of the cursor on the screen; in fact, the cursor may move right off the edge of the screen. You are not selecting a normal X-Y coordinate with this point, but an actual physical location on the digitizer, and the screen cursor is not involved.

After selecting the lower-left corner of the active area, you are asked to digitize the upper-right corner. (Only two points are required, as the active area is assumed to be a rectangle with sides parallel to the edges of the digitizer.) Once you have digitized the upper-right corner of the active area, the relationship between the screen coordinates and the digitizer coordinates is readjusted to match the new specification. Screen pointing can occur only in the new active area, and the rest of the digitizer may be used for other purposes, such as digitizer menus, as you will see later in this chapter.

Using the Digitizer to Trace Drawings

Because digitizers have their own internal coordinate systems and the actual position of the digitizer pen or puck is relayed back to Generic CADD 5.0, a digitizer can be used to trace a paper drawing into your drawing file.

You must carefully follow several steps to ensure successful tracing. First, the drawing should be taped securely to the digitizer. If the drawing has many horizontal or vertical lines, they should be aligned closely with the edges of the digitizer. If the drawing does not fit on the digitizer, you must reduce it or trace it in sections. When digitizing in sections, you must be especially careful to align the drawing horizontally on the digitizer. You might want to draw a large grid over the drawing so that you can align these grid lines with the edges of the digitizer whenever you move the drawing.

Aligning Paper and Electronic Drawings

In order to trace the drawing accurately, Generic CADD 5.0 needs to establish a relationship between the units of the paper drawing and the units in CADD. When you select points on the digitizer, these are interpreted as actual X and Y coordinates by Generic CADD 5.0. To translate the digitizer coordinate system into CADD's units of measurement, commands such as the Trace Scale command and the Drawing Align command are provided.

The Trace Scale Command

The Trace Scale command on the MENUS menu provides one means of translating digitizer units into real units. This command can also be accessed by typing **RZ** on the keyboard and is activated automatically when you use the Drawing Align (DA) command, covered later in this chapter.

The *Trace Scale* sets up a simple ratio between the paper drawing and your screen drawing. If the paper drawing is drawn at full size, the Trace Scale should be set to 1, meaning that one unit on the digitizer is the same as one unit in your drawing. If the paper drawing is one-half full size, the Trace Scale should be set to 2, meaning that one unit on the digitizer equals two units in your drawing. Since your CADD drawing uses real scale, the relationship between the scale of your drawing and the paper drawing is the same as the relationship between the paper drawing and the real object. If the paper drawing is scaled at 1/4" = 1' 0" (a typical architectural scale), the trace scale is calculated by determining the relationship between the drawing and the real object. In this case, the real object is 48 times the size of the drawing, so Trace Scale should be set to 48.

If you do not know the proper trace scale, use the Drawing Align command (see the section entitled "A General-Purpose Alternative—The Drawing Align Command" below).

Enabling Tracing Mode

Tracing a drawing on the digitizer is very different from simply moving the cursor on the screen. When you are using the digitizer for pointing, a relationship is set up between the digitizer active area and the current video screen. When you are tracing, the relationship is between the entire digitizer and the actual coordinates of the drawing. These drawing coordinates may or may not be the same as what is currently displayed on the screen.

To map the digitizer coordinates to the actual drawing coordinates (instead of the current screen coordinates), you must activate Trace Mode by selecting it from the MENUS menu, by typing **TM** on the keyboard, or by using the Drawing Align command, which activates Trace Mode automatically.

If you need to return to pointing mode for any reason, use the Trace Mode (TM) toggle again. Each time you select it, it reverses its status from Trace Mode on to Trace Mode off or vice versa. You might want to turn off Trace Mode temporarily in order to select a menu item, or to add something to the drawing that does not appear on the paper drawing. Just remember to go back to Trace Mode before you start tracing again.

A General-Purpose Alternative—
The Drawing Align Command

The Dwg Align command on the MENUS menu (DA on the keyboard) is designed to help you start tracing a drawing. It combines the functions of the Trace Scale and Trace Mode commands and adds a little extra.

When you use the Drawing Align command, you will first go through a series of steps that are similar to Trace Scale. The current Trace Scale is shown, which is assumed to be one-to-one unless you have previously specified otherwise. You are asked if this is the right scale, and if it is not, you are asked if you know the scale. If you do, you can type it, just like with Trace Scale. If you use this option, Trace Mode is not selected automatically.

If you don't know the scale, or if the drawing is not exactly straight on the digitizer, you can specify the tracing scale by digitizing two points instead. Basically, this process gives coordinate values to two points on the drawing, so that Generic CADD 5.0 can figure out the scale. In addition, it allows CADD to make an internal adjustment for any rotation in case the drawing isn't aligned exactly horizontally on the digitizer tablet.

When you say that you don't know the scale, you will be asked to select a point on the screen using the NP command. Generic CADD 5.0 assumes that you have a line already in the drawing that represents a line on the paper and asks you to select one of the endpoints. If you have such a line, you can use the third button on the pointing device to select it, or type **NP** on the keyboard when your cursor is near the point. Once you have selected the point on the screen, you will be asked to digitize the point on the tablet. Position the point of the digitizer stylus or the cross hairs of the digitizer puck over the point that you want to select and press down on the stylus or press the first button on the puck. Repeat this process for a second point.

Once you have given two points, a scale and a rotation will be calculated, and you will be asked if they are right. If so, Trace Mode will be selected automatically using these values. If not, you will be asked to digitize two more points to try again.

Notice that Generic CADD requires that you have a line in the drawing so that you can match it up with a line on the paper. However, sometimes you don't have such a line, or perhaps you want to specify your points by other means. You can type the coordinates of the two points if you like, instead of picking them with the NP command; note that you must have at least one line in the database—even a line that you have drawn and erased will do. If you want to type the coordinates instead of picking points, simply type them as usual, separated by a comma, using any units format, and ignore the prompt that tells you to use NP. After typing the coordinates, you will be asked to digitize the point on the tablet. You do this by selecting the point whose coordinates you have just typed. Repeat for the second point, or select it with NP.

Remember that unless you type the scale yourself, Trace Mode is enabled automatically when you use Drawing Align, so turn it off by typing **TM** if you want to use the digitizer for normal screen pointing.

Typically, you can use Drawing Align to set up your tracing scale and to turn on Trace Mode at the beginning of a drawing session. You can then use Trace Scale and Trace Mode whenever you need to change either of these parameters.

Tracing

Tracing drawings is similar to other ways of drawing in Generic CADD 5.0, except in the selection of points. You still use the basic Draw commands to create simple entities, which take on the characteristics set by the current Line parameters. Accuracy can still be controlled by the Grid Size (GS) and Snap to Grid (SG) commands, as well as by the Ortho Mode (OR) toggle. In fact, these drawing aids can help you to create a Generic CADD drawing that is more accurate than the one you are tracing.

You may encounter some difficulty editing a drawing in Trace Mode, because the screen does not necessarily show an exact replica of what you are tracing. If this is the case, you can issue Zoom Window (ZW) with Trace Mode active, and place the window by pointing to the area of the paper drawing that you want to have displayed on the screen.

To understand the tracing process, you must remember that you are working with three different manifestations of the drawing at one time. You are pointing to (1) scaled coordinates on a paper drawing that are being converted to (2) real scale in the Generic CADD drawing, and these, in turn, are being reconverted to (3) the varying units of the screen display, which depend on how much of the drawing is currently displayed. Of these, usually only the units in the Generic CADD drawing file are scaled at 1:1, the actual size of the object.

Tracing Versus Drawing

Be wary of the urge to use tracing as a general-purpose input mechanism for Generic CADD 5.0. Even though it is possible to create accurate drawings by tracing, in many cases it is faster and more accurate to create them from scratch without tracing.

Digitizing works best when accuracy is not crucial, or when you know that you will be editing the drawing extensively later anyway, checking and adjusting the accuracy as you edit. The real key is to analyze the drawing task and determine whether tracing is really appropriate. Digitizing is an excellent technique for transferring topological drawings to Generic CADD, for example, or for tracing the basic shape of certain products. If, on the other hand, you are the manufacturer of the product, you will probably want to create the shape using manual entry of Relative Coordinates—the most accurate of all data input techniques—rather than tracing a designer's sketch. It really depends on the application, and what will be done with the finished drawing.

Using the Digitizer to Select Commands

You've used the digitizer to point and to trace. The third use of a digitizer is to select commands. Just as commands can be selected by positioning the menu cursor on the video menu, they can also be selected by pointing to a specific area of the digitizer tablet. These areas are often identified by a digitizer overlay, which contains either the names of the commands or icons (pictures) representing the desired functions. An example of such an overlay is shown in Figure 14-1.

As with tracing drawings, several steps are required to use digitizer-driven commands. First, you must obtain a digitizer overlay. If you want to try the one shown in Figure 14-1, you can draw it in Generic CADD and then plot or print it at a scale that fits your digitizer, or you can xerographically or photographically enlarge this one. A sample digitizer menu is shipped with Generic CADD 5.0 as well.

A Menu File

The second necessary item is an ASCII file that contains, in order, the commands that you wish to execute from the digitizer overlay. The sample digitizer menu shipped with CADD uses the menu file DIGIT.MNU. This ASCII file is called the digitizer menu file (for a detailed discussion, see

FIGURE 14-1 A sample digitizer menu overlay

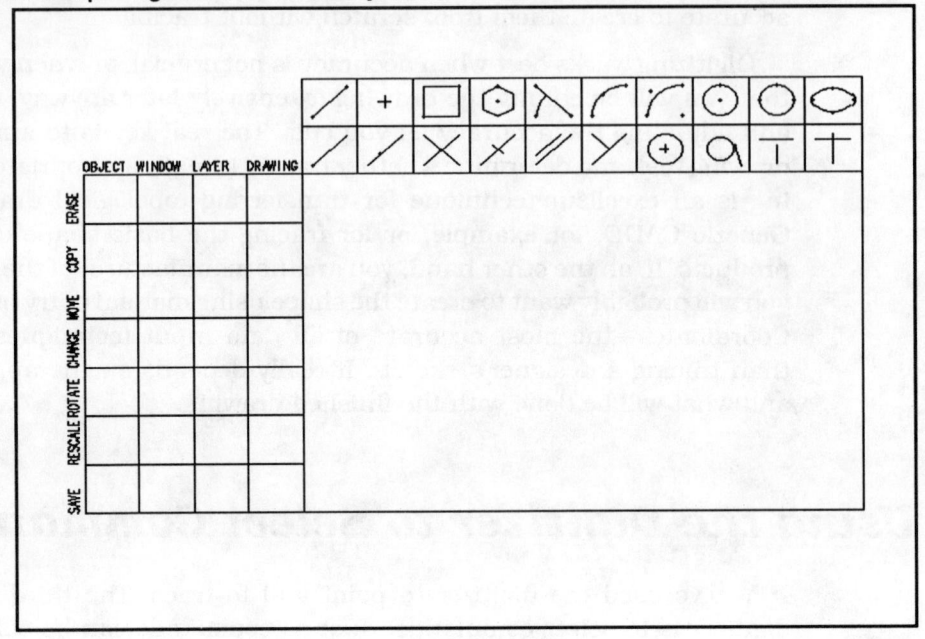

Chapter 16, "Programming Generic CADD 5.0"). If you want to try the sample digitizer menu, type the following, using any text editor or word processor that is capable of producing ASCII files.

```
m01r01c01,LI;
m01r01c02,PO;
m01r01c03,RE;
m01r01c04,RP;
m01r01c05,A2;
m01r01c06,A3;
m01r01c07,A4;
m01r01c08,C2;
m01r01c09,C3;
m01r01c10,EP;
m01r02c01,SC;
m01r02c02,SO;
m01r02c03,SI;
m01r02c04,SM;
m01r02c05,SL;
m01r02c06,SP;
m01r02c07,SN;
```

```
m01r02c08,ST;
m01r02c09,XT;
m01r02c10,RM;
m02r01c01,OE;
m02r01c02,WE;
m02r01c03,YX;
m02r01c04,DX;
m02r02c01,OC;
m02r02c02,WC;
m02r02c03,CO,Y;
m02r02c04,CO,D;
m02r03c01,OM;
m02r03c02,WM;
m02r03c03,MV,Y;
m02r03c04,MV,D;
m02r04c01,OG;
m02r04c02,WG;
m02r04c03,YG;
m02r04c04,DG;
m02r05c01,RO,O;
m02r05c02,WR;
m02r05c03,YR;
m02r05c04,DR;
m02r06c01,SZ,O;
m02r06c02,WZ;
m02r06c03,YZ;
m02r06c04,DZ;
m02r07c01,SV,O;
m02r07c02,SV,W;
m02r07c03,SV,Y;
m02r07c04,DS;
```

Some terms used by various programs to produce these files include Print to a File, Save as Text File, and Nondocument File. Be careful not to add any extra spaces not shown in the listing, either at the end of lines or between lines. Name this file DIGIT.MNU, and you will be ready to try the sample digitizer menu.

Configuring for the Tablet Menu

You will notice that the digitizer overlay is divided into three rectangular areas. Two of these areas are used for commands, and the third, blank area becomes the active area for screen pointing. The active area is set up once you are in Generic CADD, as you have seen. The menu areas must be similarly assigned, using the Setup option of the Select Dmenu command on the MENUS menu. You can get there on the keyboard by typing **SD** and then **S**.

When you use this option you are asked which menu you want to place. (Although the sample menu has only two menu areas, you can have up to ten areas at one time.) Start with number 1. You are asked to digitize the lower-left and upper-right corners of menu area 1, and then to indicate the number of horizontal boxes (columns) and vertical boxes (rows) of commands in each area. Type a number for each. The sample menu contains ten horizontal boxes and two vertical boxes in the first menu area. Repeat the Setup option of Select Dmenu for the second area. This area contains four horizontal and seven vertical boxes.

If you want Generic CADD to start automatically with the tablet menu instead of the normal video menu, use the Environment command (EN) once you have loaded the digitizer menu. The Environment command is discussed in Chapter 15, "Customizing Generic CADD 5.0." Thereafter, when you start up Generic CADD, the digitizer menu will be loaded instead of the video menu, and the video menu will not be displayed. Instead, you will be ready to use the digitizer menu.

Loading the Digitizer Menu

If you have not configured Generic CADD to load the digitizer menu automatically, you will need to load it by selecting Load Dmenu on the MENUS menu, or by typing **LD** on the keyboard. Because you have probably started up Generic CADD with the video menu active, you are warned that loading a digitizer menu erases the video menu, and you are given a chance to change your mind. If you elect to continue, you are asked for the name of a menu file. Type **DIGIT**, and press ENTER. The menu is assumed to be in the Generic CADD 5.0 directory unless you specify a pathname. If there is a file with the extension .MNU, it will be loaded.

The first command in the menu file is located in the upper-left of digitizer menu number 1. The next command will be in the box immediately to the right of the first box, and so on, until you reach the end of the row of boxes (in this case, ten commands). The eleventh command in your menu will be placed in the first box in the second row of digitizer menu number 1, and so on, until all the boxes in menu area 1 are exhausted. Because the first menu area has 20 boxes, the twenty-first command in the menu file is mapped to the upper-left corner box of digitizer menu area 2, and the remaining commands appear from left to right until you reach the end of the row, and then move on to the next row. You can see this relationship clearly if you compare the sample menu overlay with the menu file listing.

Using the Digitizer Menu

To select a command from the digitizer menu, position the point of the digitizer pen or the cross hairs of the digitizer puck within the box that contains the desired command and press the first button on the puck or press downward on the pen. Note that this button is different from the button that you use for selecting items from the video menu. The digitizer uses the first button both for selecting digitizer menu items and for pointing on the screen, to allow the use of single-button pens. When you select a command in this manner, it is activated exactly as if you had selected it from the video menu or typed its two-character code.

Because you need to go back and forth between choosing commands and selecting points on the screen, and because these tasks are both accomplished with the same button on the digitizer puck, there is a potential conflict between the two functions. Initially, Generic CADD assumes that you want to use the entire digitizer for pointing on the screen. When you have two digitizer menu areas enabled, these areas are made unavailable for screen pointing; that is, you form two "blind" screen areas where points cannot be selected. If you attempt to select points within these areas, you will get commands from the digitizer menu instead.

To solve this problem, you must reset the portion of the digitizer that is used for screen pointing using the Active Area (AA) command discussed earlier in this chapter. When you are asked for the lower-left corner, select the lower-left corner of the large blank box on the digitizer overlay, and select the upper-right corner of this same box for the next point. Once you have done this, the screen pointing area is reassigned to this box, and the conflict between pointing to the screen and selecting commands is resolved.

Activating More Digitizer Menus

When you first load Generic CADD 5.0 and a digitizer menu, either automatically or with the LOAD Dmenu (LD) command, all the commands from that menu are loaded and are active simultaneously, as long as the digitizer menu areas do not overlap. If they do overlap, the command that appears earlier in the digitizer menu file will supersede any that appear further down in the file.

For example, if you configure menu areas 1 and 2 to be in the same location on the digitizer, each containing ten boxes, only the first ten commands in the menu file are active; the second ten are hiding "under" the first ten. In order to activate the second group of ten, you must use the Enable/disable option of the Select Dmenu command on the MENUS menu, or type **SD** on the keyboard.

This command asks if you want to enable all digitizer menus, and asks you to type the number of the menu that you wish to enable or disable. You must type a number between 1 and 10 and press ENTER. You can enable or disable as many menus as you like with a single command. The list on the third prompt line is updated with each new number that you type. When you are finished specifying the menus that you want to enable, press ESC to end the command. The ability to turn on and off menu areas gives you access to several at one time without using up the entire tablet.

Switching Digitizer Menus

In some cases, the current menu might not contain the appropriate commands for your application. If you want to load another digitizer menu in place of DIGIT.MNU, you must unload, or delete, the current menu with the Menu Delete command on the MENUS menu, or with the VX command on the keyboard. Any video or digitizer menu that is currently loaded will be eliminated, so that you can load a different one. Until another menu is loaded, you will, however, have no menu whatsoever, video or digitizer. To load another digitizer menu, type **LD** to activate the LOAD Dmenu command.

Loading More Commands

On the other hand, you might start with a small DIGIT.MNU file and then want to add more commands. If DIGIT.MNU has just 20 commands in it, for example, and you load another digitizer menu with another 20 commands, these commands are numbered 21 to 40 and are assigned to the next available set of boxes.

A digitizer is a very powerful addition to any Generic CADD 5.0 installation. More than just a stationary mouse, its capability as both an accurate tracing device and its ability to activate macro commands make the digitizer a popular peripheral for CADD use. Chapter 16 contains more specific instructions on customizing Generic CADD by creating your own digitizer and video menus to take advantage of these functions.

CHAPTER 15

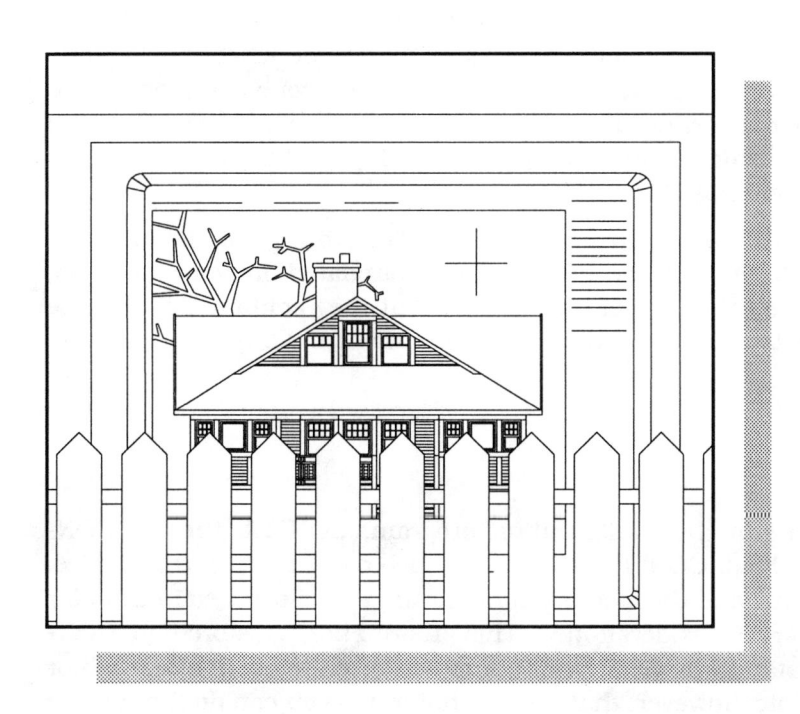

Customizing Generic CADD 5.0

You can customize Generic CADD for your specific applications using several methods. You can configure for your specific hardware combinations, and configure many of the parameters and toggles through the use of the Generic CADD 5.0 Environment command.

Custom Configurations

Now that you have had a chance to try all Generic CADD commands, you probably have a better idea of how you want to set up the configuration of toggles and parameters. As you gain more experience with Generic CADD, work with more drawing files, or upgrade your equipment, you might occasionally want to change your configuration. This is a normal part of customizing Generic CADD 5.0 to suit your hardware and your own style of working.

Generic CADD 5.0 utilized several files for storing the default configuration. These files are edited and/or updated in various ways, depending upon the type of information that they contain. All of these files must be in the same directory as Generic CADD 5.0.

CONFIG5.FIL

When you run the configuration program, CONFIG, the file CONFIG5.FIL is edited. CONFIG selects the video card, the pointing device, the unit system, and the memory configuration, as discussed in Chapter 3, "Preliminary Considerations." This information is stored in CONFIG5.FIL in standard ASCII format, and can be edited with a text editor in a pinch. Note, however, that there is not much you can do that will be useful here. If you change the name of the video driver, there is a good chance that you will need to change the values for CADD_FONT and CADD_COLORS in your AUTOEXEC.BAT as well. Values for these are documented in the Generic CADD 5.0 user guide, but it is usually safer to let CONFIG.EXE set it up for you. Similarly, if you change the pointing device, you will need to specify a new .IPD (Installable Pointing Device) file as well, and these are not documented anywhere. It is possible, however, that very experienced users may want to edit this file after becoming very familiar with CADD.

ENVIRON.FIL

This is not the file created when you use the Environment command in Generic CADD 5.0. This file updates whenever you leave CADD using the Quit command. It includes information regarding default paths, your selected plotter driver including information taken from the driver regarding number of pens, resolution, and standard sheet sizes, and similar information regarding your selected printer. Also, you will find information in this file regarding your digitizer overlay setup.

While ENVIRON.FIL, like CONFIG5.FIL, is a standard ASCII format text file, there is not much that the user can or should do to this file. Again, very experienced users may find a need from time to time to make small changes to this file, being very careful not to change the format in any way. For the most part, it is better to go to CADD, make the changes, and exit without calling up a drawing file if all you want to do is make changes to ENVIRON.FIL. This way, you can be sure that the file does not get corrupted by inadvertent changes.

GCADD.DWG

Finally, all of the toggles and variable settings in the drawing are saved by the Environment command (EN) into the file GCADD.DWG. This information is encoded, and cannot be edited or changed other than through the use of the Environment command. The information stored in this file is exactly the same as the information that is stored in every drawing file saved by Generic CADD 5.0, except that there is no drawing. This allows this file to be used when you start Generic CADD 5.0 but do not specify a drawing file.

To set up the Environment, simply start up Generic CADD 5.0 and set all of the parameters, toggles, and other settings that you wish to use when you first start up CADD. Level 3 users will be glad to know that you can turn on Manual Entry Relative permanently in this way. Almost all other settings can be saved as well, including whether or not the video menu is displayed, the size and display of the Grid, and all of the Fast options.

To save the Environment file, select the Environment command from the FILES menu or type **EN** on the keyboard. After a verification prompt, the file GCADD.DWG will be updated, and the settings that are now current will be used each time you start up Generic CADD 5.0 without a drawing file until you use this command again.

When you save a drawing, the same information is saved. Therefore, when you start up Generic CADD 5.0 with a drawing file, by typing CADD followed by the name of the drawing, all of the settings that were active when you last saved that drawing will be restored, rather than using the ones in GCADD.DWG.

Multiple Configurations

While you probably wish to avoid editing these files yourself, you may want to make copies of them to use under different circumstances. You may have different needs for configuration settings depending on the type of drawing that you are doing and whether or not you have colleagues who might also be using the same files.

You may also need more than one configuration if you use more than one video display, pointing device, or plotter with the same computer. You might, for instance, be running Generic CADD on a laptop with a built-in display that uses a different video driver and a different screen aspect ratio when you plug in an RGB monitor. Or perhaps you have several computers that normally use mice but share the use of a digitizer, which is moved from machine to machine whenever it is needed for tracing.

Both of these types of information are stored by Generic CADD 5.0 in CONFIG5.FIL. This file is updated whenever you make a change in any part of the configuration. When Generic CADD starts up, it looks in this file for information on the video display, pointing device, memory configuration, and unit system.

You can take advantage of this external storage by creating more than one version of this file. For example, if you work on a laptop computer, you might configure Generic CADD 5.0 to work with the laptop and test it to make sure that it functions properly. Select the proper video driver, and select the resolution that you want. Make sure that the other configuration options are also appropriate for your needs.

Once you are satisfied with the current configuration, copy CONFIG5.FIL to another file, substituting a mnemonic extension, such as CONFIG5.LAP. This is done at the DOS prompt, by typing **COPY CONFIG5.FIL CONFIG5.LAP** and pressing ENTER. You now have two copies of the configuration file for Generic CADD running on the laptop screen.

Now, go back to the CONFIG program and configure for the RGB monitor. Select the appropriate video driver (it is different from the one you are using with the laptop screen) and adjust the resolution and font if you have these options. When you exit CONFIG, a new CONFIG5.FIL will be created. (Don't worry about overwriting the laptop configuration because it is now in CONFIG5.LAP.) Test the configuration on the RGB monitor and make any necessary adjustments in the CONFIG program. Then, copy this new version of CONFIG5.FIL to a new file, such as CONFIG5.RGB. At the DOS prompt, type **COPY CONFIG5.FIL CONFIG5.RGB** and press ENTER. You will now have three separate configurations, each in its own file.

At this point, whenever you want to use the laptop screen, instead of going to CONFIG and resetting parameters, just type **COPY CONFIG5.LAP CONFIG5.FIL** at the DOS prompt before running Generic CADD. Similarly, to run CADD on the RGB monitor, type **COPY CONFIG5.RGB CONFIG5.FIL** before starting Generic CADD.

You can now go back and forth between the laptop screen and the RGB monitor much more easily. You can streamline the procedure even further. If you have a text editor or a word processor that creates ASCII files, you can create DOS Batch files that copy these files for you. Start a file called LAP.BAT with the following:

```
COPY CONFIG5.LAP CONFIG5.FIL
CADD
```

Make a second file called RGB.BAT that contains the lines

```
COPY CONFIG5.RGB CONFIG5.FIL
CADD
```

With these two files, you can start up Generic CADD 5.0 to run on the laptop screen simply by typing **LAP** and pressing ENTER. You can also start CADD on the RGB monitor by typing **RGB** and pressing ENTER. If you do not want CADD to start up right away when you switch configurations, just leave out the line that contains the word "CADD" in both files.

This technique can be used for several purposes. Even if your equipment stays the same, you might store configurations for different path setups, printer, plotter, and digitizer overlay setups by copying ENVIRON.FIL instead of CONFIG5.FIL. Similarly, you might want more than one version of GCADD.DWG, so that you can copy the appropriate one to GCADD.DWG and then start up CADD with a particular set of toggles and parameter values.

Clearing Digitizer Menu Areas

There is one function that can only be accomplished by editing ENVIRON.FIL. This is clearing digitizer menu areas (see Chapter 14, "Using a Digitizer"). If you have positioned digitizer menu areas in CADD, the locations of these digitizer menus are saved in ENVIRON.FIL. The locations are represented by four rows of ten numbers each, which represent two points (four numbers) for each of the ten digitizer menu areas, just above the line containing the name of the pointing device. If you wish to clear the digitizer so that these digitizer menus are no longer positioned anywhere, you must change all 40 numbers to zero. These four rows of numbers should stand out clearly in the file. Be sure that you have a backup copy of ENVIRON.FIL if you try this.

You will more likely want to move menu areas than clear them, but if your application requires clearing them, the best you can do without editing ENVIRON.FIL is to assign each to a very small area on the perimeter of the digitizer.

Macros, Menus, and Batch Files

Another good way to customize Generic CADD 5.0 is through the use of macros, menus, and Batch files. These are three different ways that Generic CADD 5.0 can be programmed to perform somewhat automated tasks using commands that you already know combined with a few extra techniques. The details of programming that apply to all three are discussed in more detail in Chapter 16, "Programming Generic CADD 5.0," so only the specifics of each are covered here.

Assigning Macros

Macros are combinations of commands and other characters that can be assigned to the press of a button. Every pointing device button beyond the first two, and combinations of SHIFT, CTRL, and ALT together with the function keys can be assigned a macro.

Macros can be assigned either with the Macro Assign (MA) command on the UTILITIES menu or from the Display Assigned Macros option on the Screen Flip menu.

If you select the Macro Assign command, you will be asked to press the key that you want to assign the macro to. This can be any pointing device button after the first two, or any function key. You can also hold down SHIFT, CTRL, or ALT as you press the function key and assign a macro to the two-key combination. Up to twelve function keys are supported, for a total of either 40 or 48 function key macros, in addition to the pointing device macros, depending on the configuration of your keyboard.

When you press the desired key or key combination, the macro currently assigned to that keypress will be displayed. If there is none, you will get a blank prompt line. The current macro can be added to, deleted, or edited. The cursor keys move around the macro line, the BACKSPACE key deletes backwards, and the INS and DEL keys work too.

The macro can be up to 255 characters, much more than will fit on the prompt line. As you continue typing or moving the cursor right or left, the macro line will slide along, allowing you to view the entire line. For more information on the characters that you can use in macros and what they do, see Chapter 16.

When you have finished editing the macro, press ENTER. To exit without changing the currently assigned macro, press ENTER. The Macro Assign command allows you to quickly create and change macros as you use Generic CADD 5.0, whenever you come to a repetitive task.

Editing macros from the Screen Flip (SF) menu is convenient if you want to see what macros you already have, and perhaps pick one to modify or simply locate an unassigned key. If you select Display Assigned

Macros from the Screen Flip menu, you will have the opportunity to display as a group all of the Pointing Device macros, the unshifted function key macros, or the SHIFT-function key, ALT-function key, or CTRL-function key macros. When you find one that you want to edit, simply press it, and it will appear on the prompt line for editing, just like with the Macro Assign command. For the combinations, you must press the appropriate key together with the function key, or you will edit the unshifted function key macro.

Once assigned, a macro may be used immediately. At the "Enter a command >" prompt, simply press the appropriate key to use the macro. All currently assigned macros are stored in a file called MACROCMD.FIL, which may be edited with a text editor if you like. This file is updated when you assign the macro. You may copy your MACROCMD.FIL for the purpose of creating multiple configurations as discussed earlier in this chapter.

Custom Menus

Generic CADD 5.0 video and digitizer menus are stored in ASCII files that can be created or modified with many text editors or word processors. Creating your own menus or modifying CADD5.MNU to perform specific tasks is another good way to customize Generic CADD 5.0.

Menus consist mostly of macros that are accessed by selecting an item on the video menu or picking a location on the digitizer (instead of using a mouse button or a function key). Chapter 16 includes more information on the specific format for menu files.

Unless you have changed the menu with the EN command, when you start up Generic CADD 5.0, the menu file CADD5.MNU is loaded, and is used as the video menu. If you either make a new file called CADD5.MNU or edit the one supplied, your new menu will be loaded instead. In this way you can alter either the name or the function of every item on the menu, remove items, or add new ones. New submenus may also be created, where you might store your own menu macros.

Various commands on the MENUS menu, a submenu of DISPLAY, allow you to load new menus after you have already started up Generic CADD 5.0. In addition, part of the memory configuration in CONFIG allows you to specify how much memory to set aside for the use of menus.

The Load Video menu command (LV) loads a menu file for use on the video menu. If there is already a video menu loaded, the new one is added to it, assuming it will fit in the amount of space set aside in CONFIG. If you want to load a whole new menu instead of adding it onto the end of the current one, use Remove Menu (VX) first. If you load a video menu when a digitizer menu is loaded, the digitizer menu will be removed. Similarly, a digitizer menu can be loaded with the Load Digitizer (LD) command. Newly loaded digitizer menus are added to those already loaded unless VX is used first, and incoming digitizer menus displace any video menus that might be already loaded. You cannot have both a video menu and a digitizer menu loaded at the same time.

Unlike function key and pointing device macros, menu items may be only 80 characters in length each, although they may be used to activate Batch files, extending the amount of work that may be done with a single menu item.

Batch Files

Batch files may also be treated as extended macros to customize Generic CADD. They may either be called manually from Generic CADD or from a custom menu item. A Batch file in this context consists of a file full of Generic CADD 5.0 commands and other special characters designed to perform a certain task. Batch files are usually used for programming when the complexity of the tasks exceeds the 80-character limit of a menu item.

From the keyboard or from a custom menu item, a Batch file is loaded with the Load Batch (LB) command or the Batch option of the Load command. Batch files may be created with a text editor or other software, using the extension .TXT. The format of Batch files is discussed in more detail in Chapter 16.

Custom Images

The Image Load and Save functions of Generic CADD 5.0 may come in handy in certain applications, where you want to show an image on the screen during a macro, menu item, or Batch file. Before selecting a

Component from the Component List, for instance, you may wish to illustrate the choices available with an image.

First, you must create the image (.GX2 file) using the Image option of the Save command, assuming that you are using a video driver that supports the use of .GX2 files. Place the components that you wish to preview into a drawing, together with any other information you might wish to see during the preview, such as the location of the reference points, the names of the components, and so on. Save the display of this drawing by using Save (SA) Image (I) and typing a filename. Do not save the whole screen, only the drawing area.

When you wish to view this image, you can load it with the Load (LO) command Image (I) option and type or select the filename. This combination of commands and a filename may be put into a macro, menu item, or Batch file for automatic recall at a later date.

This chapter has given you some methods and perhaps some ideas for how you might customize Generic CADD 5.0 to better meet your requirements. The best way to find out how you might want to customize CADD is to simply use it for your applications until you begin to run into repetitive tasks or recognize patterns in your work. You will soon see what needs to be automated. The function key macros are a good place to try out your ideas, because they can be easily edited without leaving CADD, so you can quickly test them out. Once you get them working, you might put them into menu items so that they are easier to find; this also frees up your function keys for more experimentation. You can even steal macros right out of MACROCMD.FIL and import them into CADD5.MNU if you can figure out how to do that with your word processor! The next chapter discusses the various formats, additional characters, and syntax for each of the macro types.

CHAPTER 16

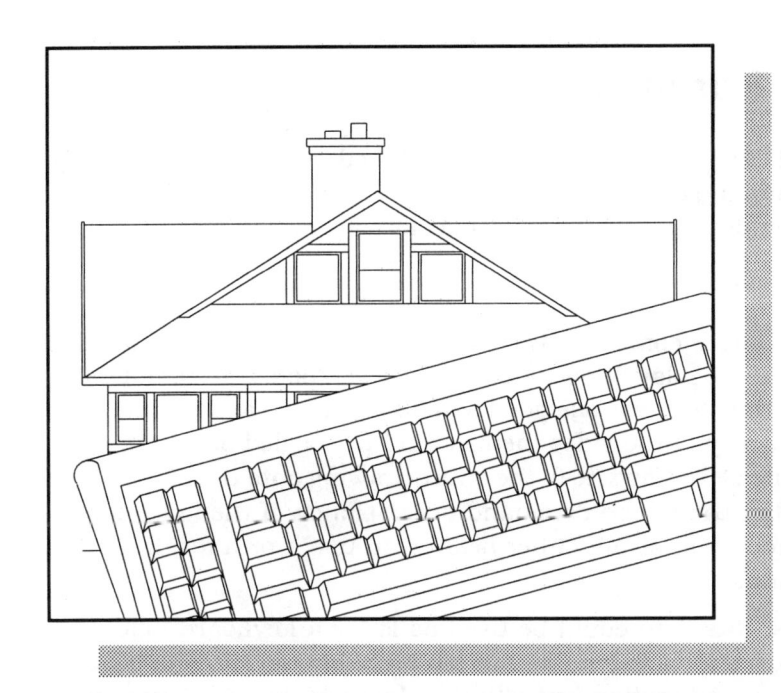

Programming Generic CADD 5.0

All of the various macro techniques discussed in the previous chapter make use of a specific format, together with some special characters used only in macros. All methods share most aspects of this format, and differ only in a few technical areas, file format, and how they are used in Generic CADD 5.0.

Macros, menus, and Batch file commands are all based upon the automated execution of a list of Generic CADD two-character commands, arranged according to these rules, and combined with the special characters discussed in this chapter.

Basic Macro Format

Generic CADD 5.0 commands can be combined into a macro by simply listing the commands that you want to execute, separating them with commas, and ending the list with a semicolon. For example:

```
VM,ZA;
```

This item simply combines two two-character codes, VM and ZA, representing the Display Video Menu and the Zoom All commands, respectively. If this item was assigned to a function key, and the key was pressed, the display of the video menu would be toggled on or off, then the screen would be redrawn to fit the entire drawing onto the newly sized screen. Note that the macro command doesn't know if the video menu display is currently on or off, either before you use it or after; it simply reverses its status.

As it stands, this item could be used as is for a keyboard macro. It could also be used as a Batch file, but it's probably too short to bother. Try putting it onto a function key with the Macro Assign (MA) command to get the hang of it.

The following simple item only requires a name to make it into a valid menu item:

```
Fit Screen,VM,ZA;
```

In a video menu, the words "Fit Screen" would show up somewhere on the menu. When you pick this from the menu, the rest of the macro is activated; the display of the video menu is toggled, and the drawing is zoomed to fit the screen. Note that the name of the command can be as long as you want, as long as the whole line does not exceed the 80-character limit, but only 12 characters fit on the video menu. Don't worry yet about where this item will show up on the menu.

Command Options

Options within commands can be included in macros also. Many commands lead, for example, to a prompt that asks you to type another letter to further define what you want to do. The Color Settings command provides a prompt asking what you want to set the color of. One of the available options is T for Text. You could make a macro item to set Text Color as follows:

CS,T;

As a menu item, this might be:

Text Color,CS,T;

Notice that all items in both the macro and the menu item must be separated by commas, and the line must end with a semicolon, even though the command isn't really done, because you haven't selected the color yet. The semicolon simply tells Generic CADD 5.0 that the macro is finished, and that it should take over from here. In the case of these items, when the macro is done, you will be at the prompt that asks you to select the color, with the menu of color bars showing if the video menu is active.

Supplying Information

Another thing that can be contained in a macro, menu item, or Batch file is data. Numeric values, point locations, filenames, and so on can all be included. To extend the previous example to specify a particular color, you might simply add the color number to the macro:

CS,T,4;

If your system uses a 16-color card such as an EGA or VGA, color 4 is red, so you might make a menu item such as:

```
Red Text,CS,T,4;
```

Since menu items come one after another in a file, you could create a partial menu file that looked liked this:

```
Text Color,CS,T;
 Red,CS,T,4;
 Blue,CS,T,2;
 Green,CS,T,3;
```

When displayed on the screen, this menu would appear as:

```
Text Color
 Red
 Blue
 Green
```

If you picked the first item, you would be asked for the color number, while picking any of the other four would automatically set the Text Color without asking you for any more information.

Interactive User Input

The previous color selection command allowed you to select the color by simply exiting at the end of the command and turning control back over to Generic CADD 5.0. In some cases, you may wish the macro to continue after you have supplied the information, so you don't want to give control back to CADD yet.

In these cases, the *tilde* symbol (~) allows you to supply a value and continue on with the macro, as in the following menu item:

```
All Colors,CS,L,~,T,~,H,~,F,~,D,~;
```

This item will ask you for the Line, Text, Hatch, Fill, and Dimension colors before returning control back to Generic CADD 5.0.

If the information that is required to be supplied by the user is a point instead of a single value, the "at" (@) symbol is used instead, as in the following macro example:

```
C2,@,MR,1,0;
```

See if you can figure it out. The first command starts a Two-Point Circle. Next, the macro pauses while the user enters a point. After the point is entered (either by typing coordinates or by picking a point on the screen), Manual Entry mode is set to Relative, and a second point, 1 unit to the right of the user-selected point, is supplied automatically. So this command creates a one-unit radius circle with the selection of a single point by the user. Note that it must be a keyboard macro and not a menu item, because it doesn't have a name. Video menu items must contain a name so that you've got something to select. In a video menu, you might try something like this:

```
Circle,C2;
 1" radius,C2,@,MR,1,0;
 2" radius,C2,@,MR,2,0;
 3" radius,C2,@,MR,3,0;
```

In a style similar to the Text Color example, one item creates a circle of user-specified radius, while the items following are self-contained. All that the user need specify is the center. While this example might seem too simple to be very useful, it illustrates the mechanics of menu items, and suggests some organizational strategies.

Other Special Characters

You have seen two special characters, ~ and @, which have special meaning when used in macros, menu items, and Batch files. There are several others that can be used for programming as well, each with its own purpose.

Escape

There are two methods for issuing an ESC in a macro. Each works best under specific circumstances. The "pound" key (#) works well for ending a Text Place or Text Line command. For example, consider this menu item:

```
3"=1',TL,@,SCALE:  3"=1'-0",#;
```

This item will issue a Text Line command, ask for a location, then type the text, 3"=1'-0". The comma acts as a carriage return here, and the pound sign issues an ESC.

The undocumented two-character command ES is useful in circumstances where the pound character doesn't work, as in ending a Line command:

```
LI,0,0,10,0,10,10,10,0,ES;
```

In many cases such as this, the two-character command PU (Pen Up) may perform the same function.

Enter

To issue an ENTER (or carriage return), use the exclamation point (!). Sticking with the text example, the ENTER key can be useful to create multiple lines of text with a single macro item:

```
3"=1',TL,@,SCALE:!3"=1';0",#;
```

This item will place the word SCALE: on one line, and the text 3"=1'-0" on the next, due to the exclamation point, which issues an ENTER in the middle of the command.

Ignore Function

Sometimes, you'll want to use a special character without having it do something special. For example, suppose you want an exclamation point in your text, but don't want it to go to the next line. In these cases, a slash in front of the special character renders it temporarily powerless:

```
No Scale,TL,@,NOT TO SCALE/! Verify all dimensions,#;
```

This item produces the single line of type:

```
NOT TO SCALE! Verify all dimensions
```

Without the slash before the exclamation mark, an ENTER would have been issued and split the text into two lines.

Directional Toggles

Going back to the very first example, suppose that you wanted to make sure that the macro actually turned the video menu display off, instead of just toggling it whichever way it wasn't. Special two-character commands exist for this purpose, Double Plus (++) and Double Minus (--). These are treated like any other two-character command, and are separated by commas from the commands that surround them. If you rewrite the macro, then, you get:

```
VM,--,ZA;
```

This macro will always turn the video menu display off, never on, and then issue the Zoom All. You might want two commands, for more precise control:

```
VM,++,ZA;
VM,--,RD;
```

Note that the macros have been adjusted somewhat to make a little more sense. When you turn the video menu on, you leave less room on the screen, and therefore will be more likely to need to Zoom All, while turning the menu off makes more room, and the Redraw lets you see what's under there. These two could go on a pair of function keys, but not on a menu, so they don't need names. How would you select the one for turning on the menu when the menu was off?

Preparation

You can see that in order to write macro or menu items that automatically respond to prompts, you must have a good idea of what the prompts are going to be. A logical procedure is to go through the process that you want to automate in Generic CADD 5.0, writing down all of the answers to all of the prompts. Many commands include "Yes" or "No" questions, which must be answered with either letter Y or N.

Digitizer Menu Items

All of the preceding rules apply to digitizer menus as well as video menus. Because the text before the first comma is essentially only a command label, you might number the commands instead of naming them, so that you can remember which box they are activated by. You could indicate the menu area, column, and row numbers in only nine characters per item:

```
m01c01r01,CS,L,~,T,~,H,~,F,~,D,~;
```

The name of this item would not mean much if you saw it on a video menu, but it might help you use the commands on a digitizer menu. If your digitizer menu is small enough that you can remember which box each command is in, you might use the same names that are on your video menu. For more detailed discussion on using digitizer menus, see Chapter 14, "Using a Digitizer."

Video Submenus

Unlike digitizer menus, on which numerous commands may be active at one time, video menus must be divided into smaller groups that will fit on one area of the screen. These submenus are generally activated from a master menu. In the standard Generic CADD 5.0 menu, CADD5.MNU, the first group of commands in the menu file is called the ROOT menu, which is a list of the available submenus, and each submenu has an entry that returns you to the ROOT menu. Though this is a fairly typical organization, you may organize your menus however you like.

To divide a menu into submenus, a pair of menu items is created: one that allows you to jump ahead to the desired submenu, and another to identify the submenu. To activate a submenu called EDIT, for example, you might have an item on your initial menu like this:

```
EDIT,**
```

This item consists of the name of the submenu, a comma, and a pair of asterisks. You do not need to end this type of item with a semicolon. When you select this item, Generic CADD looks for an item somewhere in the menu that starts with an asterisk and has the same text:

```
* EDIT
```

This entry would normally be followed by a number of commands that fit into this category. Usually following these items is an item to get you out of this menu. A simple two-screen menu for drawing and editing objects might look something like this:

```
* DRAW

Point,PO;
Line,LI;
Circle,C2;
Arc,A2;

Quit,Y,!,Q;

EDIT,**

* EDIT

Erase,ER;
Copy,CO;
Move, MV;
Change,CG;

DRAW,**
```

This is a relatively simple menu, but it illustrates how one menu can call another. When you first load this menu, only the first part, the * DRAW section, is displayed, due to the * EDIT line, which Generic CADD recognizes as a separate screen. When you select EDIT from the DRAW menu, the EDIT commands appear; when you select DRAW from the EDITS menu, the DRAW commands appear. Note that the Quit command on the EDITS menu automatically elects to save the drawing, assumes that the default name is acceptable, and then escapes to DOS by typing Q. This command will not make it to the end of the prompts if the file already exists, because you must type **O** or **R** to get beyond this point, and neither of these letters is included in this command.

Conventions

In the previous menu, you may have noticed that the words DRAW and EDIT were in all uppercase letters, while the rest of the items where in upper- and lowercase. This is an unenforced convention used on the default menu, CADD5, to distinguish between menu names and commands. When you select an item that is in all uppercase, you can expect to get another menu, while selecting a mixed-case item actually initiates an action of one kind or another. It is more than convention to skip a line below the name of the menu. If you put an item on this line, CADD won't do anything.

Do-Nothing Items

If you want to make a menu item that doesn't do anything, as a reminder or a label, for example, simply use the two-character command PU, for Pen Up:

```
DO NOTHING,PU;
```

Loading a Video Menu

There are two ways to load a video menu for use with Generic CADD 5.0. If you have elected to display the video menu in setting up your Environment file, GCADD.DWG, Generic CADD automatically loads the menu that was active when the Environment was created. Actually, only the filename is stored in the Environment, so if you update the menu in the meantime, the latest version will be loaded. If you plan to experiment with the CADD5.MNU file, it would be a good idea to make a copy of it first. STANDARD.MNU might be a good name.

The other means of loading a video menu is from within CADD after you have already loaded the default menu. In this case, you can either

Chapter 16: Programming Generic CADD 5.0

load the new menu at the end of the current menu, or you may erase the current menu and replace it with the new one. If you exceed the maximum length of video menus, established in CONFIG, the last submenus in your file will not be active. In these cases, you will need to break your menu into separate files, and erase one before loading another, or increase the amount of memory allocated to menus with CONFIG.

To erase the current menu, use the Menu Delete command on the MENUS submenu of the DISPLAY menu or type **VX** on the keyboard. The menu is cleared. Now you can load the new menu by typing **LV** on the keyboard. You are asked for the name of the menu to load. Type the name of your menu. You can also use the New Menu command, which is really a macro command that performs the same function by combining the VX and LV commands.

If you do not want to erase the current menu first, simply use the LV command to load the new menu. If the video menu display is currently off, The LV command automatically turns the menu display back on.

When you add a new video menu to an existing one, the submenus may not be accessible from your ROOT menu. To use the newly loaded menus, use the PGUP and PGDN keys, which flip through one menu screen at a time. If you construct your own menu system, you can put references on your ROOT menu that activate submenus, which may or may not be loaded, depending on what you have done previously.

If you call a submenu that does not exist, nothing happens. If two submenus have the same name, you will only be able to use the first one, as Generic CADD always looks for submenus by starting at the beginning of the file and searching downward.

You can create commands with the same name, as long as you can tell them apart. You can even include commands with the same name on the same submenu if you like. These can either activate the same or different command codes. The following submenu uses command lines with different names that do the same thing, and commands with the same name that do slightly different things:

```
* DECO

  FIRST,FS,T,DECO;
  TIME,FS,T,DECO;
==========,PU;
  Size:,TZ,T;
```

```
----------,PU;
    Small,TZ,T,1,!,TP;
      -  ,TZ,T,2,!,TP;
      -  ,TZ,T,4,!,TP;
      -  ,TZ,T,5,!,TP;
    Large,TZ,T,6,!,TP;
----------,PU;
TEXT,**
```

This menu would appear on the screen as the following:

```
* DECO

  FIRST
  TIME
==========
  Size:
----------
  Small
    -
    -
    -
  Large
----------
  TEXT
```

Note the flexibility that you have in breaking up the menu into groups by introducing nonfunctional commands or blank spaces. In this menu, the items are arranged in the order that they might normally be used. The first time that you use text, you would select either FIRST or TIME. These items have been allocated two lines so that you will be more likely to notice them when you go to the Notes menu. Both menu items perform exactly the same task: select and load the font DECO.

The group of menu items ranging from Small to Large all do the same thing except for creating a different size text. Each then goes on to start a text placement, after ending the Text Size command with an ENTER (!).

Four of the text placement commands begin with the same text—a dash preceded by two spaces—but you can tell which is which by the way that they are arranged. Generic CADD doesn't care what you call these commands, as all CADD does with the text is show it on the screen.

Long Menu Items

Each line of a menu file can be up to 80 characters long. This is true for both video and digitizer menus. Characters beyond the eightieth are simply ignored. Though 80 characters are enough for most commands, you may occasionally want to use longer macros.

To write commands longer than 80 characters, you must use Batch files with the menu. The actual commands that you want to execute would be stored in a separate ASCII file with the extension .TXT, and the item on the menu would use a Load (LO) Batch (B) command to activate this Batch file. Batch files can include pauses for user input as well as data required by command prompts, just like any other Generic CADD macro type.

Suppose, for example, that you want to create (1) a menu item that would load several components from a special directory, and (2) a menu designed for automated placement of these components. Your menu item for such a task might look like this:

```
FURNITURE,LO,B,FURN;
```

The Batch file associated with this menu item would be called FURN.TXT, and should be in the same directory as Generic CADD. It might look like the following:

```
FP,C,\CADD5\CMP\FURN\,#;
LO,C,CHAIR;
LO,C,TABLE;
LO,C,DESK;
LO,C,LAMP;
LO,C,BED;
LO,C,COUCH;
LO,C,LOVESEAT;
LO,C,DRESSER;

FP,C\CADD5\CMP\,#;
LV,FURN;
CZ,1,1;
```

Note that the Batch file returns the component path to the normal component directory after loading the furniture components from their own directory. This Batch file also makes sure that the component scale is returned to the default value of 1, as the furniture will probably be inserted at real scale. Rotation of the furniture will likely be controlled by the Furniture Placement menu, called FURN.MNU, which might look something like this:

```
* FURNITURE

facing,CR;
--------,PU;
 Right,CR,0;
  Left,CR,180;
   Up,CR,90;
    Down,CR,270;
========,PU;
Chair,CP,CHAIR;
Table,CP,TABLE;
Desk,CP,DESK;
Lamp,CP,LAMP;
Bed,CP,BED;
Couch,CP,COUCH;
Loveseat,CP,LOVESEAT;
Dresser,CP,DRESSER;
========,PU;
ROOT MENU,**
```

This menu allows you to select one of four preset directions (component rotations) or specify your own, and then place any of the furniture components, which are preloaded if this menu is accessible. If you are placing more than one component using the same direction, you would not need to select a direction each time. As usual, the last item allows you to return to the ROOT menu.

Batch files can be called from digitizer menus as well, and as you can see from this example, menus can be used to activate each other so that all of your commands need not be in a single menu file.

Including Images to Illustrate Menus

The previous example included a menu item on one menu that loaded a Batch file, which, in turn, loaded components and another menu. In the example, .CMP files, .MNU files, and .TXT files were used. To this,

Chapter 16: Programming Generic CADD 5.0

you could add one more file type, .GX2, which would allow you to illustrate the menu as well.

First, you must create the .GX2 file. Place each component in a drawing, title with the name of the component, and indicate the reference point somehow. If you have Display Reference Points turned on, the actual reference points will show. Figure 16-1 shows what this screen might look like. To create a .GX2 file from this screen, use the Save (SA) Image (I) command on the FILES menu, and call this image "FURN," to match the Batch and menu files.

To use this image file, add the following lines to the FURN.MNU file:

```
Preview ON,LO,I,FURN;
Preview OFF,RD;
```

The first of these lines loads the image file so that you can see each component and the location of its reference point. The second line erases the image from the screen by issuing a Redraw command, which returns your drawing to the screen.

FIGURE 16-1 An image for use with the Furniture menu

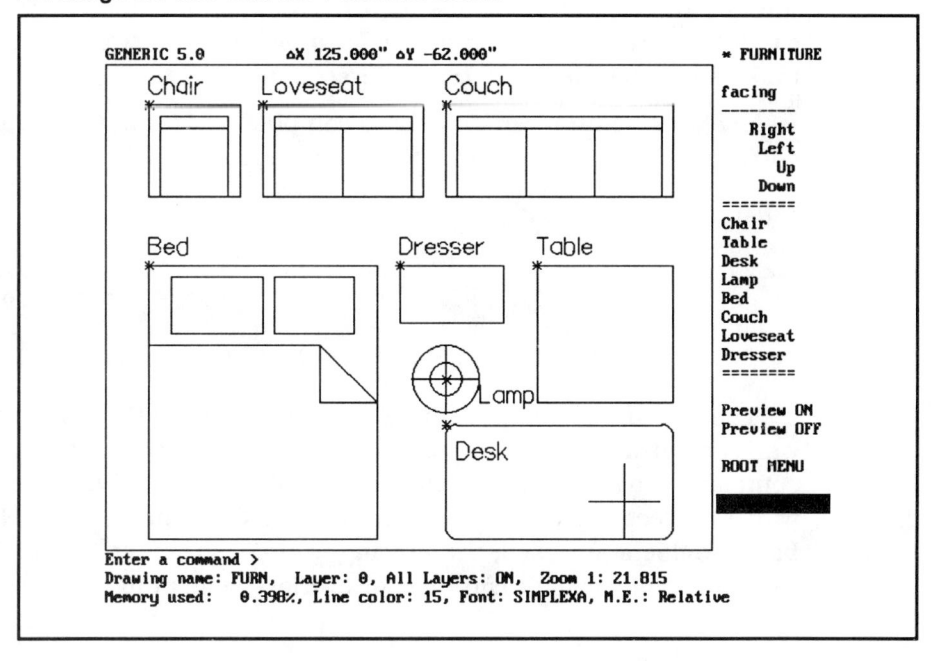

Image previews can also be useful for font selection, hatch pattern selection, or any situation when a picture is helpful. Digitizer menus can call image files in exactly the same way.

Some Useful Menu Macros

The best way to write your own menus is to keep track of the tasks that you do continually in Generic CADD 5.0, and try to automate these functions. The type of drawings and procedures that you do the most should influence which macros you create.

Here are some menu macros that you may find useful, or you may want to modify them to suit your own requirements. They may also give you some ideas on how to write your own.

Wall Intersections

Figure 16-2 shows a plan that has been drawn with double lines (L2). The manual technique for cleaning up the intersections between the interior and the exterior walls requires that you break the double line of the interior wall, and then either Trim or Fillet the two new corners to make sure that they were true intersections.

All of this manual work can be accomplished with four macros, which correspond to the direction of the intersections, as follows:

```
* WALL T's

Above,OB,@,MR,0,0,0,0,BP,0,0,MB,FR,0,FL,-9,0,-3,9,FL,9,0,3,9;
Below,OB,@,MR,0,0,0,0,BP,0,0,MB,FR,0,FL,-9,0,-3,-9,FL,9,0,3,-9;
Right,OB,@,MR,0,0,0,0,BP,0,0,MB,FR,0,FL,0,9,9,3,FL,0,-9,9,-3;
 Left,OB,@,MR,0,0,0,0,BP,0,0,MB,FR,0,FL,0,9,-9,3,FL,0,-9,-9,-3;
```

The title of each menu item indicates on which side of the continuous wall the butting wall intersects. The point picked at the beginning of the command is a point on the continuous wall, on the side where the butting wall intersects, between the two sides of the butting wall. Note that because fillets are used, the butting wall doesn't have to exactly touch the continuous wall; it can miss or overlap by as much as nine inches.

Chapter 16: Programming Generic CADD 5.0

FIGURE 16-2 A drawing with unbroken intersections of double lines

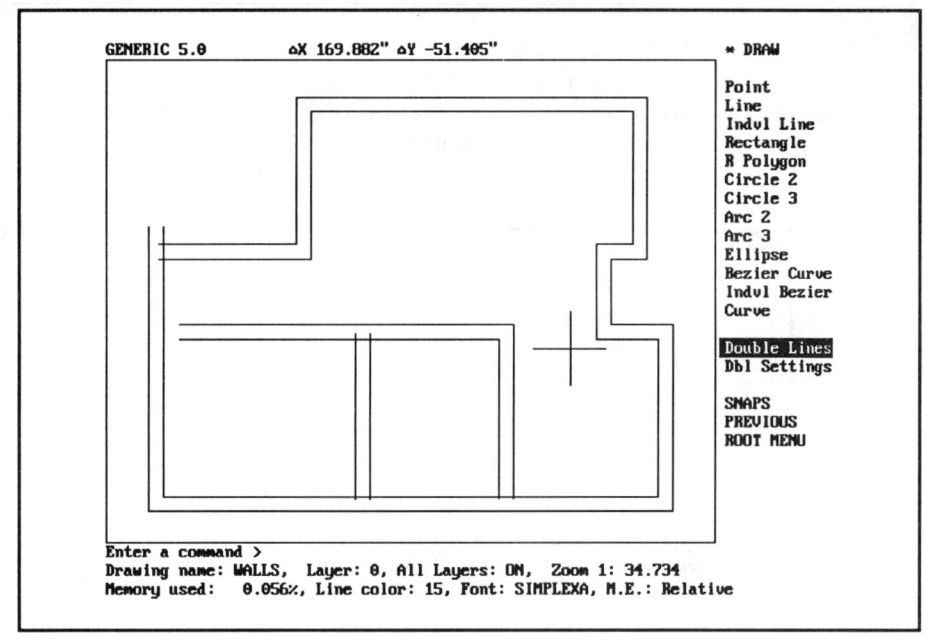

If you are using an EGA card or another graphics card that supports the extended ASCII character set, you can even use special characters to illustrate the items on the menu. The following menu items are self-explanatory:

```
* WALL T's

┬ ,OB,@,MR,0,0,0,0,BP,0,0,MB,FR,0,FL,-9,0,-3,9,FL,9,0,3,9;
┤ ,OB,@,MR,0,0,0,0,BP,0,0,MB,FR,0,FL,0,9,9,3,FL,0,-9,9,-3;
├ ,OB,@,MR,0,0,0,0,BP,0,0,MB,FR,0,FL,0,9,-9,3,FL,0,-9,-9,-3;
┴ ,OB,@,MR,0,0,0,0,BP,0,0,MB,FR,0,FL,-9,0,-3,-9,FL,9,0,3,-9;
```

Some new techniques are introduced with these macros. One of these is the use of the Basepoint (BP) command to mark a point so that you can specify coordinates relative to this point later in the Menu command. In this case the basepoint is located at the point that you first selected by positioning it at 0,0 using Manual Entry mode. After this point on the continuous wall has been located and broken, all further points are specified relative to the basepoint by using the Manual Entry Basepoint

Use of the Intersection macros

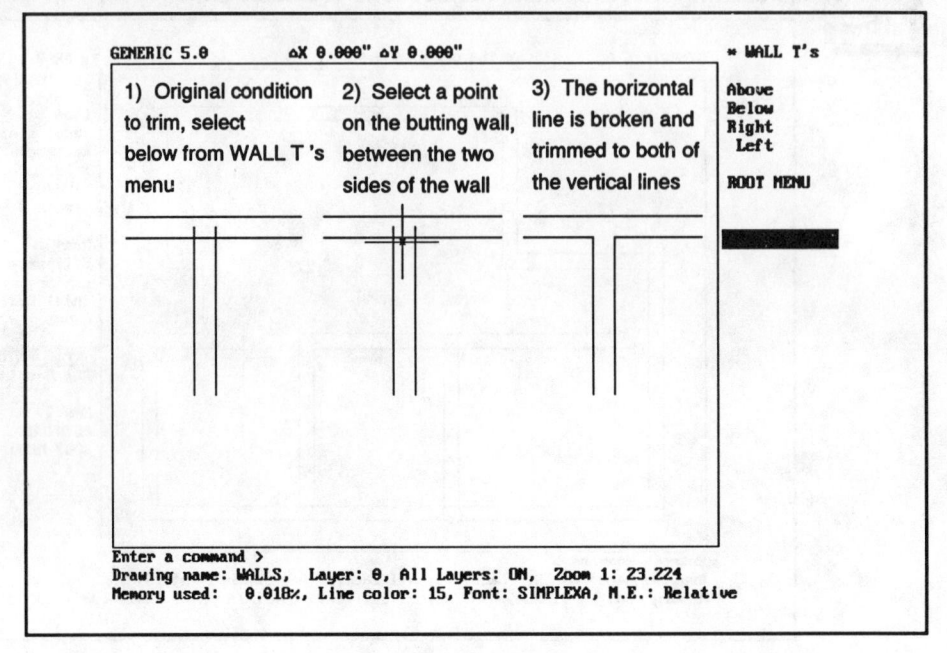

FIGURE 16-3

```
GENERIC 5.0        ΔX 0.000"  ΔY 0.000"                    * WALL T's

1) Original condition   2) Select a point    3) The horizontal     Above
   to trim, select         on the butting wall, line is broken and  Below
   below from WALL T's     between the two     trimmed to both of   Right
   menu                    sides of the wall   the vertical lines   Left

                                                                    ROOT MENU


Enter a command >
Drawing name: WALLS,  Layer: 0, All Layers: ON,  Zoom 1: 23.224
Memory used:  0.018%, Line color: 15, Font: SIMPLEXA, M.E.: Relative
```

(MB) command. This allows you to make sure that you are getting the lines that you want, regardless of the width of the wall. Figure 16-3 illustrates a typical use of this macro command.

Another technique introduced by this macro is one of generalization. You may not know exactly where the lines are going to be located, but you can estimate the thickness of a wall to be between 4 inches and 24 inches. The points specified by the Fillet command are overestimated, due to the fact that a line will probably be found somewhere in the vicinity of the point specified, and will usually be the line that you want. This command will work in most instances, except those in which another wall or an opening in either wall is nearby.

In general, this macro will save quite a bit of time in the editing process. Special cases will still require editing "by hand." What's more, these macros can be revised to work with any type of drawing that makes use of double lines that need to be trimmed at butting intersections. Simply change the values to coordinate with your typical spacings.

Openings in Double Lines

These macros are especially useful for putting doorways and windows in walls, but like the previous example, they can be modified for other applications. Simply adjust the values used here. The technique used is to add a line at each end of the opening, and then to break the original lines. Note that these particular macros are written for walls six inches thick.

```
horizontal,PU;

30",MR,SO,@,0,6,ES,30,0,0,-6,OB,-15,0,15,0,-30,0,OB,15,6,15,0,-30,0;
36",MR,SO,@,0,6,ES,36,0,0,-6,OB,-18,0,18,0,-36,0,OB,18,6,18,0,-36,0;
42",MR,SO,@,0,6,ES,42,0,0,-6,OB,-21,0,21,0,-42,0,OB,21,6,21,0,-42,0;

vertical,PU;

30",MR,SO,@,-6,0,ES,0,30,6,0,OB,0,-15,0,15,0,-30,OB,-6,15,0,-15,0,30;
36",MR,SO,@,-6,0,ES,0,36,6,0,OB,0,-18,0,18,0,-36,OB,-6,18,0,-18,0,36;
42",MR,SO,@,-6,0,ES,0,42,6,0,OB,0,-21,0,21,0,-42,OB,-6,21,0,-21,0,42;
```

The opening in the horizontal walls is created to the right of the selected point, which must be on the lower of the two lines; the opening in the vertical walls is created above the point selected, which must be on the rightmost line of the wall. If these assumptions will not always be true, you must write additional macros to cover these cases. Figure 16-4 illustrates the use of the Opening macros.

Setting Variables

Several variables in Generic CADD 5.0 depend on the scale at which the drawing is plotted. These include Text Size, Component Scale, and many of the Dimensioning Variables.

The following menu items set two of these variables, Text Size and Component Scale, by selecting a scale from the menu:

```
* SCALE

1/8"=1',TZ,T,12,!,CZ,96,96;  1/4"=1',TZ,T,6,!,CZ,48,48;
3/4"=1',TZ,T,2,!,CZ,16,16;

ROOT MENU,**
```

FIGURE 16-4 Use of the Opening macros

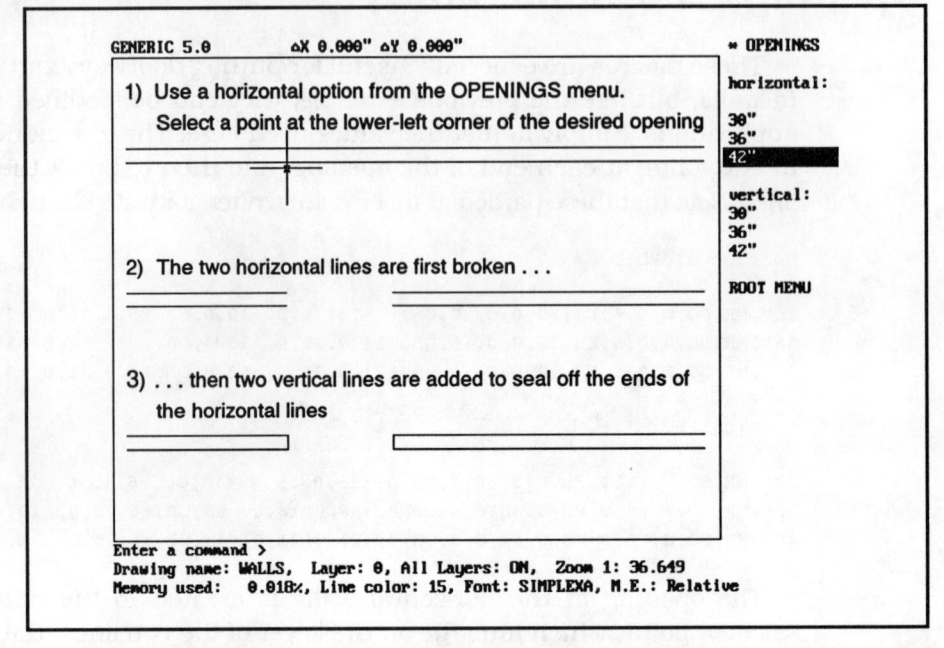

```
GENERIC 5.0          ΔX 0.000"  ΔY 0.000"                    * OPENINGS

  1) Use a horizontal option from the OPENINGS menu.        horizontal:
     Select a point at the lower-left corner of the desired opening   30"
  ─────────────────────────        ──────────────────────    36"
                                                             42"
  ─────────────────────────        ──────────────────────
                          ╆                                  vertical:
                                                             30"
                                                             36"
  2) The two horizontal lines are first broken . . .         42"
  ─────────────────────            ──────────────────────
                                                            ROOT MENU
  ─────────────────────            ──────────────────────



  3) . . . then two vertical lines are added to seal off the ends of
     the horizontal lines
  ─────────────────────┐          ┌──────────────────────
                       │          │
  ─────────────────────┘          └──────────────────────





Enter a command >
Drawing name: WALLS,  Layer: 0, All Layers: ON,  Zoom 1: 36.649
Memory used:   0.018%, Line color: 15, Font: SIMPLEXA, M.E.: Relative
```

These items make certain assumptions about the text size that you want to use. They also assume that you will be inserting components that are symbols rather than real objects. Of course, you can modify these menu items to use whatever values suit your drawing requirements or scales. The important point is that you only have to remember to set the scale once, instead of variable by variable. Similar macros could be written to set other variables, or these could be extended to cover dimensioning, attributes, and so on.

Macro Tricks

You can automate almost any drawing task with Generic CADD 5.0's macro programming capabilities. Some tasks may require that you use a combination of menu macros, Batch files, user input of points, user input of single values, and various forms of manual entry that allow you to keep track of where you are at any given time.

Chapter 16: Programming Generic CADD 5.0

One of the limitations of Generic's macro function, however, is its lack of variables. A few pseudo-variables are available: the Origin, the Basepoint, and the last point entered; you can specify future points in reference to any of these. If used carefully, these points can help you overcome some interesting programming difficulties, as seen in the wall-intersection examples. Consider the following macro, which creates the simple house shape shown in Figure 16-5 from just one user-selected point:

```
LS,200',200',ZL,MO,RE,0,0,@,MR,BP,0,0,MB;
LI,0,0,-100',100';
BP,SC,-100',0,LI,0,0,MR,100',100',MB,FR,0,BP,SM,1,0,OE,0,0;
TO,1.0,BP,SI,0,100',TO,0.25,FL,1,-1,-1,-1;
```

This Batch file will automatically start up a Rectangle command, fixing the first point at the origin. You will be asked for the second point. The rest of the drawing will be done automatically. This particular version of the Batch macro will work on almost any rectangle that is roughly the

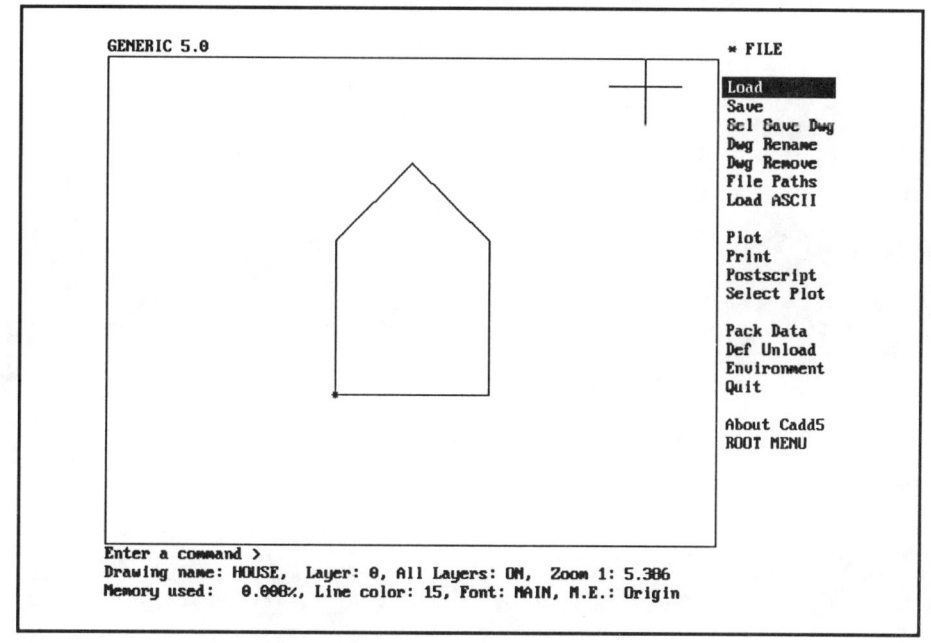

FIGURE 16-5 A house shape that can be created with the sample Batch file

size of a house. If you have Absolute Coordinates turned on before you load this Batch, you will be able to see the size of the rectangle. Alternatively, you can simply type the width and height of the rectangle at the first prompt.

If Generic CADD's macro capabilities are not powerful enough to automate your drawing procedures, you may be able to combine Generic CADD's menu or Batch capabilities with other software, as discussed in the next chapter.

CHAPTER 17

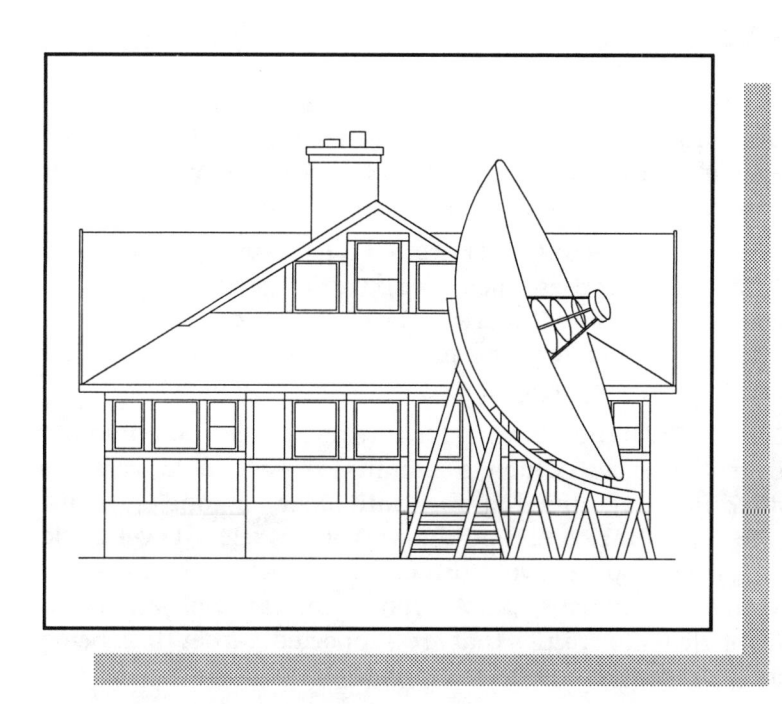

Communicating with Other Programs

Because Generic CADD 5.0 creates and reads several types of disk files, it can communicate with other software that is also capable of creating or reading these files.

Regardless of file type, Generic CADD 5.0 can send information to the disk, where it can be interpreted by other programs and it can read information from the disk, allowing other programs a channel into Generic CADD 5.0.

Communication Through Drawing Files

Generic CADD's most natural form of communication is through drawing files. Any drawing created in any version of Generic CADD using any hardware combination can be read and processed by any other version of Generic CADD, even if the hardware configuration is different.

Previous versions of Generic CADD utilized a somewhat different file format for drawing files, but these files are *upwardly compatible*—that is to say that they can be read by Generic CADD 5.0. You don't need to do anything special to load old drawing files. They can be loaded in the normal fashion, using any command that loads drawing files.

However, Generic CADD 5.0 drawing files are not directly *downwardly compatible*. To create files with which to communicate with older versions of CADD or with other programs that work with older versions of CADD, an option of the Save (SA) command allows you to select Level 3 file format. Note that when you save your drawing in Level 3 format, entities such as Associative Dimensions and Attributes that are not supported by Level 3 are exploded into entities that are supported, rather than being lost altogether.

Note For the most part, other older versions of CADD will also read Level 3 drawing files, as will most software designed to work with earlier versions of CADD. However, most earlier versions of CADD that do not support certain Level 3 entity types (such as Beziers) will simply ignore them rather than converting them to something that they can work with. Levels 1 and 2, for example, cannot interpret everything in a Level 3 drawing, such as Hatches and Fills, but for the most part, two-way communication is possible.

Sending Drawing Data to Other Software

In addition to communication between different computers running various versions of Generic CADD, drawing files can be used to send information to and from other Generic Software. The most recent version of Generic AutoConvert, for example, is capable of reading Generic CADD 5.0 drawing files for conversion to the .DXF file format.

Data Input Through Drawing Files

Other Generic Software programs can create Generic CADD drawing files, so that information developed in other programs may be loaded into Generic CADD. Generic 3D (formerly 3D Drafting) creates two-dimensional drawing files from three-dimensional viewpoints that are readable by any version of Generic CADD. Once exported from the 3D programs and imported into Generic CADD, these viewpoints become fixed, of course, and can be edited as you would any other drawing created in Generic CADD.

Some third-party programs can create Generic CADD 5.0 drawing files as well, while others create Level 3 format files. Generic CADD 5.0 can be used with either, as it imports Level 3 files with ease.

Two-Way Communication

Generic AutoConvert and IGES read and write Generic CADD drawing files, allowing other CAD programs to communicate with Generic CADD. Any program that creates either .DXF or IGES files can send drawing information to Generic CADD through the use of these programs.

A number of Utility programs are available, both as part of Generic Software's Utilities package and from third-party software developers. These perform specific functions on Generic CADD drawing files, leaving them in drawing file format so that they can be reloaded into Generic CADD with the revisions.

Communication Through Batch Files

Generic CADD drawing files are stored in a special compact format that is difficult for other software to access. For this reason and others, Batch files are provided as an access route, both in and out of Generic CADD 5.0, in the much simpler form of ASCII files.

Batch files are actually just a list of all of the commands and values that are required to create a given drawing file. When you save a Batch file from a drawing, you are actually saving a list of the commands and values required to create that drawing; when you load a Batch file, a drawing is created from these commands and values. See Chapter 16, "Programming Generic CADD 5.0," for more information on Generic's Batch file format.

Data Extraction

Because a Batch file contains all of the commands and values required to create a drawing, other software can use the file to extract this information. The other software can then change, analyze, or use this information as necessary.

As a simple example, every time a certain component is used in a drawing file, the Batch file saved from that drawing file includes a CP (Component Place) command, followed by the name of the component. External software could be written that would read the Batch file and count the number of various components for cost analysis, inventory, parts ordering, or other purposes.

Many other types of information can be extracted from Batch files. Square footages of Filled or Hatched areas can be derived, character placements can be accumulated into an even simpler ASCII text file, and so on. The data that can be extracted from a Batch file is limited only by the amount of information put into the drawing file, and sometimes you can extract more than you imagined possible. Another form of data extraction is provided by the use of attributes, discussed later in this chapter.

Data Input Through Batch Files

Chapter 16 explained how you can create your own Batch files to automate certain drawing tasks, using a text editor or word processor. Batch files can also be created by other software. Many third-party products on the market perform automated drawing tasks or transfer drawing information to Generic CADD through the use of Batch files. Batch files are popular for this task because their format is well documented, and ASCII files are much easier to create than Generic CADD drawing files.

Additionally, you can use different types of software to create intelligent Batch files for automating many drawing tasks. Spreadsheet and database programs, for example, can manipulate text and numeric data, process and sort this data, and provide user-formatted output.

Creating a Drawing with A Spreadsheet Program

Spreadsheet programs can help you create drawings automatically by manipulating numeric data through the use of formulas and by combining text and numeric data. These capabilities make spreadsheets excellent vehicles for the automation of drawing procedures. For example, you might need to make several drawings that vary only in dimension or in the number of times a certain part appears. Often, these variable dimensions or numbers can be derived from a few simple parameters.

Figure 17-1 is an example of a drawing that can be created by a spreadsheet program. The parameters for this drawing of a column are the height and width of the base; the height of the column shaft and its width at top and bottom; and the height and width of the column capital. From this information, you can make the drawing.

To create a spreadsheet program to draw the column, place titles for these parameters and sample values into the first two columns of a spreadsheet program. In the following example, assume that the spreadsheet columns are labeled with letters and the rows are numbered. The following might be your list of parameters:

```
       A                              B

01  Base Height                       36
02  Base Width                        18
03
04  Shaft Height                      72
05  Shaft Width at Bottom             12
06  Shaft Width at Top                 9
07
08  Capital Height                    15
09  Capital Width                     12
```

After you have created this part of the spreadsheet, make a sketch of a typical column and imagine how you would go about drawing it from the information available.

The base is easy. Suppose that you were to start at the Drawing Basepoint. (This will later allow you to place the Basepoint wherever you

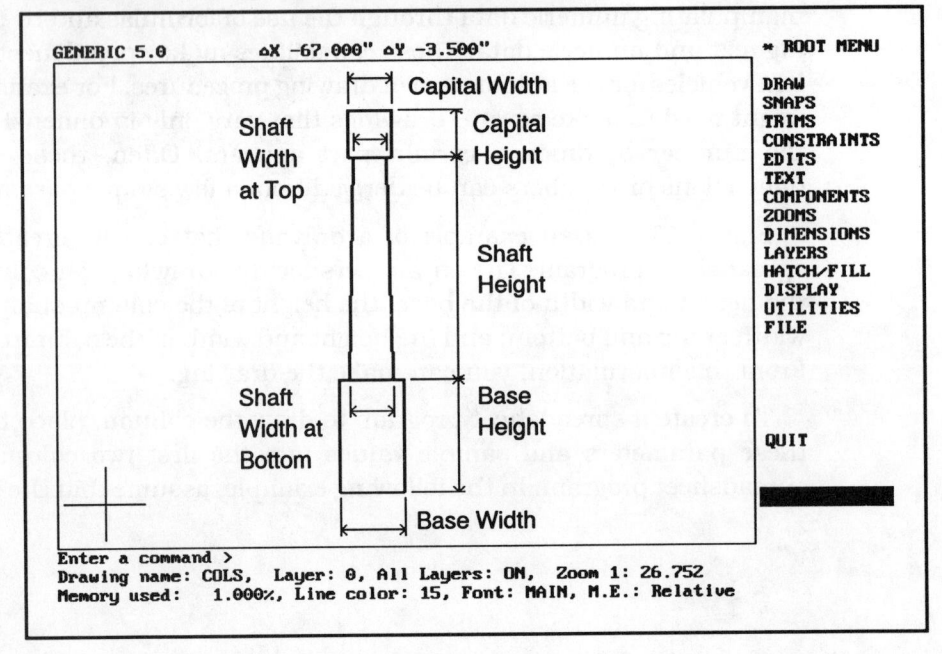

FIGURE 17-1 A column that can be created with a spreadsheet

want the column to be drawn, and then load the Batch file to run this macro.) The first step in this automated macro would be to set Manual Entry to Basepoint, using the MB command. Next, you would simply draw a rectangle that uses the Basepoint as its lower-left corner and the base width and height as its upper-right corner. If you were writing the Batch file to make this drawing instead of with this spreadsheet, the commands for this would be as follows:

```
MB;
RE,0,0,18,36;
```

But what happens if you decide to change the width or height of the base? When you write the automated macro, you should use references to the parameters in the spreadsheet instead of the actual numbers that appear there. Therefore, since the height and width of the base appear in column B, rows 01 and 02, you should replace the height and width in the Rectangle command with B01 and B02 (or use whatever column and row references your spreadsheet uses). At this point, your Batch file would look like this:

```
MB;
RE,0,0,B02,B01;
```

Of course, Generic CADD will not be able to understand the B01 and B02 values, but you can get the spreadsheet to take care of this, by putting these commands and values into some additional columns:

```
      C    D    E F    G H    I J    K
01 MB                              ;
02 RE,  0,0  ,  0,0  ,  B02  ,  B01 ;
```

By putting in B01 and B02 as formulas rather than absolute values, the values in H01 and H02 should change whenever you change the values in B01 and B02.

The next task is to draw the shaft. It is a good idea to move the Basepoint to the top middle of the base as a better reference point for the shaft, as shown in Figure 17-2. Specify a new Basepoint that is one-half the base width to the right of the current Basepoint, and above the current Basepoint by the full height of the base. The following command would do the trick:

```
BP,B02/2,B01;
```

FIGURE 17-2 The column base

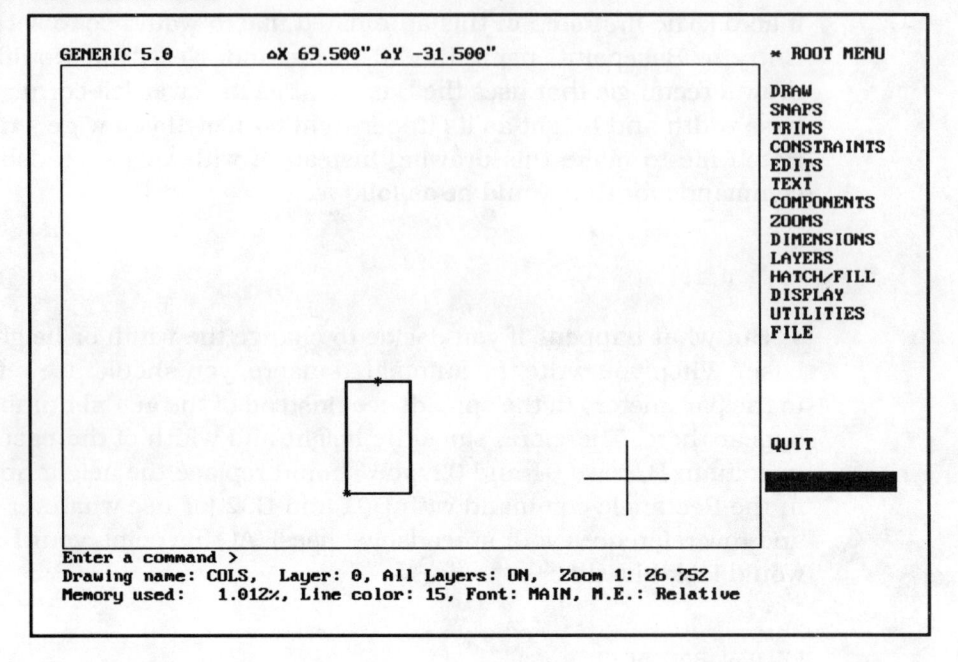

```
GENERIC 5.0        ΔX 69.500"  ΔY -31.500"              * ROOT MENU

                                                        DRAW
                                                        SNAPS
                                                        TRIMS
                                                        CONSTRAINTS
                                                        EDITS
                                                        TEXT
                                                        COMPONENTS
                                                        ZOOMS
                                                        DIMENSIONS
                                                        LAYERS
                                                        HATCH/FILL
                                                        DISPLAY
                                                        UTILITIES
                                                        FILE


                                                        QUIT


Enter a command >
Drawing name: COLS,   Layer: 0, All Layers: ON,   Zoom 1: 26.752
Memory used:    1.012%, Line color: 15, Font: MAIN, M.E.: Relative
```

With the new Basepoint in place, the right side of the column could be described as follows:

`LI,B05/2,0,B06/2,B04;`

This would draw a Line (LI) starting half the bottom column width (B05/2,0) away from the center of the top of the base (the Basepoint) to a point half the top column width (B06/2) to the right and the column shaft height (B04) above the same point. The line at the left side of the column can be similarly described, but with negative X values:

`LI,-B05/2,0,-B06/2,B04;`

At this point, the column would resemble the one shown in Figure 17-3. These three lines could then be added to the spreadsheet:

```
      C     D       E F      G      H      I J    K
03 BP              , B02/2 , B01              ;
04 LI, B05/2 , 0.0       , B06/2 , B04 ;
05 LI, -B05/2 , 0.0      , -B06/2 , B04 ;
```

Chapter 17: Communicating with Other Programs 461

FIGURE 17-3 The column base and shaft

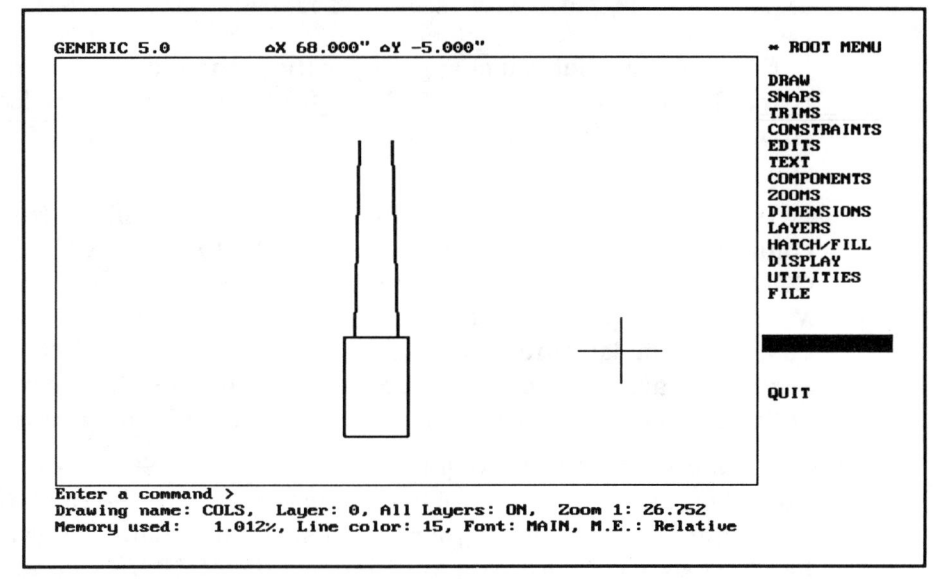

```
GENERIC 5.0          ΔX 68.000"  ΔY -5.000"                    ← ROOT MENU

                                                                DRAW
                                                                SNAPS
                                                                TRIMS
                                                                CONSTRAINTS
                                                                EDITS
                                                                TEXT
                                                                COMPONENTS
                                                                ZOOMS
                                                                DIMENSIONS
                                                                LAYERS
                                                                HATCH/FILL
                                                                DISPLAY
                                                                UTILITIES
                                                                FILE


                                                                QUIT


Enter a command >
Drawing name: COLS,   Layer: 0, All Layers: ON,   Zoom 1: 26.752
Memory used:    1.012%, Line color: 15, Font: MAIN, M.E.: Relative
```

The Basepoint would move once again—to the center of the column top, or even better, to the left corner of the column capital. This location is one-half the capital width to the left and the full column shaft height above where it is now, or:

`BP,-B08/2,B04;`

The column capital can now be drawn quite easily with a single Rectangle command:

`RE,0,0,B09,B08;`

With these last two commands, columns C through K of your spreadsheet will now look like this:

```
       C       D        E    F        G     H      I J    K

01  MB                                                    ;
02  RE,      0,0    ,   0,0      ,   B02   ,   B01 ;
03  BP,              ,   B02/2  ,   B01               ;
04  LI,     B05/2  ,   0.0      ,   B06/2 ,   B04 ;
05  LI,    -B05/2  ,   0.0      ,  -B06/2 ,   B04 ;
```

```
06 BP,            , -B08/2 , B04           ;
07 RE,  0.0    ,  0.0    , B09    , B08 ;
```

Now, anytime that you change any of the parameters in column B, the Batch file, stored in columns C through K, will change to reflect these changes. Set the values in column B to what you want, and save the spreadsheet in the usual way.

To create the actual Batch file that Generic CADD will use to draw the column, save columns C through K only to an ASCII file called COLUMN.TXT. How this is done varies among different spreadsheets. Many have an option to print to a file, or to export to an ASCII file. Before doing this, make sure that column K is right-justified—that is, the semicolons are flush to the right edge of the column. Spaces at the end of the lines may cause the Batch to work improperly in Generic CADD.

If your spreadsheet program does not save ASCII files with the extension .TXT, you may have to rename the file with the DOS RENAME command. For example, if your spreadsheet automatically gives ASCII files the extension .PRN, you must rename the ASCII file so that Generic CADD can load it as a batch:

```
REN COLUMN.PRN COLUMN.TXT
```

Once you have saved the spreadsheet in the normal way and columns C through K as an ASCII file, exit to DOS and start up Generic CADD 5.0 again. Select a line color, layer, and whatever drawing parameters you want to preset. Next, place the Basepoint at the lower-left corner of where you want the column to be drawn. Use the BP command and select a point. Finally, load the Batch with the Load (LO) command Batch (B) option, and type or select the name of the Batch file, COLUMN. The column described in the spreadsheet will be drawn.

To create more columns of varying shape, you can simply edit column B of the spreadsheet, resave columns C through K as an ASCII file, and load them into Generic CADD again. Figure 17-4 shows you the variety of columns that can be created with this simple spreadsheet macro program.

You can add additional parameters, such as the total number of columns, the distance between them, and the colors and layers of each part of the column. Number and spacing could be added by introducing two new parameters:

Chapter 17: Communicating with Other Programs

```
      A                B
11 Number of Columns   6
12 Column Spacing      60
```

The additional columns could be created with a Window Copy command, which uses the previous parameters to figure out how large to make the window, and the new parameters for the copy number and distance:

```
MR;
WC,B02/2,0,-(B09+B02+B02/2),(B01+B04+B08),0,0,B12,0,B11;
```

The Window Copy macro looks complicated, but it really just combines the various heights and widths to make sure that the window is big enough. The final five values indicate the displacement and number of copies. If you insert these formulas into the spreadsheet, you can produce a great variety of multiple-column combinations, as shown in Figure 17-5.

FIGURE 17-4 Several columns that can be created with the Column spreadsheet macro

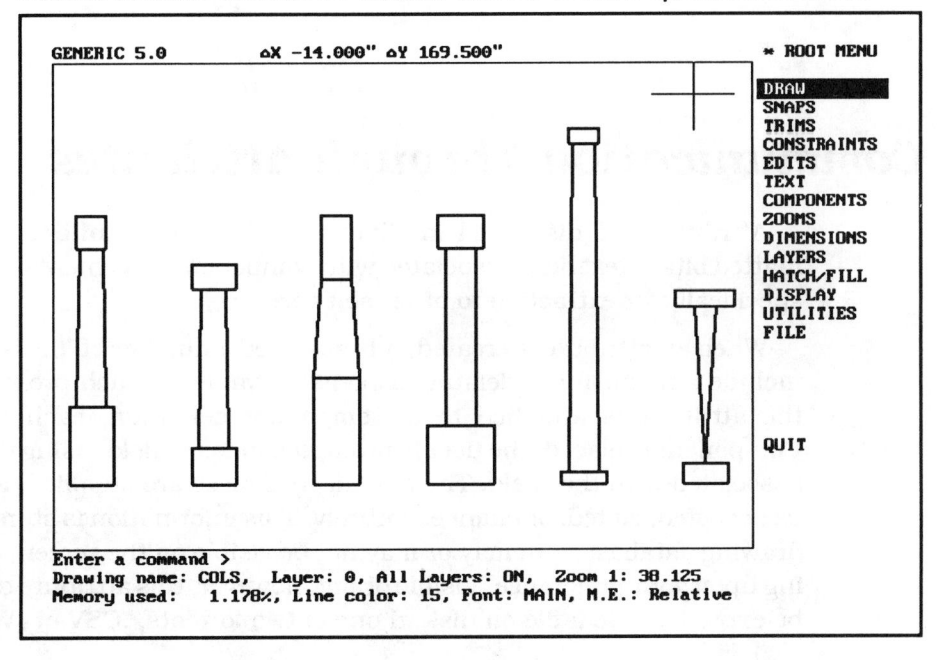

FIGURE 17-5 Different column types and spacings that can be produced with the expanded spreadsheet macro

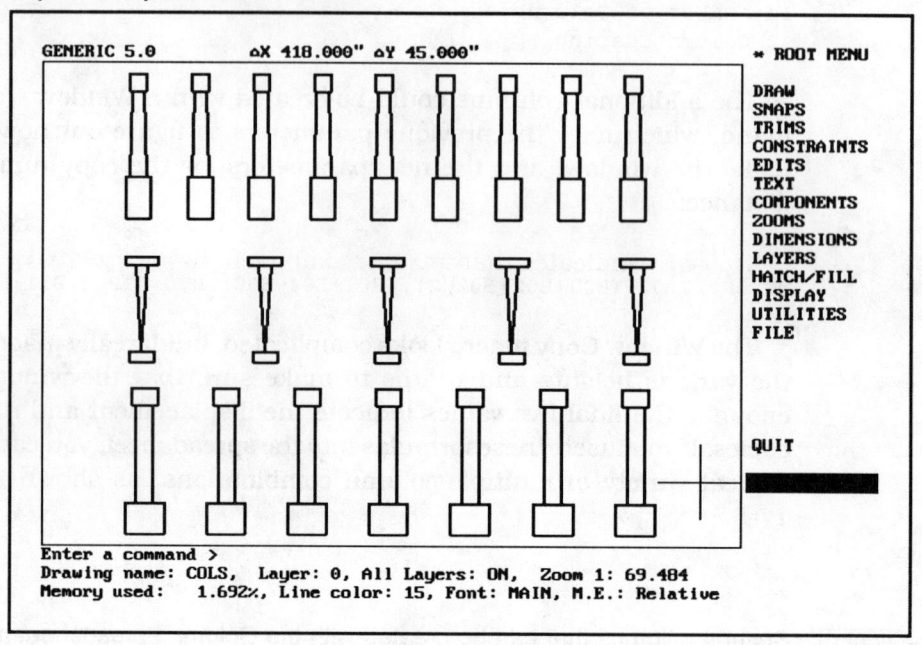

Communication Through Attributes

Attributes, as discussed in Chapter 8, "Complex Entities," are formatted bits of text data associated with component placements, designed specifically for extraction to other software.

When an attribute is created, it is assigned a number of "fields," which include a name and a default response or value for each prompt. After the attribute is attached to a Component definition, each time the Component is placed, the user is prompted for each field, using the name associated with that field. The default responses are supplied, and may be accepted, edited, or changed entirely. This information is stored in the drawing database, and may or may not be visible on the screen, depending upon your preference. Visible or not, however, this attribute data may be extracted into a file on disk in one of two formats, .CSV or .WK1.

Comma-Separated Value

CSV stands for Comma-Separated Value format, in which your data is sent out as an ASCII file containing the attribute information. This file is divided into lines of text, each of which starts with a slash and a number, followed by the data, as in:

```
/100,"CHAIR"
```

The /100 indicates that this is a component name. CHAIR is the name of the component, surrounded by quotes and separated from the first part by a comma. Each type of information sent to the ASCII file has its own number code:

```
/100 = component name
/200 = attribute name
/300 = field names
/400 = field values
```

Following this code number is a comma, and the data itself, surrounded by quotes and separated from any other data on the same line by commas.

For each attribute extracted, each of these lines will appear in the ASCII file. First comes the component name, then the attribute name, then a line containing all of the field names, and finally a line containing the field values, as in this example:

```
/100,"CHAIR"
/200,"SPECS"
/300,"Manufacture","Style","Color","Price"
/400,"Stendig","Armchair","Black","350.00"
```

This format will repeat for each attribute that is extracted. If a component has more than one attribute attached to it, the last three lines will repeat until the next component is found. The order of entries in the .CSV file will be the same as the order in which the components and their attributes were placed into the database.

These files may be used for importing into your spreadsheet, database, or other program that accepts comma-separated ASCII files. In some cases, you may need to edit the file first, or process it with other software to get it into a format that is acceptable to your application program.

Worksheet Files

The .WK1 files extracted from Generic CADD 5.0 may be loaded into Lotus 1-2-3 or other software that accepts .WK1 files, but cannot be edited with your word processor.

Your attribute data is transferred into individual cells within the workshop, in the order in which they appear in the database. Component names will use one cell, followed by the attribute name in the cell immediately below. The next row will contain each of the field names, each in its own column, followed by one more row containing the field data, in the same columns as the names. This pattern will repeat for each attribute extracted. Each attribute exported to the spreadsheet will be separated from the preceding one by a blank row in the spreadsheet, as in the following example:

```
   A                 B          C       D
1  Component Name:   CHAIR
2  Attribute Name:   SPECS
3  Manufacturer      Style      Color   Price
4  Stendig           Armchair   Black   350.00
5
6  Component Name:   CHAIR
7  Attribute Name:   SPECS
8  Manufacturer      Style      Color   Price
9  Steelcase         Secretary  Blue    225.00
```

Note that the words "Component Name:" are in the same cell as "CHAIR", and that the price figures are treated as text, not as numeric data.

Extracting Attribute Data

To send data of the type just discussed to the file of your choice, select Export from the ATTRIBUTES menu or type **XA** on the keyboard. You will get a selection prompt allowing you to choose which attributes you want to export. Attributes are selected by choosing the component placements to which they are attached. If you wish to export only the attributes attached to a certain component, you may use the Filter option to select components of a certain name. Remember that you must still use another selection method to actually select the filtered entities.

Once you have signaled the end of selection by pressing ENTER at the selection prompt, the next prompt will ask in which format you want the file created, .WK1 or .CSV. Choose one from the prompt or type the letter indicated, **W** for WK1 or **C** for CSV. The filename prompt is next, and the current drawing name with the appropriate extension is suggested. You can either accept or edit this name, and press ENTER when you are ready. The file will be created, and you will return to the "Enter a command >" prompt.

Uses of Attributes

Attributes have great potential for one-way communication with spreadsheet and database programs in particular. They make it possible to automate the creation of parts lists, schedules, and other documents based on your drawings. As the drawings are updated, new schedules or lists can be created by exporting the data again.

Communication Through Image Files

The image files produced by the Generic CADD Save Image command can be transferred to other programs, and images created by other software can be loaded into Generic CADD. These files have the extension .GX2.

Image files are less compatible between various hardware configurations and programs than drawing files because they contain specific pixel locations, colors, and so on, which may be defined differently on different hardware.

Sharing Images in CADD

In general, .GX2 files created by any version of Generic CADD using a particular type of graphics card can be loaded by other versions of Generic CADD as long as the same type of graphics card is in use. You can load a Generic CADD 5.0 image made on an EGA card into Generic 3D running on an EGA card, for example. However, you cannot load an image made on a Hercules monochrome card into any program running on an EGA card, or vice versa.

Keep in mind that when images from one drawing or copy of Generic CADD are loaded into another, no actual CADD data is transferred, only the image on the screen. This image will be wiped clean the next time that the screen is redrawn.

Transferring Images to Other Software

Image files are also used by several other types of products, including painting and desktop publishing software. Generic PaintConvert, available separately or bundled with 3D Drafting and later releases of CADD 5.0, can save files to a number of other image formats. Among the supported formats are .PCX, .IMG, .TIF, .MSP, and .BMP files. By selecting the appropriate input and output formats in the stand-alone version, or by simply selecting the output format in the bundled version, you can convert Generic drawings to any of these formats.

Communication Through Print and Plot Files

Files created with the Plot command, using an output file instead of an actual port, can often be read by other software. In particular, the PostScript Device and .EPS files are particularly useful for transferring Generic CADD 5.0 drawings to desktop publishing programs. You may find uses for the Plotter and Printer output files as well.

Two programs in the Utilities package (compatible with Generic CADD Level 3) convert Hewlett-Packard and Houston Instruments plotter files into CADD drawing files. This capability remains available as either a separate utility or bundled into CADD 5.0.

The variety of file formats that Generic CADD 5.0 can read and write, combined with the flexible file format characteristic of the DOS environment makes it possible to get Generic CADD 5.0 to communicate in both directions with almost any other PC software, either directly or through translation of the files available. The fact that real data is stored in the CADD drawing file, and not just images of the drawing, makes connections to database, spreadsheet, and other numerically-oriented programs a real one. No information need be lost. On the other hand, since Generic CADD 5.0 draws to a variety of different resolution devices, including the screen, printers, plotters, and PostScript files, image-based connections are just as viable, when the desired application demands it.

APPENDIX A

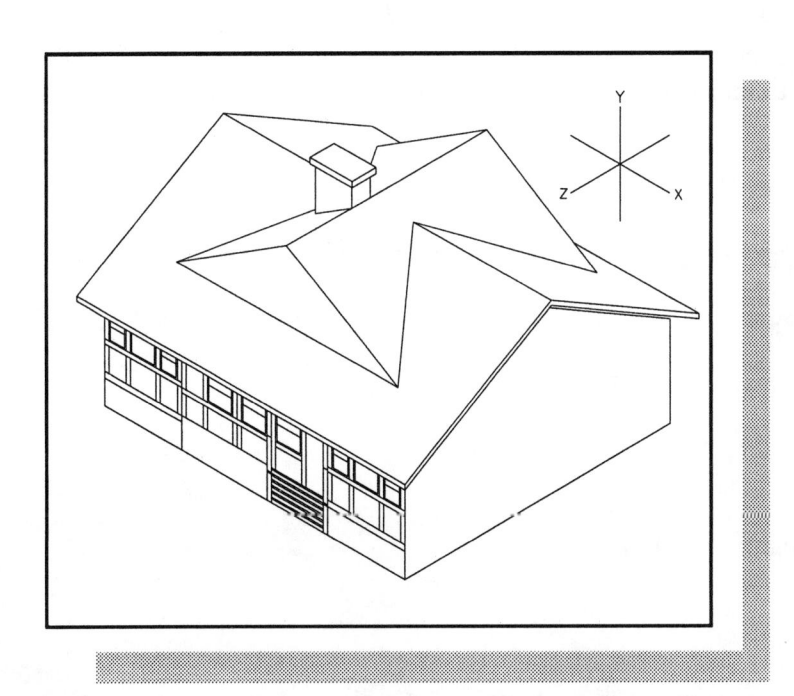

Related Software

A number of programs are designed to interface directly with Generic CADD 5.0, including other stand-alone Generic Software products, Generic Software products designed specifically to add additional functions, third-party software that has been designed to add capabilities to Generic CADD, symbols libraries developed by Generic Software and other users, and software that creates Generic CADD drawing or Batch files as its output.

Products developed by Generic Software and other manufacturers to work with Generic CADD Level 3 and earlier versions of Generic CADD can be used with 5.0 through the use of Level 3 files.

This appendix briefly describes some of these programs and how they can be used to increase the productivity of Generic CADD.

Generic 3D (formerly 3D Drafting)

Published by:

Generic Software, Inc., Bothell, Washington

Function:

3D drawing program

Description:

Generic 3D is a full-featured 3D wireframe modeling and shading program that includes an option to save drawings to Generic CADD drawing file format, allowing users of 3D Drafting to send drawings to Generic CADD for printing, plotting, or additional editing. Generic 3D also imports Generic CADD drawing files for creating 3D models using existing CADD drawings. This is a useful companion to Generic CADD in any application that deals with three-dimensional forms.

AutoConvert

Published by:

Generic Software, Inc., Bothell, Washington

Function:

Two-way translation between Generic CADD drawing files and .DXF format ASCII files

Description:

AutoConvert allows Generic CADD and Generic 3D drawing files to be sent to a program that accepts .DXF format files (a Drawing Exchange Format file popularized by AutoDesk, Inc. and supported by many CAD and graphics-oriented programs). The program also converts .DXF files to Generic CADD or Generic 3D drawing format so that drawings made in other CAD programs supporting the .DXF format may be loaded into Generic CADD. In addition to allowing file transfer between Generic CADD and other CAD programs, AutoConvert allows Generic CADD and 3D users to take advantage of numerous programs that have been designed to perform functions on .DXF files.

Symbols Libraries

Published by:

Generic Software, Inc., Bothell, Washington

Function:

Components for use with Generic CADD

Description:

Over 25 individual packages are available, each containing from 50 to 500 components organized by application, such as Residential and Commercial Furnishings, Industrial Pipe Fittings, Landscape Architecture, and Electronic Symbols I-V. Each symbols library includes an illustrated manual and placement menus, and works with all versions of Generic CADD.

Type Fonts-I and Type Fonts-II

Published by:

Generic Software, Inc., Bothell, Washington

Function:

Fonts for use with Generic CADD

Description:

Each package includes a number of fonts that can be used with any version of Generic CADD.

Translator
(bundled with Generic CADD for the MAC)

Published by:

Generic Software, Inc., Bothell, Washington

Function:

Translation between Generic CADD DOS and MAC files

Description:

Translator provides two-way translation capabilities between Generic CADD for the MAC and Generic CADD 5.0 for DOS. It also converts Generic CADD MAC files to .DXF format. Translator runs on the Macintosh computer only.

CADD Master Ray's CADD PLATTER

Published by:

WORKSHOP 3D Software, Inc., Seattle, Washington

Function:

Utilities, information, and accessories for Generic CADD and 3D users

Description:

The unofficial guide to Generic CADD, CADD PLATTER is a bimonthly publication edited by the author, and not connected with Generic Software in any way. Each issue of CADD PLATTER contains both printed and disk-based material, providing product reviews, articles, and commentary as well as utility programs, new fonts, hatch patterns, 2D and 3D components and drawing files, menus, macros, and other useful CADD and 3D paraphernalia.

APPENDIX B

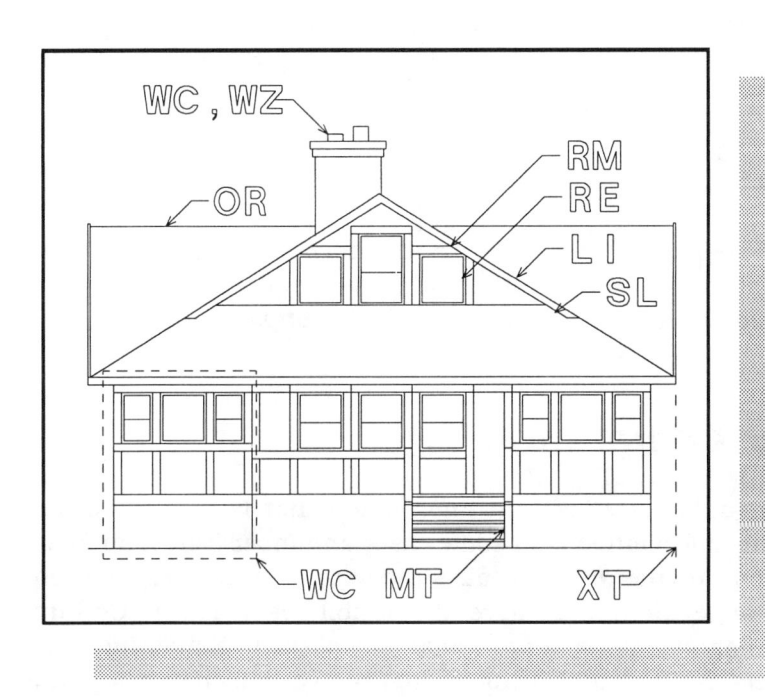

Command Summary

This summary lists the commands in the order that they appear on the Generic CADD 5.0 menu. Each listing has four elements:

- The name of the command
- Its two-character code
- The chapter or chapters in this book where the command is discussed
- The function of the command, or the command "type"

Technically, Generic CADD makes no distinction between command "type" but certain "families" of commands can be identified and defined.

The Create Entity Commands

These commands are used to place new objects into the drawing. Some of these commands create one entity at a time, while others create several new entities simultaneously (these are marked *multiple*).

The Parameter Commands

These commands preset certain information that is used by other commands. This information is in some cases a number (value) such as scale or rotation. In other cases it takes the form of an integer between 0 and 255 (range) or one of several possibilities (choice). Certain parameter commands specify a particular way of doing something (setting). Still others ask for a text string (string) such as a filename or path.

The Toggle Commands

Toggles set specific conditions to either on or off. Almost all of the toggle commands can be issued while another command is active. Most of the toggles could also be considered Parameter settings.

The Command Modifier Commands

These transparent commands modify the actions of other commands. They are generally issued after the main command, while the main command is asking for certain information. These commands generally qualify the information that you are providing.

The Edit Objects Commands

These commands change existing entities. They include commands that erase, copy, move, and otherwise modify either one entity or many (multiple).

The Database Modifier Commands

Some information stored in the drawing file (database) is not shown on the screen and does not appear on a printout. This information can be component and character definitions, named views, and other information that helps to define the drawing without being explicitly shown. Commands that modify this type of information fit into this category.

The File Input/Output Commands

These commands send information to, or retrieve information from, a disk.

The Define Complex Object Commands

These commands allow you to define your own entities, using other Generic CADD 5.0 *simple* entities. Text and Components can be created and then placed. Hatches and Fills are defined as you place them.

The Place Complex Object Commands

These commands, similar to the Create Entity commands, place *defined* objects, rather than individual entities. The defined objects only appear in the database (drawing file) once and are placed in various locations by reference only.

The Display Modifier Commands

This group of commands changes the way that the drawing appears on the screen without actually changing the drawing itself. An editing command, for instance, actually makes the drawing larger, but a display modifier only makes it appear larger.

The Program Modifier Commands

Because Generic CADD is a configurable program that you customize, it has certain commands that specify how the program works. These commands control such program aspects as use of the video and digitizer menus.

The Inquiry Commands

This type of command asks Generic CADD to obtain and display certain information, such as distances, angles, and areas, as well as drawing status information, layer usage, disk directories, and so on.

Appendix B: Command Summary

Menu	Command	Code	Chapter	Type
DRAW				
	Point	PO	4	Create Entity
	Line	LI	4	Create Entity (multiple)
	Indvl Line	L1	4	Create Entity
	Rectangle	RE	4	Create Entity (multiple)
	R Polygon	RP	4	Create Entity (multiple)
	Circle 2	C2	4	Create Entity
	Circle 3	C3	4	Create Entity
	Arc 2	A2	4	Create Entity
	Arc 3	A3	4	Create Entity
	Ellipse	EP	4	Create Entity (multiple)
	Bezier Curve	BV	9	Create Entity (multiple)
	Indvl Bezier	BW	9	Create Entity
	Curve	CV	4	Create Entity
	Double Lines	L2	9	Create Entity (multiple)
	Dbl Settings	DB	9	Parameter (values)
SNAPS				
	Close Point	SC	6	Command Modifier
	Object	SO	6	Command Modifier
	Midpoint	SM	6	Command Modifier
	Percentage	SR	6	Command Modifier
	Intersction	SI	6	Command Modifier
	Parallel	SL	6	Command Modifier
	Perpendiculr	SP	6	Command Modifier
	Tangent	ST	6	Command Modifier

Menu	Command	Code	Chapter	Type
	Arc Center	SN	6	Command Modifier
	Grid	SG	6	Toggle
	Component	GC	6,8	Toggle
	All Layer Sn	SY	6	Toggle
	Tolerance	TO	6	Parameter (value)
TRIMS				
	Trim	RM	10	Edit Object
	Extend	XT	10	Edit Object
	Fillet	FI	10	Edit Object (multiple)
	Fillet Rad	FR	9,10	Parameter (value)
	Autofillet	AF	9	Toggle
	Chamfer	CH	9	Edit Object (multiple)
	Chamfer Dist	CA	9	Parameter (values)
	Intersection	IT	10	Edit Object (multiple)
	Multi Trim	MT	10	Edit Object (multiple)
CONSTRAINTS				
	Ortho Mode	OR	6	Toggle
	Ortho Angle	OA	10	Program Modifier
	Tracking	TK	10	Command Modifier
	Cursor Free	CF	10	Toggle
	Grid On/Off	GR	6	Toggle
	Snap Grid	SG	6	Toggle
	Grid Size	GS	6	Parameter (values)
	Grid Reorgin	GO	10	Program Modifier
	Curs Move	CM	10	Program Modifier

Appendix B: Command Summary

Menu	Command	Code	Chapter	Type
EDITS				
	Move Point	MP	5	Edit Object
	Move	MV	5,10	Edit Object (multiple)
	Copy	CO	5,10	Create Object (multiple)
	Mirror Copy	MI	5,10	Create Object (multiple)
	Radial Copy	RC	10	Create Object (multiple)
	Rotate	RO	5,10	Edit Object (multiple)
	Scale	SZ	5,10	Edit Object (multiple)
	Change	CG	5,10	Edit Object (multiple)
	Break	OB	5	Edit Object
	Stretch	SS	10	Edit Object (multiple)
	Bezier Edit	BE	10	Edit Object (multiple)
	Erase	ER	5,10	Edit Object (multiple)
	Erase Last	EL	5	Edit Object (multiple)
	UnErase	UE	5	Database Modifier
	Undo	OO	10	Database Modifier
	Redo	UU	10	Database Modifier
SHORTCUTS				
	Object Copy	OC	5	Edit Object
	Window Copy	WC	5	Edit Object (multiple)
	Object Erase	OE	5	Edit Object
	Window Erase	WE	5	Edit Object (multiple)
	Object Move	OM	5	Edit Object
	Window Move	WM	5	Edit Object (multiple)
	Win Rotate	WR	5	Edit Object (multiple)

Menu	Command	Code	Chapter	Type
	Dwg Rotate	DR	5	Edit Object (multiple)
	Window Scale	WZ	5	Edit Object (multiple)
	Dwg Scale	DZ	5	Edit Object (multiple)
	Obj Change	OG	5	Edit Object
	Win Change	WG	5	Edit Object (multiple)
	Dwg Change	DG	5	Edit Object (multiple)
TEXT				
	Line Place	TL	8	Place Complex Objects
	Change	TG	8	Edit Complex Object
	Edit	TE	8	Edit Complex Object
	Char Place	TP	8	Place Complex Objects
	Insert	TI	8	Place/Edit Complex Objects
	Delete	TD	8	Edit Complex Objects
	Replace	TX	8	Edit Complex Object
	Font Select	FS,T	8	Parameter (string)
	Spacing	TS	8	Parameter (multiple)
	Color	CS,T	8	Parameter (range)
	Size	TZ,T	8	Parameter (value)
	Rotation	TR	8	Parameter (value)
	Win Create	WT	8	Define Complex Object
	Load ASCII	LA	8	Create Object (multiple)
COMPONENTS				
	Place	CP	8	Place Complex Object

Appendix B: Command Summary

Menu	Command	Code	Chapter	Type
	Create	CC	8	Define Complex Object
	Win Create	CW	8	Define Complex Object
	Scale	CZ	8	Parameter (value)
	Rotation	CR	8	Parameter (value)
	Explode	CE	8	Edit Complex Objects
	Replace	CN	8	Edit Complex Objects
	Remove	CX	8	Database Modifier
	Image	CI	8	Toggle
	Comp Snaps	GC	8	Toggle
	Explode Layr	XY	8	Parameter (range)
	Save	SA,C	12	File Input/Output
	Load	LO,C	12	File Input/Output
	Comp Dump	CD	8	File Input/Output
ATTRIBUTES				
	Create	AC	17	Create Complex Object
	Attach	AT	17	Edit Complex Object
	Detach	DE	17	Edit Complex Object
	Load	LO,A	12	File Input/Output
	Save	SA,A	12	File Input/Output
	Export	XA	17	File Input/Output
	Scale	TZ,A	17	Parameter (value)
	Display	AD	17	Toggle
	Edit	AE	17	Edit Complex Object
	Settings	AS	17	Parameter (multiple)

Menu	Command	Code	Chapter	Type
	Font	FS,A	8,17	Parameter (string)
ZOOMS				
	All	ZA	6	Display Modifier
	Window	ZW	6	Display Modifier
	In	ZI	6	Display Modifier
	Out	ZO	6	Display Modifier
	Pan	PA	6	Display Modifier
	Previous	ZP	6	Display Modifier
	Redraw	RD	6	Display Modifier
	Backwards	BR	6	Toggle
	Win Redraw	WD	6	Display Modifier
	Limits	ZL	6	Display Modifier
	Value	ZM	6	Display Modifier
	View	ZV	6	Display Modifier
	Name View	NV	6	Database Modifier
	Del View	NX	6	Database Modifier
DIMENSIONS				
	Linear	LX	11	Place Complex Object
	Angular	AX	11	Place Complex Object
	Mode	UM	11	Parameter (selection)
	Direction	UD	11	Parameter (selection)
	Proximity	PF	11	Toggle
	Radial	RX	11	Place Complex Object
	Diameter	IX	11	Place Complex Object
	Leader	LE	11	Place Complex Object

Appendix B: Command Summary

Menu	Command	Code	Chapter	Type
	Shoulder Length	LL	11	Parameter (value)
	Dim Move	UV	11	Edit Complex Object
	Dim Change	UG	11	Edit Complex Object
	Dim Tolernce	UT	11	Parameter (value)
DIM SET				
	Display	DD	11	Parameter (multiple)
	Extensions	XS	11	Parameter (multiple)
	Arrows	AR	11	Parameter (multiple)
	Font Select	FS,D	11	Parameter (string)
	Text Size	TZ,D	11	Parameter (value)
	Dim Text	DT	11	Parameter (multiple)
	Dim Layer	UY	11	Parameter (range)
	Dim Color	CS,D	11	Parameter (range)
LAYERS				
	All Layers	AL	3	Toggle
	Set Current	YC	3,6	Parameter (range)
	Display	YD	6	Display Modifier
	Name	YN	6	Database Modifier
	Hide	YH	6	Display Modifier
	Erase	YE	6	Edit Object (multiple)
	Rotate	YR	5	Edit Object (multiple)
	Scale	YZ	5	Edit Object (multiple)
	Change	YG	5	Edit Object (multiple)
	Dimension	UL	11	Parameter (range)

Menu	Command	Code	Chapter	Type
	Layer Load	YL	12	File Input/Output
	Layer Save	SV,Y	12	File Input/Output
HATCH/FILL				
	Window Hatch	WH	8	Define/Place Complex Object
	Object Hatch	OH	8	Define/Place Complex Object
	Fitted Hatch	FH	8	Define/Place Complex Object
	Bound Hatch	BH	8	Define/Place Complex Object
	Hatch Settings	HS	8	Parameter (multiple)
	Window Fill	WF	8	Define/Place Complex Object
	Object Fill	OF	8	Define/Place Complex Object
	Fitted Fill	FF	8	Define/Place Complex Object
	Bound Fill	BF	8	Define/Place Complex Object
	Fill Color	FC	8	Parameter (range)
DISPLAY				
	Line Color	LC	3	Parameter (range)
	Line Type	LT	3	Parameter (range)
	Line Width	LW	3	Parameter (range)
	Line Scale	LZ	3	Display Modifier
	Color	CS	3	Parameter (multiple)
	Fast Redraw	FA	6	Display Modifier (multiple)

Appendix B: Command Summary

Menu	Command	Code	Chapter	Type
	Coordinates	DC	3	Display Modifier (multiple)
	Num Display	NF	3	Display Modifier (multiple)
	Units	UN	3	Program Modifier
	Screen Dsply	DI	3	Display Modifier
	Ref. Points	PR	6	Display Modifier
	Con. Points	PC	3,6	Display Modifier
	Std. Points	PS	6	Display Modifier
	Redraw	RD	6	Display Modifier
	Object Drag	OD	6	Display Modifier
	Rubberband	RB	6	Display Modifier
	Highlight	HI	6	Display Modifier
MENUS				
	Load Menu	LV	16	File Input/Output
	New Menu	VX,LV	16	File Input/Output
	Remove Menu	VX	16	Program Modifier
	Display Menu	VM	16	Display Modifier
	Load Dig Mnu	LD	14,16	File Input/Output
	Select Dmenu	SD	14	Program Modifier
	Dwg Align	DA	14	Program Modifier
	Active Area	AA	14	Program Modifier
	Trace Mode	TM	14	Program Modifier
	Trace Scale	RZ	14	Program Modifier
UTILITIES				
	M E Origin	MO	3	Input Modifier

Menu	Command	Code	Chapter	Type
	M E Relative	MR	3	Input Modifier
	M E Basepnt	MB	3	Input Modifier
	Set Basepnt	BP	3	Program Modifier
	Explode	EX	10	Edit Complex Objects
	Measure	ME	7	Inquiry
	Macro Assign	MA	16	Program Modifier
	Screen Flip	SF	7	Inquiry
	Filter	EF	10	Command Modifier/Parameter
	Selection	SE	10	Command Modifier/Parameter
	Limits	LS	3	Program Modifier
	Match Params	MH	10	Command Modifier/Parameter
	Shell Exe	SH	12	Program Modifier
	View Fst Txt	TV	6	Display Modifier
	Dwg Origin	DO	10	Database Modifier
	Save Batch	SB	12	File Input/Output
	Sel Save Btc	BS	12	File Input/Output
FILE				
	Load	LO	12	File Input/Output
	Save	SA	12	File Input/Output
	Sel Save Dwg	SV	12	File Input/Output
	Dwg Rename	DN	12	Program Modifier
	Dwg Remove	DX	5	Database Modifier
	File Paths	FP	12	Program Modifier

Appendix B: Command Summary   491

Menu	Command	Code	Chapter	Type
	Load ASCII	LA	8	Create Complex Entities
	Plot	DP,1,1	13	File Input/Output
	Print	DP,1,2	13	File Input/Output
	PostScript	DP,1,3	13	File Input/Output
	Select Plot	PL	13	File Input/Output
	Pack Data	PD	10	Database Modifier
	Def Unload	DU	10	Database Modifier
	Environment	EN	15	File Input/Output
	Quit	QU	4,12	File Input/Output
	About Cadd5	G1		Inquiry

APPENDIX C

Glossary

Some of the following definitions are specific to Generic Software. These terms may have different meanings in other programs.

ABS   Abbreviation for Absolute.

Absolute Coordinates   Coordinates that are measured from the origin, 0,0, and the coordinate system in which the definition of entities is stored.

Arc   A portion of a circle. An arc is one of Generic CADD's basic entity types, defined by three points, two of which are endpoints of the arc.

Area   The amount of space contained within specific boundaries, measured in square feet, square inches, or other units.

ASCII   An acronym for American Standard Code for Information Interchange. Used to refer to a file format in which alphanumeric data is stored according to a predefined standard code. The term ASCII file is generally used to refer to text files that can be viewed with the TYPE command in DOS or edited with any simple text editor.

Aspect Ratio   The ratio between height and width. In Generic CADD, two aspect ratios are employed. The aspect ratio of the screen is calculated when you specify the appropriate values with the Screen Ratio (RA) command. The aspect ratio of text characters is specified with the Aspect option of the Text Spacing command.

Associative Dimensions   In Generic CADD 5.0, dimensions that are updated when their definition points are moved. They are said to be associative because if you make a change in your drawing, the dimensions are updated as well, even though the dimensions are not actually tied to the other entities in the drawing.

Attach   In Generic CADD 5.0, to connect an attribute definition to a component definition in such a way that when the component is placed, the attribute information becomes part of the component placement. *See also* Attribute.

Appendix C: Glossary

Attribute   A text entity that is associated with a component placement. As the component is placed, the text is entered, so that it is specific to that placement. Attributes can be extracted to an external file, which allows communication with other software.

AutoConvert   A Generic Software program for converting Generic CADD drawing files to and from .DXF (Drawing Exchange Format), a file format developed by AutoDesk, Inc., allowing transfer of data between different CAD programs.

Automate   To create and save a series of commands, known as a macro, for the purpose of speeding up the execution of repetitive tasks.

Backspace   To delete an unwanted character or space by positioning the cursor to the right of the character and pressing the BACKSPACE key. Used to correct typing errors when typing commands, specifying filenames, and so on.

.BAK   A file extension used to signify files that have been superseded by newer versions. A shortened form of BACKUP, .BAK is used if something goes wrong with the new version of the file to mitigate the amount of lost data by reverting to this earlier version.

Basepoint   A user-defined position in the drawing from which other locations can be referenced. X and Y coordinates can be specified relative to the Basepoint.

Bezier   A type of curve specified by four points: two endpoints and two control points. If the curve itself is regarded as a path between two endpoints, the two control points determine the angle at which the curve takes off as it leaves one endpoint to head toward the other.

Break   To separate a simple entity, such as a line or arc, into two parts. Normally, two points are specified, and the portion between them is removed. Breaking a circle turns each part into an arc.

Bug   An error in the way that software functions.

CAD An acronym for Computer Aided Design. Widely used to refer to a specific class of computer programs that feature creation, storage, display, and editing of accurate dimensional and geometric data, generally broken down into object primitives, such as Lines, Arcs, and so on.

CADD An acronym for Computer Aided Design and Drawing used by Generic Software as the name of its two-dimensional drawing program.

Callouts Words or characters that identify parts of the drawing: callouts are sometimes used with an arrow or other symbol to specify materials, refer to other drawings, and so on.

CGA An acronym for Color Graphics Adapter, a hardware standard popularized by IBM to add color capabilities to its system of Personal Computers. The 320x200 color and 320x400 monochrome resolutions are generally considered marginally adequate for CAD purposes, and are not supported by many CAD programs. Generic CADD supports the CGA card and clones at only the higher monochrome resolution.

Chamfer A procedure by which a third line is constructed at specified distances from the intersection of two lines to form a flattened rather than a sharp corner.

Change To alter the properties (layer, color, line type, line width, and so on) of an entity.

Character A single letter, numeral, or punctuation mark. All the characters of a particular style make up a font, and characters are always placed using the currently active font. *See also* Font.

Circle One of Generic CADD's basic entity types, defined by the location of a centerpoint and one point on the perimeter.

.CMP The file extension used by Generic CADD to identify files in which component definitions are stored. *See also* Component.

Color A characteristic of objects drawn in Generic CADD. Color can be specified whether or not you are using a color monitor. Because colors

Appendix C: Glossary

are stored by number, not name or actual hue, objects drawn using one color on one system may appear as a different color on another system that uses a different graphic standard.

.COM A file extension for certain executable programs. You can start these programs by typing the name that appears to the left of the period (you don't need to type the .COM extension).

Command A single function that has a corresponding two-character keyboard code. Although the items on the video menu may appear to be commands, they simply activate commands. Several commands may be activated from a single menu item.

Component A portion of a drawing that has been defined to include certain entities, and given a name and a reference point. Components, once defined, can be reused in a drawing, inserted at various rotations and scales, and saved to a disk file for use in other drawings.

CONFIG The program that tells Generic CADD what type of video hardware, pointing device, memory configuration, and unit system you are using.

Configure To use the CONFIG program and other features of Generic CADD 5.0 to select the default conditions under which Generic CADD will run.

Construction Point A definition point of an entity, such as the endpoint of a line, the center of a circle, and so on, displayed by a small x on the screen (if you choose). Temporary construction points are placed by certain editing commands as you select points on the screen.

Coordinates The numeric values that identify the location of a point, specified as a horizontal distance X and a vertical distance Y, measured from a selected origin. Coordinates may also be specified in distance and angle from the selected origin.

Copy To duplicate a portion of the drawing without reconstructing it. Several commands vary in the method of selecting objects to be copied, but all use prompts that ask you to select the objects, then specify the displacement, direction, and the number of copies.

Cross Hair   Two lines that intersect at their midpoint, forming a cursor that can be moved around the screen. Also, a similar mark inscribed on the plastic viewing portion of a digitizer puck to allow you to accurately select points from a drawing that you may be tracing.

Cursor   A graphic device on the screen used to aid user input. Generic CADD makes use of several cursors. The drawing cursor is a cross hair that can be moved around the screen by the mouse, digitizer puck, or the cursor control keys. Points are selected by pressing the first button on the mouse or puck, or by pressing ENTER on the keyboard.

The menu cursor appears as a solid block of color in the menu area when the video menu is in use. This block can be moved up and down with the mouse, digitizer puck, or the cursor keys, highlighting items on the video menu. These highlighted items can be selected by pressing the second button on the mouse or puck, or the HOME key on the keyboard.

The selection cursor appears as a small solid block in the prompt area whenever you are asked to select an option from the prompt area. Whenever this cursor is active, it can be moved with the mouse or digitizer puck, and the option selected by pressing the first button. The keyboard alternative is to type one of the letters highlighted in the prompt.

The text cursor appears on the screen as a horizontal line when you use the Text Place command. This line is the same width as the character that you are about to place, as calculated by the combined values of the Text Size and Aspect values. If Text Rotation is other than zero, the text cursor will be rotated to the specified angle. This cursor is moved by typing a character, or by pressing the BACKSPACE key, the ENTER key, or any of the cursor control keys on the keyboard. It cannot be moved with the mouse or the digitizer puck.

Finally, the prompt cursor appears at the end of a prompt that asks you to type a value, the name of a file, or anything else on the keyboard. This is an underline character just like the one that you get at the DOS prompt, and is moved by typing characters, pressing BACKSPACE, or by using the cursor control arrows on the keyboard.

Database Bits of information that have been grouped and organized in a particular way. A Generic CADD drawing file can be thought of as a database, because it stores information in a manner that allows you to retrieve or manipulate it.

Default The value, parameter, or situation used automatically when you do not specifically select an alternative. In Generic CADD, many defaults can be established through the CONFIG program and the Environment (EN) command.

Desktop Publishing Software used to combine and print text and graphics information in a single document. These programs generally offer a "What You See Is What You Get" (Wysiwyg) graphic interface. Generic CADD drawing files may be imported into many desktop publishing programs by plotting them to PostScript EPS files.

Detach To sever the association between a component definition and an attribute definition. *See also* Attribute and Attach.

Digitizer A hardware device, consisting of a tablet and a pen or puck, used for controlling the cursor and tracing drawings. Cursor control is through positional (coordinates) rather than the directional information you normally give with a mouse.

Digitizer Menu A system for issuing commands to Generic CADD, consisting of a plastic or paper digitizer overlay with the names of the commands and an ASCII file containing the commands. In addition to simple commands, macros may be assigned to the digitizer menu.

Digitizing The process of tracing a drawing into a Generic CADD drawing file using a digitizer. Generic CADD commands are combined with points selected on the digitizer instead of the screen.

Dimensioning A process in which lines, text, and arrows are added to a drawing to convey information about the distances or angles between points in the drawing. In Generic CADD 5.0, dimensioning is associative, meaning that all of the parts of the dimension make up a single complex entity that may change as the drawing is edited, keeping the text portion up to date. *See also* Associative Dimensions.

DIR   A command that can be typed at the DOS prompt to display a list of files on the current disk or in the current directory.

Directory   A subdivision of a disk, used to organize information stored on the disk. Normally, Generic CADD is stored in its own directory, which is further subdivided into directories for drawings, components, fonts, and so on. Also, the list of files that appears on the screen when you use the DIR command in DOS.

Disk   A device for storing files. Floppy disks are inserted and removed from a disk drive so they are portable. Hard disks store more information than floppy disks and are permanently installed in your computer.

Displacement   The distance and direction between two points, usually associated with an editing action of some kind.

Display   Another name for the video screen. Also used as a verb for showing information on the screen, as in "Display Hatches ON/OFF" or "Display Drawing Status."

Distance   The shortest measurable length between two points. The distance between two points can be displayed by using the Measure (ME) command, Distance option.

DOS   An acronym for Disk Operating System. DOS is a software program that coordinates the activities of the computer and its disk drives, allowing you to access files stored on disks. You use DOS to load Generic CADD and for a variety of file manipulation functions; it is normally started up automatically when you turn on your computer and must be running before Generic CADD can be used.

Drag   To move something across the screen. Components can be dragged when they are placed if Component Drag (CD) is on; components

Appendix C: Glossary

and text characters are dragged when you use the Move Point (MP) command.

Drawing A set of related entities stored in a single file in memory or on a disk. Comparable to a document in a word processing program or a worksheet in a spreadsheet program.

.DWG A file extension used by Generic CADD to identify drawing files. This extension is added automatically to all files that you save as drawing files from Generic CADD. Any file that is to be loaded must have this extension.

.DXF The file extension for an ASCII file format popularized by Auto-Desk, Inc. for exchange of drawing information. Generic CADD files can be converted to and from .DXF format with AutoConvert.

Edit To perform functions such as erase, copy, move, change, rotate, and scale on Generic CADD entities.

EGA An acronym for Enhanced Graphics Adapter, a video standard developed by IBM and improved by many other manufacturers. Use of the EGA card requires an EGA-compatible monitor. The 16-color 640x350 resolution of the EGA standard is widely considered to be the minimum for professional use of CADD. Many EGA clones can be run at higher resolution than the original IBM standard.

Ellipse An oblong circular shape, geometrically derived from the angled section of a cone, and one of Generic CADD's basic entities. The ellipse is defined by the endpoints of its two axes, normally of different lengths (though both may be the same, in which case the ellipse is a circle).

Endpoint The terminating point of a Line, Arc, or Curve. Each of these entities has two endpoints as part of its definition.

Entity A single object. Simple entities include Standard Points, Lines, Arcs, Circles, Ellipses, Curves, and Beziers. Complex entities are portions of the drawing that are composed of simple entities, but are treated as one object. Text Characters, Text Lines, Components, Attributes, Hatches, Fills, and Associative Dimensions are all complex entities.

Environment The status of all the parameter settings, toggles, and other nondrawing information in Generic CADD 5.0. A default environment is stored in the drawing GCADD.DWG, while the current environment is saved with every drawing file.

.EPS File A file extension used to indicate an Encapsulated PostScript file. EPS files can be created with a Plot command, usually for transfer to desktop publishing software.

Erase To remove entities from the drawing. Several commands offer methods for selecting the entities to be erased. Because erased entities are not immediately removed from the computer's memory, they can be restored in most cases with the Unerase (UE) command.

.EXE A file extension used to indicate an executable program file, such as CADD and CONFIG. Programs that are located in files with .EXE extensions can usually run by typing the first part of their name at the DOS prompt.

Extension The three letters after the period in a filename. Extensions are optional, but are often used to indicate the type of file. Some extensions used by Generic CADD include .DWG for drawing files, .CMP for components, .FNT for fonts, .HCH for hatch pattern definition files, .MNU for menus, .TXT for batch files, .GX2 for image files, and an assortment of others.

Fast Arcs A function that displays arcs as a selectable number of line segments instead of perfectly curved entities. This function can greatly speed up redraws.

Fast Text A function that displays text characters as Standard Points instead of individual characters, and text lines as straight lines. This function can reduce redraw time while still allowing you to see where your text is placed in the drawing.

Appendix C: Glossary

File   A collection of related information stored under a single name on a disk. Each drawing that you create is stored in a file, as is each component that you save, each font, and so on. Filenames can be up to eight characters, plus an optional period and up to three characters that form the file extension. In Generic CADD, extensions are standardized and added automatically.

Fill   To "paint in" a closed area with solid color. Several commands allow you to specify an area and the color of the fill. The display of filled areas can be turned on or off with the Display Fills (DF) or the Fast (FA) command, Fill option.

Fillet   An operation in which an arc of specified radius is inserted as close as possible to the intersection of two lines or arcs, tangent to each line or arc. When filleting, the arcs or lines are trimmed to meet the endpoints of the inserted arc.

Fillet Radius   The radius used by the Fillet (FL) and Auto-Fillet (AT) commands. If the Fillet Radius (FR) is too large, filleting will not occur. A fillet radius of zero simply allows you to trim or extend both lines or arcs with the Fillet command.

Filter   To select entities according to their properties rather than their location. Entity type, color, line type, line width, and other properties may be filtered.

Floppy Disk   A flat magnetic storage media that can be removed from the computer disk drive. Popular formats include 5 1/4-inch flexible disks and 3 1/2-inch disks in hard plastic sleeves. Floppy disks store from 360K to 1.4 MB of file data.

.FNT   An extension used by Generic CADD to identify font files. Font files are in a special format and must be created with Generic CADD or with special software designed for creating Generic CADD fonts.

Font   A set of definitions for each character that can by typed on the computer keyboard. A font can include the upper- and lowercase letters of the alphabet, numerals, and punctuation marks. A font other than the default font must be loaded with the Font Select (FS) command before it can be used. Generic CADD 5.0 comes with several fonts, and more are available from Generic Software and third-party sources, or you can create your own.

Fractional Value The largest denominator that you allow to be used in a display of fractional value. The allowable values are in powers of two, starting with 2,4,8,16, and so on. The larger the specified denominator, the smaller the fractions that will be displayed.

Function Key One of 10 or 12 keys on the PC keyboard that performs functions specific to the program being run. These keys are usually located either on the left side or along the top of the keyboard and are marked F1, F2, F3, and so on. In Generic CADD, macros may be assigned to these keys, either used alone or in combination with SHIFT, CTRL, and ALT, by using the Macro Assign (MA) command.

Graphics Card The hardware device that runs the monitor. This card controls the resolution and number of available colors, and is an add-on to the standard PC. Typical graphics cards that work well with Generic CADD include the Hercules monochrome graphics card for monochrome monitors, and the EGA and VGA for enhanced color monitors. Generic CADD supports a large number of graphics cards by many different manufacturers. You use the CONFIG program to tell Generic CADD which type of card you have installed in your computer.

Grid A visual aid for estimating the dimensions on the screen. In Generic CADD, the grid appears as a number of dots; you can separately control the horizontal spacing and vertical spacing of these dots. The spacing of these dots may be used to limit cursor movement to the specified interval.

.GX2 A file extension used by Generic CADD to identify image files (a record of the color of each pixel on the screen) created by Generic CADD and other Generic products. .GX2 files made on one graphics card may be loaded onto another system using a compatible graphics card.

Appendix C: Glossary

Hard Disk   A high-capacity magnetic storage media permanently installed in your computer. Generic CADD 5.0 is usually installed on a hard disk.

Hardware   The electronic and mechanical parts of the computer, such as circuit boards and chips, the disk drives, the monitor, the mouse or digitizer, the printer, and the plotter. The programs that make the hardware run are known as software. In the case of floppy disks, the disk itself is hardware, while the program stored on the disk is software. *See also* Software.

Hatch   An operation in which continuous or dashed lines are drawn through a closed area at regular intervals in one or more directions. Often the spacing in the dashed lines is arranged so as to form special shapes or figures when combined with other similar lines.

Hatchable Area   An area that is bounded by lines and arcs that meet at their endpoints. Hatchable areas may be nested in such a way that a second enclosed area inside the first (as with a square inside a larger square) is considered to be an edge of the hatchable area and so is excluded from hatching.

.HCH   A file extension used by Generic CADD to identify files that contain the definitions of hatch patterns.

Hierarchical   Organized in an outline or "tree" format. The Generic CADD video menu is said to be hierarchical because it contains a ROOT menu from which you select other menus, from which you select commands or other menus. This implies greater detail at each sublevel of the menu.

   In Generic CADD 5.0, it is possible for the user to create hierarchical organizations of drawings and component files, by having components within components, and drawings within drawings.

Highlight   To alter the display of entities on the screen so that you can tell which ones have been selected. In Generic CADD 5.0, entities are actually "lowlighted" by a technique called bit-blitting, which removes every other pixel from the display. This technique is sufficient to convey the desired information.

Image A record of the colors of the pixels on the screen. An image contains no actual CAD data, but is more like a "photograph" of the drawing on the screen. Even when an image file is loaded, the entities displayed on the screen cannot be changed, as they exist only on the screen and not as entities in the drawing file.

Incrementation To add a constant value repeatedly. In Generic CADD, the X and Y coordinates are incremented by the movement of the pointing device when Snap to Grid is turned on. If the Grid Size is 1 by 1, X and Y values increase or decrease by one unit every time the pointing device is moved a small amount.

Insert To place a text character between two existing characters. When characters are inserted, the attributes of the character to the right are taken on, but the currently loaded font is used. In some other CAD programs, the term insert applies to the placement of components, hatches, or fills. Generic CADD calls the placement function place.

Intersection A point (including an endpoint) where two or more lines, arcs, or circles meet. Imaginary intersections exist at the point where entities would meet if they were extended.

Kilobyte (K) A unit of measurement of computer data, consisting of 1024 bytes or characters. Each letter of the alphabet, numeral, and punctuation mark takes up a single byte. Numeric data is stored in a number of formats, using multiple bytes for the storage of each number.

Laser A printer technology that involves a narrowly focused beam of light passing over a charged plate in order to create an image, which is transferred to paper via carbon "toner" particles. Laser printers are currently capable of resolutions of up to 300 dots per inch (dpi), which is much greater than the resolution of most dot matrix printers.

Three basic types of laser printers are supported by Generic CADD 5.0. Hewlett-Packard and Canon formats are handled through the Printer option of the Plotting interface, while PostScript-compatible printers, such as the Apple LaserWriter series, are supported by the PostScript option.

Layer A device for linking certain pieces of information together. In Generic CADD, 256 layers, numbered 0 to 255, are available, and can be assigned names. Each entity is created on the "current" layer, but can be changed to any other layer using several commands. Information may be displayed or hidden layer by layer, and editing may be done on either the current layer only or on all visible layers.

Library A group of symbols or components. Generic Software sells libraries that consist of 50 to 300 components, menus for placing these components, and a manual that illustrates them. Symbols libraries are usually grouped by application or discipline, such as landscaping or plumbing.

Limits An arbitrarily selected "boundary" for your drawing. The limits are measured relative to the objects that you are drawing, not the size of the paper on which you print. It is not unusual, therefore, to have limits in the hundreds of feet if you are doing building plans or elevations.

Line In Generic CADD, the term Line is used in two ways. In the more specific use, a Line is a simple entity with two endpoints, created by the Line command, the implied Line command, or the Rectangle or Regular Polygon command. In more general use, any entity is referred to as a Line, as in the Line Width and Line Type commands.

Line Type A characteristic of simple entities, the Line Type determines the pattern of dots and dashes of each entity. A continuous line is Line Type 0.

Line Type Scale The Line Type scale determines the interval for repetition of the dash pattern in Line Types 11 through 19, in the units of the drawing. Line Types 1 through 9 are not affected by the Line Type scale, and Line Types above 20 are scaled by the integer value of the Line Type number divided by 10 times the Line Type scale.

Load To read a file from disk into the computer memory. Loading a drawing file causes the entity in the file to become part of the current drawing, and to be displayed on the screen. Loading a font or a component simply makes the definitions in the file accessible by other commands. Loading a Batch file causes the commands in the Batch file to be executed. Loading a menu file makes the menu items in the file available from the video menu or the digitizer menu, and loading an image file displays the image on the screen.

Macro A group of commands that can be stored and executed with one action to automate certain drawing tasks. Macros can be executed from the function keys, from the video or digitizer menus, or from a Batch file.

Match A function for setting drawing parameters by selecting an entity. All parameters that can be derived from the entity placement are matched. Note that certain parameters, such as Color and Layer, are always matched, while others, such as Text Size, can be derived only from entities that contain the desired information. Note that some entities (such as dimensions) are highly parameterized—and you may be changing a large number of parameters by matching them.

Menu A list of commands or actions. In Generic CADD, a menu is kept in a file with the extension .MNU. This file contains the words that appear on the screen and the actions that are taken when these words are selected. Generic CADD menus can be entirely redefined by the user. The second button on the pointing device or the HOME key on the keyboard is used to select an item from the video menu after a menu bar has been placed over the desired item.

Midpoint The point on a Line that is equidistant from each endpoint.

Mirror To reflect a portion of the drawing across an imaginary plane creating additional entities that are mirror images of the originals. In Generic CADD 5.0, entities can be reflected across an imaginary line at any angle.

.MNU A file extension used by Generic CADD to identify a menu file. Files with a .MNU extension contain the commands that are executed when certain items are selected from the video menu or boxes are selected from the digitizer menu. Menu files are in ASCII format and can be modified or created by the user.

Appendix C: Glossary

Monochrome A type of graphics system or monitor capable of displaying only one color—either amber, green, or white on a black background. Generic CADD can assign color characteristics to entities on a monochrome system, even though these characteristics may not be displayed at the time the drawing is created.

Mouse A device for controlling the cursor that moves back and forth on a desktop surface. An optical mouse rolls over a gridded surface and "sees" which direction it is moving. A mechanical mouse "feels" the direction using wheels that turn as the mouse is moved. Many mice currently on the market are opto-mechanical combinations.

Move In Generic CADD, an action that causes the coordinates of the definition points of an entity or entities to be displaced by a specified amount.

Object Each identifiable entity in a Generic CADD drawing is something called an object. Examples include Lines, Circles, Arcs, and other simple entities, as well as Text Characters, Components, and other complex entities.

Operating System A program or set of programs that controls the operation of your computer. In many ways, the operating system acts as an interpreter or buffer between your computer and the application software, such as Generic CADD. Generic CADD 5.0 requires DOS 3.0 or later.

Ortho Short for orthogonal, ortho in Generic CADD is a mode of operation in which cursor movement is restricted to vertical or horizontal directions, which may be user defined.

Ortho Angle The actual angle that is defined as horizontal for the purpose of orthogonal cursor movement. Vertical is simply defined as 90 degrees to this angle.

Override An action of certain commands that negates the action of other commands. For example, certain Snap commands can override both Ortho Mode and Snap to Grid if the point in question does not meet the requirements of the current mode.

Overwrite To replace one item with another, usually a file. This action occurs because you cannot have two files by the same name in the same directory. Whenever you attempt to save a file, Generic CADD checks to see if a file by the same name already exists. If it does, you are given the choice of overwriting the existing file, in which case it is replaced by the new file, or renaming the existing file, in which case its extension changes to .BAK so that there is no conflict between the two filenames.

Pan To change the part of the drawing that is displayed on the screen by moving left, right, up, down, or diagonally. When panning, the scale of the drawing as it is displayed on the screen remains the same.

Parameters Variables that control the way that Generic CADD 5.0 entities are created. Also called Settings, the parameters that control the placement of components include the standard entity parameters Color, Layer, Line Type, and Line Width as well as the special component parameters Scale and Rotation. Generic CADD 5.0 makes extensive use of parameters.

Parametric Programming A technique whereby a drawing can be created by establishing a number of known geometric relationships between entities, and by allowing the distances, lengths, angles, and so on, to vary. In Generic CADD 5.0, parametric programming may be accomplished through keyboard macros, menus, Batch files, and interfaces with other programs.

Partitioned A mode or style of dimensioning in which two or more linear dimensions are created continuously, each one starting where the previous one left off.

Pathname The complete name of a file, including the disk drive letter, any directory or subdirectory in which the file may be stored, the filename, and the extension. A colon (:) follows the disk drive letter, backslashes (\) are used to separate directories, subdirectories, and filenames, and a period or decimal point (.) is used to separate the filename from the extension. The pathname for the drawing file HOUSE in the DWG subdirectory of the CADD5 directory on the C drive would thus be C:\CADD5\DWG\HOUSE.DWG.

.PCX A file extension used by a number of software publishers to identify pixel image files. Many manufacturers follow a standard developed by Z-Soft for their PC-Paintbrush program, allowing direct transfer of files between these programs. Generic PaintConvert, supplied with Generic 3D and Generic CADD 5.0 can create .PCX files.

Peripheral A hardware device, other than the keyboard or monitor, that attaches externally to a computer. Examples include printers, plotters, digitizers, and mice.

Perpendicular The geometric relationship that exists when two lines intersect at a 90-degree angle. In Generic CADD, this definition is extended to lines that intersect arcs in a similar way.

PGDN A keyboard key normally used for cursor movement. In Generic CADD, the PGDN key moves the video menu forward one screen.

PGUP A keyboard key normally used for cursor movement. In Generic CADD, the PGUP key moves the video menu back one screen.

Pick A term sometimes employed in CAD jargon to indicate the selection of a menu item or screen location by pressing a button on the mouse or digitizer puck. For example, the ARC 4 command is so named not because you actually place four points on the arc, but because four "picks" are required, each providing a different type of information.

Pixel A single dot of light on the video monitor.

Plot A form of hard-copy output that is printed with moving pens rather than individual dots. The term plot is often used for both the process and the result. You can "plot a drawing," and the resulting drawing may be called a "plot."

Plotter A hardware device that produces hard-copy output through the action of moving pens rather than placing individual dots. Generic CADD 5.0 supports plotters made by a number of different manufacturers.

Point A single coordinate pair that has been selected for a particular purpose. Generic CADD 5.0 employs three separate definitions and on-screen representations for Standard Points, Construction Points, and Reference Points. Standard Points, placed into the drawing by the user and usually intended to be printed as part of the drawing, are represented by short vertical and horizontal line segments that intersect at their midpoints. Construction Points, which can be displayed to indicate the definition points of entities and their locations, are shown as two short diagonally crossed lines. Reference Points, used to indicate the Origin and the intersection points of complex entities, are displayed as a combination of horizontal, vertical, and diagonal line segments, slightly longer than those that make up Construction Points.

Pointing Device A hardware device, such as a mouse, digitizer, or trackball, that is used for controlling the movement of the cursor and for selecting points on the screen. The keyboard cursor keys may also be used as crude pointing devices. The extra buttons on a digitizer puck or multi-button mouse can each be assigned a command or macro.

Polar Coordinates An optional format for the display and input of coordinates, in which a distance and an angle from a selected reference origin is displayed.

Polygon *See* Regular Polygon.

Print A form of hard-copy output that is created by placing a number of individual dots onto paper. The term print is often used for both the process and the result. You can "print a drawing," and the resulting drawing may be called a "print."

Printer A hardware device that produces hard-copy output through the placement of characters or dots on paper. Generic CADD drawings can be printed on dot matrix or laser printers. A large variety of printers by many different manufacturers may be used, some at user-selectable resolutions.

Prompt A line of text at the bottom of the Generic CADD 5.0 screen that usually asks you for information. To respond to the prompt, you may be required to select a point or a menu item, type a value or a name, or answer a question by typing a number or character.

Properties Descriptive qualities of any Generic CADD 5.0 drawing entity. The properties of any simple entity includes its color, line type, line width, and layer. Complex entities have other properties as well. Text characters, for example, also have size, aspect ratio, slant, rotation, and other properties.

Proportional In Generic CADD 5.0, a system for spacing text characters so that there is an equal amount of space between all character combinations, even though the characters themselves may vary in width.

Puck A device that is attached to a digitizer tablet for the purpose of pointing to and selecting locations on the tablet, often corresponding to locations on the screen or items on the digitizer menu, selected with the first and second buttons. The puck usually has additional buttons, each of which may be assigned a command or combination of commands, called a macro.

Quit To exit Generic CADD 5.0. You have the option of saving or discarding your work as you exit.

Radial Copy To copy selected entities around an axis point a specified number of times, each time rotating the objects around the axis point by a specified angle.

RAM An acronym for Random Access Memory, the type of computer memory in which both Generic CADD and your drawings are located as you use Generic CADD. The 640K that can be addressed by DOS is memory of this type.

Redo A function that reverses the effect of an Undo command. This command is necessary because if the Undo command could undo itself, you could only undo one command at a time. *See also* Undo.

Redraw To refresh the video display. This process "cleans up" any extra or missing lines that may be left over from a previous operation and recognizes any display toggles or changes that may have been set since the screen was last redrawn, such as the use of Fast Text, Fast Arcs, and other display variables.

Reference Point   The insertion point of a complex entity such as a component or hatch pattern. Visual display is optional and consists of four short line segments, a vertical, a horizontal, and two diagonals, which meet at their centers to form an asterisk-like figure. A Reference Point is displayed at the drawing Origin when display of Reference Points is turned on.

Regular Polygon   A multi-sided figure with equal length sides and equal angles between all sides. Although the Regular Polygon command in Generic CADD asks for only a few points, a number of Line entities are actually created.

Relative   Locations to be measured from the previously selected point. Coordinates may be displayed and data may be manually entered in Relative mode if you wish.

REN   A DOS command for reassigning the name of a file. To rename the drawing file HOUSE to MYHOUSE, for example, you would type **REN HOUSE.DWG MYHOUSE.DWG** at the DOS prompt.

Rename   In Generic CADD, to replace the extension of a filename with the extension .BAK. Whenever you attempt to save a file, Generic CADD checks to see if a file by the same name already exists. If it does, you are given the choice of overwriting the existing file, in which case it is replaced by the new file, or renaming the existing file, in which case its extension changes to .BAK so that there is no conflict between the two filenames.

Representational   The quality of conveying information about real situations. Generic CADD 5.0 and CAD in general are said to be representational processes because real data and geometric relationships can be defined, stored, and re-created in a way that conveys true, accurate information.

Resolution   The number of dots available for representing information on the screen or printer. Video resolutions are usually expressed in terms of the entire screen (EGA resolution, for example, is 640x350), while printer resolutions are often expressed either in dots per inch (many laser printers operate at up to 300 dpi) or pins per character (most dot matrix printers offer either 9 or 24 pins).

Rubberbanding   A process in which an entity is continually redrawn on the screen as the cursor is moved, giving the impression that the entity is stretching as it moves. Rubberbanding is optional in many Generic CADD 5.0 commands, and is used automatically in a number of other drawing and editing commands to increase visual feedback.

Save   To store information in a file on a disk. Generic CADD 5.0 can save drawing files, font files, component files, Batch files, attribute files, and image files.

Scale   A parameter applied to a complex entity before it is placed (or during placement) that determines the final size of the entity. Each scalable type of complex entity has its own scale variable(s).

Selection   The process of picking which entities you want to work with. In Generic CADD 5.0, many commands include a Selection prompt, allowing you to select entities using your choice of techniques before continuing with the command.

Settings   *See* Parameters.

Snap   To place a point or locate the cursor based on existing points in the drawing, existing geometric relationships, or the spacing and origin of the grid. Among the Snaps available in Generic CADD 5.0 are grid and definition point Snaps, as well as geometric Snaps such as intersections, midpoints, centers, and parallel, perpendicular, and tangent relationships.

Software   Instructions that cause the computer to perform various functions. Software stored on a chip (known as the BIOS) tells the computer how to look on the disk drive for more software (the operating system) that issues prompts, receives commands, and loads and runs programs (application software such as Generic CADD).

Spline A type of curve defined by a number of points or nodes. The curve created by Generic CADD 5.0's Curve command is a spline curve that passes through the user-placed points.

Stretch An editing operation in which certain definition points are moved while others remain in the same place, changing the shape of entities.

Stylus A pen-like pointing device that works with a digitizer tablet. The stylus is usually connected to the tablet by a wire and includes a single button that is depressed when the point of the stylus is pressed downward on the tablet. A second button is sometimes present on the side of the stylus, which may be depressed with a fingertip. In order to use the video menu in Generic CADD 5.0, a two-button stylus is required.

Symbol A drawn representation of an object or concept. In this book, the term symbol is used to distinguish those items that are added to a drawing as a reference rather than as a representation of the real objects that you are drawing. Thus, notes, dimensions, North arrows, titles, and so on, are considered symbols.

Tablet The flat portion of a digitizer on which you point with a puck or stylus. Most tablets contain a very fine grid of wires that detects the presence of the pointing device and relays coordinates to the computer. Often a printed overlay is taped to the tablet to identify various areas that may be used for pointing on the screen and for selecting menu items.

.TDG An extension used by Generic Software to identify files that contain pointing device drivers that communicate technical information about a variety of mice, digitizers, and trackballs to Generic CADD 5.0.

Text Predefined complex entities that are placed according to a number of predetermined parameters. The definitions of text characters come from a selected font file. Generic CADD 5.0 implements two methods for placing text: character by character, or as a string of characters.

Toggle A command that changes a parameter from one state to another. Most toggles in Generic CADD 5.0 are switched on and off by selecting the same command.

.TPL An extension used by Generic Software to identify files that contain plotter drivers, which communicate technical information about a variety of plotters to Generic CADD 5.0.

.TPR An extension used by Generic Software to identify files that contain printer drivers, which communicate technical information about a variety of dot matrix and laser printers to Generic CADD 5.0.

Trackball A stationary pointing device similar to a mouse.

Tracking A technique available in Generic CADD 5.0 (pioneered in Generic 3D), in which the cursor is moved along each cursor axis repeatedly without selecting a new point until tracking is ended. Tracking is essentially an extension of the more typical ortho concept, but works in more than one direction simultaneously.

Transferability The quality of certain file types to be shared between various programs. Generic CADD 5.0 drawing files are transferable among different computers running Generic CADD. Generic Level 3 drawing files are transferable between Level 3, CADD 5.0, and Generic 3D. CADD drawing files are transferable to other CAD programs through AutoConvert using the .DXF file format.

In addition, Generic CADD drawing files and images are transferable to other software through plotter, printer, and PostScript files, as well as a variety of image formats.

Undo A function for reversing the effects of the last command. Normally, only drawing and editing commands (commands that add to or alter the database) are subject to the Undo command. You cannot Undo a Zoom Window, for example, for it has no effect on the database. Undo will not function after a Pack Data or any command that implicitly performs the same function, such as Drawing Erase or Origin. You can undo commands successively back to the point of the beginning of the drawing session or the last Pack Data. *See also* Redo.

Unerase A function for restoring to the screen database entities that have been previously erased. Each Unerase command restores the same number of entities that were erased by a corresponding Erase command.

Units   In Generic CADD, a variety of measurement systems are available. English units may be expressed in feet, feet and inches, or just inches. In either feet and inches or just inches, the basic unit of measurement is the inch. Partial inches may be expressed in either decimal or fractional format. Three different metric formats are also available: meters, centimeters, and millimeters.

.VGD   An extension used to identify files that contain video drivers, which communicate technical information about a variety of video graphics cards to Generic CADD 5.0.

Video Menu   A list of commands that appears on the right side of the screen, from which you can select a desired action. The video menu is used by moving a menu cursor up and down with the pointing device or cursor keys and pressing the second button on the pointing device or the HOME key on the keyboard. The actual text of the video menu and the commands associated with each text item are stored in an ASCII file with the extension .MNU.

Viewport   A term often used to describe the way that the video monitor functions as a device for displaying the CADD drawing. Often, only a portion of the drawing is displayed on the screen at any one time, as if you were looking through an opening at a small portion of a much larger drawing.

Window   A rectangular area described by placing two points on the screen with the cursor. The window is displayed as a visible box on the screen and is used for selecting items for editing, display, and other functions. Items are defined to be "in the window" only if all of their definition points fall within the rectangular area. Only the reference point of a complex entity need be captured, as this is the only definition point that it has.

Zoom   To change the portion of the drawing that is displayed on the video monitor. Most of the Zoom commands also change the scale at which the drawing is displayed on the screen.

Index

3D, Generic, 472

A

Abbreviations, standard, 45
ABS, defined, 494
Absolute
    coordinates, 75, 173-174
    defined, 494
Active, area, 407
Active Area, selecting, 407
Align, drawing, 410
All
    edit, 75, 126, 187, 321
    file selector command, 383
    snap, 126, 321
    zoom, 150
Angle
    arrow, 338
    defined, 509
    measure, 202
    ortho, defined, 509
    rotation, 131, 141
    show, 132
Angular
    dimensions, 352
    units, 63

Arc
    defined, 494
    four-point, 111
    rubber, 112
    sides, 182
    snap, 320
    two-point, 112
Arcs
    defined, 502
    fast, 181, 502
    parallel, 317
    plotted, 393
    three-point, 96
Area
    active, 407
    coordinate, 37
    cumulative, 201
    defined, 494
    digitizer menu, 416
    drawing, 36
    file selector, 380
    hatchable, 505
    measure, 201
    menu, 38
    message, 38
    printable, 386
    prompt, 38
Areas, selecting, 407

519

Arrow
    angle, 338
    dimension, 337
    display, 343
    length, 339
    location, 339
    type, 337
Arrows, dimension, 336
ASCII
    character, 447
    defined, 494
    files, 50
    load, 243
    text files, 243
Aspect
    defined, 494
    text, 235
Assign
    command, 427
    macros, 427
Associative
    about, 29
    defined, 494
    dimensions, 328
    vs. automatic, 329
Asterisks, use in menus, 439
At, use in macros, 434
Attach
    attributes, 214
    defined, 495
    extracting, 466
    file extension, 33
Attributes
    about, 29, 248
    attach, 214
    communication through, 464
    entity, 162
    loading, 379
    saving, 370
    uses of, 467
Auto, defined, 495
AutoConvert
    about, 455
    Generic, 473
    program, 455
Autofillet, command, 268
Automate, defined, 495
Automatic, drawing load, 105
Axis
    major, 108
    minor, 108
    point, 131
    radial copy, 291

B

BACKSPACE, defined, 495
Backwards
    redraw, 161
    zoom, 161
.BAK, defined, 495
Basepoint
    coordinates, 75
    defined, 495
    manual entry, 77
    use in macros, 447
Batch
    file extension, 33
    files, 51
    loading, 378
    macros, 429, 443
    path, 36
    saving, 369
    use of, 456
Bezier
    curve, 262
    defined, 495
    edit, 266
    single, 263
Beziers
    editing, 266
    multiple, 264
    single, 265
    tangent, 266
Boundary
    fill, 255
    hatch, 250, 255
Break
    command, 135

Index

Break, *continued*
    defined, 495
    object, 135, 143
Buffer, printer, 403
Bug, defined, 495
Button
    alternates, 40
    first, 40
    second, 40
Buttons
    mouse, 40
    pointing device, 40, 50

C

CAD
    as a drawing medium, 2, 14
    as a tool, 14
    characteristics, 3
    classified, 2
    compared to word processing, 9
    defined, 496
    primitives, 9
    vs. drawing by hand, 2
    vs. other drawing software, 2
    vs. painting programs, 3
CADD
    database, 20
    defined, 496
    history of, 20
    installing, 54
    PLATTER, 475
    screen, 34
    starting, 34, 59
    vs. CAD, 20
CADD.COLORS, about, 422
CADD.FONT, about, 422
Callouts, defined, 496
Card, graphics, defined, 504
Center
    plot, 402
    snap, 320
Centered, dimension text, 333
CGA, defined, 496

Chamfer
    command, 299
    defined, 496
    distances, 299
Change
    defined, 496
    dimension, 346, 349
    function, 136
    plotter pens, 395
    prompt for, 395
Character
    ASCII, 447
    defined, 496
    first, 45
    ignore, 436
    second, 46
    spacing, 233
    third, 47
Characters
    about, 29
    macro, 435
    text, 232, 237
Circle
    centerpoint, 98
    defined, 496
    radius, 98
Circles
    parallel, 317
    plotted, 393
    three-point, 119
    two-point, 98
Close, snap, 310
.CMP, defined, 496
Codes, two-character, 137
Color
    background, 163
    current, 71
    cursor, 177, 284
    defined, 496
    dimension, 331
    display, 179, 284
    fill, 249
    hatch, 249
    line, 71, 163
    PostScript, 396-397

Color, *continued*
    settings, 284
    text, 236
.COM, defined, 497
Comma-delimited, file extension, 33
Comma-separated, file format, 465
Command
    defined, 497
    repeating, 93
Commands
    keyboard, 45
    shortcut, 48
    two-character, 45, 49, 137
Commas, in macros, 433
Compatibility
    downward, 21, 366, 454
    upward, 454
Complex
    about, 28
    commands, 479-480
    define, commands, 479
    entities, 206
    place, commands, 480
    predefined, 209
Component
    automatic loading, 377
    create, 211
    creating, 210
    defined, 497
    definitions, 228
    dump, 369
    explode, 224
    file extension, 33
    files, 367
    ghost, 231
    list, 215
    load, 377
    name, 212
    path, 361, 363
    place, 216
    placing, 213
    reference point, 213
    remove, 231
    replace, 229
    rotation, 218

Component, *continued*
    scale, 221
    snaps, 231
Components
    about, 29, 210
    command codes, 46
    eliminating, 231
    exploded, 226
    loading, 376
    menu, 43
CONFIG, defined, 497
Configuration
    file, 422
    program, 422
Configurations
    custom, 422
    multiple, 424
Configure
    defined, 497
    plotter, 393
    printer, 393
Constraints, menu, 42
Construction
    defined, 497
    display, 121
    points, 82
    points, display of, 166
Continue, after quit, 90
Control, point, 262
Conventions, menu, 440
Convert, defined, 495
Coordinate
    display, 75
    modes, 173
Coordinates
    about, 25
    absolute, 37, 75, 173-174
    absolute, defined, 494
    basepoint, 75
    delta, 175
    display of, 173
    manual entry of, 76
    polar, 37, 75, 173, 176
    polar, defined, 512
    relative, 37, 75, 88, 173, 175

Index

Coordinates, *continued*
    reset, 116
    typing, 88
    using, 83
Copies, number of, 130
Copy
    command, 190
    defined, 497
    function, 129
    object, 146
    radial, 290
    radial, defined, 513
    window, 147
Create
    commands, 478
    component, 211
Cross Hairs
    defined, 498
    digitizer, 408
Current
    layer, 74, 187
    view, 297
Cursor
    color, 177, 284
    control, 322
    defined, 498
    free, 322
    keys, 240
    menu, 38
    size, 176
Cursors, multiple, 38
Curve
    bezier, 262
    command, 117
    ending, 118
    last point, 118
    points, 118
Custom, configurations, 422

D

Data
    attribute, extracting, 466
    CAD, 3

Data, *continued*
    extracting, 466
    extraction, 456
    flexibility of, 7
    geometric, 3
    graphic, 3
    input, batch files, 457
    macro, 433
    numeric, 6
    pack, 286
    painting, 3
    specifying, 6
    transfer formats, 13
    transferability of, 13
    user supplied, 434
Database
    capability, 21
    commands, 479
    defined, 499
    drawing, 20
    independence of, 21
Decimal
    places, 64
    units, 63
Default
    defined, 499
    drawing file, 423
    layer, 74
    parameters, 371-372, 423
    settings, 91
Define, commands, 479
Definition
    geometric, 7
    stored, 7
    unload, 286, 289
Definitions
    about, 288
    component, 228
Delete, text, 242
Desktop Publishing, defined, 499
Destination
    layer, 225
    output, 391
Detach, defined, 499

Device
    pointing, buttons, 40, 50
    pointing, defined, 512
    output, 390
Devices
    about, 406
    external, 21, 24
Diameter, dimensions, 353
Digitize, defined, 407
Digitizer
    about, 406
    align, 410
    as a pointing device, 406
    clearing menu, 426
    commands, 416
    cross hairs, 408
    defined, 499
    menu, 50, 413
    menu items, 438
    menu, configuring, 415
    menu, loading, 416
    menu, select, 416
    overlay, 413
    pen, 408
    puck, 407
    scale, 409
    select menu, 418
    stylus, 406
    tablet, 406
    to select commands, 413
    to trace drawings, 408
    trace mode, 410
    using a menu, 417
Digitizing, defined, 499
Dimension
    about, 332
    arrow angle, 338
    arrow length, 339
    arrow location, 339
    arrow type, 337
    arrows, 336
    centered, 333
    change, 346, 349
    color, 331
    cumulative, 347

Dimension, *continued*
    direction, 333, 345
    display, 334, 341, 344
    extension lines, 340
    fixed variance, 336
    in-line offset, 333
    layer, 331
    mode, 347
    offset above, 334
    partitioned, 347
    placement, 332
    proximity, 345
    scale, 350
    single, 347
    stacked variance, 336
    text size, 332
    tolerance, 335
Dimensioning
    about, 328
    defined, 499
    leaders, 354
    menu, 329
    parameter, 331
    style, 329
    text, 332
Dimensions
    about, 29
    angular, 352
    associative, 328
    associative, about, 29
    associative, defined, 494
    defined, 494
    diameter, 353
    editing, 346
    linear, 351
    menu, 43
    moving, 347
    placing, 350
    radial, 353
    typing, 88
    updating, 347
DIR, defined, 500
Direction
    dimension, 345
    dimension text, 333

Index

Direction, *continued*
    radial copy, 292
    rotation, 141
Directories, creating, 57
Directory
    default, 60
    defined, 500
    tree, 381
Disable, LW and LT, 182
Disk
    floppy, defined, 503
    hard, defined, 505
Displacement, defined, 500
Display
    assigned macros, 427
    color, 179, 284
    commands, 162, 480
    construction points, 121
    defined, 500
    dimension, 341
    fills, 182
    hatch, 183
    layer, 191
    macros, 198
    menu, 44, 183
    modes, 173
    screen text, 176
    text, 245
Distance
    between lines, 93
    cumulative, 200
    defined, 500
    direct, 77
    measure, 200
    offset, 129, 316
    show, 69
Distances, chamfer, 299
DOS
    defined, 500
    exit to, 99
Double
    filled lines, 272
    filletted lines, 273
    lines, 269
    width, 270

Drag
    command, 172
    defined, 500
    object, 172
Draw, menu, 42
Drawing
    about, 32
    align, 410
    default, 423
    defined, 501
    erase, 286
    existing, 60
    files, 364
    load, 373
    loading, 59
    method, 127
    new, 59, 91
    origin, 287, 306
    parameters, 71
    path, 361-362
    plot, 389
    rename, 374
    save, 365-366
    saving, 89
    scale, 132
    status, 196
Drawings
    exporting, 455
    importing, 455
Drive, file selector command, 382
Drivers, device, 24
Dump, component, 369
.DWG, defined, 501
.DXF
    creation, 473
    defined, 501

E

Edit
    all layers, 75, 187, 321
    bezier, 266
    commands, 479
    defined, 501

Edit, *continued*
   text, 242
Editing
   dimensions, 346
   functions, 182
   selection, 127
   shortcuts, 47
   text, 240-241
Edits, menu, 43
EGA, defined, 501
Ellipse
   command, 108
   construction, 109
   defined, 501
   true, 109
Endpoint, defined, 501
ENTER
   emulated, 49
   in a macro, 436
   symbol, 49
Entities
   about, 27-28
   associated, 12
   complex, 28, 206
   discussed, 21
   multiple, 262
   obsolete, 21
   predefined, 209
   selected, 279
   simple, 27
Entity
   attributes, 162
   commands, 478
   create, 478
   defined, 501
   filter, 380
   new, 27
Entry
   basepoint, 77
   manual, 76
   of coordinates, 76
   origin, 76
   relative, 76
Environment
   command, 371

Environment, *continued*
   defined, 502
   file, 423
.EPS, defined, 502
Erase
   drawing, 85, 286
   function, 129
   in a macro, 435
   object, 99
Exit, file selector command, 384
Explode
   component, 224
   destination layer, 225
Export, drawing files, 455
Extend, command, 297
Extension
   attribute, 33
   batch, 33
   comma-delimited, 33
   component, 33
   defined, 502
   display, 344
   filename, 33
   font, 33
   hatch, 33
   image, 33
   lengths, 340
   lines, 340
   Lotus, 33
   menu, 33
   offset, 340
   stretch, 341
Extraction, data, 456

F

Factor
   scale, 133
   zoom, 159
Fast
   arcs, 181
   defined, 502
   redraw, 179
   text, 181, 245

Index

File
    ASCII, 50
    commands, 382, 479
    configuration, 422
    defined, 502
    drawing, 10
    environment, 423
    .EPS, defined, 502
    import plotter, 395
    menu, 45, 50, 413
    paths, 361
    plotter, 391, 395
    PostScript, 391
    printer, 391
    selector, 380
    space, 33
Filename
    component, 377
    extension, 33
Filenames, about, 60
Files
    about, 32, 360
    ASCII, 51
    batch, 51, 429, 456
    component, 367
    configuration, 54
    copying, 57
    data, 56
    drawing, 32, 364
    drawing, use of, 454
    file selector, 380
    loading, 372, 378-379
    macros, 429
    optional, 55
    required, 54
    saving, 364, 369-370
    selecting, 381
    use of, 456
    worksheet, 466
Filespec, file selector command, 382
Fill
    boundary, 255
    color, 249
    defined, 503
    display, 182

Fill, *continued*
    fitted, 254
    object, 253
    window, 250
Filled, lines, 272
Fillet
    auto, 268
    command, 298
    defined, 503
    radius, 298
Fills, about, 29, 248
Filter
    by comparison, 282
    command, 280
    entity, 280
    method, 280
    toggling, 282
Filtering, about, 280
Fit
    plot, 402
    to sheet, 399
Fitted
    fill, 254
    hatch, 254
Fixed
    dimension tolerance, 336
    proximity, 345
Flip, screen, 195, 427
Floppy, defined, 503
.FNT, defined, 503
Font
    defined, 503
    file extension, 33
    path, 361, 363
    select, 232
Fonts, creating, 246
Format
    comma-separated value, 465
    macro, 432
    numeric, 63
Fraction
    defined, 504
    smallest, 64
Function
    change, 136

Function, *continued*
    copy, 129
    defined, 504
    erase, 129
    like, 283
    move, 130
    rotate, 131
    scale, 132
Functional, units, 63
Functions, editing, 128

G

Geometric, vs. graphic data, 3
Ghost, components, 231
Graphics, defined, 504
Grayscale, PostScript, 396
Grid
    command, 84
    defined, 504
    displaying, 68
    size, 68
    snap to, 70
    using the, 70
.GX2, defined, 504

H

Hard Disk, defined, 505
Hardware
    defined, 505
    independence, 12
    support, 13, 21
Hatch
    boundary, 250, 255
    color, 249
    defined, 505
    display, 183
    file extension, 33
    fitted, 254
    object, 253
    path, 361
    pattern, 249
    rotation, 249

Hatch, *continued*
    scale, 250
    settings, 249
    window, 250
Hatch/Fill, menu, 44
Hatchable, defined, 505
Hatches, about, 29, 248
.HCH, defined, 505
Height
    drawing, 67
    text, 236
Help, file selector command, 382
Hide, layer, 190
Hierarchical, defined, 505
Hierarchy, menu, 438
Highlight, defined, 505
Highlighting, command, 172

I

Ignore, in a macro, 436
Image
    communication through, 467
    defined, 506
    file extension, 33
    files, 445
    loading, 379
    mirror, 142
    saving, 370
Images
    custom, 429
    menu, 444
    sharing, 467
    transferring, 468
Import
    ASCII files, 243
    drawing files, 455
In, zoom, 107, 153,
Incrementation, defined, 506
Input, user, 434
Input/Output, commands, 479
Inquiry, commands, 480
Insert
    defined, 506

Index

Insert, *continued*
    text, 241
Installation, about, 54
Intersection
    defined, 506
    macros, 446
    snap, 313
    trim, 300
Items, digitizer, 438

J

Justification, text, 235

K

Key
    defined, 504
    function, 427
    function, defined, 504
Keyboard, commands, 45
Keys
    cursor, 240
    function, 50
    programming, 427
Kilobyte, defined, 506
Korner, trim, 300

L

Language, macro, 432
Laser, defined, 506
Last
    point, tracking from, 325
    selection, 279
Layer
    about, 12
    current, 32, 74, 187
    default, 74
    defined, 507
    destination, 225
    dimension, 331
    display, 191
    explode destination, 225

Layer, *continued*
    hidden, 186
    hide, 190
    list, 186
    load, 376
    method, 126
    name, 191
    save, 367
    update, 183
    visible, 186
Layers
    about, 29
    all, 75
    commands, 184
    edit, 75, 126, 187, 321
    edit all, 126, 321
    editing, 184
    explained, 30
    managing, 184
    menu, 44
    snap, 126 321
    snap all, 126, 321
Leader, shoulder, 348
Leaders, about, 354
Length
    above, 339-340
    below, 340
Lengths, extension, 340
Level 3
    compatibility, 454
    files, 366
    format, 21
    importing, 455
Libraries, symbols, 473
Library, defined, 507
Limits
    defined, 507
    drawing, 66
    hard clip, 387
    zoom, 67, 150
Line
    color, 71, 163
    command, 86
    commands, 162
    continuing, 86

Line, *continued*
   defined, 507
   display, 334
   first, 86
   function, 283
   hardware, 72
   implicit, 103
   mirror, 133
   PostScript, 396
   reference, 95
   scale, 73, 165
   scaled, 72
   text, 232, 237
   text, spacing, 234
   toggle, 194
   type, 72, 164
   type, disable, 182
   width, 71, 163
Linear
   dimensions, 351
   units, 63
Lines
   display, 344
   double, 269
   double filleted, 273
   extension, 340
   filled, 272
   filleted, 268
   offset, 274
   smart, 267
   status, 194
   using, 86
List
   component, 215
   layer, 186
   objects, 197
   selected, 279
Load
   ASCII, 243
   automatic, 105
   command, 375, 378
   component, 377
   defined, 507
   digitizer menu, 416
   drawing, 373

Load
   file selector command, 384
   layer, 376
   video menu, 429
Loading
   about, 360
   automatic, 373
Location, arrow, 339
Lotus, file extension, 33

M

MAC, translator, 474
Macro
   assign, command, 427
   characters, 435
   data, 433
   defined, 508
   editing, 417
   enter, 436
   escape, 435
   format, 432
   generalization, 448
   ignore character, 4367
   input, 434
   keyboard, 432
   toggles, 437
   variables, 451
Macros
   about, 427
   assigning, 427
   batch file, 443
   batch files, 429
   display, 198, 427
   double lines, 449
   edit, 199
   intersection, 446
   long, 443
   sample, 446
   use of basepoint, 447
   use of commas, 433
   variable setting, 449
Manual Entry
   basepoint, 77

Index

Manual Entry, *continued*
    of coordinates, 76
    origin, 76
    relative, 76
Margins
    plotter, 387
    printer, 386
Match
    defined, 508
    parameters, 283
Measure
    angle, 202
    area, 201
    command, 199
    distance, 100
Memory, freeing, 289
Menu
    area, 38
    components, 43
    configuring, 415
    constraints, 42
    conventions, 440
    cursor, 38
    default, 428
    defined, 499
    delete, 418, 441
    digitizer, 50, 413, 438
    digitizer, defined, 499
    digitizer, select, 418
    digitizer, using, 417
    dimensions, 43
    display, 44, 183
    draw, 42
    edits, 43
    explained, 49
    file, 45, 50
    file extension, 33
    hatch/fill, 44
    hierarchy, 438
    images, 429, 444
    item, 432
    layers, 44
    line length, 443
    load, 441
    load, digitizer, 418

Menu, *continued*
    loading, 440
    new, 441
    path, 361
    root, 40
    select, 416
    snaps, 42
    structure, 40
    sub, 40
    switching, 418
    tablet, 415
    text, 43
    trims, 42
    utilities, 44
    video, 38, 49
    video, defined, 518
    zooms, 43
Menus
    about, 428
    custom, 428
    memory configuration, 428
Message, area, 38
Method
    drawing, 127
    filter, 280
    layer, 126
    object, 125
    window, 125
Methods
    combined, 127
    selection, 124, 278
    shortcut, 124
Metric, units, 62
Midpoint
    defined, 508
    of a circle, 311
    of an arc, 311
    snap, 311
Min/Max, dimension tolerance, 335
Mirror
    command, 142
    commands, 133
    defined, 508
    line, 133
Miscellaneous, path, 361

.MNU, defined, 508
Mode
    dimension, 347
    ortho, 87
    trace, 410
Modeling, wireframe, 472
Modifier, commands, 479-480
Monochrome
    defined, 509
    display, 163
Mouse
    buttons, 40
    defined, 509
Move
    beziers, 266
    command, 134
    defined, 509
    drawing, 307
    function, 130
Multi-Trim, command, 302

N

Name
    component, 212
    delete, 158
    layer, 191
    view, 158
Nearest
    point, 102
    snap to, 102
Nested, definitions, 11
No, option, 49

O

Object
    break, 135, 143
    command, 172
    commands, 479-480
    copy, 146
    define, commands, 479
    defined, 509
    drag, 172

Object, *continued*
    edit, commands, 479
    erase, 99
    fill, 253
    hatch, 253
    method, 125
    place, commands, 480
    snap, 311
Objects
    commands, 479
    definable, 11
    list, 197
    number selected, 279
    select, 127
    real, vs. symbols, 8
Offset
    above, dimension text, 334
    distance, 129, 316
    extension, 340
    in-line, dimension text, 333
    lines, 274
Oops, command, 285
Operating, defined, 509
Options
    command, 433
    configuration, 58
    output, 392
    plotter, 393
    PostScript, 396
    printer, 396
    prompt, 49
Origin
    about, 389
    drawing, 287, 306
    manual entry, 76
    plot, 399-400
    uses of, 307
Ortho
    defined, 509
    snap, 87
    with cursor free, 322
Out, zoom, 153
Output
    destination, 391
    device, 390

Index

Output
    hard copy, 26
    options, 392
    scaled, 8
Overlay, digitizer, 413
Override, defined, 509
Overwrite
    a file, 90, 365
    defined, 510

P

Pack Data, command, 287
Page, setup, 400
Pan
    command, 160
    defined, 510
Parallel
    arcs, 317
    circles, 317
    snap, 315
Parameter
    commands, 478
    dimensioning, 331
Parameters
    attributes, 208
    components, 208
    default, 371
    defined, 510
    dimensioning, 208
    drawing, 71
    hatch, 20
    hatch and fill, 249
    match, 283
    placement, 207
    text, 208
Parametric, defined, 510
Partitioned, defined, 510
Pattern, hatch, 249
Path
    component, 363
    drawing, 362
    font, 363
Pathname, defined, 510

Paths, default, 56, 60, 360
.PCX, defined, 511
Pen
    digitizer, 408
    prompt for, 395
Pens, plotter, number of, 394
Percentage, snap, 313
Peripheral, defined, 511
perpendicular
    defined, 511
    snap, 317
PGDN, defined, 511
PGUP, defined, 511
Pick, defined, 511
Pixel, defined, 511
Place
    commands, 480
    component, 216
Placement, dimension text, 332
Places, decimal, 64
PLATTER, CADD, 475
Plot
    abort, 403
    about, 389
    center, 402
    command, 390
    defined, 511
    drawing, 389
    files, communication through, 468
    fit, 402
    origin, 399-400
    rotate, 402
    scale, 399, 401
    selection, 390
    start, 403
Plotter
    arcs, 393
    circles, 393
    configure, 393
    defined, 511
    file, 395
    import file, 395
    margins, 387
    number of pens, 394
    options, 393

Plotter, *continued*
  pen change, 395
  pen settings, 394
  pen speed, 304
  pen width, 394
  resolution, 6
Plotting
  about, 26
  basics, 386
  current view, 397
  fit full drawing, 399
  view type, 397
Point
  about, 29
  axis, 291
  beziers, 266
  command, 121, 134
  component, 213
  construction, defined, 497
  control, 262
  curve, 118
  defined, 497
  move, 134
  nearest, 102
  of reference, 88
  reference, 115, 132
  reference, defined, 514
  rotation, 141
  snap to, 102
  tracking from, 325
  user supplied, 434
Pointing Device
  about, 406
  buttons, 40, 50
  defined, 512
Points
  construction, 82, 166
  definition, 27
  display, 121
  display of, 166
  reference, 168
  standard, 121, 169
Polar
  coordinates, 75, 176

Polar, *continued*
  defined, 512
Polygon
  regular, 101
  regular, defined, 514
Port
  parallel, 391
  serial, 391
PostScript
  color, 396-397
  command, 390
  grayscale, 396
  line width, 396
  options, 296
Previous, zoom, 156
Primitives
  common, 9
  geometric, 9
Print
  command, 290
  defined, 512
  files, communication through, 468
Printer
  configure, 393
  copies, 393
  defined, 512
  margins, 386
  options, 396
Printing
  about, 26
  basics, 386
Program, commands, 480
Programming
  defined, 510
  parametric, defined, 510
Prompt
  area, 38
  defined, 512
  enter a command, 38
  options, 49
Properties
  defined, 513
  geometric, 7
  of an entity, 7

Index

Proportional
    defined, 513
    text spacing, 234
Proximity, fixed, 345
Publishing, desktop, defined, 499
Puck
    defined, 513
    digitizer, 407

Q

Quit
    and save, 90
    command, 90, 364
    defined, 513
    or continue, 90

R

Radial
    command, 190
    defined, 513
    dimensions, 353
Radius
    defined, 503
    fillet, 268, 298
    fillet, defined, 503
    zero, 298
Ratio
    aspect, defined, 494
    screen, 159
Ray, CADD Master, 475
Real Objects, vs. symbols, 8
Rectangle, drawing a, 81
Recursive, definition, 11
Redo
    command, 286
    defined, 513
    limitations, 287
Redraw
    backwards, 161
    command, 119, 160
    defined, 513
    fast, 179

Reference
    about, 29
    component, 213
    defined, 514
    point, 132
    points, 115, 168
    points, display of, 168
Regular Polygon, defined, 514
Relative
    coordinates, 75, 173, 175
    defined, 514
    manual entry, 76
Remove, component, 231
REN, defined, 514
Rename
    a file, 90, 365
    defined, 514
    drawing, 374
Repeat, a command, 93
Replace
    component, 229
    text, 241
Representational, defined, 514
Resolution
    defined, 514
    limitations, 13
    minimum available, 6
    plotter, 6
    video, 6
Rotate
    function, 131
    plot, 402
    window, 140
Rotation
    angle, 131, 141
    component, 218
    direction, 141
    hatch, 249
    point, 141
    text, 237
Rubberbanding
    about, 82
    defined, 515
    optional, 171

S

Save
  command, 366
  components, 368
  defined, 515
  drawing, 89, 365
  layer, 367
  selection, 367
  window, 367
Saving
  about, 360
  attributes, 370
  batch files, 369
  files, 364
  image files, 370
Scale
  automatic, 8
  command, 409
  component, 221
  conversion factor, 5
  defined, 507
  dimension, 350
  drawing, 132
  factor, 133
  function, 132
  hatch, 250
  line, 73, 165
  line type, defined, 507
  plot, 399, 401
  plot, about, 387
  real world, 5
  trace, 409
  user-selected, 8
Screen
  blank, 66
  CADD, 34
  display, 176
  flip, 195, 427
  main, 34
  ratio, 159
Search, file selector command, 383
Select
  digitizer menu, 418
  font, 232

Selected, list, 279
Selection
  about, 278
  command, 279
  defined, 515
  editing, 127
  last, 279
  methods, 124, 278
  plot, 390
  prompt, 278
  save, 367
  stretch, 130, 138
Selector
  commands, 382
  file, 380
Settings
  color, 284
  default, 91
  hatch, 249
  Plotter Pen, 394
Setup
  drawing, 91
  page, 400
Shortcut
  command codes, 46
  methods, 124
Shortcuts
  command codes, 46
  editing, 47
  filtering, 281
Shoulder, length, 348
Show
  angle, 132
  distance, 69
  units, 65
  vertex, 132
Sides, arc, 182
Simple Entities, about, 27
Size
  command, 84
  component, 221
  cursor, 176
  grid, 68
  page, 392
  paper, 386

Index

Size, *continued*
    show, 69
    text, 236
Slant, text, 234
Snap
    center, 320
    close, 310
    commands, 309
    component, 231
    defined, 515
    intersection, 313
    layers, 321
    midpoint, 311
    object, 311
    ortho, 87
    parallel, 315
    percentage, 313
    perpendicular, 317
    tangent, 319
    to grid, 70
    tolerance, 310
Snaps, menu, 42
Software
    defined, 515
    related, 471
Sort, plotter pens, 394
Space, drawing, 66
Spacing
    character, 233
    text, 233
    text line, 234
    text, proportional, 234
Speed, plotter pen, 394
Spline, defined, 516
Spreadsheet, communication with, 457
Stacked, dimension tolerance, 336
Standard
    point, 121
    points, 169
    points, display of, 169
Status
    drawing, 196
    lines, 194
    toggle, 194

Stretch
    command, 130, 138
    defined, 516
    extension, 341
    selection, 130, 138
    straight line, 131
    window, 145
Strings, about, 29
Style
    dimensioning, 329
    type, 232
Stylus
    defined, 516
    digitizer, 406
Subdirectories, creating, 57
Submenu, name, 439
Submenus, video, 438
Symbol, defined, 516
Symbols
    libraries, 473
    vs. real objects, 8, 223
System
    defined, 509
    operating, defined, 509
    options, 62
    selecting, 61
    unit, 61
    unit, default, 62

T

Tablet
    defined, 516
    digitizer, 406
Tag, file selector command, 383
Tangent, snap, 319
.TDG, defined, 516
Text
    about, 29, 332
    ASCII files, 243
    aspect, 235
    centered, 333
    characters, 232, 237
    color, 236

Text, *continued*
    command codes, 46
    defined, 502
    delete, 242
    dimensioning, 332
    direction, 333
    display, 245, 344
    edit, 242
    editing, 240-241
    fast, 181, 245
    fast, defined, 502
    importing, 243
    in-line offset, 333
    insert, 241
    justification, 235
    line, 232, 237
    line spacing, 234
    menu, 43
    multiple lines, 239
    offset above, 334
    placement, 332
    placing, 237
    proportional, 234
    replace, 241
    rotation, 237
    slant, 234
    tolerance, 335
    window, 247
Tilde, use in macros, 434
Toggle
    commands, 478
    defined, 516
    transparent, 83
Toggles, in a macro, 437
Tolerance
    command, 310
    dimension text, 335
    fixed variance, 336
    min/max, 335
    snap, 310
    stacked variance, 336
.TPL, defined, 517
.TPR, defined, 517
Trace
    command, 409

Trace, *continued*
    mode, 410
    scale, 409
Tracing
    about, 412
    vs. drawing, 412
Track, command, 323
Trackball, defined, 517
Tracking
    about, 322
    from the last point, 325
    use of, 323
Transferability, defined, 517
Translator, MAC, 474
Tree, directory, 381
Trim
    command, 296
    commands, 296
    intersection, 300
    korner, 300
    multi, 302
Trims, menu, 42
Type
    arrow, 337
    dimension, 337
    line, 72, 164
    line, defined, 507
    line, disable, 182
    plotting, 397
Types
    hardware, 72
    new, 27
    line, scaled, 72

U

Undo
    command, 285
    defined, 517
    limitations, 286
    un-, 286
Unerase
    command, 99
    defined, 517

Unerase, *continued*
    limitations, 129
Unit
    default, 62
    options, 62
    selecting, 61
Units
    angular, 63
    database, 26
    decimal, 63
    defined, 518
    functional, 63
    show, 65
    definition, 286
Unload, definition, 289
Up, zoom, 107
Update, layer, 183
Utilities, menu, 44
Utility, programs, 455

V

Value
    decimal, 63-64
    defined, 504
    file format, 465
    fraction, defined, 504
    fractional, 63-64
    zoom, 159
Variables
    macro, 451
    setting, in macros, 449
Variance
    dimension tolerance, 336
    fixed, 336
    stacked, 336
Vertex, show, 132
.VGD, defined, 518
Video
    defined, 518
    explained, 49
    menu, load, 429
    resolution, 6

View
    current, 397
    delete, 158
    named, 158
    plotting, 397
Viewport, defined, 518

W

Width
    double, 270
    drawing, 67
    line, 71, 163
    line, disable, 182
    plotter pen, 394
    PostScript, 396
Window
    copy, 147
    defined, 518
    explained, 125
    fill, 250
    hatch, 250
    inside, 125
    method, 125
    rotate, 140
    save, 367
    stretch, 145
    zoom, 155
Wireframe, modeling, 472
Working, rename, 374
Worksheet, files, 466

Y

Yes, option, 49

Z

Zeros
    leading, 65
    trailing, 65
Zoom
    all, 150

Zoom, *continued*
    backwards, 161
    command codes, 45
    commands, 150
    defined, 518
    factor, 159
    in, 107, 153
    limits, 67, 150
    out, 153

Zoom, *continued*
    pan, 160
    previous, 156
    redraw, 160
    up, 107
    value, 159
Zoom, window, 155
Zooms, menu, 43

Osborne McGraw-Hill

Computer Books

(800) 227-0900

← Tear off for Bookmark

▼ You're important to us...

We'd like to know what you're interested in, what kinds of books you're looking for, and what you thought about this book in particular.

Please fill out the attached card and mail it in. We'll do our best to keep you informed about Osborne's newest books and special offers.

▶ YES, SEND ME A FREE COLOR CATALOG
of all Osborne/McGraw-Hill computer books.

Name:_____ Title:_____

Company:_____

Address:_____

City:_____ State:_____ Zip:_____

I'M PARTICULARLY INTERESTED IN THE FOLLOWING *(Check all that apply)*

I use this software:
- ❐ Lotus 1-2-3
- ❐ Quattro
- ❐ dBASE
- ❐ WordPerfect
- ❐ Microsoft Word
- ❐ WordStar
- ❐ Others_____

I use this operating system:
- ❐ DOS
- ❐ OS/2
- ❐ UNIX
- ❐ Macintosh
- ❐ Others_____

I rate this book:
- ❐ Excellent ❐ Good ❐ Poor

I program in:
- ❐ C
- ❐ PASCAL
- ❐ BASIC
- ❐ Others_____

I chose this book because...
- ❐ Recognized author's name
- ❐ Osborne/McGraw-Hill's reputation
- ❐ Read book review
- ❐ Read Osborne catalog
- ❐ Saw advertisement in _____
- ❐ Found while browsing in store
- ❐ Found/recommended in library
- ❐ Required textbook
- ❐ Price
- ❐ Other_____

Comments_____

Topics I would like to see covered in future books by Osborne/McGraw-Hill

include:_____

Print **ISBN** from the back cover here: 0-07-881_ _ _ - _

Osborne McGraw-Hill

Computer Books

(800) 227-0900

NO POSTAGE
NECESSARY
IF MAILED
IN THE
UNITED STATES

BUSINESS REPLY MAIL
First Class   Permit NO. 3111   Berkeley, CA

Postage will be paid by addressee

Osborne McGraw-Hill
2600 Tenth Street
Berkeley, California 94710–9938